General Custer, Libbie Custer and Their Dogs

DOGS IN OUR WORLD

Dogs in Health Care: Pioneering Animal-Human Partnerships
(Jill Lenk Schilp, 2019)

*General Custer, Libbie Custer and Their Dogs:
A Passion for Hounds, from the Civil War to Little Bighorn*
(Brian Patrick Duggan, 2019)

*Dog's Best Friend: Will Judy, Founder of National Dog Week
and* Dog World *Publisher* (Lisa Begin-Kruysman, 2014)

*Man Writes Dog: Canine Themes in Literature,
Law and Folklore* (William Farina, 2014)

*Saluki: The Desert Hound and the English Travelers
Who Brought It to the West* (Brian Patrick Duggan, 2009)

General Custer, Libbie Custer and Their Dogs

A Passion for Hounds, from the Civil War to Little Bighorn

BRIAN PATRICK DUGGAN

Foreword by Paul L. Hedren

DOGS IN OUR WORLD
Series Editor: Brian Patrick Duggan

McFarland & Company, Inc., Publishers
Jefferson, North Carolina

ALSO OF INTEREST
AND BY THE AUTHOR

*Saluki: The Desert Hound and
the English Travelers Who Brought It
to the West* (McFarland, 2009)

LIBRARY OF CONGRESS CATALOGUING-IN-PUBLICATION DATA

Names: Duggan, Brian Patrick, 1953– author. | Hedren, Paul L., writer of foreword.
Title: General Custer, Libbie Custer and their dogs : a passion for hounds, from the Civil War to Little Bighorn / Brian Patrick Duggan ; foreword by Paul L. Hedren.
Description: Jefferson, North Carolina : McFarland & Company, Inc., Publishers, 2019 | Series: Dogs in our world | Includes bibliographical references and index.
Identifiers: LCCN 2018050894 | ISBN 9781476669540 (softcover : acid free paper) ∞
Subjects: LCSH: Custer, George A. (George Armstrong), 1839–1876. | Custer, Elizabeth Bacon, 1842–1933. | Dog owners—United States—Biography. | Women dog owners—United States—Biography. | United States—History—1849–1877.
Classification: LCC E467.1.C99 D84 2019 | DDC 973.8/20922 [B] —dc23
LC record available at https://lccn.loc.gov/2018050894

BRITISH LIBRARY CATALOGUING DATA ARE AVAILABLE

ISBN (print) 978-1-4766-6954-0
ISBN (ebook) 978-1-4766-3487-6

© 2019 Brian Patrick Duggan. All rights reserved

*No part of this book may be reproduced or transmitted in any form
or by any means, electronic or mechanical, including photocopying
or recording, or by any information storage and retrieval system,
without permission in writing from the publisher.*

"General Custer with His Horse Vic," from *Tenting on
the Plains* by Elizabeth Custer (Buffalo Bill Center of the West,
Cody, Wyoming, USA; F.594.C961.1893.pg212).

Printed in the United States of America

*McFarland & Company, Inc., Publishers
Box 611, Jefferson, North Carolina 28640
www.mcfarlandpub.com*

For Wendy,
who was herself a "Custer widow" for a few years,
and to Hannibal, Tezzy, Bakkeer, Calista, and Ildico's daughters—
faithful hounds all.

Table of Contents

ACKNOWLEDGMENTS	ix
FOREWORD BY PAUL L. HEDREN	1
PREFACE	3
A NOTE TO THE READER	9
PROLOGUE	11
1: Judge Bacon's Daughter	13
♦ *Tail Piece: The Havelock-Hollywood-Custer Connection*	22
2: That Custer Boy	23
♦ *Tail Piece: A Cadet and His Dog*	32
3: Armstrong Ascendant	34
♦ *Tail Piece: P.T. Barnum's Civil War Dog Show*	46
4: My Husband's Dogs	48
♦ *Tail Pieces: The Sporting Ritual of Foxhunting in America*	62
♦ *Slave Tracking and Prison Guard Dogs*	62
5: The Texas Pack	64
♦ *Tail Pieces: Libbie Custer and Persian Greyhounds—Two Degrees of Separation*	85
♦ *Dogs as Property in the 19th Century*	85
6: Kansas—Hunting Game and Chasing Indians	87
♦ *Tail Pieces: Scotch Stag Hounds and Chinese Edible Dogs— Victorian Breed Terminology*	109
♦ *Army Dogs: Birth, Sutures and Death*	109
7: Kansas and Indian Territory: Bloody Snow	111
♦ *Tail Piece: Did Armstrong Kill His Own Dogs at Washita?*	127
8: The Tourist Hunters	131
♦ *Tail Piece: Plagiarizing Lord Byron*	153
♦ *Barnum and the Grand Hoboken Buffalo Hunt*	154

Table of Contents

9: Blue Grass, Pvt. Burkman, and the Grand Duke Alexis	155
♦ *Tail Piece: Russian Wolfhounds Emigrate to America*	170
10: Paw Prints on the Yellowstone	171
♦ *Tail Piece: Sir St. George Gore's Greyhounds Populate the West*	193
♦ *Sighthounds vs. Antelope*	194
11: Fort Lincoln and the Black Hills	196
♦ *Tail Piece: California Joe and His Custer Hound*	216
♦ *Tailless Dogs*	216
12: The Last Dog Deals and the March to Little Bighorn	218
♦ *Tail Piece: Custer's First Stand*	236
13: Dog Rumors and the Last Stand Hoax	238
♦ *Tail Piece: Rusty's Improbable History*	262
14: The Widow Custer's Burden	264
Epilogue: Custer's Last Hound	283
Appendix: General Custer's Dogs in Art, Literature and Film	289
Chapter Notes	301
Bibliography	321
Index	331

Acknowledgments

There are a good number of people who have contributed significantly in their different ways to this book and I hope my acknowledgments do not seem as long as the credits at the end of a CGI film—but they are most necessary. If I have inadvertently omitted anyone, I apologize.

In my introduction, I noted that Denise Flaim, my editor at *Sighthound Review*, is responsible for sparking the tinder by asking for that one article about Custer and his deerhounds. Mara Bovsun, my editor at *AKC Family Dog*, encouraged me to write another piece, but one more from Libbie's perspective. Solidly hooked, I turned to the Scottish Deerhound community for their wisdom and Richard Hawkins and Clay Finney shared what they knew and told me I should get in touch with Stephen Youngkin, who had previously researched and written about this very topic. Stephen was exceedingly kind and sent me his files, including several rolls of microfilm (from the days when you could purchase them) containing documents from the Elizabeth Bacon Custer Collection held at the Little Bighorn Battlefield National Monument. These were out of date as the collection had expanded since the microfilm was made, but they served as a research starter until I could get to the collection itself in Montana. In his files were a number of letters from Don Schwarck, who was researching Armstrong's dog patron, Kirkland Barker. Eventually, I got in touch with Don and he generously shared some of his research with me—and even loaned me his prized Reedstrom illustration for inclusion in this book. It has been close to thirty years since Stephen and Don had their articles published, but their work still stands today as solid research and a foundation for my odyssey. In a way, they are the godfathers of this book.

Early on, I approached two well-published authors for guidance. Brian W. Dippie was not only a well-known Custer and Western historian but had written the only book that was primarily devoted to Custer's stories about hunting with his hounds—*Nomad: George A. Custer in Turf, Field and Farm*. He thought my project was unique, gave advice, and remained interested in the project from start to finish. Robert Utley also thought the project had promise and when I naively asked where to find more in print about Armstrong's dogs, he said, "keep peeling back the onion's layers." Bob was right, for the best doggy material was not in the published history books but rather in contemporary letters and journals.

From the first explorations on the topic, the California State University, Stanislaus library faculty, Maryann Hight, John Brandt, Tim Held, Laura French, and even Dean

Ron Rodriguez, were enthusiastic and unfailingly bemused by my unusual reference questions. The Interlibrary Loan staff enjoyed the challenges of my borrowing requests and never once failed to deliver—so Julie Ruben (retired), Deb Childers, and Guillermo Meraz, take a bow!

My good friend and former colleague at Stan State, Tawn Gillihan, went to some trouble to help me get needed books, did initial proofreading of the manuscript, and built an excellent web site for me. Her savvy comments reminded me that not all of my readers would be steeped in cavalry or dog lore and that better explanations were needed at certain points.

The Custers' letters were primary sources of information and three individuals were exceptionally accommodating and cheerful in providing insight and access to source documents in their archives—Cindy Hagen of the Little Bighorn Battlefield National Monument, MT, Charmaine Wawrzyniec of the Ellis Library and Reference Center in the Monroe County Library System, MI, and Khaleel Saba of the Western Archeological Conservation Center, Tucson, AZ.

For most of the manuscript's development, I did not think maps were needed as there are numerous others in the many publications about Armstrong and his campaigns. However, in explaining the book's concept to a friend, I realized that my readers should not have to put down the book to find a possibly obscure location on the web to understand the narrative. I had considered borrowing (with permission) another author's maps, but then I realized that those were all campaign and battle focused, and would not help tell the dogs' stories, so new ones had to be created. I tip my hat to the work of Charles Preppernau, my cartographer, and Gary Ellis for the deerhound drawings which enhanced the maps.

I am deeply indebted to the proofreaders of the final draft of my manuscript, my friends, Dale Kosman, Richard Hawkins, Tawn Gillihan (who came back for more), the Rev. Vincent Heier, and Frederic C. Wagner III, for not only encouraging me, but correcting, questioning, and testing my content. In particular, I owe special thanks to Dale, for he has a store of knowledge that is both broad and deep about Armstrong and the Civil and Indian Wars. He generously worked hard in guiding me through some of the more complicated or obscure portions about campaigns and battles. If there are errors in the book, they will be mine and I trust only in the nature of omission rather than commission.

For the production of this book, I must thank my editor, Natalie Foreman, who not only steadfastly believed in this project from its conception, but advised and encouraged me along a very long trail. Lisa Camp, Beth Cox, Jennifer McLaughlin and the rest of the McFarland team are also deserving of appreciation and *kudos* for their care and professionalism.

One of the challenges in researching George Armstrong and Libbie Custer is getting to primary documents in archives and collections which have direct or related information to the Custers' story. These are located in many institutions across the country and as of this writing, there is no authoritative, comprehensive directory for these resources. So, research in one archive often turned up a lead in another collection, and from that collection to another, and so forth. All of the institutions listed either provided scans of documents or images or occasionally just confirmed that they did not have what I was looking for. There were so many consulted, that it seemed logical to list them here by state rather than by category of information.

ARIZONA: The Western Archeological Conservation Center of the National Park Service (which partners with the University of Arizona and the Arizona State Museum) holds and conserves artifacts too delicate or valuable to be housed at their respective National Park locations. It is an amazing facility but one which is only open to researchers by appointment. I spent a couple of days at the facility and Khaleel Saba, Bree Hewit, and Ana-Elisa Arredondo assisted me with document requests (where a few happy surprises turned up) both during and after my visit.

CALIFORNIA: There is not much about the Custers in California institutions, but Marva Felchin of the Library and Archives for the Autry National Center of the American West spoke to me about the Custer and Keogh items in their collection during my visit. Fortunately for me, not so far down the road is the impressive collection of books on the Indian Wars and General Custer at the Henry Madden Library at California State University, Fresno and I made a number of "hunter-gatherer" trips there to acquire likely sources. While trying to find the earliest imports of Borzoi to America, Glenn Farris of the Fort Ross State Historic Park assured me that there had been none at that Russian outpost in Old California.

COLORADO: As it turned out, trying to find the D.F. Barry image of the Little Bighorn Monument with the *standing* dog (featured on a widely available postcard) was not as straightforward as it might seem. Dale Kosman gave me a couple of leads and Coi Drummond-Gehrig of the Denver Public Library's digital image collection provided the image from the original glass negative for inclusion in the book.

CONNECTICUT: Adrienne Saint Pierre, curator, and Melissa Houston of the Barnum Museum, Bridgeport, helped me on all things related to the fascinating showman, P.T. Barnum, and in particular the "English Stag Hunt" in his Hippodrome show. Elizabeth Van Tuyl at the Bridgeport History Center in the Bridgeport Public Library provided a few more pieces of that story. At Yale University, Natalia Sciarini and Rebecca Aldi in the Beinecke Rare Book and Manuscript Library kindly assisted with a couple of Armstrong's letters.

KANSAS: It took a lot to track down the elusive James "Dog" Kelley, but Sam Shipley, from the Dodge City Public Library, Janice Scott of the Kansas Heritage Center, and Kathie Bell, Curator of Collections and Education, Boot Hill Museum, Inc., Dodge City, came through for me. Sara J. Keckeisen at the Kansas Historical Society verified that there is no record of James Kelley's watch (supposedly presented to him by Armstrong) ever being in their collection. Lee Dobratz and Betty McDonald of the Ellis County Historical Society sent me a scan of the second photograph of Lord Waterpark and Sir Henry Paget in Armstrong's buffalo hunting camp, and while I ultimately chose not to include it in the book, it was useful for comparing the dogs that appeared in that pair of images (the Little Bighorn Battlefield National Monument has the other). At Fort Riley, the staff on duty at the restored Custer House pointed out the actual house where they lived and had their dogs, and at the Cavalry Museum, the exhibit on The Cavalry School Hunt Club offered further proof of the Army's passion for hunting hounds.

KENTUCKY: Joe Hardesty of the Louisville Free Public Library and Laurie MacKellar, Technical Services Librarian at the Elizabethtown Community and Technical College, both found more information for me than historians usually mention about the Grand Duke Alexis' visit to the Custers in Elizabethtown.

MASSACHUSETTS: The Harvard University Archives' reference staff sent along biographical information on Robert Tallant, one of the men who had a dog down Armstrong's staghound line.

MICHIGAN: I've already thanked Charmaine Wawrzyniec of the Ellis Library and Reference Center in the Monroe County Library System, but I will note here that in addition to their considerable collection, they also have microfilm copies of the Elizabeth Bacon Custer Collection letters. Elsewhere in Monroe, assistance came from the County Museum from Christine Kull (retired) and Caitlyn Riehle. Mark Bowden, of the Burton Historical Collection, Detroit Public Library, made me aware of the telegrams between Kirkland Barker and George Armstrong Custer, and independent researcher, Sherry Wells, did a site visit to search for mentions of dogs in those documents for me. Annakathryn Parker Welch from the Archives of Michigan, Michigan History Center, and Kimberly Schaaf in the Springfield Township Library both tried to find the fugitive image of the Custers and their pointer and the William Pywell portrait of Gen. Stanley on the Yellowstone Expedition. I hope that these images which had once been in private collections many years ago have been preserved and are still out there somewhere.

MINNESOTA: Christina Johnson of the Sibley Historic Site, Dakota County Historical Society, Mendota, gave me useful information about Gov. Sibley's Irish Wolfhounds—which surprisingly found a place in this story at the 11th hour. In my search for Libbie's favorite staghound, Cardigan, I had help from Jenny McElroy of the Minneapolis Historical Society. At the University of Minnesota, Erin George of the University Archives also contributed and Dr. Sharon Jansa, curator of mammals at the Bell Museum, made one last search in their collections for any remains of Cardigan's mount. A word to future searchers—he's not there.

MONTANA: Profuse thanks to the National Park Service staff at the Little Bighorn Battlefield National Monument. Sharon Small and Cindy Hagen assisted with access to the Elizabeth Bacon Custer Collection (an amazing archive of documents and artifacts, most of which are currently housed off-site for protection and conservation). Jerry Jasmer introduced me both to the White Swan Library and his fellow ranger (also a professor, artist, historian, and author), Michael Donahue, and it was he who first put me on to the Hardin newspaper story about Hinrich Glüsing's letter and the black dog "survivor." At the Billings Public Library, in the Montana Room, Dee Ann Redman, graciously allowed me time with the fascinating Custer Scrapbook and answered questions about its origin. Dr. Linda Olson of Minot State University shared information with me about the old inscriptions on Pompey's Pillar (nothing from the 7th Cavalry's dog owners was there). Chris Kortlander of the Custer Battlefield Museum, Garryowen, MT, published the Glüsing "black dog" letter in the local paper and encouraged my research. He gave me copies of that letter in German along with Ranier Kuhn's translation—which had originally come from Joyce Radloff in Texas, and it was she who told me about the history of Glüsing and his letter. My sister-in-law, Annette Fuchs, contributed to the analysis of the letter with translation insights and advice on the difficulties of translating not only 19th century German script but the idiom into

Acknowledgments

modern English. Finally, I have to say that being able to stand alongside the Yellowstone, Powder, and Little Bighorn rivers gave me a better understanding for the experiences of the 7th Cavalry (and operation of the steamboat, *Far West*). At the battlefield itself, I've walked the Reno Defense Site, Weir Point, the ridges and coulees around Last Stand Hill, and visited John Burkman's grave (Armstrong's dog tender), and can say that they were insightful, powerful experiences.

NEBRASKA: James Potter of the Nebraska State Historical Society and author of the article, "The Great Source of Amusement: Hunting in the Frontier Army," tipped me off to the hoax about the Irish Wolfhound at the Little Bighorn and gave me a number of potential resources to investigate the topic of Army officers and their hunting dogs.

NEW YORK: At the 5th Avenue branch of the city's public library, in the Archives & Manuscripts Department and Brooke Russell Astor Reading Room for Rare Books and Manuscripts, Philip Heslip, Tal Nadan, Kyle Triplett, and Maurice Klapwald, were extremely helpful, both on my visit and then later when I was ordering scans of documents. The American Kennel Club Library is an amazing resource for all things canine, and archivist Brynn White and her predecessor, Craig Savino, cheerfully guided me through their collection on more than one visit. At West Point, the United States Military Academy, Suzanne Christoff, Unique Resources in the Library, Marlana L. Cook, Curator of Art in the Museum, and Michael McAfee who advised me on the West Point hold. Heather Henricksen-Georghiou, of the Newburgh Free Library, did some sleuthing to find the obscure J.B. Miller, Esq., who adopted two of Armstrong's hounds after Little Bighorn. In trying to track down still more about the dog adoptions of 1876 (and specifically the staghound connection with the Thorne family of Millbrook), assistance came from Oakleigh Thorne III, Dianne McNeil and Alison Meyer of the Millbrook Local History Society, and Betsy Park of the Millbrook Hunt.

NORTH DAKOTA: In Bismarck, at the Heritage Center (State Historical Society of North Dakota), Jim Davis and Sarah Walker were unfailingly helpful during my visit and afterwards, and at the Fort Abraham Lincoln State Park (Armstrong and Libbie's last post), where Ranger Dan Schelske provided useful insights about how Armstrong's dogs lived there. Sharon Kilzer of the Theodore Roosevelt Center, Dickensen State University, kindly gave me a sound lead about Teddy Roosevelt and his hunts with descendants of Armstrong's hounds.

OKLAHOMA: Breanna Boss, student photo assistant, University of Oklahoma Library, Western History Collections, shared the original notes on the famous photo of California Joe and his dog—which established that it was *not* one of Armstrong's hounds. After I had walked the ground of the Washita Battlefield site, the ranger there was as helpful as he could be, but I imagine they don't often get questions at about dead cavalry dogs.

PENNSYLVANIA: Richard Baker at the U.S. Center of Military History at Carlisle patiently assisted with the Jacob Lyman Greene Papers about Armstrong getting a Chihuahua in Texas.

SOUTH DAKOTA: At the State Historical Society Archives in Pierre, Ken Stewart and Matthew Reitzel of their Research Room assisted with the Fort Sully Sporting Club documents and William Illingworth's fascinating photographs. Carol Hauck at the Deadwood Public Library sent me articles about Judge Ford (who features in the first dog rumor of Little Bighorn), and Patricia Andersen of the Devereaux Library, South Dakota School of Mines and Technology, checked on a couple of obscure points about the 1874 Black Hills Expedition.

TEXAS: Judy Robinson of the Hempstead Historical Society tried unsuccessfully to find information about Col. Groce, his hounds, and the hunting packs of Hempstead, and Clarence Miller and Truett Bell of the Waller County Historical Commission/ Society talked to me about the Hempstead Library holdings on the Groce family. Samantha Cook from the Austin History Center attempted to verify the story of Armstrong's dogs urinating in the state capitol building, but could find nothing beyond the article I had (such was the case with many dog stories about Armstrong—all had to be carefully evaluated and cross-checked for the likelihood of plausibility).

UTAH: At Brigham Young University, Cindy Brightenburg at the L. Tom Perry Special Collections, Harold B. Lee Library, sent me scans of a few of the original Walter Camp notes and Dr. Albert Winkler passed along to me the source of Sgt. Windolph's story about his adopted Little Bighorn Indian dog.

VIRGINIA: At Arlington National Cemetery, the historian, Tim Frank, answered my obscure question about whether any military headstones or monuments there have images of dogs, and as it turns out, Gen. Alexander Asboth's marker does have the engraved image of his dog York accompanying him into battle.

WISCONSIN: Tony Tracy of the Douglas County Historical Society in Superior was very obliging in tracking down a copy of the D.F. Barry image of the standing dog at the Little Bighorn monument and offered further help with their collection.

WYOMING: At the Buffalo Bill Center of the West, Karen Preis, Kathleen Broder, and Sean Campbell of the McCracken Library (the only reading room I know with a buffalo head to watch the researchers) all contributed to my searches, and in the Papers of William F. Cody Department, Linda Clark and Deb Adams found information for me about Cody's imported English Greyhounds (which later proved to be too peripheral to my story), and Jeremy Johnston, the Hal and Naoma Tate endowed chair and curator of Western History at the BBCW, took an interest in my research and gave me further encouragement.

UNITED KINGDOM: Ciara Farrell and Colin Sealy of The Kennel Club's Library (another marvelous place to peruse dog books and archival materials) provided long distance assistance with greyhound stud book information in the early years of this project when I thought there might be a tangible relationship between the imported English Greyhounds that both Armstrong and Buffalo Bill Cody owned (other than the latter being exposed to former's greyhounds, there wasn't). Roger Griffin of the Athlestan Museum, Malmsbury, Wiltshire, shared recondite information on Walter Powell's big game trophies and their display in Powell's community reading room.

Guidance and answers came from historians, Brian W. Dippie, Paul Horsted, Paul L. Hedren, Shirley A. Leckie, T.J. Stiles, and James Donovan, who pointed me toward the Custer Scrapbook in the Billings Public Library. My gratitude also goes out to: Lord Clifford of Chudleigh who graciously allowed me to read and quote his forebear's fascinating letters; George Armstrong Custer III who kindly gave me permission to quote letters from the Brice C.W. Custer Collection and likewise Philip Downs for his GAC letter; Peter Russell in England sent additional information on two of the British tourist hunters; Aurie Bradley contributed her expertise on the clothing terminology which

Libbie Custer used; Jessica Snow provided the lead on the P.T. Barnum National Dog Show; Dr. Lilah Pengra shared particular portions of her research on the Custers' servants in Kansas; Mary Ann Thompson secured copies of scarce articles about the Custers in Kansas; Lorne Langley advised on the Washita River Fight; Steve Tillotson posted on the web that odd portrait of Armstrong, Tom, the grizzly bear, and deerhound, Tuck; Michael Bad Hand shared his considerable knowledge about Indian sign language; and Dave Rambow of the H.H. Bennett Studio and Museum educated me about the process of wet plate photography while making tintype exposures one windy afternoon in Rapid City.

The American Veterinary Medical Association librarian, Diane Fagen, put me in touch with Dr. Ian Tizzard of the Texas A & M, Department of Veterinary Pathology, and he explained the early 19th century attempts to vaccinate dogs against distemper. My two favorite veterinarians, Dr. Jim Quinley and Dr. Suzanne Solvin, good-naturedly answered a number of my unusual questions about dog and horse medical care. Thom Ross, Glenwood Swanson, and Jerry Thomas spoke to me about their art depicting Armstrong with his dog, and Thom generously offered one of his paintings for use in the book.

For their sustained encouragement and enthusiasm for the project, without which this would have been a much lonelier journey, I must thank my colleagues at the *AKC Family Dog* and *AKC Gazette*; Mara Bovsun, Kate McCroary Jay, and Arliss Paddock, and my stalwart family and friends who always cheered me on or prodded me to keep going; Seán Duggan (who also resurrected a photograph scan for me), Annette Fuchs, Fiona Duggan Fuchs, Kevin Duggan, Jim Trayler, Lennart and Brenda Johansson, Craig and Karen Robertson, Bob and Karen Frost, Ken Bornstein, Debbie Jeheber, Sir Terence Clark, Dr. John and Lisa Hudson, Dr. Nancy Taniguchi, Dr. Gwyneth Ann Thayer, Matt and Lindsay Keevy, Victoria Dade, Henry Burnett, Jay Field, Anne Mayea, Henrik Olsgaard, Danny Carnahan, Ken and Mary Ellen Gorske, John Smith, Robert Jones, Susan Schroeder (Kansas) Susan Schroder (California), Cindy Taylor, Maryann Lillemo, Warren and Vicky Cook, Gary Roush, Dina Ericksen, Frank Borrelli, Carl Whitman, Loretta Blakeley, John Ensminger, Barb Heidenreich, Kingsbury Parker, Rick Collin, Dr. Christopher Dixon, Linda Bellile, Todd Harburn, M.D., Bruce Liddic, Dale Ramsey, Bob Reece, Lowell Smith, Rod Thomas, Richard Upton and the late Chet Nelson. In England, my cousins, the Noctors of Windsor and the Duggans of Aylesbury and Marsworth, and in my father's home town in Ireland, the Galway Duggans.

Even though he died before I began this long project, the memory of my father, Jim Duggan, and his love for history and the written word has sustained me. Sadly, my mother, Betty Duggan, and five dear ones and supporters died during the seven years of work on the book and I'm sorry that she and Jay Kappmeier, Lin Hawkyard, Richard Duggan, and Ken and Diana Allan, will not be able to read it. My steadfast old writing dog, Ildico, did not live through the completion of the manuscript, but she was in her bed under my desk for most of the work (and her daughters have figured out how cozy it is to hang out when I am writing in The Study).

And last but certainly not the least, I again have incurred a literary debt to Wendy. During the writing process we both worked and retired, judged and showed dogs, had two litters, were involved in both our local and national Saluki breed clubs, and Wendy had the idea to build me a private space for writing and all my books. Through all of this, she was patient and steadfastly believed in me and this book.

Foreword by Paul L. Hedren

In the realm of Custer and Custer books, what with new titles appearing continually, aficionados hear and repeat a common refrain suggesting that it's hard to imagine something *new*, meaning something fresh and revealing, appearing in a time-worn story altogether familiar to its students. But then, surprisingly, T.J. Stiles's Custer biography, *Custer's Trials*, appeared in 2015 and captivated the nation. Stiles provided a strikingly inventive take on a story everyone believed they knew so well, and so originally sourced and distinctive, in fact, that it earned the 2016 Pulitzer Prize for History. In truth, Stiles's case gets repeated more often than anyone would care to admit (less the Pulitzer Prize of course). And so it goes that when learning that my friend Brian Duggan was writing a book about Custer and his dogs, I smiled, wishing to be encouraging, even while inwardly hearing that old refrain. And then Brian asked me to write this foreword. I agreed. I had read those Custer biographies and figured I had plenty for comparison. Anyway, Brian's book proposed adding the dimension of dogs and maybe therein would be something fresh.

Then I read the manuscript. Brian has obviously read the Custer biographies, too, and aims in his effort at personalizations and intimacies missing from so many of them. This is Custer up close and personal, during his courtship, nightly in his battlefield camps, in his military quarters, eating trail dust on the Western frontier, and invariably, of course, with darling wife Libbie at his side. The framework of Custer's life and Army career is present, but the focus is the private, married, family man. Alone, this proves quite an endearing telling of story so altogether familiar.

Then add the dogs. It turns out that to know Custer is to come to grips with his fondness for hounds of every sort. He speaks devotedly of them in his writings. Libbie, who never had pets, does so as well. For the Custers, dogs were literally everywhere in home and field. They appear in their photographs. We thought we knew this dimension of Custer's life too. But then again, maybe not.

Here's the story of a man, a loving wife, and a remarkable passion for hounds. Theirs was no home with a couple of house or yard dogs. Theirs was a home with seemingly too many dogs, "his" and "ours," and measured by the pack ... four, six, eight. At Fort Abraham, Lincoln Custer kenneled in his back yard forty dogs. Most had the run of their quarters; all had the run of the fort. They went to the field with Custer in 1868, were on the Yellowstone River in 1873, explored the Black Hills in 1874, and were on the great campaign against the Sioux in 1876. Custer was savvy about his hounds. In the Army's world, and his, they were always great hunters, camp guards and pets, and pleasurable and welcome companions, especially for Army women whose husbands could be away for weeks and months at a time. But at the Washita they came near betraying Custer's attack. He could not allow that in 1876, and his staghounds were tied to the wagons parked at the mouth of the Powder River when the Seventh Cavalry rode away, fearing their noise would alert the Indians.

We've read their names ... Byron, Ginnie, Bowser, Turk, Rattler, Rover, Blucher, Maida, Cardigan (Libbie's lap dog), and so many more. Brian Duggan knows the breeds and gently spots throughout his narrative appropriate backgrounds on all of them. We watch the Custers nurse their sick animals, hunt with them, push them from nighttime human beds, get nuzzled when adults are trying to write. We read of Libbie's heroic efforts at a dog rescue, when burdened at Fort Lincoln in that fateful July with the disposal of the enormous pack, what Brian calls American's first great dog rescue.

This is indeed a delightfully original book about Custer and his dogs, writ large, and amounting to a thoughtful examination of one of the West's most intriguing characters, told in the light of his one true obsession.

Paul Hedren is a retired National Park Service superintendent and life-long student of Custer, Crook, and the Great Sioux War. Many times published, Hedren is now working on his twelfth book, a history of the Rosebud battle of 1876.

Preface

I entered the world of Custer via the doggy door—literally. It began when Hickory, the Scottish Deerhound, won the prestigious Westminster Kennel Club's Best in Show award.

A great many biographers and historians who write about George Armstrong Custer or Little Bighorn will say that their first exposure to him was *They Died with Their Boots On* (1941) with Errol Flynn. However, my first brush with the Custer legend occurred when I was at San Francisco State University and brought my youngest brother, Seán, on campus for a screening *of Little Big Man*. This was during the Vietnam War and, not knowing anything, I wasn't sure what to make of director Arthur Penn's egomaniacal and finally unhinged Custer. (Seán and I loved the film and to this day, either one of us can croak, "My name is Jack Crabb…" and induce howls of laughter in the other.) My second "meeting" with Custer, happened when my mother sent me from Idaho a photograph of three late 19th century U.S. Artillerymen wearing kepis and tunics, with a note that the antique dealer had "established" that these unnamed men had been with Custer at Little Bighorn (they weren't). I still did not know much about the man or the battle when my good friend, Ken Bornstein, introduced me to "Custer's Last Jump" (1976), a proto-steampunk tale by Steven Utley and Harold Waldrop, who cleverly imagined Custer with dirigibles and parachuting soldiers in the attack on Little Bighorn—and being defeated by Crazy Horse and several warriors who had been trained to fly Confederate monoplanes (don't scoff—it's splendidly researched and written). The short story was provocative and made me think a little more about Little Bighorn.

However, what made the deepest impression on me was reading author and historian George MacDonald Fraser's brilliant novel, *Flashman and the Redskins,* where Custer was portrayed as a more well-rounded person—definitely ambitious and anxious about his career, but also a good dinner companion and friend to Flashman (who manages to survive Little Bighorn as he did so many other Victorian battles—the disastrous retreat from Kabul, the Charge of the Light Brigade, and fighting on both sides during the American Civil War). Fraser's intriguing description of Custer and Flashman at Little Bighorn prompted me to vow that one day, I would follow his advice to learn something about Little Bighorn that is not found in books and "…walk across the Greasy Grass."[1]

After the Westminster Kennel Club show in February 2011, Denise Flaim, my editor at *Sighthound Review*, who knew of my interest in historical canines, asked me to write a piece about General Custer's deerhounds. I was aware that he had large hounds, and being always keen to research new aspects of canine history, I took this as a compelling reason to learn more about the man and his dogs—and finally visit the battlefield. For advice on where to begin researching, I turned to two venerable scholars, Brian Dippie and Robert Utley—who both gave me encouragement but warned, "...the infection produced by the bite of the Custer Bug was rarely fatal but nearly always permanent!" The article that resulted, "General Custer and his Hounds," won a Dog Writers Association of America award in 2012—but there was more to the story than could fit in that piece.

So, what started out as a focused slice of American history and dogs led to a second article, "Our Dogs Give Us Such Pleasure," for *AKC Family Dog*, and I was thoroughly engrossed in the lives of George Armstrong Custer and Elizabeth Bacon Custer as dog owners—as well as those of other Army officers. The personal accounts of hounds on the frontier were fascinating—and in many ways similar to some of the British officers' stories I recounted in *Saluki: The Desert Hound and the English Travelers Who Brought It to the West*. After two articles on the Custers' dogs, there were still more dog stories needing to be told.

There are so many, many biographies, military histories, and articles about George Armstrong Custer that it could well be the work of a lifetime to find and read them all. Starting to read the better-known works, I found that the topic of the Custers and their pack of dogs hadn't received much scholarly attention. My first intention was to focus on them as dog owners and collate all of their dog adventures into a kind of hunting biography. As this unfolded, it became difficult to write meaningfully about George Armstrong Custer without touching on the politics and issues of his day—secession, slavery, the Civil War, Reconstruction, and the Indian Wars. So much has been written about the man that my project at times seemed daunting and akin to writing something new about Winston Churchill or Teddy Roosevelt. Of course, dogs are not a usual topic for historians researching Custer, the 7th Cavalry, or Little Bighorn. If a bit of dog information was mentioned in one history, it had been derived from an earlier book or two, and so going back to the original letter, journal, or personal recollection—which might say rather more than the historian chose to use. All these puzzle pieces, once discovered, started clicking together in a fascinating narrative. So, rather than just a collection of Custer dog stories, the book evolved into a limited biography of both Custers viewed through the lens of dog-ownership. During the process of discovering the man himself, I came to think of George Armstrong Custer by the name that his family and good friends called him—Armstrong—so that is how I usually refer to him in this book and, in doing so, I hope to avoid invoking some of the preconceptions that are inevitable when someone mentions "Custer."

Finding the puzzle pieces was a challenge. There is no end of primary documents to research on the topic of the Custers' dogs, but they are spread through archives and private collections in at least a dozen states. Armstrong and Libbie wrote about them, and many other people mentioned their dogs in passing. In trying to track down first-hand accounts, I found nuggets but more often dust—and not a few blind alleys. There were times when, like the crusty Oracle Jones in the film *The Hallelujah Trail*, a flash of inspiration would provoke me to shout "There! I see it now!"—although I will say that my revelations were not fueled by Jones' whiskey nor accompanied by a heavenly choir singing "Hallelujah!" However, more than once Wendy likened Oracle Jones' sartorial disarray to my often casual writing attire.

The first pass at collecting details of the Custer dog life come from five published sources—Armstrong's *My Life on the Plains*, Libbie's three books, *Boots and Saddles*, *Tenting on the Plains*, and *Following the Guidon*, and their dog tender John Burkman's recollections in *Old Neutriment*. Each of these memoirs had to be carefully evaluated as they were written long after the events (except for the contemporary *My Life on the Plains* and Armstrong's letters that Libbie included in her books). Both the Custers could be vague about their dogs' names, which makes it difficult to sort out their pack population at any one point. Teasing out dog identities from Armstrong's letters can be challenging and sometimes several have to be correlated in order to find scattered references, which, when put together, named one individual (complicating this further, Armstrong re-used a couple of dog names). The Custers rarely write about dog deaths, and when a particular one stops being mentioned in their letters, it is a pretty good indicator that the dog was dead or had gone missing on the prairie—which itself was a death sentence. The only time that *all* their dogs are named at one time is when Libbie describes their initial pack of six hounds in Texas. It is well established that they had about forty dogs in the Dakota Territory (and possibly eighty in Kentucky), but frustratingly, only a few favorites appear in their letters and memoirs.

When he was in the field, Armstrong's letters to Libbie about his hunting adventures were very similar to the sort of thing any dog person would write to their spouse—"Honey, guess what Rover did today?" While on an expedition or campaign, he wrote nearly every night, when the dogs' doings were fresh in his mind. As they were not intended for publication, there were only his usual story-telling embellishments. Complementary to these are Armstrong's letters to his dog patron, Kirkland Barker, and his "Nomad" letters to *Turf, Field and Farm*, which recounted more of his hunting stories—and the latter were even more dramatic than his personal letters. As Brian W. Dippie said in *Nomad: George A. Custer in Turf, Field and Farm*, Armstrong knew how to tell a good story.

In her three books, Libbie used Armstrong's letters and her own memory to tell their dog stories (edited and excerpted for publication), and she told a few of them in her public lectures. She verified some of the dog stories with Eliza, their cook—particularly those of Byron the greyhound and Ginnie the pointer from Texas and their early years in Kansas. Pvt. John Burkman cared for the Custer dogs and horses from September 1871 until June 1876. When he told his dog stories, decades after Little Bighorn, he was a solitary, suspicious man, bitter that he had not been with his general on that last day (Burkman's mental demons eventually drove him to suicide). However, his recollections were filtered through at least two people before being published in *Old Neutriment* and must be carefully considered. Dippie notes that while Burkman does add a certain flavor to recounting dog life in the Army with the Custers, he is often unreliable or vague as to date and place, and his stories need crosschecking.

Besides those five books, in several archives and collections around the country, there are letters, telegrams, journals, interviews, and photographs—many of them unpublished and, which as primary documents, had pieces of the dog story. Newspaper and sporting magazine accounts of Armstrong's doings sometimes mention the dogs, and those were useful in establishing definite dates. Other sources of dog information are the incidental mentions of the Custer pack by the officers, troopers, and civilians who came in contact with them, but these tend to lack details and are often merely an aside in their letters or memoirs—such as when Capt. Albert Barnitz wrote his wife from the field, "...General Custer arrived (with his hair cut short, and a perfect menagerie of Scotch fox hounds!)...."[2] The Custers' dog ownership predates the American Kennel Club, so there were no show catalogs, studbooks, or pedigree registry where lineage and ownership can be traced (although there are hints that had Armstrong not been killed in 1876, he might have been enthusiastic about exhibiting in the fledgling Westminster Kennel Club show in New York).

Another primary source of information, although one not available to most historians, is the experience of living with dog packs, small and large, for over fifty years. I'll note here that their general behavior as a domesticated species doesn't change from century to century, so, when I observe my dogs seeking out a sun-warmed fence in the winter, arguing over a bitch in season, dashing across a field for the joy of running, or nuzzling my hands while I'm writing, I know that dogs in the 19th century did the same.

Following on that line of thinking, I made a point of visiting four significant locations where Armstrong had his dogs. Up on the hill at Fort Riley and across from the parade ground, I saw the stone house where the Custers lived on his first command in Kansas (the actual quarters are in use but there is a nearly identical, restored building nearby which serves as their Custer House museum). The officers' quarters are grouped closely together and there would not have been much room for a kennel-shed or fenced yard—but then his pack was comparatively small at Fort Riley. How different was the wide-open, Fort Abraham Lincoln in North Dakota—the Custers' last post and where they kept some forty staghounds and foxhounds. There is a great deal of space between the officers' quarters with open country behind them, and more than enough room behind the houses for outbuildings (which the period photos do show). Bounded on the east by the Missouri River, and with hunting grounds to the west and south, Fort Lincoln would be a perfect place for a large pack of hounds. Its parade ground is even bigger than that of Fort Riley and it was easy for me to visualize the hounds basking in the sun, visiting the horses picketed outside the long stable buildings, trotting back and forth on their errands, and chasing the post's cats. The only time Armstrong took his hounds into battle was in the attack on Black Kettle's village on the Washita River. I walked the field, putting together battle maps with the surrounding terrain to figure out where the 7th Cavalry's dogs would have been executed and how the movements of Armstrong and his troops led to the death of his deerhound, Blucher. Lastly, I trekked out to the Powder River Supply Depot site—the last place that Armstrong was with his hounds before he died at Little Bighorn. The place has not changed much since 1876 and imagining the rows of tents and cooking fires, stacks of supplies, and even the garbage dumps full of discarded tin cans and wooden crates for rations was not at all difficult. Somewhere on that field, Armstrong's four staghounds slept in his tent—taking over his cot when he was writing one of his last letters to Libbie.

There have been only a handful of serious works on the Custers and their dogs. In 1974, Paul L. Hedren, investigating the whereabouts of Cardigan, Libbie's favorite staghound (which was stuffed and on display in a museum), published his findings in

Research Review: The Journal of the Little Big Horn Associates. The James L. Pope monograph, *Custer and His Dogs* (1990), is a basic psychological analysis of his relationship with them but only goes as far as the dog mentions in Libbie's three books. Deeper and more useful studies came from Stephen D. Youngkin who wrote three articles covering Armstrong's Scottish Deerhounds in *The Claymore: Newsletter of the Scottish Deerhound Club of America* (1991) and did much to ascertain the final fate of Cardigan. Don Schwarck was the first to research Armstrong's relationship with his friend and dog patron, Kirkland Barker, and published this in the *Research Review* (1992). In 2011 and 2012, Scottish Deerhound owner Sandy MacAllister relied solely on published sources but did spread out further than Libbie's books for four short articles for *The Claymore*. On the wild and woolly internet, blogs and articles about Armstrong's dogs pop up constantly, but these are also pulled from Libbie's and Burkman's recollections, and consequently shallow and often repeat error and myth. Paul Andrew Hutton talked about the "remarkable disregard for historical fact" in the shifting of Armstrong's image over the years from victorious Army hero and sagacious frontiersman to an arrogant, brutal tool of white exploitation in the West.[3] With the easy willingness to believe he killed his own dogs at Washita, I'd say that Hutton's "remarkable disregard" would also apply to the facts about Armstrong as a dog owner.

Without repeating my bibliography, I'll note here that the *principal* authors I have relied upon are John M. Carroll, Brian W. Dippie, James Donovan, Lawrence A. Frost, Jerome A. Greene, Richard G. Hardorff, D. Mark Katz, Shirley A. Leckie, Marguerite Merington, Jay Monaghan, Arlene Reynolds, Edgar I. Stewart, T. J. Stiles, Gregory J. W. Urwin, Robert M. Utley, Glendolin Damon Wagner, Jeffry D. Wert, and James Willert. Some of these have their distinct *caveats*—for instance Merington censored and edited the Custers' letters. Some readers may object that more use was not made of other authors, but for the purpose of this canine narrative, these were the ones whose research proved the most useful.

About Armstrong's military battles, with the exception of the attack on Black Kettle's village on the Washita River (where Armstrong actually had two of his hounds), I have chosen not to go into the details of Little Bighorn and Civil War battles, as those have been so well covered by many other eminent historians that I would only be repeating their words—and battle tactics are not really relevant to the dog story. That said, I do relate a few of Armstrong's actions in the Civil War as it is important to understand the reasons for his rapid promotion and fame as a cavalry commander—which in turn led to being appointed second in command of a famous regiment. (It is interesting to speculate briefly that if history had played out differently and Armstrong had *not* been a lieutenant colonel of cavalry stationed on the frontier, then would he have still had his large hunting pack of forty hounds?)

About the Battle of Little Bighorn, historian Edgar I. Stewart observed in 1957, "It has become almost completely engulfed in myth and legend, and the blood spilled on that eventful Sunday has been exceeded many times over by the ink from the fountain pens of historians and military experts who have written about it."[4] In the intervening six decades, there has been even more ink produced on the battle. Some of my first research thoughts after reading Burkman had to do with placing Armstrong's hounds on the battlefield, but once I learned they were definitely not there, Little Bighorn would have less emphasis in this story. As to the stories of a dog on Last Stand Hill, while I had not originally intended to devote an entire chapter to them, they kept popping up in disparate and fascinating places. Naturally, there were a great many rumors on the internet concerning Armstrong's dogs at Little Bighorn, and most of these were clearly nonsense derived from cursory readings of Burkman's stories. By the time I had counted a dozen dog rumors, it was clear they had to be addressed in an analytical manner. While there are many compilations of eyewitness accounts, diary entries, and troop movements for Little Bighorn, no one had ever collected all the dog survivor stories before. Originally I thought that a chronological listing would reveal the evolution of the rumors (or perhaps even reveal some truths) but this did not pan out as I thought it might. With that hypothesis discarded, I looked at the rumors afresh and saw that when either the dog type or owner was considered as a primary grouping, certain patterns *did* emerge and so the twenty-five rumors are in categories—where indeed some story "growth" can be seen. So, keeping in mind Stewart's comment about the amount of ink already written, here is some fresh ink on the dog stories from Little Bighorn.

Now, as this book is largely about Armstrong, it may seem unusual that I have started the book with Libbie Custer's girlhood. However, in reading everything I could on the Custers' life with dogs, her voice is, at times, louder and more clear than Armstrong's—and she lived to write probably more about them than he did. As I end this story with Libbie the widow remembering her life with Armstrong and their dogs, it seemed fitting to begin with the story of a girl who had no pets at all.

Lastly, readers of *Saluki* will remark that in both it and this volume, I have ended with a stuffed dog in a museum. That Florence Amherst's first Saluki, Luman (imported to England in 1895), and Libbie's favorite hound, Cardigan, were both mounted and placed on display in museums is not so unusual as the Victorians and Edwardians used to do that sort of thing for dogs which they considered important. It was an entirely unanticipated, marvelous coincidence that I was able to write about the similar and final chapters of both these hounds.

A Note to the Reader

Armstrong: As I mentioned in the Preface, rather than "Autie" (Libbie's pet name for him), or the more public and formal "Custer," I have chosen to use "Armstrong" because that was what his friends and family called him—and I wanted to avoid the almost instant polarization that comes with just the use of his last name. (As a toddler, he could not pronounce, "Armstrong" but could say, "Autie," so that was what his family called him as a boy.) Where it was important to give his military rank, I have used his surname as it was commonly used, for instance in newspaper accounts or letters which usually refer to him as "General Custer."

Army Ranks: For the sake of clarity, I have used officers' permanent, *functional* Army ranks so that regimental command structure is more easily understood. The ranks and honorary titles of the 19th century American Army can definitely be confusing. Officers might have a rank of captain, and yet have been awarded an honorary higher rank or "brevet" for gallantry or leadership. Officers were frequently given temporary command ranks such as Brigadier General above their regular rank, just as Capt. Custer was promoted to Brigadier General of Volunteers—ranks for the state Volunteer troops being separate and different from Federal or U.S. Army ranks. For instance, Armstrong was *both* a Major General and Brevet Major General of U.S. Volunteers and a Lieutenant Colonel and Brevet Major General in the U.S. Army. To add to the potential muddle, it was common for an officer to be called by his highest brevet rank as a courtesy—even if his regular Army rank was lower. In Armstrong's case, I do use his brevet and temporary ranks during the Civil War as they are indicators of his rapid and fortunate promotions.

Nomenclature: During Armstrong's time, regimental numbers were expressed as both "7th" and "Seventh." I have used the former as it makes the mentions of various regiments easier to find in the text. The sub-units of both cavalry and infantry regiments are called here "companies," as this was the proper term until 1883, when "troop" was adopted for the cavalry. Of lesser importance is the issue of "bugler" vs. "trumpeter." Infantry had the former and cavalry the latter, but in common usage at the time, "bugler" was used for both, so I have chosen to continue with that term. For Indian bands, tribes, and even nations, whenever possible, I have identified the specific group such as Kiowa, Southern Cheyenne, Crow, Arikara, Oglala, etc. In geographic terminology, Little Bighorn is commonly used today for both the river and the battlefield, although in the late 1800s, locals called it the Little Horn River or the Little Big Horn—and of course, each tribe had their own name for it.

Transcriptions of 19th century handwriting: Regarding the excerpts from period letters (which were private correspondence and not intended for publication), for the most part, I have left them as written to give a flavor of their author's character. In the interest of improved readability, I have occasionally added punctuation and smoothed out the Victorian habit of capitalizing important words (Armstrong was particularly inconsistent with both of these). For quoting colorful vernacular, particularly in John Burkman's and Eliza Brown's quotes and transcribed stories, I have chosen *not* to interject [sic] every time there is a phonetically spelled word so that the flow is not interrupted.

Dog Breeds and Types: When breeds are specifically named, they are capitalized, such as English Greyhound or Newfoundland, whereas names in lowercase are references to types—greyhound, bull-dog, staghound, pointer, and so forth. The Custers and others were erratic about breed names and often used just the descriptive, "stag hound"—which could mean either pedigree or crossbreed. When Armstrong and Libbie were definitely referring to their purebred deerhounds, they used "thoroughbred," "full blooded," or just "blooded" to make their point but then often switched right back to "stag hound." Another convention I've used is the use of sighthound, staghound, and foxhound—each properly two words, but which the dog world nearly always combines into one.

Prologue

June 12, 1876, Powder River Supply Depot, Dakota Territory
(Thirteen days before the Battle of Little Bighorn)

Surrounded by his sleeping staghounds, Lt. Col. George Armstrong Custer of the U.S. 7th Cavalry was up well before the sun, writing another long letter to his wife. Breakfast would have to wait as his news was going in the mailbag for the steamboat's run down to Fort Lincoln. His hopes for the campaign were churning in his mind as he put his private thoughts for his wife, Libbie, on the thin writing paper. Annoyed with General Alfred Terry for sending Major Reno off to scout for the Sioux, he worried that his subordinate might get close enough to provoke them into scattering—or actually start the battle they wanted. Armstrong concealed his feelings in front of the other officers by dismissing Reno's chances of finding them. If his reconnaissance confirmed the absence of Sioux in that particular area, then Armstrong and his whole regiment would split off from the Dakota Column to find Sitting Bull and Crazy Horse, and the defiant Sioux—but it should have been *his* scout.

Less than a month out of Fort Abraham Lincoln, Armstrong was missing Libbie. He still had a faint hope that she might be able to come upriver on a supply steamer to visit him before the column moved beyond the banks of the Yellowstone River. Libbie had been asking him to be more mindful of his personal safety and not stray from the column to go hunting with the dogs. Her request was easy enough to oblige as Terry had banned all hunting a couple of days before. Tuck, a great wiry-coated, long-legged, Scottish Deerhound, came over and laid her head on his lap for an ear scratch. It was her habit to ask for affection while he was writing and it was hard to ignore seventy pounds of insistent leaning and soulful eyes. Of Armstrong's hounds, she was the only one keeping vigil with him. Lady, Kaiser, and Swift were curled up and still asleep in the dawn's chill.

Armstrong had a lot on his mind. He only just made it back from the Belknap hearings in Washington in time to ride out with his regiment. President Grant had considered his testimony to be personally disloyal and wouldn't allow Armstrong to rejoin his regiment. With the start of the expedition growing near, only General Terry's intercession persuaded Grant to reconsider—but made it clear that Armstrong would have no higher command than his regiment and *nothing else* in the column. Still smarting from Grant's rebuke, Armstrong knew his Army career and reputation depended upon a victory against the Sioux. In addition to Terry's Dakota Column heading west, General

George Crook's Wyoming Column was moving up from the south while Colonel John Gibbon's Montana Column headed east to converge on the area where the Indians were believed to be, and bottle them up. Each column wanted first crack at the Sioux to either defeat or return them to their reservation. For Armstrong to triumph personally, he needed this to be a clear 7th Cavalry success—despite the simmering discord with some of his officers.

Terry, Crook, and Gibbon were facing a typical Indian War tactical problem—to find and engage the Sioux before they could disappear into the difficult terrain of the Wolf and Big Horn Mountains. Armstrong knew there would be probing actions in the uncharted land to find a trail. For this, the Army relied on Indian scouts whose tribes were hereditary enemies of the Sioux and a few white scouts who were roughly familiar with the area. Mobility and speed would be needed for pursuit over twisting rivers, through wide and narrow ravines, and over steep divides. Sooner rather than later, the infantry and cumbersome Gatling guns would bog down the march. It was a job for the cavalry—*his* cavalry and no mistake.

Armstrong's column was to consist of some 650 horse soldiers (officers and enlisted men), civilian mule packers and translators, Indian scouts, and one newspaper reporter. For a reconnaissance in force, rations and ammunition would have to be transferred from the lumbering supply wagons to the more agile pack mules. Rattling sabers (glamorous but not overly useful) and bulky tents would be left behind along with the officers' trunks at the Powder River Supply Depot. As much as he loved their music, the brass band would stay so their horses could be re-mounts for the fighting men. While he was thinking this through, Tuck's ears had gone unscratched and she impatiently shoved her master's hand with her wet nose—and that reminded him of one more troubling problem—the dogs.

The staghounds had been on expeditions before and could easily keep up with the horses. The rangy hounds earned their keep by catching meat for the pot and needed nothing other than clean water and a bed at night. Along with Armstrong's brothers, Tom and Boston, nephew Autie Reed, and brother-in-law, Lt. James Calhoun, the dogs were a part of his campaign family and adored their master. They had always accompanied him with no great problems—except at the Washita fight, eight years before, where an arrow had killed young Blucher.

Armstrong had become a more experienced Indian fighter in the eight years since then and was supremely confident about his 7th Cavalry, which he boasted were invincible on the plains—even against the mighty Sioux. Still the question gnawed at him, "Should the dogs come along?"

Chapter 1

Judge Bacon's Daughter

"I have told the girls that they may play and laugh to their heart's content, promenade, and walk in good weather. But must not ride after fast horses, and no boat rides, and have as little to do with fast young men as is consistent."
—Judge Daniel Bacon[1]

For a woman who, along with her husband, General George Armstrong Custer, would eventually own forty dogs, Libbie Custer's formative years were astonishingly free of the canine species. In fact, the only animals she had any contact with were a few kittens (briefly) and a pony for riding lessons.

Mr. Bacon Chooses a Town and a Wife

Daniel Stanton Bacon was the son of physician-farmer Dr. Leonard Bacon and Elizabeth Clift, of Howlett Hill, Onondaga County, New York. Dr. Bacon wanted a college education for Daniel, but with eight children and limited means this was not possible. Being a resourceful and optimistic young man with a teaching certificate, at the age of twenty-four in 1822, Daniel went to the frontier to be a teacher and find growing towns with opportunities in real estate and government.

America was not yet a wide country and transportation within it was limited to steamboat, horse-drawn coach, horse, or walking. The Erie Canal would not be completed until 1825, and railroads were not practical until after 1830. Traveling west from Syracuse, Daniel reached communities of Peru and Sandusky, Ohio—and then left the States for the Michigan Territory. He accepted a lucrative teaching appointment in Bloomfield. In the spring of 1823, Daniel relocated south to Monroe, a settlement with a bank, constabulary, churches, schools, saw mills, breweries, tanneries, and a newspaper. Purchasing a farm, he acquired cash from the timber cleared to plant fruit orchards. In the evenings, Daniel Bacon studied law.

Monroe was near the mouth of the River Raisin and had long been a settled area. Its European roots dated from a land transaction in 1785 between the Potawatomi people and a French officer in the American Army. French colonists named it *Riviere au Raisin*, but with increasing numbers of American settlers, it was called River Raisin, Raisinville, and Frenchtown, and was christened Monroe in 1817—the year that James Monroe became the fifth president and visited the area.

By 1832, Bacon farmed, taught school, and helped his neighbors with legal advice.

Respected for his integrity and knowledge, he was elected as a school inspector and county supervisor.[2] Bacon bought and sold land, increasing his wealth, and was appointed associate judge and probate judge as well.[3] In 1835, his fellow Michiganders voted him to the Territory's Legislative Council, which was preparing for statehood (achieved in 1837). Judge Bacon was President of the Merchants and Mechanics Bank, a circuit court judge, and had run for Lt. Governor of the 26th state in the union.[4]

He was a deeply religious man who believed that success in life came from education, hard work, and community involvement. Of course, the right marriage partner could help make this success happen, but Bacon would not take a wife unless every comfort could be provided for her. At the age of thirty-nine, he finally felt up to the task and found twenty-two-year-old Eleanor Sophia Page of Grand Rapids. Sophia shared his values and was a confident, industrious young woman. She saw no objection to marrying a prosperous man sixteen years older than herself. Major Abel and Zilphia Page were upstanding, church-going members of their community who valued education, and all their daughters had attended a fine ladies' seminary. As it turned out, both the Bacons and Pages could trace their families back to the *Mayflower* colony. The courting couple was affectionate but not demonstrative. Judge Bacon's letters to Sophia (and everyone) were pragmatic as evidenced by this one sent in early 1837.

> The navigation of Lake Erie is open so as to admit boats from Buffalo. But for the pecuniary embarrassment in the East the coming season would be a prosperous one. My feelings for you have undergone no change since I saw you. It is therefore unnecessary to give you further assurances of my friendship and affection.[5]

In June of that year, Judge Bacon asked the Pages for permission to marry their daughter. They were married on September 12, 1837. Before marriage, Judge Bacon had been consumed by his work and lived an abstemious life. Preferring to be unfettered by the domestic obligations of a homeowner, he rented rooms in hotels or boarding houses. Fortunately, Sophia would excel at running a household. Their first child, Edward Augustus, was born on June 9, 1839, and Bacon had a two-story house built in central Monroe. It was white with green shutters and a long porch on two sides. In the yard, surrounded by a white picket fence, there were fruit trees. His law practice, business, and civic duties kept him busy but he was still a loving father. He had great hopes for Edward, who was a big, healthy boy but somewhat contrary. In a letter to his father, Judge Bacon wrote with parental pride and frustration: "...he requires looking after, for he is mischievous, disorderly, and unmanageable."[6]

When Sophie took Edward to Howlett Hill, Bacon was worried about her parents' ability to regulate his child and wrote to her:

> Life with grandparents is apt to be unfavorable to the discipline of children. Bear in mind that Edward is wild, ungovernable. I fear his young uncles may not control him in their rambles and that he may fall from fences, trees, into the canal or Lake.[7]

It is telling that he used words like "discipline," "ungovernable," and "control" within that one paragraph. Judge Bacon needed obedience and was not getting it from his son. His daughter was much more of a comfort to him.

Elizabeth Clift Bacon was born on April 8, 1842. Named after Bacon's mother, she would always be called Libbie. She was a beautiful child with chestnut brown hair and blue-gray eyes. Between the ages of ten and twenty, her parents had her sit for at least nine portraits—eight of them were photographs made in the town's "Daguerrean Room" and one painted by a local artist.

The Bacons would have more than their share of tragedy. Their third child, Sophia, died in infancy. When Edward was seven, his father's fears were realized when he crashed through a wooden step at the back door, seriously injuring his spine. A nurse was hired, and Edward was a year in recovering. During an outing in a wheelchair, the thoughtless woman took him to a neighborhood stricken with contagion and into the house of a recent victim.[8] Edward died of cholera or diphtheria on April 11, 1848. That same year, Sophia gave birth to Harriet, who died at six months. Libbie was now the sole focus of her parents who were understandably overprotective with their only surviving child.

Raising Libbie

Libbie's childhood was much the same as that of any middle class girl in young, urban America. Her parents taught her obedience, truthfulness, and respect for God, family, and country.[9] She played with dolls and learned to sew clothes for them, hosted her little friends for tea parties or in play sessions, enjoyed supervised outings, and went to church. From her mother (whose health had been delicate since Harriet's birth), Libbie learned charity toward the unfortunate, the love of fashionable clothes, and the essentials of keeping a journal. Throughout her girlhood, she was an avid reader and devoured *David Copperfield*, *Pickwick Papers*, and the chivalric romances of Sir Walter Scott.

Libbie was never a problem child but after a certain threshold of girlish misbehavior, she would be locked in a bedroom closet as punishment. Rather than crying or fighting (or contemplating her bad behavior), Libbie happily discovered she could nap in the clothesbasket. After learning their punishment was actually counterproductive, her parents locked her in her room while the sun was shining and her friends were playing. Again, Libbie found these punishments to be great opportunity for catnaps—but now in her bed. After she married Armstrong, her knack of being able to nap as needed was one of the traits that allowed her to thrive gracefully with the cavalry in the much less comfortable conditions of the frontier.

When Libbie was about eight, she was enrolled in the Young Ladies Seminary and Collegiate Institute in Monroe. It offered not only the equivalent of a four-year college education for older girls, but elementary schooling for younger ones. The director and principal was the Rev. Erasmus J. Boyd, a widely regarded educator whose personal influence was such that the school became known as Boyd's Seminary. It attracted boarding students from other states and during its inaugural term there were 112 enrolled students.[10] Libbie would have a broad and liberal education. Bible instruction happened after each Sunday service, and from the seminary, English, French, literature, history, arithmetic, domestic arts, drawing, and penmanship. She had music and singing lessons—although she was an indifferent pianist despite the birthday gift of an upright piano.

On Libbie's ninth birthday, her father gave her a diary to record daily events, but confusingly said that she might not be good enough at writing and postponing entries for a while would be best. A year later on her tenth birthday, Libbie dutifully took up her journalistic pen. With only the occasional inkblot, she began to record her life—school, illnesses, smallpox vaccination, weather, visitors, births and deaths, presents, and the doings of her parents. Sophie took an interest and with no secrets between mother and daughter, she would suggest grammatical corrections or dictate a particular entry. Here and there Libbie would make a doodle and sometimes only note, "Nothing of special interest has transpired today" or "I have spent the day about as usual."[11] Libbie showed a flair for writing and recorded news from the telegraph and community, including the arrival of P.T. Barnum's Menagerie and Museum show featuring General Tom Thumb (which she was not allowed to attend), a local suicide, and a steamboat collision. She could be witty and once described a teacher's lecture on the human skeleton, saying that the anatomical manikin was a "womankin!"[12]

Libbie's girlhood was almost entirely uncontaminated by pets. The one brief exception was a cat—for which there was no real affection. Whether feral or pet, cats were a necessity to protect pantry and kitchen stores from mice and rats. Apparently, the Bacons had such a cat as Libbie noted on April 19, 1852, "we have had an addition to our family—six kittens and one which died." Her tone in the three entries about the cat is purely factual and she never names it. When Sophie was to go away on an extended visit home in May, Judge Bacon arranged for Libbie to board at the seminary, closed their house, and rented a room for himself. All Libbie had to say about the cat and kittens, was that they were "carried away."[13]

Libbie's only girlhood mention of dogs occurred that same month when she wrote that "three mad dogs" had been roaming around town for several days and that her friends playing on her swing had left early in fear of them.[14] Hydrophobia (rabies) was untreatable, and death was a horrible combination of respiratory failure, dehydration, and paralysis, so the girls had good reason to be afraid. (In New York City, policemen were authorized to shoot "mad" dogs on sight.)

Another Sorrow

When Libbie was twelve years old, her mother died and was buried next to Edward, Sophia, and Harriet under the family's stone pillar in Woodland Cemetery. Libbie's diary had been neglected for five months, but two weeks after her mother's death on August 12th, she poured her anguish onto its pages. She wrote of how her mother died looking at her portrait (apparently Libbie was not allowed in the sick room), about the black coffin with screw fasteners on the lid, and how she was now her father's only comfort. In the midst of the passage, she noted factually that her mother was the second person in town to die of bloody dysentery.[15] Husbands and children were expected to formally mourn for at least twelve months. Mourning clothes were somber with veils for women and black armbands for men. Social activities were reduced and letters written on black-bordered stationary. Certain Libbie would find consolation among his wife's family (and not disposed to try housekeeping for himself and his daughter), Judge

Bacon sent Libbie with Sophie's sister, Harriet, back to Grand Rapids and then on to Howlett Hill. Their house was closed up and Bacon moved into the Exchange Hotel. Libbie's last diary entry about her mother's death was, "Our pleasant home is to be broken up. But I must try and bear up under my great trial." Two years later she would append, "Nor is my grief elayed [sic] now, in the year 1856."[16]

The aunts and cousins at Howlett Hill welcomed Libbie and it was a good place for recovery. Her relatives often remarked, "Libbie Bacon has no mother!" or "Poor motherless Libbie Bacon" and made many allowances for her. Libbie was quick to capitalize on this sympathy and admitted years later making shameless use of it to avoid anything she did not want to do.[17] At summer's end, Boyd's Seminary became Libbie's home. She shared a room and parlor with Miss Thompson, one of the teachers, and was allowed a modest garden plot for flowers. While she sorely missed Sophie, her cooking and homey traditions, Libbie was ever adaptable. The atmosphere of learning and feminine comradery was one that she enjoyed and appreciated. Her father visited regularly but on the first Christmas day without Sophie, he did not stay long and Libbie had Christmas dinner with her classmates. At the end of term, she would return to Howlett Hill and often spent her summers there. In the fall of 1858, her 16th year, Judge Bacon arranged admission for Libbie at the Auburn Young Ladies Institute in New York—a select school whose focus was religion and culture, with enrollment limited to twenty-five girls.

Boarding School and a New Mother

That same year, Judge Bacon was persuaded by a friend that it was time to remarry. The idea of a second marriage had been considered as disloyal to Sophie, but after being introduced to an eligible widow in Tecumseh—and doubtless desiring a return to domesticity with Libbie—the sixty-year-old Judge Bacon changed his mind. Rhoda Wells Pitts was the childless widow of the Rev. Samuel Pitts who had died of consumption in 1855. Originally from New Bedford, Massachusetts, Rhoda at forty-nine was smart, practical, financially comfortable, charitable, an industrious housekeeper, and good looking. She was perfect for Bacon, and so a long distance courtship began between Monroe and Tecumseh.

Preparing for the wedding in February 1859, Bacon moved the tenants out of his house and had some repairs done. Until the work could be finished that summer, the newlyweds boarded and Libbie continued to live at the Young Ladies Institute or at Howlett Hill—where she had a thoroughly good time at neighborly parties with food, dancing, and sing-songs. Her uncle allowed Libbie and the children to milk a placid cow, and Judge Bacon had a pony sent from Monroe so that Libbie and her cousins could learn to ride sidesaddle. Even though she knew the house repairs were costly, Libbie ordered two new dresses and sent the bill to her father. She explained this by saying that a higher standard of dress was required in Howlett Hill. Much as he had tried to regulate Edward, Bacon feared that Libbie's comparatively loose leash with "those unrestrained aunts" would not prepare her for "a little control" in his new household and hoped Libbie and Rhoda would become as sisters.[18]

Despite the adjustment difficulties one might expect between a stepmother and her new daughter, Rhoda and Libbie liked each other almost instantly and became very close. She was a good cook and Libbie would fondly remember Sunday dinners with "those juicy steaks, smoking muffins, and all the delicacies my Mother knows so well to prepare…." The attachment between the two was evident when Libbie told her cousin, Rebecca Richmond, "Mother and I laugh and grow fat."[19]

Judge Bacon enjoyed the domesticity and laughter in the house. He set out a small vegetable garden, built a grape arbor and patio, tended to two cows and two pigs, and hired a man to cut firewood.[20] His office (and central Monroe) was only a short walk so he did not keep a horse. Libbie returned to Boyd's Seminary that fall but she developed a worrisome illness. Fearing that it might be consumption or a prelude to it, the doctor could only prescribe bed rest and nourishing meals as a cure. Libbie would miss many months of her schooling. In the fall of 1860, she was back at the seminary, but as she had been absent for nearly a year, graduation would have to be put off—a delay which she resolutely accepted. For older girls, literature was an important topic and Shakespeare's plays were a mainstay. They were taught composition, drawing, philology, history, "Moral Science," chemistry, and anatomy. Prof. Kellogg was an unusual woman in those times to be able to teach chemical experiments and human anatomy. Libbie noted she had a child's skeleton and an anatomical manikin—which frightened a younger classmate into crying.[21]

That fall, Libbie became close friends with Nettie (Mary Annette) Humphrey, the only daughter of General Levi S. Humphrey, Bacon's old friend and mercantile partner from the early days of Monroe who had returned to build a hotel. Nettie was two years older than Libbie and they got on famously. The older girl loved gentle intrigue and would later play an important role in Libbie's courtship.

Southern Secession and Courting

Libbie had always been a lovely girl and by the time she was fourteen, she was a beauty with pale complexion, an enigmatic smile, sparkling gray eyes, and a vivacious personality. Already attracting male attention, she learned to gracefully rebuff greeting kisses from married men. By eighteen, she had reached her full height of 5'4" and was considered one of the prettiest girls in Monroe. She was now allowed modest activities outside of home, church, and school. Escorted by her father or a respectable young man to evening lectures or concerts, she and her girlfriends also attended the Literary Society meetings, where poems and essays were read. Libbie had occasional sleep-overs at her friends' homes and there were carefully chaperoned parties with boys. The family attended a special "New England" supper at Humphrey's hotel and afterwards strolled to City Hall for a Literary Society reading. Libbie noted in her diary that there was music and dancing after the papers were read but *"of course* we went home."[22] At another hotel social event, Libbie was asked to dance and though enjoying herself, she retreated upstairs to sit with the women because she knew her father wouldn't approve. Afterwards, she and Nettie entertained each other by play acting and recitations.[23]

At the end of December 1860, South Carolina had formally seceded from the Union, capping off a long feud with the government which began with the state's avowed right to dispute federal tariffs and expanded to their right to hold slaves. The president-elect was Abraham Lincoln, known to oppose slavery in any new states admitted to the Union, and it was feared other states would follow South Carolina. At New Year's Day gatherings of Monroe's families and neighbors, there was worried talk about federal intervention in South Carolina and even the possibility of a "Civil War." By the first week in February, six states had joined South Carolina: Mississippi, Florida, Alabama, Georgia, Louisiana, and Texas.

Four days after Libbie's nineteenth birthday on April 8th, the Confederate States of America opened fire on Fort Sumter from Charleston's shore batteries, and after a lengthy bombardment, the commandant surrendered. On April 15th, President Lincoln called for an army of three-month volunteers from loyal states to reinforce the Federal Army against the Rebellion. Not willing to send troops against their neighboring states, Virginia, Arkansas, North Carolina, and Tennessee joined the Confederacy—which also claimed parts of the southwest. That left twenty-one states and large areas of the western territories who were loyal to the Union.

Monroe was in a state of patriotic fever as men enlisted and prepared for shipping out. Flags flew everywhere and the women formed a Society for Knitting and energetically produced socks and underclothing for the soldiers, as well as linen havelocks to protect their necks from the sun.[24] (See this chapter's *Tail Piece*.) Uniforms were all the rage and civilian *beaux* paled in comparison to their dashing competition. Libbie was selfishly glad that her father was too old. Otherwise with his patriotic fervor, he would have enlisted to fight for the Union. After she returned from her summer holiday, Michigan already had several volunteer regiments and the 7th Infantry was encamped at the fairgrounds and its adjutant was Libbie's friend. Invited to the Officers' Grand Military Dress Parade, Judge Bacon (who well knew of the allure of young officers) would not let her go—but apparently she did get to see the soldiers drilling and on parade.[25] The eligible gentlemen of Monroe were becoming scarcer and those remaining men all seemed to be too forward or licentious. Libbie became quite skilled in artfully declining invitations for dubious outings and dodging physical and verbal overtures. She was

A tintype of twenty-year-old Elizabeth "Libbie" Bacon in 1862—the year she graduated from school and met 2nd Lt. George Armstrong Custer. The photographer painted a delicate blush of pink on her cheek. Courtesy of the National Park Service, Little Bighorn Battlefield National Monument, LIBI_00295_010703.

genuinely sweet and quite popular with both women and men. There was plenty of male interest, but Libbie remained flirtatious and non-committal with her *beaux*.

Libbie did have one persistent suitor, Mr. Dutton, whom she liked and thought she might be able to learn to love—but she felt no spark for him. Judge Bacon approved of sedate horseback rides with Mr. Dutton. And while he was gallant, attentive, and probably good husband material, she considered him to be vaporish and uninteresting—and oddly remarked that his hands were rather small for a man. Like most girls, Libbie dreamed of romance but understood the value of a pragmatic marriage where love could grow. As she was finishing school, this dilemma occupied much of her thoughts for she wanted to be certain she was in love. In January 1862, Libbie had hopes of being valedictorian for the commencement but knew she had to keep up her "school-digging" for that to happen. In a diary entry about Dutton as a potential husband, she resolved, "I must go and study and not think so much of males."[26] A week after her twentieth birthday, she declined his offer of a deeper relationship.

A Memorable Party

Libbie's "brain work" paid off, for in June, she had the highest grades and earned valedictorian. For commencement, the eleven graduates were required to wear white and Rhoda made Libbie's a dress of muslin. With her father's clear and steady elocution as a model, Libbie read an original composition, "Crumbs," at the lectern. The *Detroit Free Press* reprinted it, praising her writing style, sensibility, and good humor.[27] There must have been a great deal of speech-making, remarks, prayers, and hymns in the stately ceremony, for it lasted nearly five hours. In the large crowd were many of Sophie Bacon's friends, and from Grand Rapids, cousins Rebecca and Mary Richmond, and grandfather Abel Page. Judge Bacon and Rhoda were greatly moved at Libbie's achievement, and thinking about Sophie, he wrote to Mrs. Richmond, "Thankful I am that I have been able to give Elizabeth an education, knowing what would have been the wishes of her mother."[28]

Libbie could once think again about men and suitable matrimony. As her biographer Marguerite Merington so aptly put it, "Her main preoccupation from that time onward would be to find a husband—or, more modestly, to be found by a husband acceptable to herself and family."[29] That summer for Libbie was one of fun and suitors—and free from a looming return to school. Rebecca and Mary stayed in Monroe for three weeks and while girlish merriment ruled, her father forbade boat rides, fast horses and fast young men. As patriotic as Judge Bacon was, he did not believe that a soldier could be a suitable son-in-law. They might be maimed or killed in battle, certainly never became wealthy in the Army, and were believed to be prone to gambling, drinking, and rakish behavior. Pragmatically, he encouraged Libbie to consider only civilian suitors—and she tended to agree with him. That September, she was first bridesmaid at the marriage of her friends Mary Landon and Joe Dansard. It was customary for the wedding party to travel with the couple for part of the honeymoon and Libbie went with the Dansards to Trenton before going on to Grand Rapids to visit the Richmonds.

As it happened, two regiments of Michigan Volunteers were bivouacked nearby. Libbie was introduced to several officers and among them, Capt. Drew, with his big mustache, caught her eye. Unlike some of his fellows, he was serious and not given to flattery. Despite her father's admonition, Libbie was attracted to the dashing Capt. Drew and had changed her opinion of soldiers: "he is something—my style of man."[30]

Libbie was back with her parents in November and was invited to what would be a life-changing event—a Thanksgiving party at the seminary hosted by the Rev. Boyd and his wife. The young ladies wore colorful evening dresses but Libbie chose a plain brown dress with lace trim. Attending were men from nearby cities, but in particular, one Mr. Henry Munson Utley of Detroit was there. Utley had a university degree and worked for the *Detroit Free Press*. It was he who had "Crumbs" reprinted in the newspaper. Libbie noticed with pleasure that his gaze followed her as she moved around the room. Unassuming and a trifle shy, Utley was introduced to Libbie, who was impressed by his academic background and his being a writer who admired her writing. There was a spark in that tinder until a minister came over to talk to Utley. Libbie politely excused herself and while walking across the room, spoke to her friend, Conway Noble, but became annoyed with him over some triviality. Noble tried to lighten her mood: "Shall I introduce Captain Custer?" Libbie agreed only to escape Conway.[31] (Henry Utley, 1836–1917, would have been an interesting match for Libbie, the scholar. He earned a master's degree, wrote for Detroit newspapers, authored three books, and was city librarian and president of the American Library Association.[32])

Captain George Armstrong Custer, late of General McClellan's staff, was another bashful young man who had been admiring Libbie. He was taller than average, slender but solid. He had blue, bedroom eyes, a very fair complexion which freckled in the sun, and curly reddish-blonde hair, anointed with cinnamon oil and worn long to his collar. Fashionable mutton-chop whiskers and mustache completed the picture. He wore a blue uniform with brass buttons and gold embroidered shoulder straps, white collar and neck tie, crimson sash, and dress sword. Very dashing in his uniform, Armstrong might have been the only man there who had seen combat.

After Conway made the introduction, there was an awkward pause—but Libbie was socially adroit and knew not to let a conversation falter—particularly with a man. Her standard conversational jump-start was to ask, "And what do you *really* think of Higher Education for Women?"[33] However, for an officer, a question about the war or his advancement was a reliable starter.

"I believe your promotion has been very rapid?"
"I have been very fortunate."[34]

And that was all they said to each other that night. While he was smitten with her, Libbie was not impressed with him—although having strong family ties to Monroe, the captain's promotions and war exploits would have been noted in the newspaper. Likewise, Libbie was a popular young woman, so the two were doubtless aware of each other before they were formally introduced at the party. Curiously, she said little else in her diary for that day except having met Capt. Custer. Biographer Lawrence Frost would note that six lines of her writing below that entry were later torn out.[35]

Tail Piece: The Havelock-Hollywood-Custer Connection

The havelocks thought to be needed by Civil War soldiers were lightweight "curtains" suspended from the cap to protect the neck from the sun. Named after Sir Henry Havelock, KCB, who popularized them in the tropical heat of the Indian Mutiny of 1857, they are most famously associated with the French Foreign Legion in North Africa but were first adopted during the ill-fated Maximillian Affair in Mexico (1861–1867).

Despite the patriotic labor of American women, havelocks were impractical in wet weather, useless in the cold, and not at all popular with American troops. George Armstrong Custer did not wear them, but in the film *Fort Apache* (1948), the Custer-like martinet, Lt. Col. Owen Thursday (Henry Fonda), wears a havelock with his kepi. After Thursday dies in a "last stand" massacre, Capt. Kirby York (John Wayne) becomes commander, adopting the havelock as a symbol of his leadership and regimental tradition.

Chapter 2

That Custer Boy

"Her sons talked dog to her...."—Libbie Custer[1]

If Libbie Bacon's upbringing as an upper middle-class, only child was measured and respectable, then George Armstrong Custer's was the polar opposite. Armstrong, as his family called him, was the son of a blacksmith turned farmer, and one of several siblings in a raucous, doggy household where pranks and scuffles were commonplace. There was minimal schooling, authority was always questioned, and there was no fixed ambition for the boys other than helping their father with the farm, securing a job or buying their own farm, and flirting with girls. The Bacons were Presbyterian and the Custers were Methodist—a difference which mattered a great deal in small communities. The gulf between the two families was even greater because Judge Bacon was a soft-spoken but firm member of the Republican Party which opposed slavery, while Emanuel Custer was an equally staunch Jacksonian Democrat who did not own slaves, but believed a man had a right to own them if he so chose. Emanuel was well known for loudly declaiming his political views at the slightest provocation. The differences between the Capulets and Montagues paled in comparison.

The Extended Custer Clan

The Pennsylvania/Maryland/Ohio Custers were descended from Paulus Van Haren Küster, who immigrated from northwestern Germany to Germantown outside Philadelphia in the late 17th century.[2] Emanuel Henry Custer was born in 1806 in Cresaptown, Maryland, near the border of Pennsylvania and would migrate to the rural community of New Rumley, a little over 100 miles south of Cleveland, Ohio. Emanuel's uncle, Jacob Custer, blacksmith and founder of the hamlet in August 1813, persuaded his nephew to join him in his prospering smithy in 1825.[3]

Emanuel Custer and his first wife, Mathilda P. Veirs, had three children, Hannah (who died in infancy), Brice William, and John A. In 1835, seven years after their wedding, Mathilda died. Within a year, Emanuel married the recent widow Maria Kirkpatrick (née Ward), whose husband had died within a few months of Mathilda's passing. (Mathilda and Maria may have each had another child who died in infancy.)

It was a tiny community, and mutual bereavement, necessity, and proximity initially brought the two single parents together, but a genuine and lasting love bloomed for them. Maria had three children from her previous marriage, David, Lydia Ann, and John, and as she had the larger house, Emanuel and his children moved in.[4] He was highly regarded in the township and elected as their Justice of the Peace and appointed as a trustee for the New Rumley Methodist Society.[5] Despite his stern looks (his long chin beard increasing that effect), Emanuel was a loving husband and father.

In 1836, the year they were married, John A. died at the age of three. They had other children but suffered more infant tragedies. Maria and Emanuel had seven of their own, but the first two died in infancy, leaving George Armstrong as the eldest (born December 5, 1839), followed by Nevin Johnson in 1842, Thomas Ward in 1845, Boston in 1848, and their last child, Margaret Emma, born in 1852 when Maria was forty-four.[6] Armstrong had fair skin and curly blonde hair, and as a toddler could only pronounce his name as "Autie." After he grew up, his family and friends called him Armstrong—although to Libbie he was always "Autie."

With brothers and sisters from three marriages between two mothers and two fathers, Armstrong would say that he often had to calculate how the kinship worked for a particular sibling. The entire family considered everyone on equal footing—"Outsiders knew no difference between full or half brothers and sisters, and they themselves almost resented the question."[7] Armstrong and Tom were especially protective of Nevin, a weakly child. Tom was as boisterous and as fun loving as Armstrong and the two were very close. Boston, the youngest boy, idolized them both.

In the spring of 1849, Emanuel traded his smithy for an eighty-acre farm a few miles to the northeast.[8] The house was more rustic than their town home and the land was not the best for farming, but with hard work, they sustained themselves. It was a rollicking, laughing household where noisy wrestling matches, chases, and scuffles frequently ended inside the house—often with consequences to the furniture. Pranks and booby traps were constant and only their mother was safe from them. Emanuel was often the victim of his boys' tricks and he gave back as good as he got with no hard feelings. The irrepressible and impulsive Armstrong loved practical jokes—and if they were cleverly played on him, then so much the better.

Never having a lot of money, somehow Emanuel and Maria always managed the essentials for the children—food, clothing, basic schooling, and a nurturing home. The children slept in a communal bed in the loft. It was tightly packed and warm, but edge sleepers were in peril of being inadvertently pushed out and having to struggle back in or invoke parental intervention as little Tom once did after being ejected, moaning plaintively, "Where am I to sleep?"[9]

Maria Custer suffered from delicate health and settled on Armstrong as her favorite child and in turn, he was devoted to her. What she lacked in means was compensated for with acts of kindness—happily sewing and cooking for her children. Books were bought occasionally at the expense of other luxuries, and Armstrong read these voraciously. The Custer children learned honesty, self-reliance, and the value of work and temperate habits. When Armstrong was a grown man, he thanked his parents in writing for being taught these virtues.[10]

Always Talking About Dogs

The Custers were practicing Methodists, and education was a family value. Debate was encouraged despite Emanuel's quick and immovable opinions on any topic. The boys learned that superior numbers, fast talking, and tactics could drown out his dinner table pontifications—and he never seemed to mind being outnumbered. The healthy give and take imbued the Custer boys with confidence and a sense of self-worth. Maria's sympathy was generally with Armstrong and her boys. As one of the eldest, Armstrong frequently challenged his father's views (sometimes just to be contrary), but always sided with him when it came to canines. Maria tried to control the number of dogs brought home by pleading for a higher doggy standard and pointing out that the incoming curs had "no pedigree."[11] (Emanuel was as almost as guilty in this as the boys.) Such a position was futile against the patriarch and their dog-loving sons. The merits of scent hounds, bird dogs, bull dogs, and mongrels were such common conversational topics between the boys and Maria that Libbie would write, "Her sons talked dog to her so much that one would be very apt to be educated up to the demand for an authenticated grandfather"[12]—meaning she could recount three-generation pedigrees. The number of "Rovers" and "Towsers" never declined, but Libbie hinted that Mother Custer was able to choose a better bred dog of her own in later years.[13] Despite affection for his own dogs, Armstrong could be boyishly mean to someone else's. While at West Point, more than once he tied a tin pan to the tail of a professor's dog.[14]

All the Custer boys learned to ride bareback even when "their little fat legs were too short to describe a curve on the animal's side."[15] From the time Armstrong could wear britches, he was at ease with horses and could even stand on a horse's back as it trotted around the paddock.[16] Libbie remembered that Emanuel was a strong rider—like a centaur in the saddle and in his younger days he had "ridden after the hounds" (fox hunting) in Maryland and Virginia.[17] When his sons were old enough, he took them on coon and possum hunts—which required at least one trail hound to follow the scent and tree the quarry. Armstrong would say he had hunted fox in Ohio and deer and turkey in Michigan but never specified as to whether these hunts were in his youth or when he was on leave from the Army.[18]

Education in Monroe

Six years of schooling was sufficient to teach reading, writing, and simple arithmetic, and education was finished by the age of twelve for rural children. Armstrong was an indifferent student when the subject did not interest him. He figured out how to skate through by producing what the teacher wanted with minimal effort. Rather than see his son become a hardscrabble farmer, Emanuel and Maria thought he might be suited to one of the "learned professions."[19] His brothers were bigger and better able to help their father, so Armstrong could be spared from farm work. Emanuel heard good reports from his daughter and son-in-law about post-primary education in Monroe. Besides Libbie Bacon's progressive school, the Boyd Seminary, there was the highly commended Boys and Young Men's Academy, where principal Alfred Stebbins prepared his pupils for college.

In 1846, Armstrong's half-sister, Lydia Ann Kirkpatrick, had married farmer David Reed, and moved from New Rumley some two hundred miles northwest to his home in Monroe, Michigan. Lydia gave birth to her first child, Marie, in 1848, but was still sorely missing her family. In 1852, when Armstrong finished school, Emanuel and Maria sent him to the Stebbins Academy where he could keep Lydia company (at least until she had more children). Always excited by novelty, the thirteen-year-old Armstrong was entirely agreeable to the arrangement, so he packed his bag and rode with his father to Monroe. The Reed home would become a happy extension of his family and Armstrong would always be close to Lydia. She had two more daughters, Lilla Belle in 1854 and Emma in 1856. Her fourth child, Harry Armstrong, was born in 1858 and named after his doting uncle. "Autie" Reed would eventually die with his four uncles, Armstrong, Tom, Boston, and James Calhoun at Little Bighorn.

Despite the Stebbins Academy's higher standard of education, Armstrong was still able to game the system by doing a quick review of the material before delivering an in-class performance—which gave the impression of competence. Armstrong's knack for quick study when motivated would serve him well at West Point and as a commander during the Civil War. At the time of Armstrong's enrollment, the United States had recently won the Mexican War (1846–1848), and General Winfield Scott was the lion of the day. Schoolboys were infected with military fervor and, too young to enlist, devoured accounts in newspapers or read books with military history. Armstrong's schoolmates admired his ability to hoodwink the schoolmaster by reading novels hidden behind an open textbook or under the desk lid—and get away with it a fair amount of the time. One of his favorite authors was an Irishman, Charles Lever, who wrote picaresque military novels such as *Charles O'Malley, the Irish Dragoon*, *Jack Hinton*, and *The Guardsman*. In *Charles O'Malley*, the hero joins the dashing 14th Light Dragoons to fight in the Peninsula Wars while carousing, drinking, and even fox hunting—possibly not an altogether unfair depiction of a British officer's regimental life at that time and one which certainly appealed to Armstrong and his fellows. (*Charles O'Malley, the Irish Dragoon* was published serially in *Dublin University Magazine* a year before its appearance in 1841 as the two-volume novel which Armstrong read.)

Armstrong was a natural athlete who did well in competitive sports—although he disliked swimming and rowing. With natural charisma, his classmates considered him the leader in fun and hijinks. The dormitory room he shared with his chum, Edward Merrill, was a staging area for students sneaking out after hours.[20] Armstrong was breezing through his classes and began thinking about a job. He knew teachers had steady work (and some prestige) and probably figured that teaching classes would be as easy as taking them. In Ohio, a prospective schoolteacher only needed basic education and a certificate of passing a knowledge test. Armstrong ramped up for the examination by taking extra courses and received his certificate on March 28, 1856.[21] As a teacher, he earned a handsome wage of $25 a month plus his board.[22] Armstrong was proud to take his earnings home to his mother as a gesture of thanks for all that his parents had done to give him an advanced education.

A Fork in the Path

It is no surprise that his students delighted in the fun-loving Mr. Custer. One of his pupils remembered that "He liked music, playing the accordion himself, and was socially inclined ... he was so jovial and full of life that everyone enjoyed themselves."[23] Teachers were unofficially part of a town's leadership structure, and their schoolrooms were often used for public meetings. While Armstrong liked his new status in the community and being the center of attention in his classroom, for him teaching was somewhat drab and tedious. During the summer months, when students were home for the harvest work, there was no pay, so he took a job making furniture. Teaching, however fun it might be, was not going to fulfill his ambitions.

Armstrong began to think about the Army. An officer's pay was steady and better than that of a teacher, but admittance to the U.S. Military Academy at West Point needed the endorsement of a Congressman—who usually favored the sons of fellow party members. The Honorable John Bingham (Republican) was the man to persuade, and that was not going to be easy for the son of a clamorous Democrat. Armstrong's father and half-brother David supported him, but Maria had to be persuaded it was a good career move for her favorite son. (Congressman John Armor Bingham, 1815–1900, would be the special judge advocate in the trial of the Lincoln assassination plotters.)

In May 1856, Armstrong began writing to Bingham asking for advice on securing admission to West Point. He was determined to serve his country as an officer and acknowledged he was a Democrat, but believed Bingham would appoint deserving candidates *regardless* of their politics. Always the strategist, Armstrong thought if West Point would not have him, he would "work my way through one of the great Eastern colleges, and qualify myself as a teacher, educator." Bingham recalled in his memoirs that he was impressed by the frankness and originality of the young man's letter and eventually agreed to be Armstrong's sponsor.[24] Congressmen could only nominate one name per year and Bingham already had a young man ahead of Armstrong.

Armstrong's sincerity and Bingham's interest aside, historian Shirley Leckie suggests it is also possible that a Republican friend of Emanuel may have advanced Armstrong's case to Bingham, and also that his appointment may have actually come about because of an awkward romance. While seventeen-year-old Armstrong was teaching, he boarded with Alexander Holland and became enamored of his daughter, Mary Jane "Mollie," who welcomed the attentions of the handsome schoolteacher, two years her junior. They exchanged daguerreotype portraits—and in Armstrong's, he posed with Mollie's photograph.[25] Holland disapproved of him as a suitor for he attended rowdy Democrat meetings, drank liquor, and wasn't a good social match for Mollie. After Armstrong's note asking her to meet "at the trundle bed" was discovered by Holland, it was apparent that they had been doing rather more than just talking. Armstrong was summarily booted out of the house. Undaunted, he persisted and even arranged to meet Mollie secretly at the home of a complicit neighbor. Worried that a hasty marriage might become necessary, Holland seems to have asked Bingham to support Armstrong's West Point application—but probably said nothing about separating the two lovers.[26]

Armstrong continued writing to Bingham, met him at least once, and even went to Republican rallies to further his case. Bingham was persuaded and wrote to the admissions office at West Point about Armstrong. In February 1857, Bingham confirmed Armstrong's appointment and instructed him to report to West Point in June for his entrance examination. Knowing that mathematical proficiency was required at West Point and it was not his best subject, Armstrong crammed in a few math courses. Of the 108 boys who took the entrance examination in 1857, only sixty-eight passed and could take the second test. This was a six-month evaluation of the candidates in military encampment and the classroom.[27] Armstrong passed this as well and could now expect to graduate with the Class of 1862. He left his family and dogs behind and took up the life of a cadet.

A Bedeviled Life

Officially the United States Military Academy, West Point is located fifty miles north of New York City on a high bluff overlooking the Hudson River. It had been an artillery fort during the Revolutionary War, and its strategic location prevented British ships from sailing upriver as they had to slow down to negotiate the dogleg bend. After the war, it became a training center for artillery and engineering, and it was a natural location for the nation's Military Academy. In 1802, the campus welcomed its first class of cadets. Rich in tradition, West Point was (and still is) an imposing collection of stone and brick buildings which house the same facilities a university would have—classrooms, library, dormitories, mess and assembly halls, ballroom, infirmary, chapel, administrative offices, housing for faculty, and athletic fields. However, unlike at a university, there is weaponry, a massive parade ground known as "The Plain," and military graves and memorials. It is a place of tradition, duty, and order.

From arrival through graduation, cadets jumped to the drum roll which signaled each activity of their day. Everything was to be done double-time in immaculate uniforms and gleaming brass buttons. The rigorous, five-year program was designed to create a cadre of junior officers skilled in leadership, tactics, weaponry (musket, saber, and artillery), horsemanship,

Cadet George Armstrong Custer doubtless borrowed the civilian pocket pistol from the photographer's martial props for this photograph, circa 1860. National Portrait Gallery, Smithsonian Institution, NPG.81.138.

and engineering. The military arts and science were grounded on a liberal arts foundation of the classics, philosophy, ethics, English, French, Spanish, military history, mathematics, chemistry, geology, drawing (useful for mapmaking), and even dancing to ensure the cadets were socially skilled gentlemen at the regular dances or "hops." Sunday was the only respite from the twice-daily routine of precision drilling.

The new cadet was issued a musket and sword, but used his government allowance to purchase clothes, textbooks and writing materials. The distinctive uniform consisted of a black shako with brass badge, a gray tunic with tails and rows of brass buttons, trousers (gray wool for winter and white cotton for summer), white leather shoulder belts, gray overcoat, black shoes, and shirt with collar and black stock. To properly keep all this in good repair, a cadet also purchased a clothes brush, sewing materials, boot blacking, whitening compound, and brass polish. The only time he could be out of uniform was in his quarters after hours. During the summer, they hauled their gear down to The Plain and camped for three months. Demerits or "skins" were given for unsoldierly behavior, which ranged from being untidy to neglect of duty. Dirty shoes or being unshaven were worth one demerit while being absent from any duty could earn five. Accumulating 200 demerits in one academic year (or 100 in six months) could get the cadet bounced out. Upperclassmen hazed their juniors—waking them at night, messing up rooms, giving them menial errands, or even making them polish their equipment. Armstrong's first biographer, Frederick Whittaker, quoted a poem about the harassment of unfortunate plebes and one pun summed it up succinctly: "But soon you share the fate of the ham—that is, you're nicely 'deviled.'"[28]

Cadets were forbidden to have pets and none of Armstrong's classmates say he kept dogs, but an unsubstantiated rumor in a 1959 magazine article declared he brought three hounds to West Point—but had to find a farmer to keep them nearby.[29] Perhaps coincidentally, in the 1941 film *They Died with Their Boots On*, Armstrong is erroneously depicted as entering at West Point for the first time with his pack of foxhounds. (There was a cadre of dogs belonging to the staff and almost three years after he graduated, Libbie wrote about their visit to the Academy, "Everyone was delighted to see Autie. Even the dogs welcomed him."[30]) Presumably the professor's dog which Armstrong had bedeviled with tin pans was not one of those. (See this chapter's *Tail Piece* for a rare image purporting to show Cadet Custer with a dog.)

Armstrong wanted to graduate but not without with his fair share of *Charles O'Malley* amusement. As he had gamed the schools in New Rumley and Monroe, Armstrong quickly began to test the military system. Well liked by his fellows (his closest friends were Southerners) Armstrong was nicknamed, "Fanny" because of his girlish, blonde curls. One of his friends thought him a thoroughly decent person but probably "too clever for his own good."[31] Armstrong soon became the lord of mischief, and fun came first, second, and third. Closely watched by wary instructors, his exploits were admired and abetted by his fellow cadets. He skillfully played The Demerit Game—always keeping his accumulated black marks just under the expulsion threshold until they were erased for the next six months. Some demerits could be expunged with "punishment tours"—marching guard duty with a musket for tedious hours in all weather. Armstrong spent a fair amount of time drilling off minor infractions that way for sixty-six Saturdays—nearly a third of all of his Saturdays at West Point.[32] He once earned fifteen skins in one day, but to be fair, most of these in four years were the result of absent-mindedness, carelessness, or boyish hijinks.

Armstrong was frequently late to and absent from muster calls, meals, inspection, duty, classes, drill, and more. He got demerits for being poorly groomed or out of uniform, having a dirty musket or a sloppy room, trifling, talking, smoking, stealing food and cooking in his room, sneaking out at night, and using the wrong horse at cavalry drill. He once showed up enthusiastically for riding class while on sick report, and it cost him three skins. While the demerit system may sound like a draconian camp for musket-carrying Boy Scouts, the U.S. Military Academy was trying to produce officers worthy of rank and respect. Armstrong's class standing was far below average yet he did pass his classes, and always stayed under the limit of 200 demerits per year. (In *Cadet George Armstrong Custer: Demerits & Academics*, Tom O'Neil cataloged the collection of transgressions from Armstrong's official West Point records.[33])

When he wasn't sneaking out for night carousals, Armstrong read adventure novels from the library and developed a lifelong habit of staying up late to write long letters. To his parents and half sister, Lydia-Ann Reed, he wrote about life at the Academy, his comrades, and his concern about the looming threat of war. He continued to write Mollie and in November 1858, boldly asked to have a "sleep" with her on his next summer leave, assuring her many other unmarried couples they knew had already been intimate. Mollie's reply was encouraging and he asked her to plan the tryst where they would be uninterrupted.[34] In January 1859, Armstrong wrote to Mollie and, according to biographer T.J. Stiles, used their private nickname for her genitals, saying plainly he knew "Miss Lizzie" better than anyone and had done more to her than anyone, and essentially promised the remaining intimacy which was the prerogative of a *husband*—and signed the letter "H----d."[35] Apparently, they did have "that great sleep" while on one of his leaves, and he continued to write, but Mollie lost interest in the long distance relationship.

During the 1859 summer furlough, Armstrong contracted gonorrhea—almost certainly from a prostitute in New York City, as had many cadets before him. He was treated with one of the standard remedies of the day—probably silver nitrate or one of the other equally unpleasant metal-based compounds administered by urethral injections. The treatments targeted the symptoms of burning urination and discharge but did not kill the specific bacteria (which was not identified until 1879). The symptoms might be mitigated by the injections or disappear spontaneously. However, the bacteria remained in the urogenital tract, typically scarring it and causing sterility. Fortunately for Armstrong and the cadets, no demerits were given for catching the "clap." (The U.S. Army did not formally recognize and begin to address the prevention of venereal disease until 1912.[36])

His behavior in class was continually poor and he was certainly free from the student's malady, "cram-stunt," a mental defect due to over-study.[37] Desperate to pass a previously failed exam, he broke into an office to copy or steal the test. Interrupted in the act, Armstrong escaped but not before being identified. Luckily (and curiously), he was not expelled for cheating.[38] One of his more famous pranks was prompted by his fellows wanting to disrupt Spanish lessons. In class, Armstrong asked in apparent innocence, "Professor De Janon, may I ask what 'the class is dismissed' is in Spanish?" When the teacher gave the translation, he stood up and led his fellow conspirators out of the room.³⁹

Political discussions were off-limits but in 1860, the cadets were debating states' rights and whether or not slavery would be permitted in new states joining the Union. The Republican presidential candidate, Abraham Lincoln, knew this philosophical and political issue had already divided the country. As national events proceeded, their debates became more heated and positions deeper entrenched. Could Lincoln possibly beat Democrat Stephen Douglas in the election and, if so, how would that affect the slave states? Would they secede from the Union? For the Southern cadets contemplating leaving West Point, it was a terrible dilemma with honor and duty on both sides, and it was compounded by loyalty to home, family, and friends—not to mention the loss of their diploma and Army career.

Emanuel had taught Armstrong to believe in a strong presidency with a government free of political elites where voting was the privilege of white, adult males, and slaves could be owned if state laws allowed it. These views were further reinforced by the opinions of his Democratic Southern friends. Every cadet understood that if war happened because of secession, they might well face each other on the battlefield. To Armstrong, more worrisome than the issue of slavery was the thought of the nation tearing itself apart. His duty was always clear to him, having sworn "true faith and allegiance" to the United States of America, and to obey the orders of the president and his superior officers. However, Armstrong knew *if* he graduated, that he would be a junior lieutenant with low pay. Always strategizing, he wrote the governor of Ohio and offered his services in a Volunteer Regiment fighting with his fellow Buckeyes—and where he was likely to have higher rank and pay than in the Federal Army.

Abraham Lincoln was elected 16th president in November 1860, winning out over Democrats John C. Breckinridge (Southern Democrat), Stephen Douglas (Northern Democrat), and John Bell (Constitutional Union Party). South Carolina promptly seceded the following month and was joined in February by six states to form the Confederate States of America. Starting with Lincoln's victory, the Southern cadets began a steady withdrawal from West Point as they felt greater loyalty to their home states. Lincoln was inaugurated on March 4, 1861, and on April 12, South Carolina's troops demanded possession of Fort Sumter in Charleston Harbor. The commander refused and only after a thirty-four-hour bombardment, the fort's flag was hauled down. The war had begun. To bolster the Federal Army, Lincoln called for volunteer regiments from the states loyal to the Union. The need for officers to train and drill the mushrooming Army caused West Point to graduate the Class of 1861 a month early. The Class of 1862 had another year of instruction ahead, but the most critical courses were condensed and crammed into one month to produce a *second* Class of 1861. Armstrong now had a compelling reason to be serious—if he failed he would have to return home in disgrace to try the volunteer regiments. Ramping up his quick-study skills, he and his friends buckled down, studying night and day. He passed his examinations with the lowest rank in his class of thirty-four, but he didn't care as any passing score made a graduate, and a graduate was an officer. (Historians have noted there were graduates with worse academic records but, to be fair, Armstrong's class standing might have been somewhat better if the Southern cadets had not left and reduced the class by about half.)

The commencement ceremony for the second Class of 1861 took place on June 24 and the graduates were dispatched to their different assignments. Champing at the bit to be off, Armstrong was still waiting for orders by the 29th when he was assigned as Officer of the Guard. This consisted of overseeing the cadet sentries and their immediate superiors. That evening, a fracas broke out between two cadets, but rather than stopping it, Armstrong encouraged a "fair fight." As a senior cadet, he knew better than to allow the fistfight and was caught in the act. His court-martial took place six days later.

For his defense, Armstrong wrote a four-page, rambling letter in which he declared the fight was a trifle, that he had acted boyishly and shouldn't have, and suggested that his four years' "hard work" should be considered because he wanted to fight for the Union.[40] Despite his defense and favorable testimony, he was found guilty of neglect of duty and conduct prejudicial to good order and military discipline. Doubtless the court had in mind the Army's pressing need for officers and only gave him an official reprimand.[41] Armstrong's luck never seemed to fail.

On July 18th, a letter arrived with his commission as a newly minted 2nd lieutenant in the 2nd U.S. Cavalry and orders to report to the Adjutant General. Traveling to Washington, Armstrong made a hurried stop for a few hours in New York, where he posed for an ambrotype in his cadet's uniform and went to a military outfitter to purchase the blue uniform, saber, pistol, and spurs which were proper for a junior lieutenant. When he arrived at the War Department, the talk was all about the armies gathering twenty-five miles away for the first major battle of the war. The place was Manassas, but a stream gave the battle its more common name—Bull Run.

Tail Piece: A Cadet and His Dog

In the Billings Public Library, Montana, the Custer Scrapbooks are a treasure trove of newspaper and magazine clippings about George Armstrong Custer and Little Bighorn. The two scrapbooks are actually old encyclopedia volumes with the clippings pasted on the pages. Unfortunately, many are undated or unattributed, but a few dates here and there suggest the clippings were collected prior to the late 1940s, and at least one article does coincide with the 70th anniversary of the Battle of Little Bighorn.

Pasted over the entry for "India" are trimmed photos from a magazine spread with a painting of Cadet Custer with a dog. Accompanying this image (which resembles a heavily re-touched photo) in the clipping are eight well-known photographs of Armstrong.[42]

Marlana Cook, Curator of Art, West Point Museum, writes about this image,

> It is from a series of paintings created for West Point in 1937 by Joseph N. Colgan under the Easel Division of the WPA Federal Art Project of New York City in 1937. In the paintings, Colgan inserted notable graduates, however, their portraits are not necessarily accurate/

A 1930s painting purported to show Cadet Custer with a dog. This was published in a 1940s article entitled, "Here is Custer." The image was captioned: "George Custer at West Point (*right*), class of 1861, was snapped with fellow cadet on eve of Civil War." There is a slight resemblance to the youthful Armstrong but the uniforms and equipment are not correct for the period and, given the prohibition against pets on campus, the depiction of him with a dog is fanciful. Originally on display at West Point, the painting's location is currently unknown. Custer Scrapbooks. Montana Room, Billings Public Library, Billings, Montana.

> identifiable. There is no credible historical accuracy to the subject matter other than the uniforms depicted. Therefore, there is no historical record of Custer with a dog at West Point.[43]

The current location of the original painting is unknown—but there is a certain irony about Cadet Custer being depicted with a dog in the one place where he absolutely could not have had one.

Chapter 3

Armstrong Ascendant

"I have got another dog...."—Capt. George Armstrong Custer[1]

Reporting to the Adjutant General's office, Armstrong waited until two o'clock in the morning on July 21 for his orders. He was to join the 2nd Cavalry under Brigadier General Irwin McDowell, Commander of the Army of Northeastern Virginia, but the intake officer asked Armstrong if he wanted to meet the Army's General in Chief, Winfield Scott—"the Grand Old Man of the Army" and venerated hero of the Mexican War. What would any young officer do but say, "Yes, sir." In a nearby room, Scott and several members of Congress were pouring over a map of where the armies were going to converge—Centreville and the rail junction of Manassas.

Scott, at 71 years, could no longer sit a horse but was still imposing—huge in both height and circumference, his bulk emphasized by his blue coat with double row of gilt buttons, massive gold braid epaulets and gold braided cuffs and collar. It was a historic moment of sorts—the most senior officer in the Army meeting the newest "shavetail." (The term was used for new officers or those who lacked experience. Army mules unbroken to harness had their tails partially shaved as a warning they might be troublesome.) Armstrong was impressed when Scott actually shook his hand and asked if he wanted to train recruits or, "...is your desire for something more active?"[2] It was the sort of perfunctory question that generals ask when expecting only one answer. Armstrong responded correctly, that he wanted to be on the front line. Knowing full well that unassigned horses were scarce in Washington, Scott said that if he could get a horse and was not afraid of a twenty-five-mile, night ride, he should report back at seven o'clock that evening to take dispatches to General McDowell at Centreville. Armstrong could not believe his luck—personal orders from a general after being commissioned less than 24 hours before. Now all he had to do was find a horse.

Hours later, Armstrong felt as if he had worn the soles off his boots by asking at every livery stable and barrack for a horse to requisition or borrow. The civilian horses were also gone as spectators were flocking south to see the first battle on American soil since the War of 1812. With the looming prospect of admitting failure to General Scott, by chance, he ran into a soldier from West Point who was in a flying artillery battery. The gunner had been detailed to bring his captain's spare horse to Centreville before the fighting was expected to begin. The situation was perfect for Armstrong, so he persuaded the artilleryman to delay until after he had Scott's dispatches. With probably the only available horse in Washington, Armstrong and the gunner set off along the dark road.

Baptism

It was the middle of the night when Armstrong arrived at McDowell's headquarters. By flickering campfires and the glow from lanterns within tents, he saw men talking, lounging, and bustling on errands—all waiting for orders to march. He expected to deliver Scott's dispatches to General McDowell but was disappointed to be relieved of them by a staff officer. When offered breakfast for himself and food for his horse, Armstrong refused the former as he supposed was expected of a gallant soldier. Dismissed by the officer, Armstrong accepted another breakfast and devoured steak, Virginia cornbread, and coffee. (Years later, he would remember how good his first breakfast as a fighting soldier tasted.[3]) With no further orders from a general, he gave the borrowed horse back and secured another. In the darkness, Armstrong found his way to Company G of the 2nd Cavalry, already formed on the road and waiting to advance.

Armstrong always bridled at inaction but would learn that waiting was inevitable whether for orders, troop movements, ammunition, reinforcements, the enemy's advance, or indecisive generals. In this case, the 2nd was waiting for the opening maneuvers so that they could play their part. The Federals were on one side of the stream, Bull Run, with the Confederates opposite—each having about 18,000 troops which made the odds even. McDowell would make twin feints to provoke General Beauregard's counterattack, and when the Rebels committed their troops, he would send two divisions (including the 2nd Cavalry) to hit Beauregard's flank—catching them between hammer and anvil.

At least that was the plan until Beauregard did his own out-flanking on McDowell's army and whipped it. The Federals fled in disarray, leaving guns behind at Bull Run—a mark of their desperation, for it was a matter of universal artillery pride that cannon were never abandoned. It was a triumph to capture a gun, and likewise, a regiment's battle flag or a general's personal possessions. The most senior Union general down to the youngest drummer boy were certain they would handily beat the Rebels and march directly to Richmond, the capital of the Confederacy. The South had a similar view, but the Battle of Bull Run (Manassas to the Confederates) demonstrated to the North the serious consequences of raw, untrained troops, uncoordinated units, and poor intelligence.

Bull Run scarcely offered any opportunity for glory, for Armstrong wisecracked he had "reached the front just in time to run with all the rest."[4] Still, he did behave creditably when retiring his company in good order (his was one of the last formed units to leave the battlefield) and avoided the shellfire which blocked their retreat over a bridge by finding a fording place for his regiment.[5] It was a small thing but fodder enough for the Northern press to take some sting out of the defeat. (Later, Congressman Bingham would make much of the heroism of "my boy Custer."[6]) When the 2nd Cavalry finally reached Arlington Heights near Washington, Armstrong wrapped himself in his waterproof, stretched out under a tree, and "from fatigue, hunger, and exhaustion, I soon fell asleep, despite the rain and mud, and slept for hours without wakening."[7] Going thirty hours without food taught him that seasoned soldiers never turned down a meal or a nap. He had come out of his first battle with skin and honor intact. Three days earlier he had been idle at West Point, and now he had led troops in combat.

Armstrong could have easily missed the opening battle of the war if he had not been serendipitously presented to Lt. General Scott on the spur of the moment and miraculously found a horse. He was a lucky man and knew it.

* * *

George Armstrong Custer's Civil War career has been so very thoroughly covered by historians that only events as they pertain to the canine focus of this book (including the promotions which gave him privilege) will be related here. Suffice it to say that his energy, daring, initiative, and personal charm won him rapid promotions. He believed in doing reconnaissance himself (whenever possible), developing a plan based on that intelligence, and using surprise and speed to hammer a disorganized enemy (it is worth noting that these are also the essentials for executing a good practical joke—at which Armstrong excelled). At a time when many generals were content to command from the rear, Armstrong preferred to be leading the charge. His men were loyal and showed their pride by wearing their own versions of the red neckerchief he affected as a general. Of course, Armstrong got a black eye occasionally, but he never lost a battle in the war.

Custer Luck and the First Dog

After the defeat at Bull Run, the 2nd Cavalry was withdrawn to Washington to strengthen and man the city's earthworks for the expected Rebel siege, but they were generally idle while waiting for something to happen. McDowell was replaced by Major General George B. McClellan, and the Army of Northeastern Virginia was renamed the Army of the Potomac to mark this change. "Little Mac" had a glowing service record, for he was second in his class at West Point (and later an instructor), served on Winfield Scott's staff during the Mexican War, was a military engineer, knew railroads, and had been an observer with the British Army in the Crimean War.[8] There, McClellan studied European military equipment and tactics, designed a cavalry saddle, and seemed just the man to reorganize the Army into a machine that could fight through to Richmond. (The McClellan saddle was adopted by the Army in 1859 and remained in use through World War I.)

There were other shifts in leadership. Brigadier General George Stoneman, a dog man, was made chief of cavalry. Philip Kearney, Brigadier General of Volunteers, arrived in Alexandria, Virginia, with four New Jersey regiments but no staff, so Armstrong was detached to be Kearney's aide-de-camp, and later "assistant adjutant general."[9] On one mission, he and three hundred men stealthily tried to capture some important Confederate officers on a picket line. A few shots were exchanged, and the inexperienced Federals hastily retreated in half the time it took them to get there. Armstrong likened the operation to a boyhood raid on an orchard or melon patch and having the feeling that the owner and his dog were wise to the plans and waiting for them.[10] He gave his report directly to Stoneman (who kept his pointer bitch at headquarters) and was interviewed by three newspapermen looking for a story.[11]

In October, Armstrong became ill and went home to recover and spent considerable time in Monroe with his sister, Lydia Reed. The recuperating "hometown hero" was feted, invited to luncheons and social gatherings, and pressed for firsthand news of the war. Libbie Bacon had seen the young cavalier and disliked both his long hair and the flashy yellow lining of his overcoat. One day, Armstrong was with some old school chums and took far too much drink onboard, raucously singing and laughing as they swayed past the Bacon house. From the window, both the judge and Libbie made note of the disgraceful behavior. Lydia was shocked at Armstrong's condition as he staggered home. When he was sober, she talked seriously to him and extracted his promise to give up drink. Moved by his sister's concern as well as realizing that drink could be an obstacle to his goals—and disliking the loss of control—Armstrong kept his word and never again passed a drop through his lips.

For four months Armstrong was on sick leave, and surely Monroe grew weary of a hero who lingered away from the battlefront. While he was gone, McClellan—whose war "mantra" was preparation, training, and supplies—reorganized the pre-war horse units (dragoons, mounted rifles, and cavalry) into numbered regiments, and Armstrong's 2nd Cavalry became the 5th U.S. Cavalry.[12] When he was fit for duty in February 1862, Armstrong rejoined his regiment under Stoneman, who was pushing toward Manassas. Armstrong led his first charge and scouted, probed, and skirmished with Rebels as they withdrew from Centreville. He and several officers cautiously scouted an intimidating, well-armed, earthen fort, discovering the Rebels were long gone and the massive "cannon" in the embrasures were blackened tree logs set up by the crafty Rebels. Dubbed "Quaker guns," their illusion had caused McClellan to delay his advance even with superior numbers. Greatly embarrassed, President Lincoln now had to weather the scandal of the Quaker gun affair to support McClellan—who had missed almost certain victory because of poor intelligence and hesitation.[13] (In the spring of 1862, P.T. Barnum exhibited a captured Quaker gun from Centreville at his American Museum in New York City.)

With the 5th Cavalry, Armstrong acquired his first campaign dog. In a six-page letter to his parents dated March 17, 1862, he praised McClellan and talked about a skirmish, the unreliable food supply, and sleeping without a blanket in the rain. His postscript was brief—"I forgot to tell you I have a black foxhound which I got at Manassas."[14] Armstrong got a dog after having only been in the Army for only eight months—with half of those on sick leave.

Soldiers' Dogs

In May 1862, the Great Showist, P.T. Barnum, exhibited a captured Rebel dog called "Jeff Davis" at his First National Dog Show in New York City. The dog had been taken two months earlier at the battle of New Bern, North Carolina, and given the name as both a jab at the President of the Confederacy and so that the regiment could jokingly brag they had captured Jeff Davis (see this chapter's *Tail Piece*). Dogs were common enough in both armies, but officers tended to have personal pets while soldiers (or sailors) had collective pets which could be company or regimental mascots. It was comparatively easy for an officer to keep a larger dog on campaign as each had an orderly to help look after them. General George Stoneman was photographed twice at headquarters with his pointer in 1862. Brigadier General Alexander Asboth had York, a St. Bernard-type, who was always by his side.[15] *Frank Leslie's Illustrated Newspaper* had an engraving of them at the battle of Pea Ridge in March 1862. (This image is engraved on Asboth's tombstone—arguably making York the only dog on a military headstone in Arlington National Cemetery). General Rufus Ingalls, Chief Quartermaster for General Ulysses S. Grant, owned a Dalmatian who was photographed at least three times in 1864 and 1865.[16] Soldiers had their dogs too—the collar tag of Curly, the water spaniel of the 11th Ohio Volunteer Infantry had this witty inscription: "I am Company A's Dog, Whose Dog are You?"[17] (This persistently popular phrase for dog collars seems to have originated with a collar given to the Prince of Wales by Alexander Pope in the early 1700s which was wittily inscribed "I am his Highness' dog at Kew; Pray tell me, Sir whose dog are you?"[18])

A dog was a bit of home to a soldier in blue or gray—a warm furry being to care for and distract him from sore feet, short rations, bad weather, and his dangerous life. As a benefit, dogs were instinctive, around-the-clock sentinels whose sharp hearing and scent detected intruders long before their masters could. Pvt. Lyman J. Seeley of the 13th Vermont Infantry described how their dogs and even horses helped with night guard on a captured ford on the Occoquan River: "Sometimes the pickets are aroused by the footsteps of horses, or the barking of dogs which show the guerrillas are ranging the country on the other side of the river, trying to secure something from our army to feed themselves with."[19] For dogs, Army life could be heaven. There were frequent marches with new territory to explore. Tidbits from mess tins were always offered along with kind words and pats, and there was always a choice of which soldier to snuggle with at night. Tony, the mascot of Battery A, 1st Illinois Light Artillery, saw eighteen months of hard campaigning between Paducah, Kentucky, and Larkinsville, Alabama. The little dog was in four battles and twice wounded before finally going missing or getting killed. One of the soldiers wrote of him, "He owns no one master, but all."[20]

When Armstrong looted his new dog at Manassas (taken from a farm or Rebel), he was at the headquarters of the Army of the Potomac in Fairfax, on the road to Centreville. He knew hounds at home but there were many regional types of scent hounds throughout the South—all purpose-bred and trained to follow a hot or cold trail while "giving tongue" (baying) to lead the hunters to the quarry. The color black would be very unusual for a typical foxhound which is white with an overlay of brown and black markings. More than likely, Armstrong had a Virginia Black and Tan, which had brown or tan points on their feet and muzzle, and long ears. These "black hounds" were common in Virginia and Ohio River Valley. Davy Crockett was said to have hunted bear, cougar, and varmints with them.[21] It is possible his dog was a black Plott Hound, but at that time, the breed was localized to North Carolina's western mountains, which had yet to be penetrated by the Union Army. (Virginia Black and Tans were recognized by the American Kennel Club [AKC] in 1945 as the Black and Tan Coon Hound.)

Armstrong wrote his parents nine days later on the 26th but said nothing else about his dog, as he was preoccupied with the business of getting his company's men, horses, and equipment aboard boats. In a 19th century version of the D–Day invasion, McClellan had assembled nearly 400 paddlewheel steamers, schooners, and barges and filled them with men, horses, artillery, and wagons to move from Washington to Fortress Monroe, from where they would launch a major attack.[22] Armstrong's hound would have been left at headquarters in the care of his servant or an officer friend. His "black fox hound" was the first of several dogs that he had during the war. The next dog was only months away.

Trenches and Balloons

The following month, he was detached from the 5th Cavalry to assist Lt. Nicholas Bowen, the topographical engineer on staff for General W.F. "Baldy" Smith. A siege was starting on the Rebel entrenchments at Lee's Mills on the Warwick River, and there was a lot of counter-fortification needed.[23] Given Armstrong's Academy grades, he was probably the least suitable officer for the Topographical Engineers—although overseeing soldiers digging trenches and making bullet-stopping fascines (bundles of tree branches) and gabions (tall baskets filled with dirt) was well within his capabilities. First, Armstrong had to organize the burial of dead soldiers who had been killed in the work of building earthworks—the very job he was to supervise. There were no coffins for the bodies, only their blankets as shrouds. It made a profound impression on Armstrong and in a letter to Lydia, he wrote, "Some were quite young and boyish, and looking at their faces, I could not but think of my younger brother."[24] He was glad to move on to the labor of building earthworks.

Junior staff lieutenants get oddball assignments and Armstrong was no exception. He was ordered to make aerial ascensions to observe enemy positions. The Army had six balloons filled with chemically generated hydrogen gas. General Fitz-John Porter had gone aloft to make reports but experienced a terrifying flight over enemy lines when the tether broke. Fortunately, the wind blew Porter's balloon back to safety, but "Baldy" Smith would no longer risk a senior officer for observations at 1,000 feet. An expendable junior lieutenant would do—and that was Armstrong. Nervous for his safety, he made his first ascent sitting on the floor of the reinforced willow basket. Armstrong did not like leaving the ground, but he followed orders. Equipped with field glasses, compass, notepad, and pencil, he made night ascensions to count Rebel campfires to estimate their numbers. One dawn, where there had been Rebel troops camped previously, Armstrong could see no morning fires. He correctly surmised the Rebels had withdrawn in the dark and reported this to General Smith—who had heard this from two escaped "contrabands" (the Federal term for escaped slaves). Never comfortable as an aeronaut, Armstrong did see the intelligence value in this new military technology, although later it never seems to have occurred to him that aerial reconnaissance would be useful for finding Indians or buffalo herds. After the war, during a buffalo hunt in Kansas, his balloon experience would be something in common with P.T. Barnum (who offered regular tethered balloon ascensions at his museum and saw great potential in aerial travel).

Reassigned to earthbound duties again, Armstrong and Lt. Bowen were at the headquarters of General Fitz-John Porter. Together with General Porter's staff, the two men posed on May 20 for a photograph in front of a tent amidst scattered bottles

2nd Lt. Custer visiting General Fitz-John Porter's staff in May 1862. Armstrong is on the right with the terrier, and his immediate superior, 1st Lt. Nicholas Bowen, is reclining on the left. The little dog's name is not known but clearly, Armstrong wanted it next to him for the photograph. Armstrong already had a "black fox hound" at this point. Prints & Photographs, Library of Congress, LC-B811-389.

and cups—presumably from a convivial meal. Armstrong, propped up on his elbow, lies on a blanket and affectionately strokes a bristle coated, terrier. Whether it belonged to him or someone else is not known. What is significant about the image is the obvious affection between Armstrong and the little dog.

McClellan and More Dogs

Four days later, he was back in the saddle and reconnoitering for the Army's chief engineer, Brigadier General John G. Barnard. Armstrong had no hesitation with wading creeks and rivers (where he was vulnerable to snipers) to determine where they could be forded. Characteristically, Armstrong never thought about his safety when there was work to be done—or just trusted his luck. On May 24, elements of the 4th Michigan Cavalry and supporting infantry were stalled at the flooded Chickahominy River where

Rebel marksmen waited to pick off the Federals attempting to ford between wrecked bridges. Finding a suitable new crossing was a subtly shifting equation with variables of depth, current, solidity of river bottom, and steepness of the banks—and width to accommodate several horses. Ordered to jump in and test the bottom, Armstrong found a ford—deep but manageable if rifles and cartridge pouches were held above water. He went on to scout the Rebel positions and then pointed the way for the 4th Michigan, shouting, "Go in Wolverines, give them hell."[25] For three hours, there was hot skirmishing, and the Rebels fell back. At the end of the fighting, Lt. Bowen praised Armstrong by citing him as the first to cross the river and the last to leave.[26]

The report of Armstrong's successful reconnoiter caught General McClellan's attention. He quizzed Armstrong and was impressed enough to offer him a staff position of captain. Armstrong would later say that the Chickahominy River "was almost literally a stepping-stone for my personal advancement."[27] (Armstrong's exploits are frequently exaggerated, and McClellan himself inflated the incident by calling it, "a desperate act of gallantry on the banks of the Chickahominy."[28] On the internet, wilder versions have him shouting from mid-stream, "That's how deep it is, Mr. General!"[29])

Armstrong was promoted to 1st lieutenant in July, while retaining the temporary staff rank. Loyalty to McClellan was a potential problem as his chief was continually butting heads with President Lincoln over the management of the Army of the Potomac. McClellan waited for more men, training, supplies, and weapons. Perhaps none of these were unreasonable requests, but nothing was being accomplished to justify them. His lack of progress toward Richmond (only 100 miles away from Washington) caused Lincoln to ask frequently about the delays. There was always some excuse—insufficient or untrained troops, worn out horses, low supplies, unfinished fortifications, poor weather, and bad roads. Exasperated, Lincoln quipped, "If General McClellan don't intend to do something with the Army of the Potomac, I should like to borrow it for a while, provided I can see it can be made to do something."[30]

Between May and August 1862, Armstrong posed again with a dog for a portrait—this one by the famous Civil War photographer Matthew Brady. In the stereo view, Armstrong wears an undress, double-breasted sack-coat and on the ground is a fashionable topee (sun helmet). The black and white dog of indeterminate gender (perhaps a retriever or large spaniel) lies on a rug and from the look of its legs, has been in wet grass or a creek. As Armstrong arranged for the photograph, certainly the dog is his own. In fact, an Ohio schoolteacher, who had taught his younger siblings, confirmed this. (This photograph is often said to be Armstrong as a general but the Library of Congress dates it to the summer of 1862 when he was still a 2nd lieutenant. Likely the confusion of his rank in this image arises from subsequent printings and labels of the photograph *after* Armstrong had attained general rank in 1863.)

In an interview, Lucy Carpenter (neé Hewlett), remembered vividly the "wonderful, big, shaggy, black and white dog General Custer brought home with him once." The dog had crossed Rebel lines during a fight and "sought out Gen. Custer as his friend and protector." Armstrong said they had been through fourteen battles together, and after one exhausting reconnoiter, the dog had saved him from capture. He and his squad had dismounted to rest and slept until the dog bit and tugged at his master's arm. Awakened by the pain, Armstrong spotted a large group of Rebels but was able to get his men safely away. Mrs. Carpenter said, "The dog was idolized by the Custer family as long as he lived."[31] So, this dog, the black hound, and the terrier, could make at least three dogs which Armstrong owned during the first years of the war.

The Battle of Antietam on September 17 was technically a Union victory but in reality a bloody, tactical draw. Armstrong was delivering McClellan's orders and probably did no fighting. Afterward, in one of his characteristically long letters, he wrote to Lydia, on Sept. 21, "You are perhaps, in doubt whether I am still among the living or numbered with the dead. These few lines will show you I belong to the former."[32] He described in detail about being given special leave to attend the wedding of Capt. John "Gimlet" Lea, C.S.A., a West Point friend. Back in May, Armstrong went out of his way to help Lea when he was wounded and captured. Lea vowed to remember the kindness and gave Armstrong a note saying that if Armstrong was taken prisoner, he should be well-treated.[33] Since then, Lea had been paroled and was recuperating in Williamsburg

Armstrong in camp during the summer of 1862 with a gun dog lounging on a rug. Armstrong's fashionable topee (sun helmet) is on the ground by the wet dog. While the gender and name of the dog are unknown, it is likely the one which an Ohio schoolteacher not only remembered hearing stories about, but saw on one of Armstrong's visits home. (Some sources have this image of Armstrong as a brigadier general, however, the photograph is authoritatively dated to the summer of 1862, when Armstrong was a 2nd lieutenant.) Prints & Photographs, Library of Congress, LC-B811-2344.

with his fiancée and her cousin. When McClellan and his staff arrived, Armstrong rode over to visit, taking along his servant and dog. He had always enjoyed the easy ways of the Southern cadets, so he settled in admirably with Lea's group—telling war news, joking, singing Southern songs, flirting with cousin Maggie and hinting that for her favor, he would become a Confederate. Lea's wedding was moved up by a week so that Armstrong could stand as best man.[34]

In an offhand remark, he gives the name of one of his wartime dogs. After Antietam, McClellan's headquarters were shifting weekly, and Armstrong was trying to predict where his chief would finally settle. Armstrong told Lydia that he traveled from Yorktown to Fortress Monroe to Baltimore by boat and listed his entourage: "…having with me 'Rose,' my two horses and servant."[35] From Baltimore, he and Rose went on to Washington to wait for McClellan.

Now, Rose was a puzzle for Frederick Whittaker, who churned out a glowing biography less than six months after Armstrong's death in 1876. Libbie had loaned Whittaker a considerable number of Armstrong's letters and had to clarify that Rose was a dog rather than a paramour or camp follower. Whittaker called the dog "old Rose" and noted that Armstrong always had dogs—even as a lieutenant.[36] His use of "old" with the dog's name suggests that Libbie had told him something about Rose's age, loyalty, or even campaign history (much as Armstrong's men affectionately called him "Old Curly")—or it might be just be Whittaker's effusive prose. Little can be deduced about Rose from the letter other than her presumed gender and that she was a good traveler. The black and white dog (which was male according to Carpenter) could not be Rose, so perhaps she was the Manassas black hound or the terrier—or even another dog. Unfortunately, Whittaker says nothing about Armstrong's other Civil War dogs.

After the Quaker Gun Affair and the second defeat at Bull Run, Lincoln removed McClellan as General in Chief of the Army but left him with command of the Army of the Potomac. After the nominal victory at Antietam, Lincoln issued a preliminary version of his Emancipation Proclamation on September 22. He visited the battlefield on October 3 and was photographed with McClellan's staff and Armstrong.[37] Still in the doghouse with the president for poorly managing his forces at Antietam and neglecting to pursue and destroy Robert E. Lee's smaller force (as well as paralytic caution and previous failures), McClellan was replaced by Major General Ambrose Burnside in November. As he no longer had staff, Armstrong's appointment as captain ended. Once again a lieutenant, Armstrong secured leave and someone to take care of his dogs, and he went to Monroe. November 1862 proved to be a month of both dejection and exhilaration, for he had lost his rank and McClellan but would meet the beautiful Libbie Bacon.

Fortress Libbie

Part of the Custer mythology has Libbie and Armstrong as sweethearts from childhood who "met" when she was swinging on the gate as he walked past her house. Libbie called out, "Hi, you Custer boy!" and then dashed inside with embarrassment.[38] In fact, their first social interaction occurred at the Thanksgiving party at Libbie's seminary. After leaving McClellan, Armstrong had "neglected" to remove the captain's bars from his shoulder straps—nor did he make a correction when he was introduced as Captain Custer. When Libbie remarked upon Armstrong's rapid promotion, he was an unassigned lieutenant.

Despite Libbie's coolness (or perhaps because of it), the twenty-three-year-old lieutenant was smitten. He discovered her routine to be near her—carrying parcels, opening gates, or holding his umbrella over her when it was sleeting—a particularly gallant gesture which Libbie admired.[39] An ardent suitor, Armstrong went to the same church services she attended even though he was not a Presbyterian. Libbie liked the attention but kept her emotional distance. She did not ask him into the parlor or accept his invitations, but always thanked him for his courtesies. She wrote her cousin Rebecca that she has "the escort of one of General McClellan's staff whenever I put my nose out of doors" and to a friend, "I don't care for him except as an escort."[40] She still disapproved of his cinnamon-scented, blonde locks, garish yellow shoulder straps, trouser stripes, and overcoat lining.[41] It may seem surprising that the patriotic and well-educated Libbie did not know that yellow was the cavalry's signature facing color just as light blue, red, and green respectively denoted Infantry, Artillery, and Medical, but she admitted paying little attention to the war. "The clash of arms and glitter of the soldiery only appealed to me as it did to thoughtless, light-hearted young girls still without solider lovers or brothers…."[42] Despite her initial opinion, later she proudly regarded Armstrong's long hair and yellow cavalry facings as the hallmarks of a noble cavalier.

Judge Bacon and Libbie and had long since talked about the unsuitability of soldiers as husbands.[43] In war, there was a fair chance they could be killed or go missing in action—leaving a widow and children with a meager pension. Perhaps worse, a soldier could be maimed and receive only a pittance as compensation. Glory did not pay rent or buy food, and peacetime officers could only expect promotions at a glacial pace. Soldiers, even married ones, were frequently regarded as rakes who drank, gambled, and whored. At the time, Libbie had no interest in "following the drum." Judge Bacon did not approve of Armstrong because he was a soldier, Methodist, Democrat, and from a lower social class (despite Bacon's own farming background).

Early in December, Armstrong returned to Washington but still without assignment, promptly wrangled leave to return and press his suit. He continued to walk down Libbie's street (Judge Bacon counted "forty times a day"), and Libbie encouraged him by tossing a bag of candy to him after choir practice.[44] Perhaps remembering her attraction to the mustachioed Capt. Drew, Libbie began to respond to Armstrong's persistent attentions. By the end of the year, he had brought up the topic of marriage and declared that he could talk to no one else for an hour without "feeling lonely."[45] Libbie's feelings for him were warm but not intense—and she did have other *beaux* jostling for her attention.

Armstrong's suit was not making progress and he switched tactics—resorting to some gentle competition. He began squiring Fanny Fifield (an incorrigible flirt) around town but continued to see Libbie at social gatherings and on her errands. She was certain that she had Armstrong's true affections. Judge Bacon felt that his flirtatious manner with Fanny (or so he perceived it to be) while seeing his daughter and that old drunken episode were not the behaviors of a serious suitor. Armstrong was regarded as, "One of those mustachioed, gilt striped and button critters" who was after "our Libbie."[46] When Bacon took his daughter and her friend to the station for a visit to Toledo, Armstrong was there to assist her on the steps onto the car (difficult to manage in voluminous, hooped skirts) and hand up her luggage. Judge Bacon was angry at this liberty and wrote that she had been *too* friendly with him. Libbie fired back that he had done the same for the other ladies. She liked Armstrong "very well," and he was a nice escort to rely upon. Being dutiful, she did promise her father not to be seen in public with him, and said she had told Armstrong not to meet her. Every inch her father's daughter, she had a lawyerly loophole: "But I did not promise *never* to see him again." "Do not blame Capt. Custer," she wrote, "He has many fine traits and Monroe will yet be proud of him."[47]

Libbie and Armstrong could not entirely avoid each other. It was customary on New Year's Day for gentlemen to call on their friends to wish them well and chat. Libations were provided, and Libbie remarked that it was a temperate man indeed who resisted drinking or "cramming" at every house. Armstrong, still a teetotaler, was one of the callers, and Judge Bacon could not refuse to receive him on the occasion.[48] As it happened, he was an enthusiastic supporter of McClellan and a keen student of the war's progress, so he sought out Armstrong to learn more details. Despite his initial dislike, he was impressed by Armstrong's knowledge and gravitas when it came to military matters. Like fathers before and after, Bacon was unaware of all that was going on between Libbie and Armstrong. Despite his view that he was an unsuitable match for his daughter, an unlikely, war-focused friendship developed between the two men.

Regardless of Fanny, Libbie nourished Armstrong's courtship (as well as three other suitors), but random meetings were not enough. Her close friend, Nettie Humphrey, was still living at her father's hotel and when Libbie went to visit her, she often ran into Armstrong, as it was a gathering place for the men of the community. Nettie conspired to help the couple as a courier for their notes—while pursuing her own romance with a former infantry officer, Jacob Greene. Through Nettie, Libbie gave Armstrong a cased, ambrotype portrait of herself—a most sincere gesture. Armstrong wrote letters to Nettie which were really for Libbie. The two women read them, and Libbie would dictate the reply. Armstrong's leave ended in April 1863, and he joined McClellan in the East where the latter was writing a defensive report as former commander of the Potomac Army. McClellan had a knack for embellishment and self-aggrandizement, and from that, Armstrong learned official reports, newspaper coverage, and influential friends helped win promotions and favorable opinion. (Maj. Gen. Alfred Pleasonton would also reinforce this public relations strategy for Armstrong.) After his assistance with McClellan's report was done, Armstrong was given clerical work in Washington where he had little to do but "idleness and theatergoing."[49] There was plenty of time to compose long letters to "Friend Nettie."

Fanny kept up her antics with men—even hinting that she was to marry Armstrong. Libbie knew this to be untrue because of his professed fidelity. She was dismayed at the reckless flirting,

> Fan is now crazy over the vilest looking man, a perfect rake. He stared me right in my face yesterday. He owns a leopard dog and I hear he is a dog breeder.... He is a healthy looking fellow—and maleish. But of course, dresses elegantly as all that style of men do.[50]

The rake, who seems to have been a sleazy version of *Gone with the Wind*'s Rhett Butler, had a Catahoula Leopard Dog, native to central Louisiana. Originally a Choctaw tribal dog, white settlers used them on crop-destroying razorback hogs. The breed has brindle striping, spots, and patches (hence the name "leopard dog") and frequently has eyes that are unnerving shades of blue, gray, green, or hazel. (The Catahoula has been the state dog of Louisiana since 1979 and was recognized by the AKC in 2009.) Such a dog from the South would have been most unusual in Monroe at that time, and together with its ill-mannered "dog breeder" would have been avoided by respectable young women. It is telling that the normally charitable Libbie described the man as "vilest looking" and a "perfect rake." Every farm had at least one dog, and Monroe men kept bird dogs and trail hounds, but breeding dogs for sale was not highly regarded in good society. That Libbie was repelled by the "dog breeder" suggests strongly that she and Armstrong had not yet talked about his dogs.

Ordered to leave his desk job and return to the front, Armstrong missed being in the fight at Chancellorsville (April 30–May 6, 1863), where the Federals were badly beaten by Lee and the Army of Northern Virginia. Maj. Gen. Joseph Hooker (Burnside's replacement) was rightly blamed for the defeat, and he blamed Gen. Stoneman for mismanaging the Cavalry Corps. Armstrong wrote to his parents, saying the whole Army was asking for McClellan to be reinstated and, the following week, wrote again with dog news.[51] "I have got another dog, a hound pup about two months old. One of my men got it from an old negro woman."[52] He talked about accepting a staff position with Maj. Gen. Alfred Pleasonton, naming one of his two horses Harry after his favorite nephew (Harry "Autie" Reed) and said that he acquired a waif. Johnny Cisco was a hungry boy of about twelve years who showed up in camp and attached himself to Armstrong as a servant. The lad was fed and dressed in cast off uniform parts and did laundry, cooked, and was "so fond of the pup he takes it to bed with him."[53] Once again, Armstrong does not give a name or say much about the dog, but in saying, "I have got *another* dog," he implied that it was an additional dog or a replacement—perhaps even both. With the black hound, the black and white dog, the hound pup, and depending upon the ownership of the small terrier and Rose's identity, the pup would be Armstrong's fourth or fifth wartime dog.

Later that month on May 20, he wrote to Judge Bacon asking for the "honor" of a letter in return.[54] Along with war news, Armstrong was methodically revealing aspects of his serious character to Bacon. More and more impressed, Bacon was still unaware of Libbie's correspondence with Armstrong. In the aftermath of Chancellorsville, Hooker resigned and was replaced by Maj. Gen. George Meade, who relieved Stoneman of the Cavalry Corps and replaced him with Maj. Gen. of Volunteers Alfred Pleasonton on June 22, 1863. Armstrong was made Pleasonton's aide-de-camp, and the appointment was a feather in his wide-brimmed hat, but there was a finer one soon to come.

Tail Piece:
P.T. Barnum's Civil War Dog Show

Phineas Taylor Barnum was famous in his own time for exhibiting General Tom Thumb, the Feejee Mermaid, Jenny Lind "the Swedish Nightingale," Jumbo the Elephant, and for his traveling circus, "The Greatest Show on Earth." In his New York City museum of unusual, educational exhibits, he staged baby shows with cash prizes to draw people into his museum and invented the first National Dog Show in 1862.

The one-week show began on May 12 in his American Museum, and the grand prize winner, a giant, crop-eared Siberian Bloodhound (Great Dane), was chosen the first day so that people could see it and the other winners for the extended, three-week duration. Barnum also arranged for topical exhibits to entice the war-curious public—a wax figure of Jefferson in women's underwear, the Quaker Gun, and the Rebel dog, "Jeff Davis," which was captured at the battle of New Bern by Capt. De Hart of the 9th New Jersey Regiment.[55] The *New York Times* waggishly remarked upon, "that extraordinary breed—unknown here until about a year ago—the 'rebel' dog..." who looked harmless but was hardened and reckless and needed to have his dinners confiscated and be threatened with hanging at the end of the dog show.[56] The hyperbole was amazing:

> On this side of the Atlantic so fine a collection of dogs has never been dreamt about before. From the gigantic Siberian bloodhound to the most diminutive of rat annihilators, dogs of all sizes, and of every variety nearly under Heaven, send in delegations.[57]

One thousand dogs on display represented forty "distinct breeds" and was the, "GREATEST NOVELTY IN THE WORLD!"[58]

However, Barnum's second dog show in 1863 was not as profitable as the first, and the war had lost its initial novelty, so he moved on to circus and arena shows. Still, the Great National Dog Show was the first of its kind in all the world (the national dog shows in England, Germany, and France not occurring until 1863). Barnum's show concept was borrowed for the Centennial Dog Show in Philadelphia in 1876. The following year, the fledgling Westminster Kennel Club held their first dog show at Gilmore's Garden (Barnum's old Roman Hippodrome), which would be renamed Madison Square Garden. From that day to this, the name of the famous Westminster Kennel Club show would be synonymous with Madison Square Garden.[59]

Chapter 4

My Husband's Dogs

"And when the tent was pitched, stealing under the flap, crawling under the bed, only discovered by [their] licking, snuffling, and snorting."—Libbie Custer[1]

General Pleasonton's cavalry brigades needed more daring leadership, and three young officers seemed to fit the bill. Two days before the battle of Gettysburg, he promoted captains Elon Farnsworth, Wesley Merritt, and George Armstrong Custer to the temporary rank of Brigadier General of Volunteers. It was "Custer's luck" working away, for in one swoop, Armstrong had leap-frogged to a brigadier and got a whopping pay raise. Not yet twenty-four, he was the youngest general in the Army—and for better or worse, he was called "The Boy General" for the rest of his life.

He was given the Michigan Cavalry Brigade—the Wolverines. With Libbie and his family connections there, it was his adopted home, so Armstrong was glad to be commanding fellow Michiganders. At his age, he was certainly a little insecure about changing from commanding a company of 100 men to 3,000. However, Armstrong did have particular views on a leader's appearance (possibly inspired by Charles Lever's Napoleonic dragoons and Sir Walter Scott's knights). Urgently needing a symbol of his new rank, Armstrong cobbled together a uniform which would become his signature. His black velvet jacket had a star on each shoulder, swirling gold braid loops on the sleeves (similar to Confederate uniforms), and was fastened with a double row of buttons in pairs (the single star and paired buttons of a brigadier). Under the jacket he wore a sailor's jumper with exposed, wide blue collar and white stars on the points, a red necktie, and a black broad-brimmed hat with a silver star. Saber, spurs, high boots, and his long ringlets completed the highly theatrical picture. The press loved it, and Armstrong was favorably likened to a pirate, a cavalier, or the musketeer, D'artagnan.[2] After Gettysburg, Armstrong's published portrait reminded Libbie of a brigand, and she was shocked that he had shaved his whiskers.[3]

The regulation elements of a general's uniform were extremely difficult to conjure up in the field, much less having the uniform tailored, so either Pleasonton had tipped off his protégé about the promotion or else Armstrong had stashed away uniform pieces for some time—although as lofty as his aspirations were, he could hardly have predicted the jump from captain to brigadier. Biographer Jeffry Wert suggests his hope for general rank as being the most probable—and indicative of both Armstrong's faith in certain promotion and the forethought given to his command persona.[4] Somewhat outlandish by Union Army standards and comment-provoking, it accomplished what Armstrong needed. Like a medieval knight's heraldic crest and surcoat, it made him recognizable as a general to his men and the enemy from afar.

General Robert E. Lee's Army of Northern Virginia was moving out of its home base and through the Shenandoah Valley corridor to bring the war north of Washington. He intended to disrupt the Federals' plans for their summer campaign as well as secure food in Pennsylvania. The clash would come outside the small town of Gettysburg in July 1863. Rebel cavalry had been far superior to that of the Federals, but Armstrong took on J.E.B. "Jeb" Stuart's brilliant cavalry, famously shouting, "Come on you Wolverines." His charge prevented Stuart from attacking the Union rear and helped turn the tide. When Armstrong's horse was shot (the second in three days), a Wolverine killed the attacker and pulled Armstrong up onto his horse. The Michigan Cavalry Brigade distinguished themselves with honor, although they sustained more casualties than the Confederate cavalry. (Armstrong had eleven horses shot from under him during his life.)

Just eight months after meeting Libbie, Armstrong's success at Gettysburg earned him an immediate promotion to the regular Army rank of major (to be confirmed by Congress). As a tribute to "Old Curly," his troopers started wearing the red neckerchief. Armstrong proved to be an aggressive and tactical commander always at the forefront of any action. He and his men captured prisoners, cannon, supply trains, and battle flags. With his battle victories and distinctive appearance, George Armstrong Custer was a "rock star" in the Army. Writing about his Civil War record, historian and historical novelist, George MacDonald Fraser, noted he "...was spectacular in an age which did not lack for heroes."[5] Armstrong had found his purpose in life.

Confusion in the Ranks

The mid–19th century American Army system of awards and ranks can be confusing. At the beginning of the Civil War, no medals were given to officers, and the reward for commendable gallantry or a victory was a "brevet" promotion to the next higher rank. Being awarded a brevet was strictly honorary and carried no pay increase but did entitle the officer to be called by his highest rank (a major breveted to colonel, was addressed by the latter rank even if he did not command as a colonel). In this way, Armstrong as a Brigadier General of Volunteers was awarded a brevet major in the Regular Army for success at Gettysburg. Both the Regulars and Volunteers did this—confusing the issue further when an officer held different ranks in both. (After the war, it was common enough to have a couple of brevet generals in a regiment commanded by the regular colonel.) So, when Armstrong was Bvt. Brigadier General of Volunteers, he was still a Regular Army captain. In the same month as Gettysburg, the Congressional Medal of Honor (established in 1862) was authorized for officers, "for acts of valor above and beyond the call of duty." (Armstrong's brother, Tom, would be the first to receive two Medals of Honor.)

The General's Entourage

While officers routinely had servants and pets (usually not more than one of each), generals had an entourage consisting of staff officers—adjutant/chief of staff, aides-de-camp, orderlies, color bearer and often specialist officers, as well as a cook, hostler, and personal servant—either a striker (a soldier who got extra pay for the job) or sometimes a paid civilian or a freed slave. Inevitably one of the staff was the "dog robber"—a curious military term for one who excelled at special errands and all kinds of "acquisitions." (In the British Navy, both "dog robber" and "dogsbody" were terms for a junior officer assigned to drudge work.) Often, newspaper reporters and sometimes photographers accompanied a general's staff. After Gettysburg, Armstrong recruited Nettie's *beau*, Jacob Greene (now a cavalry captain), to be his adjutant general. Armstrong preferred a close circle of friends and family around him, and he wanted his brother, too. Tom was a corporal in the 21st Ohio Infantry, but Armstrong had no available staff positions. It would take over a year of lobbying to create the position and get Tom promoted so he could join his brother's staff as a 2nd lieutenant the following autumn. In Amosville, Virginia, Armstrong needed a cook (presumably unhappy with his current one), and out of a group of contrabands, he chose Eliza Brown.[6] Along with other slaves from her plantation, she had run away because she wanted to see what this "freedom" was all about. The two got on well—Armstrong liked her cooking and Eliza enjoyed the perks of better food and good naturedly bossing the "Ginnel" around. Despite being lonesome for her family and people, Eliza would be loyal to him and Libbie for many years. At this point, Armstrong's dog entourage *could* have consisted of the black hound, the little terrier, the black and white dog, and the hound pup—and one of these might or might not have been Rose. He rarely wrote about their deaths, so it is difficult to be sure of his dog roster at any one time.

Besieging Judge Bacon

At the battle of Culpeper Court House in September 1863, Armstrong and his Wolverines went up against Jeb Stuart's cavalry again and soundly beat them with a saber charge against the Rebel center to capture cannon, prisoners, and Stuart's headquarters (with his waiting dinner). During the charge, an exploding shell killed Armstrong's horse and a fragment tore through his boot leather to make a painful gash in his calf. That wound meant a twenty-day leave to see Libbie.[7]

Judge Bacon, the protective father and patriot, had a problem. His daughter's suitor, who had been publicly drunk and behaved like Casanova, was now a general and a war hero. Armstrong hoped his promotions would change Bacon's opinion, and he had maintained a neutral correspondence with him, although at least once, he delegated his aide-de-camp, Lt. James Christiancy, to write with purely military news.[8] Knowing Libbie's parents still opposed Armstrong as a suitor, Nettie looked for opportunities to improve the judge's opinion of him—while continuing as letter courier. Fanny had been stirring the pot of intrigue with hints that Armstrong would marry her, and Libbie knew the two had been corresponding.[9] She professed to be indifferent but privately was conflicted as Armstrong had been all but declaring his love outright to her in his letters. Ultimately, she gave the benefit of the doubt to Armstrong. When they finally had a chance to talk, he dispelled any worries and professed his sincere feelings. Armstrong had been proposing to Libbie for nearly a year but was always refused because of Judge

Bacon. Won over by his latest proposal, she agreed. Libbie must have been certain of winning her father's consent, but the next move was entirely up to her long-haired, *beau sabreur*.

Armstrong was supposed to have asked for and received both Emanuel's and Judge Bacon's consent to become engaged to Libbie. Without Bacon's approval there was no hope for the lovers as Libbie would never disrespect her parents by eloping. Apparently, the word reached Bacon, and he took pains to avoid being alone with Armstrong where the question could be asked. On October 5, Armstrong was taking a train back to his command, and well-wishers came to see him off—including Judge Bacon. The two men spoke about his Army prospects, but the platform was unsuitable for what Armstrong needed to say. At the last instant, he asked if he could write to Bacon on an important matter. No father of an eligible daughter could misunderstand those words, but Bacon could only answer, "Very well!"[10]

Strategically, Armstrong would ask only for permission to write to Libbie and this was granted. At last, they could freely send letters to each other, and Libbie called Armstrong "My more than friend."[11] In addition to his romantic feelings, Armstrong's letters contained news from his brigade where, naturally, he was the hero of his own accounts—detailing actions, narrow escapes, and captured trophies. In their letters and during his periodic leaves in Monroe, Armstrong and Libbie talked about their hopes, his ambitions, camp life, and horses—but his dogs do not seem to have ever been a topic.

Armstrong began to carefully put forward his case as good husband to Judge Bacon, citing integrity, temperance, self-reliance since the age of sixteen, and his future. Bacon began to soften, and when Armstrong finally did ask for consent to become engaged, he declared it in such a weighty matter that weeks or even months were needed to deliberate.[12] With his cherished daughter and her general besieging him from two sides, it was inevitable that "Fortress Bacon" would surrender. A ceremony was planned for the spring of 1864, but Armstrong rightly pointed out a spring wedding would leave no time for a proper honeymoon tour as campaigns would be re-starting with improving weather. Libbie felt it was improper to show unmaidenly haste to satisfy an impatient fiancé: "If I am worth having am I not worth waiting for?"[13] Unspoken was the real possibility that the longer they delayed, the greater the chances were of Armstrong being killed before their wedding. At last, Tuesday, February 9 was selected (the last day before Lent), the Presbyterian church was reserved, and Armstrong applied for marriage leave.

The future bridegroom was champing at the bit to get married, but Libbie still showed virginal diffidence. Not only was it unseemly to appear *too* eager, she needed time to assemble her trousseau. She traveled to Detroit for dresses made by professional seamstresses, sent to New York for silks, but made her own nightgowns and undergarments on a treadle sewing machine. Armstrong expected her to ride with him and asked her to order a riding habit. After hearing nothing further, he asked about the habit and Libbie assured him that it had been ordered.[14] Thinking ahead, she prudently bought a waterproof cloak with armholes and which buttoned from head to ankle over her fashionably large skirts.

The church was packed with family and friends and the evening ceremony went off without a hitch. Armstrong wore his dress uniform and Libbie was a vision in all-white silk and lace, with orange blossoms crowning her veil. It was the custom for the community to view the wedding gifts on display in the bride's home. With the amount of silverware the newlyweds were given (including dinner service from the 1st Vermont Cavalry and a tea set from the 7th Michigan Cavalry) and three hundred people trooping through for the reception, Judge Bacon fretted all night long about burglary.[15]

Marriage, Diplomacy and War

On their honeymoon, Brigadier General and Mrs. Custer were accompanied to Cleveland by the whole bridal party (including Jacob Greene and Nettie Humphrey). Separating from their friends, the Custers made stops in New York to visit Libbie's relatives and snowy West Point. There, Libbie was enchanted with the grounds and buildings and understood why her husband loved it so. The professors, staff, and cadets greeted Armstrong enthusiastically, and Libbie wrote her father about their warm welcome—particularly from the West Point dogs.[16] (This was Libbie's first mention of her husband and dogs.) An older professor and several young plebes flirted with her, and on the train to New York City, Armstrong silently glowered—like an "incarcerated thundercloud." Libbie's assurances that it was harmless *and* not of her doing did no good. Finally, she let him have it: "Well, you left me with them, Autie!"[17] Armstrong explained he was accustomed to long periods of silent thought from his punishment tours as a cadet and she shouldn't mind his "silent seasons." Years later, Libbie wrote that when he had a career problem to think out, "...my husband threw himself on the broad couch facedown, the dogs gravely climbing up and packing themselves around him... it was a deliberate process with him, and after the whole question had been given his deepest thought, he sprang to his feet, the dogs ready for play, the same buoyant boy he was as a cadet."[18]

The marriage leave was cut short with orders to return to his brigade. Libbie decided to go with him to Stevensburg, Virginia, and they took up residence on the upper floor of his headquarters. There she first met Eliza, his servant Johnny Cisco, and presumably his campaign dogs. Eliza handled all the housekeeping, which was just as well. Apart from dressmaking, Libbie had not been taught how to run a household. She was fine with the arrangement and had no intention of becoming domestic as Armstrong didn't want her saddled with chores which might prevent her from joining him in some activity.[19] The two women got on well, and Eliza delighted in organizing things for Libbie and Armstrong. Not quite what Libbie was expecting, their farmhouse quarters had a hodgepodge of furniture augmented by Army gear. Still, Pleasonton gave excellent dinners for his staff and commanders, and Libbie was tickled pink to ride in a plush, silver-decorated carriage (Armstrong's war booty) with a trooper escort rather than a less comfortable Army ambulance.

By the end of February, the war was already heating up, and Armstrong sent Libbie to Washington. There, like other Army wives, she roomed in a boarding house to be as close to him as possible as well as to the earliest news and casualty lists. Washington was populated by women in somber clothes—from waiting spouses like herself to officers' wives doing subsistence clerical work to widows petitioning for pensions. The only col-

The nucleus of the Custer Clan: Armstrong, Tom, and Libbie. Tom was like a younger brother to Libbie, and she loved their affectionate nickname for her: the Old Lady. The photograph was taken in January 1865, not quite a year after they were married. Armstrong wears his major general's uniform and has his famous slouch hat in hand. Prints & Photographs, Library of Congress. LC-USZ62-114798.

orful dresses in the capital were those of the prostitutes who were doing a land office business. Libbie was careful to dress sedately and not walk alone on certain streets for fear of being mistaken for one of the "ten thousand."[20] As a woman, she could have no career, but by her charm and wit, she bloomed as an advocate for her husband's career. Historian Shirley A. Leckie described the couple as having a "strong physical attraction binding them together, they had formed a partnership, committed to moving the boy general up the ladder of success."[21] As a general's wife and favorite of Senator Zachariah

Chandler, Libbie was invited to official functions and social affairs. Heeding both her father and husband's advice, she avoided talking politics (Army and government) and kept the conversation light or patriotic as the circumstances called for. Where Armstrong's forte was warfare, Libbie was equally a master of diplomacy, and at teas, dances, and other social occasions, she never said an uncharitable word about anyone. Always mindful that the men she met in Washington could influence her husband's promotions and post-war Army career, Libbie was socially adroit and without giving offense, could deftly avoid a lecherous kiss or hug from a tipsy senator. She kept any conversation from stalling and danced when asked. President Lincoln charmed her and she proved a good "straight man" for his quips.

While socializing could be pleasurable, the heat and humidity in Washington during the summer were difficult and the over-full hospitals, maimed soldiers, and the seemingly endless funerals made the place even more of a trial.[22] Libbie was appalled by the glass-eyed, stuffed dogs, staring out from embalmers' windows as advertisements for their art.[23] Everywhere there were wounded soldiers, and she was too fretful to attempt her normal creative outlets of writing and drawing. Unable to tolerate long periods in Washington, Libbie escaped to Armstrong in the field whenever it was safe and manageable—once even surprising him by showing up unbidden, and Armstrong would say, "I knew nothing of her coming until I heard she was at Harper's Ferry. It is all I can do to keep her from coming out right to camp."[24]

The leadership in the Army continued to change. Shortly after Armstrong was recalled to duty, Lincoln promoted Ulysses S. Grant to lieutenant general in charge of all the Union's armies. Unhappy with Pleasonton's record, Grant installed General Philip Sheridan as commander of the Cavalry Corps. "Little Phil" intended to use the cavalry more strategically rather than just for reconnaissance and flank attacks as they had been previously. Sheridan and Armstrong were a perfect match, and the two would become lasting friends.

In May 1864, Armstrong fought in the Battle of the Wilderness and at Yellow Tavern made a brilliant charge where "Jeb" Stuart, was mortally wounded. At Trevilian Station in June, Armstrong was beaten in a hot fight where he and his men were suddenly surrounded. Other units came to his rescue, and they fought their way out, abandoning Armstrong's baggage train. Eliza, Johnny Cisco, horses, and presumably the dogs were captured. Somehow Eliza (and presumably Johnny and the dogs) escaped and rejoined Armstrong. Along with his personal gear, he lost his valise with Libbie's ambrotypes and letters. (Their mildly erotic correspondence indicated a passionate and imaginative love life.) Armstrong had to tell her the letters were probably read by the Rebels—and cautioned about any future double entendre regarding their lovemaking. Libbie countered that she shouldn't have to refrain as there could "be nothing low between husband and wife." While Armstrong agreed in principle and believed that no gentleman, Southern or Northern, ought to be reading a couple's private letters, he did make her promise to avoid passionate euphemisms because he hated to think of a stranger being amused by the letters.[25] (Armstrong's pet names for Libbie were, "My Little Army Crow," "Darling Durl," "Rosebud," and "Sunbeam"—and he was her "star" or "my boy.")

Grant had instructed Sheridan to pursue Jubal Early's corps in the Shenandoah Valley and to torch the fertile corridor so it could not feed Early, the Rebel Army, or

Richmond. It was a previously unthinkable kind of warfare—a "total war" which affected civilians and their ability to feed themselves. Regrettable, but it was deemed absolutely necessary when fighting guerrillas on their home ground. The campaign spanned the harvest, lasting from May through October. Between September 26 and October 8, Sheridan's men confiscated livestock and torched every barn, mill, and store of grain they found. It would be remembered by the residents as "The Burning." The total war tactic was also used by Sherman on his infamous March to the Sea in Georgia—and years later, he would order it to crush the independent tribes of the Plains.

On September 10, Libbie took the train from Washington northwest to Sheridan's headquarters at Harper's Ferry. Armstrong rode sixteen miles from the Berryville camp to spend the day with her. Unbeknownst to him, she intended to stay two weeks, and he arranged a hotel room and would return to see her when he could.[26] Nine days later, Armstrong and his brigade fought the third battle of Winchester (near Harpers Ferry), and on October 9, commanding the 3rd Division, he beat his West Point friend General Thomas Rosser, at Tom's Brook—capturing his baggage. (Armstrong sent Rosser a note through the lines saying his tailor should do a better job as the uniform fit him poorly.) At Cedar Creek on October 19, Armstrong and Merritt's brigades effectively bottled up Jubal Early's cavalry. The victorious Armstrong was promoted to Major General of Volunteers, and Sheridan sent him to present their captured rebel flags at the Capitol. Unaware he was coming to Washington, Libbie was in New Jersey when she learned on October 23 she had missed Armstrong and was heartbroken. The ceremony was to be delayed, and when he learned where she was, he grabbed a train to Trenton and surprised her, bounding up the stairs with thudding boots and clanking saber. The morning after their reunion, they returned to Washington for Armstrong's ceremony.[27]

At this point in their marriage, it is unclear precisely what Libbie thought about Armstrong's dogs, but she did strenuously object to his pet raccoon, Dixie, sleeping on his pillow and said as much. He wrote back and talked about Dixie's antics, a pet squirrel captured from Rosser, and Eliza's goat. He assured Libbie the disgruntled Dixie was now relegated to the foot of his bed.[28] (Like many soldiers, Armstrong knew the value of a warm critter on a cold night, and during winter campaigns in Kansas he had his dogs for body heat.)

At the end of October, Armstrong was well settled in Winchester for the winter, and with Sheridan's approval, he asked Libbie to join him,

> You must make up your mind to fewer comforts than you now enjoy. You will lead a real soldier's life. Do not come if you do not desire it.... Bring riding-habit, one small trunk. You will not need any nice dresses this time.

Libbie replied, "I love luxury, dress, comfort. But, Oh, how gladly I will give them up. I can be ready in a day or two. I can hardly wait."[29] She was there within the week. Armstrong devised a prank and met her on the platform wearing a Confederate uniform—slouch hat, overcoat, and trousers and as Libbie put it, "looking every inch a rebel."[30] His captured carriage was there for her with an escort of 150 troopers with his banner bearers. All this delighted Libbie, who knew the cavalry was not just for show as there had been guerrilla action in the area by Mosby's Raiders—partisan Rebels who were wreaking havoc on supply lines and communications.

Libbie followed Armstrong's packing instructions to the letter—almost. She brought one or perhaps two calico dresses for mornings, an afternoon dress, her riding habit, and presumably her waterproof. She chose deliberately plain clothes because she did not think an Army camp was "an appropriate place for display."[31] Libbie would teach herself to pack light and fast so she could move with the brigade on a moment's notice—although she could not pull her shoes on as quickly as soldiers did their boots. Libbie was said to always have her hat on and boots buttoned so she would not be left behind.[32] (Shoes were buttoned with a slender hook and getting both done took some minutes.)

She was introduced to living in a tent—admittedly a general's tent-complex, rather than a soldier's pup tent (also called "dog tents"), but it was still canvas. In a circle of evergreens, there was a bedroom tent, another for a reception with a floor made from a barn door, and Eliza's nearby tent was their dining room.[33] Libbie noticed only some of the soldiers had tents—the rest had made log huts or dugouts with wooden chimneys for protection from the winter rain and snow. Sometimes there were commandeered houses which she and Armstrong could use, but Libbie came to love tent life when the weather was at all decent. She wrote to cousin Rebecca,

> It seemed so strange at first to sleep in a tent, like sleeping out of doors; almost no furniture, the free winds of heaven playing with the walls. But oh, so exciting, a fascination about it. A soldier's life is glorious.[34]

Of course, what Libbie meant was that a *general's* life was glorious—she had yet to see any carnage.

Headquarters, 1st Brigade of Horse Artillery, Brandy Station, Virginia, in the winter of 1863–64. There was a strong culture of dogs in both Union and Confederate armies, and while there are no Civil War photographs of the Custers with dogs, this image of a husband, wife, and fellow lieutenants is not atypical of camp scenes. (Officers had the luxury of being able to keep bigger dogs than those of their men.) Prints & Photographs, Library of Congress, LC-B8171-7582.

The romance of being a soldier's wife began to dissipate when faced with the practicalities of Spartan camp life and being left with Eliza when her husband was working or fighting. "I had countless surprises and genuine scares in that bewildering life," she wrote. "I was afraid of everything at first and never got over some of the frights, not at all the sort of wife for a 'warrior bold.'"[35] Despite Libbie's accustomed ease of life at home and the boarding house, she adapted surprisingly quickly to being an officer's wife. "But, Father, I assure you, in this age of delicate females, none is better adapted to army life than your daughter."[36] To be near Armstrong, she came to terms with canvas shelter, rationed food, rough comforts, pre-dawn reveilles, breakfast by candlelight, washing in basins, and mud—which was hard on skirts and shoes. When there was to be a battle, Armstrong sent her and Eliza to General Torbert's headquarters near the main body of the Army, where they would wait with ready carriage just in case.

The Old Lady and Her Husband's Dogs

Armstrong wanted Libbie to ride with him, and her riding habit had been made in military style in dark green cloth with the bodice accented with cavalry-yellow piping and a single row of brass buttons. The very full skirt covered her down to the ankles (modest trousers were worn underneath so that legs could lock around the saddle's pommel and leaping horn). Libbie sported a black velvet jockey hat with red plume and leather gloves and had a long riding whip to reach back beyond her draped skirts to the horse's rump. At Armstrong's request, the jacket's sleeves had gold Austrian knots to match those of his own uniform.[37] To further mark her as the Boy General's wife, Libbie wore the metal badge he adopted—a cross *pattée* with an inverted, five-point star as the top arm of the cross. Written on it was "Custer" and the motto from the great seal of Michigan—"*Tuebor*" (I will defend).

Riding in camp was rougher than the Sunday pleasure outings in Monroe or Howlett Hill. It took practice to adjust to an English-style, side saddle, which did not have the more generous, secure, Western-style cantle. With a borrowed horse, she began to jump ditches.[38] In Libbie's prior life, horses appeared saddled for riding and disappeared afterwards, and she knew nothing of feeding, watering, grooming, and doctoring horses (or dogs). She had not been exposed to the full experience of life with animals, and her husband owned several horses and dogs.

> Love and admiration for horses was awakened for me at our first camp. The horses were picketed so near, to protect them from capture, that when eating their forage, they seemed under the canvas of our tent. In a long, cold storm I know my husband would gladly have taken his idolized animal in our tent, if there had been room.[39]

For the first time, Libbie was surrounded by horses and hounds—and Armstrong had considerably more privilege in his campaign lifestyle with regard to dogs than he did when he was a shavetail lieutenant.

After over a year of politicking and cajoling, Armstrong finally got his brother on staff, and Tom arrived at Winchester a few days after Libbie. She liked the handsome young man and treated him like a younger brother. Away from camp, Armstrong and Tom had billeted themselves with a Pennsylvania Dutchman whose wife worried about them stealing their meager belongings. After a couple of days, the fellow apologetically told the Custers they could no longer stay, "You see, I'm willin' but 'the old lady,' she kicks agin it." And from then on, Armstrong and Tom would talk about her "kicking agin" something which might be fun. Libbie, at twenty-two, was delighted to be called "the Old Lady."[40]

Libbie's Civil War memoirs and notes can be rather vague and frustrating for historians trying to reconcile a date or location, or identify a person (she frequently used an initial instead of a surname). Libbie's few dog notes (written decades afterwards) date from after joining Armstrong's brigade in Winchester. Always an excellent observer, in her first passage about dogs, Libbie described how they suddenly appeared at the end of a march.

> And the secluded dogs that crawled forth when the wagons were parked. Crowded for hours into the smallest space, smothered, thirsty but almost with human understanding that they were contraband, that if they barked or whined they would be separated from their adored master, and dog lovers know that they have died from that grief. Out of a crevice in the packed wagon the dog leaped at the end of a march, shaking himself, frisking about his owner, growling if anyone came near his possession. In the winter camp the education of a dog went on famously and his tricks were part of the campfire amusement and, oh, the comfort to a homesick man. When the marching orders came he knew as well as humans that he was infra dig and was silent and subdued, hidden without a thump of the demonstrative tail.[41] [Libbie was facile with language and expression, and uses "infra dig" as a shortened version of *infra dignitatem*, meaning beneath one's dignity—anthropomorphically suggesting the dogs knew their precariously low status.]

With this reporter-like prose, Libbie does not seem to be describing her husband's dogs. Later, a hint of affection creeps in when she writes about crossing the "roaring, boiling" Potomac River at Harper's Ferry, over a long pontoon bridge, which was only planks laid precariously on flat-bottomed boats, all tied together. While the teamster lashed furiously at the mules, she cowered in the bottom of the wagon through the crossing. Almost safely across, the wagon stalled on the steep bank and had to be hauled up by men with ropes. There was a happy reunion with the dogs afterwards, but how they got across that torrent seems nothing short of a miracle.

> The dogs, who had swum the river, with their noses, [were] shaking water over me in their rejoicing over the feat we had accomplished, whining with pleasure, putting their paws on my shoulder in excitement, or snuggling their shaggy wet sides against me. And when the tent was pitched, stealing under the flap, crawling under the bed, only discovered by [their] licking, snuffling, and snorting.[42]

As survivors of the crossing, Libbie and her husband's dogs now had something in common. From her account, Armstrong had at least two dogs which were strong enough to swim the river. Clearly, Libbie was not bothered by their friendly, wet greetings and rather amused by the dogs' affection for her. It is possible she misremembered Harper's Ferry as the crossing but what is unmistakable is the glimmer of feeling for the dogs. Unfortunately, neither Libbie nor Armstrong seem to mention their campaign dogs again (or give them names)—but then the war was keeping them busy.

In the presidential arena, Sheridan's recent successes in the Shenandoah Valley had greatly helped Lincoln's campaign for re-election. He bested McClellan in the November 1864 election and his second inauguration was scheduled for March. Sheridan was generally dissatisfied with his officers in Winchester and decided that their wives (there on extended visits) were distracting them from their duties.[43] They were all ordered to leave except Libbie Custer—who had charmed Sheridan when they first met in July.⁴⁴ The wives left, Libbie stayed—and presumably acquired clothing suitable for the coming winter.

Sheridan could not grant the customary Christmas leave to Armstrong as he was needed for his regular duties and to preside over a court martial of two deserters who had turned spy. He did get a short leave after Christmas, and following a grand send-off banquet hosted by Sheridan on Sunday, January 1, he, Libbie, and Eliza dashed home to Monroe via Washington and New York City. They visited P. T. Barnum's American Museum in lower Manhattan (near today's site of the 9/11 Memorial). As a girl, Libbie had not been permitted to see Barnum's traveling show, but with her husband, she could. The five-story, wooden building was crammed with oddities, human "wonders of nature," art, dioramas, personalities in wax (including the one of Jefferson Davis in petticoats), automatons, the Feejee Mermaid, Egyptian mummies, and an exotic menagerie. Eliza's reaction to the family of mummies and the fat lady was apparently comical enough that Libbie later noted it for one of her lectures.⁴⁵

They returned to Winchester that month with Rhoda Bacon and Rebecca Richmond. Judge Bacon was reaping the benefit of a famous general as a son-in-law, for Armstrong sent him a railroad pass to Winchester so he could see something of the war. While the in-laws were visiting, he had them join Libbie and his staff for a photo on the steps of the mansion which served as headquarters, and Tom posed with a little dog in his lap.⁴⁶ The Bacons and Rebecca stayed to the end of February when they and Libbie traveled to Washington for the festivities of Lincoln's inauguration on March 4. It was a good time for them to leave, as Sheridan was gearing up to push through the Shenandoah. For this advance, the wily "Little Phil" had in mind a *ruse de guerre* in which dogs would play a part.

Outfoxing Jubal Early

Winchester was situated between Washington and the mouth of the Shenandoah Valley which, for the Confederates, had been bread basket, refuge, and a highway for attacking northwards. The Federals had been plagued by Mosby, "the Gray Ghost," and his guerrilla raiders—who were so effective that Grant ordered their summary hanging if captured. Sheridan organized a counter-guerrilla force of some sixty scouts called Sheridan's Raiders (also called Jessie's Scouts), led by Lt. Col. Henry H. Young of Rhode Island. Young, who as Chief of Scouts was assigned to play Mosby's ruthless game, and both sides changed uniform colors when needed. As it happened, Young had his foxhounds with him.

It was still winter and neither army expected to do much fighting while the weather was poor. Early's Confederate units in the valley had been given home leave to obtain better rations and shelter. Sheridan was going to move on Early before he could reassemble his troops—but there were known informants, pretending to be Northern sympathizers in camp, and his preparations would be reported to Mosby and Early. Taking advantage of this, Sheridan created a plausible ruse. Although the beloved fox hunts of antebellum Virginia and Maryland had come to a virtual halt, when there was nothing else to do in winter, both Union and Confederate officers staged fox hunts with hound packs assembled on the spot. Sheridan, himself an old hunter, had his officers plan a "grand fox-chase" for the last day of February. It was carefully arranged for the spies, to see the "leash" of red foxes caught for the hunt along with the large pack of fox hounds owned by Lt. Col. Young.[47] Libbie noted over the course of a week, a great show was made of shoeing horses, refurbishing tack, and "the men entering into every preparation with great enthusiasm and in constant confabs with the darkies who were of course up in the haunts of the foxes."[48] Had Armstrong not more important work to do for Sheridan, he would have loved being in on the fox hunt as a good joke on the Rebels. (Despite the war, hounds were still important to Southerners as evidenced by a dog deal in 1864, where two six-week-old fox hound puppies from Dr. Thomas Y. Henry in Charlotte, Virginia, were taken nearly six hundred miles to Col. George Lawrence Forsyth Birdsong in Upson, Georgia. These were the foundation of the famous Buchanan-Henry-Birdsong foxhounds.[49])

Two days before the Rebels believed the grand fox hunt was to happen, Sheridan unleashed his cavalry. Armstrong's and Brigadier General Thomas Casimer Devin's divisions advanced rapidly with artillery, pontoon bridge materials, and a supply train. There were rations for fifteen days—the estimated time needed to clear out the Rebels.[50] (It was possibly the first time a hunt had been used for a strategic military purpose, but definitely not the only instance. In 1918, a group of British officers, prisoners of war in Yozgat, Turkey, covered a mass escape by an organized hare hunt with the native Saluki hounds they had been allowed to keep for coursing hare.[51])

Sheridan's war machine rolled southwards and on March 2, at the Battle of Waynesboro, Armstrong made a frontal charge against Jubal Early's defenses and followed with a flank attack. The Rebel force collapsed, with Early just barely escaping. The captured flags were to be presented in Washington and though Armstrong was too busy to attend the event, Libbie and Rebecca went to the ceremony. In his office, the Secretary of War, Edwin Stanton, recognized Libbie and introduced her as "the wife of the gallant general." As each flag was presented it was attributed to "Brevet Major General Custer commanding," and she was delighted when people pointed and said, "That's the wife of Custer!"[52] But there were still battles to be fought, so Libbie made a replacement for his personal banner in time for the last hurrah of the war. Larger than the first, it was swallow-tail in shape with white crossed sabers on a red and blue background with her stitched initials on one of the points.[53]

In the final week of March, Sheridan and Grant joined their armies against Lee's Army of Northern Virginia and things began to snowball. Armstrong got his banner just as the Battle of Dinwiddie Courthouse was beginning on the 31st. It was only a partial victory for Sheridan. Lee was encouraged but withdrew to Five Forks. Sheridan pressed them again and on April Fool's Day, the Union won. Tom Custer was in the fighting and awarded a pair of Congressional Medals of Honor and a brevet colonelcy for capturing a battle flag at Namozine Church, and three days later at Sailor's Creek, repeating the feat. There, a bullet tore through the flesh of his jaw and cheek, narrowly missing the jugular vein. On the afternoon of April 8, there was a fight at Appomattox Station. Armstrong's division captured three of the four supply trains there and, after being shelled all day, they charged at night and captured prisoners, wagons, and guns. The Rebels were surrounded near Appomattox Courthouse, and at dawn they tried to break out, but Lee quickly recognized his worn out army was no match for the Federals. So terms could be discussed, he sent forward a white flag, and Armstrong happened to be in the right place to receive it. There was a slight disagreement over whether this was a truce or a full surrender, and if the latter, whether Armstrong, as a brevet major general of volunteers, was entitled to receive the surrender of an entire army—which he surely wanted for his credit.[54] Despite some uneasy moments, that was the beginning of Robert E. Lee's surrender.

The Little Table at Appomattox Courthouse

The victor would normally designate the meeting place for surrender but Grant generously allowed Lee this privilege. Wilmer McLean's home was chosen as it was near Appomattox Station and also the local courthouse. (Ironically, McLean had relocated there after his home had been destroyed at the First Battle of Bull Run.) Grant and Lee with their senior generals (including Sheridan) gathered in the parlor to discuss terms. The two men were old friends from West Point and reminisced about the Mexican War while officers from both sides sought out friends across the lines. Writing at a small table with spiral-turned legs, Grant drafted the terms of capitulation. They were very generous—the Rebels would not be charged with treason, they could keep their horses and mules for farming, were given badly needed food and the officers kept their side arms and personal baggage. Lee signed the document on a larger table and it went back to Grant for his signature. The men shook hands and parted to arrange the ceremony where the Army of Northern Virginia would formally hand over their muskets, cannon, and regimental flags.

With those two signatures, the Appomattox Courthouse had suddenly become a historic place, and Grant's staff knew it. There was a rush for parlor souvenirs, and from McLean they purchased everything from furniture to candlesticks to carpets. For $20 in gold (approximately $250 in today's dollars), Sheridan bought the small table Grant had used. As a mark of his esteem, he gave the table to Armstrong for Libbie, along with this note,

> My Dear Madam,—I respectfully present to you the small writing table on which the conditions for the surrender of the Confederate Army of Northern Virginia were written by Lt. General Grant—and permit me to say, Madam, that there is scarcely an individual in our service who has contributed more to bring about this desirable result than your gallant husband.[55]

Armstrong thought this was wonderful, bounded down the steps like a schoolboy, and rode off with the table balanced precariously on his head.[56] (Kept for years by Libbie, the table and its parlor companion are now in the Smithsonian National Museum of American History.)

However, the war was not entirely finished as there were still other Confederate units fighting in the South, and President Jefferson Davis was a fugitive. Far from Armstrong's mind just then was any notion of what he was going to do in peacetime. There was another mission brewing for him and in assigning it, Sheridan would unintentionally open Armstrong's eyes to an entirely new aspect of fun with dogs.

Tail Pieces: The Sporting Ritual of Foxhunting in America

In 18th century England the elements of fox hunting became fixed and ritualized. Ostensibly, the reason was to eliminate predation of poultry—and the hunt served that purpose, but an exciting chase with friends following a pack of baying hounds was also fun. As the Colonists evolved their own lifestyle, keeping a foxhound pack was one of the marks of landed gentry—although with American egalitarianism, anyone who could afford hounds kept them. The Colonists hunted fox, deer, raccoon, possum, and skunk, and in some areas, lynx, mountain lion, wolf, and bear—selectively breeding for local terrain and quarry. The relative isolation of population centers led to over seventy different strains of foxhounds.

This type of social hunting afforded the renewal of acquaintances and community standings, and discussions of politics, business, and local gossip. There were formal hunts with a leadership structure and casual ones as simple as a free-for-all chase. In a typical hunt, the men (it was not uncommon for women to hunt in the South) gathered for a dawn breakfast and would ride off with the hounds to find a trail in the brush. The Master of Fox Hounds had absolute authority and was assisted by the Huntsman and Whippers-In who managed the dogs. Each hound man controlled his pack by blowing a particular call on a horn or with a dog whip—cracked as a warning to stay put. When the foxhounds struck a scent, they would give chase, barking and howling. Their "music" or "tonguing" allowed the hunters to follow their own packs. A chase might go twenty to thirty miles and sometimes continue on the next day. After the conclusion, there would be another gathering for refreshments and stories of the day.

Slave Tracking and Prison Guard Dogs

There was a dark side to the dogs of the Civil War. The notorious Confederate prisons at Andersonville, Libby, and Castle Thunder had ferocious tracking hounds which intimidated and ran down escaped prisoners. (Estimates of prisoner deaths on both sides by starvation or disease run to 56,000. Armstrong's friend from Monroe, Jacob Greene, was in Libby Prison and barely survived.) During the 2nd Seminole War in Florida (1835–1842), the Army actually imported "Cuban bloodhounds" and handlers to track the Seminole in the swamps. Unpopular with Congress and the public, it was a sound military idea but poorly implemented, and the project failed spectacularly.[57] Landowners in the South imported these hounds as well as using their own game-hunting trail hounds to track and terrorize slaves. If a plantation owner did not own a trail hound or two, there were men who would hire theirs out for a slave hunt.[58]

With advent of the prisoner of war camps there was suddenly a need of dogs to find escaped prisoners and it was easy enough to re-train slave hunting hounds. This was known and depicted in magazines in the North, and the hounds became a symbol not only of the hated institution of slavery but of the rebellion. The dogs were an easy target for vengeance and during Sherman's total war in Georgia, he ordered his men to kill any tracking hounds they found. Sometimes soldiers adopted these dogs (and other animals) but more often they shot or bayonetted both scent hounds and pet dogs indiscriminately.[59] Of the pack of hounds which guarded prisoners in Andersonville, eleven were killed by liberating soldiers, and two were sent north. One died, but the most terrifying of the lot, a large Cuban Bloodhound named Spot, was kept as a curiosity.[60] The twin Richmond prisons, Libby and Castle Thunder, shared a fierce "Russian bloodhound" named Hero (possibly Nero) who, like Spot, also had a heavy body and cropped ears. Hero was also taken north as a novelty.[61]

Chapter 5

The Texas Pack

"Libbie's admiration for dogs is second only to that for her horses, the latter ranking next to her affection for her nearest relatives."—Armstrong to Libbie's parents[1]

By the end of the war, Libbie was tolerant of her husband's canine dabbling, but his next command would change that. He was to be a civil peacekeeper—not a subject taught at West Point. More tedious than campaigns, it required a fine balance of diplomacy and both martial and civil law. Fortunately, Armstrong found a substitute for the excitement of war in hunting with the sombrero-wearing, good old boys of Texas and their hounds.

The morning after Lee's capitulation, Washington awoke to church bells and cannon salutes even though other Confederate units hadn't yet surrendered. Senator Chandler personally invited Libbie to join him, and the Committee on the Conduct of the War and their wives, to travel to Richmond. Libbie packed as quickly as if she were on campaign again. The party went by train to Fortress Monroe, boarded President Lincoln's gunboat and steamed up the James River to Richmond. At City Point Libbie asked Admiral David Dixon Porter to telegraph Armstrong that she was going to Richmond.[2]

There, Libbie toured President Jefferson Davis's abandoned home under the housekeeper's watchful eye, inspecting their furnishings. Mrs. Davis had taken the silver and linens but Libbie though it odd that she had left a sewing machine and a small dog belonging to their young son, Jefferson Davis, Jr. That night, Mrs. Custer slept in the President of the Confederacy's bed and on the next, in his wife's bedroom. On April 11th, Armstrong, "tanned but thin and worn," woke her up.[3] Their reunion was doubly joyous as they knew the Union would be victorious. Later, they joked about Libbie arriving in Richmond ahead of Armstrong—who had taken four hard years to get there.[4] With the war all but over, there was soon going to be nothing for Brevet Major General Custer to do—and he had never been a peacetime soldier.

There were still Confederate units in North Carolina, the Trans-Mississippi, and Texas. A few loyalists developed a plot to decapitate the government and encourage the Rebels who were still fighting. On the evening of April 14, the actor John Wilkes Booth entered the president's box in Ford's Theater and shot Abraham Lincoln. One man botched an attempt on Secretary of State, William Seward, and another lost his nerve, failing to attack Vice President Andrew Johnson. Lincoln was taken to a house where his long body had to be laid diagonally on the bed. The president died on the morning of April 15—the day that Armstrong's promotion to major general was confirmed.

The unthinkable assassination shocked the nation but didn't paralyze the government or the Army's victories. Grant was already talking to Sheridan about finishing the war in the Southwest. The latter wrote to Armstrong on May 7 about going to Texas with a cavalry command.[5] Two days later, President Andrew Johnson declared the war over despite some scattered fighting. Jefferson Davis was captured on May 10 and the last battle was fought in south Texas on May 12 and 13—but the very last surrender was that of the C.S.S. *Shenandoah*. The Confederate raider was out of communication while capturing whalers along the Pacific Coast. After Captain Waddell heard the news, he sailed to Liverpool and surrendered the *Shenandoah* on November 6, 1865.

Eliza Brown, Libbie and Armstrong Custer, April 1865. Armstrong, looking a little haggard at the end of the war, wears a fairly plain major general's tunic with his signature red necktie, and Libbie wears her military-style riding habit and velvet jockey cap and holds her riding whip. Both are wearing Armstrong's personal pin with the *"Tuebor"* motto ("to protect"). Eliza, the Custers' cook and housekeeper, was frequently included in their photographs. Courtesy of the National Park Service, Little Bighorn Battlefield National Monument, LIBI_0019_00562. Original tintype attributed to William Frank Browne.

There was to be a celebratory, Grand Review of the Army in Washington on May 23 and 24. While the Confederate forces in Texas were finished, another threat loomed along the Rio Grande. Mexico's colonial French government under Emperor Maximilian had been collaborating with Texas Confederates along the border, and it appeared they were going to use post-war unrest to reclaim by force territory lost in the Mexican War. At the same time, Maximilian's Legionnaires (the French Foreign Legion) were fighting Benito Juarez's Nationalist troops. A strong American presence was needed to meet the threat of Mexican troops crossing the Rio Grande. (Sheridan's force included his fox hunting, Chief of Scouts, Col. Henry Young, who would be killed in an ambush by renegade ex–Confederate soldiers and Mexican rancheros on the Rio Grande.[6])

Armstrong was to follow Sheridan after the Grand Review on the 23rd. At the head of his cavalry division, his thoroughbred, Don Juan (a dubiously obtained spoil of war), bolted at a drum flourish just as he was saluting the dignitaries. Armstrong lost his hat and saber as the race horse galloped down Pennsylvania Avenue. (General Alexander Pennington, who witnessed the incident, said races in Virginia were started by a drummer which accounted for Don Juan's sudden launch.[7]) The crowd applauded thunderously. Depending on how people felt about George Armstrong Custer, the incident was an accident or shameless grandstanding.

Gone to Texas

Armstrong skipped the second day of the Grand Review and headed out to assume his command, the Cavalry Division, Military District of the Southwest, but he hadn't told Libbie the assignment in Texas might expand into a Mexican campaign. He, Libbie, Eliza, and his picked staff (including Tom and Capt. Jacob Greene—still haggard from Libby Prison) went briefly to Monroe and then headed south on May 31 by train and steamboat.[8] The horses, Custis Lee (named for General Robert E. Lee's eldest son) and Jack Rucker, came with them, but none of Armstrong's campaign dogs, which if still alive, would have had been left with brother officers. Whether his horses were in a livestock car or on the deck of a riverboat, it was Armstrong's habit to check them often to ensure they were not suffering from long confinement.[9]

Arriving in New Orleans in June, Armstrong and Libbie shopped and dined in French restaurants, and she delighted in tasting lobster, crab, and shrimp. For souvenirs, they had their portraits painted on porcelain vases.[10] They met retired General in Chief, Winfield Scott, who was in poor health but glad to see his former messenger had general's stars. The immense Scott could not rise to meet Libbie, and she felt sorry for him.[11] Armstrong spoke with Sheridan at his headquarters in the French Quarter and learned that he and his friend, Wesley Merritt, were to have 4,000 cavalry each in Houston and San Antonio. To the border hotbed of Brownsville, where the Mexican government was colluding with ex–Confederates, a large force was assigned with additional infantry for Galveston and Houston.[12] At Alexandria, Louisiana, Armstrong would assume command. He and his staff took passage on a Red River steamer, but it wasn't the same as the plush cruise on the Mississippi. The boat was smaller and the crooked, muddy river was laced with dangerous snags. The banks were lined with trees which dripped moss, and with little to see, Armstrong and Tom amused themselves by shooting alligators.

Many of Alexandria's homes had been damaged or abandoned during the war, but a large house was found for headquarters and the Custers. Armstrong's cavalry were veteran volunteers—the 1st Iowa, 2nd Wisconsin, 7th Indiana, and the 5th and 12th Illinois.[13] The men were not happy as they had volunteered to fight for the duration of the war. It was over and their families and occupations needed them. The climate was oppressively hot and humid and made worse by mosquitos and fever. Uniform and equipment resupply was substandard and the appalling rations came from swindling contractors. Their meat was chiefly gristle and fat or bristled hog jowls with tusks, and the hardtack was riddled with weevils.[14] When they marched to Texas, cattle were driven with the column and beeves slaughtered daily, but with no time to age, the beef rations were nearly inedible. The poor food prompted the men (who felt entitled as victors) to steal livestock, eggs, butter, and vegetables. Their officers, possibly sympathetic to the troopers' plight, turned a blind eye to the thefts. This fanned an already smoldering resentment against the occupying Army.

Almost immediately, Armstrong received citizen complaints about the thefts. With reconciliation a firm goal for President Johnson, Sheridan wanted no resentment by the local population. He gave strict orders that his Army was not to live off the land as in wartime. Armstrong prohibited foraging and overreacted with punishments. He declared there was no time for courts martial or civil trials, and perpetrators would be convicted, have their heads shaved, and, "twenty-five lashes upon his back, well laid on."[15] Armstrong had no right to order these punishments as they were illegal, to say nothing of being harsh and capricious. All soldiers had the right of due process through a court martial, and flogging had been abolished in 1861.[16] Standard punishments ranged from the mild (extra guard duty, being dismounted on the march, or cleaning kitchens or latrines) to those which humiliated and caused pain. Of the latter, men carried logs in endless circles, were spread-eagled for hours on a wagon wheel, or sat astride a narrow board for hours on end in the sun. Deserters were shot at and if captured alive, tattooed and sentenced to hard labor—often with a twenty-five pound iron ball shackled to their ankle.[17]

Despite bad rations, soldiers could only get food from the quartermaster and make private purchases from the locals. When produce was for sale, the officers usually got there first. Army medical supplies were deficient and with mosquito-borne breakbone or dengue fever, troopers pooled their wages to purchase quinine. Resentment and indiscipline continued. These regiments were used to an informal style of soldiering, and if they didn't see the reason for an order, both officers and men might question it. They wrote petitions and talked openly of mutiny—they hadn't volunteered to be policemen in Texas (much less fight in Mexico). A few soldiers took shots at unpopular officers, and some deserted. All this infuriated Armstrong, whose Wolverines and 3rd Cavalry Division had been obedient and loyal to him. Appeasing complaining soldiers was unthinkable so discipline increased while morale declined—but becoming a martinet without first knowing his men was a mistake. A newspaper article accused him of "gross inhumanity" by "a system of tyranny and oppression ... unparalleled in the history of the war."[18] The formerly brilliant Boy General was becoming known as a commander who cared little for his men. There were murmurs of a death threat, but Armstrong insisted to Libbie that "barking dogs do not bite." Still, to ease her mind, he placed a revolver under his pillow, although he later confessed that he never loaded it.[19]

Sheridan approved of Armstrong's draconian methods (and their results) and gave him a new title—Commander of the Cavalry Forces of the Department of Texas. He continued to bestow confusing title changes until Armstrong was Chief of Cavalry of the Department of Texas—a position he held until February 1866.[20] His men called him Old Curly, but not with the Wolverines' affection. He would soon earn new nicknames—Iron Butt and Hard Ass—because he could ride tirelessly for hours and also for his stern discipline.

At the end of July, Armstrong's force set off to Hempstead, sixty miles northwest of Houston. From Alexandria, the distance was 240 miles but because of the heat, the column only traveled about fifteen miles per day instead of twenty. Libbie rode Custis Lee or sat in her ambulance drawn by four matched gray horses.[21] Normally pulled by four mules, the tall Rucker wagon with high sides had better spring suspension than ordinary wagons (which might only have springs on the driver's seat). Designed for wounded men, there were two leather or canvas covered benches which could be converted into a bed. Four people could be seated comfortably and eight if necessary. A canvas roof with curtains gave protection from sun and rain, and suspended underneath the body was a bucket for watering the mules and a keg of water. Armstrong had it fitted with canvas pockets for Libbie's personal needs such as her needlework and book, and there was a box for her lunch meal. One of the soldiers made a leather cover for her canteen with "Lady Custer" stitched in yellow silk.[22]

The Gulf climate was sticky hot, so for comfort's sake, Armstrong was persuaded by Libbie to cut his hair short. It was nothing like campaigning in Virginia. The column, with its supply train, ambulances, and pontoon bridge components, marched southeast through dry, breezeless pine forests that made Libbie feel claustrophobic. The weather, exertion, and diet were a trial for all. Diarrhea, boils, and fever plagued the men while horses suffered from saddle sores, glanders, flies, and hoof ailments—and if a horse could not be ridden, its owner had to walk.

Water was scarce and biting insects (red ants, ticks, chiggers, fleas, centipedes, scorpions, and mosquitos) pestered them constantly—and there were venomous rattlesnakes, water moccasins, and copperheads. While Libbie loved "tenting," the omnipresent bugs and snakes drove her to sleep in the ambulance. Because there was no way for a lady in skirts to modestly climb into the tall ambulance or get down, Armstrong would gallantly lift her each time. Sleeping late was never an option with the cavalry. Reveille was well before dawn so that ablutions, breakfast, roll call, sick call, saddling, and packing up were completed and the column moving soon after first light. Armstrong would not risk his wife being called a "feather bed soldier" and roused her to breakfast by candlelight (Eliza was already up and cooking). Libbie learned quickly that dawdling would keep the column waiting while daylight was burning—and she did not want to be resented. Dressing unassisted was quite the process for a Victorian lady. If she was riding in the ambulance that day, she had to don undergarments, petticoats, corset, skirt, bodice, bonnet, and button her low-rise boots. Her mirror was broken early in the march and so her toilette was all done by feel. She gave up trying to fix her hair and combed it back to be tied behind her neck or confined in a net. Libbie was quite proud that she learned to bathe and dress in only seven minutes inside the ambulance (surreptitiously, Armstrong once timed her) and considered it high praise when he introduced her to other officers, "Oh, I want you to know my wife; she slept four months in a wagon."[23]

Always impatient, Armstrong never waited for his column to start its lumbering march. He, Libbie, and a staff member or two would briskly ride ahead and spend the morning scouting the next campsite. Armstrong kept a shotgun in a saddle holster and shooting game birds was a daily activity that kept him from being bored and provided variety for dinner. He never got tired of seeing new landscape, and choosing that night's campsite was a privilege he always reserved for himself. Finding a good site was a challenge as cavalry camps needed fresh water, open space, grazing, and fuel for fires (when there was no firewood or brush, dried buffalo dung was burned). Generally, by midday, Armstrong would have made his decision and sent someone to guide the column in. Their afternoons on the road to Hempstead were idle and they napped or read under shade trees or canvas stretched out from the ambulance. On one siesta, Libbie accidentally left her gold-braided riding jacket on a branch and it was not missed until the column was moving the next day. Fortunately Libbie had a second, plainer one and Armstrong joked that a traveler discovering her fancy jacket would think a circus had passed through.[24] When Libbie got to Hempstead, she made a replacement—this time double-breasted with brass buttons in threes and velvet cuffs in the style of the major general's tunic which Armstrong wore. For the full effect, she substituted Armstrong's kepi for her jockey cap.

Southern Hospitality

They arrived in Hempstead on August 26 after marching nineteen days. Armstrong chose the grounds of a large cotton plantation with the musical name of Liendo. He had his men camp on its western boundary, the former prisoner of war compound of Camp Groce (pronounced "gross"). Armstrong's headquarters were set up near the house, which was owned by sixty-year-old Col. Leonard Waller Groce, who was indignant at the intrusion on his property. Groce's granddaughter, Sarah Groce Berlet, remembered the family story about the arrival of the troops at dinner time. "They heard the rumbling of the wagons, clatter of horses hoofs, and before one could realize it, soldiers in Federal uniforms were dismounting and stretching their tents in front of the gate."[25]

The wealthy Groces were from southern Virginia and came to Texas via Georgia and Alabama. Inspired by Stephen Austin's plan to colonize Texas, Jared Groce was one of his original Three Hundred settlers, moving there in 1822 with a wagon train and nearly a hundred slaves. He built the Bernardo Plantation, which produced cotton for the New Orleans market and purchased the first cotton gin in Texas.[26] Both Jared and his eldest son, Leonard, supported the Texican revolution against the Mexican government in 1836, but Col. Leonard Groce seems to have been a "courtesy" colonel as there is no record of military service. Leonard established Liendo Plantation in 1853 on a part of Bernardo. The house was a white, two-story, clapboard building featuring verandas with balustrades on both stories, brick chimneys, and green shutters. The cooking facilities in the kitchen were Texas-sized and could roast a whole beef.[27] On the front gable, Groce had placed a bronze Texas star and the date, "1853."[28] (The reconstructed Liendo Plantation is now a Texas historic landmark.) By 1858, Hempstead was developing nicely on Groce land. The community had a government, school, church, hotel, shops, newspaper, a two-line train depot, saloons, and modest bordellos.[29] Despite growing prosperity, it had the unsavory nickname of "Six-Shooter Junction" due to gunfights and murders.[30]

On the Custers' arrival, Groce's wife, Courtney Ann, graciously offered Armstrong and Libbie a room in their home, but the Custers preferred to sleep under canvas. Three tents were set up to face into a ten-foot-by-ten area covered with fresh hay. Leafy branches were placed on a constructed pergola to give deeper shade for the midday siesta. It was a breezy location and, being away from the trees, had fewer mosquitos.[31] While the days were beastly hot, the evenings were warm and perfect for socializing. As they only had "two camp stools and a bucket," the Groces loaned them furniture—including their best rocking chair for Libbie.[32]

When the threat of Mexican invasion collapsed, Armstrong's mission in Hempstead became one of civil peacekeeping, mostly dealing with outlaws and crimes against the freed blacks. The community was eventually glad to have the initially unwanted Federal troops. Gangs of bravos and ex-Confederates had turned to brigandage and bushwhacking, but the Army proved to be an excellent deterrent. Sheridan looked in on Armstrong and with him was Father Custer, whom Armstrong put on the Army payroll as forage master—a job characterized as "little to do and fine pay."[33] Emanuel was glad to see his sons, and his arrival sounded the bell for another round of audacious pranks. There were two other arrivals from Monroe—Carrie Lyon (Capt. Farnham Lyon's wife) and Nettie—Libbie's friend who had married Capt. Jacob Greene, Armstrong's assistant adjutant general.

Despite their enforced role as hosts, the Groces were gracious and gave the Custers vegetables, fruit, milk, preserves, and occasionally, a roast of mutton—and even loaned them dishes when Armstrong and Libbie had a large dinner party.[34] The Colonel visited, spending many an hour chatting under the arbor and trees trailing Spanish moss. When Libbie fell sick, Mrs. Groce nursed her in the house. The warmth of Texas hospitality was extended to Armstrong too, although in a different fashion. With his gregarious temperament and partiality towards Southern lifestyle, he was soon on good terms with Groce, who introduced him to the cotton planters who were the community's leaders. Sagaciously, Armstrong made the best of this opportunity, for he understood the benefits of political networking. They invited him on a deer hunt which would change his and Libbie's lives.

Whoop 'em Up!

Armstrong, Tom, Emanuel, and some of the staff attended that first hunt, of which Libbie wrote, "Each planter brought his hounds, and I remember the General's delight at his first sight of the different packs—thirty-seven dogs in all—and his enthusiasm at finding that every dog responded to his master's horn."[35] Afterwards, they gathered to review the day's maneuvers over a saddlebag meal and recalled previous exploits of hounds and quarry, mishaps, and the "one that got away." Seeing Armstrong was eager to be included, Groce gave him six foxhounds named Rattler, Sultan, Jupiter, Brandy, and Tyler (the sixth was killed early on and never named by Libbie). Doubtless Col. Groce had more hounds as no serious dog man will give away his best hunters or breeding stock. (Groce's Tyler was perhaps named for John Tyler, Virginian, tenth American president, and Confederate congressman, who supported the annexation of Texas.)

Armstrong, keen to be a houndsman, practiced blowing hound calls on a carved steer horn. (In England and the Eastern states, dog horns were traditionally brass or copper, but steer horns were convenient for Westerners.) Tom, with a foxhound of his own, followed his brother's lead, and their antics in trying to master the calls made Libbie laugh, and no amount of her good-natured ridicule could stop Armstrong, who indignantly said, "I am obliged to practice, for if anyone thinks it is an easy thing to blow on a horn, just let him try it." The brothers' cheeks grew red and distended, their eyes bulged, and their bodies contorted as they tried to master both volume and melody—with the hounds in a circle, yodeling with full force. The two Custers would "leap into the saddle, lift the horn in unconscious grace to their lips, curbing their excited and rearing horses with the free hand, and dash away amidst the frantic leaping, barking, and joyous demonstration of their dogs."[36] (Armstrong's dog horns have sold at auction for under $10,000, but in the 1980s, one of them realized $19,000.[37])

The blasts from the dog horn could travel a few miles, and Libbie could often hear the progress of the hunt from her tent at Liendo.[38] An experienced houndsman could recognize the individual voices of his own dogs amongst the baying of several packs. Libbie noted dryly that "giving tongue" was too mild an expression for their "wild cries and cavernous howls."[39] The hounds' earsplitting "music" was not just confined to hunts. Like all dogs, Armstrong's foxhounds would vocalize when a stranger or animal approached or when lonely or missing one of their pack—and males howled incessantly when separated from a bitch in estrus. Libbie was used to the couple of dogs Armstrong kept while on campaign in

A contemporary engraving of a foxhound, which, along with a greyhound and pointer, was one of the three types of dogs that the Custers had on Reconstruction duty in Texas. The foxhound type has changed very little since then. This one has an initial shaved into its coat as an easy way for a huntsman to identify his own hounds in a multi-pack hunt. Edward Jesse's *Anecdotes of Dogs* (1870).

Virginia, but with six hounds, it was a noisy life but not a displeasing one—"Our dogs give us such pleasure, though it took me some time to get used to the din they set up when Armstrong practiced on the horn."[40]

From all accounts, he was one of those people whom horses, dogs, and children immediately like. As if they were human, he spoke to his hounds with courtesy and affection, and in "dog talk," would explain when he was too busy for them or why they could not ride with him—and Libbie said their "canine family" seemed to understand.[41] Social hunting appears to have been entirely new to Armstrong, and even though officers had fox hunts during the lulls in the war, he never mentions participating in any. Libbie's description of his enthusiasm upon seeing thirty-seven assembled hounds surely indicates it was his first hunt—and it hooked him for life.

In Texas, they rode for comfort, not to impress, and yet with great style. The elite, longhaired ranchers had Mexican-style, silver-ornamented, tall saddles and large-roweled spurs, and leather quirts dangling from their wrists. With trousers tucked into high boots and a fancy shirt, the men had a colorful *poncho* or *serape*, tightly woven of waterproof wool. They openly wore pistols on their belts, and the Custers had never seen armed civilians before—or horses with brands (apart from the Army's practice, branding was unknown in the North). Besides hunting with hounds, the other Texas custom Armstrong adopted was the broad-brimmed hat—sombrero or "wideawake."

Hunting was unpredictable and a potentially dangerous business for hunters, horses, and hounds. Ditches and burrows could trip a galloping horse or hound, potentially causing it to break leg or neck—and accidental gunshot wounds were not unknown. In starting a hunt, they would ride toward timber or brush, with the foxhounds casting about for scent, and striking a trail, the pack would tear off in full cry, with the hunters following. When the deer was brought to bay by the pack, it would kick and slash while the hounds tried to grab hock, neck, or ear. With luck, the deer was quickly killed with a clean shot. If the deer was driven onto the prairie, the pursuit shifted from brush scramble to a flat out chase. Built for endurance, foxhounds couldn't catch a deer or jackrabbit speeding away—but a greyhound could.

Sometime in late October or early November, Armstrong acquired Lord Byron, a pedigreed English Greyhound named after the English poet. The Custers say nothing about his origin, apart from Libbie telling Rebecca Richmond the hound was from Detroit.[42] The most likely source was Kirkland C. Barker, a Detroit mayor, businessman, and sportsman who became friends with Armstrong during the war and who would later give him a pair of Scottish Deerhounds. Greyhounds were an uncommon breed in America then as scent hounds were better suited for hunting deer, fox, coon, and possum in the hilly thickets and forests of the East. However, in the 1820s and 1830s, officers at Fort Crawford (Prairie du Chien, Wisconsin) and at Fort Dearborn (Chicago) coursed wolves and deer with greyhounds.[43] Decades later, in the 1850s and 60s, officers at Fort Union, New Mexico, and Fort Kearney, Nebraska, hunted on the prairie with them.[44] The leggy, deep-chested, long-muzzled hound with keen eyesight was eminently suited to spotting game at a distance and running it down in a burst of speed. Providing both sport and table meat, they were a status symbol for officers.

Greyhounds had been hunting deer and hare in Europe since the Middle Ages, and the breed appealed instantly to Armstrong (who was a cast iron snob), for it was not only the fastest breed known, but the hound of European nobility. Byron's cunning and nerve delighted Armstrong as they were the very qualities wanted in a hunting dog. There was another quality Custer admired in men, horses and dogs and that was "sand" (guts). Byron had sand, and a "damn your eyes" attitude—for he never backed down from a dogfight. The greyhound became Armstrong's favorite—despite his brazen thievery of dinner meat.

That Byron was "to the manner born" obviously made a great impression, for in her writing, Libbie described him as high-bred, noble, stately, aristocratic, patrician, and even royal highness. To her eyes, he was peerless in form and manner—"a superb greyhound, his head carried so loftily as he walked his lordly way among the other dogs, that I thought he would have asked to carry his family-tree on his brass collar, could he have spoken for his rights."[45] Armstrong wrote very little about their pack in Texas but Libbie was more expansive, and Byron is the only hound she told stories about. In fact, in her second book, *Tenting on the Plains*, Byron crops up fifteen times while the rest of the pack are only named once.

Riding with Byron was always an adventure. When a jackrabbit popped up in the chaparral, it could escape into cover, but if one was started at the edge of the prairie, Armstrong shouted, "Whoop!" to the hound and, "Come on!" to Libbie.[46] It was difficult to keep up with her husband but Libbie was always game. She described Byron in full chase:

> When he started for a run, with his nostrils distended and his delicate ears laid back on his noble head, each bound sent him flying through the air. He hardly touched the elastic cushions of his feet to earth, before he again was spread out like a dark, straight thread.[47]

When a greyhound pressed close on a jackrabbit, it would dodge and zigzag—and even head for obstacles to shake off the pursuit. A clever hound compensated for each change of course and pressed harder still. When the greyhound finally closed the gap, he would reach down to snatch at the jack with powerful jaws and break its spine or neck. (Experienced pairs of sighthounds would try to drive the jack into their partner.) Nothing was certain—jacks often escaped, and hounds suffered cuts, torn pads, and dislocated toes. A jackrabbit ran from coyotes nearly every day and knew all the bolt-holes. Hounds might not catch them if they were inexperienced, tired, or unlucky. Byron caught a respectable number and would carry the jackrabbit in his mouth back to Armstrong.

The speed and audacity which made Byron a good hunter (desirable military qualities as well) also made him a good thief. Once at their headquarters compound, Byron snatched a large piece of meat out of a boiling kettle and streaked away through a hail of boots, sticks, and rocks. Armstrong watched the whole thing, secretly delighted at the canine prank, and tormented Eliza about the latest accomplishment of "her favorite." Libbie and Eliza thought the thieving part of Byron was "hateful" for he would steal "his master's dinner just as readily as the neighbors'."[48] He grabbed Eliza's main course many times as it was ready to be served and, "after he'd gorged hissel... hidin' from the other dogs, and burying it in jest such a stingy way you might 'spect from such a worthless, plunderin' old villain."[49]

In camp, Armstrong's habit was to sprawl out on his bed when he wanted to think or relax. Byron expected to join him on the clean bedding despite Libbie's protest. He was always invited by his master, and Libbie quoted a typical scenario:

"Certainly," my husband used to say, sarcastically; "walk right up here on this clean white spread, without troubling yourself to care whether your feet are covered with mud or not. Your Aunt Eliza wants you to lie on nice white counterpanes; she washes them on purpose for you."[50]

Eliza fumed at the mud on her sheets and if she raised her voice toward the dog or moved to get him off, Byron would bare his fangs. Armstrong initially sided with Byron and watched how the contest went—much like the fight he allowed at West Point. When Libbie wanted to lie down on her bed, she would take the broom, her "woman's weapon," and try to push the dog off the bed. Invariably, she would fail, and be taunted with a silent lip curl and glimpse of teeth. Pretending to sleep, Byron allowed Libbie to squeeze into bed with her back against his feet, but he would push her toward the edge with his legs until Libbie had to stand up. At that round in the fight, Eliza would admonish Armstrong. "*Now* see what you've done. You keer more for that *pesky, sassy* old hound than you does for Miss Libbie. Ginnel, I'd be 'shamed, if I was you. What would your mother Custer think of you now?"[51] (The author, when a teenager, had an identical experience with his Irish Wolfhound puppy, who would unconsciously stretch out his legs and shove his master off the bed.)

By then, Armstrong had seen enough and gave Byron a kick, knocking him off to make a place for Libbie. The bed battles were such powerful memories for her that she devoted more prose to them than Byron's hunting or thieving. As to Eliza's threat, Armstrong's mother "had been in the midst of too many happy scuffles, and the center of too many friendly fisticuffs among her active, irrepressible boys, in the old farm-days, for the mention of her name to restore order in our turbulent household."[52] Neither Libbie nor Eliza ever bonded with Byron.

> The tribute that a woman pays to beauty in any form, I gave to Byron, but I never cared much for him. A greyhound's heart could be put into a thimble. Byron cared for the General as much as his cold soul could for anyone but it was not to be compared with the dear Ginnie: she was all love, she was almost human.[53]

This new dog was the result of diplomacy.

Libbie's First Dog

After settling in to Hempstead, Armstrong, as a quasi-magistrate, resolved a potentially serious misunderstanding between two neighbors, so he and Libbie were invited to the plaintiff's home. They were a genteel couple from Virginia but Libbie was surprised at their ramshackle, bare-log house. Still, they had a piano, nice furniture, and good china and linens. In gratitude for Armstrong's help, the couple presented the Custers with a Virginia ham, four game chickens, two turkeys, and a "valuable full-blooded pointer" named after their home state.[54] Ginnie was a sweet and loving dog who took to the Custers right away. She was by their side whether hunting, riding, or just strolling, and while Libbie would write that she was "*en rapport* with her master at all times," it is obvious there was a special bond between her and Ginnie.

> She received us exactly in the spirit with which we approached her, responded, with measure pressed down and running over, to our affectionate demonstrations, and the blessed old girl never sulked if we dropped her to attend to something else.

Libbie expressed her feelings for Ginnie by quoting the English novelist and poet, George Eliot (the pen name of Mary Anne Evans), who wrote in 1857, "Animals are such agreeable friends! They ask no questions, they pass no criticisms."[55]

Elizabeth Bacon Custer, whose life had been dogless until she married, was now a dog lover like her husband—and *her* dog was allowed on the bed. Whenever Libbie protested Byron's head on the pillows or his mucky feet on the sheets, Armstrong noted that no bedding was too clean for Ginnie, even if she was dirty.[56] Libbie now took an active role in doctoring their dogs. Ticks were a nasty problem for people and dogs as they carried disease and with their heads buried under the skin, could cause infection. Their pack acquired ticks from the brush and the job was never ending—Libbie would sit on the dog, trying to calm it while Armstrong applied his tweezers.[57]

While Libbie thought Ginnie was the "dearest, chummiest sort of house-dog," she was a good hunter—regularly flushing quail out of bushes and cacti (which scratched her wagging tail). The country was flat and they could ride at will, fording streams and pushing through thickets. The prickly vegetation was a hazard to Libbie's clothing—brambles were always snagging her riding habit or the drooping Spanish moss catching her hat. While Libbie tried to ride around, Armstrong would just plough through the brush.[58] Father Custer came along on the hunts and one of the farmers gave him a "bulky old cur." Emanuel appreciated Bowser as a companion. In contrast to the hounds in the pack,

> The dog looked as if he were a make-up from all the rough clay that was discarded after modeling the sleek, high-stepping, springy, fleet-footed dogs of our pack. His legs were massive, while his cumbersome tail curled over his plebian back in a tight coil, until he was tired—then, and only then, did it uncurl. The droop of his head was rendered even more 'loppy by the tongue, which dropped outside the sagging jaw. But for all that, he lumbered along, a blotch of ungainly yellow, beside our splendid thoroughbreds....

Emanuel staunchly defended Bowser and assured his sons he'd match him against "any of their new-fangled, unreliable, highfalutin' lot."[59]

Libbie, the new "doggist" in the Custer clan, was already enchanted with the idea of pure-blooded canine superiority. Not without affection, she described Bowser among their hounds,

> ... and there in the midst, panting and faithfully struggling to keep up, was the rough, uncouth old fellow, too absorbed in endeavoring not to be left behind to realize that he was not all that a dog could finally become, after generations of training and breeding had done its refining work.[60]

Not untypical for Victorian thinking, in that passage and the ones about Byron, Libbie anthropomorphizes, suggesting the dogs are self-aware to the point where the greyhound knew he was noble but Bowser was too low-born to understand his lack of pedigree. Still, Bowser was loyal to Emanuel and, like a veteran prizefighter, he knew enough not to be provoked into a dust-up—a virtue which Libbie applauded.[61]

The Hunting Life

On the first deer hunt with Armstrong's new pack, there was a mishap. Pairs of men had been stationed along the brush cover so at least one would have a shot at a deer being flushed. Tom Custer was one of these, and after a long period of no activity, he heard the baying hounds approaching. The deer burst out of the brush, bounding toward him and he fired—killing both the deer and one of his brother's foxhounds.[62] Armstrong was philosophical about it but couldn't resist the opportunity to "guy" his brother by saying, "Oh, Tom's a good shot, a sure aim—he's sure to hit something!" The joke continued for years and every time there was a newspaper story about some hapless hunter having shot an unintended target, Armstrong would pointedly leave it for Tom to see.[63]

The Custers had been at Liendo for just over a month, and Libbie had taken to the easy Texas lifestyle as if she had been born to it. She loved the warm weather with its freedom from heavy clothing, lazy days, and conversations with the gentry. Armstrong took to wearing his white, Sunday suit after working hours on weekdays—it being more comfortable than his wool uniform. On October 5, he wrote to Libbie's parents about their happiness, her good health and expertise with horses, and even his thoughts on the negro's place in post-war America (fine for them to be free farmers, tradesmen, and even soldiers—but not voters or leaders). Armstrong also spoke of their dogs and hunting.

> We hunt a great deal he [Emanuel] being very fond of it. Saturday we went deer hunting with a pack of twenty dogs. Tom and Captain Lyon each shot a nice deer. We sometimes have four kinds of game upon the table, last night a party of us went coon hunting. We caught two coons, two opossums, and one polecat. We did not go far from our camp, in fact Libbie, who of course remained at home, could hear the baying of the hounds as we hunted the coon. I keep six dogs all large hounds. You may imagine this expense, on the contrary no expense whatsoever is incurred. They are supported on the waste meat obtained at the butcher, as we kill six or eight large beeves daily. I expect to have a pack of fifteen or twenty hounds to hunt with this coming winter & I can keep this number at no expense whatever. Libbie's admiration for dogs is second only to that for her horses, the latter ranking next to her affection for her nearest relatives. The dogs in this country are not trained by the voice of their master but by the blast of a horn which can be heard a distance of up to three or four miles.[64]

Significantly, Armstrong dissembles when he says their daughter was "of course" not riding on hunts when in fact she had (and would hunt when they got to Austin). Ten days after that letter, Armstrong wrote to his brother and sister, and talked about Libbie on a coon hunt—which she herself describes in *Tenting on the Plains*.[65] (Libbie seems also to have neglected to disclose this in her letters home.) Also noteworthy is Armstrong's certainty that Judge Bacon will not approve the cost of fifteen or twenty hounds, and pointedly states twice that they won't be an expense because they are fed on the scraps of government beef. (This passage comes directly from Armstrong's letter of Oct. 5, 1866; however, in *The Custer Story*, Libbie's friend and biographer, Marguerite Merington, has edited this passage considerably—omitting nearly all the material on hunting and dogs—but leaving the line about Libbie's admiration for dogs.[66])

Armstrong had begun collecting hounds and progressed from Groce's six to some number approaching twenty. The division's ambulances were commandeered to "bring in any blooded hound that could be heard of within twenty miles."[67] By the time they left Texas, Libbie reckoned there were twenty-three dogs about their house and "most of them ours."[68] The dog use of the ambulances became another camp gripe as about half were kept two miles away at headquarters for the convenience of Armstrong, his staff, and the three wives.[69] (Marching to Hempstead, two of the eleven ambulances were used for Libbie and the Custers' baggage.) The disgruntlement increased when Armstrong started using one for sport. To save his dogs' strength, he let them ride to and from the hunting grounds.[70]

Civil peacekeeping left Armstrong with considerable time on his hands. His leisure was filled with pleasure rides, hunting, and horse racing on both the Hempstead track and one that he had built outside camp. He had three racehorses with a small mulatto boy as his jockey. He often organized races—which his detractors claimed a commanding officer shouldn't be doing. Libbie told her cousin about this new enterprise, "But no one could object with reason to an Army race—They are conducted with such order—I don't approve of betting tho' and am so thankful neither Tom nor Aut bet."[71] Despite Libbie's belief, Armstrong did wager on horses, and while he did not swear, smoke, or drink, gambling was a vice he could never quit. Racing and breeding thoroughbred horses became a passion, and Armstrong's dream of owning a racing stable and stud farm began in Texas and would be further encouraged in Kentucky.

Texas Longhorns

Armstrong occasionally loaned his dogs to his officers when he could not go with them. Pvt. Samuel Isadore Grey (sometimes Samuel J. Grey) and Pvt. Lyons, young troopers from the 7th Indiana Cavalry, were Armstrong's orderlies. As such, they were in daily proximity to Libbie and the hounds. Once when Armstrong was off on inspections, Grey and Lyons (who had no orders) went off hunting. After shooting one jackrabbit on the prairie, they heard a deep rumble and felt the ground vibrate—like a train laboring up a grade. From out of a dust cloud burst a herd of wild longhorns heading their way. The men took shelter in an old cattle pen, and after several hours, the herd wandered off. Grey and Lyons hurried back to camp, arriving about 2 a.m. At breakfast, the delinquents were summoned to the command tent. Caught in the wrong, they hoped Libbie might moderate Armstrong's temper—which she was known to do.

Armstrong was furious, but after hearing about the longhorns he turned attention to the potential threat. Without vaqueros, the herd was a danger to everyone—particularly to some officers and wives who were off on a pleasure ride. Armstrong had the orderlies saddle up to find and warn the riders—who had two of his "prize greyhounds" on loan for coursing jackrabbits. (While Libbie mentions only Byron in Texas, Grey's account suggests another greyhound had been acquired.)

Grey and Lyons struck the party's trail and rode after them. Nearing timber, they heard shots and looked up to see a jackrabbit scudding toward them with the greyhounds on its tail. The trio disappeared and from out of the timber came the joyriders. It took some talking before they understood about the danger but the menacing dust cloud in the direction of the greyhounds emphasized Lyons' warning. The orderlies set off to catch the hounds knowing the only way to stop a heated chase was to shoot either the jack or the dogs—but as Grey would say, "Nothing is certain until the hangman springs the trap."

Lyons figured the jack would eventually circle back to shake off the dogs, so they rode and searched while the dogs barked in the distance. Sure enough, the jack hove into sight with hounds close behind, heading again for the men. Lyons' second shot killed the jack, and he snatched it by its legs—the greyhounds stopped to sniff their dead quarry. Chests heaving and tongues lolling, they were blown, and one had injured a leg. Grey padded the pommel with his blanket roll, and Lyons hoisted up the dog. They rode back with both hounds and the jack, imagining the longhorns behind each rise as the sun set. Reaching camp, the injured greyhound was handed down to a grateful Armstrong.

After breakfasting on the jackrabbit, the orderlies were peppered by Armstrong's questions. He wanted to know every detail about the longhorns and his greyhounds. Digesting all this, he determined something must be done about the herd—but they had wandered off to become someone else's problem.[72]

Ladies' Hunts

Hunting deer involved crossing the Brazos River at first light and the wild chases often lasted until dusk. This rough hunting wasn't considered safe for Libbie, Nettie, or Carrie. So the three wives weren't entirely left out, moonlight coon and possum hunts were arranged for them. When the quarry was eventually treed, a black attendant (brought along for this purpose) climbed up to dislodge the varmint, and it would almost inevitably fall to its death amidst the dogs below.[73] Libbie quite liked the excitement and camaraderie of hunting but did not care to be in at the kill.

In Monroe, a coon hunt was not ladylike but Libbie could see no objection to them. She did, however, draw the line of propriety in Austin when she met a wealthy and refined woman who rode alone with her gun and hounds, and once famously captured a wolf with her lasso. In town, the huntress/socialite wore expensive dresses, jewels, and French hats. Part of Libbie's disapproval came also from the woman's home. Her plantation had thoroughbred horses, acres in cotton and a mill, but Libbie thought the house a hovel as it was only a one-story, plastered log building with breezy gaps between the walls and the ceiling.[74]

Armstrong threatened to get another breed of dog. Eliza had been instructed that no one was to be turned away hungry from his tent but she was secretly feeding a number of disappearing vagrants. At one point, he noticed a path from the cook tent into the weeds and jokingly threatened to get bloodhounds to find out how many were eating for free. Armstrong knew full well about slave-tracking bloodhounds and it is somewhat appalling that he even jokingly suggested this to Eliza, a former slave. He never followed through and, as it turned out, two of the freeloaders were "wretched little ragamuffins—one, of the poor white trash, and the other a negro..." who had depended on the meals for so long that the Custers took them on as servants. The little blonde boy was given the special job of keeping the tent, bedding, and Libbie's clothing free of scorpions and centipedes.[75]

Armstrong's dog collecting had nearly doubled the initial pack, for Libbie wrote home saying, "I forgot to tell you that our nine dogs sleep round our wagon at night, quarreling, growling, snoring, but I sleep too soundly to be kept awake by them."[76] The dogs' nocturnal ruckus caused Armstrong to get a long wagon whip to snap at them whenever they got stirred up so he and Libbie could have quiet.[77] At this point, they had Byron, the five Groce foxhounds, and probably a few more acquisitions (Ginnie, as a "house" dog, may not have been included in the total). Libbie's addendum about their nine dogs hinted at her full life with dogs—of which her father would probably disapprove. By the time they were settled in Austin, they had twenty-three dogs—a few more than Armstrong had told Judge Bacon he intended to have.

Puppies in Austin

On November 13, Sheridan sent Armstrong's force 100 miles west to Austin. Libbie was thankful as it was getting too chilly to sleep in the ambulance and it would be warmer in the city. As on the march to Hempstead, Libbie alternated between her ambulance and riding Custis Lee. Ginnie and the foxhounds flushed birds and jackrabbits, and Byron coursed the latter. When the sun was harsh or the dogs were tired, into the ambulance they went.

Many years later, a surgeon and a provost marshal would give affidavits that Armstrong used the best ambulances for his dogs while sickly men had to ride in unsprung, freight wagons. One trooper swore that he ordered two sick men out of an ambulance so his dogs could ride, and the men died in Hempstead.[78] Confusingly, all these men declared the incidents were on the march from Alexandria—which was impossible as the Custers brought no dogs to Texas. As these notarized affidavits were made more than twenty years afterward, it is most likely the march to Austin the veterans were remembering. Nonetheless, Armstrong's dogs' riding in ambulances was added to the complaints against him, which included horse races, bad rations, lack of proper uniforms, and cruel discipline. His reputation was changing. He was now a callous commander who cared little for his men and more for his own privilege and the comfort of his dogs—and he would be accused again of putting his dogs before his men in Kansas.

The Custers and the column's advance party came to Austin in mid–November 1865, and the town turned out to see the Yankees. For their headquarters, Provisional Governor Andrew Jackson Hamilton offered the unoccupied the Blind Asylum.[79] A spacious stone building, it offered a parlor for Armstrong and Libbie, and private rooms for the married officers. No matter how good the air circulation was in the high-ceiling rooms, Libbie thought they were stuffy and missed sleeping outside. Ginnie was allowed a bed outside the Custers' room and the other dogs were kept in the stables. (Bowser slept on Emanuel's bed which did not "render our father's bed as downy as it might have been."[80]) The Custer pack mysteriously decreased in size from nine, for on November 17, Libbie wrote that they have "five dogs, a coop full of turkeys, another coop full of chickens, and some famous game chickens in the yard."[81] (The Blind Asylum is preserved today as the Arno-Nowotny Visitors' Center at the University of Texas, Austin.)

One morning, Libbie and Armstrong missed hearing Ginnie's wake up call—tail thumping on the floor. Her bed was empty, so Armstrong scrambled into his clothes and soon came back with the news that Ginnie was under the servants' quarters with "seven other little Ginnies." The war hero, General George Armstrong Custer, eagerly wriggled into the crawl space and handed out the puppies to Libbie. Nothing would do but for the mother and her "pulpy, silken-skinned little rolls" to be placed in the Custers' bed to be admired and lovingly inspected. Libbie would refer to the happy event as "Altering the Dog Census."[82] They were delighted but knew Eliza would go on the warpath when she learned there was a litter in the bedroom—and she did. "Did I come way off down in this here no 'count country to wash white counterpanes for dogs?" At each blast from the indignant Eliza, Armstrong would answer by talking sweetly to Ginnie. It was a defense which even Eliza could not best and he wore her down. With Eliza settled, the officers and wives trooped in to pay court to the puppies and Ginnie—who responded by offering her paw.[83]

It is surprising that neither Libbie nor Custer was aware Ginnie had come into season, been bred, and swelled with pregnancy and milk over the nearly three months between estrus and birth. Libbie might not have connected what she knew about human pregnancy to Ginnie's growing condition, but for farm-boy Armstrong there seems to be little excuse—perhaps he was just too distracted to notice. These were the first puppies in the Custer pack and if Ginnie had made Libbie a fledgling dog person, then her puppies sealed the deal. For the childless Custers, their dogs would become their surrogate family. Armstrong doted on the puppies, and when two became ill, he searched for cures in his dog book. With the little ones cradled in his arms, he walked the floor all night—rubbing and soothing, and talking to them, but despite his best exertions and remedies, they died. When the rest of the pups were old enough for outdoors, Armstrong was like the Pied Piper with Ginnie at his heels and the five puppies trailing behind her. Libbie teased him about the dignity of the commanding officer with such an absurd parade—but Armstrong did not mind the puppy procession or her chiding.[84]

The Custers and Austin society quickly became comfortable with each other. The leading citizens and planters became glad of the military presence, and it was easy duty for the cavalry. Austinites were bemusedly tolerant of the rambunctious Custer pack—and forgave them (as the story goes) for bursting into the State House and lifting their legs while Armstrong was visiting there.[85] (The author was unable to verify this story and while it is probably apocryphal, any owner of male dogs will vouch for its possibility.) There were dinners, sociables, horse races, and pleasure rides. With their friends, the Custers would ride across the Colorado River to Mount Bonnell for picnics (sometimes with the cavalry band), and hunting on the low-ground. Libbie rode along on jackrabbit hunts and wrote to Rebecca, "The great sport here is chasing hares across the prairie" and likened them to the English hare but because of its tall ears, the locals called them a "mule head rabbit."[86] Others called them jackass-rabbits or simply, jackrabbits (technically the black-tailed jackrabbit, sub-species *lepus californicus texianus*). The jack relied on speed and agility to evade pursuit and could sprint in bursts of 35 to 45 miles per hour. This was Byron's forte as a greyhound in good condition on favorable ground could just match that speed in a 1,000-yard run.

Byron was the only Custer dog photographed in Texas, and that happened three times. The first two images of him, clearly taken in the same location, are tintypes which author D. Mark Katz dates to October 18, 1865. In one Byron is seen with the Custers and in the second with Armstrong and Carrie Lyons. There was a considerable amount

If an officer's wife did not ride, her life on a frontier post could be pretty tedious. This engraving was made for Frances M. A. Roe's *Army Letters from an Officer's Wife, 1871–1888* and can suggest Libbie Custer's coursing experiences in Texas. Frances was married to 2nd Lt. Fayette Washington Roe (3rd U.S. Infantry) and had a special greyhound named Hal. The Roes hunted at Fort Lyon, Colorado Territory, with the officers' greyhounds.

of gear needed for photography—not only the wooden camera and tripod but a mobile dark room. For the wet plate process, exposure times were necessarily long—perhaps three to seven seconds (depending on the light). In 1865, to capture a good image of a dog, it would have to be well trained or tired enough to hold still. Byron is blurred considerably in one photo and his head is hidden in the other. Libbie never notes his color but the tintype of her riding with Armstrong and Byron was gently colored by the photographer. Trees and grass are pale green, the horses are brown, Armstrong's trousers are light blue, and his hat and saddle blanket are brownish-yellow. As Byron was also tinted that shade, likely he was fawn or tan.

The third photograph of Byron was on the steps of their headquarters in Austin sometime in November. Armstrong gathered his staff, Libbie, Tom, Jacob and Nettie Greene, Emanuel, Eliza and a few others to pose on the front steps. Byron stands alongside Armstrong and Libbie, with his hindquarters facing the camera (in a second, closer photo of the group, Byron has wandered off). Even though the Custers owned him for a few years longer, no other photos of Byron are known.

At the end of January 1866, Armstrong's assignment was finished. Texas was more stable than it had been after surrender and a large "Army of Observation" was no longer needed. He had expected his wartime rank of major general of volunteers might cease and he would revert to a captain in the 5th U.S. Cavalry—not an easy thing for

Libbie and Armstrong pleasure riding in Hempstead, Texas, October 1864. Byron, their lordly greyhound, moved during the exposure and is almost entirely blurred out. Armstrong has already adopted the Texas fashion of a broad-brimmed, *sombrero*-style hat and wears his major general's coat. Libbie wears a cavalry kepi with her riding habit—the full skirts of which were always catching on thorns and bushes. The original image is delicately colored with transparent paint, and Byron is a brownish-yellow—a fair indication that he was fawn or tan in color. West Point Museum Collection, United States Military Academy.

Armstrong, particularly with the pay decrease from $8,000 per year to $2,000. However, he was glad for the coming leave and expected that Sheridan would secure him a permanent promotion and assignment.

Armstrong made a last, unusual effort at dog collecting. He had sent his adjutant, Jacob Greene, to ask Texans as to how their state was faring in Reconstruction and learned they were determined to get back at the government and reinstate slavery. Greene was in San Antonio chatting with community leaders when Armstrong wrote on January 8, 1866, warmly congratulating him on his promotion to lieutenant colonel and sharing some news. As an afterthought, Armstrong asked, "If you have an opportunity to procure me a full blooded Chihuahua dog do so, a full blood should not weigh over three or four pounds."[87] A diminutive Chihuahua would have been a new type of dog for the Custers. (Custer biographer T.J. Stiles says the request was essentially a last minute one as Armstrong knew he was leaving in three weeks.)

Bordering southwest Texas along the Rio Grande, the state of Chihuahua had given its name to the little dog. (Chihuahua City was the seat of Benito Juárez's exile Nationalist government.) Originating in ancient Mexico, this ancient Toltec-Aztec breed was imported into the States in the mid–1800s.[88] Armstrong and Libbie had visited Greene in San Antonio in mid–December and presumably saw Chihuahua dogs there. It was a scarce breed outside of Mexico and southern Texas, and was not seen at dog shows until the 1880s. Armstrong's comment on the dog's weight may have been about shipping costs, although there was no rail connection between Austin and San Antonio. More likely, he wanted a true lapdog for Libbie rather than a larger cross-bred. (Chihuahuas debuted at the Westminster Kennel Club Show in 1885 under the category, "Miscellaneous (or Foreign Class) Dogs or Bitches under 25 Lbs."—along with two Chinese Cresteds, three Mexican Hairless, and the son of a famous New York police dog.[89] Chihuahuas were recognized by the AKC in 1904.)

Adios to Texas

In early February, the Custers and their entourage headed for Monroe. There was not much the Custers had to do in the way of packing as they had been living in tents with only essentials. Armstrong sold his racehorses, and their milk cow was returned to its lender. His twenty-three hounds were a problem. It was one thing to transport their

Mrs. Carrie Farnham Lyon and Armstrong in Hempstead, Texas. In this photograph, Byron is standing still but his head is bent down and concealed behind his body. Carrie's husband, Capt. Farnham Lyon, was initiated into the Hempstead hunting fraternity by being drenched with deer blood after his first hunt, but somehow, Armstrong avoided the same treatment. Courtesy of the National Park Service, Little Bighorn Battlefield National Monument, LIBI_0019_00274.

four best horses (Jack Rucker, Custis Lee, Phil Sheridan, and a newly acquired, blooded mare, "Fanchon"), but so many dogs would be difficult to ship—not to mention keeping them in Monroe. Libbie said, "It was a trial to part with the elderly dogs, which were hardly worth the experiment of transporting to the North, especially as we had no reason to suppose we should see another deer, except in zoological gardens."[90] So, the pack was broken up and given to brother officers or the local hounds-men. Only the two favorites, Lord Byron and Ginnie (and apparently a couple of foxhounds), went to Monroe.

The Custers entrained for Galveston and then sailed to New Orleans on a former blockade runner, with the horses and dogs in stalls below decks. The ship steamed into a hurricane and was tossed like a cork—straining rigging and timbers. Everyone was seasick and terrified of drowning. Armstrong knew that on cavalry transports, when it became necessary to jettison weight to save the ship, the horses would be hoisted up with block and tackle and dropped overboard—and if it came to that, Byron and Ginnie would be sacrificed (if they hadn't already drowned). Luckily, the battered ship with all passengers and animals made it safely to New Orleans. Once again, the Custers had a shopping and gustatory holiday before taking a riverboat north.

The Blind Asylum in Austin, Texas, which served as Armstrong's headquarters in November 1865. The Custers had a large room upstairs, and Ginnie the pointer was allowed to sleep outside their bedroom. Byron is on the steps next to Armstrong and Libbie, and looking left toward Tom Custer. Behind Tom to the left is Libbie's matchmaker from Monroe, Nettie Greene (seated), and Eliza Brown is in the doorway. On the right side, leaning against the pillar on the right is Emanuel Custer and on the bottom step is Capt. Jacob Lyman Greene. The building still stands at the University of Texas, Austin. Courtesy of the National Park Service, Little Bighorn Battlefield National Monument, LIBI_0019_00484. Enlargement section of the original wide-view image.

Texas made strong memories for Armstrong and Libbie, although the passing years tended to soften the struggles with biting insects and snakes, the blazing heat of summer and the "northers"—the strong, cold winds of winter. Libbie fondly remembered the hospitality of the Groces, the friendliness of the deer-hunting fraternity and the charm of their "tall tales."[91]

TAIL PIECES: LIBBIE CUSTER AND PERSIAN GREYHOUNDS—TWO DEGREES OF SEPARATION

When Libbie accompanied Senator Chandler to Richmond, at City Point, Admiral David Dixon Porter telegraphed Armstrong about his wife's arrival. Porter, also a dog man, kept his pack of foxhounds aboard his flagship, the steamboat U.S.S. *Black Hawk*.[92] He was the second son of Commodore David Porter, a naval hero who had fought pirates in Barbary and the West Indies and the British in the War of 1812. (Porter was the adoptive father of Admiral David Farragut—"Lincoln's Admiral.") David Dixon's father was the first American *Chargé d'Affaires* to the Ottoman Empire who introduced Persian greyhounds (Salukis) to the United States in 1832 (see illustration in Ch. 9).[93] The unusual breed was recognized by the AKC as "Saluki" in 1927—partially due to the sustained excitement about King Tutankhamun's tomb, which had been discovered five years earlier.

DOGS AS PROPERTY IN THE 19TH CENTURY

At the conclusion of the week-long, second Great National Dog Show in 1863, P.T. Barnum had arranged for an auction so New Yorkers could "obtain choice dogs of any breed."[94] It is strange for us now to read about someone selling or giving away an adult dog to a friend or comparative stranger, yet in the 19th century it was commonly done. At that time, dogs in America (and Western countries) were not universally regarded as pets in the way they are now. Apart from lapdogs or upper class house pets, dogs were property and, like livestock, expected to earn their keep whether by guarding and herding flocks of sheep, reducing the rat population, pulling carts, defending the homestead, or hunting game. Generally, only urbanites of some means could afford to regard dogs as pets.

While there was often affection between master and dog, it would not have occurred to the master (or greatly concerned them if it did) that a dog would have any strong feelings about being shifted to a new owner. While enlightened Victorians believed dogs felt pain as humans did and anthropomorphized their imagined feelings, dogs were first and foremost, property. Fortunately, dogs, even old ones, can be extremely adaptable. In time, with considerate treatment and affection, the dog could adjust—although until acceptance of the new home, it might need to be watched or tied up to prevent it from running away.

Chapter 6

Kansas—Hunting Game and Chasing Indians

"I had several fine English greyhounds, whose speed I was anxious to test..."
—George Armstrong Custer[1]

Armstrong and Libbie were home in March 1866, and Rhoda was shocked to see her daughter's lustrous brown hair lightened from the Texas sun and her fair complexion now ruddy. They moved in with his parents who lived near the Bacons. Maria Custer was delighted to have her boys at home—and her daughter-in-law as well. Emanuel routinely woke them by releasing the dogs to leap up the stairs and pounce on their beds, all the while bellowing that it was past time to be up. His sons and Libbie liked sleeping late when not on campaign, and at these intrusions, Armstrong and Tom shouted for hot water, the morning paper, the barber, the boot-black, and cocktails, demanding to know, "What sort of a hotel do you keep, anyway?"[2]

At Loose Ends

Armstrong went to Washington to deliver a speech to Congress about the progress of Reconstruction in Texas, as well as to lobby for promotion and a posting—both hard to come by in the post-war economies, even for a hero. He wanted prestige and money, although he would always say to Libbie, "For you and you alone I long to become wealthy, not for the wealth alone, but for the power it brings. I am willing to make any honorable sacrifice."[3] A number of his Army friends had resigned to enter politics or industry. Armstrong wasn't really suited for these—even as a vice president merely lending his name to a company. He toyed with the idea of diplomatic service and also applied to be Inspector General of U.S. Cavalry. Finding nothing in Washington, Armstrong wanted to see what his favorite city might offer him.

By April 1, he was in New York, living it up, networking, and squiring around his wife's friends to restaurants, theater, and parties. He wrote Libbie often, giving accounts of his doings and tried to describe the latest fashions in dresses and hats. Somewhat perversely, he also described joking with the *Nymphes du Pavé* (assuring Libbie it was only for "sport") and described a baroness whose dress was so décolleté that, "I had not seen such sights since I was weaned."[4] When Judge Bacon died of cholera on May 18, Armstrong left his city amusements and returned for the funeral.

In Washington, Armstrong had applied to Señor Don Matias Romero, the Mexican minister, for the post of Adjutant General in the Mexican Army. The grapevine had it there were increasing efforts to eject the French from Mexico, and Benito Juarez's Nationals needed experienced officers. Romero was playing both sides of the fence by serving his government while recruiting for Juarez. The post of Adjutant General had prestige and cash pay—$16,000 in gold coin—twice Armstrong's former salary as a major general (he was only earning $2,000 as a captain).[5] He was agreeable but stipulated that at Mexico's expense, he would recruit and equip his own force of American soldiers.[6]

Both General Grant and Secretary of War Edwin Stanton were willing to give Armstrong a year's leave, and Grant even wrote a letter of recommendation. Sheridan thought the rebellion could be quickly finished but advised Armstrong it wouldn't be a good situation for American involvement.[7] Libbie, who almost certainly couldn't go with him to Mexico, was decidedly unhappy. However, Secretary of State William Seward (on behalf of President Johnson) denied the leave. Seward was rightly concerned about a serving American officer leading Nationalist troops in a rebellion against the Mexican government.[8] Armstrong could either resign from the Army to fight in Mexico or stay put as a captain and hope for something to turn up. Even for wealth, Armstrong would not leave the Army without hedging his bet—much to Libbie's relief.

By July, he was languishing as an unassigned captain, and Grant recommended him for the lieutenant colonelcy of the 9th Cavalry while Wesley Merritt was offered the same in the 7th Cavalry.[9] Despite his circumstances, this posting was *not* what Armstrong wanted. With the growing need for soldiers to protect the settlers and railroad steady encroachment on the lands of the Plains Indians (even those guaranteed by treaty), Congress increased the number of cavalry regiments. The 9th and 10th were composed of black troopers with white officers, and with the 24th and 25th "U.S. Colored" Infantry, they were known by the Indians' name for them—Buffalo Soldiers.

Even though a lieutenant colonelcy (second in command) in the 9th Cavalry was an excellent promotion for an unassigned captain, Armstrong didn't want to command black soldiers (he would have taken a white infantry regiment or state militia before that). He was still hoping to find something better and looked to politics—and this would serendipitously lead him to a new variety of canine enthusiasm.

Being friendly with the Southern cadets at West Point, Armstrong favored bringing the South back into the Union as President Lincoln had expressed in his second inaugural address, "With malice towards none, with charity for all ... to bind up the nation's wounds ... and achieve a just and lasting peace among ourselves and with all nations." He had been trading opinions on Reconstruction in the newspapers and due to his war and Texas experience, on August 9 he was appointed vice president of the Michigan delegation to the National Union convention in Philadelphia.[10] It appears that while Armstrong was at the planning meeting in Detroit, he renewed his wartime acquaintance with the Honorable Kirkland C. Barker, a former alderman who had just completed a two-year term as mayor (Barker had taken office in January 1864). He was a large, heavy man with receding hairline and a bushy goatee, and at forty-seven, he was twenty years older than Armstrong. Besides being a wealthy businessman (he founded the American Eagle Tobacco Company's forerunner), he was a Mason, a Knight Templar, a commodore in the Great Lakes Yacht Club, president of the Detroit Audubon Club, held office in the Horse Association of America, and owned a stud farm.[11] Barker also kept hunting hounds. Libbie wrote, "He is so fond of dogs & horses and hunting. Autie and he are great friends...."[12] The Barkers were gracious hosts who did not mind spending money for their friends' enjoyment. That month, Barker invited the Custers to be their guests—for Armstrong to go muskie fishing with him and for Libbie to stay with Jeanette, his wife, at their country house.[13] There was some sort of dog activity going on in July 1866, for Armstrong wrote to Libbie on the 17th saying, "...all the pups died from distemper except two."[14] These may have been puppies from Ginnie's Austin litter (which would have been about seven months old), or they might have been Barker's. More than that is unknown, but that winter or the following spring, Barker would give Armstrong two English Greyhounds.

Political Waters

The summer was fast burning away, and Armstrong still had no definite prospects apart from a regiment he didn't want. Feeling entitled to at least a colonelcy, on August 13, Armstrong bypassed Sheridan and Grant and wrote directly to President Johnson, as his Commander in Chief, requesting a *full* colonelcy in a cavalry regiment or, failing that, a colonelcy in an infantry regiment—but only with "*White* troops."[15] Johnson declined to involve himself in Army matters but did ask if Armstrong would join him on an important "campaign." Always willing to curry favor with the influential, and having an eye toward a political career, he accepted. Meanwhile, Sheridan persuaded the reluctant Grant that Armstrong be allowed to trade appointments if he could. Wesley Merritt was willing, and swapped his 7th Cavalry for the 9th.[16]

There was a vigorous debate in the North about what to do with the Southern states. The options more or less boiled down to punishing them for rebelling and taking away their governments or Lincoln's "prodigal son" philosophy, where they would be welcomed back in the Union with full rights—apart from slavery. The question of what to do with the former slaves continued to be a vexing issue, and whether or not negro males should have the vote was hotly argued. Armstrong, whose views were not atypical of a segment of the population, felt they made satisfactory soldiers with supervision but in no way should be trusted with the vote. (Despite his views, he had affection and loyalty for Eliza. Once in an Ohio restaurant with no place for blacks or servants to eat, he insisted she be served while seated with his family.[17])

President Johnson, a native North Carolinian, naturally favored full reconciliation and believed he could persuade Americans with a speech-making tour through a number of states. To further impress the public, the "Swing Around the Circle" tour had members of his cabinet, the Mexican Minster, the highest officers in the Army and Navy—General Grant and Admiral Farragut—and the heroic icon, General George Armstrong Custer.

Despite Judge Bacon's recent death and Libbie being in mourning for two years, Armstrong persuaded her to come along. They were able to join Johnson's party at Manhattanville, New York, in time to steam up the Hudson to West Point. The Custers seem to have taken Byron the greyhound along, as biographer Jay Monaghan notes the hound was with them at Manhattanville.[18] (Unfortunately, Monaghan gives no source for this, and Libbie doesn't note it anywhere.) Johnson's tour was not a success, and his party was often confronted with catcalls and demonstrations. It ended disastrously on September 14 when temporary seats erected at the Johnstown station in Pennsylvania collapsed, injuring hundreds of people. Johnson and his party tried to assist, but the rail schedule forced their departure—giving the impression that President Johnson abandoned civilians in a crisis. The Custers and Byron left the tour early so Armstrong could attend the Soldiers and Sailors Convention in Cleveland on September 17. Armstrong's Michigan supporters encouraged him to consider Congress, but having just seen for himself that politics was more than speeches, dinners, and applause, he wisely declined to stand for office.

Off to Kansas with the Horses and Dogs

Armstrong's successive leaves (beginning at the end of April) had prevented him from taking up his post with the 7th Cavalry at Fort Riley, and he had been assigned it back in July. His continuing delays wore out Grant's considerable patience and on September 24, he ordered Armstrong to join his regiment "without delay."[19] On October 8, he and Libbie boarded the train in Monroe, and with them came pretty Anna Darrah, one of Libbie's bridesmaids, Eliza and the mulatto jockey from Texas, their trunks, their dogs, and their thoroughbred horses; Jack Rucker, Phil Sheridan, Fanchon, and Libbie's pacer, Custis Lee. Armstrong's prized stallion, Don Juan, won races at the Michigan State Fair in June, and could have brought $10,000 if he hadn't died of a stroke after the fair.[20] This was a blow which meant Armstrong wasn't going to have his racing stable just yet.

The Custer dog contingent now consisted of a couple of Texas foxhounds, Barker's two greyhounds, Ginnie, Byron—and a new addition, Turk the bull-dog. The details about the Custer pack are again vague. Frederick Whittaker said they left Texas with only, "one or two of the finest dogs" but Libbie wrote they went to Kansas with "…several hounds given to the General by the planters with whom he hunted deer in Texas…" and Byron and Turk.[21] Curiously, Libbie does not mention Ginnie in the move to Fort Riley, and yet she was with the Custers. Turk had been given to them and was "the ugliest white bull-dog" Libbie ever saw. He had a twisted, lumpy tail, bowed legs, and a heavy muzzle but was affectionate and loyal. In shape and form, he was opposite of Byron, and the two had fights over who was to be the alpha dog (Turk won these). Inspired by him, Libbie drew a picture for Armstrong of a pipe smoking, bull-dog.[22]

Turk and Phil Sheridan adored each other. The dog would nip playfully at the colt's legs and Phil would lift him off the ground by the scruff of his neck. Their reunions were enthusiastic and Turk would sleep with Phil whether in a stable or boxcar stall. When Armstrong and Libbie took him for a drive, he was confined to the buggy to prevent him dashing off toward any dog who challenged him. If there was any lingering doubt about Libbie's being a dog woman, it is dispelled in this wonderful passage about Turk:

> When we came home to this ugly duckling, he usually made a spring and landed in my lap, as if he were the tiniest, silkiest Skye [terrier] in dogdom. He half closed his eyes, with that beatific expression peculiar to affectionate dogs, and did his little smile at my husband and me by raising what there was of his upper lip and showing his front teeth. All this with an ignoring of the other dogs and an air of exclusion, as if we three—his master, mistress, and himself—composed all there was of earth worth knowing.[23]

The Custers had an ugly, but affectionate, white bull-dog named Turk, similar to this one, who constantly feuded with Byron and Old Rover, the foxhound in Kansas. Unlike the pedigreed Bulldogs in show rings today, bull-dogs of the 19th century were more athletic and had longer muzzles, necks, and legs, and their heads were less broad. Edward Jesse's *Anecdotes of Dogs* (1870).

In bull-baiting, the bull (frequently chained), tried to gore the bull-dog trying to bite its nose or lip—immobilizing it with pain. The best dog for this was short and muscular, with powerful jaws and a pugnacious temperament. Different from the English Bulldog seen today, these had longer muzzles and legs, and almost any squat and powerful canine could be fairly called a "bull-dog." Bull-baiting was outlawed in England in 1835, but as the breed's popularity increased, so did a compression of body type—morphing into today's Bulldog. Exhibited at the first Westminster Kennel Club show in 1877, they were recognized by the AKC in 1896.[24]

Always competitive with his brother, Tom got his own bull-dog named Brandy. The two dogs hated each other and in one terrible fight, Brandy managed to clamp his jaws on Turk. Attempts to pry them apart failed—including that of one officer who bit one of Brandy's toes. The infuriated bull-dog took no notice until Tom finally shoved a carbine under his collar and twisted it until Brandy couldn't breathe and released Turk. After that, it was everyone's job to keep the two enemies apart.[25] (Armstrong had wangled Tom a promotion to 2nd lieutenant in the infantry and then got him into the 7th as a 1st lieutenant.)

To get to Fort Riley, the Custers would travel by rail from Monroe through Detroit, Chicago, and St. Louis to Fort Leavenworth, and from the end of the line, by wagon to Fort Riley. Like today's airline passengers worried about luggage, Armstrong was concerned the car with his horses and dogs might get side-tracked in Chicago's massive rail yard. In writing to the Northern Pacific Railroad superintendent, he invoked Barker's name to get his stock car attached to a morning passenger train arriving in St. Louis at the same time as they would.[26] Barker loaned the Custers his private railroad car to share with his daughter, niece, and a couple of friends going to the Southern Relief Fair in St. Louis.[27] Armstrong had orders to join his regiment posthaste, but he dawdled, taking full advantage of the St. Louis stop.

Raising money for the Confederate widows and orphans, the Southern Relief Fair had exhibits, food, art (including works by Western landscape painter Albert Bierstadt), livestock, horse races, and costumed "knights" tilting at rings which reminded the Custers of the jousting in Sir Walter Scott's *Ivanhoe*. They attended a play in St. Louis and met the lead actor Lawrence Barrett, who would become Armstrong's close friend. He never missed an opportunity to see Barrett on the stage if he was anywhere near a

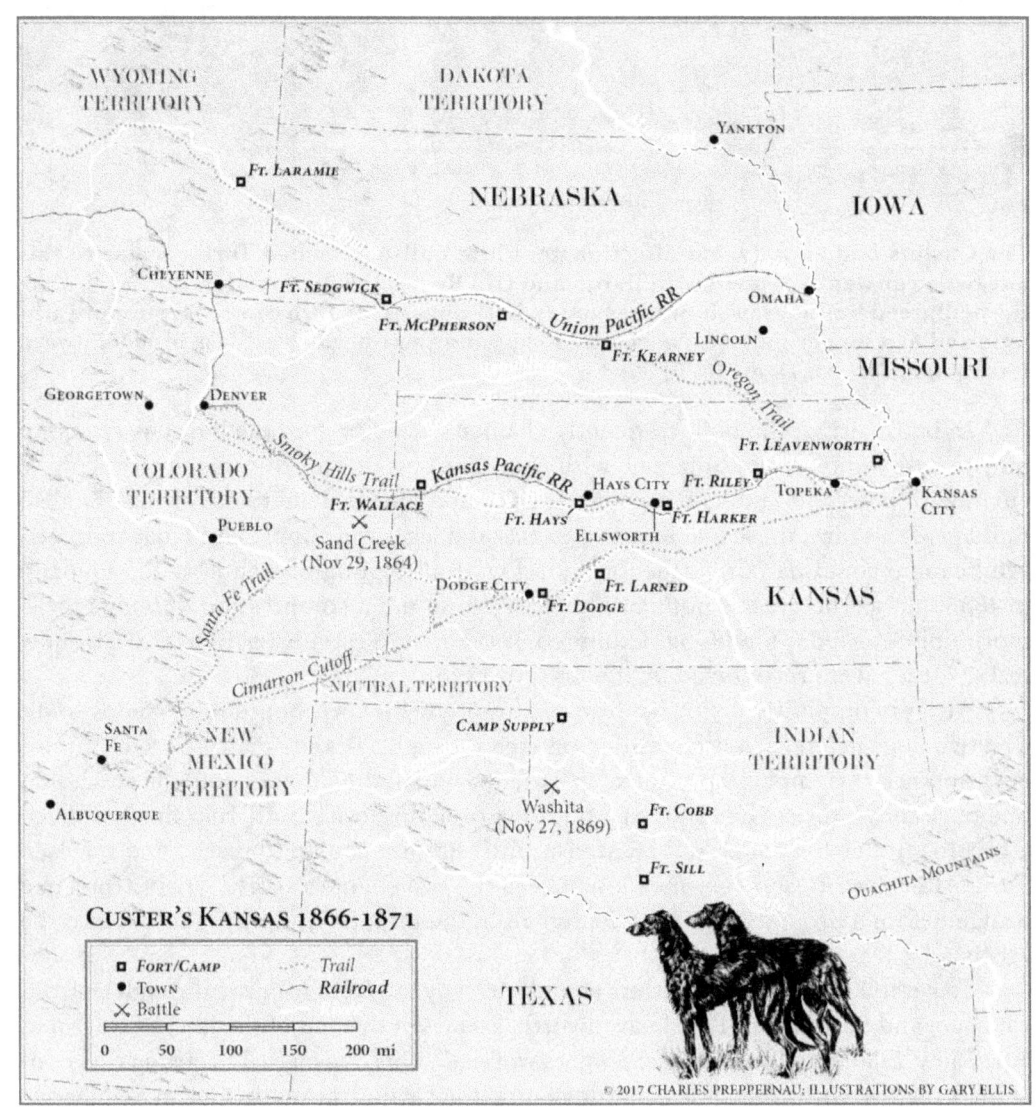

Custer's Kansas 1866–1871

performance. Armstrong loved theater and could immerse himself in the performance and weep or laugh as the actors emoted.

Fort Riley

In 1866, the young state of Kansas jutted out from the Eastern states into the Territories of Nebraska and Colorado and the Indian Territory (which would become Oklahoma in 1907). Kansas was the edge of the frontier, for buffalo were still hunted and white men could be killed by Indian war parties. On their journey, the Custers stopped in Kansas City, the last big town before "the Great American Desert," to buy supplies and a few luxuries. At the end of the line past Fort Leavenworth, a wagon and ambulance were waiting to take them ten miles to Fort Riley. Their horses were tied behind the wagons but Byron and Turk rode in the ambulance with Armstrong, Libbie, and Anna. The track was rough and, bouncing on the slippery leather benches, they often fell on the dogs ensconced in the narrow space between the seats.

They rolled into Fort Riley at dusk on October 16, and Libbie waited in the wagon while Armstrong reported to acting commanding officer Major Alfred Gibbs, a comrade from the Late War. While Libbie was worrying about quarters for all of them, including Anna, Eliza, their Texas jockey, the horses and the dogs, a fight erupted. Byron and Turk, who had been behaving in Armstrong's presence, noisily tore into each other between the benches. Terrified, Libbie wrapped her fingers around Turk's chain and pulled toward the door while Anna hauled Byron away on the other end. Hearing the noise, Armstrong dashed out, yanked the "burley brute" from Libbie and threw him to the ground.[28] Not the best way to start at a new post—and Libbie was further distressed when she learned they had to be the Gibbses' guests that evening because their own house wasn't ready for them. Peggy Gibbs was gracious, and she and Libbie would become close friends—despite Peggy's antipathy toward the Custer dogs.

As lieutenant colonel, Armstrong was now the commanding officer, and the next day, they moved into the C.O.'s house, only to be "ranked out" a couple days later when Col. Andrew Jackson Smith arrived and claimed the quarters as was his right. Armstrong then bumped a less senior officer from his quarters. While bachelor officers were used to packing up and living where they needed to, the frequent shuffling of houses because of seniority was a trial for wives and children—particularly when they had decorated the house to their satisfaction. Married quarters were generally duplexes constructed of stone with either separate entries or one common entry hall. There was a large parlor, dining room and kitchen. Tom Custer and Anna Darrah had their own rooms upstairs, and Eliza's was adjacent to the kitchen. Outside there was a stable, cow shed, and chicken coop. The Custers quickly came to be known as bumptious neighbors, for there was all manner of horsing around between the brothers and Libbie—chases up and down stairs, barricading the furniture—and all the while, the dogs barking at the happy fracas. The rumor went around the garrison that Armstrong was beating his wife. Libbie was acutely embarrassed but Armstrong thought it a very good joke.[29]

Fort Riley was one of six posts guarding the western push of the Kansas Pacific and Union Pacific Railroads, as well as the pioneer roads—the Santa Fe and Smokey

Hill trails, and the trailheads for Oregon and California. Libbie was expecting a fort with moats and battlements and was surprised that Fort Riley was a widespread collection of sandstone buildings. Palisades were not as important in protecting the fort from Indians as were regular cavalry patrols. Riley's fortified blockhouses could withstand any siege barring artillery, and its stone barracks, stables, and storehouses were fireproof. Despite protocol, the parade ground was far from sacrosanct and frequently a short-cut for dogs, mounted men, and wagons, and a cow even pastured there.[30] (In 1887, Fort Riley became the official U.S. Cavalry School and continues today as a major Army post.)

A regiment's colonel was often away from post on business, so command responsibility went to the lieutenant colonel. In that role, Armstrong met the officers of the 7th at Fort Riley. In the closed, seldom changing environment of a regiment, jealousies over promotion, favoritism, and personal bias could cause animosity and even feuds. The 7th's officers soon formed into lasting factions—those whom Armstrong liked and those who didn't like him. The "Custer Circle" was composed of lieutenants Myles Moylan, William Cooke (a tall Canadian with drooping side whiskers), Algernon E. Smith (called "Fresh" Smith to distinguish him from former sailor Henry Walworth "Salt" Smith), Thomas Weir, Tom Custer, and later Capt. Myles Keogh (an Irishman, dog fancier, and veteran of the Papal Wars in Italy). Keogh may have been an early member of Armstrong's dog circle, for in 1867, he wrote home that life at Fort Wallace was boring enough that only the daily flag raising was a relief—and "the great event" of "my dog Spot having seven little puppies." In an 1868 letter, he mentions sending five dogs from New York to Kansas by rail.[31] These dogs came from the home of Enos Thompson Throop Martin in Auburn, New York, who also had a "friendly stag-hound" named Maida.[32] Keogh and Nelly Martin were fond of each other, so he (and sometimes Armstrong) frequently visited the Martin home where Maida greeted them at the door. There are other hints that Keogh was a hound man. He carried "a heavy cane having a silver dog's head for a handle" and used it on the troopers in his company.[33] (In 1892 Maj. Henry Inman wrote "A Hunt with Custer" for the *Kansas City Journal*, describing a wolf hunt with staghounds near Fort Harker in March 1868. The participants included Inman, Armstrong, Keogh, Generals Sheridan and Sully, and from the Custer Circle, Capt. Yates and Lts. Cooke and Weir. Inman tended to interweave facts and fiction, and it is hard to determine actual dog ownership from the story.)[34]

Outside Custer's Circle, Majors Alfred Gibbs and Joel Elliott (who was with Armstrong in Texas), and Captain Louis M. Hamilton (Alexander Hamilton's grandson) were fairly neutral. Armstrong's chief opposition would be Major Wickliffe Cooper and Captains Frederick Benteen, Robert West, and Albert Barnitz (who served under Armstrong during the war). Virginia-born Frederick Benteen (a dog man himself) had been a lieutenant colonel in the war and as historian Jeffry Wert described him, "His bravery and capability as an officer were unquestioned, but while he had a backbone of steel, he possessed a soul of vinegar."[35] Benteen immediately sized up Armstrong as an upstart, and the two never got along. Aside from personality conflicts and jealousies, alcoholism was rampant on Army posts. For Cooper, Keogh, West, and Weir, their fondness for the bottle sometimes caused problems. Armstrong knew he had to appear impartial in his decisions and instructed Libbie that she mustn't discuss post politics at social affairs or have favorite officers. As the commander's wife, she was the leader of post society and expected to be a diplomatic and gracious hostess to all. Fortunately, Libbie had learned those lessons well in Washington. (While waiting for Armstrong, Gibbs had done much of the organization of the new regiment, and the formation of its band is variously attributed to Gibbs, Keogh, or Armstrong. The latter two are generally credited with adopting the Irish drinking song "Garry Owen" as the regiment's signature tune, as both knew it during the War.[36] The 7th's other favorite was "The Girl I Left Behind Me.")

* * *

The surprising force of the Kansas wind caused Libbie and the ladies no end of embarrassment when their voluminous skirts were blown up over their heads while walking. Armstrong solved the problem for Libbie by getting small lead bars and bird shot to be sewn into her hems—thus making her dresses even heavier but more manageable in the wind. Life for Libbie and other Army wives on the frontier was always something of a trial. While some of the better posts (like Fort Leavenworth) had plenty of comforts for officers and their families, many only had rudimentary housing. Whatever the lifestyle of the post, women endured their husbands' long absences and uncertain returns, erratic mail and newspaper delivery, and lack of easy access to commercial goods and medical care. Well-settled regiments could have a reading library but the 7th's shifting assignments didn't allow for that. Books were heavy and took up valuable space on the march, although Armstrong always had his small library with him—military studies and history, a few novels, and his textbook on dog care. Life on the frontier was difficult. The boredom in a rigid, isolated community was punctuated by prairie fires and flash floods—and the terror of Indian raids. It was not talked about often, but the women understood that their husbands or a trusted officer would put a "mercy bullet" in their brain rather than let them be captured alive for "outrage" (rape), torture, and slavery.

And yet, officers' women—who could live safely back East—opted to endure hardships with husbands and brothers. The wives had to manage housekeeping and cooking (often with short rations), entertaining guests on a shoestring, and frequent housing upheavals and relocations. Keeping maids was a struggle, and as the few unmarried females on post never waited long for proposals. Infant mortality and raising and schooling children were concerns for parents. Post life had happy occasions as well—religious services, evening sing-alongs, holiday celebrations, amateur theatricals, and regular dances or "hops." Social riding was important, for if women did not ride or talk horses, they missed out on a central element of Army life—not to mention seeing any country beyond the post's boundaries. For a few adventurous women, Libbie included, riding and hunting on horseback with their dog was a thrill not to be missed.

In December 1866, Libbie wrote to Rebecca, saying they had "...five dogs, cow & chicken coops. So you see we are comfortable."[37] These seem to have been Byron, Ginnie, Turk, and two foxhounds. The favorites slept in the house and when their master and mistress donned riding clothes in the morning, the dogs "leaped and sprang about the room, tore out into the gallery, and tumbled over one another and the furniture in racing back, and such a din of barking and joyful whining as they set up—the noisier the better for my husband."[38]

Blowing his horn and snapping his dog whip, Armstrong would work the pack into a frenzy, shouting "Whoop 'em up! whoop 'em up!"[39] The melee continued outside and joyously infected the horses. Armstrong would lift Libbie into the saddle and ride off with their dogs and an orderly. It was a delight for Libbie despite her husband's prank of galloping alongside her and reaching over to hoist her off the saddle. Libbie thought she was like a circus rider and remarkably changed from a quiet girl brought up in a quiet home.

The territory around Fort Riley was perfect for riding and hunting buffalo, deer, antelope, jackrabbits, wolves, and game birds. Hunting was considered to be practical training for warfare, as it involved strategy, scouting, stalking, and riding and shooting skills. It was aristocratic fun (albeit with hazards) and put meat in the pot. Danger could come from rattlesnakes, wolves, wildcats, warring Indians, and accidents. Experienced hunter Lt. Col. Richard Irving Dodge wrote, "A thousand accidents may happen to a sportsman which are serious only when he is alone." Dodge knew of incidents when hunters never returned—one man going after buffalo fell into a chasm, broke his leg, and starved to death alone. The poor fellow's remains were found three weeks later.[40]

First Contact with Indians

The rumor mill had been buzzing that there would be an expedition early in 1867. The 7th Cavalry was to be part of Major General Winfield Scott Hancock's mission to negotiate better relations with the Sioux and Southern Cheyenne after their understandable retaliations against settlers for treaty violations. The bad rations doled out by Indian agents compounded the tribes' treaty grievances. The Army expected the Indians might fight rather than talk, so the expedition went prepared for both. It was a different kind of enemy and warfare—absent from the West Point curriculum. Certainly, it was new to Hancock, who distinguished himself at Gettysburg. Indian fighting was learned by hard and bloody experience where carelessness was often fatal. The Plains Indian tribes were hardy, fierce warriors, and merciless captors. Yet, they were tender with their families and highly valued community welfare and harmony. Living off the land and going wherever they pleased, warriors and whole villages could seemingly disappear at will. They had a completely different ethos and world view difficult for the white man to understand, and yet they could be staunch allies or terrible enemies—depending upon whether or not they trusted you. Naively, Hancock thought they could be intimidated into peaceful behavior by a show of force. He could not have been more wrong, for they led him on a wild goose chase all that summer.

It would be the 7th's and Armstrong's first foray against Indians. His dog pack had increased since December and he brought along his two greyhounds, Lu, a female, and Sharp, a male—and foxhounds Rover, Fanny, and Rattler (a common name for hunting dogs; this was not the Rattler from Hempstead). The latter two were inexperienced hounds, and this was Rattler's first hunt. Byron is not mentioned after his Fort Riley fight with Turk and was dead or missing by this point. Staying home with Libbie were Ginnie, Turk, and some new additions to the pack about which little is known—setter puppies.

In the last days of March, Hancock's expedition rode west from Fort Riley. When fully assembled at Fort Larned, there were six companies of the 7th, one company of the 37th Infantry, and an artillery detachment, making a force of about 1,400 men. While the column was on the march, scouts would take mail bags back and forth between the column and the nearest fort—avoiding Indians by riding at night and resting under cover in daylight. (James Butler "Wild Bill" Hickok was one of these.) Libbie and Armstrong wrote each other daily but because the letters often had to be relayed between posts before reaching their destination, there would be worrisome gaps of no letters which suddenly ended with several all at once.

Every officer had an orderly to attend to laundry, meals, fires, and myriad other tasks. Commonly called "strikers," they were paid a small salary, could be excused from duty, had access to better food, and often had early notice of upcoming orders. Armstrong's strikers principally took care of his dogs and horses. On the first day out, he wrote Libbie that the dogs were "behaving admirably" but worn out from the march and swimming a creek. They were snoring around the sheet metal stove in his tent as he wrote. Libbie had packed a large dinner of ham, chicken, biscuits, pickles, and coffee, which Armstrong enjoyed with two friends under dog supervision—"The old hound Rover took his place alongside the table at dinner, as naturally as if he had been accustomed to it all his life."[41] (His description suggests Rover was acquired in Kansas rather than coming with them from Monroe.)

When he stretched out on his cot, Rover, being the alpha dog, claimed the space nearest his master's pillow, while Lu slept at the foot and Sharp fitted in between. The two younger dogs, Rattler and Fanny, slept on folded canvas near Rover. Exhausted, they seldom moved—their noisy breathing punctuated by snoring. Col. Smith once found Armstrong in a morning nap surrounded by dogs and had a good laugh at him. He explained, "they were great company to me, and are as completely domiciled in the tent, as if 'to the manor born.'"[42] Armstrong's tent mate had no objections—and certainly with all those bodies, they were warmer at night than officers in dogless tents.

On the march, when the dogs were fresh, they ranged out searching for moving game—the greyhounds stopping on rises to scan the horizon while the foxhounds snuffled in bushes and burrows for fresh scent. They trotted alongside their favorite men and horses and would go joyously scudding up and down the column on important dog errands. They chased antelope and jackrabbits, and if a jack was not caught by the greyhounds, Rover would trail it all day if not called off. (Whether or not any of Armstrong's hounds could catch a healthy adult antelope was an ongoing debate.) The dogs were fed with the unwanted meat from game or else shared rations of bacon and hardtack. A recent buffalo carcass would provide a meal but prairie dogs were not eaten by the hounds. The communal rodents would stand on mounds by their burrows making tiny barks at the mounted men and dogs and would dive into their holes, leaving Lu and the other dogs puzzled as to their sudden disappearance. Some prairie dog "towns" were vast enough to be "prairie dog republics." Despite elements of comedy and cuteness, prairie dog territory was potentially dangerous as the horses could collapse the burrows and break a leg.

Armstrong's dogs were not the only ones as there were a number of dogs belonging to soldiers and companies in the column. Three days out from Riley, Armstrong wrote Libbie jokingly that if he ran across any nice dogs, he would send them via express to Mrs. Gibbs—who didn't like dogs but, sharing quarters with the Custers, put up with the annoyances of their pack.[43] In his letters, he repeatedly told Libbie the expedition would be successful and he'd be home soon—but then he was not yet savvy about Indians. Hancock directed the Indian agents at Fort Larned to arrange a meeting with several local chiefs for April 10. The column arrived on the 7th and camped outside the cluster of stone buildings, but on the day, the chiefs were absent as their tribes had been delayed by a snowstorm and an impromptu buffalo hunt—winter food being more important than meeting white soldiers, which could always happen another day. Unfamiliar with tribal ways, Hancock wouldn't accept these reasons, decided they were deliberately evading him, and gave orders to find the combined Sioux and Cheyenne villages farther along the Pawnee River. After a near-confrontation with the warriors, Indian Agent Wynkoop arranged a meeting with two chiefs, Bull Bear and Roman Nose, but the women and the children, justifiably fearing a sneak attack, quietly moved out of the area. Armstrong was sent to stop any further escapes and found the village hastily abandoned, but still with "…dogs of all sorts, sexes, sizes, and colors."[44] In one teepee, they found a simmering pot, and Armstrong thought it a good joke that Dr. Coates (who wanted to taste Indian food), declared the stew delicious but was repulsed upon learning it was dog.[45] There were two abandoned inhabitants remaining—a feeble, old man and a recently brutalized, half-breed girl. "Those Indian men did me bad!"[46] Armstrong swore to punish the perpetrators but knew the odds of identifying and catching them were slim.

Hancock, provoked by the vacated village, burned it. He sent the cavalry off in pursuit of the Sioux and Cheyenne, and any other Indians they could catch. Armstrong and his officers quickly learned Army horses, heavily burdened with gear and rider, and dependent upon grain, could not catch warriors on their ponies—which were smaller and lived quite well on prairie grass. That was the beginning of the summer of chasing Indians—or as Armstrong exaggerated, "an Indian War."

Shortly after camping at Fort Larned, the officers were out hunting near the column when a jackrabbit popped up and streaked away with Armstrong and his five hounds after it. He had neglected to properly tighten the saddle girth and it came loose, sliding down Phil Sheridan's side and pitching him onto the prairie. Five miles later, they started another jackrabbit, and with everyone watching, a dozen dogs from the column joined Armstrong's pack in the course. Sharp led, followed by Lu and three or four other dogs with Rover, Rattler, and Fanny bringing up the rear. After nearly a mile, the greyhounds were on its tail and Sharp near enough for a take, but the jack leapt to one side and sped off in a different direction. Sharp could not check himself and ran past before being able to turn. With this lead, the jackrabbit distanced the pack—the whole lot disappearing in the undulating prairie. They all returned except Fanny, who was last seen far away and clearly lost.[47] Armstrong was used to dogs going missing and turning up later, so he didn't search for her. She never found her way back and died on the prairie.

During the wait for the Sioux and Cheyenne chiefs to come in for talks, a blizzard dumped nearly a foot of snow on the ground. To prevent the picketed horses from freezing to death, they were whipped by night guards to keep them stamping and moving. Many of the officers were unprepared for the bitter cold, but Armstrong's dogs were keeping him toasty, for, as Libbie put it, he and Tom "…shared their own blankets with them when caught out in a cold snap, or divided short rations with the dogs they loved."⁴⁸ One freezing night, an officer begged the loan of a dog as he couldn't get warm. Armstrong gave him Old Rover because he was large and, once sleeping, would not budge until daybreak. Armstrong took the hound into the fellow's tent and settled him by pretending to sleep alongside Rover with the man on the other side. When the dog snoozed off, Armstrong went back to his tent. Only afterwards did he remember Rover snored and was prone to twitching his legs and "thumping his cumbrous tail" (which Libbie thought were signs of dream hunts and battles with Turk). Later that night, Armstrong went to check on the "portable furnace" and saw the man sleeping on his back making awful noises with Rover sprawled across his chest, snoring and snorting. In the morning he asked for a different dog, "as he did not expect to have a bedfellow which would climb up over his lungs and crush all the life out of his body." Armstrong collapsed with laughter upon his bed.⁴⁹

On Tuesday, April 16, the day after Armstrong left to find the Sioux and Cheyenne, the column was encamped near Walnut Creek, and he rode out at dawn. There had been antelope grazing a few miles away, and he was eager to try Lu and Sharp against the fastest mammals on the prairie. Mounted on Custis Lee, he brought along the foxhounds, Rover and Rattler, but was accompanied only by his chief bugler, Sgt. King. It was a risky thing to do, for no seasoned frontiersman would have gone off alone in unfamiliar and dangerous country. Armstrong had never been tested by Indians but was cocksure of himself. Typical of a tenderfoot, he reckoned because the Indians hadn't been seen recently, it was safe. What the frontier scouts said about the Apaches was also true of the Plains tribes: "When you see Apache 'sign,' be keerful; 'n' when you don' see nary sign, be *more* keerful."⁵⁰

The Unfortunate Buffalo Hunt

Two miles from camp, Armstrong spotted the white rumps of a small herd of grazing antelope. All the dogs were sighted, but the greyhounds left Rover and Rattler in the dust, following a scent trail. While Sharp fell behind in the chase, Lu overhauled the antelope after four miles but couldn't catch one (Armstrong estimated the distance). Sgt. King on his plodding Army horse couldn't keep up with the thoroughbred and greyhounds and fell so far behind that he headed back to the column. After a futile chase, Armstrong recalled Lu and Sharp. The two foxhounds were missing, and while he figured Rover would be fine, he had doubts about young Rattler. As the greyhounds were coming in, Armstrong spotted a large buffalo some distance away and, having never hunted one before, he went after it with the greyhounds.

There were two types of buffalo hunters. One type was the professional wanting meat or hides and who used powerful rifles to pick off grazing buffalos one by one. (Before his Wild West Show days, William F. "Buffalo Bill" Cody killed thousands to supply railroad workers with meat.) The other was the sportsman who wanted excitement. Their standard method of hunting involved galloping alongside a buffalo at the edge of the herd and firing a revolver into the chest. Six-shot pistols typically were .36 or .44 caliber with small black powder loads, so a hunter carried spare pistols as it could take twelve, eighteen, or even twenty-four slugs to stop a buffalo. If the horse was trained to close with the buffalo, the rider could use both hands for his repeating rifle—typically the Spencer carbine, Winchester, or Henry (which, as the Rebels used to say, "...can be loaded on Sunday and fired all the week"[51]). Lt. "Bill" Davis, brother of Gen. Jefferson Columbus Davis, was hunting near Fort Griffin, Texas, and stabbed a running buffalo with his saber, but it disappeared with the sword sticking out of its side.[52]

Armstrong was armed with two .36 caliber percussion revolvers, and this hunt was going to be tough work for him and his dogs. After a run of three miles, Sharp overtook the buffalo and broke its stride, allowing Armstrong to ride up and draw his pistol. Both horse and beast were getting winded, but he jockeyed alongside and was in the act of pulling his gun hand up when the buffalo swerved into Custis Lee. Armstrong pulled the reins with both hands to bounce the horse away and accidentally pulled the trigger. The bullet went through the back of the horse's neck and into its brain. Lee dropped like a stone and pitched his rider headfirst over the saddle bow. Stunned but unharmed, Armstrong lay there for an instant before getting up with revolver still in his grip. Facing him was a snorting buffalo taller than a horse and weighing twice as much. Lu and Sharp were blown and still far away. On foot with only a pistol, it was a desperate situation for he could be gored or trampled as easily as the bull flicked its tail. His bullets couldn't penetrate the massive skull but if the dogs caught up and put the buffalo at bay, he might be able to get a heart shot—but it would still be a close shave. The balance tipped unexpectedly in his favor when the great bull turned and galloped away, leaving Armstrong in possession of the field—but not the victor. (When Libbie Custer published *Tenting on the Plains* in 1887, the famous Western artist Frederic Remington contributed a drawing of the buffalo face-off.)

Disoriented on the featureless prairie, Armstrong was not sure where his command was, and the dogs were nowhere in sight. Lee was dead, and there was no way he could haul saddle, bridle, and personal gear on foot, so he set off toward his best guess for the column's location. Describing this to Libbie, he joked about his predicament, "But now came the time to try men's *soles*." After about two miles, Armstrong spotted the tops of Army wagons heading his way, so he sat down to wait. The column was surprised to find him sitting alone on the prairie. He explained, and soldiers went back to retrieve his equipment from Lee's body. Someone loaned him a horse, and he was back in action—and later that day, he did kill a buffalo with his revolvers. Pvt. John Ryan of M Company, a generally reliable memoirist, was with the column and misremembered finding him seated on his saddle. (Ryan also thought he had the larger staghounds with him.[53]) Somewhere on Armstrong's solitary walk, Lu and Sharp found him. Old Rover made his way to the column after three hours, but Rattler was never seen again.[54] Armstrong figured the wolves got him—they probably got Fanny, too. He dreaded having to tell Libbie that while struggling to shoot the buffalo, he accidentally shot her favorite horse, but as it turned out, she had already heard the news from someone else.

Armstrong's account of the incident changed with time. The first version was in his April 20 letter to Libbie and is perhaps the most accurate.[55] At Barker's urging, it was next a letter to *Turf, Field and Farm* on September 21.[56] Armstrong's flair for adventurous prose under the pen name "Nomad" established him as a premier Indian fighter, hunter, and hound man in his *Turf* letters. (It didn't take long before *Turf's* readership knew the identity of Nomad.) Armstrong's final version appeared in *The Galaxy* April 1872, with more Indian menace for the general public. It and his other stories of that period were published serially in *The Galaxy* and subsequently included in his partial autobiography, *My Life on the Plains*, in 1874.[57] (*The Galaxy* featured distinguished writers such as Mark Twain, Henry James, and Walt Whitman and was absorbed by *The Atlantic Monthly* in 1878.)

In the first account, the hounds are all named and they have a specific role to impede the buffalo. As Nomad, he has the generic "half a dozen hounds" and commands the greyhounds to intercept the buffalo and slow it down for him. When Nomad is stranded, there is a hint of worry about Indians until he spots dust from his column (previously it was canvas wagon covers). In *The Galaxy*, Armstrong included more Indian menace, and the pack is now "several fine English greyhounds," who are called to *follow* him after the buffalo for "mile after mile." Though his thoroughbred is not fresh, Armstrong still outdistances the hounds (including the ride out, chasing antelope and the buffalo, and the walk, he covered a lot of mileage that day). Interestingly, in this version, it was his hounds' whining and stares toward the horizon which guided him to the column. Once again, there is dust, but this time it might be cavalry, buffalo herd, or a war party, so Armstrong and the hounds hide in a ravine until he sees a guidon's stars and stripes.

"Custer luck" had saved his neck but not Custis Lee, Rattler, and Fanny. Armstrong still went hunting with his remaining three dogs, Lu, Sharp, and Rover, and got replacements for the two lost hounds. Libbie recalled Armstrong's standard response to any kind of loss, "When that's gone, we can get another."[58] When he described Custis Lee's death to Libbie, he closed with detailed descriptions of the men at Lookout Station who had been burned to death by Indians and then partially eaten by wolves (just what Libbie *didn't* want to hear).[59] From that station, Armstrong and his men went to Fort Hays, with him planning a way to be reunited with Libbie. The 150-mile march was done in a grueling four days, exhausting his men and horses. (Armstrong always took an almost perverse delight in telling "too much" to Libbie. In New York, he had written about flirtations with prostitutes and female admirers, and in Kansas, he meticulously described the beauty of a Kiowa girl.[60])

Setter Dogs (Briefly) and the Irksome Separation

Libbie, still at Fort Riley, wrote on April 18 with news from the garrison. One black soldier had shot another, and their ammunition was confiscated (Libbie was never comfortable around black soldiers—she had been accidentally fired upon by one on guard duty). She wrote that Major Gibbs had arrived to put the garrison in order, and he was chiding her about the volume of letters the Custers were writing. She worried about him pursuing Indians and distracted herself by making and mending clothes. Turk the bull-dog was admired by the dog *cognoscenti* who offered to buy him, but Libbie and Eliza knew despite his ferocity, he wouldn't be much of a fighter as his teeth were worn down from gnawing on his chain. "Dog sorrows are pretty hard..." Ginnie had a litter of puppies who all died, and their disconsolate mother dug two burrows for herself (Eliza thought she was burying herself with grief) but Libbie wrote, "the setter puppies are doing well."[61]

English, Irish, and Gordon Setters were very popular as most outdoor men kept a pointer or setter for hunting game birds, and the first local dog shows in America were strictly pointer/setter affairs. That the Custers never named the setter puppies in their writings (only mentioning them twice) indicates they weren't significant dogs for them. Likely, the puppies were given away or died early from any of a number of hazards—distemper, accident, or just going missing. (Setters were three of the first nine breeds [all bird dogs] recognized by the AKC in 1878—the others being the Pointer, Chesapeake Bay Retriever, and Clumber, Cocker, Irish Water, and Sussex Spaniels.[62] A persistent internet rumor has Armstrong owning Chesapeakes, but there is *no* evidence to substantiate that claim.)

Rover, Lu, and Sharp were still with him on April 30 when he acquired a pet beaver. "Medicine Bill" Comstock took him to Beaver Creek, where he killed a beaver and wounded a large wildcat.[63] Armstrong fancied himself an epicure but thought beaver had a "...fatty, lamp-oil taste connected with it which to my mind would be agreeable only to a Lapplander [sic]...."[64] Always one for novelty pets, Armstrong adopted a young beaver and like Dixie, the raccoon, it followed him around the tent and slept in his bed—cuddling under his nightgown. Doubtless Libbie was appalled. Devilment was never far from his mind, particularly with Eliza, and he intended to tell her the beaver's tail was once round but had been run over by a wagon. Armstrong joked about getting Eliza an Indian for a husband who didn't need laundry or buttons sewn, and only wanted one kind of cooking—"stewed puppies."[65]

By the beginning of May, there had been no Indian sightings around Fort Hays for days, and a few officers decided to go buffalo hunting, taking six troopers and dogs. Capt. Benteen accidentally shot both his own horse and E Company's "buffalo dog" while the latter was biting the nose of a bull at bay. About half the party got lost and didn't return until the next day. The wounded dog was brought back, and Armstrong thought it would recover. In the wake of Custis Lee's death, he pointed out to Libbie that Benteen also managed to shoot his own horse in a buffalo melee.[66]

Armstrong had a hard time being separated from Libbie and their marriage bed. He persuaded Hancock that she, Anna Darrah, and Eliza could safely join him at Fort Hays (Benteen and Barnitz also intended to send for their wives). On May 4 he said she could go with Col. Smith, who would be coming from Fort Riley to rejoin his regiment. She would travel by ambulance and was instructed to bring lightweight calico dresses, have a chicken crate made, and to be sure Turk and the setters were kept on leashes when passing through town.[67] (Ginnie seems to have stayed at Fort Riley, and this was the last mention of their setter dogs.) Armstrong wrote again on May 7 and 9, urging haste as he would not be at Fort Hays for long. He asked for their two croquet sets (table top and lawn), 100 lbs. of butter, lard, potatoes, onions, vegetables, and fruits. Armstrong hinted cryptically at a passionate reunion—"I know *something* much, very much better and be sure you bring it along. *I am entirely out at present*, and have been for so long as to almost forget how it tastes...."[68]

At Fort Hays, a rather poor collection of log and adobe huts, Armstrong set up the bivouac for his exhausted cavalry near Big Creek, about a half mile from the post. Unfortunately, the grazing was poor and the rations bad—some of the hardtack was Army issue from 1860. Without vegetables and fruit, scurvy broke out. Tempted by the gold mines in Colorado Territory, many soldiers deserted, taking their horses and guns. Disheartened by the inability to come to grips with the Sioux and Cheyenne, and furious at the desertions, Armstrong retaliated with harsh discipline. As biographer Jeffry D. Wert wrote, "In his first independent operation with the Seventh Cavalry, he had lost the quarry—a Civil War hero outwitted by Indians."[69] His mood worsened because Libbie wasn't there. Despite dismal conditions, amusements were staged for the officers and men—a foot race, horse race, and a buffalo hunt where two teams of officers competed for the most kills. The tongues (a great delicacy) were used to prove each team's count. Armstrong's hunters won, twelve to ten, and the losing team gave a champagne banquet for all the hunters.

Shortly before Armstrong's orders came through, Libbie, Anna, Eliza, and dogs (definitely Turk and possibly the setter pups), arrived at the camp in mid–May to find Armstrong had arranged a tent complex with bedroom, guest room, sitting room, dining room, his orderly's tent, and a cook tent for Eliza. Armstrong had to ride out on June 1 for a circular scout which would take him to Fort McPherson (Nebraska) and Fort Sedgwick (Colorado) and then back through Fort Wallace (Kansas) to Fort Hays. He arranged for "Medicine Bill" Comstock's services again. Comstock knew the territory and Indian culture intimately, was a skilled tracker, and spoke a few dialects and knew sign language. So deeply steeped in tribal lore, everything for him had good or bad medicine (even horses and field glasses)—and hence his nickname. Theodore R. Davis, a reporter with the 7th, said no Indian was half as superstitious as Comstock—who even fastened a medicine collar on Cuss, his large "evil looking dog."[70] (Cuss was supposedly named for Custer.) Armstrong, still a novice to Indian ways, was savvy enough to get Comstock talking in order to soak up information. (Sometimes confusingly called "Wild Bill," Comstock was still working for the Army when he was killed in uncertain circumstances in August 1868.)

Terror on Big Creek

Armstrong left with 350 men, twenty wagons, and Lu and Sharp. Rover and the other dogs stayed with Libbie in her new canvas home. Less than a week after he left, the area was hit with violent storms. For two days, wind, rain, and lightning hammered the camp, slackened briefly, and then pounded them for another two days. At first, the tents held up to the wind and rain, but the creek swelled rapidly—some thirty-five feet—and overflowed the banks. Amidst lightning flashes and rising water, soldiers helped Libbie and Eliza carry their possessions to slightly higher ground. The center ground of the Big Creek loop surrounding the Custer tents became an island in the rushing torrent. In the midst of the storm, Rover and Turk broke their chains and murderously went for each other's throats. Libbie and Eliza stood helpless until several soldiers tried forcing the dogs apart. At last, one strong man choked Turk enough to make him unclench his jaws. The bleeding combatants were dragged apart and re-chained, and the soldiers returned to saving the tents.

Men, trees, and large chunks of the creek's bank were washed away. Terrified by the storm and the cries of drowning men, Libbie and Eliza struggled to loosen tent ropes for life lines, but their freezing hands couldn't undo the knots. They spotted one man, stuck in the fork of a tree and near death with water swelling over him. Miraculously, Eliza got her clothes-line looped around him and together with Libbie, hauled him up to higher ground. Seven men on horseback drowned in rescue attempts—but the women saved two more with Eliza's clothes-line. Rover and Turk continued to eye each other while the flood was threatening the fort itself. The officers improvised a rescue boat out of a box wagon. If the flood appeared to be getting worse, they would lash Libbie, Anna, Mrs. Gibbs, and Eliza to the Gatling guns—which, at over 400 pounds each, would prevent them from being swept away—or get them drowned.

After a long, panicky night, the morning was clear. Everywhere there was water, mud, camp debris, and the occasional body. They had a day's respite before the storm and flood hit again—nearly as bad and ending around midnight of June 8. Armstrong was heading for Fort McPherson and would not know about the flood on Big Creek for days. The canine belligerents, Turk and Old Rover, survived.

The Hard March

Armstrong thought his scout was going reasonably well until Major Wickliffe Cooper committed suicide. An alcoholic with a pregnant wife and desperately unhappy to be away from her, he believed himself badly used by Armstrong, sinking deeper and deeper into a liquor-fueled depression, until he shot himself on June 8. Armstrong, still a teetotaler, somewhat callously used the opportunity to lecture his officers on alcohol abuse while lamenting the loss of Cooper. Describing the tragedy to Libbie, the thought of Cooper's widow being alone seemed to affect him greatly.

In his desperation to be with Libbie, Armstrong was about to blot his career with a huge judgment error. After ten days on the trail, he arrived at Fort McPherson and immediately asked General Sherman if his wife could join him. Libbie knew a reunion was brewing but had no idea where or when. Sherman was agreeable but *after* Armstrong returned from Fort Sedgwick. The news delighted Libbie as she might be able to accompany Wild Bill Hickok on his dispatch run to McPherson. She liked Hickok— "Physically, he was a delight to look upon. Tall, lithe, and free in every motion, he rode and walked as if every muscle was perfection...."[71] However, the Fort McPherson rendezvous couldn't happen as Armstrong was never in one place for long. His column headed south to the Republican River on the 17th—and he told Libbie to intercept him at Fort Wallace, his destination after re-supplying at Sedgwick. Then Armstrong began to play fast and loose with his orders. He was supposed to have gone to Sedgwick but instead, sent Lt. Samuel Robbins with wagons and escort to get supplies at Fort Wallace, and if Libbie was there, return with her. Maj. Elliott was dispatched to Fort Sedgwick for any new orders from Sherman. A minor skirmish with Pawnee Killer's Sioux band (Armstrong's first combat with Indians), concerned him enough to send Capt. Myers

6: Kansas—Hunting Game and Chasing Indians

and a detachment to reinforce Lt. Robbins' wagon train where Libbie *might* be a passenger.

On June 26, Meyers met Robbins' returning supply train during another Indian attack, and the day after, they rejoined the column (Libbie was not with them). Elliott returned to the column from Sedgwick. While Sherman's orders gave Armstrong some latitude, having been resupplied, he was supposed to be heading back to Kansas and Fort Wallace—but he was worried about Libbie, for he didn't know if she was at one of the forts or in transit by rail or ambulance. Equally on his mind was the possibility of scoring a victory against war parties raiding in the area. At the beginning of July, he rode north by the Republican River toward the River Platte and Fort Sedgwick. Champing at the bit to complete his mission and get to Libbie, "Hard Ass" pushed his men—expecting them to match his own endurance. With water scarce, the wide valley was the driest, hottest land in Kansas and the animals suffered terribly. The easy first day's march on July 4 took them to a spring, but it was sixty-five dry miles to the next watering hole, so leaving at midnight, they made a grueling ride to get there. Armstrong dryly noted in his memoir, "Many of the dogs accompanying the command die of thirst and exhaustion."[72] Luckily, Lu and Sharp made it through the Kansas furnace.

When they reached Riverside Station, forty miles west of Fort Sedgwick, on July 5, they rested. On the 6th, Armstrong received a telegram with new orders to return to Fort Wallace because it and other settlements on the Smokey Hill Trail had been recently attacked. He was informed that Lt. Lyman Kidder with a 2nd Cavalry escort had been sent from Sedgwick toward the Republican River to deliver these orders to him. Unfortunately, Armstrong and Kidder completely missed each other on the prairie. Disgruntled at the thought of backtracking on that harsh trail, thirty men deserted at night. The next day, at 5 a.m., the column started for Fort Wallace, but ten men deserted in daylight—five on horseback and five on foot. Incensed, Armstrong ordered them brought back, alive or dead. The riders got away, leaving the walking deserters shooting at the detail, who returned fire. Three deserters were wounded, and one later died. Armstrong had them confined in a springless wagon. In front of his men, Armstrong ordered that there be no medical care for the deserters. (Dr. Coates dressed their wounds at the next watering hole.) Armstrong kept pressing toward Fort Wallace—later saying he had "great anxiety" about Kidder and his men.[73] That day, they marched twenty-four miles and had to dig for drinkable water.

The next day, the column rode through the crimson and yellow of "prickly pear country"—low, bulbous cacti which stretched for miles across the landscape. Armstrong got his dogs into a wagon, but they jumped out and "...went along the column pricked at every step by the sharp thorns." The cactus was tough on man and beast, and Davis, the reporter from *Harper's Weekly*, wrote after two days of struggle, "I do not think there was a man in the entire command that would have willingly gone through it again."[74] Armstrong's greyhounds would have been in the wagons, and of that march, one trooper said bitterly, "He thinks more of his dogs than he does of us."[75] (As in Texas, Armstrong used his multi-knife's tweezers to extract cactus thorns from paws.[76])

Despite the hardships, there were a considerable number of critters besides the dogs—young antelopes and wolves being the "chief stock now on hand" according to

Davis. He recorded that the field menagerie consisted of four orphan antelopes (their mothers had been killed for meat), eight young wolves "principally of the coyote kind," as well as eagles, ravens, prairie-dogs, jackrabbits, owls, and fangless rattlesnakes. Armstrong bragged that as soon as the prairie wildlife collection was complete with a buffalo calf, elk, beaver, black-tailed deer, and "a musical specimen of the buffalo wolf of the big gray kind," he would ship them to New York's Central Park menagerie.[77] (Frontiersman believed there were two varieties of wolves—the "buffalo wolf, as tall as an ordinary greyhound" and the smaller "prairie wolf," mistakenly called "coyote." True coyotes were thought to be native only to Texas and Mexico.[78])

Accompanying Davis' article was an illustration of the "Camp Pets of the Seventh United States Cavalry," done prior to the dog-killing march. It showed Armstrong sitting amidst greyhounds (Lu and Sharp), a collared bull-dog, two other dogs, three wolves (or coyotes), antelopes, jackrabbits, a bald eagle, a hawk improbably perched on a saber hilt, and what appear to be beavers in the distance. While Davis drew this and other images of the 7th in the field, the engraving artists at *Harper's* turned the sketches into printing plates and imaginatively filled in details. The strict accuracy of the published image is different from the sketch, as all those "pets" never lounged together harmoniously. Davis included himself with notebook and pencil in the portrait, sitting

The 7th Cavalry's menagerie in Kansas as sketched by Theodore R. Davis, who sits next to Armstrong petting an antelope. Nearby are the greyhounds, Lu and Sharp, and a bull-dog who may be Turk. While the officers and troopers of the 7th did collect many pets, this group of wolves, coyotes, antelope, jackrabbits, hawk, and bald eagle (and apparently beavers in the distance) would never have been loose together like this. *Harper's Weekly*, August 17, 1867.

alongside Armstrong.[79] The "Camp Pets" engraving was published along with a gruesome trail scene by Davis in August. Six days after the deserters were shot, and once again in cactus country, the decomposing bodies of the luckless Lt. Kidder and his command were found on July 12, bristling with arrows and mutilated, with at least one man burned to death. Davis sketched the corpses, they were buried quickly, and the march to Fort Wallace continued.

A number of cavalry dogs wandered off looking for better conditions, and Davis noted, "As far as dogs are concerned the regiment has been unfortunate, losing more than it could replace by the most persistent stealing from ranches and trains."[80] Armstrong gives no further word of Lu and Sharp, but the following summer, Tom Custer confirmed they died of heat exhaustion: "I have fully come to the conclusion that Grey hounds [sic] cannot stand the plains as you know the General lost two from the same curse last summer."[81] (The letter's recipient is unknown but possibly Kirkland Barker.)

Libbie was not at Fort Wallace when Armstrong arrived on July 13, nor was there word of her location. He agonized for a day about what to do and, in the end, put his wife above orders. Leaving Maj. Elliott in charge, he took three officers (including Tom) and a detachment of seventy-two men with the freshest horses, and on the morning of the 15th, headed for Fort Hays—one of the few places where Libbie could be. A deserter decamped with Custer's spare horse, and a sergeant and six men were ordered to get him. Attacked by Indians, they suffered one killed and another seriously wounded. Despite this news from the detail, Armstrong violated a basic trust of the Army. Certain both men were dead, he refused to backtrack for rescue or burial regardless of threatened mutiny. (The wounded trooper survived and was later rescued.) Armstrong was in a sweat to get to Hays and pushed his exhausted men 130 miles in under sixty hours. Reaching there on the 18th, and not finding Libbie, he left his worn out men. Armstrong, his orderly, Tom and Lt. William Cooke took two ambulances to Fort Harker where he could catch a train to Fort Riley. The next day at 2:30 a.m., Armstrong woke up his commanding officer, Col. Smith, told him about his "supply run" and said that he was going to Fort Riley. Groggily, Smith agreed and went back to sleep. Armstrong arrived there in the morning and found Libbie. She would always remember that "…one, long perfect day. It was mine, and—blessed be our memory, which preserve to us the joys as well as the sadness of life! It is still mine, for time and eternity."[82]

Col. Smith realized what Armstrong had done and telegraphed him to return to his command at Fort Wallace. The next train was not for two days, and when the Custers arrived, Armstrong was immediately placed under house arrest. Smith's charges were: absent without leave from his command (going off to Fort Harker); conduct prejudicial to good order and military discipline for the forced march of exhausted men and horses to Fort Hays on personal business (and using ambulances and mules for the same reason); and failing to pursue the Indians who ambushed his men or return to recover or bury their bodies. An additional charge of "Conduct prejudicial…" had specifications about his orders to shoot deserters and inhumane treatment after wounding them.[83] In late August, General Grant approved the charges and ordered a court martial, which convened at Fort Leavenworth on September 15.

Court Martialed and Adrift

As he did with West Point exams, Armstrong shifted into study mode. He borrowed law books and searched fervently for a precedent or loophole which would help his defense. Taking a break from this on September 9, he wrote a long Nomad letter to *Turf* about the unfortunate hunt with Custis Lee, but also touched on the Hancock Expedition (published September 21, 1867). His next letter, written on September 29 while the court was in progress (published October 12), covered the buffalo hunt contest. He was determined to win a complete acquittal, and Libbie, the judge's daughter, assisted by copying pages and pages of statements to aid Armstrong's defense. She never forgot he risked both his life and Army career to find her at Fort Riley and would forgive him much because of it.

His counsel and former classmate, Capt. Charles Parsons, had him pleading not guilty to all charges and specifications. Armstrong justified everything by claiming Fort Wallace had cholera and was in desperate need of medicine and supplies, and hence his forced marches to obtain them. The deserters were treated harshly to prevent other desertions (and Sherman had wanted strict discipline). As witnesses gave statements and were cross-examined, Armstrong's claims unraveled. Capt. Keogh, who commanded Fort Wallace, confirmed it had a month's worth of supplies and had not yet experienced cholera.[84] As he did in his court martial at West Point, rather than speaking on his own behalf, Armstrong wrote a long closing statement for his advocate to read.

On October 11, Armstrong was found guilty of all charges—although exonerated from criminality with respect to the ambulances and treatment of the deserters. (His wagon-riding dogs were not mentioned in the witness testimonies.) The court suspended him from rank, command, and pay for one year. Grant approved the sentence on November 18 and thought it lenient under the circumstances. Libbie wrote to Rebecca that it was difficult to lose his "pay proper" of $95 per month but that "…a soldier's emoluments amount to more than his pay, so we have enough to live on."[85] Sadly, Armstrong now believed his own humbug about Fort Wallace needing supplies because of the cholera, and he railed against the verdict. Libbie, who didn't know the truth behind his dereliction of duty, stood loyally by him. Both were convinced he had been persecuted by Gen. Hancock and Col. Smith. Armstrong, who was frequently his own worst enemy when he thought himself wronged, tried to get public opinion behind him. In the next two months, he lashed out in the papers and charged Capt. West with drunkenness on duty. Found guilty, West retaliated with civil charges against Armstrong for the deserter's murder. (That case was dismissed in January.) The 7th's officers were already starting to take sides because Armstrong had abandoned men on the march. The petulant attack on West further divided them. Armstrong wrote three more Nomad letters before the end of the year describing the burning of the Cheyenne village and the futile pursuit of the Indians—all suggesting Hancock was to blame for the expedition's failure.

As much as he could, Sheridan stood by his disgraced favorite and generously offered Armstrong and Libbie the use of his home at Fort Leavenworth for the winter. With no responsibilities during his suspension, the Custers socialized, did what they pleased, and enjoyed their dogs. Lu and Sharp were long dead on the trail, but Rover, Turk, and Ginnie were still with them.

Armstrong had time on his hands and began to pen his Civil War memoirs for paid installments in *The Galaxy.* He told a friend he was now like the ever-optimistic Mr. Micawber from *David Copperfield,* "...waiting for something to 'turn up.'"[86] As it transpired, Barker and Sheridan would oblige him.

Tail Piece: Scotch Stag Hounds and Chinese Edible Dogs— Victorian Breed Terminology

Before show competitions and national kennel clubs, dog types or breeds were named by their function (retriever), origin (Newfoundland), or even after the breed's inventor/patron (Gordon Setter). The emphasis was on purpose rather than being purebred. The term "lapdog" is perfectly descriptive as is "feist" for dogs with feisty temperaments. "Stag hound" could mean the Scottish Deerhound or a cross-bred lurcher or even the English staghound (a taller type of foxhound). In Britain, "stag" was the male red deer, while in the States, the term encompassed both large deer and elk, but American hunters never called their dogs "elk hounds." Some of the more colorful names for vanished dog types include, the Cuban bloodhound, Siberian mastiff, the Great Bruno (derived from the St. Bernard, Newfoundland, and Alpine Shepherd), Adirondack Deer Hound, Whitlock Shaggy, Clydesdale Terrier, and the Turnspit dog—which walked on a kitchen treadmill to turn roasting meat. Perhaps the most blunt name which combined both origin and function was Fanny the "Chinese Edible Dog," exhibited at the Westminster show in 1878.[87]

Army Dogs: Birth, Sutures and Death

Medical care for dogs was basic and derived from a few American or English books on the topic or sporting magazines and folklore. In a regiment, the owner of an ailing dog could consult the farrier, surgeon, and veterinarian, although the latter was only trained for horses and mules.

Birth control consisted of separating males from bitches in estrus if puppies weren't wanted. Mother dogs frequently whelped on their own without problems but in larger breeds, such as greyhounds, puppies were often killed by their mother rolling over on them. Unwanted puppies (and kittens) were drowned—in a bucket or a weighted sack thrown into a pond or river. As cruel as this sounds, Victorians believed drowning was peaceful because the facial expression frequently resembled that of a sleeper.

Skin diseases were cured with salves or horse cures. Lacerations that weren't gaping and which could be licked by the dog were allowed to heal on their own. Cuts or tears were sutured with thread or horsetail hair, and puncture bites from wolves, foxes, and skunks, frequently abscessed and needed to be lanced for drainage. (Before antibiotics, wound infections were usual and "laudable pus" was considered to be the first stage of healing.)

There were no cures for hydrophobia (rabies), and dogs showing symptoms were promptly shot. Distemper was not always fatal, and a strong puppy or adult might survive with careful nursing (the term was used for many diseases not yet fully understood). Poison became a danger when cattle ranchers started baiting carcasses with strychnine or arsenic—which killed wolves and dogs equally well. Broken leg bones could only be set, splinted, and the dog confined to heal. A cracked rib would heal on its own, but there was little hope for a fractured pelvis or skull.

In spite of all these hazards, dogs are amazingly capable of self-healing. Near Fort Harker, one of Armstrong's loaned greyhounds was accidentally shot during a hunt, the slug going from rump to shoulder. The men couldn't bring themselves to euthanize the dog and left him by a stream to die. Two weeks later, the hound walked into camp.[88]

CHAPTER 7

Kansas and Indian Territory: Bloody Snow

> *"...Blucher and Maida, two splendid specimens of the Scotch staghound, who were destined to share the dangers of an Indian campaign and finally meet death in a tragic manner—"—George Armstrong Custer*[1]

Suspended from the Army, Armstrong downplayed his punishment as a "temporary retirement from active duty."[2] No longer separated, he and Libbie were not writing letters, so the trail of Rover, Turk, and Ginnie grows fainter during this time. The Custers spent winter and spring at Fort Leavenworth enjoying pleasure rides, hunting, card parties, hops, and socializing, and cousin Rebecca came out in January and stayed for three months. In March 1868, Custer and Libbie were briefly in Monroe and made a social call to nearby Dundee, where they posed for a photograph with three friends and an unidentified pointer.[3] The dog's position next to Libbie suggests it was Ginnie. If so, she was the only Custer dog to be photographed in a studio.

In April, they were back at Fort Leavenworth and despite Libbie's belief that their dogs didn't bother anyone, there were complaints about theirs and others. Gibbs, then post commander, issued General Order No. 6 on April 18—"On and after Monday the 20th *inst* [this month] all dogs found running loose in the Garrison will be shot by the Guard."[4] Interestingly, Gibbs, who was on good terms with Armstrong, had their friend and post adjutant, Lt. Moylan, send a copy of the order addressed to *both* Custers. (The order to shoot unleashed or stray dogs was not unusual on Army posts. At Fort Sill, noisy dogs caused the adjutant to order twice a year—always ignored—for all of them to be tied up at night.[5])

They were back in Monroe for a visit, intending to return to Leavenworth in the summer. Armstrong probably left his dogs at the fort. He enjoyed fishing with Kirkland Barker on Lake Erie and hunting game birds in the marshes of Monroe (a bird dog such as Ginnie would have been essential). The Custers and Barkers were now great friends, and the latter frequently hosted them on his yacht and at home. Barker was already advocating the merits of Scottish Deerhounds as good hunters and offered a couple of pups when they were old enough. Armstrong, who never turned down a dog, enthusiastically accepted. In early July, he left Libbie in Monroe and briefly went back to Leavenworth, taking along Ginnie. Tom Custer, out in the field with Maj. Elliott, wrote Armstrong with the scant news of their Indian hunting but more about his hunting exploits. The brothers were already planning a buffalo hunt for Barker and

111

The Custers, Mrs. Rose Flint (dark dress), and an unidentified couple in a studio portrait in Michigan, March 1868. (Armstrong was still on suspension after his court martial.) That the pointer was included in the portrait and lies on Libbie's skirt strongly suggests that it is Ginnie, her "dearest, chummiest sort of house-dog." From Ernest L. Reedstrom's *Bugles, Banners, and War Bonnets* (1986).

Armstrong hoped Tom could get a young antelope and buffalo for him and the Detroit Audubon Club—as well as prairie dogs for their sister, Maggie Calhoun. Tom's greyhound, Witch, had managed to catch and hold a wolf but couldn't kill it until Brandy rushed in. Tom was now keen on sighthounds and knew his brother was going to get deerhounds from Barker. In July, he wrote, "Armstrong, I want you to write as soon as you get this letter and promise me one of those stag hounds if you get three, for I want one so much."[6] When Armstrong left Fort Leavenworth for Monroe, Ginnie stayed behind.

Later that month, Tom, Witch, and Brandy were catching up with supply wagons going from Fort Leavenworth to the new Big Creek camp (Fort Hays had been relocated after the flood). After only six miles, Witch overheated and collapsed. Tom tried to revive her with water and whiskey, hoisted her onto the saddle, and carried her for a couple of miles. She died despite his efforts. "I don't know of anything that I could have lost that would have made me feel any worse about, except Brandy (I would have willingly given my horse instead)." Witch's death, combined with the loss of Lu and Sharp, would convince Tom and Armstrong that greyhounds were not best suited for prairie hunting.[7] Greyhounds were so keen that if more than one antelope appeared, they would run successive courses and could sprint themselves to death. (This was noted by other greyhound owners.) During that same march, Brandy (who had walked much farther than Witch that day) ran into buffalo and caught a calf until Lt. Nowlan could shoot it. (If the wagons had not been full they would have taken it into camp.[8]) Witch's body was carried to Big Creek in a wagon, and Tom would have buried her in a quiet spot. In the letter fragment describing Witch's end (probably sent to Libbie), he said he would tell Col. Parsons about her death—which suggests the close connection of previous owner or even her breeder.

"The most perfect creature under heaven..."

Sometime in late summer, most likely in Monroe, Armstrong got his brace of Scottish Deerhounds. He called the female Maida, after Sir Walter Scott's favorite hound, a Scottish greyhound-Pyrenean shepherd cross named after a Napoleonic battle. The male's name, Blücher, was a tribute to the tough-as-nails Gebhard Leberecht Blücher, Prince of Wahlstatt and Prussian field marshal, who came to Wellington's aid at Waterloo. (Armstrong soon dropped the *umlaut* in Blücher's name.) A third Deerhound, named Flirt, was acquired but possibly not from Barker. Frederick Whittaker wrote that Armstrong purchased these deerhounds which were "...bred in Canada from imported dogs, and afterwards received a present of another, imported dog."[9] (Even though Whittaker had borrowed Custer's letters, his biographical version of Armstrong's deerhound acquisition is a montage of fact and myth.)

Scottish Deerhounds originated from the rough-coated greyhound types which became favorites of clan chiefs and Scottish nobles for hunting red deer in the rugged Highlands. Stalking the stag for hours early in the morning and quietly trying to get close for a good shot was hard work. If the wounded stag bolted, the deerhounds were slipped to pursue and bring it to bay until the hunters caught up to give the *coup de grâce* with a bullet or long dirk. Tall and agile, with both a wiry overcoat and a soft undercoat, deerhounds could handle rough terrain and poor weather. With the advent of long-range rifles and high-velocity cartridges, the need for a deerhound was beginning to diminish in the early 1800s. At the time of Armstrong's acquisition, the breed was kept only by Scottish estate owners—and increasingly by affluent English for dog shows. (The Scottish Deerhound was recognized by the AKC in 1886. Today, they are blue-gray in color with perhaps a splash of white on the chest or toes. Before the 20th century, yellow, sandy-red, tawny, or brindle were not uncommon. Maida was brindle and Blucher off-white.)

Sir Walter Scott declared deerhounds to be "the most perfect creature under heaven" and included them in his historical novels—which the Custers knew well. Armstrong, a would-be cavalier, considered deerhounds the most suitable hound for the West. Their romantic history appealed greatly to him—and he called them variously Scotch stag hounds, or Scotch deerhounds, deerhounds, or staghound/stag hounds. (When he writes about his stag hounds it is difficult to tell if he is referring to his purebreds or his cross-breeds, but he often uses "pure blood" or "blooded" or even "thoroughbred" to differentiate.)

Field Testing the New Hounds

General Hancock's failed attempt to stop the Indian problems in 1867 made the Kansas frontier worse—and settlers' intrusions weren't helping. Indian retaliations continued, and women were taken captive and property destroyed—all providing justification for Army intervention. Phil Sheridan had replaced Sherman as the commander of the Department of Missouri and was at Fort Hays. He wanted Armstrong with him and petitioned Grant for an early end to his suspension. On September 24, he wired Armstrong that Generals Sherman and Sully and most of the 7th's officers asked for him (the latter was perhaps exaggeration or flattery). "Can you come at once?" The request was tantamount to exoneration and puffed up Armstrong considerably. Before hearing *officially* that he was restored to rank, he took the bit in his teeth and went to Fort Leavenworth.[10] Ginnie was waiting for him when he arrived on October 2. He wrote Libbie about how good it was to be back in his comfortable, big house again.

> Jennie the pointer, is lying at my feet as I write. She was overjoyed to see me and has followed my every movement since my arrival. The house is ready for you and you can come in as soon as you like.[11]

(While Libbie always wrote "Ginnie," Armstrong apparently used "Jennie"—but in transcribing her husband's letter, she didn't correct his spelling.)

From Monroe, Armstrong brought his horses and new deerhounds, Blucher, Maida, and Flirt. The foxhounds, Old Rover and Fanny, and an unidentified bitch named Rosa seem to have been waiting for him at Leavenworth with Ginnie. (Turk is not mentioned on this campaign—nor was he ever photographed.) From there, he entrained for Fort Hays where Sheridan gave him command of a strike against the Indians with the details yet to be decided. Two companies of volunteer Kansas cavalry were to go along—but the snow prevented them from joining the 7th before the attack. Leaving

Hays at 6 a.m. on the 5th, with a two-company escort, Armstrong pushed his detachment, horses, and dogs hard, riding ninety miles to Fort Dodge in two days. Since leaving Monroe, his horses had been in the livestock car for twenty-eight consecutive hours with only one feed, and yet they handled the trek well enough.[12] The day after arriving he wrote Libbie that he wanted her at Leavenworth, and there she could keep Mrs. Gibbs company.[13]

On the 8th, Armstrong wrote Barker with the first news of his new hounds. "…Maida is lying by my side, Rosa and the other bitch are a few feet further off. Blucher and the little hound are on the bed, all sound asleep and tired from their march of ninety miles." Maida handled the long march better than the others. The deerhounds and foxhounds had unsuccessfully coursed an antelope and wolf, and both times, Armstrong followed closely to prevent them from getting lost. Enticing Barker, he listed the local game: buffalo, bear, deer, antelope, turkey, geese, ducks, jackrabbits, etc. Apart from Old Rover, the dogs were new to the prairie and needed training—"I know there is sport ahead for me after the dogs get a little broken."[14] With Barker's nomination, Armstrong had been unanimously elected to honorary membership in the Audubon Club on September 1—but as the notification just missed him in Monroe, the secretary telegraphed again on October 7, and the message reached him in the field.[15] This and his *Turf* fame validated him as a premier hunter.

On October 10, Armstrong made a grand entrance into the 7th's camp, fifteen miles south of Fort Dodge. "…General Custer arrived (with his hair cut short, and a perfect menagerie of Scotch fox hounds!)…" wrote Capt. Alfred Barnitz to his wife Jennie, using Armstrong's honorary rank.[16] Because there had been a couple of minor skirmishes with war parties, Armstrong immediately sent out three patrols—which were unsuccessful in finding anything. Tom was glad to see him and told Armstrong about Brandy tackling a skunk (also called polecats or prairie dandies) and when trying to separate them, he got "enough perfumery to last him for several months." Armstrong dryly noted that hundreds of miles out on the prairie wasn't the place to need new clothes. Tom was reduced to begging for spare clothing but managed to make a Custer prank out of the reeking circumstance. He and Capt. Hamilton entered a crowded tent and when the smell was noticed, Tom said, "Some dog has been killing a skunk. I wonder where the d--n brute is!" While everyone was talking about the awful stink, Tom and Hamilton struggled not to burst out in laughter. When they could no longer stifle themselves, the joke was revealed and they went off to try another tent.[17]

In camp was the famous scout, Joseph "Moses" E. Millner, known as "California Joe." A native Kentuckian with a colorful past, he finally adopted the Kansas frontier, leaving his wife and sons in Oregon. Joe knew the land and tribes, preferred a mule to a horse, and had a black dog. He wore cavalry trousers, an overcoat, and a wide hat, habitually drank and smoked a pipe—his dark hair and beard obscuring most of his face. (Armstrong thought well of California Joe, and a few years later would give him a rare gift—one of his staghounds.) Civilian scouts were paid $75 a month and fed. They ranged far ahead of the column to find the best path, water, or Indian sign—translating tribal speech or sign language, and relaying dispatches and mail. In a hurry to find and punish *any* Indian village, Armstrong offered $100 to the scout who found one. As savvy as civilian scouts were, it usually took Indians to find Indians, and this time it was Osage warriors who were happy to work against their hereditary enemies, the Southern Cheyenne and Sioux.

By the 18th of October, Armstrong and his men were some 40 miles out from Fort Dodge when they had a brief dust-up with Indians a couple of hours after making camp. Despite Armstrong joining in with his rifle, only two ponies were killed and he told Libbie he was remembering his promise to not put himself too much in danger. Armstrong was already referring to his regiment as being "on the warpath." When there was scant possibility of action, the cavalry otherwise occupied themselves by shooting the area's abundant wild turkeys. Armstrong's new deerhounds were learning to course as well.

> Now I want to tell you about my splendid stag hounds. The other day Maida caught a Jack Rabbit alone. Yesterday she and Blucher took hold of a buffalo and today as we came into camp, Blucher started a wolf, caught it alone, seized it across the back and never relinquished his hold until the wolf was dead. The latter was not even able to bite him once. Within half an hour afterwards a Jack Rabbit was started near camp. My three stag hounds and two other gray hounds [sic] went in pursuit. We could see the chase for nearly a mile. Then they disappeared over a hill. In a few moments, the dogs were seen returning. Blucher had the Rabbit in his mouth, bringing it back to camp. The officers are constantly trying to buy the stag hounds off me. I wish Eliza was out here to make some nice rolls instead of the solid shot our cook girls use.[18]

Lt. Thomas Ward Custer in dress uniform wearing his two Congressional Medals of Honor (circa 1872). Tom always followed his brother's lead and had greyhounds in Kansas, and he would pester Armstrong and Libbie for a Scottish Deerhound. Courtesy of the National Park Service, Little Bighorn Battlefield National Monument, LIBI_0019_00197. Photographed by J. F. Coonley of the Y. Day studio in Memphis, Tennessee.

Armstrong wrote a sportsman-like account of these hunts to Barker and noted, "...of the many dogs that are in this regiment, there is but one that will attack a wolf and he needs to be encouraged. Don't you think that this is a pretty good for a pup?" This was about Blucher, whom he also identified as the "white dog."[19] (Armstrong uses "wolf" for both wolves and coyote.) In the jackrabbit course, an officer followed his own greyhound and found the pack returning, and Blucher had the large jack in his jaws. Armstrong wrote to Barker and Libbie, "What do you think of a stag hound as a retriever?" (Despite Armstrong's remark, it is common for sighthounds to return with the jackrabbit.) One officer offered him $50 for the little hound bitch (even though Flirt was lame) and another offered $100 for all three deerhounds. Armstrong declared he wouldn't sell them—even for $1,000. "Maida is lying asleep on my bed at this moment, they all sleep with me every night and travel by my horse's side every day. They are my constant companions day & night."[20]

There was quite a bit of enthusiasm for the deerhounds, which were "…daily marvels to their proud owner,"[21] and Tom tried again to get one through Libbie. Annoyed, Armstrong wrote,

> Tom pesters me daily about giving him one of the stag hounds. He says that you wrote to him that he should have one. I tell him that they are my dogs not yours and that if you bring any out, you are likely to dispose of them as you see fit. Yet I might as well talk to a mule. You have had some experience in determining how persistent a Custer is when seeking any thing he really desires.[22]

At this point, Armstrong clearly considered the three deerhounds as *his* dogs and the letter suggests Barker had been asked for more deerhounds (or there were others in Monroe) and that Libbie would be bringing them with her to Fort Leavenworth.

A Chance for Glory

The continuing failures to confront the tribes finally decided Sheridan on a winter campaign. It was known by experienced officers that Indians (both war parties and villages) could not be caught by encumbered cavalry unless surprised and unable to quickly move. During the snowy winter, the plains tribes hunkered down in secluded river valleys to wait for spring. Dawn attacks tipped the odds for the Army, and that tactic had worked several times—perhaps most notably in Col. Patrick Connor's 1863 attack on a Shoshone village in Wyoming Territory and Col. Chivington's infamous massacre of a Cheyenne-Arapaho village at Sand Creek in 1864. With the winter attack, Sheridan ordered the total war strategy used in the Civil War to eliminate their ability to wage war (and ultimately their way of life and existence). All warriors were to be killed and women and children taken hostage. The lodges (teepees), clothing, food stores, and possessions would be burned and their ponies killed. Anyone escaping the destruction had to survive without shelter, clothes, food, or transport. The government naively thought "punishment" of a single village would be a lesson to every other band and tribe—and force all to sue for peace.

Armstrong was keen to make a name for himself as an Indian fighter and wrote out his hopes to Libbie. As Sheridan's instrument, he was to "…punish the Indians and bring them to a lasting peace." Egotistically, he assumed all the tribes (predominantly Southern Cheyenne, Arapaho, and Kiowa) would unite against him. Cocksure, he wanted a battle or a village—a success in either would get him back to Libbie.[23] Two days later on October 26, Armstrong expressed frustration about their separation—but he had barely been gone a month. There would be no chance for a mid-campaign tryst as he had contrived during the Hancock Expedition.

He ordered drilling and target practice (the latter was surprisingly unusual on the frontier), and selected the best shots for a detachment of forty sharpshooters. Libbie sent him wool underclothing, and he had the regimental saddler make extra large saddle bags to free him from the baggage wagon. Flannel and wool union suits (long johns) were worn underneath wool uniforms and overcoat, and lucky troopers might have buffalo fur boots, coats, mittens, or caps. There was little protection for horses except at night when they had blankets of condemned tent canvas. (The ubiquitous dogs had only their fur.) The first photograph of Armstrong's Scottish Deerhounds was taken at Fort Dodge. Armstrong stands at the entrance of his Sibley tent with his Spencer carbine, and chained to stakes are Flirt (sitting), and recumbent Blucher and Maida—and a captive pelican. Many years after Armstrong's death, Libbie would annotate the margin of the photograph, identifying Maida and Blucher, and noting the former was "pure Scotch stag" and the latter "part stag & bull."[24] It was a metaphor for Blucher's strength and courage—and the second time that he was likened to the pugnacious breed, for Barker was told about Blucher holding onto a wolf "like a bull dog."[25]

The month before attacking Black Kettle's village on the Washita River, Armstrong and his first Scottish Deerhounds were in camp at Fort Dodge, Kansas, November 1868. Given to him by Detroit businessman Kirkland Barker, the hounds are, from left to right, Flirt, Blucher, and Maida. Armstrong sometimes called Blucher "the white dog" in his letters, but the deerhound was probably a light cream color. He was shot with an arrow at Washita. On the right is the captured pelican, which was shipped to Barker but died en route. Courtesy of the National Park Service, Little Bighorn Battlefield National Monument, LIBI_0019_00576. Possibly photographed by W. S. Soule.

"Custer luck" momentarily lapsed when Armstrong was seriously injured in a casual camp encounter. On October 28, Maj. Elliott brought his horse over to him to see if he could tell its age. While Armstrong examined the teeth, the horse reared up, slamming a hoof into his head. Stunned, and almost certainly concussed, Armstrong was bleeding from a deep cut over his left eye. The doctor closed it with sticking plaster and bandaged his face "securely to prevent taking cold." (It was believed that open wounds could induce chills and fever.) Swathed in bandages, he could only see out of one eye and was restricted to his tent. He joked about Uncle Sam paying him to do nothing but write to his wife. Sheridan had promised, "furloughs will be given to every enlisted man who does well," and impatient to be with Libbie, Armstrong was figuring out a loophole which would allow him (as an officer) to claim the reward. Being "brilliant" or "decisive" on the campaign should qualify—but how to do that quickly was the trick. After telling Libbie about his injury, campaign expectations, and his hope for leave, he closed with, "You must hope then as I do, that we may be successful in finding a village. Should I be able to do so I would be home at Leavenworth within three weeks after."[26]

As part of the preparation for the "Indian War," Armstrong gave a highly unpopular order. The regiment's horses were to be "colored," where the companies would swap mounts until each had one color—bay, sorrel, brown, black, gray, and the least senior company commander would get the mismatches. After years of bonding and shared hardships, it was like forcing a man to trade pet dogs with his neighbor. The order was thought capricious and a sign of their lieutenant colonel's vanity; however, there was a sound reason for it. The cavalry elite of England and Europe (and some Federal regiments in the Late War) sorted their units by color for easy recognition in battle—thereby aiding the commander in tactical decisions. It also made a better display on parade, and Armstrong was ever mindful of both his and the 7th's image. The troopers hated exchanging their old friends for strange mounts—especially just before a campaign—and this didn't help Armstrong's reputation as an uncaring commander.

The Campaign Begins

On the eve of the National Election, Barker wrote back about the deerhounds, "You can hardly imagine how elated I am to know that you are so pleased with the dogs. Their performance is really wonderful. I hope you will not lose any of them." After some chatty news about Libbie's visit with them and her plans to leave for Leavenworth, Barker asked for Indian souvenirs for the Audubon Club and expressed his desire to hunt the prairie with Armstrong as his guide. "I can raise another litter of staghounds if you think there is any probability of you wanting them. I know you will not sell any. Fanny had 6 pups night before last." Barker urged him to resume letters to *Turf, Field and Farm*—but did not mail the letter until the following day (November 4) so he could comment that General Grant seemed to be winning the presidential race.[27] (Voting was largely ignored by soldiers as they could not vote away from their homes.) From Barker's gently admonishing comment about not losing the deerhounds, it is clear he was familiar with Armstrong's history of dogs going missing.

Armstrong rode out on election day to select the next campsite. He took all four dogs, Blucher, Maida, Rover, and Fanny. (Flirt the deerhound was still lame from cutting her foot on a broken bottle.) Less than a mile out, they spotted a large wolf and started after it. The foxhounds, Rover and Fanny, dropped behind as the two young deerhounds and Armstrong chased the wolf for three quarters of a mile. Maida was able to grab it and the two fought wildly until Blucher joined in to finish the wolf.

> Blucher and Maida were perfectly Savage [sic], each time they closed their powerful Jaws [sic] I could hear the bones crunch as if within a Vice [sic]. There did not seem to be a bone left unbroken when the dogs had finished him. All the officers and men were watching the chase from camp.

Returning to camp, all four hounds chased a jackrabbit, and Armstrong claimed he had never seen a horse race as exciting.

> I am delighted with my dogs. They surpass my highest expectations. All four are lying on my bed or at my feet. I have to keep a stage whip along side my pallet as I used to do in Texas as they are inclined to be cross and bark in the night.[28]

All that was in Armstrong's letter to Libbie on November 4, and he gave more details to Barker four days later. He covered Maida's previous timidity in hunting and her tumbling fight; the fact that neither deerhound had more than slight scratches ("...although a wolf is considered an ugly customer for two dogs..."); the jackrabbit course of two miles; and that "they [the deerhounds] are growing finely and have not reached their best speed by far."[29] Armstrong was learning deerhounds were tough, had more stamina, and could stand winters better than greyhounds. Mindful of his promise to send wildlife specimens to the

Kirkland C. Barker, the prominent Detroit businessman and sportsman who was Armstrong's staunch friend and dog patron. *American Biographical History of Eminent and Self-Made Men,* **(Michigan volume).**

Audubon Club, he had the pelican (which an Osage scout had stunned and caught) crated and shipped off as his first installment. Despite Armstrong's assurances of good health, it died before reaching Fort Leavenworth, so Barker sent the pelican to a taxidermist. In a macabre gesture (not considered such at the time), Armstrong promised, "I hope to find a village in two or three weeks, and if I do, look out for scalps [sic]."[30]

Snow Blood

The Indians were believed to be south in the Wichita Mountains in Indian Territory near the Texas border. Some ninety miles south of Fort Dodge, a palisaded depot was quickly built for the expedition and unimaginatively named Camp Supply. To the lively tune, "The Girl I Left Behind Me," the 7th set out from there on November 23 in a blizzard with nearly two feet of snow on the ground and sleet in the air. The column consisted of between 800 and 900 men and the attendant supply wagons and mules. Only the officers were allowed tents (with minimal personal baggage), and the men were sleeping in the snow, fully clothed with only their blankets. There were plenty of dogs, and one photo of twenty-nine officers taken during preparations at Camp Sandy Forsyth shows Armstrong with a staghound, and three or four other dogs with Tom Custer petting one of them.[31] Armstrong took only Blucher and Maida, leaving the others behind at Camp Supply. Fanny and Flirt ("the little hound bitch") vanished from Armstrong's narratives after November 4 when he noted Flirt's foot injury and her lameness. (He owned two foxhounds named Fanny, and the flirtatious Fanny Fifield may have been his inspiration. Both hounds went missing or died.) Rosa and Ginnie stopped being named in letters after early October. In Armstrong's correspondence over the years, when specific dogs cease to be mentioned after having been in the field, they were likely dead—and going missing on the prairie resulted in death sooner or later. The only two dog deaths Armstrong wrote about were "Good Deaths"—the Victorian concept of dying well for a noble cause, which conveyed honor and quasi-martyr status. For Armstrong, whose lifestyle was hard on canines, the ultimate way for a hound to end its life was in the hunt. (Old Rover managed to outlive a number of his pack mates.)

Bundled against the cold, the column plodded in the snow, the troopers periodically walking to keep blood circulating in their feet and, for the same reason at night, the horses were whipped to keep them moving. Sharing his conical tent (warmed by a small stove) with Lt. Moylan, Armstrong slept wrapped up with Blucher and Maida. The hunt for Indians was serious business, but he indulged himself by testing the hounds on buffalo. He singled out a bull to chase, but the deerhounds were too close to risk a pistol shot. They struggled in the drifts, with the deerhounds getting battered, until at last, the buffalo turned at bay. Blucher clamped onto his throat while Maida tried to bite his shoulder. With the bull thrashing his head, stamping, and kicking, Blucher's vise-grip was getting him trampled. Dismounting, Armstrong waded in, slashing the bull's hamstrings with his knife and finally shooting it.[32]

Ranging out from the column, Maj. Elliot's scouts and three companies found a recent campsite and then a war party sign on November 26. As they followed the trail by moonlight, more evidence pointed toward an Indian presence. Fearful any time wasted would increase the column's chance of being discovered by foraging warriors, Armstrong left the supply train with a guard of eighty men. With seven wagons and one ambulance, the column marched through snow lit by the nearly full moon.[33] After midnight, they cautiously advanced up to a ridge and the scouts reported that they heard dogs barking up ahead. As war parties didn't travel with dogs (barking would alert an enemy), it was speculated they were approaching a hunting party until they heard the tinkle of a bell (commonly tied on ponies' manes) and a baby crying—which indicated a village.

Unlike an Army post, Indians in winter camp didn't normally have night sentries but might have a few young men watching the pony herd which combined with the village's dogs to make a reliable alarm system. Armstrong's tactical problem was to ensure that hundreds of troopers and horses got within striking distance without sabers, canteens, carbines, and lumbering wagons alerting the village (not to mention the unfamiliar smell of white men). The lodges were nestled on a wide "bench" on the opposite bank of the Washita creek. Officers' call was done verbally, and Armstrong revealed his plan to separate into four wings and strike from three sides. The men took a day's rations in their haversacks and one hundred rounds for their carbines and pistols. The clanking sabers and steel scabbards were left in the wagons.[34] Lt. James Bell with the supply wagons was ordered to follow behind and arrive after the attack started.

There was no attempt to ascertain the tribe's identity, and Armstrong only learned later it was the peace chief Black Kettle's village of Southern Cheyenne who, despite having been almost entirely massacred at Sand Creek four years earlier, were known to be generally friendly toward the whites. In fact, Black Kettle kept a white flag on a long pole which was to be raised at the first sign of soldiers.[35] At that point, there was no way to determine who they were—and it really didn't matter to Armstrong which tribe would become Sheridan's example. Uncharacteristically, he didn't order a wider reconnaissance (which would have been difficult, even in moonlight), but had he done so, he would have known about Cheyenne, Arapaho, Comanche, and Kiowa villages not so far away.

Maj. Elliott with Capts. Benteen and Barnitz and three companies would circle left around hilly ground and attack from the northeast. Capts. Thompson and Meyers would approach from the right (southwest) with four companies, splitting into two squadrons as they approached the village. From the south, Armstrong would hit the village center with four companies, the sharpshooters, Indian guides, and civilian scouts. The dawn attack signal would be the band playing "Garry Owen." If one of the wings was discovered while waiting, they were to start the shooting. As the officers were preparing to move to their positions, some of column's dogs were squabbling and already starting to bark in response to the distant village dogs. There was a serious concern they would start a noisy chain reaction and waken the village. Steeling himself, Armstrong ordered the dogs to be killed silently—either by strangulation with a lariat or by muzzling them and slitting their throats. Capt. Barnitz would later confirm this highly unpleasant business in his journal.[36]

Cavalrymen accepted putting a horse out of its suffering with a bullet in the brain but that was hard for the owner, so usually a comrade would do it. Armstrong's order to kill their dogs didn't sit well with the troopers but, had they not done it, someone else would have—and perhaps not as kindly as could be managed. One of the favorite dogs of M Company was a little black dog named Bob who was "as harmless as a kitten." A dim-witted trooper hammered a 15-inch steel picket pin through Bob's head, leaving him for dead in the snow.[37]

Armstrong's Scottish Deerhounds were exempt from that order—even though they were starting to bark at the dog commotion. Pvt. William C. Stair, K Company, watched Armstrong wrap an apron over the head of one of the hounds, trying to muffle both its hearing and noise.[38] It would have been difficult for Armstrong to muffle both hounds, and presumably his orderly or dog tender was helping him—but once the shooting started, barking dogs wouldn't matter anymore. (The apron belonged to Mrs.

Courtenay, the officers' quarrelsome Irish cook—the only white woman on the campaign.[39])

The companies moved to their positions around the village periphery, and the men waited quietly for dawn, cold to the bone in their damp uniforms. Some stood with their horses and calmed them, others sat huddled, talking in hushed tones, while some tried to sleep. Armstrong, who could sleep anywhere, lay down in the snow, pulled the half-cloak of his overcoat over his head, and napped for an hour—probably alongside Blucher and Maida as was his custom. He woke two hours before daybreak and moved through his men, offering encouragement and getting a feel for their readiness. As night faded into dawn, a bright golden light appeared above the horizon. Armstrong and others thought it was a rocket sent up by Elliott or Thompson to signal a problem—or even an Indian signal. Once the light rose above the haze, they realized it was a rising star. Armstrong declared it a good omen and named it "The Star of Washita." He issued another grueling order—his men were to remove their overcoats, haversacks, and canteens so they were unencumbered for the fight. It was bitter cold and when they grumbled, Armstrong snapped, "Stop that noise—it will be hot enough for you inside of an hour."[40] The overcoats and gear were piled up by a wagon within covering fire from his wing, with a few troopers to guard them. This order would lead to the death of one of Armstrong's deerhounds.

The dawn attack at Washita was not the complete surprise Armstrong wanted. Emerging from his lodge at sunrise, the warrior Big Man was alerted by the barking dogs.[41] The uneasy ponies were making noise, and Barnitz's men in the right wing startled a few guards in the herd but held their fire as the Indians ran toward the village. When Barnitz pressed forward, he heard a rifle shot from the lodges.[42] Armstrong's signal to fire followed after that shot, but the band could only manage the first few bars of "Garry Owen" before their instruments' valves seized up with the cold. After an opening fusillade, the soldiers charged the village. (Lt. Edward Settle Godfrey said the tune was played after Armstrong ordered buglers to sound the charge—but that the instruments did freeze up.[43])

The sharpshooters picked off men and boys and women as they came out to fight or escape. The four wings charged across the shallow Washita, up onto its bench and into the village, firing at anything moving. Chief Black Kettle and his wife Medicine Woman (who both escaped death at Sand Creek) managed to get on his horse but were shot down crossing the icy stream. Armstrong with his command group rode through the village blasting away and then took position on a knob overlooking the swirling melee. With him and his staff were non-combatants—a few officers and non-coms, six white scouts, his bugler, orderly, and Armstrong's bodyguard of ten sharpshooters.[44] The interpreters, cooks, scouts, and strikers came over after fighting subsided. Presumably one of the strikers had Blucher and Maida on leash.

The fight was not all one-sided, and the warriors fought back and inflicted casualties. Lt. Hamilton took a bullet in his heart and Capt. Barnitz was gut shot. With a mass of his abdominal tissue protruding from the exit wound, he was not expected to live. Overwhelmed by battle confusion and blood lust, some troopers shot women and children until Armstrong (remembering Sheridan's orders) stopped them. The Osages were harder to stop, and they killed and mutilated a number of women and children.[45] With black powder smoke, gunfire, human screams, barking dogs and neighing ponies, the attack was generally going as Custer anticipated. (Arthur Penn's 1972 film *Little Big Man* gives a fair depiction of Washita from the Cheyenne experience.) After hearing the distant gunfire, the other villages' warriors began gathering about 10 a.m. to investigate.[46] Unbeknownst to Armstrong, Maj. Elliott gathered seventeen volunteers and rode to the east, shouting, "Here goes for a brevet or a coffin!"[47] Other than trying to engage a group of warriors, his rash behavior remains unexplained, but historian Lorne Langley makes a good case for Elliott having spotted the white captives, Mrs. Clara Blinn and her toddler Willie, being hustled away by Indian women and attempting a rescue.[48]

Aftermath and a Dead Hound

After the shooting stopped, four of Armstrong's men were killed or dying and fifteen were wounded (including Tom Custer, slightly). Elliott and his men were still missing but presumably would return. Armstrong's inflated estimates of casualties for the village (approximately 250 to 300 people) were just over a hundred males killed and fifty-three women and children taken prisoner. Armstrong would increase the kill number to 140 based on his captives' testimony. Scout George Bent, a mixed blood Cheyenne, formulated his own reckoning of fatalities from tribal oral histories and came up with twenty-nine warriors killed. (Others put the casualty number somewhere between those high and low figures.[49]) The Cheyenne men who escaped into the surrounding woods and hills watched in frustration as women and children were corralled while the lodges were ransacked to "inventory" war-making materials (gunpowder, bullet molds, and lead). They found settlers' personal items which were held up as presumptive evidence that Black Kettle had been raiding.[50]

Everything—lodges, clothing, food—was to be burned. Armstrong ordered no souvenirs were to be taken to encumber their departure. Doubtless some trinkets were pocketed. Lt. Godfrey found a beautiful buckskin dress decorated with elk's teeth and considered it but ultimately threw it on the fire, figuring no exceptions would be allowed. Nonetheless, Armstrong took a buffalo hide shield, beaded buckskin dress, pony saddle, and for Barker, the scalp of Little Rock.[51] Other scalps were taken from the dead. Armstrong chose a specimen lodge for his personal collection.[52] As they were constructed of a dozen or more buffalo hides, a lodge with its poles made a heavy bundle for a supply wagon, and the rest were burned. Historian Paul Hedren described the Army's method of wrecking a village—the lodges were burned by stoking the cooking fire, throwing in anything combustible to get it blazing, and then pulling down the poles to collapse the lodge onto the fire. Everything the soldiers could lay their hands on was thrown in.[53] The bonfire was poked and stirred over time until nothing was left unburned.

The officers, scouts, and village women were allowed to take a number of the best horses and mules from the herd of 875 (according to the official count).[54] The remaining ponies presented a problem. While they were valuable, Armstrong could not risk slowing down his march home with the massive herd—which the warriors would try to recover. Nor could he leave them for the Cheyenne to recapture. The only other way to comply with Sheridan's orders was to kill them. At first, they were to have their throats cut to save ammunition, but the smell of white men badly spooked the ponies, so the Cheyenne women were ordered to round them up with California Joe directing the operation. Lt. Bell's arrival with the wagons provided the necessary ammunition for the slaughter. The ponies were pressed up against an embankment at the south side of the village, and two companies began firing into the herd. The screaming ponies did not always die quickly—or even that day. It took two hours to complete the ghastly task. A number of the village's panicking dogs were also shot.[55]

It is not precisely clear where Blucher and Maida were during the fight. They may have both been with Armstrong's orderly at the command overlook or back with the guards on the overcoats and equipment. It is highly improbable the hounds were with Armstrong when he charged through the stream and village. After the fight stopped, Blucher and Maida seem to have been retrieved, for Armstrong says while the troopers were busy burning lodges and slaughtering the herd, Blucher was with him in the village. About mid-morning, when the neighboring warriors were gathering on the ridges and Lt. Bell was loading up the overcoats, a band of warriors attacked and drove his guards off. About this raid, Armstrong wrote anthropomorphically that Blucher, "seeing them riding and yelling as if engaged in the chase [hunt], dashed from the village and joined the Indians, who no sooner saw him than they shot him through with an arrow."[56] (Maida, who had been timid in her first hunts, was safely through the battle.)

Killing Blucher served no purpose for the Indians other than an expression of rage. Dogs belonging to soldiers and settlers were often killed in fights. At the Fetterman Massacre in 1866, a terrified dog belonging to the ambushed column was shot with an arrow after the last soldier was dead.[57] During the Second Seminole War in 1839, sutler James B. Dalham was killed during a raid on his trading post, and his Irish Setter defended the body until it was shot.[58] If Armstrong's account is taken at face value, Blucher got away from his master, racing approximately a mile and a quarter back over the creek toward the attack on the overcoat pile. Given the geography of the battlefield, vegetation along the Washita banks, and distances involved, it is almost impossible that Armstrong, in the village or on the knob, actually saw Blucher killed. He wrote about this years after the battle and for his story combined geographical knowledge obtained upon three different times at Washita. What Armstrong knew at the time was only that Blucher was missing in action along with Maj. Elliott's party. However, Armstrong had much bigger problems on his hands. The day was ending and he had dead, wounded, and missing men. Killing the ponies was taking longer than expected, as was the lodge burning. The loss of overcoats and haversacks deprived his center wing of warmth and food. The column's supply train, while many miles away, was guarded by only eighty men. If Armstrong was cut off from the wagons, his men could be in much the same predicament as the fleeing Cheyenne who had lost their buffalo robes and winter food. On top of all that, a counterattack was brewing on the hills.

Knowing he had to get out of the valley, Armstrong formed ranks and, with the band playing "Ain't I Glad to Get Out of the Wilderness," boldly marched toward the distant knots of menacing warriors. It was a very "Custer" sort of move and accomplished exactly what he intended. Thinking their villages were to be attacked, the warriors took off. At sundown, Armstrong reversed the march, gathered his wounded along with the captives, and headed out to rejoin the wagon train. Time was pressing. Armstrong marched without learning what happened to Elliott (or Blucher). This was the second time Armstrong chose not to attempt a rescue or recovery of his men's bodies and it would further damage his reputation as a leader.

He had achieved his goal in quickly finding a village to punish and now considered his "Indian War" to be over. After arriving in Camp Supply on December 2, he wrote as much to Sheridan along with a brief but glorified description of the battle, the inventory, and casualty counts. Sheridan, buying his subordinate's hyperbole, praised the destruction of Black Kettle's village as a great victory—despite Armstrong's abandonment of Elliott. Armstrong wrote Libbie about his triumph and the peace which would result from it. He did not say anything about Blucher.

Elliott and his men were now presumed missing and dead. Capt. Barnitz astonished everyone by not dying from his terrible wound and resumed his journal entries about the battle. Not quite two weeks after the attack, Armstrong and the 7th were back at the now macabre site but with Sheridan and the wayward 19th Kansas Cavalry. Several Cheyenne bodies had not yet been taken away for ritual burial, and the Indian dogs were slinking around, feeding off rotting pony carcasses which were attracting wolves and coyotes at night and vultures by day. The mutilated, arrow-ridden bodies of Maj. Elliott's party were found in a "last stand" circle, and the 7th's casualty list went up to twenty-two.[59] Farther out were the white captives, Clara Blinn and little Willie, who had been brutally killed to prevent their rescue. The frozen bodies of Elliott, Clara and Willie were loaded into wagons for proper burials while Elliott's men were taken a distance away to a high place overlooking the river and buried in a mass grave. (The Snakey Bend or Custer Bend Cemetery was recognized in 1893 and also has civilian burials.) Armstrong held a faint hope that Blucher was still in the area, surviving on rabbits or carrion. It was not until Armstrong's second return to Washita in March 1869, that he found the deerhound's bones near the location of the overcoat pile.[60] Blucher had died the Good Death along with Hamilton, Elliott, and the regiment's other casualties.

Many in the 7th believed Elliott and his men might have been saved, if only Armstrong had ordered a reconnaissance—or he should have attempted a body recovery. This apparent callousness drove the faction wedge deeper between the officers—who now wondered if they might be the next to be abandoned. The baptism of combat didn't unite the 7th as Armstrong hoped, but there was more soldiering to be done before anyone could claim Sheridan's promised leave. At Fort Cobb on Christmas Eve, Armstrong spent Christmas and New Year's Eve with his campaign family, Tom, Maida, and Old Rover.

The execution of the dogs was not important enough to be included in the official account of Washita. Today, one might wonder whether it was a good decision to have allowed them on a march into battle, but soldiers and dogs were inseparable. Not very long afterwards, Quartermaster Henry Inman talked about the dogs in the 7th Cavalry and the 19th Kansas: "...and there was every breed and every size in camp, for the average American soldier loves a dog and keeps as many as he can..."[61] Strangely, it never occurred to officer or trooper until the critical moment that the dogs might give them away. Still chasing the tribes in early 1869, Custer's Osage scouts discovered a campsite, but the column's barking dogs warned the Cheyenne, who quickly escaped—the precise situation which Armstrong tried to avoid at Washita.[62]

The harsh dog deaths (and probably Blucher's conspicuous absence) sparked rumors that Armstrong and Tom had killed their own dogs before the attack. As no one would actually claim to have witnessed the killings, the stories appear to be barrack rumors. Blucher and Maida were the only dogs Armstrong took to Washita, and as the former was killed with an arrow and the latter shot in a buffalo hunt the following year, clearly *neither* was strangled by its master. Given Armstrong's fondness for his dogs, that these Scottish Deerhounds were a gift from Barker, and his status as commander of the expedition, it is not credible he would have killed his own dogs—no matter what the circumstances. Shortly after Little Bighorn, and four decades after Washita, a couple of troopers would claim that Armstrong strangled his own dogs (see this chapter's *Tail Piece*). Armstrong's leading antagonist, Capt. Frederick Benteen (Elliott's friend), wrote shortly after Washita that Armstrong shot ponies and dogs, endangering troopers in his line of fire.

> Our chief exhibits his close sharp-shooting and terrifies the crowd of frightened, captured squaws and papooses by dropping the straggling ponies in death near them. Ah! He is a clever marksman. Not even do the poor camp dogs of the Indians escape his eye and aim as they drop dead or limp howling away.[63]

Given Benteen's open animosity toward his commanding officer, little credence is given to the accusation. He also wrote anonymously to a newspaper, blaming Armstrong for Elliott's death. Armstrong confronted his officers about the letter, and Benteen admitted to writing it. Furious, Armstrong threatened to horsewhip him but rethought his position and backed down.

In a testament to canine recuperative powers (and bungled execution), poor Bob, the little dog whose head had been spiked, amazed the regiment by showing up at Camp Supply a few days behind the column. He followed the column's tracks nearly a hundred miles through snow and miserable weather to get home. John Ryan recalled how with careful nursing the dog recovered, but two years later, poor Bob was tricked by a drunken soldier into jumping out the window of a moving train.[64] Soldiers don't like men who hurt their dogs, and Sgt. Ryan did not record the fate of the malefactor.

Aside from the baptism of fire, casualties, faction rift, and newspaper outcry about the Cheyenne casualties, Washita put an unusual mark on the regiment. When Armstrong and Sheridan returned to the remains of Black Kettle's village, a few puppies were rescued by troopers. Armstrong noted in 1874 that some of those dogs or their descendants were still cherished by his 7th Cavalry.[65]

Tail Piece: Did Armstrong Kill His Own Dogs at Washita?

Forty years after the battle, a few soldiers gave hearsay testimonies about Armstrong killing his dogs. Only one of these men claimed to have witnessed *any* interaction between Armstrong and his deerhounds (usually called greyhounds by the troopers).

Capt. Barnitz's journal entry about the order to silence the dogs is included here, followed by the existing "dog-killing" testimonies.

Capt. Alfred Barnitz, G Co. in Maj. Elliott's left wing, says that after orders given for the wings to move out,

> ...a number of dogs belonging to the command, *followed* [emphasis added], and as it was feared that they would alarm the Indians, prematurely, some of the men were directed to strangle (or muzzle) them, with lariat ropes, and dispatch them with knives.[66]

Barnitz's account indicates the dogs were to be left at the first assembly point, and saying they belonged to the "command" would suggest the "kill" order came from Armstrong rather than a company officer. Later, Barnitz, writing in 1889, made an enigmatic comment about his company moving into position and being "...beset by half a dozen of large fox hounds belonging to the [Indian] band, and their baying might, without doubt, have been heard for miles in the still air...." In the next sentence, he says, "We found to our surprise, that the [regimental] band, which should have remained with General Custer, was through some misconception of orders, following us...."[67] The band was sent back, and Barnitz continued waiting for Benteen. The bracketed inserts of "[Indian]" and "[regimental]" are those of editor Robert Utley and leave room for interpretation—particularly as Barnitz interchangeably used the terms "village" and "Indians" rather than the ambiguous "band." Clearly the second reference is to the brass band (who were supposed to be with Armstrong), and as he *specifically* says "fox hounds ... baying" (not Indian dogs), then his first use of "band" must also refer to the musicians. That the appearances of the noisy fox hounds and brass band are adjacent in Barnitz's narrative is another argument for the hounds belonging to them—however he doesn't say if these foxhounds were "silenced."[68]

Sgt. John Ryan, M Co. (also in Maj. Elliott's left wing), *heard* that Custer had killed his dogs.

> I recollect where we advanced to the highest ground in that vicinity. The companies had some dogs with them and General Custer also had some of his hounds with him. When the Indian camp was discovered Custer thought that our dogs might alarm the Indian dogs and arouse the camp. I *understood* at the time that Custer had to kill a couple of his hounds" [emphasis added].

Ryan does describe Bob being killed.[69] All this was written forty years after Washita in 1908 and published serially in Ryan's local newspaper the following year. An articulate and usually reliable memoirist, the Irish-born Ryan died in 1926 at age 81.

Pvt. William C. Stair, K Co. in Armstrong's center wing, only saw his commander trying to *muffle* his dog. Walter Camp, collector of Indian War eyewitness accounts, summarizes this portion of his interview with Stair:

> Wm. C. Stair says that Custer tied the dog's head in a woman's apron which happened to be taken along for some reason. Says he did not see the dog strangled although it might have been afterward. The dog had been answering the barking of dogs in the village.[70]

Stair apparently didn't know or couldn't remember that the officers had Mrs. Courtenay as their cook. Camp's interview with Stair is undated but would have taken place between 1908 and Stair's death at nearly 86 years of age in 1916 (Camp's interviews with Little Bighorn survivors and other soldiers were conducted between 1908 and 1924).

Pvt. Dennis Lynch, F Co., was a sharpshooter in Armstrong's center wing. Lynch's interview by Camp says, "Custer had a valuable greyhound that was barking when he heard Indian dogs bark & Genl & Tom Custer choked him to death with a lariat."[71] Note that Lynch does not say he actually saw this—and in fact there are some obvious errors in his story. He said the Indian scouts were Delawares and Custer fired a skyrocket to launch the attack. Camp interviewed Lynch in 1908 and 1909 (at ages 60 and 61) and also collected Little Bighorn campaign stories from him. (On detached duty, Lynch missed that battle.) He died in 1933.

Josephus Bingaman, F Co., 19th Kansas Cavalry, claimed to have been near enough to have seen the bodies of Armstrong's dogs on the pile of overcoats and haversacks. "The soldiers had thrown luggage down and the Indians destroyed it and Custer's greyhounds lay on top of the luggage shot." The interviewer, Judge Eli S. Ricker, noted at this point, "all of which was seen by the narrator personally."[72] As the 19th Kansas was *not* at the battle, Bingaman is describing the 7th's part as someone told him—and then goes on to talk about what he saw at Washita, *two weeks* after the battle. From Bingaman's wording, it is clear he saw dead dogs on or near the pile of gear, but he doesn't say he witnessed them being killed. Whether they were "shot" by bullet or arrow is obscure, but Armstrong wouldn't have risked a gunshot to stop his dogs from barking and alerting the village. He only had two deerhounds at Washita, and Maida survived the battle, so it is difficult to believe there was more than one dead "greyhound" on the overcoat pile. The casualty and prisoner numbers which Bingaman gives for Washita are also off by noticeable margins. His story was told to Ricker sometime between 1903 and 1919. Bingaman died in 1931 at age 87.

An anonymous trooper, claiming to be a three-year veteran of the 7th Cavalry at Washita, chimed in along with the many stories about Armstrong after Little Bighorn, and told a newspaper reporter in September 1876 his opinion of how desperate and determined General Custer could be.

> It was five or six years ago that we had a fight with the Chippewas on the Washita river, the expedition being led by Custer. For a long time, the General had with him on the plains three magnificent Scotch grayhounds [sic], for which he would accept no price. Twenty miles from the Chippewa's village we struck the trail. It was in the evening and before proceeding on the march, Custer ordered that the grayhounds be placed in the wagons, which were not to accompany the detachment. This was done. We took up our line of march and found the village on the Washita at midnight, the inhabitants being wrapped in slumber, and all about the camp silent, Custer concluded to wait until daylight to make the charge, and after commanding silence all along the line, sat upon his horse like a statue waiting for the first indication of dawn. While sitting thus a slight pattering on the ground attracted his attention, and upon looking down he perceived through the gloom one of his hounds crouching at his horse's feet, the dog having escaped from the wagon and followed his master. The Indian village was swarming with dogs and Custer knew it. He also knew that if his hound emitted the slightest yelp or bark, it would agitate the entire canine force of the camp, put the Indians on their guard, and probably frustrate the object of the expedition. Slipping gently from his horse, he grasped the dog's throat with both hands, and slowly and quietly choked him to death. So silently and quickly was it done that in the gloom that prevailed, only a few soldiers standing in the immediate vicinity, perceived the desperate action. With the exception of his last fight, this engagement on the Washita was one of the most desperate ever fought on the plains and resulted in a grand victory for the "creeping panther," the name by which Custer was known among the Indians.[73]

As with the accounts of Ryan, Stair, Lynch, Bingaman, and Barnitz, this fellow does not say he witnessed Armstrong strangle his hound, and it must be remembered that the informant's words were filtered into newspaper prose. For a supposed participant, this account is riddled with enough incorrect details to cast doubt on the whole story—which Armstrong had described in *My Life on the Plains* in 1874.

The supposed 7th Cavalry veteran (easy to claim without a name) says it was five or six years before Little Bighorn (Washita happened at the end of 1868, so the gap is more like seven and a half years), and they were fighting the Chippewa (Ojibwe) who lived on the northern plains and Canada and around Lake Superior, yet any trooper present (or even a newspaper reader) would have known they had attacked a Southern Cheyenne band. Apart from that, the strangling of a nearly man-sized dog who is panicking and fighting for its life, is far from a "quick" or "silent" kill. It would take about three to four minutes of complete oxygen deprivation to render the dog unconscious to the point of ceasing to struggle, silence, and then death. With a nearly full moon such a desperate struggle would have been seen by more than a few soldiers. As to the Washita attack being "one of the most desperate ever fought on the plains...," it was a "desperate" fight for Black Kettle's people, but it certainly wasn't for the cavalry. There are other inconsistencies, but nothing more is needed to discredit the story.

CHAPTER 8

The Tourist Hunters

"The dogs ... did not fear the bull, nor did they know how much more reason they had to fear the bullets."—Chicago Tribune, September 26, 1870[1]

In the first week of 1869, Armstrong was stuck at Fort Cobb, itching to get back to Libbie. The 7th and the 19th Kansas Cavalries were occupied for a couple of months trying to find and raid the Cheyenne and Kiowa. Unlike the former urgency to punish a village, this was a focused hunt, and Armstrong actually prevented the 19th from attacking just any band they found. Perhaps the most important mission was to rescue two captured women. Even though winter snow made it easier to track Indians, the same conditions were hard on soldiers and their horses. Often on short rations, when the last of the hardtack, bacon, and game were gone, they ate their played-out mounts. No matter how hungry Armstrong was on a "horsemeat march," he claimed he wouldn't eat horse or mule—but if truly starving, he might think about eating his dogs' ears, "...and as they trotted along in front of him, quite happy over their mule breakfast, he looked longingly at these devoted friends, but with a hope that he might be spared the necessity of mutilating them."[2] Libbie doesn't say he was kidding, but with Armstrong's penchant for jokes, it is almost certain. (On the march to Little Bighorn, Armstrong wrote Libbie that the Crow scouts would loyally fight for him because he never gave up a trail and would eat mule when necessary.)[3]

Fortunately, Armstrong never had to dine on canine ear leather. In mid–March, they finally caught up with the Cheyenne band who had the captives. Armstrong took three chiefs hostage and threatened to hang them if the women were not surrendered. Indians abhorred strangulation as it was not a warrior's death but how dogs were killed for cooking (clubbing was another method). Mrs. James Morgan and Sarah White were released to Armstrong, who now claimed a success and refocused himself on getting to Libbie. On the route to Camp Supply, he stopped at Washita on March 24 for the final act of the Indian War. There, Armstrong found the last unrecovered casualty of the attack—Blucher's bleaching bones.

Camping on Big Creek Again

Libbie and Armstrong were reunited at Fort Leavenworth on April 9. At the end of the month, the regiment was to bivouac at Big Creek near the relocated Fort

Hays. While Libbie could be as industrious as anyone, she did appreciate *dulce far niente*—"the sweetness of doing nothing." She was glad to be living outdoors again where dress was more relaxed than in post or town, and she didn't have to worry about doing her hair every morning. The liberating atmosphere of camping was always appealing, and she frequently talked about their happy "bedouin lives" [sic] in a "rag house." Maida, Old Rover, Turk, and the rest were equally pleased with tent life.

Camping had two primary benefits—the horses grazed on prairie grass instead of hay, and the men could escape the stuffy heat of their quarters. Hays City, with its lynching railroad trestle and Boot Hill cemetery, was not so very far away. Echoes of frequent gunshots would cause the soldiers to say, "There goes another poor fellow with his boots on."[4] The wooden buildings in Hays City had such thin walls that bullets often penetrated both sides. For fire fighting, large water barrels were placed at intervals on the main street—and also served as shelter from gunfights. During a shoot-out at the station, Armstrong and General Miles could only take cover inside and wait until the shots stopped.[5]

In camp, the soldiers' pup tents were set up in rows with their horses on picket lines nearby—after saber-armed troopers cleared the area of rattlesnakes. Sergeants and officers had tents at the end of their company street. Near the soldiers was the sutler selling tobacco, liquor, tinned food, and clothing. Closer to the command campground was the "Opera House," a log and board structure built for entertainments like band concerts, minstrel shows, and clog dancing, but which also had a billiard table.[6] Separated from the tent lines and parade ground was the commander's camp set in an oxbow bend in the creek and surrounded by trees. There was a large tent for dining and entertaining; two each for the Custers' sitting room/office and sleeping quarters with wooden floors set on rocks, a cook tent for Eliza, a teepee for Henry (Libbie's ambulance driver) and his dog, a guest tent, and even a raised platform with railings at the back of the sleeping tent which Tom Custer called the "beer-garden." The ends of their tents were left open at night for the breeze, and Libbie remembered,

> The dogs of course, ran in and out at will; no one ever thought of repressing them. The best we had was not good enough for them. We knew their step, even, and could distinguish ours from the others in camp.[7]

Of the pack that spring, the only ones named are Maida and Turk, but Old Rover and Flirt were there—as were two more deerhounds from Barker.

Sgt. John Ryan, who had seen some of the 7th's canines executed at Washita, described the dogs at the Big Creek Camp:

> Custer at this camp had a number of thoroughbred hounds, English stag hounds, gray hounds [sic], blood hounds, and beagle hounds. About every company in the regiment had a few dogs, from the little cur up to the huge mastiff. General Custer used to enjoy himself very often hunting buffalo, antelopes, deer and other small game. It was fun to see these hounds start a prairie wolf, better known as a coyote, a jack rabbit or a deer. The stag hounds would generally take the lead and the whole pack of hounds would be strung out, from the stag hound to the little cur, trying to overtake the animal they were pursuing, and if the animal would turn out to the left or right in his course the hind dogs would try to cut him off.[8] [Ryan was with the 7th Cavalry for just over ten years and it's possible his 1908–09 memoirs melded the Custer packs in Kansas and the Dakota Territory.]

Ryan provides an interesting insight into hunting practice, for a mixed pack was useful for different kinds of game. Scent hounds would track and signal the quarry's location with their "music," terrier-types would flush it from cover or dig out a burrow, and the long-legged hounds would run the final chase. (In England this was called a "bobbery" pack, after a Hindi word for ruckus or noise.) Ryan remembered three of the dogs' names, Jude, Duke, and Topsy, Tom Custer's favorite.[9] Still following his brother's lead and occasionally trying to top him, Tom had stationery made with an almost heraldic-style seal consisting of a blue dog whip "T" surmounting a "W" of black sabers, with a black cavalry spur "C" for Thomas Ward Custer.[10]

In contrast to his aristocratic crest, Tom's tent décor was quirky and bohemian. It was hung with Indian trophies—feather bonnet, shields, war shirt, bear claw necklace, and scalps on willow frames. He took pride in his live rattlesnakes—big ones kept in hardtack boxes. Tom delighted in showing them to nervous visitors like Libbie. Second only to snakes for inducing fear in The Old Lady was Brandy, Tom's bull-dog. Libbie described him as having red eyes and plenty of teeth, and called him "the greatest fighting dog of the regiment"—partially for his battles with Turk. If Brandy and the rattlers were not enough to unsettle Tom's visitors, there was often a pet wolf chained near the entrance.[11] So great was the number of pets kept by everyone, Libbie called it "an animated 'zoo.'" Various prairie dogs, raccoons, porcupines, wildcats, badgers, and young antelopes and buffalos combined with "any number of mongrel dogs." There was a burrowing owl and Dixie the wolf (with Armstrong's raccoon and beaver also named "Dixie," clearly it was a popular name). Libbie referred to the wild pets as "ours" but they really belonged to the Custer brothers. Dixie watched Eliza's chickens and would chew anything in his tether's range—tablecloths, linens, and even greenbacks from Armstrong's wallet. The smell of dinner meat and his howling attracted other wolves, and if the Custer hounds were off hunting they would prowl through camp. Once Libbie awoke to hear unfamiliar padding through their tent and pressed Armstrong to investigate with his pistol. He reassured her it was just a large dog but in the morning, confessed it was a wolf but he hadn't wanted to ruin her sleep.[12]

The Custers' hounds had free run of the camp, napping in the sun, visiting friends, investigating smells, and mooching food. Meat was hung from tree branches to age but always up above the highest leap of the deerhounds. Eliza had to fend off voracious dogs when lowering a haunch and keep them away from her chickens. Libbie, with a twinkle in her eye, wrote,

> ...our trial was the rapacity of the dogs. They always seemed to be caverns, and at no hour could we eat without being surrounded by a collection of canines of all ages, which turned up their large appealing eyes to us, contesting in this pathetic manner every mouthful we took.[13]

As had Byron in Texas, the Kansas deerhounds stole dinner meat often enough that a striker had to be detailed to guard the Custers' table during meals.[14] If Armstrong didn't keep the hounds occupied, they went off hunting on their own. Once, four ran down a buffalo eight miles away from camp. Lufra, Juno, Maida, and Blucher drove a large buffalo to bay, and a rancher killed it.

> They had probably been running it for several miles. I call that pretty good work for green dogs. I took them with me the other day, and it was sport. Juno sprang right at the nose the first time she ever saw a buffalo. Lufra took the ear, and Blucher got hold of the side. Juno is as savage as a tiger, and so is Lufra.[15]

(Armstrong often reused dog names so this is Blucher II. Lufra was a deerhound in Sir Walter Scott's *Lady of the Lake*, and Juno was queen of the Roman gods.)

There were less dangerous activities. Annie Gibson Roberts noted on July 4 a coon hunt was arranged for the ladies and followed by an evening patriotic hop in Fort Hays.[16] Libbie encouraged her cousins, Armstrong's sister, Maggie, and their single friends to visit them. She liked playing matchmaker, and the eligible women had many attentive officers. Annie Roberts and her Aunt Fannie (married to Maj. George Gibson, commanding at Fort Hays) stayed at the Big Creek camp in 1870, and despite the considered opinion that hunting buffalo was too dangerous for women, Annie killed two herself. The handsome Capt. George W. Yates won Annie's heart, and they were married in 1872. (Yates would die on Last Stand Hill with the Custer Clan.)

The dogs accompanied the officers and their wives on pleasure rides, "from the lofty and highborn stag-hounds down to the little 'feist' or mongrel of the trooper ... his sides panting with the speed he had [to exert] to keep up." Anything which moved was fair game for the dogs, but tackling skunks got them sprayed—and they bounded back to climb on the beds, chairs, and Libbie's lap. Their exuberant mood was crushed when

> ...all their friends started hurriedly to their feet, seized sticks, chairs, anything to hurl at them, shouting wildly, "Get out! Get out, you brutes!" while only that morning we had exhausted our vocabulary and coined words to tell them what darlings they were. Of course, followed by every available missile, they beat a retreat, but not for any great distance. Perfectly unconscious why they were not as acceptable at night as in the morning, they sat in a grieving semicircle some distance out in front of the tent, and reproved us by pitiful inquiring whines, by short interrogatory barks, by wagging tails and sinuous bodies, trying by their expressive motions to argue us out of our hard-heartedness.[17]

There were two photographs from the Big Creek Camp which captured Maida and another deerhound at the Custers' dining tent. One shows the Custers and several people in chairs with Capt. Weir to the left. A careful look at the blurry shapes to his right reveals the shapes of two hounds' rumps—one recumbent and one standing with its head in Weir's lap.[18] In the second and more well known image, Armstrong and Libbie are dining while Maida lies nearby.[19] Her head is blurred, but Libbie would later have Maida's head, neck, and collar painted in—possibly for publication. Her retouched head was copied from the photograph of Armstrong with the three hounds at Fort Dodge.[20] (A reasonably talented artist, Libbie might have done the retouching herself.)

The 7th Cavalry's new colonel, Samuel D. Sturgis, resumed command in May 1869, and no matter how well they got along, Armstrong chafed at any close management. He had blooded the 7th but could never be the "alpha dog" as long as he was second in command, so he continued casting about for postings with better pay and more autonomy. In June, Armstrong was rejected for the post of Commandant of Cadets, West Point.[21] (A post which would have been highly ironic, given his demerit history and being academically last in his class.)

Thanks to his letters to *Turf, Field and Farm* and Davis' article on the Hancock Campaign, Armstrong's reputation as an Indian fighter and big game hunter grew by leaps and bounds. The onslaught of visitors keen to kill buffalo began after their arrival at Fort Riley in 1866. Libbie noted the young "Prince Ourosoff [sic], nephew of the Emperor of Russia" had come to see the "Great American Desert."[22] It was the beginning of a stream of greenhorns after a buffalo trophy, a glimpse of Indians, dinner with General Custer, or a handshake with Wild Bill Hickok, the famous marshal of Hays City. The months following the Washita Campaign were calm, but the visitor onslaughts of 1869

Armstrong and Libbie dining in their compound at Big Creek in the summer of 1869 (note the croquet mallets on the right side of the tent). Maida moved during the exposure and her blurred head has been painted in. She was accidentally shot and killed during a buffalo hunt that year. Courtesy of the National Park Service, Little Bighorn Battlefield National Monument, LIBI_0019_00496. Photograph by W. J. Philips of Preston, Missouri.

and 1870 caused Libbie to tell Rebecca, "We have had so many buffalo hunts this summer for strangers who come with letters to Autie, that it is such a bore to us. We tremble at every dispatch for fear it announces buffalo hunters."[23]

Hunting Buffalo

The West, with its seemingly unlimited supply of big game and rapidly growing railroad, became a shooting gallery for holiday sportsmen and trophy-seeking tourists. Buffalo were the quarry of choice for tourists, recreational hunters, or professional meat and hide hunters. The tourists wanted trophy heads for home or their favorite saloons. Many dilettante hunters shot buffalo from trains, and as the engineer would seldom stop, the carcasses were useful only to wolves, coyotes, and vultures (dried bones were sold to fertilizer manufacturers). All played their part in nearly eradicating the buffalo from North America, and the U.S. Government helped. In 1881 when they finally considered protecting the fragmented population of northern buffalo, General Sheridan protested, "The destruction of this herd would do more to keep Indians quiet than anything else that could happen."[24]

In a style which could be considered extravagant today, Washington subsidized hunting vacations for politicians, influential businessmen, and foreign visitors. An Army post would furnish tents, firearms, food, liquor, horses, guards, servants, and just about everything else—it would even arrange shipment of trophy heads and hides. If the tourists took any meat at all, it would be just the tongue and a few choice cuts from the hump for that night's meal. (For the Plains tribes, hides became a winter robe or a lodge skin. Meat was dried and preserved, horns were made into spoons or dippers, bones became tools and even gaming pieces, and bladders carried water.)

The parties of hosted hunters ranged from one to ten or more—and sometimes with an entourage of spectators. With dignitaries and celebrities, frequently reporters came along. Armstrong always had his deerhounds, greyhounds, and foxhounds with him and, as the dogs were a novelty, newspapermen seldom failed to mention them. "Calling for his horse, an animal worthy to bear so gallant and fearless a rider, he sprang into the saddle and was off at full speed, with a pack of stag hounds bounding around him."[25] (Just as Armstrong's rifle was always "trusty," his hounds were "faithful" and did a lot of "bounding" whenever reporters were present...)

Armstrong's routine for his guests varied little. Having some notice of their arrival, patrols would be sent to locate a nearby herd. Armstrong's scouts sometimes cheated by driving a herd closer to camp so they could hunt without the inconvenience of a long ride (and probably to get it over with sooner). Wisecrackers in Hays joked about Armstrong corralling buffalo for his guests to kill.[26] Visitors would be met at the station and driven in ambulances to guest quarters at the post—or if early enough to get in a hunt before sunset, taken directly out to meet the waiting trooper escort. A guest was given the best horse available and a brace of pistols and assigned a trooper. Sport hunting was simple to describe but difficult to execute. The escort would cut out a bull, and the tenderfoot would race alongside, aiming for the woolly chest, just behind the shoulder. The hunter would thumb-cock the hammer and fire six times. Generally, a second pistol was used, and if needed, the trooper handed over a third and fourth pistol. Even with the buffalo hemorrhaging, it could still gore horse and rider. If the guest was a bad shot or incompetent rider, the trooper sometimes fired his heavy caliber carbine to end the chase. When blood flowed from the nose and mouth, the buffalo's heaving lungs were bleeding and death was close. Turned at bay, there was still danger from horns and kicking hooves. The guest would administer the *coup de grâce*, and then cut off the tail for a fly whisk souvenir. The tongue was removed by cutting up between the massive jawbones, and the tender hump was carved up and loaded in a wagon. If a wall-trophy was wanted, the massive head was field dressed with salt for shipment to a taxidermist.

As Armstrong had done in Texas, he rested his hounds in an ambulance while driving out to the herd and back. (Experienced hunters led their best buffalo horses to save them for the hunt.) Charles, the son of Mary Kercheval (the Custers' black servant), rode in the hay-filled ambulance with the hounds and remembered them continually licking his face.[27] The hounds would be set on jackrabbits and antelope to entertain the guests and in the hunt would help bring a wounded bull to bay. Man, horse, and hound could be badly injured or even killed. Libbie remembered "Autie losing many a shot because he was afraid he might kill the dogs as they held the buffalo."[28] Falls were perhaps the most common accident—and sometimes lethal to both rider and mount. Shooting horses accidentally was common enough—in one of his Nomad letters, Armstrong admitted to killing three horses in hunts that year.[29] In his hunt stories, seldom was one concluded without an injury—and there was still the danger of Indian raids. Charles Messiter, an Englishman hunting in Nebraska Territory, discovered the mutilated bodies of a major and four soldiers who had gone hunting. They had been dead two weeks and no one knew what became of them.[30] Always aware of this peril, Armstrong detailed sizeable escorts to protect his guests. After the hunt, the riders returned with the injured hunters and tired hounds in ambulances, and wagons loaded with meat and trophies. Besides buffalo steaks, meals frequently featured game including antelope, sage grouse, and wild turkey. There were toasts, hunt stories, sing-alongs, and pranks by the Custer brothers. In the morning after breakfast, there might be another hunt. When the guests could boast at least one kill, they would be taken to the depot.

Sport buffalo hunting with pistols was a dangerous business and there was no end of hazards to rider, horse, and hounds. Injuries and fatalities ranged from broken bones and concussions to being gored and accidentally shot. *Harper's Weekly*, **July 6, 1867.**

During May 1869, Col. Nelson A. Miles of the 5th Infantry was in command at Fort Hays, and Armstrong introduced him to buffalo hunting. The two rode out with Libbie, Mary Miles, and two other women—who would all claim to be the first women to hunt buffalo. General Miles had the bonus excitement of watching Armstrong's staghounds course jackrabbits in the prairie grass, and at a midday halt for lunch,

> The dogs sat around the outside of the circle, disputing, as usual, with their hungry eyes, every mouthful we took and jumping for the bones that were tossed to them. Then the two generals poured from the keg containing the only water we might see during the whole day, a little for each hound, and in return got an affectionate lick from the rough but loving tongues, and a gambol of grateful delight as they sprang off for the march.[31]

During a run by both men with a hound snapping at the bull's hindquarters, it spun around and tossed the dog thirty feet. Limping and moaning, he started off for home—some twenty miles off (Libbie doesn't say if the dog was recovered).[32] Miles and Mary enjoyed riding with the Custers, and later, Miles would have his own staghounds—possibly from Armstrong. "I came to look on my horses and dogs as friends and companions."[33] (Miles' orders to stop the Ghost Dance movement in 1890 resulted in the Massacre at Wounded Knee—a tragedy he greatly deplored.)

Besides Miles, Armstrong's list of V.I.P. hunting guests included P.T. Barnum, Kirkland Barker, and Governor McCook (Colorado Territory) with General Smith, the U.S. assistant postmaster general. Historian Blaine Burkey suggests Armstrong also hosted Generals William Tecumseh Sherman and James A. Garfield (who would be elected the 20th president in 1881).[34] There were many more to follow—including a number from across the Atlantic Ocean.

America was no stranger to English "pilgrims"—the more famous included Charles Dickens, Rudyard Kipling, Robert Louis Stevenson, and Oscar Wilde. The West had seen wealthy English hunters like Sir William Drummond Stewart, 7th Baronet of Blair and Balcaskie, and Sir St. George Gore. Stewart fought as a dragoon in the Napoleonic Wars and stayed six years in America in the 1830s—returning again in the early 1840s. Gore, the 8th Baronet Gore of Magherabegg, Donegal, spent nearly three years hunting in the late 1850s and brought his horses, staghounds, foxhounds (and kennel-man), servants, personal gunsmith, and fishing fly tier. The Fort Kearney officers said, "Lord George Gore came with forty horses, forty servants, forty guns, forty dogs and forty of everything else."[35] He traveled in the highest style with premium liquor, tinned delicacies, and custom wagons (which foreshadowed today's motor homes) and hired Jim Bridger and a company of mountain men. He hunted everything that walked, flew or swam—and left many hounds with the Army on his return to England.

Several of the English hunters wanting buffalo trophies had already hunted big game in Egypt, Africa, and India. Despite the American Wars of 1776 and 1812, Englishmen liked the Yankees who, in spite of their democratic way of life, were partial to foreign nobility—and still looked to England for the best horses and hounds. For those whom Armstrong hosted in 1869 and 1870, it was their first time in America, and they all thoroughly enjoyed themselves. The notables included Baron Waterpark, Sir Berkeley Paget, Members of Parliament Walter Powell and Samuel Graves (and Graves' two sons), John Ainsworth, T. Sutton Townsend, M.D., William Goodwin, and two other unnamed (and presumably less scintillating) gentlemen. To various degrees, they were all fox hunters and dog men, but Paget and Powell presented Armstrong with imported Scottish Deerhounds as thank-you gifts.

In late August 1869, Col. Sturgis and Armstrong received letters from Lt. General Sheridan and Maj. General Schofield giving them two weeks' notice about two Englishmen keen to hunt buffalo. Sturgis deferred the arrangements to Armstrong. Their train arrived on Tuesday, September 7. The pair was taken to Fort Hays before heading out to the hunt camp in the morning.[36]

The Peers

Henry Anson Cavendish, 4th Baron Waterpark (1839–1912), was the same age as Armstrong. He was well educated, spoke French and German, and had served in the Foreign Office. In 1863, he inherited the Irish peerage, Waterpark, and began a life devoted to travel and hunting. He stalked deer in Scotland, fished for salmon in Labrador, rode with the famous Meynell Foxhounds, and spent a year hunting in India before coming to America. He had estates in the north of Ireland and England and would become co-master of the Meynell Hunt.[37] While in New York, a socialite (known to Armstrong) wagered Waterpark that he wouldn't be able to kill even one buffalo in Kansas. He and his friend, Paget, determined to settle the wager by going there.[38]

The Right Honorable Sir Augustus Berkeley Paget, G.C.B. (1823–1896), was a handsome man of forty-six with long but sparse side-whiskers. He was a distinguished diplomat with service at embassies in Europe, Egypt, and Greece. Paget had notable military connections which Armstrong appreciated, for his uncle was Field Marshall Henry William Paget, Marquess of Anglesey and Earl of Uxbridge—a dashing cavalry commander in the Napoleonic Wars, as well as being first cousin to Lord George Augustus Paget of Crimean War fame.[39]

Armstrong said Waterpark was "...like most Englishmen, passionately fond of the chase and its necessary attendants—good horses and dogs." Paget was admired for his famous military relations and connections to the turf.[40] Dressed correctly for sport in England, both wore tweed suits, although Paget made a concession to the warmer weather by wearing a white linen coat. Libbie, who had been prepared to count them as "snots," found them

> ...charming & unassuming gentlemen—delighted with everything done for them and able to rough-it with anyone who had been years out here." They were good riders despite their "awkward appearance.... They "took" to Autie as they are so fond of hunting & horses & dogs ... we have had some other "highnesses" out here before this party, but they were not to compare with the last.[41]

At Hays City, a trainload of nearly 150 Ohio sightseers with reporters and a photographer happened to unload the day before Waterpark and Paget arrived. Some of the 7th's officers invited them on the hunt, and Armstrong revised arrangements to include his audience of fellow Buckeyes. The cavalry and Ohioans joined forces at Fort Hays and formed an unlikely caravan of troopers, Army wagons, ambulances, private buggies, coaches, springless wagons, and the occasional mounted civilian. The eager civilians carried every manner of firearm—from venerable muskets to shotguns to breechloaders. In their excitement, several had forgotten their ammunition.[42] Young Frank Talmadge, one of the Ohioans, described the start from Fort Hays.

> The band, its members dressed in blue uniforms, with brass instruments, mounted on white horses, was on the parade grounds, flags were flying, orderlies galloping too and fro. Custer, with his pack of deer hounds, a lord on each side, took his position in front of the band, then ordered "Forward, march!" passing outside the reservation, the band playing "God Save the Queen" in compliment to the titled Englishmen, the honored guests of the hunt.[43]

On the ride out, Armstrong's hounds spooked a herd of antelope and tore off in pursuit with their master following.

> He gave an Indian war-whoop—every horse and dog understood it meant a dash—a run at full gallop. No horse could be restrained; the only safety was to proceed with him.... The hounds were running low, their breast bones scraping the ground.[44]

Some of the officers, Waterpark and Paget rode after the hounds—which weren't really expected to catch the fastest mammal in North America. After running a couple of miles, they gave up the chase and the hounds began returning singly and in pairs. Adjutant Myles Moylan's horse punched through a prairie dog warren, crashing both man and mount. Surprisingly, only Moylan's shoulder and ego were bruised. Arriving in camp, the hunters decided on a pre-dinner run at a large herd a few miles away.[45]

The over-eager civilians ultimately did more chasing than killing. The serious hunters rode up in a line and, when the herd bolted, each man chose his bull, and rode after him, banging away.[46]

Despite Libbie and Mary Miles claiming the title of first women buffalo hunters back in May, Armstrong wouldn't let women hunt. Confronting him, Miss Talmadge from the Ohio contingent (traveling with her father and brother) insisted on being allowed to hunt. After wearing down Armstrong and demonstrating her considerable riding skills and pistol marksmanship, she killed two bulls herself—and was heartily cheered. Libbie was content to stay in camp or follow the hunt with Henry her ambulance driver who, intent on being in at the death, drove at breakneck speed over the prairie—jolting Libbie and the reporters alarmingly. On the second day, soon after leaving camp and breakfast, the deerhounds demonstrated their speed when

> ...a fine one [jackrabbit] broke cover right in front of our horses. I had half a dozen stag hounds with me, most of them young dogs. With a tally-ho that might have done honor to an English fox chase, a dozen well-mounted gentlemen, including Lord Waterpark and Paget started with the dogs.[47]

Maida, Armstrong's favorite deerhound, caught the jack on the run and mightily impressed the Englishmen—who likened the jackrabbit to the English hare (*lepus europaeus*).

Injuries over the three-day hunt were not insubstantial. Two men and horses were tossed by bulls. Armstrong was thrown and his horse gashed—only the saddle blanket and felt pad saved the horse from being torn by the other horn. The band leader dislocated his shoulder, the *New York Times* correspondent was thrown as his horse jumped a ditch, and one reporter was missing for hours. The *Ohio State Journal's* man insisted someone else had shot his horse in the neck, although from the bullet hole's angle, Armstrong joked the shot must have come from a balloonist.[48] By tradition, the penalty for being "policed" (a horseback fall) was a basket of champagne, and Libbie told her friend, Laura Noble, that "...we have had considerable wine to drink this summer—forfeit wine."[49] Not even Armstrong was immune, for on one hunt, his galloping horse collapsed a prairie dog warren, stumbled and catapulted Armstrong to the ground, breaking his carbine. The horse ran off, and Armstrong walked back to be taunted and buy champagne.[50] (The other prairie hazard was buffalo wallows, where compacted, hard mud caused horses to slip and fall.)

Armstrong and Tom would often fake Indian attacks by having a detachment race toward camp, kicking up dust, shooting and whooping like a dime novel war party. The officers would drive off the raid, and the guests eventually were let in on the joke. The Englishmen were thrilled with their "Indian attack" and would have happily done some real fighting. Paget carried a Galand-Sommerville revolver which Armstrong and Tom greatly admired. Patented in 1868, it was the latest innovation with a double-action trigger and a lever mechanism for cartridge extraction which made it easy to fire and reload. (Apart from the self-cocking Starr revolver, all American pistols were single-action—thumb-cocked before the trigger could be pulled.) For sport buffalo hunters, pulling the trigger to cock *and* fire had distinct advantages when galloping. Paget promised to get one for Armstrong—as well as a hound.

Around the campfire, Armstrong, Libbie, and the officers listened to stories of

Waterpark's big game hunting and the military exploits of Paget's family. At the Charge of the Light Brigade, Lord George Paget famously smoked a cheroot while attacking Russian cannons in the Valley of Death,[51] and at Waterloo, there was the Marquess's apocryphal exclamation when grapeshot tore off his leg at the knee—"By God, sir, I've lost my leg!"—to which the Duke of Wellington replied, "By God, sir, so you have!" (The Marquess was fitted with an artificial leg and became a field marshal.) Armstrong had studied both battles at West Point, but hearing accounts from a relative was better than reading a text or novel. With the conversation about American and British wars, gun merits, horses, hounds, and hunting, Armstrong became like an old friend with both men, but Paget was impressed with his host's deerhounds and foxhounds and offered to give him "a specimen of its pure stag hounds, selected from one of the best packs."[52]

Waterpark and Paget had "a very jolly time at Hays."[53] The kills on the last evening totaled eighty-one, with nine between the two Englishmen (Armstrong had seven). Riding back to Fort Hays, the party killed six more buffalo. With his love of literature by Charles Dickens, Sir Walter Scott, and Charles Lever, Armstrong was an Anglophile before he met Waterpark and Paget, and hobnobbing with the pair drove the nail deeper. Upon leaving, they invited the Custers to visit them in England. They went to the Rocky Mountains, toured the Mormons' Salt Lake City, San Francisco, and Yosemite Valley. On their return, Armstrong planned to meet them in Chicago and take them to meet Kirkland Barker in Detroit.[54]

On September 12, just after they left, Armstrong, wrote *Turf* about the "grand buffalo-hunt just concluded" (his letter was published on the 24th). A habitual name-dropper, Armstrong took pains to write a goodly amount about the noble qualities of Lord Waterpark and "Lord Paget." (Armstrong got Paget's title wrong. It was "Sir," but British titles confused most Americans, who used them interchangeably.) Excitedly, he announced Paget's coming gift and stated he would breed this imported deerhound with his stock to produce a superior coursing hound. Armstrong threw down the gauntlet for "owners of gray [sic] or stag hounds" to beat his stag hounds in a hunt. He invited *Turf*'s editor to join a hunt and challenged Barker to host the Englishmen for duck shooting and a sail aboard his yacht.[55] (He also offered a hunt to the *New York Citizen* editor.) Of course, to produce his crossbreed hunting stock, Armstrong would have to first get the new deerhound. (In America and England, the cross-breed he wanted was called a "stag hound," "long dog," "lurcher," or "hot-blooded" hound—pedigreed hounds were "cold-blooded.")

With his letter to *Turf*, Armstrong sent along three card-mounted photographs taken by W.J. Phillips of Preston, Missouri. Magazines couldn't print photographs unless converted to drawings on engraved steel plates, so the editor described them in detail. One showed the camp tents and wagon park; the second was of the hunt group with the two noblemen, Armstrong, Tom, Libbie, Miss Talmadge and her father, and several officers of the 7th. There were eighteen people and three blurry dogs in the photo. Two of them, sizeable light-colored dogs, are resting by Libbie and Tom (in a second photo there were fewer people and the dogs had moved). Armstrong, in buckskins and beard, and with a darkish dog beside him, reclines on the ground reading a copy of *Turf*.[56] (The editor commented he had gained weight since the war and the beard made him look less boyish.[57])

A rare photograph of dying but still dangerous buffalo at bay. Armstrong can just be seen on the horse with the white blaze nearest the buffalo and his pack of hounds (blurred) can be made out by the horses' legs. Libbie had ten dogs included in the engraving of this image for *Tenting on the Plains*, but five to eight can be seen here. She thought it a modern wonder that a photograph of such a critical moment in the hunt could be made. Taken near Big Creek Camp in September 1869. From left to right: an orderly, Lt. Henry Nowlan, sutler Hill Wilson, Capt. Thomas Weir, Lt. James Bell, Lt. Francis Gibson, Lt. Col. George A. Custer, Capt. Frederick Benteen, Lt. Tom Custer, Capt. William Thompson, and Charley Thompson. Courtesy of the National Park Service, Little Bighorn Battlefield National Monument, LIBI_0019_00498. Photograph by W. J. Philips of Preston, Missouri.

The photographer risked his life to take the extraordinary third photograph. A buffalo at bay is surrounded by horsemen and a hound pack. (The hounds and some riders are blurred with motion.) Armstrong is closest to the bull, which had taken six bullets in its chest. With the bull standing there, lungs heaving, bleeding, and unpredictable, W.J. Phillips (almost certainly with his assistant and an armed trooper or two) daringly carried his camera and tripod around to the opposite side and took an exposure of the hunters and hounds behind the wounded bull.[58] The *Turf* editor dryly noted that the photographer must have worked very fast.[59] Historian Brian W. Dippie adds some clarification gleaned from Libbie herself, who stated the photo was actually taken on a hunt a few days *before* the Englishmen arrived.[60] Libbie knew the image was unique and in 1887 had it engraved for her second book, *Tenting on the Plains*. It is arguably the only period photograph of a buffalo hunt where the quarry isn't dead. Libbie said of it,

> I have a photograph of a buffalo at bay and the party of hunters around him while the camp photographer takes his picture—Isn't it a most curious item in this desert land so far out, that a buffalo hunt should be photographed? But I think this is the first time that the art has been called into use at a buffalo hunt.[61]

In September 1869, near Big Creek, Armstrong and Libbie entertain Lord Waterpark and Sir Henry Paget. There are three hounds in this photograph—one can be seen lying next to Armstrong who is reading a copy of *Turf, Field and Farm*. Two light-colored hounds are at the feet of Tom and Libbie. Left to right: Armstrong, Miss Talmadge (who killed two buffalo), Frank Talmadge, Capt. William Thompson, Lord Waterpark, Sir Henry Paget, Lt. Myles Moylan, Capt. Thomas Weir, Lt. James Bell, Col. Samuel Sturgis, Lt. William Cooke, Lt. Henry Nowlan, Libbie Custer, Tom Custer, Mr. Smith, Mrs. Godfrey (Lt. E. S. Godfrey's wife), Capt. Brewster, and Mr. Talmadge. Edward S. Godfrey papers, Special Collections, USMA Library.

The Right Honorable Kirkland C. Barker

The month after Waterpark and Paget departed, Barker finally came for his grand buffalo hunt—although a dog tragedy would sour his experience. He brought with him to Fort Hays eight Detroit and New York businessmen and a couple of retired Army officers. Leaving Detroit on October 1, Barker and company traveled in high style in his Pullman Palace salon and sleeping cars appointed like exclusive gentlemen's clubs—all polished wood and upholstered furniture with the best food and service. Quite a contrast to the camping ahead.

Barker's friends were Judge W.G. Beckwith, president of the Michigan State Agricultural Society; John B. Southerland, superintendent of the Michigan Central Car Factory (railroad); Jefferson Wiley (iron business); Samuel Lewis of Detroit, "a gentleman of leisure"; Gen. Rufus Lombard Howard; Maj. Horace Gray; Charles Hack, sportsman; and a *bon vivant* Irishman from Canada, J. H. Morgan.[62] Almost certainly, Generals Schofield and Sheridan had *not* requested these men be treated at Army expense. It was the season when cavalry left field camps for their winter stations. In fact, the 7th was supposed to be marching the 300 miles from Fort Hays to Fort Leavenworth just then, but because of Barker, Armstrong requested and was granted a postponement from Schofield. (Armstrong knew about Barker's plans in mid–September.[63]) It is tempting to suspect that if his request had been denied, he would have found some military excuse to delay the march to go hunting with "K.C.B."

Barker's party arrived at Hays City on October 8 and were loaded into ambulances and buggies and taken to base camp. There, in starting for the hunting camp, most of the guests changed into riding clothes with the less adventurous sticking to ambulances. The band played "Garry Owen" as they set out and the "...prancing, high-mettled steeds, the glistening arms, the well-bred pack of stag-hounds, formed a cavalcade and occasion long to be treasured in the memory of the beholder."[64] Another likened it to a medieval baron's march to a battle or hunt. Jefferson Wiley wrote to the Detroit *Post* and in florid Victorian style, described a deerhound course on the twelve-mile march to camp.

> But hear that ringing cry on the right! And what rider is that in the advance, followed by many others? "That is General Custer." How his voice rings out in the clear prairie air! And at what a terrific speed he dashes on! Hurry up, hounds! but give that rabbit a moment's time, and he will find safety in the first prairie dog hole he reaches. And now, rabbit, hounds, and riders disappear down the ravine, and we know not the end until General Custer rides quietly up and throws a large hare into our ambulance.[65]

Barker was delighted with the speed and cunning of the hounds. Of Armstrong's six on that hunt, Maida (his favorite) was the only one named.

> To give our visitors an opportunity to witness the great speed of the antelope and American hare, or as it is best known on the plains, the buck rabbit, I took with me from camp about half a dozen fine staghounds, including two lately sent from Michigan by K.C.B. Foremost among all of these was my favorite dog, the companion of my long and terrible marches of last Winter [the Washita Campaign]. She who by day trotted at my stirrup, and at night shared my camp couch.[66] [When writing the press, Armstrong frequently started dog stories with, "I took with me (*some number of*) staghounds."]

The half-mile long column reached camp at sundown. Always mindful of Indian attacks, the camp was set up in a defensive square with officer and guest tents and picketed horses in the center and surrounded by trooper tents with wagons for the second perimeter. (During the day, the horses were grazed and watered outside the square.) Around the campfire with drinks, cigars, and their best after-dinner stories, the men voted to name the raucous site "Camp K.C. Barker." (As it happened, Camp Barker was adjacent to the recent Waterpark-Paget camp.) Among Armstrong's officers were his fellow dog fanciers—brother Tom and Lt. Algernon Smith. In the morning, the officers selected reliable buffalo horses for guests who had never hunted on horseback. Horses who could carry the hefty weights of Barker and Beckworth (each about 230 lbs.) were hard to find. (Pvt. J.C. Pickens, who was Barker's trooper, called "the Principal Michigander ... rather corpulent."[67]) After horse and escorts were assigned, stirrups adjusted, cinches tightened, guns loaded, and their hats tied on their heads, they were ready. Unfortunately, a trooper had taken Barker's assigned horse and exhausted it while finding the herd. Another horse, not as substantial and with indifferent riding qualities, was found for him. The column set out—hunters, trooper escorts, officers, wagons, and two ambulances for injured riders and tired dogs.[68]

Barker rode with Armstrong, Tom, and Pickens—who was not to shoot any buffalo but did turn one for Barker.[69] The Easterners hunted about as expected and bagged twenty-four buffalo on the first day despite accidental pistol discharges which luckily didn't injure anyone. Still, there were the usual contusions and wounds. A buffalo rammed Major Gray and his horse into a creek. One soldier's horse was superficially gored and another shot in the hoof. Barker himself came close to being a casualty. On the substitute, skittish horse, he began firing into the left flank of a buffalo. Dropping back to cross behind and attack the right side, he passed too close (Pickens said Barker's shots were high and he couldn't control his horse). The bull turned and slammed the horse's rear—and it leapt violently away in panic, pitching Barker headfirst on the hard ground. As the bull slewed around to charge the unconscious man, Armstrong and six men rode up and scared off the buffalo.[70] (Pickens killed Barker's buffalo with his pistol—and was surprised he was never reprimanded for it.[71])

Barker was having difficulty breathing, and when the Custers got to him, they used "restoratives" from a saddle flask (whiskey or brandy) to revive him. After fifteen suspenseful minutes, Barker, his eye turning black and cheek swollen and bruised, recovered. Someone offered a savvier (but lighter) buffalo horse for him. Barker gamely rode toward the herd, singled out another bull, and after twenty-two shots from four revolvers, finally got his buffalo. The bull collapsed and suffered the indignity of Barker clambering on top of it to give three cheers while it was bleeding to death.[72]

That night, there was more feasting and drinking, and pranks were played on anyone who imbibed too much and passed out.[73] Armstrong, a firm teetotaler, slept safely in his tent with his deerhounds. The following day was Sunday, and the hunters welcomed the Sabbath to recuperate. On Monday's hunt, there was a dangerous jam of Gen. Howard's revolver, and J. H. Morgan very nearly shot himself. Armstrong related the hunt's highlights in a long letter written on November 8 and published in *Turf* on the 19th. He included references to Sir Walter Scott's romantic novels and, in fine dramatic style, interrupted his suspenseful tale of Barker's injury to describe Gen. Beckwith's hunt—and then returned to Barker's situation, adding further excitement by describing the progression of pistols and shots needed to finally kill his buffalo. After two days of hunting, they had scored fifty-three bulls, several injuries, one dose of skunk spray, and one fatality—Maida. In the last two paragraphs, he described the tragedy.

On the first run on the *first* morning, Armstrong's deerhounds dashed off on their own instead of sticking close by him. Out of sight, they brought a bull to bay and several hunters rode over for the kill. The hounds clustered around the buffalo, barking, snapping, and darting in, trying to get a bite hold somewhere. Maida dived into the fray and clamped onto the throat. The over-zealous hunters cut loose with a fusillade of lead—and she was killed by a trooper's carbine.[74] When Armstrong finally rode up to see the silent hunters surrounding the dead hound and buffalo, the hapless trooper was doubtless quaking in his boots. They had all played a part in the accidental death of General Custer's favorite hound—his patron's gift. The irony cannot have been lost on Barker who gently admonished Armstrong the year before about his bad luck with dogs: "I hope you will not lose any of them."[75] Armstrong doesn't say what happened to her body, but as his special dog, it is highly likely Maida received a trooper's grave in the field.

Officers' bodies were always carried back to the post, but soldiers could only expect a shallow grave near where they died. Because wolves and coyotes could dig it up for food and Indians were believed to unearth bodies for scalps, measures were taken to obliterate the grave and mask the smell of decomposition. A bonfire's ashes and smoke obscured the grave, or picketed horses trampled the ground and left manure. If there was hurry, wagons were driven over the grave. (Ineffective efforts included digging below "wolf smell," piling rocks on top, or strewing broken glass to cut up wolves' paws.) In print, Armstrong was silent about her burial—and, diplomatically, said nothing about what happened to the unlucky trooper.

Blucher's and Maida's deaths were the only two Armstrong ever wrote about—and he only showed sorrow for hers. "Words fail to express the grief occasioned by the untimely death of so faithful companion"—and Libbie wrote that her husband's heart was pierced with "a pang of sorrow for almost an irreparable loss."[76] Although Maida's death happened on the first day, Armstrong dramatically saved her death for the closing of his *Turf* letter, where he penned a tribute.

> *Poor Maida, in life the firmest friend,*
> *The first to welcome, foremost to defend:*
> *Whose honest heart is still your master's own,*
> *Who labors, fights, lives, breathes for him alone.*
> *But who with me shall hold thy former place,*
> *Thine image what new friendship can efface.*
> *Best of thy kind adieu!*
> *The frantic deed which laid thee low*
> *This heart shall ever rue.*[77]

Armstrong was a good teller of frontier stories, and although no poet, he was extremely well read and plagiarized two poems from the English poets William R. Spencer and Lord Byron. Stephen D. Youngkin, a Scottish Deerhound owner and Custer scholar, identified the first four lines of his tribute as copied from the famous epitaph Lord Byron had carved on the monument for his Newfoundland, Boatswain.[78] Custer historian Donald P. Schwarck identified the final three lines as those from Spencer's *Beth Gelert: or The Grave of the Greyhound*, where Llewelyn mistakenly slays his own hound, believing it to have killed his infant son from the bloody bedding. Only then does he discover that the blood came from a wolf that Gelert killed to protect the sleeping child.[79] The sentiments of both poets are sincere, so Armstrong may be forgiven for borrowing from the best to express his emotions for Maida. (Libbie published nothing about her loss but did repeat the tribute in *Following the Guidon*.)

Shortly after Barker's hunt, the 7th began breaking camp for the season. The commotion always caused great excitement among everyone as well as dogs and horses.[80] The whole process took about four hours, and after the Custer tents were packed, under their tent floor was discovered a nest of "essence peddlers" (skunks). Libbie was triumphant in saying, "I told you so!" about the nocturnal noises she'd been hearing but wondered why the dogs hadn't detected them.[81] On October 13, the regiment left Fort Hays for cold weather quarters at Fort Leavenworth—marching to save the expense of rail transportation. From there, the companies were distributed to several Kansas forts so as not to use up all the hay and grain at any one post.

That winter, the Custers were apart as Armstrong visited his parents, saw Barker in Detroit and Sheridan in Chicago, did Army business in Washington, and looked for business opportunities in New York. Tom and William Cooke traveled with him, and the two dashed up to Ontario to visit the latter's family. Armstrong was granted leave for November but then extended it to January 10, 1870. He left Libbie at Leavenworth with Bowers, his principal striker and dog tender, and a second orderly named Bishop. The temperamental Eliza had finally exasperated Libbie and, after an insolent episode, was sent away. Libbie was happy to have Mary Adams as the new cook along with her son, Charlie. Mary was a good cook, easygoing, and didn't give away food. Libbie was not entirely alone for her cousin, Rebecca, lived in nearby Topeka, and there were the other officers and their wives for company. Still, she couldn't have been happy while her husband was off in the lights and bustle of the big cities.

Armstrong wrote Libbie from Monroe on December 14 with his news and that Jacob Greene had re-married (his first wife Nettie, Libbie's matchmaking friend, had died in 1868). Inexplicably, he instructed her, "Tell Bowers to take good care of Maida."[82] As she had been dead barely two months, Armstrong's reference to her is a puzzle. One doubtful explanation suggests he mistakenly wrote her name when he meant another (as the first Maida had no puppies, this Maida couldn't have been her daughter). The most likely answer is that Armstrong reused the name—which he was known to do. Neither Armstrong or Libbie give any hints about this second Maida's parentage.

By mid–January, Armstrong was back at Leavenworth working on *Galaxy* articles. The Custers expected to spend another summer in tents and Libbie was speculating which young ladies could visit and liven up camp for the bachelor officers. Their circle entertained themselves with sociables, riding, hunting, trips to Hays City for concerts, and weekly hops at the Custers' home. For the fanciest hops, the arsenal hall was decorated with panoplies of swords and rifles; flags and patriotic bunting; howitzers with pyramids of cannon balls; and portraits of generals and presidents. The band platform, under a saber canopy, was set on a base of cannon balls. Armstrong loved supervising these details, and for a masquerade ball at his home on Wednesday evening, March 9, he pulled out all the stops. The front and back verandas were enclosed with canvas and the carpets covered with still more canvas—making the house look festively exotic in lamplight. There was even a "green room" for donning costumes. The women made salads, sandwiches, cakes, sweets, and favors. Rebecca was visiting at the time and she estimated fifty people in costume attended with dancing going on until five in the morning.[83]

For Victorian costume parties, biblical, Greek, Roman, and Medieval figures were always in vogue, as were characters from literature and cultural stereotypes. Libbie was Mrs. Partington (a scatterbrained, writer); Maggie Custer was The Owl; Miss Crouch was a Tambourine Girl; Capt. George Yates was a Yankee School Boy; and Lts. Henry Nowlan, Myles Moylan, and James Bell came as a monk, Romeo, and a Turk. Col. Sturgis was an Old Vegetable Huckster, and Armstrong (inspired by Waterpark and Paget), made a grand entrance as an English huntsman.[84] A master of Fox Hounds (and Whipper-In) traditionally wore a scarlet coat with brass buttons, light-colored riding trousers, riding boots, and either a black, jockey-style cap or a top hat. Very fond of amateur theatrics, for this costume Armstrong only needed the coat as he already had a "topper," dog horn, and whip. Likely, he got a second use out of his Huntsman costume, as a week later was the masquerade Purim Ball in town, and the officers were all attending.[85]

In early April 1870, Libbie and three visitors (Rebecca, Armstrong's sister Maggie, and a schoolmate from Monroe, Julia Thurber) played a parlor game with personality questionnaires. Libbie chose horses and dogs as her favorite animals.[86] When first married, she tolerated her husband's few dogs on occasional visits with him during the war. In Texas, she was bemused by the small pack of foxhounds and greyhound—but found her first "heart dog" in Ginnie the pointer. After three years and a few months in Kansas living in close quarters with deerhounds, greyhounds, foxhounds, setters, pointers, and a bull-dog, Libbie was a confirmed dog person.

The following month, Armstrong and five companies of the 7th were back at Fort Hays for the season. That summer and fall, there were more tourists and, annoyingly, citizens who assumed their taxes entitled them to free use of Army facilities. They visited the posts in flocks, insisting on hotel accommodations in the barracks and to be squired on buffalo hunts.[87] They got to be so persistent that Armstrong often hid, leaving Libbie to entertain them—but he never avoided Englishmen and hosted seven more that year.

The Doctor and the Industrialist

Thomas Sutton Townsend (1847–1918), a London physician, and John Stirling Ainsworth (1844–1923), a wealthy mine and mill owner from Cumberland (both in their early twenties), had their "Custer Buffalo Hunt" on May 23. They thought the prairie wonderful and deemed the hunt "...like our fox hunting but <u>rather more</u> exciting."[88] Armstrong, Libbie, and Tom were at the top of their form and charmed their guests. Both men had their buffalo heads shipped home. They were fascinated by the pet rattlesnakes Tom kept and, being of scientific and public-spirited minds, Townsend and Ainsworth decided the Zoological Society of London should have specimens. Tom caught two and shipped them to Ainsworth. (Englishmen abroad were always looking for new species or oddities for the London Zoo or British Museum. In 1835, the only Persian greyhound [Saluki] in England, Zillah, was on lonely display in the London Zoo.[89])

After leaving Kansas, Townsend and Ainsworth went to Salt Lake City to get an opinion of Brigham Young and the Mormons ("...poor deluded creatures, I'm sure—but nevertheless flourishing and earnest") and then to San Francisco. There, Townsend received notice of his father's death on the day after their buffalo hunt when they had drunk the Queen's health in Armstrong's tent (coming from an American, it was a meaningful gesture to an Englishman). Townsend declared their happy time with Armstrong would always be associated with "my dear & excellent father's memory."[90] Townsend parted company from Ainsworth in San Francisco and made the trip to Liverpool in an amazing sixteen days. (Nine of those were on the Atlantic crossing, and in Jules Verne's *Around the World in Eighty Days*, published in 1873, fictional Phileas Fogg also took sixteen days to make the same journey.) Ainsworth traveled to Harvard College where he met Henry Wadsworth Longfellow and Ralph Waldo Emerson,

"...and some others of your great men."⁹¹ Both men began a warm but sporadic correspondence with Armstrong, exchanging photographs, personal news, travel stories, and the doings of Generals Sheridan and James Forsyth as observers in the Franco-Prussian War. On September 12, from his shooting lodge in northern Scotland, Ainsworth sent his thanks to Armstrong, Libbie, and Tom—and noted that only one rattlesnake was installed in the London Zoo as its companion had died before reaching New York City (the shipping agents noted this on the crate).

> We had a good deal of <u>dislike</u> to opening the box when he did arrive, and I finally sent him off direct to the Zoological Gardens. The buffalo heads, do you know, <u>never turned up</u> and I could not make out what had become of them. But I look forward to shooting another with you some day.⁹²

Both he and Townsend lamented the loss of their souvenirs from the delightful time they had with the Custers (who were welcome in England anytime).

As had Waterpark and Paget, Ainsworth brought his own English revolver which the Custer brothers admired. For a thank-you gift, he and Townsend bought one for each brother (the pistol's manufacturer was never noted), and in February 1871, the cased revolvers were sent to Fort Leavenworth along with photographs of the two men.⁹³ Armstrong confirmed the delivery of the pistols, and Ainsworth replied, "I am glad the revolvers reached you & that you like them. My own is lying in its case waiting, I hope, for a day in your company before the buffalo are all exterminated."⁹⁴ Ainsworth was aware of the massive slaughter, and like most hunters, wanted to get his trophies while he still could. (There would come a time when scarcity necessitated the manufacture of fake buffalo head trophies for saloons.) Armstrong would have fine, London-made revolvers from Paget as well as Townsend and Ainsworth, and at Little Bighorn, he was carrying "two Bulldog, self cocking, English white handled pistols, with a ring in the butt for a lanyard."⁹⁵ (The British Bulldog, debuted by the Webley firm in 1872, was a compact, short-barreled pistol designed to fit in a gentleman's overcoat pocket. It fired a man-stopping slug in three heavy calibers.)

Ainsworth kept tabs on Armstrong's doings by subscribing to an American newspaper and getting his articles in *The Galaxy*—usually sending them on to Townsend. From the latter, Armstrong received a copy of his article, "A Buffalo Hunt in Kansas," published by *The Field* in September 1871. Thoughtfully, Townsend also sent information on the "Tube Well"—a British Army, portable ground water pump used in Abyssinia.⁹⁶ Armstrong thought enough of both men to include their addresses in his pocket diary.⁹⁷ (Ainsworth would later serve in Parliament, be knighted, and in 1917, become the 1st Baronet Ainsworth of Ardanaiseig, County Argyll.)

Goodwin of Yokohama

William Goodwin was so grateful for his buffalo hunt that he attempted to repay Armstrong with an exotic dog. He wasn't a big game hunter like Waterpark and Paget, for he talked about being "...passed off as a hero on the strength of my buffalo hunt & the dangers of the plains" (the Indians were Armstrong's "coffee colored friends."⁹⁸) From Yokohama in November, he apologized for not being able to send a "Japanese dog" as he could,

...find none that were worth sending anywhere. There seem to be only two sorts—curs & poodles.... I can't for my part see what people have admired in the poodles for they seem to be delicate & peevish little wretches & by no means handsome. Like a good many things in Japan, they have been over-described & made much of.

Goodwin went on about the modernization of Japan and marveled at *bonsai* trees, but he dismissed Yokohama's curios and porcelain as being inferior to those of San Francisco. He liked the Japanese people and compared the entire country to a garden.[99] (It is unclear why Goodwin was in Yokohama, although the British-owned Hongkong and Singapore Banking Corporation, HSBC, opened a branch there in 1866.)

Commodore Matthew Perry had brought specimens of the "Japanese dog" back to the States for himself and President Franklin Pierce in 1854.[100] The breed was the Japanese Spaniel and, exhibited at the earliest dog shows, it became a popular lap dog. It is not clear whether Armstrong or Goodwin came up with the Japanese Spaniel idea, but like the "full blooded Chihuahua dog" which Jacob Greene tried to get, the Oriental dog was intended for Libbie. (Recognized by the AKC in 1888, the Japanese Spaniel was appropriately renamed the Japanese Chin in 1977.)

Parliament on Holiday

Arriving in New York in early September were members of Parliament Walter Powell (Malmesbury), Samuel Robert Graves (Liverpool) and his sons, and Thomas Hughes (Lambeth)—the author of *Tom Brown's School Days*.[101] Graves was a ship owner and merchant, and Powell, a truly beneficent community leader whose family wealth came from mining and shipping coal, was an avid horseman who rode to the hounds, drove four-in-hand coaches, gave magic lantern shows to the public, and would become a ballooning enthusiast. Both were after buffalo.

Graves' enthusiastic sons were just over twenty but still called "the lads" by their father. Armstrong made usual arrangements for the party and, like all his guests, they were thrilled with the hospitality, action, and buffalo trophies. Despite the Custers growing weary of their numerous hunting guests that year, Libbie pronounced these two "so agreeable" and "...refined gentlemen who appreciated everything."[102] Of course, the deerhounds were on the hunt, and when Powell offered Armstrong a purebred from the Highlands, he accepted like a shot. (Powell's buffalo head along with his other big game trophies was mounted in the Malmesbury Reading Room he built for his community.)

During the hunt, Graves became enchanted with prairie dogs and asked if he could have some for the London Zoological Gardens. Pvt. Bowers was tasked with digging up a burrow to catch a few. They were stashed in a barrel partially filled with dirt and shipped off. Powell and Graves were the last of the Custers' British hunters in Kansas, but three years later, Armstrong would host two more in Dakota Territory.

The Politicians and the K.P.R.R.

Armstrong took leave in September and went with 125 dignitaries on a Kansas Pacific Railroad excursion celebrating the completion of their line from the Missouri

River to Denver. Armstrong got many perquisites, including free passes, from the railroad—probably through his friendship with Col. Charles Burleigh Lamborne, Civil War veteran and secretary of the Kansas Pacific. The excursionists enjoyed the trip and made plans to return to the Rockies the following summer "with our guns, dogs, and—God bless them—our wives."[103] They stopped at Fort Hays, where Armstrong treated Governor McCook of the Colorado Territory, General Smith, the U.S. assistant postmaster general, and several others to a two-day buffalo hunt. *The Chicago Tribune* correspondent rather oddly likened the dashing vision of Armstrong on horseback surrounded by hounds to a picturesque painting of Arabs and camels. The hunt went about as usual, but McCook was rammed off his horse and menaced by the buffalo. Several shots were fired at it, and Armstrong released his hounds. They tore in, securing holds on the buffalo's neck, shoulders, and hamstrings. At that point, the riders poured a lethal barrage into the buffalo. Miraculously, none of the hounds were shot—that time.[104]

The Great Barnum

As the season ended, the deluge of hunters lessened, and it was about then when Libbie complained to Rebecca about being fed up with buffalo hunts—reckoning they had 200 visitors.[105] One more had to be accommodated before leaving for winter quarters. The celebrated impresario and showman Phineas Taylor Barnum was "...buffaloing out West."[106]

Armstrong welcomed P.T. Barnum at Hays City but detailed Capt. Hale to manage the buffalo hunt for "The Great Showist" and his party. Barnum had recently turned sixty but was game for the experience. He managed to shoot one bull but became quickly disgusted with the wanton slaughter. Prints & Photographs, Library of Congress, LC-BH82-4961.

Precisely when Barnum first met the Custers is not known, but in 19th century America, social spheres were smaller and more fluid, and it was easy to meet famous people. The Custers visited his American Museum on their honeymoon in February 1864 and with Eliza in January 1865. Libbie had been impressed with the exhibits and particularly with Eliza's overboard reaction to the mummy family.[107] Barnum was often in the museum greeting people, and if Armstrong and Barnum didn't meet on either of those occasions, it may have happened at the *Vanity Fair* Masquerade Ball in April 1866. In a Thomas Nast drawing of the event, both the Devil (Armstrong) and P.T. Barnum were represented.[108] If none of those, then Barnum definitely met the famous Indian fighter at Fort Hays.

In October, Barnum and nine businessmen wrangled a hunt invitation as part of an investigation into Kansas land and cattle investments for the National Land Company.[109]

> "General Custer, commandant at Fort Hayes, was apprized in advance of our anticipated visit, and he received us like princes. He fitted out a company of fifty cavalry, furnishing us with horses, arms and ammunition. We were taken to an immense herd of buffaloes, quietly browsing on the open plain. We charged on them, and, during an exciting chase of a couple of hours, we slew twenty immense bull buffaloes, and might have killed as many more had we not considered it wanton butchery."[110]

Despite the sometimes negative perceptions of animal treatment in his menageries and circuses, Barnum did his best to keep them humanely and even helped the founder of the American Society for the Prevention of Cruelty to Animals, Henry Bergh, to establish a branch in Bridgeport, Connecticut.

Armstrong had indeed made the arrangements but either had pressing work back at Fort Hays or was worn out from hosting guests. He turned the hunt over to Captain Owen Hale of K Company and stayed home with his dogs. (Hale was a veteran of Washita.) This absence was atypical of Armstrong, who was always present if there was a celebrity or the prospect of business. Barnum noted Capt. Hale's capable management of the hunt in a full newspaper account, and said as he had killed one large bull and helped to kill three more, "…it seems cruel and wicked to murder large numbers of these huge beasts, and make no useful disposition of them."[111] It is ironic that Barnum, the era's master of hyperbole and promoter of hoaxes like the FeeJee Mermaid and the "Oldest Woman in the World," was perhaps the only tourist to accurately assess the hunts as pure slaughter.

For a sixty-year-old who was more used to the sidewalks of New York and Bridgeport than riding the prairie, Barnum gets credit for being game enough to try the dangerous sport. (See this chapter's *Tail Piece* for Barnum's first encounter with buffalo.) Although they never hunted together, Barnum was probably invited to a dinner at the Custers' compound at Big Creek. The deerhounds and foxhounds made an impression on him which, in five years, would result in another dog gift for Armstrong. The two had much in common. Both were Anglophiles and egomaniacs with nearly insatiable appetites for spectacle and novelty—and they were gifted storytellers with an instinctive knack for self-promotion. They got on like old chums, and in 1875, Barnum would thank Armstrong for "past courtesies" over the years.[112] While the favors weren't specified, Barnum was keen to have Indian trophies for his museum, and Armstrong had certainly provided these to his friends.

The Winter of Discontent

With Barnum's departure, the 7th broke camp and headed for their winter stations. There was scuttlebutt they were to be split up and distributed around the South for Reconstruction duty. Armstrong, still uncertain about any promotion, applied for an extended leave to investigate business opportunities. Detachments of the 7th were to be garrisoned at Fort Hays (Tom's company) and at Fort Harker (Capt. Myles Keogh and Lt. William Cooke). Officers Weir, Hale, and Yates were away from Leavenworth for a while. With Armstrong going East after this disappointing scatter of the Custer clan, Libbie knew a Leavenworth winter was going to be dreary and difficult. Only Mary, Bowers, and the dogs would be around the house. There would be the usual hops and social events, but without Armstrong, pleasure rides would be far fewer. Libbie decided that she too, wanted to go East for the holidays.[113]

It was toward the end of 1870 that the seemingly ideal marriage of the Custers was having problems. Libbie was alone at Fort Leavenworth. There is scant evidence from her but Armstrong's contrite letters make it clear he had wronged her—and she coolly chose not to forgive him. It might have been gambling (cards and horse races), but Libbie was generally tolerant as long as she thought his losses weren't excessive. Historian Shirley A. Leckie's insightful analysis of their existing letters offers a more probable answer—that Armstrong had committed at least one infidelity.[114] It took a number of months and apologies before they got back on an even keel. (Libbie's principal biographers, Marguerite Merington and Lawrence A. Frost, either misunderstood the import of those letters or ignored their implication to preserve the couple's image.)

* * *

On December 1, Samuel Graves sent Armstrong a warm letter from his home, Wavertree Grange in Liverpool. He wished the Custers a Happy New Year and thanked them for their pleasant "scamper across the prairie." His letter touched on English, American, and European politics and the troubling Franco-Prussian War. The prairie dogs were a more amusing note. "Bowers will be interested in learning that the dogs are safely housed in the Zoological Gardens and have become great favorites." And at least one was shortly to give birth to a litter.[115] Both Sir Berkeley Paget and Walter Powell would be true to their word about the Scottish Deerhounds. Armstrong took Paget's advice to heart about keeping the breed pure—abandoning his notions about cross-breeding and becoming a staunch advocate for "full blooded" hounds.

TAIL PIECE: PLAGIARIZING LORD BYRON

When Lord Byron's Newfoundland, Boatswain, died of rabies in 1808, he stipulated (against strenuous objections) that he was to be buried with his dog on his estate's lawn. Fifteen years later, Byron died of fever in Greece, and his body was brought home and, against his instructions, buried in the family crypt. Boatswain's monument on the lawn has Byron's lengthy epitaph (from which Armstrong borrowed for Maida). Perhaps the most moving tribute to a dog ever written, it begins and ends with these well-known lines:

> Near this spot,
> Are deposited the remains of One
> Who possessed Beauty without Vanity
> Strength without Insolence
> Courage without Ferocity
> and all the Virtues of Man without his Vices...
>
> ... To mark a friend's remains these stones arise;
> I never knew but one—and here he lies.[116]

Barnum and the Grand Hoboken Buffalo Hunt

In 1843, Barnum purchased a few scrawny, young buffalos in New Jersey. Over the next week or so, he placed announcements in the New York papers about a buffalo herd seen roaming closer and closer to the city. At the peak of public interest, Barnum announced they had been captured, and he would display them and demonstrate cowboy roping techniques in Hoboken for free. Admission was indeed free—but Barnum had quietly hired all the Hudson River ferries and made a fortune off the Manhattan crowds determined to see buffalo at no charge.[117]

CHAPTER 9

Blue Grass, Pvt. Burkman and the Grand Duke Alexis

"Custer thought it'd be great to breed pedigreed dogs and sell 'em. Wall, he raised 'em. By the time we left Kentuck fur Yankton we musta had 'round 'bout eighty."—Pvt. John Burkman[1]

A year after his buffalo hunt, in September 1870, Paget sent a chatty letter to Armstrong apologizing for the delay in writing but full of his news and British affairs and good tidings about the deerhound. He and Waterpark had a wonderful time and wanted to return to Fort Hays one day. "How is 'Wild Bill'? Has he been shot yet?" The two Englishmen met Wild Bill Hickok as newly elected Marshal of Hays City and sheriff for Ellis County soon after he killed two men. Despite his moniker, Wild Bill was a cool hand in a gunfight, and his reputation as a dead shot made him a dime-novel legend in his own time.

Paget asked after Col. Sturgis and the officers, wanted to know if Indians were better fighters than white men, wondered if he'd be scalped on his return, and requested Indian trophies. He talked about the foxhunting injuries he and Waterpark had sustained, shooting and fishing, a hunting party with the Prince of Wales, the loss of their new ironclad, *H.M.S. Captain*, and the recently begun Franco-Prussian War. He sent his and Waterpark's warm regards to Libbie—"I hope she is flourishing"—and asked for a photo of the Custers.[2] (All the officers were following the war news as it was the first armed conflict in Europe since Napoleon's defeat in 1815 and the Crimean War of 1854, and new weapons and tactics were anticipated.)

He went on to tell Armstrong he hadn't forgotten the cased Galand-Sommerville revolvers which his gunsmith—"the best man in London"—was making for Armstrong and Tom. It was a handsome gesture of appreciation, for a presentation revolver was perhaps the ultimate gift for officers and sporting gentlemen. The gun was blued steel and had cleaning tools, oiler, and twenty-five cartridges—all nestled in green velvet cutouts within a wooden box fitted into a monogrammed leather case.[3] (Tom Custer's cased Galand-Sommerville sold at auction for $77,000 in April 1995.) However, the best news was about the promised hound.

> I have also a Deer hound that I have bought for you. He is the best breed in Scotland. He is very fast. Has been "entered" at Deer and shown great pluck—I could have sent you a more handsome dog which I have got, but remembering your bitch, think that the one I am going to send to you will make the best crop—his name is "Grime" and will be invaluable to you on the Plains. I shall

send him and also the pistol to L.P. Morton of N. York with instructions for him to send them on to Fort Leavenworth to you. At some later date I will send you another dog and bitch if you will promise me to keep the breed pure. You will then I believe be the only man in America that has got it.[4]

In those days, dogs traveled in wooden crates and on ships, often confined in the hold. (Because of the heat, British ships going to India had foxhound kennels on deck.) Dogs were confined for long periods, but kindly agents at ports and rail depots could take the dogs out for exercise, relief, and food. They still fared poorly on long trips—assuming they didn't die or get loose. (In 1877, it cost £5.00 to ship a dog from England to New York[5]—over $500 in today's dollars. "Pinnacle Jake" Snyder noted that in the mid–1890s, it cost a whopping $36 each [$900 today] to ship five Russian Wolfhounds from Boston to northeastern Wyoming by rail.[6])

Grime could have arrived in New York as early as October 1870. He was sent to Levi P. Morton, who would ship him to Armstrong—probably through Col. Lamborne of the Kansas Pacific. There seem to have been no difficulties with Grime's immigration. When Libbie was eighty-four, she noted they had been sent other hounds from British officers serving in Canada upon their return to England.[7] (Paget knew Morton through his banking firm L.P. Morton & Company and the London branch, Morton, Rose, and Co. Morton was also a politician and President Benjamin Harrison's vice president in 1889.)

Silver Mining in New York

Armstrong had left Libbie at Fort Leavenworth in November. In Washington, he sat on a "Benzene Board," reviewing the fitness of officers. He attended plays in New York, returned to Monroe to settle Judge Bacon's estate and spent Christmas with his parents. He visited Barker and was back at Leavenworth in time for New Year's Eve with Libbie. Off again to New York on January 11, he traveled with his captured bear cub, intending to donate it to the Central Park Zoological Gardens' haphazard collection of animals in the old armory. He regretted giving up the bear but knew he couldn't keep it at his next post—which the rumor mill said was in Kentucky. Armstrong had secured a sixty-day leave to explore business prospects. He got three extensions and was away from his regiment for nearly eight months—hedging his bets again by leaving Army options open. During this long hiatus from the 7th, Armstrong returned to Leavenworth several times.

As the grapevine had predicted, orders came through in March that the companies of the 7th Cavalry were to be stationed in nine Southern states on Reconstruction duty—chiefly to bring order to communities plagued by lawlessness and Ku Klux Klan terrorism. The regiment left Fort Hays at the end of May, taking a week to get to Louisville where they would be split up. Company M with Tom Custer and his dogs went first to Darlington, South Carolina, and eventually to Oxford, Mississippi.[8] Sgt. Ryan was there with Tom and remembered that he had two favorite dogs with him—one of them, Topsy, was taught tricks by the men and frequently slept under Ryan's bunk.[9] The 7th's headquarters were at Elizabethtown, Kentucky. Armstrong had hoped his headquarters could be in Lexington or Louisville, which were more cosmopolitan and racing-oriented cities. Having a grand time in New York, he was in no hurry to get to provincial Elizabethtown.

Armstrong rubbed elbows with socialites, actors, artists and writers, and generally lived high on the hog. In an intriguing hint of what Armstrong might have been like in middle age, he wrote Libbie he had "grown so corpulent" that he needed suspenders to keep his trousers up.[10] He told her about the latest dress fashions, hairstyles, and his social activities. Repeating his teasing letters from New York and Washington in 1866, Armstrong talked of outings with Miss Clara Louise Kellogg, a famous soprano, the marital peccadillos of his New York friends, a nubile blonde flirting with him, and a young woman's blatant overture and her disappointment he was married—all while professing love for Libbie with assurances of his fidelity.[11] Given their recent marriage difficulties, it seems odd Armstrong would bedevil Libbie in this self-centered, passive-aggressive fashion, but then he did have his callous streak and always was able to mentally separate his love for Libbie from what he perceived as harmless flirtation.[12]

The celebrated Indian fighter and buffalo hunter had easy entry to the social circle of bankers and investors. Armstrong hoped to find his way into an investment scheme which would generate a substantial return despite his having little to invest. August Belmont and Col. Jairus W. Hall (an Ann Arbor man and colonel of the 4th Michigan Infantry) were developing the Stevens Lode Silver Mine outside of Georgetown in Colorado Territory. (Armstrong and Hall could have known each other from Michigan, the Civil War, or Reconstruction duty in Texas.) They pitched the investment opportunity to Armstrong who claimed to know the area.[13] He had indeed passed through Georgetown on the Kansas Pacific excursion and was impressed by the mineral wealth there—not that he had knowledge of prospecting or mining, but Armstrong knew there was excellent hunting and fishing there and friendly Utes. He had once hoped for a posting at Fort Garland.[14] Armstrong's reputation as a "frontiersman deluxe" who had actually seen Georgetown was considered qualification enough to be the mine's manager. He had no funds to invest but purchased shares on credit by paying a fraction of their value. He was able to persuade several affluent men to buy in, also with nominal down payments, including John Jacob Astor, Jr., James H. Banker, William R. Travers, and August Belmont.[15] These men were so wealthy, they would have been equally content with either the loss of token investments if the mine failed or the profit if it panned out.

Armstrong's part was to drum up backers with capital, and he and Hall would co-manage the Stevens Lode Mine. To entice an investment from railroad magnate and financier James "Diamond Jim" Fisk, Jr., Armstrong sent him a military-trained horse from his stable at Fort Leavenworth.[16] As it happened, Levi Morton (the banker and deerhound transfer agent) was one of the potential investors who received Armstrong's pitch, but he politely declined.[17] (James Fisk and his partner Jay Gould actually caused the Black Friday stock market crash of 1869, making millions themselves but ruining many businessmen.) Unfortunately, as he did in school and West Point, Armstrong tried to skate through the work, assuming that his name and schmoozing investors would produce the capital to work and expand the mine, and someone else would oversee the actual operations. Neither happened—and Armstrong never visited the mine. Eventually, the whole scheme began to collapse, but as late as June 1875, he was still working with Hall to salvage their investments by selling the mine for a share of future profits. For some reason, Armstrong, who rarely gave his dogs to anyone outside his clan, was sending some of his hounds to Hall in Chicago.[18] The reason for this dog deal is obscure, but it is evocative of Armstrong's attempt to curry favor with "Diamond Jim" with a gift horse.

The Pack in Elizabethtown

Armstrong's second Scottish Deerhound import arrived in New York at the end of April or early May 1871. On House of Commons stationery, Walter Powell wrote:

> I am very pleased to say that I have at last got what I believe to be a really good deer hound. The Head Forester of Mar Forest, one of the principal deer Forests in Scotland, got him for me, and gave him two good runs after deer. I enclose you one of his letters that you may see what he says.[19]

That letter was dated April 25, 1871, and Samuel Graves had made the arrangements for the deerhound to be shipped from Liverpool to a Mr. Riff in New York City.[20] Riff would transfer the hound to Col. Lamborne who then sent him by rail to Armstrong. The letter from head forester Alastair McDonald was written at Old Mar Lodge on April 5 and confirmed sending the "staghound" to Graves in Liverpool. McDonald also said that he had given the hound another run in the forest—where it chased a deer three miles, cornered it, and then bolted in to bite its throat for the kill. "No dog could [have] done better," said Alastair proudly.[21] Incongruously, Armstrong named that deerhound Possum.[22] Stags were only hunted with male deerhounds. Their shoulder height was typically just under 30" compared to the stags' 40" to 50" and 200 to 300 pounds. Powell had high hopes the hound would do well for Armstrong and invited him and Libbie to England for the hunting season as a partial repayment for "the magnificent sport you showed us with the buffalo."[23] They would not meet again. Powell became a ballooning enthusiast and, on an ascent in 1881, was blown out over the English Channel and disappeared. (Mar or Marr Forest was 60,000 acres in Aberdeenshire with granite mountains, glens, and streams and was estimated in the 1830s to have some 3,000 deer.[24] Old Mar Lodge belonged to James Duff, the 5th Earl Fife, who rented it to the Duke of Leeds, a hunter and breeder of Scottish Deerhounds. McDonald as estate forester could have gotten Possum from either peer.)

Armstrong continued his travels, and by June, Libbie was in Monroe and met him there briefly. Then he was off to the Saratoga races but asked her join him at the Barkers' in Grosse Ile toward the end of July.[25] In August, Armstrong was in New York attending the theater and working on the Stevens Lode investments as his leave was expiring. General Sheridan returned from observing the Franco-Prussian War and was in New York on September 1. Armstrong had just enough time to meet him and hear about the Prussian victory before leaving for Kentucky.[26] While in Pisa, Sheridan had taken part in a "driven" hunt arranged for him by King Victor Emanuel. A pack of sixty to seventy hounds and huntsmen drove a herd of deer through a fenced "funnel" past a hunting stand where Sheridan shot eleven at close range with a double-barreled shotgun.[27] He considered it to be no sport for a hunter, and Armstrong would have agreed with him. With no more leave extensions possible, on September 3, Armstrong rejoined his command as lieutenant colonel at Elizabethtown with only two companies. After a perfunctory appearance, he dashed up to Monroe to collect Libbie and planned to return via Louisville to purchase horses for the Army.[28] (Victorious armies became military fashion trendsetters, and after Kaiser Wilhelm I defeated the French, the American Army adopted Prussian-style uniforms and helmets in 1872. Armstrong even named one of his staghounds Kaiser.)

While Kentucky had been a Union state, it was home to a large population of Southern sympathizers and ex–Confederates. Apart from procuring government mounts in the finest horse country, the mission didn't thrill Armstrong, as it was essentially political—enforcing tax laws on legitimate distilleries, stopping illegal ones, and quelling the Ku Klux Klan's outrages against freed slaves and white sympathizers. It was like civilian peacekeeping in Texas but with U.S. marshals. There was no glory, and a trooper remembered it as "pretty dull soldiering."[29]

Armstrong's two companies of the 7th joined one company of the 4th Infantry in Elizabethtown. With no Army post, private buildings had to be rented, which meant that barracks, stables, guardhouse, hospital, and parade grounds were scattered around town. The officers lived in boarding houses, and "Aunt Beck" Hill rented rooms to the Custers.[30] Later, the Custers would share a house with Lt. Algernon Smith and his wife Nettie.[31] Smith was in Armstrong's circle and would eventually be given at least one staghound. (Aunt Beck's house was restored and donated to the town by her relatives in 1932. Now named the Brown-Pusey House, it serves as museum, library, and community center.)

Elizabethtown was nothing like Leavenworth—or even Monroe. It was rural and very poor. Libbie declared to Maggie Custer, "Everything is old, particularly the women.... The dog is sweet sixteen and can scarcely walk.... The most active inhabitant of this place is a pig." She noted that two, three, and four people would ride one horse bareback and "Everybody in Kentucky drinks."[32] The wooded hills of central Kentucky were a far cry from the horizon at Fort Hays, but for Libbie, the disadvantage to living in town (even a small one) was losing the Bohemian lifestyle she had come to love. Now, she had to fix up her hair daily and conform to social convention with different dresses for day and evening. The fact that E-town (as it was called by the locals, or Betsy-town by the Custers) received only scant attention in Libbie's published memoirs is evidence that the posting was no great experience.

They found ways to occupy themselves. Libbie threw herself into making clothes for herself, Armstrong, and Tom on her sewing machine.[33] Armstrong worked on his series of articles for *Galaxy* magazine (the New York competition for Boston's *Atlantic*). The Custers and their dogs sorely missed the freedom of the prairie. Libbie never said how many dogs they took to Kentucky, but it was probably a dozen or more—and again, because Armstrong wasn't on an expedition, there appear to be no letters between them which record their dogs' adventures and misbehaviors. The only dogs named in Elizabethtown were Old Rover, Driver and Ferguson the foxhounds and Lulu the deerhound—whose origin is unknown. While Libbie never explicitly says Lulu was a deerhound, in *Boots and Saddles*, she called her puppies "thorough-bred"—a term *only* used for their deerhounds.[34] (Libbie confirmed in her books the presence of both Rover and Lulu after leaving Kentucky.) For the Custers, not mentioning a particular dog might mean it was dead, missing, given away, or just that it wasn't doing anything noteworthy. After Texas, when their pack was re-expanding, it becomes harder to pin down names and quantity. They left nothing like a kennel history, and their pedigrees were lost. The two gift deerhounds from England were presumably in Elizabethtown, but Turk, Flirt and Barker's gift brace are not mentioned again—and yet the Custers had an enormous breeding population of staghounds and foxhounds by the time they left Kentucky in 1873.

Pleasure rides with the dogs were perhaps more meaningful in Elizabethtown where there were few Army couples, no band music, and not as many social opportunities as at Fort Leavenworth. The Custers' rides were confined to roads and meadows, and they had to be careful about letting the dogs run loose. Confined to the stable kennels for much of the time, the dogs weren't allowed to roam free. There would be no coursing jackrabbit and antelope, and the only hound sport Kentucky offered was hunting coon, fox, and deer. Armstrong participated in these, but they weren't the caliber of the hunts he had described in *Turf, Field and Farm*.

Armstrong was more disconnected from Sheridan than he cared for. He must have felt left out when he heard of the "millionaire's hunt" which Sheridan arranged in the very month Armstrong's extended leave ended. It was just Armstrong's cup of tea—a high-style buffalo hunt for twelve dignitaries and Army officers which lasted ten days. Buffalo Bill Cody was there to lend his expertise at Fort McPherson, Nebraska. Maj. Eugene A. Carr (a greyhound man) assigned Capt. William Henry Brown (breveted major) and one hundred 5th Cavalry troopers as the escort. Sheridan joined the hunt and brought his own greyhounds, including Cinch, an imported English bitch. Capt. Brown brought his greyhound to make a total of five on the hunt. Their hounds also rode in ambulances to keep them fresh for coursing jacks and antelopes.[35] Ironically, the sumptuous hunt finished near Armstrong's recent post, Fort Hays.

Nomad and Old Neutriment

Racing in the South had been put on hold during the war but afterwards, it bloomed prodigiously—and Elizabethtown was on the edge of Bluegrass Country where thoroughbred horse racing was business, recreation, and a way of life. One of Armstrong's duties was periodically inspecting and approving horses and mules for purchase. This required travel but still left him ample free time. Apart from the lack of prairie adventure and city lights, being an Army horse expert was a job which actually suited Armstrong, as he had time to conduct his own research at tracks and stud farms. He had caught the horseracing bug in Texas, but in Kentucky he was fever stricken. Armstrong easily embraced the culture and was sure that he could substantially augment his pay with thoroughbreds.

Historian Brian Dippie chronicled Armstrong's sporting life and observed, "Precious little has been written about Custer's stint in Kentucky—perhaps because precious little happened—".[36] During Armstrong's time there, he wrote five letters to *Turf*, but unlike the thrilling descriptions of his hunts and Indian exploits, he was reduced from being the hero of his narratives to a mere observer. He reported on track records, pedigrees, sale prices and winnings and devoted a third of one long letter to travel reviews—touting "Blue Grassonians" with their warm hospitality, excellent mutton, purest bourbon (he was still a teetotaler), and beautiful ladies who preferred to be blonde.[37] His dogs were scarcely mentioned in these letters, but the pack was growing. In the course of his socializing with the horsey set, he met Henry Price McGrath, who had started in the casino business and owned "McGrathiana"—500 acres of stud farm near Lexington. McGrath presented Armstrong with two foxhounds named Ferguson and Driver, who were excellent on deer.[38] (McGrath owned Aristides, the first Kentucky Derby winner, and McGrathiana would become the famous Coldstream Stud.)

For whatever reason, Armstrong's former strikers, Bowers and Bishop, were not with him in Kentucky, and a new one was needed to care for the horses and hounds. He chose Pvt. John W. Burkman, who was a simple illiterate man of few words but was devoted to the Custers and their animals. Libbie wrote affectionately about him as

> ... the strangest contrast to the whole party—dashing cavalryman, mettlesome horse, and rollicking dogs. Indeed, he seemed so much out of place in a cavalry camp that I always wanted to ticket him "Lost, strayed, or stolen." He was slow of speech, thought, and movement but in affectionate fidelity he was to be trusted above the gayer and more active trooper.... His horizon encompassed two horses, some dogs, and one yellow-haired officer.[39]

Born on January 10, 1839, Burkman was from Germany but on his enlistment papers declared he was from Pennsylvania in order to prevent any Army difficulties. (Armstrong was born the same year.) During the Civil War, Burkman was in and out of the Army serving volunteer hitches in the 5th Missouri Mounted Infantry, where he seems to have been a teamster. At age twenty-eight, he enlisted with the 7th Cavalry, A Company, in 1870 and then re-enlisted in September 1875 in L Company. He was a loner with no real friends and in Dakota would acquire the nickname "Old Neutriment" because of his bottomless appetite. He and Armstrong got along because of their mutual love of the horses and dogs. There is a distinct character to Burkman's rambling stories about the dogs, and while he may confuse places and dog names, the essence of Armstrong and Libbie and their dog life is there—"They was the orneriest pups you ever shook a stick at.... Seemed like they could think of more ways of gittin' into mischief and

A slow man of few words but deeply loyal to the Custers, Pvt. John Burkman ("Old Neutriment") was Armstrong's striker and dog tender from late 1871 through June 1876. Courtesy of the National Park Service, Little Bighorn Battlefield National Monument, LIBI_0019_00175. By Orlando S. Goff, Fort Lincoln, Dakota Territory, circa 1877.

raisin' hell general. But Custer and Miss Libby set great store by 'em."⁴⁰ He and Armstrong often argued but always settled on good terms. Burkman's special job was to take care of him on campaign. To the day he died, Burkman would be plagued with guilt that he didn't die on Last Stand Hill with his general. (The author of Burkman's memoirs retold his stories in an approximation of his colorful speech.)

In addition to the dogs, Burkman had charge of Armstrong's horses (both campaign and racing)—including Libbie's current favorite, Phil Sheridan. The striker quickly won her maternal affection through a simple but most considerate act. The Custers often made trips to Louisville, Lexington, Cincinnati, and Monroe, and while they were away on one of these, Phil Sheridan died. On their return, Burkman showed Libbie the shady green valley where he had the horse buried.⁴¹ Deeply touched, Libbie was steadfastly loyal to Burkman for the rest of his life. (Neither Burkman nor Libbie makes mention of the tremendous effort required for several men and horses to haul a dead horse from the stable to the countryside—and then dig a pit for him. Burkman remembers Phil dying on the march to Fort Rice, Dakota Territory, in the spring of 1873, but Libbie's memory is certainly more reliable.)

Armstrong and Libbie had talked for some time about his retirement and starting a stud farm in Bluegrass Country.⁴² Armstrong got a jump-start on becoming a "turf-man" by buying two race horses, Frogtown and Bluegrass. Along with trying to produce track winners who commanded large stud fees, he planned to breed hounds and sell their puppies. Burkman had his own version about how Armstrong got started with purebred dogs. "Wall, the General started out with one hound, a thoroughbred bitch some Englishman sent him as a present."⁴³ Before Maida was killed Armstrong had intended to breed her to Paget's deerhound, but there were Lulu and other bitches for his new stud dogs Grime and Possum. Of course, in order to profit from a purebred litter, a breeder has to be willing to let the puppies go.

> Trouble was when come time to sell 'em. 'Peared like he never could bear to part with one o' 'em hounds. Bein' full-blooded they could have made him a lot o' money, but if a buyer 'ud come along Custer'd get red in the face and hedge and stall, talkin' fast, tellin' a dozen reasons why he couldn't sell jist then.⁴⁴

Armstrong would often get out of a dog sale by having to "confer" with Libbie or else declare that they and the mother would miss the puppy too much. Offers of cash seldom topped his emotional attachment to them, and Burkman warned that if he kept every puppy, they would eat them out of house and home. Once, after refusing to sell one of Lulu's pups for the princely sum of $500, Armstrong said (in Burkman's words), "They's more in life than jist money, John. They's friendship, too, and faith. Lulu trusts us."⁴⁵

Not even a favorite dog could stay with them in Aunt Beck's boarding house, so they were kept at the company stables. Burkman made their food, bedded them down at night, and exercised them daily by riding with multiple dogs leashed in braces. If the weather was decent, Libbie rode with Burkman and the pack. More than three or four pairs of dogs at once would have been unmanageable, so Burkman must have taken them in relays (or perhaps had troopers assisting him). These outings often caused problems for the town residents and Burkman, for while the dogs were normally peaceable, they would furiously go after the dogs, cats, and pigs they came across. More than once, Libbie and Burkman made private restitution to spare Armstrong from the trouble. (The second Blucher may have been in this pack, for Bleuch, as Burkman called his favorite, was a terror when it came to strange dogs.)

One day, they came upon a fellow in a buggy with his bird dog. Burkman saw the trouble coming but was powerless to stop it. The pack's ferocious barking spooked the horses—and each man tried desperately to control them while swearing like muleskinners. The road dust swirled into a cloud, and Burkman could no longer restrain the hounds—"Might as well try to hold in a hurricane." When it was over, the poor bird dog had been torn to pieces. The man threatened to sue, demanding to know whose "hell-hounds" they were. Burkman refused to say and retreated with the story to Libbie. Ever the diplomat, she immediately paid a visit to the fellow who, as it turned out, was a friend of Armstrong's. He willingly backed off on his lawsuit threat, and she persuaded him to take one of their next puppies as partial recompense.[46] Armstrong was unaware of the conspiracies to shield him from these incidents. Nor did he notice the number of puppies being slightly reduced periodically—but then Armstrong can't have been close to every one of them.

Most men didn't pay attention to the estrus cycles of their dogs or confine bitches when in season, so doubtless there were both accidental and planned litters—a lot of them. Grime and Possum brought a welcome infusion of fresh blood into Armstrong's kennel—along with an aristocratic cachet. By the time the Custers were transferred from Kentucky in the spring of 1873, Burkman reckoned they had about eighty dogs. A pack that size could never have been managed by two people, but a lieutenant colonel could order soldiers to help with their care. With so many dogs, not all of them got as much attention as they wanted, and they were always jostling for a friendly word and ear scratch. Armstrong, Libbie, and Burkman each had their favorites—and the laconic striker summed up his relationship with the pack: "The General's hounds give me considerable trouble most of the time."[47] That would continue in Dakota Territory.

With the addition of Grime and Possum (who curiously aren't mentioned in his hunting stories), Armstrong had two proven hunters in his pack—which should have included the recent deerhounds from Barker and others of his own breeding. He boasted that he probably had "...the finest pack of Scotch staghounds in this country...."[48] Armstrong reported to Powell and Graves that he was quite happy with Possum. Graves wrote back, "Powell and I often refer to our day with the Buffalos—he is quite well and be glad to hear that 'Possum' has turned out well...."[49]

His Serene Highness Meets Uncle Sam

By January 1872, Armstrong was bored with cooling his heels in Elizabethtown and itching for action worthy of a cavalryman. Once again, Sheridan came to his rescue with a telegram version of the "Boots and Saddles" bugle call. The son of the Russian Tsar was on a three-month tour of the States which had begun in late 1871, and after a considerable round of diplomatic and civic functions, industrial tours, balls, and receptions, he wanted buffalo. Sheridan tasked Armstrong and Buffalo Bill Cody with staging a full Western experience to entertain His Imperial Highness, the Grand Duke Alexis.

The government would spare no expense, and that hunt would result in a unique addition to Armstrong's pack.

America's relationship with the Tsar was very friendly, for the government had bought the entire Alaska Territory from Russia in 1867 for $7 million. The Alaskan purchase greatly helped Russian finances and prevented the British from expanding the Dominion of Canada to Russia's back door. America was grateful for the Baltic Fleet's visit in 1863—a gesture of "...Russia's solidarity with the Union at a time when Britain and France were leaning towards recognition of the Confederacy."[50] It was most important that the Grand Duke be favorably impressed by America. (The unpopular purchase of the Alaska Territory was called "Seward's Folly" or "Seward's Icebox" after Secretary of State William Seward.)

Grand Duke Alexis Alexandrovich Romanov (1850–1908) was the third son of Tsar Alexander II, whose Romanov lineage stretched back to Peter the Great and beyond. (He was the uncle of the last tsar, Nicholas II, executed in 1918 after the Bolshevik Revolution.) Alexis was a tall man, good looking, with a thin mustache, long sideburns, and bedroom eyes. He was cultured and spoke Russian, French, and very good English. "You must experience everything in life" was his personal motto. He was considered the handsomest man in the Imperial family and an "International *bon vivant.*"[51] Alexis had a great fondness for hunting, champagne, and beautiful women—but not necessarily in that order.

Russian Grand Dukes were directly related to the Tsar and expected to have military careers. Alexis was a lieutenant on the armed steam frigate *Svetlana* (he would later become grand admiral of the Navy but was too focused on his own pleasure to take the post seriously). When not on military service, wealthy royals had little to do but entertain themselves, and hunting was a prime diversion. Alexis had shot bear and other game, and his relatives had hunted wolves and stag with Russian Wolfhounds, which were seldom seen outside of Russia. (Properly named *barzoi* at the time, the dog was called by function and place of origin—"Siberian or Russian Wolfhound/Greyhound/Deerhound/staghound" or, more elegantly, the "fan-tailed greyhound.")

In August 1871, the *Svetlana*'s squadron sailed into New York harbor. The sedately dressed Grand Duke was a bit of a disappointment to Americans who were expecting regal raiment.[52] The affable royal was feted in New York City, although in Washington there was no White House reception because of a current impasse with the Russian minister. Apart from shabby treatment in the capital, Alexis was well received in America. Traveling in a suite of five palatial Pullmans, he had two sleeping cars, a drawing room car, and commissary and baggage cars.[53] Special timetables were made for his train and the lines cleared for his tour of several states. In every city there was an onslaught of feminine attention and dalliances.

Before Alexis even landed in America, the famous Western landscape painter Albert Bierstadt suggested to General Sherman that he might enjoy the unique experience of hunting buffalo. After funding for the grand hunt was approved by Secretary of War William Belknap, Sheridan was delegated to make it happen.[54] He tasked Armstrong and Cody to be in charge of the hunt itself while he planned the overall logistics of the two-day "hunting campaign" in Nebraska with military precision. The previous September after returning from Europe, Sheridan and his staff arranged the "millionaires' hunt."[55] Cody was Sheridan's choice for shepherding hunting dignitaries around the Plains. (In the fall of 1872, he and his friend John "Texas Jack" Omohundro were guides for Alexis Windham Thomas Wyndham-Quinn, the 4th Earl of Dunraven—another wealthy tourist hunter.[56])

The 2nd Cavalry provided the necessary troops, ambulances, spare horses, and supply wagons loaded with tents, carpets, stoves, and firewood. Luxuries included silverware, gourmet food, cigars, liquor, and champagne—crates and crates of champagne. To ice the already extravagant cake, Sheridan arranged through intermediaries for Chief Spotted Tail's band of friendly Brulé Sioux to put on a colorful display of warfare, hunting, and dancing. (Spotted Tail's fee for his tribe's participation was a thousand rations of tobacco and ten thousand rations each of coffee, sugar, and flour.[57])

On January 13, Alexis' special train arrived at the North Platte Station, and there he met Cody who was wearing one of his fancy buckskin coats trimmed with embroidery.[58] From there, the ducal party and entourage rode out in carriages led by Cody as scout. (He and Sheridan knew that area from the millionaires' hunt.) After a full day of travel, the column reached a large military camp on Red Willow Creek named in honor of Alexis. The Stars and Stripes were flying, and the band struck up the Russian national anthem—but Armstrong was missing. His ambulance had broken down, but before a search party could be dispatched, the "Hero of the Plains" jauntily walked over a ridge with his buffalo rifle on his shoulder.[59] (Cody and Armstrong both knew how to make an entrance.) He was also familiar with the area, as he had blazed a trail through it during the Hancock Expedition.[60] Armstrong had further cause to remember the trail, as his two greyhounds Lu and Sharp had died there of heat exhaustion.

The following morning, after riding out on snowy ground to locate the herd, Armstrong and Cody instructed Alexis on the sport. There were a few dwindling herds of European bison left in Poland and Russia, but they were stalked rather than shot from a galloping horse, so this would be entirely new to Alexis. To help ensure his success, Cody loaned him Buckskin Joe, his best buffalo horse. According to the decorum of royal visits everywhere, Alexis was to have the first kill before anyone else could hunt, and there was great relief when he got his bull and cut off the tail for a fly switch. Fortunately, Alexis never injured himself, but his assigned trooper was nearly killed when his horse tripped in a prairie dog hole and threw him.[61] The expedition went very much as had Armstrong's other tourist hunts—although this one had a loftier tone with better food and more liquor. In the evenings, there was feasting, drinking, and singing, and Cody and Armstrong regaled the grand duke's company with tales of the Civil War, wild hunts, and Indian fighting. Being hastily summoned from Elizabethtown, Armstrong did not have his usual hunting clothes and gear.[62] Nor did he have his striker, horses, and hounds. However, he piqued Alexis' interest by talking about coursing his hounds on the prairie, which contrasted greatly with Russian hunts for hare, fox, and wolf, which were huge affairs with nobility, servants, beaters, and sometimes dozens of wolfhounds (often loosed from moving sleighs)—where the goal was to capture the bayed wolf alive by forcing a stick between its jaws and tying its muzzle shut.[63]

In a buffalo hunt with the Brulé warriors, Alexis was astonished to see them kill a bull with a single razor-sharp arrow which passed clean through the chest, and he

Armstrong and the Grand Duke Alexis Alexandrovich Romanov with his little dog. This photograph was taken in 1872 after the ducal buffalo hunt in Nebraska. Armstrong lies on a buffalo hide with his sport-converted Model 1866 "Trapdoor" Springfield rifle. A buffalo tail fly-whisk is artistically draped over the wooden branch above him. Alexis wears a European hunting suit, holds a large caliber revolver in one hand, and cuddles a dog in the other. Alexis would send Armstrong two Russian Wolfhounds, and when he returned to America in 1877, he brought along his own dog—but nothing is known about the little fellow in this photograph. Prints & Photographs, Library of Congress. LOT 11156-5.

asked for one as a souvenir. Spotted Tail's band danced and sang and staged a mock tribal battle. The Russians loved it, but such things were unnerving for soldiers whose friends and relatives had been killed by war parties.[64] After two days, Alexis had four kills to his credit with trophy heads, hides, and tails to decorate his St. Petersburg mansion. The group headed by train for Colorado where at Alexis' insistence, they had another hunt. He bagged five more buffalo—and shot six from the train on their return to Kansas.[65] Alexis got on famously with Armstrong, and in St. Louis, the two posed for studio photographs with guns on display—Armstrong in buckskins and Alexis in a double breasted woolen suit—very reminiscent of a German *jäger*, for he wore the short sword used by European hunters to deliver the *coup de grâce* to wounded stag, boar, and bear.

Alexis' party (now including Armstrong) returned east and, after leaving Louisville, headed south to see Mammoth Cave. On the way to Cave City, the train stopped briefly in Elizabethtown where Alexis inspected Armstrong's horses and hounds. The two spent so much time talking about them that they had to skip the planned civic function to get to the cave on time. This peeved the Elizabethtown locals somewhat—although they were pleased *they* had a visit from the grand duke—who had ignored

The greyhound types known in Europe and America in 1881—standing, Persian Greyhound (Saluki), the diminutive Italian Greyhound, English Greyhound, and Scottish Deerhound. Lying down, the Siberian/Russian Wolfhound (Borzoi). Excluding the Italian and Persian Greyhounds, Armstrong had the other three breeds.

the waiting citizens of Cincinnati.[66] (Despite the newspaper accounts confirming he was traveling with Alexis, a local version has Armstrong riding up horseback to meet the train with a leash of hounds.[67])

Naturally, Libbie charmed Alexis, and she was invited to join the rest of the tour, taking in Memphis and enjoying Mardi Gras in New Orleans. (Alexis was the second member of the Imperial family the Custers had met, for they had hosted Prince Ourosoff [*sic*], at Fort Riley in 1866.[68]) For Libbie, the New Orleans holiday was a tonic, and she enjoyed the whirl of fancy dinners, sleeping late, and being served coffee and rolls in bed.[69] They parted company on February 19 when Alexis entrained for Mobile, Alabama, and from there sailed to the *Svetlana* at Pensacola, Florida. The squadron went to Japan before reaching Vladivostok, where Alexis took the train across Siberia for home. He was in St. Petersburg in December—sixteen months after departing. Summarizing what the public remembered about Alexis' visit, one editor quipped, "He loved also our buffaloes and our belles...."[70] In the papers, the reported number of his buffalo kills varied between a sarcastic "one" to the preposterous "hundreds."

Alexis liberally gave large sums of money and expensive gifts to Americans who had helped make his trip memorable, and Libbie noted, "The royal purse has no string." He donated money for the poor in New York and Boston and a princely $5,000 for the homeless victims of the recent Chicago fire.[71] After he returned home at the end of 1872, ducal presents continued to be sent overseas, and Alexis asked a relative to send two wolfhounds to Armstrong. (The Grand Duke Alexis' first cousin, the Grand Duke Nicholas Nikolayevich—not to be confused with his father of the same name—established the renowned Perchina Kennels which boasted wolfhounds, English foxhounds, and Russian harriers.[72])

Publication, Vaccination and New Orders

After Alexis departed, the Custers ended their luxurious vacation, returned to Elizabethtown, and then went up to Monroe for a wedding. Maggie Custer married the handsome Lt. James Calhoun on March 7. Armstrong had already expanded the Custer Clan by helping his brother Boston to get a position as forage agent (the same easy job which Emanuel Custer had in Texas) and, later that summer, arranged for his new brother-in-law to be transferred into the regiment. The rest of 1872 was fairly humdrum. Armstrong wrote *Galaxy* articles and his war memoirs and dabbled with his thoroughbreds. There were horse-buying trips and intermittent efforts to salvage the Stevens Mine. Letters from Townsend, Ainsworth and Graves went back and forth between Kentucky and England, and Armstrong's former guests sent him news of their doings and European politics, and he reciprocated. (Townsend and Ainsworth still hadn't found their buffalo head trophies.) All the Englishmen said repeatedly how much they enjoyed their "scamper through the Great West."[73]

By August 1872, Graves was convinced that Armstrong's published adventures would be popular in England and began writing to him about getting him published—American copyright laws permitting. (His articles about Indian wars and hunting began appearing in the *Galaxy* in January that year, and the complete series was published as *My Life on the Plains* in late 1874.) Graves found a publisher who was confident that a book by Armstrong would sell very well in England. Armstrong sent some "specimen chapters," but they were lost in the mail. So he could put together a proposal, Graves kept after Armstrong to re-send them along with a "photograph of yourself in war or hunting gear on horseback."[74] He did all the legwork, securing the publisher's approval based on the replacement chapters and calculating the book's price, but he could never get Armstrong to make a definite proposal about the content and form.[75] His correspondence with Graves was erratic even though he was considerably less busy than he was at Fort Hays—and given his passion for writing, it's unclear why Armstrong did not produce the materials (copyright was no longer an issue)—unless it was that the paid *Galaxy* pieces were fully occupying him. Despite four months of Graves' energetic work and a willing publisher, the whole effort to get Armstrong published in England collapsed in late 1872 and Graves gave up trying.

Armstrong's extended horse-buying trips were hard for Libbie—who seems to have forgiven the 1870 offenses. He was in New Orleans when she wrote to "My Darling Autie" after Thanksgiving, saying several times how lonely she was without him.

> Today has been about a week long.... Now my surroundings are pleasant—all our household litter is again about me—books, brackets, pictures, whips & dog horn—but I am so alone. I know that day by day, I depend more upon you.

Libbie referred to herself as "your little snoozy poozy" and included news of their community, fixing up the house, the coming winter cold, the need for an honest maid, and she said that Frogtown's illness was affecting his track time. She signed the letter, "Your Own Loving Bunkey, Libbie." Apparently, there was no significant dog news.[76]

As it turned out, Armstrong finally did have something doggy for *Turf*. His last Nomad letter with dog and hunting exploits was published in November 1869, and after a three-year dearth of anything remarkable to say about his dogs, he suddenly had a triumph. In his last letter to *Turf* from Kentucky in January 1873, Armstrong covered the previous autumn's Louisiana Jockey Club meet and told a slightly lurid story of how the track winner and stud horse Lexington escaped castration when the knife slipped and cut the man's hand instead of the testicles. In the final paragraph, Armstrong boasted about his successful distemper vaccination program.

"Warwick" had written a scholarly letter to *Turf*, complete with citations, about the proven unreliability of trying to prevent distemper in dogs by variolation with cowpox matter.[77] The two diseases had similar symptoms, but no one knew that distemper's cause was a microorganism. In 1798, Dr. Edward Jenner had been successful using cowpox vaccinations to prevent smallpox in humans. He was the first scientist to distinguish distemper from hydrophobia and had tried unsuccessfully to prevent canine distemper by cowpox inoculations on the 5th Earl of Berkeley's foxhounds.[78] (Death by distemper was miserable but dogs that survived it had immunity—and were consequently valuable.) Based on Jenner's successes, the British Army and Navy began smallpox inoculations, and Americans soon followed suit. There was increased interest in inoculation by scientists attempting to prevent bovine anthrax, fowl cholera, equine grease heel, cowpox, horsepox, and canine distemper. Controversy seethed about which techniques worked or didn't—or whether any worked at all. Typically, cowpox or grease heel matter or an infected dog's nasal mucus was introduced into the puppy via the nostrils or a snipped hole in the skin. Of course, Armstrong had an opinion on the topic. He told Warwick and the readers about his method and predictably began, "I have probably the finest pack of Scotch staghounds in this country, and each year had lost many valuable dogs from distemper, until I concluded to try vaccination." He even said sometimes most of a litter died from distemper—the first time he ever admitted this in print. Armstrong doesn't say which inoculation matter he used but advocated the "operation" on young dogs just inside the foreleg in the armpit where it was difficult to lick the resulting painful scab. He ended with the proud statement, "One of my bitches dropped a litter of eleven. These I caused to be vaccinated as soon as old enough, and every one of them grew finely and are still alive and well."[79] Distemper vaccinations were interesting enough for dog men but, on the whole, fairly humdrum. However, in ten months' time, Armstrong would again have hunting epics for *Turf*.

One day in February 1873, Armstrong received word from Lt. Smith, his adjutant, that the 7th was being transferred to the Dakota Territory. As he usually did with happy news, he bounced around the room, sweeping Libbie into his arms—waltzing and knocking over furniture. Libbie confessed she had to get an atlas to find out where Dakota was and was crestfallen to learn that it was so close to the "British Possessions," it might as well be Lapland. When the laughter subsided, they began packing.[80] Kentucky had been no place for the Custers or their deerhounds. Armstrong was to regroup the regiment, move it to Dakota, and prepare for an expedition. On the way to Fort Rice, he would meet serious hound men—the Sporting Club of the 22nd Infantry.

TAIL PIECE: RUSSIAN WOLFHOUNDS EMIGRATE TO AMERICA

Russian Wolfhounds are believed to have originated in the late 1700s when nobles crossed Persian Greyhounds (Salukis) with larger, more thickly coated hounds in the Caucasus.[81] Beginning in 1845 with a gift to Queen Victoria, they began appearing outside of Russia.[82] Breed history has the first Russian Wolfhound imported to America from England in 1889. However, Russian Wolfhounds had been hunting on the American prairie since the early 1870s. In 1872, Mr. McDonald made a hunting trip across the prairie toward Denver with an oxen-drawn wagon and two "beautiful Russian stag hounds."[83] (They were speedily recognized by the AKC in 1891, and the breed name changed to Borzoi in 1936.)

In 1878, a British rancher by the name of Smith used three "Siberian wolf hounds" on the wolves killing his cattle in Nebraska.[84] Western ranchers went to great lengths to obtain them, and in 1897, Fort Riley's hunt pack had four which were also exhibited at dog shows. (In 1887, Fort Riley became the U.S. Army's Cavalry School, which in 1895 formed the Cavalry School Hunt with a drag-hunting pack of foxhounds.) Curiously, the 27th Infantry became "The Wolfhound Regiment" after it was given a Borzoi mascot in recognition of their fight against the Bolsheviks in Siberia from 1918 to 1920.[85]

Chapter 10

Paw Prints on the Yellowstone

"He had a habit of throwing himself prone on the grass for a few minutes' rest and resembled a human island, entirely surrounded by crowding, panting dogs."
—Katherine Gibson Fougera[1]

Moving a self-sufficient cavalry regiment out of the States was a migration of semi-biblical proportion. Libbie estimated there were eight or nine hundred men and as many horses. The men, horses, mules, ambulances and supply wagons were first priority, but also necessary were rations and forage, massive amounts of personal luggage (of which officers were allowed considerable), weapons, saddles, ammunition—and equipment for surgeons, veterinarian, blacksmith, carpenter, farrier, and saddler, as well as the regimental records. The wives, civilian servants, laundresses, and a sutler had to be accommodated, as did Libbie's caged canaries and mockingbirds, a cat or two—and the ubiquitous dogs.

The 7th Cavalry was to escort a survey expedition and protect construction crews of the expanding Northern Pacific Railway from warring Indians. The scattered companies assembled in Louisville and Memphis where steamboats carried them to Cairo, Illinois. There, the reunited regiment was loaded onto trains heading for the territorial capital, Yankton (South Dakota), taking over a week to get there. Passenger cars were up front and livestock and flatbed cars at the rear. In a stock car, Burkman was tending to the Custers' horses and the deerhounds Lulu, Blucher II, and Tuck (and presumably other hounds including Rover, Grime, and Possum). Lulu had been mated in Elizabethtown, and her belly was swollen with puppies. Several times daily, the train halted for watering the horses, and Libbie remembered, "My husband and I always went on those occasions to loose the dogs and have a frolic and a little visit with our own horses." Local children delighted to see a general playing with dogs.[2] From Yankton, the regiment would march over 400 miles north in dodgy spring weather along the Missouri River's eastern bank to Fort Rice, south of Bismarck. (The silt-laden Missouri River or "Big Muddy," was described as "...too thick to drink and too thin to plow"—a catch phrase also applied to the Colorado and Platte rivers and the Rio Grande.)

Libbie's thirty-first birthday (April 8) was celebrated on the train with steaks and macaroons hastily obtained at a stop. Lulu gave birth to nine puppies in her car, which the Custers went back to admire. She was given extra food and a special bed, but when Burkman opened the car door for air, she leapt out and disappeared on the prairie. Making his way forward, he reported Lulu's escape. Armstrong was furious, believing

Burkman had been asleep on duty. He actually stopped the train to search for Lulu—but with no luck.[3] Burkman did his poor best for the newborns—keeping them in a basket and feeding them hardtack soaked in water.[4] At a watering stop, Armstrong came back with a smile on his face to check on the puppies and admitted he knew Lulu's escape wasn't Burkman's fault. "Everything right between us John?" Burkman agreed and later said, "Seemed like you couldn't hold a grudge agin Custer when he kept lookin' at you that way and smilin'."[5] The incident became a running joke between them. After the birth of subsequent litters, Burkman reported to Armstrong with a salute, "I have the honor General, to say that Ginnie has nine puppies." Armstrong would give a solemn look and ask, "Did any of them get away?" Burkman answered, "No," while trying to hide his laughter.[6] (Burkman wouldn't have known the Texas Ginnie, so there was a second dog of that name.)

The regiment unloaded at Yankton on the 10th and 11th—"Sich brayin' and bayin' and whinerin' and hollerin' and cussin' you never heerd, the men workin', the officers gallopin' back and forth, given' orders."[7] The territory's capital was a disappointing collection of wood houses, rutted roads, and a "frame hostelry called a hotel... little more than a glorified barn..." with equally poor furnishings.[8] Armstrong was unhappy with the original ground and moved the whole camp farther away from town.[9] Libbie got off the train and could only stare at the empty prairie, which Burkman described as "Cactus, and prairie dogs and rattlesnakes and the wind—allus [sic] and furever [sic] the wind."[10] The Custers' luggage was arranged into a corral to confine puppies and "half-grown dogs." The weather was warm with rainfall, but during the night the wind came up, the temperature dropped and the rain became sleet and snow "...comin' down thicker'n molasses in January."[11] On Monday the 14th, the ground was thick with snow and a proper blizzard was blowing up. It went from bad to worse.

The tents were blowing down, so Armstrong and Libbie settled in a small, unfinished log house, fortifying it against the wind and snow with bedding, luggage, and carpets. To Burkman, it was "...jist an empty hut, dirt floor, no stove—nothing, and the logs so far apart you could throw a cat through."[12] Armstrong gave his officers and men permission to shelter with the Yankton civilians, but he stayed at the snow camp with Libbie and their servants, Mary and Ham, and Burkman. As the snow drifts piled higher, several troopers joined them, and mules and hogs tried to force their way inside—threatening to collapse the walls. Uncharacteristically, Armstrong became too sick to walk, and Libbie had to dose him with medicine. There wasn't much food, but Mary heated up hardtack and beans with candles from the train. The Custers' chained dogs curled up under wagons, and Burkman scrounged bacon and hardtack for them—and then made the decision to loose them to find better shelter. By then it was dark and still blowing snow. Despite a candle in the shack's window, Burkman became disoriented and sleepy in the drifts. In the beginning stages of hypothermia and thinking he was going to die, he suddenly felt a shaggy body next to his leg and heard a whine. Blucher (Bluech) led him to the shack, and in telling the story, Burkman was convinced the hound was looking for him—and it was lucky he had unchained the hounds.[13] Periodically, Libbie would hear a dog howling outside—but when they opened the door, it had disappeared. (In Dakota Territory, stables were built near houses, and in winter, a rope was strung between them so that during a snowstorm a rancher wouldn't lose his way.[14])

With little food, for thirty-six hours the small group withstood the blizzard. Troopers took hay to the horses (many froze to death), and Burkman got food to the hounds. Strangely, he had stashed Lulu's puppies in a basket under a wagon, but as the snow worsened, he nestled them in a packing crate with an Army blanket and left the lid open a crack for air. On one of his trips through the drifts, he found the crate buried with the puppies dead and dying and was unable to save any (Burkman didn't know that newborn puppies cannot regulate body temperature and depend upon their mother's body for warmth). The ground was frozen, so he tenderly wrapped the puppies in a blanket and put them deep into a drift to hide them from coyotes—at least for a while. Burkman knew many soldiers who did not have burials as good as that one.[15]

The storm subsided, Armstrong got better, and one of the laundresses had given birth in a tent in the snowstorm. Eleven of the Custers' hounds (and Lulu's puppies) died. It is extremely curious that Libbie did not insist their favorite dogs and the newborns be brought inside as both humans and dogs would have benefited from the combined body heat. Blucher, Tuck and other hounds somehow survived the blizzard, but the Dakota weather would continue to be a trial for the hounds. It took four days to dig the camp out of snow, and Libbie learned Dakota weather was "eight months of winter and four of very late in the fall."[16] ("The Custer Storm of 1873," as it became known, paralyzed the area for two days.[17])

Armstrong inexplicably became sullen and went a tear about discipline—ordering hours of drilling and "make-work" labor. There were desertions, and officers complained to Col. Sturgis, who then rejoined his regiment but said nothing to Armstrong. After twenty days of repair and recuperation, they marched north on May 7 in the usual formation—beef herd and wagons at the rear, column of fours in front with scouts on the flanks, all led by Armstrong and the band.[18] Libbie and Maggie Calhoun rode with the column, with an ambulance available for them and the dogs. Steamboats carrying regimental supplies and forage leapfrogged them up the river, generally rendezvousing each day. Seeing that Armstrong's hounds were an obstreperous lot, Asel Keyes, who managed "citizen transportation" on the steamboat *Miner*, gave him "...a long whip with which he could chastise his dogs from the saddle."[19] Presumably this was welcome, for Armstrong had been using a wagon whip to keep his hounds in line since Texas.

Marching to Fort Rice

The regiment entered the reservation of the Yankton Sioux (Ihanktonwan Dakota) on May 12. The first village had many dogs which ran out to confront the strangers—barking, snarling, and biting at the legs of the horses, mules, and cattle. Armstrong ordered his pack to be tied up in wagons. Unhappy with menacing village dogs, they howled and barked, raising an awful din which lasted until the column was away from the village. It was a peaceful reservation, but troopers itching to forcefully stop the Sioux dogs were restrained by their officers.[20] The same problem happened at Greenwood, and again Armstrong's dogs were tied in wagons. By then, the troopers were growing angry at this perceived humiliation, and when they pressed for permission to shoot,

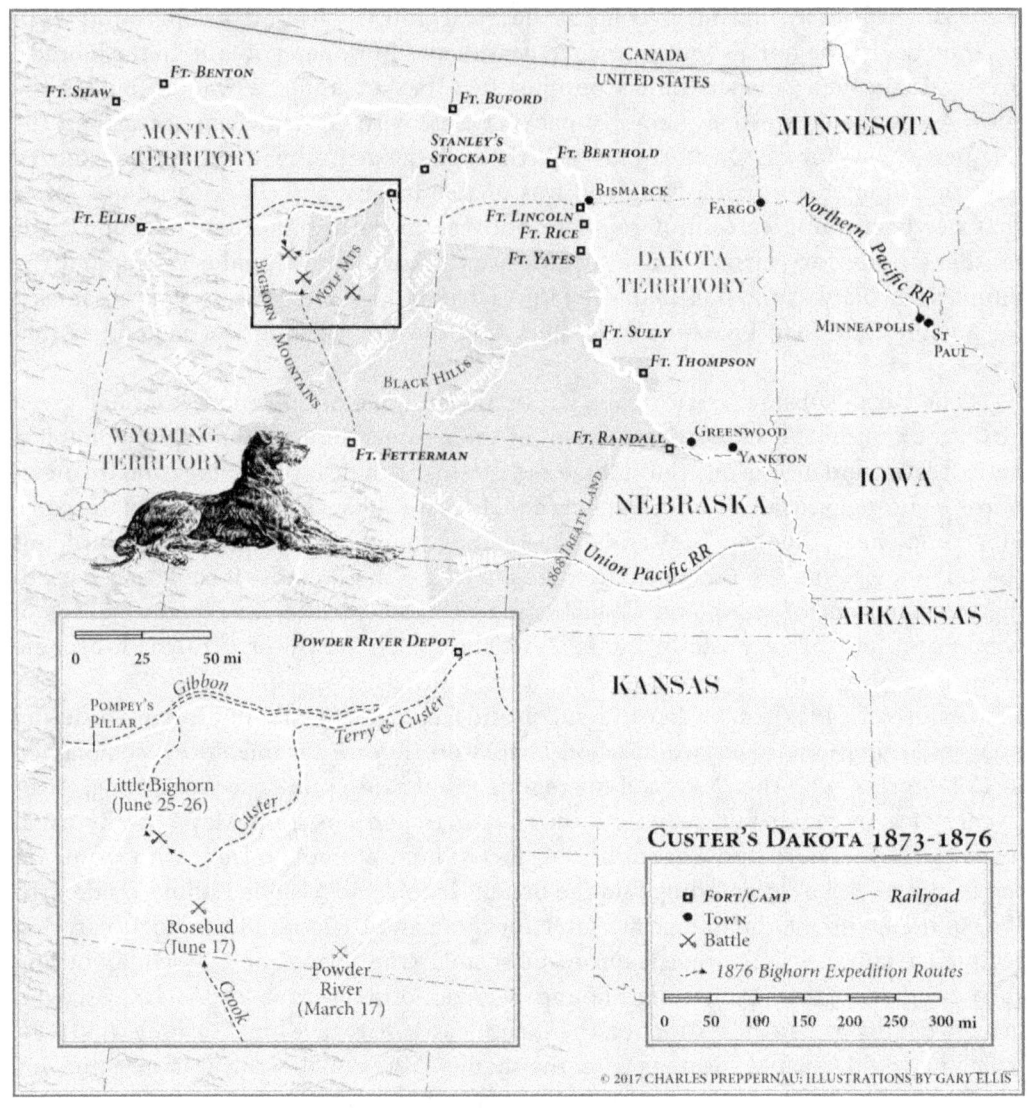

Custer's Dakota 1873–1876

with seemingly no alternative, the order was given, presumably by Sturgis or Armstrong. They fired at any dog approaching the column.[21]

The 7th's first blood in Dakota must have been a *déjà vu* moment for the Washita veterans when those village dogs were shot. Boys and girls wanting to save their pets dashed out from houses into the line of fire. Mothers tried to rescue their children amidst gunshots, terrified horses, shouting soldiers, screaming women, and barking dogs. An uncounted number of Sioux were accidentally killed—probably including women and children. Horrified at the carnage, the headman of the reservation sent word out to the other villages who cleared out to avoid the horse soldiers who killed people and dogs.[22] The 7th marched on, not bothering to count the dead.

Armstrong, wearing a red flannel shirt, buckskins and a wide-brimmed hat, was always in the lead with Libbie not far away but comfortably out of the column's dust. With the next fresh water always uncertain, she learned not to drink between halts but did save water for the hounds who were usually parched from continual activity. On the noon halts to water nearly a thousand horses and eat lunch, Burkman cleared the ground of rattlesnakes with his saber and rigged canvas between two wagons for shade with another piece for a ground cloth. Riding sidesaddle for hours was hard on Libbie's legs, and she was glad to stretch and lie down. The Custers would have their meal (Burkman often cooked a freshly shot prairie chicken), and afterwards Armstrong and hounds would sleep together in a pile. Blucher, Tuck, and Lady would curl up beside Libbie who staked out the deep shade under a wagon: "...I had to dislodge a whole collection of dogs, who soon find the best places for their comfort."[23] Armstrong could nap in sunlight, but if he and Libbie were far from the column (always with an escort), he would construct Indian-style shade for their naps. With willow saplings, he made a rectangular framework, bending the tops toward each other and loosely weaving them together. With a couple of saddle blankets thrown on top, they had shade. First Libbie would nap, then Armstrong, and then the dogs.[24] (This temporary Indian shelter was called a *wickiup*, and when soldiers found these in abandoned villages, they often mistook them for dog kennels.)

Armstrong still reserved the right to select each night's camp, and the regiment's process for setup followed the same process each day. It was fast and efficient but, to the untrained eye, seemingly chaotic with "...hustle and bustle, hounds and horses," orders, jokes, band tunes, mules braying, and Armstrong everywhere, dashing back and forth on his horse.[25] Tenderfoot Katherine Garrett remembered when Mess Call sounded, the dogs, horses, and mules all made a huge noise.[26] The Custers had a large canvas fly under which they spent their evenings. Both read books, and Libbie mended clothes—always with the dogs around them. As Burkman put it, "You never seen him anywhar without a half a dozen trailin' at his heels or fightin' for a place in his lap."[27] Their tent had two folding chairs, their bed (a mattress atop three planks on two short sawhorses), a washbowl, and a bucket. A mirror hung from the tent pole, but the wind kept it constantly moving, so as she had on the marches in Texas, Libbie did her hair without it.[28] A seasoned campaigner, she wore one dress in camp and her riding habit for the day's march. She knew not to complain about things or keep the column waiting.

While the Missouri's east bank was supposedly safe from war parties, a close call for Libbie happened on the march to Fort Rice. She was out hunting with Armstrong when he dashed after the hounds chasing a deer, leaving her with one of his friends. They rode on, keeping an eye on the younger dogs so they wouldn't stray, and stumbled upon young warriors sitting quietly in the underbrush capture (the officer had ignored the Indian warning signs). Libbie was terrified. Not only was there a threat of capture, but to prevent it, the officer would shoot her. The warriors, with rifles in hand, mounted their ponies, but the officer coolly told them many soldiers were nearby. The Indians were persuaded and left peacefully.[29] (The possibility of a preemptive "mercy killing" by a friend was understood by all officers' wives, sisters, and daughters on the frontier—but rarely talked about.)

Armstrong and Tom continued to play jokes on each other and the civilian guests.

Katherine Garrett, the sister-in-law to Lt. Donald McIntosh, was nervous about sleeping with only canvas between her and the prairie. Tom suggested a padlock on the tent to keep her safe, and she agreed. Armstrong ordered one to be installed while poker-faced officers stood by waiting for Katherine to realize she had been "guyed."[30] She remembered there were "hordes of dogs" in the 7th, and Armstrong and Tom owned forty of them.[31] (Forty is the standard number given for Armstrong's pack in Dakota and a good number in story-telling. Ali Baba had Forty Thieves, Moses was on Mt. Sinai for forty days and nights, Christ fasted for forty days in the desert, and so forth.) The dogs were all tied up at night, but once Katherine sensed a dog in her tent (which were all supposedly tied up) and called every dog name she remembered, including Brandy (who would've been at least six years old), but without result. It took her offered hardtack, ran out and was shot by the sentry. It was a wolf, and the noise roused the camp and dogs.[32] Duplicating Libbie's wolf experience on Big Creek, doubtless Katherine wished she could have padlocked her tent.

The troopers might only see Armstrong's dogs from afar while they were marching (or even on the post), and while foxhound, setter, and bull-dog types were well known, most were unaware of the distinctions between the sighthound breeds. If a dog had long legs, a long nose, a deep chest and a narrow waist, it was a "greyhound"—regardless of whether it was one, or a Scottish Deerhound (often gray in color), Russian Wolfhound, or a cross-bred staghound. Sometimes they were just "hounds." Sgt. Charles Windolph of H Company said, "Custer went in for dogs pretty heavy" and called them "a small pack of wolf hounds."[33] Whatever they were called, their chases after game within sight of the column were a bit of entertainment.

Keeping within easy range of the Missouri, but cutting across its oxbow bends, they marched generally north. There was no trail and soldiers were continually worked to get the wagons through—clearing paths, hauling them up and down gullies, and even building bridges when the creeks were too deep. Armstrong, Tom, and their hounds were always hunting, and fifteen-year-old bugler Louis E. Hills of E Company described Tom's staghounds coursing jackrabbits as a "wonderful sight." When the hounds closed on the speeding jack, it would abruptly turn, leaving the slower turning hounds behind—briefly. One jack, a veteran of many a wolf pursuit, surprised three staghounds by suddenly stopping and flattening on the ground. Each hound tried to snatch the jack as they galloped over it, but all stumbled, turning somersaults and crashing, while the jack got up and ran away.[34] (Hills' account of the 1873 Yellowstone expedition was published in the *Journal of History* in April 1915, but the coursing details in his original manuscript were omitted.)

Armstrong frequently left the column, going off with the hounds to shoot deer, bear, buffalo and the ubiquitous antelope. Going after a bull elk, Blucher ran it down, grabbed hold, and despite being injured by kicking hooves, he refused to let go until Armstrong finally shot it. Burkman described poor Blucher II as being "torn up considerable" as he lay still and bleeding afterwards. Libbie gave him water from her canteen, holding his big head on her lap and soothing him. A feeble tail wag encouraged them. Blucher was too large to hoist onto a saddle and they struggled to walk him slowly back to camp. He was settled on Libbie's bed and his cuts washed and doctored. Fortunately, the next day, "he was real pert again."[35]

Presumably with guidance from Armstrong's dog book, the regimental surgeon and veterinarian, the Custers became ersatz veterinarians for their dogs and on the march took care of cactus thorns, porcupine quills, cuts, and even dog fight wounds. Thorns were continual problems even after the dogs learned to walk around the low-growing bulbs of prickly pear cacti. The Custers were given a hound named Lucy Stone, who would sit in the road, howl, and offer up her thorn-filled paw for help. Armstrong had a habit of captioning dog behavior by speaking for them—and in this case, Lucy Stone said, "If you please, sir, since you chose to bring me into a land of bristling earth like this, will you please get down immediately and attend to my foot?" Such an appeal was never unanswered, and Armstrong would dismount, sit with the dog cradled in his arms and use the tweezers on his multi-tool pocket knife to remove the thorns.[36] To try and prevent thorn injury, Burkman and Libbie took old boot leather and made "mittens" for them.[37] The same thing was done during the Yellowstone expedition when they went lame or when they would look so intently for cactus that they missed chasing game.[38] (Lucy Stone, 1818–1893, was a famous suffragist, speaker, and abolitionist who scandalously insisted on keeping her maiden name after marriage. The dog's previous owner had named her, and presumably it was a joke.)

Libbie's ambulance was always the "hospital" for sick, injured, or foot-sore dogs. Old Rover the foxhound (who had survived being in the Custer pack since 1867), had epileptic fits but was always coddled through them by Armstrong. Sick dogs were allowed in their tent, no matter how full it was.

> While we were all getting accustomed to the new climate, it was of no use to try to keep the dogs out of my tent. They stood around, and eyed me with such reproachful looks if I attempted to tie up the entrance to the tent and leave them out. If it were very cold when I returned from the dining-tent, I found dogs under and on the camp-bed, and so thickly scattered over the floor that I had to step carefully over them to avoid hurting feet or tails. If I secured a place in the bed, I was fortunate. Sometimes, when it had rained, and all of them were wet, I rebelled. The steam from their shaggy coats was stifling; but the general begged so hard for them that I taught myself to endure the air at last. I never questioned the right of the half-grown puppies to everything. Our struggles to raise them, and to avoid the distemper which goes so much harder with blooded than with cur dogs, endeared them to us. When I let the little ones in, it was really comical to hear my husband's arguments and cunningly-devised reasons why the older dogs should follow. A plea was put up for "the hound that had fits"; there was always another that "had been hurt in hunting"; and so on until the tent would hold no more. Fortunately, in pleasant weather, I was let off with only the ill or injured ones for perpetual companions. We were so surrounded with dogs when they were resting after the march, and they slept so soundly from fatigue, that it was difficult to walk about without stepping on them.[39]

Cardigan, "a great cream-colored, stag-hound," closely bonded with Libbie, who indulged his oversized need for cuddling. While Libbie sat on her camp stool, Cardigan, wagging his tail, would plop his chest onto her petite lap and scramble up with his hind legs until she was holding his entire body on her legs. Happily, he "...closed his eyes in a beatific state and sighed in content while I held him, until my foot went to sleep and I was cramped with his weight."[40] Burkman pronounced "Miss Libby" to be "...jist as foolish about the hounds as he was."[41] (Armstrong named Cardigan after Lord Cardigan, leader of the Charge of the Light Brigade during the Crimean War. As to the hound's lap-crushing affection, the author has had that same experience with his Irish Wolfhounds and Salukis.)

The Fort Sully Sporting Club

The near 400-mile march from Yankton to Fort Sully took sixteen days, and before they got in sight of the fort, the commanding officer sent the Custers a gift of ice and fairly recent newspapers. On May 22, Armstrong camped four miles below the fort and rode in to report to Col. David S. Stanley who was commander of the post and of the 22nd Infantry, and Armstrong's superior on the coming Yellowstone expedition.

Fort Sully (near modern Pierre) was built in 1866 after the first Fort Sully, thirty miles to the south, was abandoned due to poor location. Sully was the standard stockade fort with two block houses at diagonal corners, allowing defenders to enfilade the walls. As the worry of Indian attack had decreased over the years and the garrison expanded, some non-essential buildings, such as the granary, wash houses, ice house, and band quarters, were built outside the walls. The 22nd had been there long enough to make it as comfortable a frontier post as was possible. Sully was well maintained and had fresh dairy products and baked goods, poultry, a good band, and a library. Despite these amenities, Libbie hated the thought of being snowbound inside walls for the long winters.[42] The Custers and officers were well treated and, naturally, hunting was discussed. If Armstrong thought he was a savvy hound man (and he was—in his own fashion), he was a dilettante compared to the officers of the 22nd Infantry.

Col. David Stanley of the 22nd Infantry and Fort Sully Sporting Club. Armstrong presented Stanley with a purebred Scottish Deerhound before they left Fort Sully on the 1873 Yellowstone expedition. There was a certain rivalry between Armstrong and the Fort Sully hound men over the hunting performances of their respective packs. From William Pywell's stereo view in Lawrence A. Frost's *Custer's 7th Cavalry & the Campaign of '73* (1986).

Col. Stanley and his hunting officers kept a pack of "thoroughbred Grey and Fox Hounds," bred them, and occasionally imported staghounds from England. Coursing was such a big part of their life in Dakota that in April 1871 they formed the Sporting Club of the 22nd Infantry. It was governed by democratic rules and a constitution, and Stanley was elected president with Lt. Col. Elwell S. Curtis and Maj. Joseph Garland Whistler as first and second vice presidents. Capt. Javan Bradley Irvine served as secretary and treasurer.[43] They started off with sixteen active member officers and grew to over twenty. Their regular meetings were on Saturday evenings in Irvine's parlor. There, they voted on all aspects of their hounds—acquisition of new ones and disposal of the inferior, which hounds were to be hunted or bred, and how the puppies from a litter were to be distributed. Typically, the meeting concluded with music and a few songs, and Irvine's young son, Javi, was allowed to attend. (Unwanted hounds were sent upriver, away from the bigger towns, to be sold—probably to buyers who couldn't be particular.) Irvine produced precise minutes and ledger entries showing monthly income (dues, contributions, and income from the sale of antelope, wolf, and coyote pelts), expenses for food and kenneling, pay for the strikers who cared for the hounds, costs incurred finding a stolen hound, and a club subscription to *Turf, Field and Farm*. In the month that Armstrong arrived, they had a healthy balance of $51.46 (about $950 in today's dollars).[44]

Irvine's secretarial records are an excellent insight into 19th century Army hunting. He has the ancestry of their greyhounds (some of which extended twelve generations back to England), with notes about which Army posts they came from or were sent to and some of their deaths. Irvine copied pedigree notes for their hounds from the authoritative *The Greyhound: Being a Treatise on the Art of Breeding, Rearing, and Training Greyhounds for Public Running; Their Diseases and Treatment* (1853) by John Henry H. Walsh—a surgeon, dog man, and sports writer who used the famous pen name "Stonehenge." Several Fort Sully greyhounds were descended from those left behind by the tourist hunter Sir St. George Gore. One greyhound, Spot, was a grandson of Master McGrath, the celebrated triple-Waterloo Cup winner, and others came down from notable English coursers such as King Cob, Figaro, and Bedlamite. Stanley himself owned Pencawon, descended from King Death, the Waterloo Cup winner of 1864. The pedigreed Sully hounds were hard workers who hunted wolves, antelope, jackrabbits, badgers, and red fox. Irvine kept detailed notes of courses and game caught and sent the records to *Turf, Field and Farm*. (Armstrong was never overly bothered with record-keeping apart from his kill totals and marksmanship distances.)

The Fort Sully officers had read Nomad's hound exploits in *Turf* and the newspaper accounts of the Grand Duke Alexis' buffalo hunt. In April 1872, Armstrong, Sheridan, Maj. Gen. Winfield Hancock, and greyhound breeder Mr. John Given of Keokuk, Iowa, were elected as the first honorary members of the club. Also voted in was Bvt. Brig. Gen. Thomas L. Crittenden, commander of the 17th Infantry.[45] (His son Lt. John Jordan Crittenden III would be killed at Little Bighorn.) In November 1872, William Tecumseh Sherman, the lofty commanding general of the Army, was proposed for honorary membership, but "…after a free conversation and interchange of opinions, it was the conclusion of the Club that the General, not being a sporting man, it was not advisable to elect him."[46] Irvine's minutes don't show Armstrong ever responding to the letter about honorary membership, but clearly on his discovery of their coursing hounds at Fort Sully, there was some rivalry. In a rare instance of canine beneficence (or one-upmanship), Armstrong presented Stanley with one of his "fine, thoroughbred, stag hounds."[47] Armstrong and Stanley agreed on a coursing match before the 7th Cavalry was to march the last 250 miles to Fort Rice. To make the competition fair, there would be referees, and each side would hunt within sight of each other so the coursing was on equal ground. The winner would be decided by the fastest courses and/or the most game caught. Doubtless, wagers were made. (While on the Yellowstone expedition, Stanley left Armstrong's gift deerhound with Irvine and Javi. When hunting with their other hounds, a wolf was spotted, but the deerhound wanted to play with the lead greyhound and distracted the pack from the escaping wolf. Clearly, that deerhound was no loss to Armstrong.[48])

Sixteen-year-old Javi described the match in his diary entry for Thursday, May 29. It was originally planned for the previous day, but a howling rainstorm caused the hunt to be postponed. Fort Sully Club entered eight hounds: Gipsy (Irvine's bitch), Harry, Louisa, Echo, Frisky, Drew, Fanny (Stanley's greyhound from imported stock), and one other. When the time came to start out, the hounds left behind saw the assembled horses through the cracks in the kennel boards and became so frantic that two or three more burst out to go with them. Col. Stanley met Armstrong and Tom at noon (Javi persisted in calling Tom "Sgt. Custer"). Armstrong had seven of his hounds, and Javi admired his handsome black horse and "very pretty horn"—and was surprised he had *three* orderlies.[49] Lt. Will Wirt Daugherty, Irvine, and Javi had the Sully pack, and Stanley and several officers would be observers. The hunters and spectators rode out to good hunting ground, but it was full of rocks and stony gullies—the Cheyenne Bad Lands.[50]

Surprisingly, they had no luck and were returning when a jack jumped up in front of Armstrong while the Sully hounds were a distance away. Three of Armstrong's hounds raced after it, but the other hounds were unsighted and ran wildly about, searching for something to chase. Gipsy, the mother of several Sully hounds (and the fastest), was playfully visiting Armstrong's hounds and too far away to join in.[51] Irvine rode with the Sully hounds, but despite their reputation as daring cavalrymen, the Custer brothers chose not follow.[52] The jackrabbit ran the hounds out onto the prairie and disappeared with them. It was next seen heading back toward the hunters on the other side of a ravine with the hounds a quarter of a mile behind. Echo and Louisa ran it down the ravine and up a hill—finally turning it into Frisky who made the kill.[53] It was the luck of the hunt, good or ill, that the jack had not maneuvered itself into Armstrong's hounds. Score one in favor of Team Sully.

Heading back toward the fort through the Wolf Ground, they placed the hunt groups a hundred yards apart. Gipsy was lagging behind and saving her energy when a jackrabbit jumped up squarely between both packs, took off with a good lead, and then zigzagged to throw off the hounds.[54] Louisa was close behind, but Gipsy quickly took over the lead with Harry following on her heels and the other Sully hounds behind. They ran the jack up a ridge with Harry forcing sharp, evasive turns. Tom galloped ahead of Irvine and Javi, but they overtook him. The speeding jackrabbit eventually ran out of sight and escaped. At that point, Tom was a third of a mile behind the chase and the other riders even farther away. The run was "splendid" and covered about two miles.[55] Final score of the day, Team Sully one, Team Custer nil.

The only casualty was Harry, who had gorged on meat right before the hunt and became sick from exertion on a full stomach. They carried him to water and had to get a wagon for him. Javi's diary entry was ecstatic: "...during the whole run, every one of our dogs were ahead of Col. Custer's dogs!" and "Col. Custer did not see how our dogs could beat his: he thought his were very fast before he saw ours run!"[56] Irvine made the formal entry in the Club's book for the four-pound jackrabbit taken that day—"Turned by Echo and Louisa and caught by Frisky. Custer's pack in rear."[57]

Neither of the Custers recorded which of their hounds ran, but Armstrong was seldom a good loser when it came to hunting. Libbie noted only that Fort Sully had "some fine greyhounds" and there had been a few hunts—tactfully avoiding saying there had been a contest and who lost.[58] (At age sixty-six, Javan B. Irvine, Jr., told this story from memory in *Outdoor Life*, May 1923, but some details were different from his diary entry of 1873. Descriptions of 19th century courses are rare, so Irvine Jr.'s earlier and more accurate account is used here with portions of his later version to complete the story.)

The next day, Armstrong, troopers, and hounds were marching to Fort Rice, but he decided to leave pregnant Old Flora behind. She had been bred on the day they arrived at Fort Sully (probably unintended) and was due to whelp when he would be off on the expedition. Irvine and Javi kept her, and she had a whopping litter of twelve puppies on July 24.[59] Javi does not say what breed she was, but given Armstrong's protectiveness about his deerhounds, Flora was probably a foxhound or a greyhound. She doesn't seem to have been retrieved by Armstrong.

On June 9, Fort Rice was sighted on the west bank of the Missouri, and the Custers, their hounds, horses, and luggage were loaded onto a "rickety old ferry boat" to cross the river.[60] Fort Rice was another stockade-blockhouse garrison but with log and board shacks for quarters. An infantry post (which had been attacked once), it was the starting point for Gen. Sully's 1864 and 1865 Northwestern expeditions, the Yellowstone surveying expeditions of 1871 and 1872, and one of the signing sites of the 1868 Lakota Sioux Treaty.[61] (Commonly known as the Fort Laramie Treaty of 1868, the treaty entailed the Sioux promising to live within land set aside for them—including their sacred Black Hills—and the government promised they would be unmolested.) Unlike the Kansas forts Libbie knew, Rice was a bachelor post with no quarters suitable for the women—or officers willing to move out. The 7th's next station, Fort Abraham Lincoln, was still under construction. With no viable alternatives (the fledging Bismarck was still a rough place), Libbie went home until Armstrong could get settled after the expedition, and the other wives left as well.

They camped well away from the stockade, expecting to be there only a short time before Stanley arrived with his "dough-boys" from Fort Sully. While waiting, Armstrong and his favorite officers (with Burkman) would hunt antelope and deer. William Vose Wade, a woodcutter at Fort Rice, complained that Armstrong's hounds were eating rations from the commissary and were cared for by a soldier at government expense. Supposedly, the agency Sioux complained about the "yellow-haired man" whose dogs were taking their game. One disgruntled trooper told Wade, "them damned dogs are getting more good beef from the beef herd than we are."[62] (Woodcutting was a booming business, and the region's deforestation resulted from the massive amount of firewood needed for the stoves of towns, forts, and ranches throughout the winter—as well as fueling river steamers. The steamer *F.Y. Batchelor* was loaded with 22¾ cords for a 250-mile run from Bismarck to Fort Buford.[63])

Wade and his partner were cutting wood a few miles north of the fort, and Armstrong's foxhounds frequently showed up on their own, following deer trails in the trees and howling at night. The deer had been plentiful, but after the hounds started going to the timber, the woodcutters were less sure of their meat supply. A pair of hounds were shot dead by two of these men, and after Armstrong missed them, word got out that they'd been killed. He was furious and ordered the "murderers" be found and locked in the guard house to await punishment. No one ratted out the woodcutters, and eventually Armstrong gave up—but declared, "...if another of his dogs was shot or stolen, he would hang every d—d one of us."[64] (Despite his carefully anonymous account, one is tempted to suspect Wade knew too much about the incident to have been entirely innocent. A polished version of this appears in Wade's memoirs, *Paha Sapa Tawoyakie*, published in 1965.)

The 3rd Yellowstone Expedition

As in the two previous expeditions of the same name, the purpose in '73 was to push westward by surveying the potential railroad path through the Sioux country. Scientists would go evaluate the suitability of the land for settlement, ranching, and mining. The Army was protecting the surveying team and finding locations for new forts—all groundwork for taking Sioux treaty land. Col. Stanley was in command—which included his 22nd Infantry and Armstrong's 7th Cavalry, and a detachment of artillery. (Capt. Irvine commanded Fort Sully in Stanley's absence.) The column was composed of nineteen companies of infantry and ten of cavalry totaling nearly 1,500 soldiers, 353 engineers, teamsters, and assorted civilians, and 450 cattle.[65] Accompanying the expedition were the scientist "bug hunters"—two professors who were to make biological and geologic notes and collect animals and fossil specimens. William R. Pywell was documenting the expedition with photographs, and a reporter would send his stories to Bismarck with the official dispatches.

Armstrong had deerhounds Tuck, Blucher II, Maida II or III, Cardigan, and possibly others. In addition to Burkman, his personal orderly was Pvt. John H. Tuttle, of E. Co., considered the regiment's best shot. Tom Custer had his own hounds

Lt. Algernon Emory "Fresh Smith" Smith was one of the favored few who had one of Armstrong's staghounds. He brought it along on the Yellowstone expedition and together with Armstrong's pack, it went missing for seventeen days and traveled nearly 200 miles before being found. Courtesy of the National Park Service, Little Bighorn Battlefield National Monument, LIBI_00011_07166. Photographed by D. F. Barry, 1873–76.

and Lt. A.E. Smith had brought along his staghound—almost certainly a gift from Armstrong. The rest of the pack was left at Fort Rice. The Fort Sully officers had four of their best—full brothers Given and Sweep, Donovan, and George.[66] Given was the best hunter, Sweep wasn't as fast but had more endurance, and Donovan and George each had two antelopes to their credit. (Libbie's Cardigan may have been a cross-bred staghound—she is never clear on this point.)

The civilian surveyors were under the charge of former Confederate cavalry general Thomas Lafayette Rosser—Armstrong's good friend from West Point and occasional adversary during the Late War. The two spent many happy evenings together talking of their cadet escapades and battles where they alternately captured each other's personal baggage. Armstrong brought along Mary Adams to cook her excellent meals for him and his circle. General Sheridan sent Lt. Fred Grant as his representative. The president's son was only two years out of West Point but was on Sheridan's staff. Despite Fred Grant's tendency to be slightly inebriated most of the time, he was affable and got along easily with Armstrong.

There were two Englishmen, twenty-two-year-old Lewis Clifford and twenty-year-old Lewis William Molesworth, who purchased their own "outfit"—wagons, mules, horses, rations, and gear, and, according to Capt. Grant Marsh, their own pack of hounds. Clifford was the son of the 8th Baron Clifford of Chudleigh, and Molesworth's father was Sir Paul Molesworth, 10th Baronet of Pencarrow. The wealthy young men were traveling with their St. Louis friend Robert Graham Frost (the son of Confederate Brig. Gen. Daniel Marsh Frost). The three had become friends while at London University. Like the Englishmen Armstrong had previously hosted, Clifford and Molesworth were keen to see the unspoiled West with its game and Indians. (The former would become the 9th Baron Clifford of Chudleigh and the latter the 11th Baronet of Pencarrow, Cornwall.[67])

The Honorable Lewis Clifford and his friends hoped to get to Fort Benton, Montana Territory (and perhaps farther), hunting and fishing on the way. While staying in St. Louis, they heard of the military expedition to Sioux country and by pure chance met Col. Stanley on a steamboat. Clifford was a genial and polished fellow and was soon invited to join the expedition. At Fort Rice, they hired a cook and a driver/servant and paid exorbitant prices for a wagon, two mules, three riding horses, camping gear and rations.[68] Clifford was told to buy *two* pistols, for as fellow Englishman Morton Frewen was told in Texas, "You don't often want a belt full of hardware but when you do you want it like hell."[69] Clifford was impressed with the Army but described the mule drivers as a "villainous looking set."[70] These were indispensable men who moved cargo across the West. Variously called mule skinners, mule-whackers, bullwhackers, freighters, and teamsters, they were known for giving sweetheart names to mules, for spewing foul language and inventive curses, and for their "feist" dogs. The bearded and habitual tobacco chewers took pride in getting stubborn mules to pull wagons by skillfully using a "blacksnake"—a long braided leather whip—to tickle the lead mule's rump. Clifford wrote about the expedition to his parents at Ugbrooke House in Devon, and while he talked about shooting antelope (only bagging two in the first days), not once are hounds mentioned. So, whether or not the Englishmen had hounds is uncertain—but one curious fact adds a facet to the mystery. In the Fort Sully Sporting Club book, inserted at the back of the pedigrees is an eleven-generation pedigree for an English bitch named Sady Molesworth dated 1873.[71] She is not in any of their breeding or hunting records, so Sady was *not* of the 22nd Infantry. (Her sire and dam were Tancredi and Tantivy—both known in the English coursing fraternity.)

The expedition started on June 20, 1873, and the men expected to rendezvous on the trail with the slower moving survey group who left Fort Abraham Lincoln on the 18th. From various accounts, bad weather, dust, and clouds of voracious mosquitos were the chief characteristics of the march. Game was plentiful and a welcome change from salt pork or bacon, and tough beef was slaughtered every other day. Only a day out from Fort Rice, Armstrong's hounds caught antelope, and he was shooting two to four a day.[72] Energetically riding far beyond Stanley's gaze, he was both hunter and unofficial scout. Inspired by the "bugologists," Armstrong became an enthusiast, collecting fossils, petrified wood, and minerals for the Ann Arbor college (University of Michigan)—if Libbie didn't mind letting the specimens go.[73] Being free from Army responsibilities while seeing new landscape was precisely Armstrong's cup of tea.

The sportsmen paid close attention to the hounds' performance—each group looking for their pack to best the others. Clifford later told Capt. Grant Marsh of the *Key West* (one of the three steamboats ferrying their supplies upriver) how Lt. Daugherty's favorite "deer-hound" pup, two-year-old Given, "of exceedingly hazy and uncertain lineage," was not expected to do much by the other officers of the 22nd. Clifford was mistaken about Given as he was pure greyhound, sired by Spot, the son of Master McGrath, the great Irish champion. His English dam was Gipsy, with a pedigree almost as distinguished.[74] (Clifford believed Given was so named because he was *given* to Daugherty, but in fact he was named for John Given of Keokuk, Iowa—honorary member of the Sporting Club.) Soon after departing Fort Rice, the hunters spotted two jackrabbits, and the eager officers unleashed all the hounds. Given went through the pack like "a torpedo-boat through a fleet at anchor," killed one jack then finished the other before the rest could catch up. After that, Given's speed and endurance was the byword—particularly compared to the other hounds' performance when they stumbled across grazing antelopes—and despite being in among them, the antelope scattered and leapt over the hounds, and not one was taken. On one prairie chase, Given ran down a healthy antelope, a feat which Clifford declared to be "unprecedented."[75] By the end of the expedition, Given had taken twenty-three antelope and was proclaimed "...equal if not superior to any dog in the United Kingdom."[76] (See this chapter's *Tail Piece* for the debate about hounds catching antelopes.)

The ever-curious antelope were attracted to the white covers of the wagons and came close to the column—sometimes even dashing through formation gaps. This inevitably caused "promiscuous firing." Clifford noted, "One or two of the bullets struck the ground in front of the general which caused him to ride down the line swearing, and put two or three men under arrest."[77] (Only Stanley was called "general" by Clifford.) One of the "bug" men was shooting in camp—supposedly at a rare species flying by—and "the general threatened to put him in alcohol and send him back to the president."[78] Tom Custer's dog, Bender, had been killed by—a stray shot on the second day of the march. All that blasting away resulted in Stanley's order prohibiting game shooting within the column and the creation of a special hunting unit.[79] Naturally, Armstrong claimed the role of chief hunter and selected a few crack shots to accompany him and his hounds each day. He kept a meticulous tally of his game bag for the next Nomad letter.

After camp was made in the afternoons, Armstrong often went outside the lines with his hounds to nap on the grass. Rosser had given Armstrong and Stanley each a sixteen-foot square wall tent from the Northern Pacific Railroad.[80] (Two troopers shared a pup tent, and the officers had conical "Sibley" tents.) When his luggage was unloaded each day, the large tent was comfortably furnished with Armstrong's cot, rug, trunk, footlocker, lantern, small stove, washstand, folding chair and portable writing desk—leaving plenty of room for dogs. It was Armstrong's habit to spend his evenings surrounded by them, writing long letters to Libbie—frequently with several daily installments in one. He talked about the landscape, his marksmanship, the officers, his Dakota assignment, bringing Libbie back out, and which young women they knew who could liven up the post's society. Armstrong was missing the marriage bed and penned erotic innuendos, promising Libbie a vigorous reunion.[81] He wrote in small script on thin stationery, and his letters frequently ran thirty or forty pages, with one hitting a whopping eighty. After Armstrong told Tom he ought to be writing to Libbie, his brother joked he could have nothing to tell her "...after she receives that *book* from you."[82] After his official dispatches reached the nearest post, they were relayed by telegraph—and he was so wordy, the Army docked his pay $23.57 for exceeding his monthly limit. The *Forest and Stream* editor dryly noted that with money from his *Galaxy* articles, the fine should cause him no trouble.[83] Libbie always worried about him taking risks and, as she did on each of his expeditions, she extracted a promise that he wouldn't stray too far from the protection of the column. However, Armstrong's hunting accounts indicate he applied his own semantics to the precise meaning of *too far*. Still, he reassured The Old Lady in his letters that he wasn't taking any chances—and honestly didn't think he was.

The special correspondent from the *Bismarck Tribune* filed a dispatch on June 28th, noting

> GEN. CUSTER IN BUCKSIN [sic] hunting jacket, and familiar broad-brimmed hat, beneath which streams his flowing locks, and accompanied by a fine pack of hounds, has indulged in the sport with great zeal and success. Others have taken part in the hunt, and as operations are mostly visible from the column, they are watched with great interest, and have materially relieved the tedium of the march.[84]

Based on the reporter's description, the newspaper artists engraved a dramatic print of Armstrong on horseback, officers, and a huntsman slipping five foxhounds. To save time and money, this was almost certainly a recycled engraving of a Civil War fox hunt. A version of Mathew Brady's well-known profile of Armstrong in his slouch hat was added to the engraving—although he does not look particularly dashing.[85] The large illustration was captioned,

"READY TO CHASE THE ANTELOPE"
"'Stand like greyhounds in the slips, straining upon the start.' SHAKESPEARE."

This piece of publicity was choice enough to be saved in Libbie's box of clippings. Armstrong should have enjoyed being linked to *Henry V*, from which the rest of King Harry's quote is more famous—"The game's afoot; Follow your spirit: and upon this charge, Cry 'God for Harry! England and Saint George!'"

"Whoop 'em up!" This illustration was based on a reporter's description of Armstrong and his hounds on the expedition and captioned with a famous line from Shakespeare's play, *Henry V*. This is almost certainly an engraving of a Civil War foxhunt. Armstrong's head is the famous Mathew Brady portrait superimposed on the leader's body (he did not ride a white horse), and foxhounds are shown rather than staghounds. Libbie preserved this carefully in her box of newspaper clippings, and it has not been published since its first appearance in 1873. Courtesy of the National Park Service, Little Bighorn Battlefield National Monument, LIBI_00019_03501.

Mother nature not only provided dust, flooded creeks, and mosquitos to plague the expedition, she also hammered them from above. In late June, a lightning storm quickly darkened the sky and pounded the column with hailstones the size of "large marbles" which raised welts and cut flesh. Taking what cover they could, some men sheltered under bushes and held anything over their heads—including a bucket. Horses and mules, terrified with pain, tore out of their harnesses and ran loose. The storm lasted a long ten minutes, covering the ground with three inches of hail. When it subsided, wagons and surveying equipment were damaged. The casualties, besides a great number of dead antelope not far from the column, were thirty mules, six horses (dead or needing to be shot)—and one of the staghounds.[86]

After seventeen days there was a command incident which could have cast a shadow over the whole expedition. Stanley was known to be "a squat, humorless, peevish alcoholic ... the antithesis of Custer." His drinking frequently impaired his judgment, and Rosser had warned Armstrong about this. The friction began with a dispute over the sutler, Armstrong's cook Mary, and of all things, her small camp stove. Stanley got it into his liquor-fogged head that Mary cooking breakfast was holding up the march every morning and ordered the stove discarded. Armstrong employed a number of cadet-style dodges to make it appear he had complied. The situation escalated when Armstrong went off with his cavalry instead of assisting the infantry in building a pontoon bridge. Finally, the simmering pot boiled over when Stanley made the petty accusation that Armstrong allowed a civilian (Lt. Calhoun's brother) to ride an Army mount. He fired back that Stanley himself had given one to the reporter and so had established the precedent. That did it. Stanley had Armstrong arrested and confined to his tent on July 8. As a symbol of his disgrace, he rode at the rear of the column—"leading the pelican." Armstrong bore it with good spirits, and two days later, he received Stanley's sober apology.[87] The two sportsmen reconciled, and Armstrong genuinely seems to have borne no grudge against Stanley, although Libbie would.

To help the column through unfamiliar territory, forty Arikara scouts looked for landmarks and signs of other Indians. The Arikara tribe (also called Arikaree or Ree) were hereditary enemies of the Sioux and did not mind working for the Army. The scouts didn't speak English, so several linguistically and culturally savvy white men were hired to interpret. One of the scouts was Bloody Knife, the son of a Hunkpapa Sioux warrior and an Arikara woman. The boy was raised in his father's village but after his death, he grew up an outcast.[88] Bloody Knife hated the Sioux and was glad to get paid for a chance to do them a bad turn. As a scout, he had a uniform tunic and trousers, a bandana around his neck, and a shapeless hat but wore moccasins and carried a brass-tack decorated repeating rifle. Armstrong respected his exceptional talents as a scout, and his loyalty, and he liked him—despite his tendency to be moody and temperamental. The two spent many hours "Seated on the grass, the dogs lying about them, they talked over portions of the country which the general had never seen, the scout drawing excellent maps in the sand with a pointed stick."[89] Bloody Knife would be killed in the opening shots at Little Bighorn.

The hounds' exploits weren't the only thing relieving the daily monotony. The Sioux gave them diversion as well, and in their first clash, Armstrong was caught napping—literally. On August 4, he was ahead of the column with Tom, Capt. Myles Moylan, Lt. Charles Varnum, and eighty-six men from A and B companies. Exploring along the river, Bloody Knife found the trail of a war party. It was a hot day, and Armstrong called for a late-morning halt in a grove near the mouth of the Tongue River. The men were dozing when a small group of Sioux creeping along the bank opened fire, surprising the sentries. (Armstrong had been caught asleep by the enemy during the Civil War when his black and white dog alerted him to a Rebel force. See Ch. 4.) Armstrong, Tom, and a few men rode after them while Moylan mounted the rest to follow. After a couple of miles, Armstrong halted to reconnoiter when some 300 Sioux appeared and started shooting. He and his orderly got back to his detachment, whose volleys scattered the warriors. Moylan arrived as the Sioux were re-grouping. Armstrong moved the companies to a dry streambed where they could take cover below the bank but still have a field of fire. One warrior wearing a stovepipe hat (believed to be a chief or holy man) charged and was shot through his chest.[90] The soldiers repulsed a number of attacks until the Sioux fired the tall grass—always a sign their usual strategy wasn't working. Running low on ammunition after three hours of shooting, Armstrong had the men charge the Sioux. As it had at Washita, the audacious tactic worked and the Sioux vanished. Sadly, downstream during the fight, the Memphis sutler Augustus Baliran, the veterinarian Dr. John Honsinger, and Pvt. John Ball were killed by a group of thirty Sioux.[91] Ball was filling his comrades' canteens with water at the creek, and his body was not quickly found. Baliran and Honsinger were watering their horses when ambushed. Their bodies were carried away from the scene for a burial service by Father Valentin Sommereisen, a Roman Catholic priest traveling from Fort Rice who happened to intersect the column.[92]

Three days later, the column (now on the alert) came across war party trails and that of a village on the move. Stanley ordered Armstrong to take seven companies and follow it.[93] (Presumably, his hounds were chained up back with the main column.) The village trail led across the deep Yellowstone (near the confluence of the Bighorn River), where the troopers could no longer follow. At dawn on the 11th, from across the Yellowstone, the Sioux opened fire. The troopers scrambled into a firing line in a cottonwood grove and opened up. While the 7th's heavy horses couldn't cross the river, the Sioux ponies could, and warriors swam them across to assault both flanks while firing continued from the river. Bugler Louis Hills remembered the bullets sounding like a "swarm of bees" as they ripped through trees, causing pieces of leaves to flutter down on the defenders.[94] Clifford and company, rapidly learning why a "belt full of hardware" was a very good thing, observed the fight with two of Stanley's aides and the *Tribune* reporter. Armstrong's marksman orderly, Pvt. Tuttle, had young Hills watch while he picked off warriors across the Yellowstone.[95] While sighting his next target, Tuttle was shot through the head.[96] Armstrong rode up and down, maintaining order and giving encouragement—astonishing the reporter who later remarked upon his coolness.[97] What had worked with the Sioux once was worth trying again. The band was sheltering in a ravine, and Armstrong ordered Bugler Hills to get them up on a small hill and play.[98] Always solicitous of overseas guests, he invited the "casuals," Clifford, Molesworth, and Frost, to join the attack, and Clifford rode right alongside Armstrong. In front with the guidon, Armstrong and his other orderly had their horses shot from under them.[99] Grabbing another horse, Armstrong and the 7th charged at full speed to "Garry Owen." (Clifford noted this all looked "quite theatrical."[100]) That charge and a couple of artillery rounds from the Rodman guns in Stanley's rapidly approaching column caused the warriors to retreat back across the river.[101] Tuttle and three wounded men were the Army's only casualties. His body was sewn in canvas and carried in a wagon for a day before he was buried—with a bonfire to hide his grave.[102] Armstrong and the 7th were starting to learn just how tough and clever the Sioux were. This was the last horse Armstrong would have shot from under him.)

Pompey's Pillar on the Yellowstone River was named in July 1806 by Capt. William Clark during the Lewis and Clark expedition to honor little Jean Baptiste "Pompy" Charbonneau, the toddler son of Sacagawea and Toussaint Charbonneau, fellow expedition members. Since Clark's discovery, the Pillar developed a reputation as a monumental stone tower, but Lt. Charles W. Larned, F Co., 7th Cavalry, dismissed it as "a wicked swindle; in fact, a dumpy rock seated on a sand bar in the middle of the Yellowstone River."[103] (Capt. Clark's carved name and date on the Pillar is the only existing physical evidence from the Lewis and Clark Expedition.) In the second week in August,

Stanley's column camped on the north bank there for a couple of days. They had just been through another bad hailstorm and were worn out. As it would be the last chance for bathing and laundry on the march home, Stanley declared it a rest day.[104] There, the expedition had its last and slightly comical skirmish with the Sioux.

Early on the morning of Saturday the 16th, soldiers were washing their clothes—completely naked so every stitch they owned could be laundered simultaneously. While their clothes were drying on bushes or driftwood, they bathed, swam, and relaxed. About 8 o'clock, shots from across the river caused the "Call to Arms" call to be sounded, and the naked and half-clothed soldiers raced to get their clothes and rifles. Having caused a disruption (and subsequent jitters), the Sioux disappeared. It was hardly a skirmish, and Stanley called it a "ludicrous incident"—but admitted it might have gone far worse.[105]

The day after, several staghounds went "absent without leave." They weren't noted as missing until camp was made on the Razor Creek that afternoon. There are conflicting stories about how they got lost. Lt. Smith (who owned one of them) recorded it was a particularly hot day, and several of the hounds would walk no farther and flopped down under clumps of sagebrush to get shade as the column passed them.[106] Armstrong told Barker that five had gone missing after chasing an elk.[107] Perhaps it was a combination of both circumstances.

Clifford's party left the expedition on August 19. Stanley was sending two of his best scouts, "Lonesome" Charley Reynolds and Gilman Norris, off to Fort Benton via their supply depot, Stanley's Stockade, with dispatches, letters, and the *Tribune* reporter's story, "The Yellowstone War."[108] Since Fort Benton was one of the places the three friends originally wanted to reach, they went with the scouts, traveling at night. They arrived across the river from Fort Benton and swam across—arriving at the fort on the 23rd "...with no luggage but our rifles & blankets & wet through to the middle."[109] The three rode an uncomfortable stagecoach drawn by two "half-dead" horses to Helena, where they separated. Molesworth and Frost went East but Clifford went to Yellowstone Lake and Salt Lake City before heading back to St. Louis.[110] Stanley wrote his wife about the Englishmen and Frost: "They have had an Indian fight, have killed all kinds of game, including buffalo, and now seek new adventures. They are clever fellows and very much liked."[111] Armstrong noted in his official report that all three gentlemen fought in the charge "with great gallantry."[112] If Clifford and company did have hounds—borrowed or bought—they would have been left with the column.

Lost Hounds and Nomad's Elk Hunt

Continuing on toward the expedition's end, the cavalry was away from the column again and heading for the stockade on the Yellowstone near Glendive Creek. On September 3 they struck a creek with potable water, and Armstrong ordered "Water Call." While the horses were watered, and kegs and canteens filled, the officers were astonished to see Lt. Smith's staghound trot out of the woods, drawn by the familiar smells and sounds of horses and soldiers. He had been gone seventeen days and on his own had traveled some 190 miles in search of his master.[113] If that was not lucky enough, the next day, the column arrived opposite Stanley's Stockade and learned that Armstrong's four staghounds were waiting for him. A boat was sent over to retrieve them and he found the hounds "sleek, fat and unconcerned."[114] He wrote to Kirkland Barker,

> ...five of our dogs got lost over two hundred miles from this point [the stockade] in a chase after elk—we gave them up as lost forever. When we arrived here day before yesterday, imagine our surprise at finding our dogs here, they having arrived here two weeks ago only four or five days after they were lost and having traveled through over two hundred miles of barren, uninhabited country, subsisting on what they could pick up from our old camps. This beats all dog stories I ever read, fortunately I have hundreds of witnesses to attest to the truth of the story.[115]

As Armstrong's missing dogs were usually never seen again, this occasion was something of a triumph. If the story of the lost hound pack, their homing instinct and trek in the wilderness was as special as Armstrong said it was, it is curious he never wrote about it as Nomad—but the incident was definitely eclipsed by his next hunt.

Shortly after the reunion with the wayward hounds, Armstrong added a magnificent elk to his trophy bag. No longer a mere "observer" of sport for *Turf*, he recorded his triumph in an entertaining letter published on October 17, 1873. Nomad gave a brief explanation about having been in Kentucky with no proper hunting stories to tell and then touted his marksmanship, citing the total numbers of species he'd killed and the yardages of his shots—ranging from 150 to 630 yards, with an average for antelope of over 250 yards. (Armstrong had a companion, frequently Fred Grant, to pace off the distance for verification.) Before he got to the meat of his letter, Armstrong comically related how he was keeping a porcupine and wildcat in crates inside his tent until they could be sent to the Central Park Zoo to join his bear. After whetting his readers' appetite, he went on to describe the hunting zenith of the expedition—a battle with a huge elk.[116]

He had been two miles out from camp, riding with the newly retrieved Maida, Blucher, Cardigan, and a couple of others, and seeing a magnificent bull elk, he wounded it with a rifle shot. It took off running with the staghounds and Armstrong in pursuit. The stag jumped into the river, taking a stand in water too deep for the staghounds to touch bottom. Undaunted, they swam toward the elk, who then moved deeper up to his shoulders and slashed away with his antlers. Blucher and Cardigan leapt through the river onto the elk while the others attacked front and rear. Blucher struggled across the back and locked his jaws onto an ear. Infuriated with pain, the elk submerged in a frantic effort to drag the hound under water. Cardigan, Maida, and the others were still fighting, and it looked certain the dogs would drown. From his position twenty yards away, Armstrong sighted his rifle—maneuvering for a clear shot at the fighting elk. When he realized one or more of his dogs could die by drowning or by his bullet, he acted quickly. Death by rifle was the cleaner of the two, and he searched desperately for an opening. Momentarily, the elk's loin was clear, Armstrong fired and it sank into the water. Happily, the hounds were unharmed. He likened the battle to one of Sir Edwin Landseer's engravings of a stag at bay in the Scottish Highlands.[117] He took the homage a step further, as a famous 1851 Landseer painting of a red stag was entitled *Monarch of the Glen*, while Armstrong named his trophy "King of the Forest."

He sent his orderly back for a wagon and men to help move the large elk back to camp. They laid it on the grass by Armstrong's tent and late in the afternoon, William

Sir Edwin Landseer, R. A., originally painted "Stag at Bay" in 1846. Two years later, it was engraved as a print which proved extremely popular in both the United Kingdom and America. Armstrong knew it well and it is perhaps the best visualization of Cardigan, Blucher, and Maida battling his elk in the water. He likened his hounds' fight with the "King of the Forest" to this popular engraving. Courtesy of the Royal Collection Trust / © Her Majesty Queen Elizabeth II 2017. RCIN 815291.

Pywell brought his wagon-darkroom over and made glass-plate photographs (including a stereo view) of Armstrong posing with it, wearing his black hat, buckskin jacket, blue fireman's shirt with signature red necktie, and rifle in hand. They estimated it was fifteen hands high, eleven and a half feet from nose to hind foot, and after removing the internal organs, that it weighed over 800 pounds. (While the date of this elk hunt is generally given as September 6, 1873, Armstrong wrote letters to both Barker and Libbie from the Yellowstone Stockade on that day noting the elk was killed *prior* to the 6th.[118])

Normally, he would have kept only the head, but he was persuaded by the professors that this could be the most spectacular mounted elk in the States (or so Armstrong claimed) and decided to have the whole elk mounted, but he knew it was too big for his Fort Lincoln or Monroe houses. His "comdg. officer in Monroe" had the right of first refusal of hunting trophies before he offered them to friends, so he asked Libbie if he could send the *"ne plus ultra"* elk to Barker along with other specimens for the Detroit Audubon Club. (On the other hand, Tom Custer sent mounted antelope heads to women he was trying to impress.) Armstrong was learning taxidermy from the professors—or at least how to skin and field dress a specimen—and he and his orderly stayed up long after "lights out," practicing.[119] The elk head, rack, and hide were sewn up in canvas and stowed away in a wagon. Armstrong wrote right away to Barker, describing the hunt and saying the scars from his hounds' fangs could be seen on the elk's ears and flank—and then, "Secure any good deer or fox hounds you can."[120]

As Armstrong was writing about this to *Turf*, the staghounds from the elk hunt were "...gathered near my camp-stool, some hugging the fire, others at my feet, while

Maida, my favorite, has exercised her prerogative and stretched herself at full length on the buffalo covering of my camp-bed."[121] (The first Maida died in fall 1869 and a second Maida was at Fort Leavenworth during the winter of 1869–70. It is not clear if the elk hunt deerhound is Maida II or III. Confusingly, Armstrong refers to every Maida as "my favorite.")

The main body of the expedition briefly rejoined the cavalry at the stockade, and with friendlier territory ahead, on September 12 Armstrong's regiment separated to escort the engineers to Fort Lincoln. They arrived at dusk on the 21st—a ramshackle sight with worn out and patched clothes; dented band instruments; mineral specimens; fossilized wood, bones, and sea shells; pressed flowers; and a forest of elk and antelope horns strapped to the tops of wagons and ambulances. They had been ninety-five days in the field, covered some 935 miles (probably a low number as the odometer wagon often didn't work) and averaged just over thirteen miles a day.[122] (The hounds logged even more miles, as they were always running up and down the column and going off on chases.) Both Stanley and Armstrong filed reports which glowingly described the region's potential for water, grazing, timber, and game—in other words, settlement.

Armstrong would linger at Fort Lincoln for a month to get six companies of the

Armstrong with the "King of the Forest" elk back in camp. He shipped the head, rack, and hide (bearing the fang marks from his hounds) off to Kirkland Barker to be mounted in the Detroit Audubon Club. Courtesy of the National Park Service, Little Bighorn Battlefield National Monument, LIBI_00111_01998, photographed by William R. Pywell, 1873.

7th settled and supervise the finishing stages of the post's construction. He wrote two triumphant articles which returned his name to the public eye—the "King of the Forest" letter to *Turf* and a longer one about "The Yellowstone War" to *Galaxy*. Then Armstrong headed home to collect Libbie and return with her before winter snows blocked the railroad.

During this period, Armstrong's two special dogs were Tuck and the current Maida. In what is perhaps the most genuinely moving passage he ever wrote about his dogs (even topping his ode to Maida I), Armstrong left no doubt he loved them—Tuck in particular. In a seventy-page letter which was not for *Turf, Galaxy*, or a New York paper, he wrote Libbie from the Heart River camp on the expedition's outbound trek.

> I think am going to become more warmly attached to Tuck than any dog I have ever owned. She is if anything, even more affectionate than Lulu, and so fast, she can outstrip Blucher as if he was a cur. I think I told you of her catching a full grown antelope buck and pulling him down after a run of over a mile in which she left all the other dogs far behind. She comes to me almost every evening when I am sitting in one of my large comfortable camp chairs listening to the band or joining with the other officers in conversation. First she will come and lay her head on my knee, as if to ask if I am too much engaged to notice her, a pat of encouragement and her fore feet are thrown lightly across my lap, a few moments in this posture and she lifts her hind-feet from the ground, and, great, overgrown dog that she is, quietly and gently disposes of herself on my lap, and at times will cuddle down and <u>sleep there for an hour at a time</u>, until I become so tired of my charge that I am compelled to transfer her to mother earth, and even then she resembles a well-cared for and half-spoiled child, who can never be induced to retire until it has been fondled to sleep in its mother's arms. Tuck will sleep so soundly in my lap that I can transfer her gently to the ground and she will continue her slumber, like a little baby carefully deposited in its crib. As I write she is lying at my feet—she makes up with no other person.[123] [Lulu was the deerhound who inexplicably leapt from the train. Marguerite Merington edited the above passage considerably for her book, *The Custer Story: The Life and Intimate Letters of General George A. Custer and His Wife Elizabeth*.]

TAIL PIECE: SIR ST. GEORGE GORE'S GREYHOUNDS POPULATE THE WEST

During the early 1800s, one can find occasional accounts by Army officers about hunting with greyhounds and, despite two recent wars with England, Americans were avid followers of English sport. A trickle of blooded greyhounds had been exported to the land of *E Pluribus Unum*, but these weren't enough to explain the large population of greyhounds which appeared in the post–Civil War Army. Enter the greyhound nexus—Baronet Sir St. George Gore, who went West in 1854 on a three-year hunting expedition with a small army of personal servants and mountain men in Colorado, Wyoming, and Montana. He had some forty greyhounds, foxhounds, and deerhounds and gave a number of his sighthounds to Army officers. At Fort Union, New Mexico, and Fort Kearney, Nebraska, in the late 1850s and early 1860s, cavalry officers hunted with Gore-descended greyhounds[124] who were passed on to other posts around the West—including the Fort Sully Sporting Club.

SIGHTHOUNDS VS. ANTELOPE

Armstrong insisted that his hounds could bring down antelope when there was an ongoing debate as to whether a greyhound or deerhound in condition could run down a pronghorn antelope (*Antilocapra Americana*). The fastest land animal in the hemisphere, they could reach fifty-five miles per hour at a burst or thirty-five m.p.h. over several miles, compared to a top greyhound sprint of approximately forty miles an hour over two thousand yards. Of course, antelope could stumble or be turned into another hound, but the opinion was that unless the antelope was young, sick, or in foal, no hound could catch a healthy adult.

Before Capt. Alfred Barnitz soured on Armstrong in Kansas, he witnessed his commanding officer's two greyhounds hunting antelope many times but never once saw them catch an antelope. "The chase would be kept up for two or three miles, then abandoned as useless."[125] Lt. Charles W. Larned wrote of the herds of curious antelope which followed the 1873 Yellowstone expedition column and provided hunters with easy pickings, noting, "The dogs catch the *young* [emphasis added] and afford many an exciting chase."[126]

Lt. James Calhoun remarked how antelopes could run with a mortal wound which would have stopped a deer or elk. "I have seen numbers wounded in such a manner that their entrails hung to the ground but even after such circumstances they would run faster than a horse until they fell exhausted by loss of blood."[127] G.O. Shields confirmed the gut and chest wounds which an antelope could sustain and still run for a hundred yards or more.[128] Often times, it seems the antelope was shot and then run down by the hounds—but some hunters neglected to mention this when bragging. The officers on the Yellowstone expedition set their hounds on antelope but "...had no hope that any could be caught unless previously wounded." When Lt. Daugherty's greyhound Given caught an adult antelope, Lewis Clifford declared the feat "unprecedented."[129] Paradoxically, the Fort Sully Sporting Club records for 1872–73 showed their best hounds (including Daugherty's Given) took thirty-six antelopes as well as thirty-three jackrabbits and fifty-six wolves. The 1873–74 season recorded only two antelopes but fifty-four jacks, thirty-two wolves, and other game.[130]

Sometimes lack of experience may have disadvantaged the hounds. Wild Bill Hickok was a guide for Col. James F. Meline's trek in 1866. Near Fort Kearney, Meline slipped his greyhound after an antelope, and Hickok rode after them. He came back to report that "...if the greyhound had been trained he could have caught the game." Apparently it had overtaken the antelope but plopped down to wait for Meline.[131] Lt. Col. Richard Irving Dodge, an eminent authority on hunting in the West, had seen antelopes "deliberately" leading greyhounds through prickly pear cactus or scatter so the hounds could not combine on one.

> I have never yet seen a single greyhound pull down an unwounded antelope. I have heard numbers of owners of such dogs say that their dog could and would do it; but, when I have gone out to see, something has always happened to prevent the dog's execution of the feat on that particular occasion.[132]

Perhaps the best story on the topic comes from Maj. Luther North, who told the story of how Col. Eugene A. Carr, on the Republican River Campaign in 1869, bragged to the doubtful Buffalo Bill Cody that his greyhounds could catch antelope. To prove it, Carr set them after one which handily outdistanced the greyhounds and disappeared over a ridge. The hounds gave up and were returning when Cody remarked dryly, "General, if anything the antelope is a little bit ahead."[133]

Chapter 11

Fort Lincoln and the Black Hills

"My favorite, a great cream-colored stag-hound, was named 'Cardigan.' He never gave up trying to be my lap-dog."—Libbie Custer[1]

If the Custer dog story was seeded in Texas and budded in Kansas, then it bloomed in Dakota. At Fort Abraham Lincoln, they had forty *working* hounds—deerhounds, staghounds, foxhounds, and a greyhound or two—and as much prairie for rambling upon as man or dog could want.

It is not clear when Armstrong got his Russian Wolfhounds from Grand Duke Alexis, who did not get home from his diplomatic cruise until December 1872. The brace of exotic hounds could have arrived at Fort Lincoln in the fall of 1873 or spring of 1874. Armstrong named the female Madgie and the male Stanley—perhaps after Col. Stanley. The hounds had black and tan coats—thick enough to protect them from cold on the Russian steppes. They were mature dogs, with Madgie born in 1871 and Stanley in 1870.[2] Curiously, neither Armstrong, Libbie, nor Burkman mentions these two in their writings, and yet they did not disappear. (Duke Alexis sent at least one more of his wolfhounds to America, for in 1914 a red one was exhibited at the Westminster Kennel Club Show.[3])

The new fort was south of Bismarck on the west bank of the Great Missouri. Fort Abraham Lincoln was hastily being built with green wood when the 7th arrived, and they would continue to camp until it was finished (Armstrong lived in his wall tent). It was situated below Fort McKeen, a slightly older infantry post, high on a bluff overlooking the river. McKeen was protected against Indian raids by blockhouses and three palisade walls (a fourth was unnecessary because of the precipitous slope). Fort Lincoln was designed for cavalry and situated on the flat ground between the bluff and the Missouri. As was standard, the buildings were arrayed around the parade ground. The stables were located near the river to facilitate the daily watering of eighty-eight horses in each long building. As with all Army posts, it was meant to be self-sufficient with housing, offices, hospital, corrals, guard house, officers' club, Indian scouts' quarters, granary, ice house, bakery, sutler, and buildings for the carpenter, blacksmith, saddler, etc. Later a playhouse and photographer's studio were added. A fair amount of open space was needed for long stacks of hay and firewood. (Prodigious quantities of wood were needed to get a fort through the winter. In 1873, William Wade and his crew were contracted to provide 2,000 cords of wood for Fort Rice.[4]) The post also had a vital but seldom mentioned building—the dead house. It stored the coffined bodies of people who died when the ground was frozen. The concept was not new to Libbie—there was a dead house at Fort Hays, but it was even more necessary in the colder latitudes of Dakota. Libbie never says what happened to staghounds who died in winter. There was one cemetery for soldiers, civilians, and Indian scouts on their scaffold burials.

A row of wooden two-story houses (each shared by two married couples or bachelor officers) faced the wide parade ground and the river beyond. A larger house at the center by the flagpole was the commanding officer's. Meant for entertaining, it offered a generous parlor, but otherwise it had the usual configuration of a kitchen above an underground storeroom, with bedrooms on the second floor and attic above. The kitchen had a large stove for cooking and heating, and the parlor and each bedroom had a brick fireplace. Behind officers' row, the gently sloping hills rising up to Fort McKeen were perfect ground for romping dogs.

The Custers had their own produce garden with a tall board fence to prevent staghounds from damaging the precious vegetables.[5] (Once an epic grasshopper swarm wiped out every vegetable on the post.) Their grounds were enclosed with another tall fence to contain the dogs. A woodshed also housed curing meat, and there was a kennel. Capt. Irvine's greyhound kennel at Fort Sully was built of rough-sawn wood slabs.[6] Armstrong's was the same, probably made by the carpenter and Burkman. It was unheated, but with ample straw bedding, the dogs would nestle in and curl up together for warmth. On very cold nights, Libbie took young pups to bed with her, and Burkman remembered, "Their quarters was allus full o' dogs. Most of the time they was two or three sleepin' cross the foot o' their bed."[7]

The commandant's home was the officers' social center with regular hops, gatherings of Armstrong's favorites, sewing bees hosted by Libbie, and, as the Custers usually had a marriageable young woman staying with them, the bachelor officers always found reasons to come calling. The troopers had similar entertainments—theatricals, clog dancing, music sessions, foot races, horse races (which included the officers), and a team game growing in popularity—"Base Ball." Off-post, the soldiers cut loose at Point Pleasant or "Whiskey Point" across the river. It was a crude satellite of Bismarck existing solely to separate the soldiers from their money via whiskey, gambling, and prostitution. Point Pleasant was reached by a carelessly handled "ramschackly" ferry boat—which was even more nerve-racking when there were ice floes. Libbie thought the hamlet a "wretched little collection of huts."[8] Liquor-fueled arguments over cards caused gunfights, and casualties were not unknown.

A few miles upriver and on the opposite bank was Bismarck, consisting of thirty buildings (mostly log shacks) and two hundred people in January 1873. After Fort Lincoln was occupied, Bismarck boomed. There were 1,200 citizens, a newspaper, rail depot and engine yard, hotels, restaurants, shops, churches, doctors and lawyers, gunsmith, and eighteen saloons.[9] As it had in Texas, Armstrong's command served as an auxiliary to the local marshals and occasionally assisted in bringing criminals to justice.[10] (Originally called Missouri Crossing to mark the Lewis and Clark connection, in 1872 the town was named Edwinton after a railroad engineer and in 1873 renamed for Chancellor Otto von Bismarck to attract German settlers and investments.)

Officers' Row under construction in the fall of 1873 at Fort Abraham Lincoln, Dakota Territory (from the original glass plate negative). The commanding officer's house is third from the right and has a different design plan than the others. Armstrong lived in the tent out back while it was being finished. The photographer's assistant and buggy are seen in the foreground, and on the parade ground, a flock of sheep can just be seen grazing. The Missouri River is in the distance. South Dakota State Historical Society, South Dakota Digital Archives. 2015-11-15-313.

Fort Life with Dogs

Winters were long and deep, and the regiment's routine was adjusted to match the climate. Sentries were allowed to wear buffalo fur overcoats, mittens, over-boots, and hats over their wool uniforms and overcoats, and in bitter cold they only walked their post for fifteen minutes at a time.[11] Frostbite was a common problem, and the surgeons often amputated fingers and toes. Both the Custers and their dogs had difficulty adjusting to the extreme cold.[12] When the hounds were released from their kennel on frosty but sunny mornings, they would find east-facing walls and fences and stand there, happily absorbing the sun's rays and the reflected heat from the wall. The Scottish Deerhounds and Russian Wolfhounds withstood the cold much better than the short-coated foxhounds and greyhounds.

In warm weather, soldiers would fill water kegs and barrels from the river and deliver them to the post's quarters. When the Missouri was frozen, blocks of ice were sawn and stacked in wagons. In the dead of winter, water could be as precious as it was in the desert. Sometimes it was so cold the men couldn't work, which meant no water apart from snow melted on stoves. Two water barrels were kept out back of each building, one for drinking and cooking and the other for washing—and they were used to douse house fires. The drinking barrel had a tight-fitting lid to keep out the windblown dust and grass and to prevent the dogs from slobbering in it.[13] In warm weather, mosquito larvae in the barrels produced clouds of the "night pirates" who could bite through a layer of clothing. People covered themselves in heavy clothing and veils and slept under netting. The livestock had only smudge pots for some protection from the mosquitos, and Libbie wrote of the cattle unable to feed and dying of exhaustion. "The poor dogs dug deep holes in the side of the hills, where they half smothered in their attempt to escape."[14]

For all the time they were at Fort Lincoln with a photographer regularly on post, it is surprising more images of the Custers' hounds haven't come to light. Armstrong did have several photographs taken of the officers and wives posed on his porch steps, but unlike at the Blind Asylum in Austin or the compound on Big Creek, none of their dogs wandered into the camera's view. In a photograph Libbie treasured, the always-serious Burkman posed with the elements of his world, Armstrong's horses Dandy and Vic, with four "Scotch Staghounds" from the pack lying around them.[15] The image of Burkman with horses and some of the pack is one of two existing images of their dogs on the post. (A second, less well known version exists. In that one, the photographer has shifted his position slightly, for less of the two hills northwest of Officers' Row can be seen—and there are *five* hounds lying behind the horses. This image was first published in *Custer's Indian Battles* by Charles Francis Bates in 1936.[16] As Bates collaborated with Libbie, that photograph was one she mentioned in a letter to Burkman in the 1920s.[17])

Burkman had charge of the Custers' hounds as usual but all forty couldn't possibly have been kenneled at their house. Lt. Algernon Smith and Tom had their hounds—although the latter would have been sharing bachelor quarters. That many dogs were likely parceled out amongst the Custer Clan or slept in the stables with the horses. (At that time, Armstrong's trusted circle of officers consisted of lieutenants James Calhoun, William Cooke, Frank Gibson, Benny Hodgson, Donald McIntosh, Algernon Smith and captains Tom Custer, Myles Keogh, Myles Moylan, George Yates, and sometimes Thomas Weir. Conspicuously absent from his clan were most of the senior officers.)

Burkman considered the hounds' lot to be the same as the soldiers, "But they was army dogs and army life means bein' tired and footsore and thirsty and hungry and jist marchin' on."[18] When game was caught on the march, they gorged themselves but often went hungry in-between feasts, and if it was a "dry camp" with no creek, there might only be a little water for them. At Fort Lincoln each day, Burkman boiled a large kettle of mush, composed of meat scraps, bones, grease, hardtack, and anything else from the kitchen. Like dogs everywhere, they preferred "what they considered dainties from the family table." At meal times in Kansas and Dakota, a crescent of dogs whining and barking sat around the kitchen door waiting for scraps. Mary did not have Eliza's temper and refrained from hurling objects and colorful insults at the beggars.[19] Occasionally, the adults and half-grown pups fed themselves by going hunting "on their own hook" and returned with the leader carrying a jackrabbit.[20]

Burkman was in the habit of tethering the dogs for their meals to prevent fights and food stealing. Once, the entire pack went missing after dinner. Burkman was unaware of this until one of his fellows alerted him in the mess hall. Nervous about interrupting the Custers at their dinner party, he went searching in the dark. Blucher and Tuck always seemed to be the ringleaders, so Burkman figured if he found them, he'd find the rest. Away from the fort, he heard squealing pigs and spotted the pack running toward him with bloody muzzles. In the morning, Burkman found the black farmer whose pig had been killed by the dogs. With all the noise he'd heard, Burkman was surprised it was only one pig, but he made restitution with poker money he'd recently won.[21] (From Burkman's description, it's clear this happened at Fort Lincoln, but he says there were eighty dogs—which was his tally for the pack in Kentucky.)

That many dogs produce a considerable amount of feces daily. Burkman probably took care of the Custers' yard, but there was a lot more needing cleanup. For mild infractions such as disobedience, slovenliness, getting drunk, etc., soldiers chopped firewood, shoveled horse manure (no end of that), or "policed" the grounds by picking up trash—and that could mean dog excrement. This was a fact of life which was seldom written about, but Col. Benjamin H. Grierson of the 10th Cavalry (one of the Buffalo Solider regiments) was one of the few to note that problem. His new post in Fort Concho, Texas, was generally unkempt, and he declared the three-foot-high weeds all over the place were "…actually a blessing since they hid the numerous deposits left by dozens of dogs."[22]

While they could cause a lot of trouble, the Custers' hounds helped with a problem every cavalry regiment experienced. Enormous quantities of hay and grain were stored all year round, and mice and rats were a constant problem. The post's cats (both pet and feral) kept the rodent population in check. These cats had litters continually, but dogs and the occasional coyote or fox regulated the feline census. This was the natural order of things, but Burkman had to chain up the dogs periodically so they did not kill *too* many cats—or other small animals.[23]

Dogs continually delighted Armstrong and inadvertently caused him to laugh when as commander he shouldn't have. Deerhounds, greyhounds, and wolfhounds are not barking breeds (unless provoked), but the foxhounds were always making a loud ruckus. One foxhound used to annoy the bugler sounding calls by dolefully howling while sitting next to him.[24] The Custers thought this was very funny, and Libbie fondly remembered, "The bay of the hounds was always music to the general."[25]

They were exercised daily on rides, hunts, and their rambles around the post with Armstrong—"Whar-ever he went they went too, pesterin' us considerable."[26] From the Custers' writings, it's pretty clear that Blucher II (Bleuch) was the alpha dog who deferred to Armstrong as the true pack leader. Similar to the regiment, a large pack will have a commander and string of subordinates. Below the alpha were the betas or the sergeants of the pack. From there, dominance decreased down to the submissive junior dogs, bitches, oldies, and sick dogs. Each morning, when released from the kennel, the pack would greet and sniff to check status—assessing who was on top, weak, in season, or challenging the hierarchy. Periodic rechecks happened throughout the day. The alpha male kept the pack orderly by asserting authority over the lesser males—claiming food, bones, fertile bitches, and attention from the Custers. Usually, the pack leader's signals (raised hackles, stiff neck, and growl) were enough to put a junior in his place, but sometimes a dust-up settled the matter. Fights between males were bad enough—usually ending with minor wounds and submission. When competing bitches fought, they were less likely to stop after the loser submitted by rolling over to display her belly, and injuries were worse. The Custers learned that beyond feeding, watering, and doctoring, a large pack took deft social management.

Beginning with the march from Yankton and continuing in their life at Fort Lincoln, dog personalities and quirks began to stand out. Blucher, the powerful hunter and leader, was strangely averse to long pieces of metal—rifles, sabers, pitchforks (probably someone had hit or menaced him with one). When seeing the threat in a man's hand, he groveled on his belly, whining and whimpering. Burkman said they never figured out why he behaved that way. Blucher was his favorite (and he believed Libbie's as well), and Burkman always used to get extra kitchen scraps for him.[27] During the Dakota years in her memoirs, Libbie declared Blucher to be her husband's favorite—although in his own letters he declared Tuck and Maida II or III as having that honor. Armstrong was probably greatly attached to all three—and/or possibly fickle enough to favor whichever one was meeting his expectations of the moment.

Despite Burkman's assertion about Blucher being Libbie's favorite, it was Cardigan who was her special dog. His sweet habit of climbing into her lap had endeared him to her, but a prolonged period of nursing cemented their bond. As it transpired, Cardigan had been separated from the hounds at Fort Lincoln for some extended period (Libbie doesn't elaborate as to why), and the Custers made the mistake of putting him in the kennel without a gradual reunion on neutral ground. Having been out of the pack for too long, Cargidan was perceived as an outsider, and the males attacked him. It was a terrible fight with the raging hounds standing on their hind legs and tearing into each other. Trying to separate several large dogs in blind fury was dangerous, and Libbie didn't say how the fight was stopped, but Cardigan got the worst of it and came away with large gaping wounds in his sides. He became Libbie's house dog during his months of healing.[28]

Dakota Hunting

Hunting was different than it had been in Texas or Kansas. Libbie remembered, "The weather seemed to grow colder and colder as the winter advanced—from 20° to 30° below zero was ordinary weather."[29] It could get lower, and one of the frontier jokes was that a person needed to fix the ends of two thermometers together to see how far the mercury was dropping. Like any good huntsman, Armstrong worked his pack according to their talents, the local game, and the weather. The land around Fort Lincoln was not antelope or buffalo country, but black-tailed deer, jackrabbits, wolves, coyotes, and foxes were plentiful. During the winter, when the post was frozen, hunts were considerably less social occasions. Hunting parties were generally safe from Indians—who tended to hunker down in their winter camps until spring. Armstrong and Burkman in buffalo fur coats, and perhaps an officer or two, assembled the foxhounds in front of the house, and Libbie waved farewell from the porch (if the weather was not too difficult, she would ride with them). Blasting away on his dog horn, Armstrong worked the pack in the brush and timber along the river until they struck a hot trail, and then, baying like crazy, the hounds ran the quarry down. Returning home with a deer slung over the orderly's saddle, Armstrong would blow his horn to re-gather the now satisfied and quieter pack.

In winter, the wolves and coyotes used to prowl very near the post, and Libbie could watch them from her window. One snowy morning, the staghounds were released from the kennel for exercise and, spotting a coyote, they flew after it and over the hills to the west. The snow was too deep for a horse, so Burkman slogged after the dogs on foot. He found them with the dead coyote and struggled to drag the carcass back to their woodshed. Armstrong was delighted with the hounds' prowess, and Libbie wanted the pelt made into a robe. The coyote was not large enough, but Burkman, wanting to please her, hauled back every fox, coyote, and wolf caught that winter so she could have a luxurious fur comforter.[30]

When the snow melted in late spring and the game was out on the prairie, the sighthounds came into their own, and the hunts resumed a social nature. Released from their kennel, the hounds swirled around officers, orderlies, and horses, greeting their favorites. Armstrong was dashing in his knee-high "troop boots," fringed buckskins, blue flannel shirt with long red necktie, and a broad-brimmed hat with "a slight mark of his rank."[31] (This would have been a major general's twin stars—his rank during the war.) His preferred hunter was Dandy, who loved the dogs and they him. With the barking, neighing, shouted jokes and commands, horn blasts, and goodbyes from the ladies, Libbie said not a word was intelligible.[32] Blucher would leap up to Armstrong's saddle and could nearly jump over the horse entirely. Shouting "Whoopla!," the hunters rode out, and in fair weather, sometimes a few women went along—typically wearing military-style riding habits with brass buttons and "pillbox" caps sporting the 7th's badge. The deer were frequently close enough to the fort that Libbie never stopped hearing Armstrong's horn.[33] When the foxhound's yodeling stopped, the hunt was over, and on their return, the hounds frequently had injuries which needed doctoring by the Custers.

The catalog of injuries included lacerated or bruised feet and legs, cuts from brambles, cactus thorns in their pads, and porcupine quills in their mouths. Libbie noted their "English hounds" (presumably Grime and Possum) took a while to learn about porcupines which bristled with long barbed quills and, when attacked, took refuge in dens or trees. After novice dogs tried one, they retreated with pin cushions of quills in their faces and paws. If not removed, the painful barbs would eventually corkscrew deeper into the body—causing infections and even penetrating the organs. The dogs' welfare always came first, and Armstrong never took the time to change his dirty hunting clothes before surgery. Libbie sat on the dog and held its legs, looking the other way while Armstrong used his clasp-knife's tweezers to get at the barbed quills which had to be pushed through the flesh for removal or cut out. Removing quills took a long time but the dogs learned to hold still and always seemed grateful when it was over—"licking the general's hand as he praised them for their pluck." If one of the foxhounds came over to Libbie, "...shaking his great, velvet ears and wagging his cumbrous tail," Armstrong would point out he was a recent patient paying his surgical bill the only way he could—with gratitude. Old Rover from Kansas had epileptic fits, and when feeling one coming on, he would scratch and bark to be let in the house. Armstrong would sit with Rover on the floor, petting and talking softly to him while the hound shook uncontrollably and salivated. When the fit passed, Libbie claimed that Rover's tail would feebly wag as thanks for Armstrong's care.[34]

Game was plentiful, and there was almost always a saddle of venison hanging in the woodshed. When Armstrong had enough meat for his household, he shared with his officers and men—who were always glad for relief from beef and salt pork.[35] Sometimes his hounds made more work for him. Armstrong and his pack once went calling to deliver a quarter of venison. Before any conversation in the parlor got going, there was a "tremendous scuffle and growling" heard in the attic. The officer investigated and found that nine of Armstrong's hounds had followed through an open door and dashed upstairs to tear apart the hanging joint. The ruined meat necessitated a hunt the next day to replace it for his neighbors.[36]

The one disadvantage to spring and summer hunting (and riding farther away from the fort) was the increased possibility of running into troublesome Indians. Libbie remembered on a mild day in spring, the body of a white man was found in the area where she and Armstrong had been riding earlier. The unfortunate man had been staked out and disemboweled—and that was on the supposedly safe side of the Missouri.[37] For just that reason, an escort would go along with hunting officers and sometimes on pleasure rides. So great was the fear of a torture death by Indians that new soldiers were advised to "save the last round for yourself"—but such dire straits rarely happened near a military reservation.

Armstrong and Libbie settled into winter life at Fort Lincoln. His Civil War moniker of "Old Curly" had long since dropped out of use, and he was now "Yellow Hair" to the soldiers at the fort or "Jack" from the "G.A.C." initials on his trunk. There was no library yet, but there were books which the officers brought with them. Old newspapers from travelers were eagerly passed around. With no campaign news, little doing around the post, and irregular mail and news, gossip tended to dominate luncheons and dinners. During winter, stoves and fireplaces were filled with wood before bedtime so the rooms would be warm all night long—frequently an orderly or servant would add more during the night. One evening in the first week of February, the Custers had retired early, as

Armstrong was tired from a long hunt in the snow. Libbie awoke to smoke and the roaring sound of a chimney fire. Armstrong ran upstairs as the chimney exploded and blew a hole in the attic wall. (The poorly made brick chimney had leaked and ignited the petroleum insulation paper under the plaster.) Soon the roof was on fire. He tried dowsing it with water, but it was too far gone. The sentry fired an alarm shot, and Armstrong bundled Libbie and young Agnes Bates out of the house. Refusing to allow his men inside, in his nightshirt and vest, Armstrong started pulling their belongings out of the ground floor, which troopers then dragged to the parade ground. There was no pumping fire engine, and water barrels were frozen, so the house burned to the ground. Fortunately, there was no wind; otherwise, embers would have set the downwind houses ablaze.[38] Libbie doesn't mention their hounds, but someone had released them from the kennel before the fire reached it.

Armstrong had saved a fair amount, but Agnes lost all her clothes and Libbie lost most of hers, as well as linens, china, and silver. What Libbie mourned most was a scrapbook of Civil War clippings about Armstrong and a wig made from his locks which she wore at masquerades.[39] The officers' wives gladly gave them clothes, and eventually, Libbie and Agnes replaced their wardrobes with catalog orders and shopping trips to Bismarck and St. Paul. For housing, Armstrong commandeered one side of Tom's duplex bachelor quarters. That spring, Armstrong supervised the construction of the new house. At

The Custers' house at Fort Lincoln, rebuilt after the fire of February 1874. Out back of the kitchen (just visible behind the main house), there was a woodshed and a kennel. New trees were planted in front and, with their leaping staghounds in mind, Armstrong had tall board fences built to prevent them from escaping. Left to right, Leonard Swett, W. C. Curtis, Libbie Custer, Lt. James Calhoun, Miss Emma Wadsworth, Lt. Col. George A. Custer, Lt. Tom Custer, Mrs. Margaret Calhoun, Lt. Richard Thompson, Miss Nellie Wadworth, and an unnamed soldier. Courtesy of the National Park Service, Little Bighorn Battlefield National Monument, LIBI_00019_001899. Photograph produced in 1875 by Orlando S. Goff, Fort Lincoln, Dakota Territory.

Libbie's request, it had a south-facing bay window in the parlor for her potted plants and bird cages. Armstrong delighted in designing his own library which also served as an office.

That room was a snapshot of Armstrong's life and just as theatrical. It was filled with trophy heads—a Dakota buffalo, deer, a few antelopes, some jackrabbits, a snowy owl perched on deer antlers, a sandhill crane on a pedestal, an eagle, a fox, and a grizzly bear rug in front of the fireplace. There were two portable bookshelves for his small but precious library and one shelf full of old copies of *Galaxy, Turf,* and *Forest and Stream*. Racks held binoculars, map cases, gloves and kepi, dog horns, riding whips, spurs, hunting knives, and the engraved Spanish-made saber captured from a Confederate officer. In one corner was a gun stand containing four pistols, a Winchester, Springfield carbine, shotgun, and even an old flintlock musket. Propped against the wall near the bookshelves was an oversized map of the North American continent. There were photographs of Libbie in her wedding dress, Lawrence Barrett, the actor, Generals Sheridan and McClellan, the well-known Brady profile of Armstrong in his slouch hat, and a thermometer.

On his crowded writing desk (really a small table) there were two plaster statues which had meaning for him: "Wounded to the Rear/One More Shot" and "Letter Day." The former depicted two wounded soldiers stopping for a last shot, and the latter, a soldier writing home. (They were frequently chipped and broken during moves, but Armstrong always glued them back together.) There was his desk set with inkstand, a kerosene lamp, framed photos, and a sculpture of a foxhound's head. Stored under the desk was his personal footlocker.[40] Libbie joined him periodically to read or sew. The room's camp chairs had beaver or mountain lion pelt covers, and against one wall was a wide couch covered with a brightly colored Mexican blanket from their time in Texas. It was Armstrong's refuge—a "man cave" for reading, writing, and thinking, and his favorite hounds were always welcome there.[41]

Stealing the Black Hills

The Custers managed their first Dakota winter, which Libbie said, "got colder and colder." Armstrong and the 7th Cavalry were ordered on another exploration, but this time he was in command. Summers are late in the Dakota Territory, and the Custers originally planned to leave in mid–June to move through unmapped areas in the Black Hills to locate sites for military posts. Sheridan needed a new western fort from which to strike at the Sioux and Northern Cheyenne refusing to live on reservations. Secondarily, the expedition would assess the region's gold bearing potential. Sacred to the Lakota Sioux, the Black Hills were rich in game and water. As part of the Great Sioux Reservation, their Black Hills had been guaranteed to them in perpetuity by the Fort Laramie Treaty. (Called *Ȟe Sápa* by the Lakota, the dark pine forests of the hills appear black from a distance.) The comparatively quiet discovery of gold in 1874 by trespassing prospectors and the subsequent rumor mill started an influx of miners who cared nothing for the Sioux's right to live there unmolested. The Army was to keep civilians out of the Black Hills but, like trying to hold water in a sieve, that task was doomed from the start. Trespassers caught by the Sioux were tortured and killed—which presented the Army with the unresolvable paradox of enforcing the law with white trespassers *and* trying to punish the Sioux for defending what was rightfully theirs.

The 1874 expedition was similar in size and composition to that of 1873 with scientists and mining experts to assess the land and potential mineral wealth, photographer William Henry Illingworth (whose stereographic views would be included in the Army report), and correspondents for the *Bismarck Tribune*, the *Chicago Inter Ocean, St. Paul Press, St. Paul Daily Pioneer, New York Tribune*, and *New York World*. It was expected that gold would indeed be found and of course, each newspaperman wanted to send the headline, "Gold!" Naturally, Armstrong's pack with its leaders, Blucher, Tuck, and Cardigan, went along. He left the rest with Libbie and detailed Pvt. Keevan, a house orderly who was fond of whiskey, to care for them and her. (Armstrong never mentions Grime, Possum, Stanley, or Madgie on either of the two Dakota expeditions.) William E. Curtis from the *Chicago Inter Ocean* boasted, "His leash of hounds is probably as large and well-bred as any in the country..."[42] Another correspondent noted, "There are 12 or 15 grey hounds with us..." and that they could catch jackrabbits, but the antelope always outdistanced them.[43] Col. Luther North of the Pawnee Scouts acknowledged the hounds took jackrabbits but disputed their ability to catch the pronghorn—"I saw antelope run away from General George A. Custer's pack of wire-haired Scotch stag or greyhounds in the summer campaign of 1874.... They chased antelope many times and never caught one, although the General said they had caught many."[44] For a dozen hounds to be with the column, there must have been more than just those belonging to Armstrong and Tom. Lt. Algernon Smith, as quartermaster, had the Herculean labor of supervising the wagons, civilian teamsters, livestock, provisions, and equipment. There is no record of whether or not Smith took his wandering staghound along. In fact, there is little reported about the hounds on this trip.

The column consisted of just under a thousand men. There were ten companies of the 7th Cavalry and the band, two companies of infantry, Santee Sioux and Arikara scouts, an artillery detachment with three Gatling guns and a three-inch, Rodman rifled gun, the usual teamsters and various civilian employees. There were over a hundred wagons, spare horses and mules, and 300 beeves. The engineering unit under Capt. William Ludlow was to clear roads and build temporary bridges. (Ludlow was one of the combatants in the cadet fight which Armstrong allowed at West Point.) The scouting contingent had Bloody Knife, Lonesome Charley Reynolds, and Col. Luther North (who had some vague scientific assignment). Two practical miners, Horatio Ross and William McKay, were to assess the gold potential.[45] Of the scientific men, there was Prof. Newton H. Winchell (Minnesota's official geologist) and Prof. Aris B. Donaldson who taught rhetoric and English literature at the University of Minnesota, but who signed on as botanist and correspondent for the *St. Paul Daily Pioneer*. A protégé of Yale University's paleontology professor, Othniel Charles Marsh, George Bird Grinnell was a zoology graduate student called "professor" by courtesy, and he filled out the "bug hunter" contingent. (O.C. Marsh was a renowned paleontologist who fought a back-stabbing battle over fossils with rival Edward Drinker Cope from the Academy of Natural Sciences of Philadelphia in the "Bone Wars." Grinnell had been with Marsh on his 1870 fossil hunt in Wyoming and by 1874 was well qualified for Armstrong's expedition. Both Ludlow and Armstrong respected Grinnell and after the Black Hills expedition, he returned there with Ludlow in 1875 but declined Armstrong's invitation for the 1876 campaign into Sioux country.)

Lt. Fred Grant was along again (and no soberer) accompanied by Maj. George Alexander "Sandy" Forsyth as Sheridan's representatives (the latter was Armstrong's commanding officer in Kansas). Lt. James Calhoun was the acting assistant adjutant general. Armstrong's brother, twenty-five-year-old Boston, was forage master (the same easy job which Emanuel Custer had in Texas) and Lt. Calhoun's brother, Frederick, was hired on as master of transportation.[46] One of the officers was Lt. Edward Settle Godfrey, who would become an expert on the Battle of Little Bighorn and provide a small yet significant puzzle piece in the Custer dog story. Armstrong thought the expedition would be one long picnic and tried unsuccessfully to persuade Lawrence Barrett, his actor friend, to come along.[47]

The departure was delayed by the time it took to gather wagons, mules, and supplies. General Alfred Terry postponed it a bit longer because he wanted the 7th to have the new Model 1873 "Trapdoor" Springfield carbine—a breech-loader whose copper cartridges fired heavy bullets accurately to 300 yards and which had a maximum range of 1,000 yards.[48] The men were also issued with the new Colt 1873 Single Action Army revolvers (famously known as the "Peacemaker"). On Thursday, July 2, the massive column was ready and to "The Girl I Left Behind Me," they left Fort Lincoln. (Some accounts say it was "Garry Owen," but the column was *very* long, and the band had ample time for many tunes.) Armstrong's expedition would march 883 miles in sixty days.

On the second day, the men saw an antelope herd and there was a tremendous scramble to see who could kill the first one.[49] On Saturday, the third day out, there was another wild fusillade at a herd of fifty antelope with one gunner abandoning his Gatling gun to run blasting after them. The team of four horses spooked and ran off with the heavy gun, which flipped over, trapping two horses on the ground. They were unharmed, but as punishment the gunner walked at the dusty rear for a day. After that calamity, any firing within 500 yards of the outer flank companies was banned.[50] Armstrong declared he would authorize hunting parties and reserved much of that duty for himself. Col. North recalled, "While General Custer was always telling of the great shots he made each day he hunted, he didn't seem to care much about hearing of any one else's doing good shooting."[51] (It is a little surprising that Armstrong didn't anticipate the problem of "promiscuous fire" from the incidents of the Yellowstone expedition.)

The long march was characterized as little but hot wind, dust, undrinkable alkaline water, dysentery, and Sioux alarms. Armstrong strove to make the expedition a success—and for him, that was not only as a good commanding officer, but also in finding the gold.[52] He wrote his usual extended letters to Libbie, continuing them on subsequent evenings until there was a sufficient volume of dispatches, newspaper stories, and letters to risk a mailbag run by scout. Armstrong instructed Libbie to keep any newspaper stories as he was sure they would be valuable someday.[53] (Lonesome Charley Reynolds was chiefly relied on for delivering the mail, and he supposedly had his horse's shoes nailed on backwards to fool Indians. A slightly different version from two reporters said he used leather booties on the hoofs to muffle the sound and obscure the tracks. Whichever method Lonesome Charley used, it worked.)

Libbie had extracted the usual promise from her husband to not put himself at risk. Toward the end of the Yellowstone Expedition she stated her requirements:

> I do not feel worried about your hunting. I even want you to hunt on every occasion but oh I do so beg you will not grow lax. Don't ever for my sake take less than 25 men for I know you must be closely followed by Indians.[54]

For this summer's march, Armstrong reassured her that he never ventured outside the lines without an escort of at least seventy to eighty troopers and a handful of Indian scouts.[55] Libbie did get some concessions from him; however, preventing Armstrong and his hounds from hunting ahead of the column would never be possible. While not a military subject for the adjutant's official record of the expedition, Lt. Calhoun faithfully recorded his brother-in-law's hunting kills and captures of porcupines, rattlesnakes, jackrabbits, badgers, prairie owls, and an eagle. These Armstrong called his "annual menagerie."[56] Unfortunately, several died while confined in packing crates. Despite Calhoun's meticulous records, he didn't write about the hounds. Perhaps they were so mundane a part of the 7th Cavalry that few bothered anymore to note them in letters and journals.

The first dispatch in the *Bismarck Tribune* on August 5 proclaimed,

> Every day the General may be seen in buckskin and broad-brimmed hat, accompanied by his faithful hounds. Every day the officers feast on antelope which abound here in great numbers.... Gen. Custer's pack of full blooded Scotch stag-hounds take an important part in the chase, and the few Englishmen in the command are supremely happy when they are in full chase after a jackrabbit or antelope.[57]

That was the last mention of the hounds, for in the next issue of the *Tribune* on August 12, the gold strike was prematurely announced.[58] Afterwards, Armstrong's Scotch staghounds could not compete with "GOLD!" for headlines. Apart from the photographer, William Illingworth, who was born in England, there were no Englishmen on the expedition, as Armstrong, the name-dropping Anglophile, would have talked about anyone significant from across the Atlantic. (It is possible he mentioned Clifford and Molesworth to the reporters and they got their facts mixed up.)

After dinner in camp, there were occasionally band concerts, recitations, sing-alongs, and always card games. A couple of times on rest days, teams for base ball were organized and the Actives of Fort Lincoln played the Athletes of Fort Rice with the 7th's veterinary surgeon as the umpire.[59] For the officers, writing letters or making journal entries was one of the primary evening activities. While Armstrong enjoyed staying up late to write dispatches and letters, most of the others bedded down not too long after sunset, for "Reveille" sounded at 2:45 a.m., breakfast was finished by 4:10 when "General" sounded (the call to break camp), "Boots and Saddles" at 4:35, "To Horse" at 4:55, and finally, "Advance" at 5 o'clock.[60] Sometimes, officers sent news of the expedition to the papers in what could be considered an early form of blogging. In fact, Armstrong had been paid to send expedition stories to the *New York World*. (Lt. Charles Larned's descriptive letters were published in the *Chicago Inter Ocean* during the Yellowstone expedition.[61]) It never occurred to the Army (or anyone else) that they shouldn't be broadcasting column strength and direction during the Indian Wars. (Getting useful enemy intelligence from newspapers was a common occurrence during the Civil War.)

* * *

Finding "fossilferous" bones and "petrefactions" of wood was all the rage.[62] Grinnell's first significant fossil find was a leg bone bigger than that of an elephant—four feet long and one foot in diameter at the largest end—but it crumbled upon excavation with pick and shovel.[63] Much to his annoyance, Armstrong rarely let the column stop long enough for Grinnell to properly explore cliffs and outcrops for fossil beds. Nonetheless, Armstrong enthusiastically stashed a petrified tree trunk and mineral specimens in his ambulance.[64] His other favorite pastime (besides taxidermy) was conspiring with Tom to play pranks on "Bos," their youngest brother. At twenty-five, tenderfoot Boston was exceptionally gullible but took the jokes with a good spirit. Once they convinced Bos to soak a certain stone in water, as it was a "sponge rock" and would eventually become soft and pliable—until he caught on after several days.[65]

Armstrong had only been gone for thirteen days when he wrote Libbie from the newly named Prospect Valley near the Montana Territory line. Apparently, Armstrong's bed planks had been left behind at one camp and for the rest of the expedition, his mattress went on the ground, wet or dry. Characteristically, he accepted the minor hardship and didn't complain. The letter also revealed his affection for the dogs. "As I write, ~~the dogs surround me:~~ Cardigan is sleeping on the edge of my bed. Tuck at the head & Blucher near by."[66] (The strikethrough was Armstrong's, but Libbie included it in her edited version of his letter in *Boots and Saddles*.[67] This seems to be Libbie's only published dog note taken from Armstrong's Black Hills letters.) Burkman, who persisted in referring to Tuck as a male, said, "Tuck was the General's favorite, I reckon 'cause that dog didn't have time fur anyone but Custer."[68]

The miners, Ross and McKay, were testing every stream they crossed and finally panned out flecks of "color" in late July or early August. Although the precise date and quantity were and are still disputed, no man would be rich on what was found. Gold fever hit the column, and Charley Reynolds left on August 5 with a sack of mail and the much-anticipated story. The next edition of the weekly *Bismarck Tribune* (August 12) proclaimed with several headlines on one page:

"GOLD!"
"Gold and Silver in Immense Quantities"
"CONFIRMED!!"
"Gold Bearing Quartz Crops Out in Every Hill"
"FIFTY PIECES OF GOLD AS LARGE AS PIN HEADS FROM ONE PAN."[69]

Homecoming

Having found the precious yellow metal, Armstrong turned toward home on August 7, and that day, he shot his first grizzly bear—although there is some dispute about whether he or Capt. Ludlow or Bloody Knife actually made the kill shot since all of them hit it.[70] Armstrong claimed the kill, declaring it "a most exciting hunt and contest."[71] He had Illingworth take glass plate photographs of him, Ludlow, Pvt. Noonan, and Bloody Knife posing with the eight-foot carcass.[72] Engineer William R. Wood said he, Ludlow and his orderly first shot the bear which was later shot by Armstrong and Bloody Knife. After seeing Armstrong with "his" trophy, Ludlow told Wood, "…remember this: we have seen no bear."[73] Clearly, it was a confused hunt, for Pvt. Theodore

Ewert claimed Illingworth (who was considered an excellent hunter as well as photographer) was in on the shooting and Armstrong was exaggerating, as it was merely an old cinnamon bear.[74] Sgt. John Ryan remembered several of Armstrong's hounds sleeping around the bear while the photographs were being taken, and a napping greyhound can indeed be seen in the image.[75] There were no letters to *Turf* about this trophy, but perhaps being one of four hunters shooting a grizzly was too mundane when compared to Armstrong's previous exploits—although he did tell Libbie, "I have reached the height of a hunter's fame—I have killed a grisly [sic]."[76] Confusingly, Armstrong implied he had taken a grizzly bear while on the Yellowstone expedition.[77] He would add this bear's head to his library wall and lay its pelt by the fireplace.[78] The Illingworth photograph of Armstrong's grizzly was engraved for the newspapers—but the sleeping hound was omitted.

Bloody Knife, Pvt. Noonan, and Capt. Ludlow are behind Armstrong, and at the left of the grizzly is a sleeping greyhound. Armstrong's tent is behind the group, and the photographer's distinctive wagon is in the background. Just above Noonan's shoulder are trophy elk antlers in the grass. This photograph was the basis for a rather poor painting commissioned by Armstrong (see Appendix: General Custer's Dogs in Art, Literature and Film), South Dakota State Historical Society, South Dakota Digital Archives. 2015-11-30-307.

From his field menagerie, Armstrong sent a badger, porcupine, jackrabbit, two marsh hawks, and sundry rattlesnakes to the Central Park Zoo.[79] Doubtless because of the academics on the expedition, Armstrong broadened his preference for donating his specimens from the Detroit Audubon Club and Central Park to include the University of Minnesota's fledgling Natural History Museum. He sent them the skins of "two antelopes, male and female, a deer with young, an elk head, a badger, a grizzly bear with young, a weasel...."[80] (As will be seen, this museum has a singular significance in the story of the Custers' dogs.)

Bloody Knife, Armstrong's favorite scout, points at Armstrong's map on the 1874 Black Hills expedition. Unidentified are the two Arikara scouts, the soldier (who *may* be Pvt. Burkman), and the deerhound and sleeping greyhound. Libbie commissioned a drawing based on this photograph to illustrate her book, *Following the Guidon*. Courtesy of the National Park Service, Little Bighorn Battlefield National Monument, LIBI_00011_004321. Unknown photographer and date.

Illingworth also took what is probably the most iconic photo of Armstrong the frontiersman and hound-man. Wearing his buckskins, the bearded Armstrong sits in a camp chair in front of his wall tent alongside Bloody Knife, two other scouts, and a heavily bearded soldier. Artfully displayed are Armstrong's single-shot, hunting rifle, knife, and cartridge belt. Beside the men are Armstrong's deerhound and greyhound. Unfortunately, no precise information about the location or date has been discovered, but it is the one of the last known photographs of Armstrong with his dogs.[81]

Sioux warriors had been watching the column the whole way, and as the adage went, when you don't see Indians, that's when you should worry—and the soldiers did. Despite the fears of Libbie and the troopers, the few encounters with Sioux and Cheyenne were entirely benign, and the Ree scouts became angry with Armstrong because they weren't allowed to take Sioux scalps in one small village.[82] The only casualties on the expedition were two privates and one sergeant who died from diarrheal diseases (the two doctors were not well-regarded by anyone) and one trooper who was killed when a festering dispute erupted into pistol shots. There were a few injuries—notably one teamster who fell off his seat during a difficult creek crossing, and the wheel of his five-ton wagon broke his leg in two places.[83]

On the return, they crossed long stretches of recently burned prairie which probably had caught fire from unquenched campfires on their first passing or less likely, a Sioux attempt to harass the expedition.[84] The horses needed grass, so to get through the scorched land, Armstrong had them marching hard—thirty miles a day for five consecutive days. It became necessary to move the lame, sore-backed, and played out horses and mules to the rear of the column.[85] If there was no improvement, they were dispatched with a "kindness bullet" which ensured that Indians would have no use of the horses. Armstrong's hounds were as tired and footsore as the horses and men, and biographers Jay Monaghan and Frederic F. Van de Water both say during the Black Hills expedition, he had sick men in ambulances booted out to make room for his hounds.[86] While he had in fact done this in Texas, in Kansas, on the march to Fort Rice, and probably on the Yellowstone expedition, neither of the two authors gives a source—and Van de Water was definitely anti–Custer. Whether the ambulances were occupied by the hounds or not, they were being used to transport the black cooks and Armstrong's collection of fossils, owls, porcupines, and rattlesnakes. (The two cooks were Sarah Campbell, called "Aunt Sally," and Armstrong's personal cook, a man named Johnson.) Frederick S. "Antelope Fred" Snow drove Armstrong's ambulance and twenty years later remembered it being full of his "curiosities," and he worked hard to keep it within easy reach of Armstrong. Snow said there were four ambulances, and at one point they were so full of sick men that many had to ride in the Army wagons.[87] Pvt. Ewert partially confirms this in his statement that two privates dying of dysentery and other sick men had to be carried in unsprung wagons.[88] Undoubtedly, Armstrong's dogs rode in his personal ambulance.

Days before the expedition returned, the pro-expansionist editor of *Bismarck Tribune* boldly stated each of its miners was finding $100 of gold per day and, "The very fact that Custer is in command at Ft. Lincoln guarantees immunity from the depredations of hostile bands to a country hundreds of miles in extent." The editor described how easy it was to get to the gold country and essentially promised the protection of prospectors by the government since it had been responsible for the discovery of gold.[89] A more enticing invitation to trespass on Sioux treaty land can hardly be imagined. Armstrong had barely shaken the dust off when a *Tribune* reporter interviewed him about the gold and the rest of the expedition. He claimed familiarity with mines in Colorado, which he said were similar to parts of the Black Hills. Armstrong fully endorsed the reports about gold—but it was his layman's opinion about appearances. Happily giving directions for prospectors and assurances of easy travel with no fear of Indians, Armstrong contradictorily said the land was unused "neutral ground" which the Sioux denied to those who wanted its resources.[90]

The cat was out of the bag. Newspapers were flashing the story across the country and debate raged over the amount of worthwhile gold found, the value of the Black Hills for settlement, and, echoing the anti–Custer sentiment after Washita, opening Sioux lands for Army incursion. Col. William Hazen (one of Armstrong's defense witnesses at his West Point court martial) had served in Dakota long enough to know something of the region, and he took grave exception to Armstrong's assessment of the land for settlement. The print duel between Hazen and Armstrong (who always took disparagement personally) got tremendous coverage in newspapers. Professor Winchell said he never saw any gold—but then his particular assignment was all the other mineralogy on the expedition.[91] The debate raged back and forth to no avail. With the country in a recession due to the Panic of 1873, the merest mention of the yellow metal sparked memories of the 1849 California Gold Rush. The dam burst, flooding the Black Hills with civilians despite the 1868 Treaty and the Army's attempts to keep them out. By the end of 1875, some 15,000 prospectors intent on their own fortunes stormed into the sacred land along what the Sioux now called "The Thieves' Road."[92] (In fact, the Lakota word for someone of European descent is *wasi'chu*, one meaning of which is "he who takes the best." As it turned out, there was indeed "Black Hills Gold"—a term which continues to be used by jewelry stores in the region.)

As a direct result of treaty violations on both sides and the 7th Cavalry's defeat at Little Bighorn, in 1877 the U.S. Government enacted a law which "purchased" the Black Hills, but no record exists that the Sioux nation were ever paid—even if they had wanted to sell. The United States Supreme Court ruled in 1980 the Sioux were entitled to damages with interest from the theft of their land. "The sum, uncollected and accruing interest, now exceeds $1 billion. The Lakotas would rather have the Black Hills."[93]

Libbie was following the expedition through the newspapers' accounts and Armstrong's letters, but the scout-delivered news was necessarily slow and irregular. Her life at the post, and indeed those of the other wives, consisted of watching for scouts and keeping occupied with sewing clothes (thriftily not wasting any fabric), writing poetry, drawing, and leading social activities for the officers' wives. It had been extremely hot and windy, and a plague of grasshoppers interrupted the tedium for a while—and there was always the chance of Indians with uncertain intent riding onto the post. About the only exercise she could safely take were short evening walks with the dogs and Keevan.[94]

When the news finally came that the 7th would soon arrive, Libbie was beside herself with anticipation. Armstrong stopped the column twelve miles away so the men

The Black Hills expedition just before returning to Fort Lincoln in August 1874. Several of the wagons are sporting quantities of antlers, and the photographer's wagon is in the foreground. In the inset, Armstrong is seen on the right with his hand on his hip, wearing a black hat and buckskins. To the left of him by the line of wagons, there is a recumbent staghound near the white horse. South Dakota State Historical Society, South Dakota Digital Archives (2015-11-30-305).

could clean up, the Ree scouts could don their finery, and Illingworth could take a few last photographs. In two images of the formed wagon train, what may be a staghound can be seen lying down next to a single white horse at the top center of both.[95] On August 30, they entered Fort Lincoln in four columns, with antler racks bristling on the wagons and "Garry Owen" playing. Above their shaggy beards, the men's faces were ruddy, and their trousers and blouses had been worn, torn, patched—and patched again. As they rode past the houses, the officers fell out to greet their wives. Hiding tears of relief and joyous laughter, Libbie rushed out of the house to meet her Autie. Pvt. Ewert snidely noted, "Mrs. General Custer came to meet her husband, but just as she came in 'catching' distance, she 'fainted?'"[96] It was another of their joyous homecomings, and upon Armstrong's entrance into his house, Keevan the orderly (who had promised to remain sober all summer while looking after Libbie), considered his orders discharged and announced his intention to go on a "tremendous 'bum.'"

> How any one could get drunk in so short a time was a mystery. The general had hardly removed his buckskin-coat before the old fellow stumbled up the steps and nearly fell in the door, with his arms full of puppies that had arrived during the summer. The rejoicing was too general for misdemeanors to be noticed. The man was thanked for his watchful care over me during the months past, and advised to find a place to go to sleep in as soon as possible.[97]

The Custers' days at Fort Lincoln were generally happy despite the difficult life in Dakota Territory and the never-achieved wealth and independence which Armstrong craved. He had regained his national fame and was popularly known once more as an Indian fighter, frontiersman, hunter, a judge of horses and dogs, and now, the man who found gold in the Black Hills. Libbie was happy, for a Victorian wife's contentment was supposed to come through her husband from his love and success, and their children, although she contented herself with only the first two. Armstrong considered himself blessed—he had a regiment occupying five different posts in Dakota, and he was a superior hunter with excellent horses and dogs. Lying on the bearskin rug in front of the library fire, Armstrong told Libbie he was the happiest man on earth and would not change places with anyone.[98]

The fall of 1874 finished quietly for the Custers, and aside from trips to St. Paul and attending Fred Grant's wedding on October 20 in Chicago, they opted to winter again at Fort Lincoln despite its frozen isolation. While in Monroe, they persuaded the Rev. Boyd (Libbie's former principal) to allow his daughter, Florence, to come with them as Libbie's companion.[99] In addition to introducing a marriageable, young woman to the post's society, Armstrong wanted more hounds. On Monday, October 26, Armstrong wrote a cordial letter to a friend and brother officer, "Captain Elliott Gray, Tecumseh, Mich." (thirty miles west of Monroe) wanting to know if he could get some foxhounds by the following Tuesday.

> I expect to return to Dakota in two or three weeks and am anxious to procure two or three fox hounds for deer hunting There are none to be had around Monroe but some people have suggested that you might have some or could get me some. I do not want them too young to run this winter. If you can do anything for me in this dog line please do so.[100]

Despite Armstrong calling him a captain, Gray was a lieutenant in the 7th Michigan Cavalry Regiment and had been one of Armstrong's staff officers. He was boarding some of Armstrong's thoroughbreds in Tecumseh and seemed likely to know if good foxhounds were to be had in the area. Whether or not he was able to oblige Armstrong remains unknown.

To liven up their winter gatherings, the Custers rented a piano from St. Paul and bought a harp. There were parlor games (including billiards), sing-alongs, weekly receptions, hops, frequent concerts, charades and theatricals in improvised costumes—and for Armstrong, winter hunting with the hounds. His collected *Galaxy* articles from the Kansas campaigns were published in December as *My Life on The Plains or Personal Experiences with Indians*. At age thirty-five, Armstrong was now a bona fide author. He spent much of his time in his study reading and writing more articles—often napping on the couch with a hound as his pillow.[101] There were no orders for an expedition in 1875, and Libbie was looking forward to a quiet summer with her husband at home.

Meanwhile, in New York City, P.T. Barnum was inventing a thrilling new show which would result in Armstrong's last dog acquisition.

TAIL PIECE: CALIFORNIA JOE AND HIS CUSTER HOUND

That Armstrong gave California Joe one of his sighthounds is certain. His family called it a deerhound, while a hound expert (who had seen it hunt) declared it a greyhound—making this a confusion of functional name vs. breed name. A well-known 1875 photograph shows California Joe reclining on the grass with his Sharps rifle and large black dog, but according to the caption given by his grandson, Joseph E. Milner, that was *not* one of Armstrong's hounds.[102] Family history has it that Joe met Armstrong at Fort Lincoln after a long scout in November 1875 and was presented with the hound.[103] Likely the date is off by some months, as Armstrong was in New York by then. Joe named the hound Kentuck in honor of his birthplace, and loved hunting deer with him.

TAILLESS DOGS

The Arikara scouts at Fort Lincoln lived according to tribal customs as much as was possible. In Libbie's condescending observations about their lifestyle (which were typical of white observers), she noted their "tailless dogs." Curiously, she also observed tailless dogs kept by the Southern Cheyenne captives at Camp Supply after the attack on the Washita.[104] It seems unlikely that two disparate tribes living nearly a thousand miles apart would have produced breeds of tailless dogs—and no Western observer has recorded that Indians docked their dogs' tails. At both Fort Lincoln and Camp Supply, these tailless (or at least short-tailed) dogs were kept by Indians living in proximity to white men, so that is likely the explanation. In 1873, a macabre "tail docking" incident occurred when two men from the 20th Infantry and their setter became lost near the Canadian border. Desperate after three days without food, they cut off the dog's tail, roasted and ate it, giving the bones back to the dog. They were determined to spare the setter long as possible and eating the tail stalled the need to eat the whole dog. Fortunately for all, they struck a trail and made it back to camp—where the newly missing tail was attributed to a bear attack.[105]

CHAPTER 12

The Last Dog Deals and the March to Little Bighorn

> *"'Tuck' regularly comes when I am writing, and lays her head on the desk, rooting up my hand with her long nose until I consent to stop and notice her."*
> —George Armstrong Custer, Powder River Depot, June 12, 1876[1]

New Year's Day, 1875, ushered in a quiet spring and summer at Fort Lincoln—apart from a few incidents to interrupt the monotony. Armstrong's military duties were largely administrative tasks, drilling the men when the weather was fair, and meeting with the Sioux reservation chiefs to hear complaints of short rations issued by the Indian agents.[2] In December at the Standing Rock Agency (south of Fort Rice), Lonesome Charley Reynolds heard Rain-in-the-Face, a Sioux warrior, boasting of his kills—including Dr. Honsinger and Baliran. Capt. Yates, Tom Custer, and a detachment arrested him, and he languished in the guardhouse for four months while the legal niceties of prosecuting an Indian under white law for killing soldiers and a civilian were debated. The judicial dilemma was neatly (but unsatisfactorily) resolved when Rain-in-the-Face and a civilian hay thief escaped one night with outside assistance.[3] Also a gang of thieves had been sneaking onto the post at night and stealing grain, which was then sold on the sly (clearly, no dogs slept at the granary; otherwise, they would've alerted the sentry). Armstrong received information about the thieves and, sidestepping Bismarck constabulary, his troopers found Army grain in the barns and warehouses of the miscreants—including that of the mayor.[4] Still, petty criminals and an escaped prisoner or two were tame stuff for a lofty cavalry regiment.

The Silver Mine and a Dog Deal

The Black Hills gold feud with Hazen, Armstrong, critics, and supporters continued into 1875. A second foray was to happen that summer, and it looked as if it would be Armstrong's expedition. Scenting more gold-strike news, the *New York Herald* badly wanted the scoop and offered to pay Armstrong for each of his letters published under a pen name.[5] As it turned out, the expedition was assigned to Col. Richard Irving Dodge of the 23rd U.S. Infantry. (Dodge, a dog man himself, would write *Plains of the Great West and their Inhabitants*—a substantial volume on Indians, game, and hunting practices.) So, with no military operation, 1875 was the Custers' first idle summer at Fort

Lincoln. It was a happy time for them—at least it was for Libbie as her Autie was not going in harm's way.

> ... it is impossible to express the joy I felt that there was to be no summer campaign; and for the first time in many years I saw the grass grow without a shudder. The general began the improvement of the post with fresh energy, and from the drill-ground came the click of the horses' hoofs and the note of the bugles repeating the commands of the officers. As soon as it was warm enough, several charming girls came out from the States to our garrison to visit us. They gave every one pleasure, and effectually turned the heads of the young officers.[6]

On April 27, Armstrong escorted Florence Boyd back to Monroe and then went to New York to drum up tangible financing for his mine. He and Jairus Hall had started the Stevens Lode Silver Mine enterprise in late 1870 and five years later, they were still struggling with nearly every aspect—the title, insufficient operating funds, debts, the unsuitable foreman, and ownership disputes over areas within the mine. About the only thing uncontested was one 450-foot gallery which was clearly theirs. Hall still believed the mine would produce handsomely if only its ills were cured with money.[7] He was not only trying to get this off the ground but other mining projects as well, and he traveled back and forth between his home in Hall Valley, Colorado, and Chicago and New York—all the while suffering from neuralgia. He worked on the practical difficulties of the mine and expected Armstrong to secure funding from investors.[8] Letters went back and forth between the two men until a doggy twist was introduced into the scheme.

From Jackson, Michigan, Hall wrote on May 20, acknowledging Armstrong's last letter and saying that as the current mine issue was still undecided:

> ... I will only write about the dogs—which I desire you to send to me in care of W. S. Salisbury, 34 Monroe Street, Chicago. If you start things as soon as you get home, they will be in time to go with me the last of next week. If this finds you in Chicago send me a note and it will be unnecessary for me to telegraph to Lincoln.[9] [Wilber S. Salisbury, tailor by trade, was Hall's friend and perhaps a business associate—in 1880, the latter witnessed a patent application for Salisbury's improved exhaust-draft nozzle for steam boilers.[10]]

Now, Armstrong was not the man to give his dogs away to just anyone, but like the Army horse for "Diamond Jim" Fisk, "Custer's hunting dogs" may have been another investor inducement. They hadn't arrived in Chicago by June 3, so Hall wrote from there about now trying to sell the mine since he had acquired full title. Despite its crippling debts, he felt it was a good property and a modest profit could be realized for both of them. He nudged Armstrong about the shipment: "I hope the dogs will arrive in time for me to take them on with me."[11] The trail of this particular dog deal vanishes, and whether or not Armstrong ever sent the dogs (or why) is unknown, and they never found the needed funding for the mine.

A Great Loss

On Thursday, May 20, Kirkland Barker was preparing the *Cora*, the largest cabin yacht on Lake Erie, for his club's regatta, and his two-man crew and a fifteen-year-old boy were using a borrowed yacht, *Mattie*, to bring in *Cora*'s ballast to the shipyard where she was laid up. With Barker at the helm, they sailed down the Detroit River alongside the island of Grosse Ile. The water was already rough with wind, and Barker had changed course when a fiercely blowing squall hit them. With six tons of lead on *Mattie*'s deck, she heeled over and sank in thirty feet of cold water.[12] Barker and the crew were drowned within sight of his home on Grosse Ile. Later reports said Barker suffered an attack of apoplexy (stroke) while at the helm.[13] Armstrong learned of his friend's death while in New York trying to resuscitate his silver mine.

Barker's widow, Jennette, had to figure out something for her husband's kennel of dogs. In a transfer whose details are uncertain, three of Barker's Scottish Deerhounds, Daisy, Fanny, and Kirk, were sent to Mr. Edwin Thorne and his nine-year-old son, Oakleigh, of Millbrook, New York. This likely benefited the widow. (Sometime before, Armstrong had sent a couple of his own deerhounds to Grosse Ile for Barker's breeding program.)

Edwin Thorne, a wealthy farmer and horse breeder descended from the old Massachusetts settlers, seems to have taken an interest in helping young Oakleigh make a foray into the dog breeding business. (In 1856, it was estimated that the dog trade in New York City amounted annually to nearly $100,000 with tens of thousands of dogs sold.[14]) Kirk had been mated to Fanny in the spring—possibly before Barker's death—and was bred to Daisy toward the end of June. The Thornes planned to sell the rare-breed puppies by capitalizing on the celebrity names of Armstrong and Barker.

Scotch Deer Hounds for Sale
I HAVE FIVE DOG WHELPS OF August 26. Sired by Kirk, bred from General Custer's stock by the late Hon. K. C. Barker, Detroit out of Daisy. She was by Mr. R. Hoe, Jr.'s, imported Spring, out of Fanny, bred by the late Hon. K. C. Barker from his old stock. Price, boxed and delivered at express office at six weeks old, $25 each. Will sell Daisy after whelps are weaned. Price $50.
Oakleigh Thorne
Millbrook, N. Y.[15]

There could not have been a great run on these five pups as the ad in *Forest and Stream* ran eight times from October 7 through December 16. Months later in June 1876, Edwin and Oakley still had Custer-Barker deerhounds.

Back to Fort Lincoln

When Armstrong returned to Fort Lincoln, he brought with him Emma and Nellie Wadsworth, two more eligible young ladies who would enliven social doings at the fort. Far from big cities, Army women accepted wearing out of date or even threadbare clothes. It was hard for them to stay current with the fashions in ladies' magazines such as *Harper's Bazaar* or *Godey's Lady's Book*. When traveling east and arriving at urban rail stations, the inadequacy of their post clothes became embarrassingly obvious, and nearly always the first purchase was at a dress shop. Anyone heading for St. Paul, Chicago, Detroit, or New York would have their friends' shopping lists pressed upon them. Clothes signified social standing and even regimental affiliation. Following Libbie's example, women on post often wore military-style riding habits—showing *esprit du corps* with regimental badges. In a photograph from a summer pleasure ride, Libbie wears her jockey hat, and the Wadsworth sisters wear top hats with ribbons and the 7th

12: The Last Dog Deals and the March to Little Bighorn 221

A riding party along the Missouri River at Fort Lincoln in 1875. There are three hounds (blurred from movement) at the horses' feet. Left to right the riders are Capt. Cooke, Miss Emma Wadsworth, two Indian scouts, Lt. Col. George A. Custer, Miss Nellie Wadsworth, Capt. Tom Custer, Libbie Custer, Mrs. George Yates, and Lt. Winfield Edgerly. (The two Indians next to Armstrong are not named.) Courtesy of the National Park Service, Little Bighorn Battlefield National Monument, LIBI_00011_000221. Photographed by Orlando S. Goff, Fort Lincoln, Dakota Territory.

Cavalry's crossed saber badges. There are three hounds with the riders—and this is the last image of Libbie and Armstrong with any of their dogs.

Armstrong had not written to *Turf* in a long time. Doubtless his normal enthusiasm as Nomad was dampened by the loss of Barker, but on August 23 (published on September 3), he wrote a response to "W.H.S." who had advocated cross-breeding pointers, setters, or hounds for deer hunting. Armstrong objected to the idea, citing his Texas experience with crossbreds. As a novice, he had indeed favored a concoction of breeds but since had changed his mind and staunchly insisted "half-breeds" hadn't the stamina for a chase lasting more than a couple of hours. With a high-pitched, discordant voice, they lacked the proper "deep-toned bass" or "clear bugle tones" of a hound. Armstrong admitted that crossbreds were suitable for flushing deer. He boasted about his purebred Kentucky foxhounds, Driver and Ferguson, who could find and run down a deer in less than an hour. Armstrong conceded that a satisfactory hunting dog could be made by crossing a foxhound bitch with a "Scotch deer-hound" dog to produce a large, fast dog with a scenting nose but snobbishly noted, "I have in my kennel Scotch deer-hounds, fox-hounds, and pointers; but I prefer to keep them pure."[16]

Merely expressing views on breed purity was not the hallmark triumph Armstrong wanted for letters to *Turf*, so he closed with a story about one of his two favorite mounts, the thoroughbred, Vic. The horse had gotten out of his stall one night and fallen down a thirty-two-foot deep stable well. Vic was stuck for several hours before he was found and winched up showing only minor scrapes. Armstrong put a racetrack spin on the accident and declared, "Considering the distance and direction of the course, and the conditions of this performance, I believe Vic's exploit is unequalled."[17]

Five of the Custers' deerhounds basking in the sun while Pvt. Burkman poses with Armstrong's horses, Dandy and Vic, for a photograph. The image gives some idea of what it was like to live with a pack of hounds at Fort Lincoln. Libbie almost certainly loaned this photograph to Charles Francis Bates for inclusion in his book, *Custer's Indian Battles* (1936). A slightly different version of this photograph is held by the Little Bighorn Battlefield National Monument—LIBI_00011_000173.

New York for the Last Time

Toward the end of September, Armstrong secured two months' leave and headed east with Libbie, Tom, and Lt. Cooke. They made the usual stop in Monroe to visit family (his parents were nearly seventy), and then Libbie was off to see her relatives in Grand Rapids and upstate New York, while Armstrong, Tom, and Cooke enjoyed the bright lights of New York City. The two young men absorbed everything the city had to offer for dashing, single gentlemen. Once again, Armstrong fired up his efforts to finance the boondoggle mine and made his social rounds until Libbie could join him.

He received a leave extension in November and the second in January due to snow blockage on the lines. On December 5, Armstrong celebrated his thirty-sixth birthday in New York. Approaching middle age, he was no longer the Boy General but still fairly trim—although city high life tended to put pounds on him. His reddish-blonde hair (now cut short) still curled and his soup-strainer mustache was as bushy as ever (with eyebrows to match)—but his hairline was receding and he had a bald spot. Though their finances didn't allow the latest cut in civilian suits, Armstrong was still a social lion—but he disappointed many people by not resembling Buffalo Bill Cody, Wild Bill Hickok or Captain Jack Crawford with their buckskins and long hair.

He received more invitations than he could handle, and sometimes Libbie had to nudge him into accepting important ones. They dined with two notable British tourist hunters—Major Sir Rose Lambart Price and the Earl of Dunraven. Armstrong had socialized frequently with Price, who had seen a fair deal of campaigning in East Africa, India, and China with the Royal Marines and had just completed an extended hunting and fishing tour of South and North America which he would later write about. Armstrong would invite him on the Sioux campaign, but because of unforeseen circumstances, he left with his regiment before Price could get there.[18] Windham Thomas Wyndham-Quin, the 4th Earl of Dunraven, and the Custers met for a luncheon in the studio of their mutual acquaintance, the painter, Albert Bierstadt, who had been commissioned by Dunraven to produce several paintings. (Either Libbie misspelled Dunraven's name or biographer Marguerite Merington could not read her handwriting, for in the latter's book, it came out as the "Earl of Sunracen."[19])

Lt. Col. George Armstrong Custer in civilian clothes on his last visit to New York City, three months before his death at Little Bighorn in June 1876. Photographed by José M. Mora. Courtesy of the National Park Service, Little Bighorn Battlefield National Monument, un-cataloged image.

The Custers saw their friend Lawrence Barrett and reconnected with the ever-interesting P.T. Barnum. There is not much written about their relationship apart from Barnum's buffalo hunt at Fort Hays, but historian Shirley A. Leckie summarizes their connection succinctly: "Five years later, in appreciation for their kind hospitality, he [Barnum] sent Libbie and Armstrong three English hounds."[20]

The Last Dog Deal

After P.T. Barnum's buffalo hunt in 1870, he and Armstrong became friends or at least cordial correspondents, and they may have strengthened their friendship during Armstrong's long leave in 1871 when he spent considerable time in New York. Barnum was always interested in Indian artifacts for his museum, and Armstrong had been generous in providing friends with those as well as fossils and zoological trophies. Whatever the reason, Barnum considered himself indebted to the Indian fighter. In the spring of 1874 and during the Black Hills expedition, the two were corresponding about Armstrong's expectations for it. He mentioned to Libbie that he told Barnum about Boston taking to life on the plains "as if he were bred to it." Barnum wrote back saying, "...it must run in the blood." In that same letter, he sent Libbie Barnum's first letter to the *New York Tribune* about the Black Hills.[21]

Seven months after first meeting Armstrong at Fort Hays, Barnum re-invented his "edutainment" business as Barnum's Grand Traveling Museum, Menagerie, Caravan, and Circus. He opened in Brooklyn—coining the now famous phrase, "The Greatest Show on Earth."[22] Barnum's agents had been scouring Europe for acts and curiosities, and he developed performances which mimicked English events like the Lancashire Races and the Donnybrook Fair.[23] However, it was not long before he tired of the static show and looked for something with bigger thrills to draw in crowds. During the early months of 1874, he renovated a vacant train station in the Flatiron District of Manhattan and turned it into Barnum's New Roman Hippodrome. The arena show featured exciting horse events and pageantry on an oval track and center performance area, and the acts were changed often. (The Hippodrome would later become Gilmore's Garden, which in turn became the first Madison Square Garden.)

On the nightly bill was the Great Congress of Nations, gymnastics, performing strong-men, Roman-style racing, ladies hurdles and chariot races (two and four horses), ostrich herding, an elephant trot, lassoing Texas longhorns, twenty-one free-performing horses, a race with monkey jockeys on Shetland ponies, wild Indians and Mexican rangers.[24] As an additional attraction, there was his famous menagerie of exotic animals and sometimes tethered balloon ascensions. When attendance lagged, Barnum would introduce a titillating act where actresses wore tights and exotic costumes—"The Grand March of Amazons" or "The Vision of Houris."[25] Nonetheless, the wild races were the most talked about features, for the accidents were sensationally reported in newspapers and increased attendance.

> There were two hurdles four feet high of brush. The horse took them smoothly, but when on the second field, one of the riders fell, and was dragged several feet by the animal. Instantly the audience rose to its feet again, and it was not until she had been carried out of sight by the attendants that it regained its composure sufficiently to sit down again.[26]

There were seventeen acts in the program, but the grand finale was "The Renowned English Stag Hunt" complete with red-coated master of hounds and his assistant, the whipper-in, imported English staghounds, the ladies and gentlemen of the hunt, and a live stag.[27] ("English stag hounds" were taller and longer than foxhounds to better run after stag. Barnum called his pack "stag hounds" and "fox hounds," but preferred the former because it sounded more impressive.) Like Armstrong, everything Barnum did was the biggest, fastest, and the best. He published a $5,000 challenge to the public, "That I am the only man who ever imported packs of English hounds, whippers-in, and all the paraphernalia for a representation of an English Stag Hunt in a Hippodrome in America." The act was so popular, he bought a second pack and sent it out with his traveling version of the Hippodrome show.[28]

The thrilling show opened in late April 1874 to excellent reviews and ran through November 1875. Given Armstrong's passion for theater, horses, dogs, and his friendship with Barnum, it would have been highly unusual if he *didn't* take in the Hippodrome show at least once. (In New Orleans, Armstrong and Grand Duke Alexis attended Dan Rice's arena circus with equestrians on trained horses, acrobats, gymnasts, and clowns.[29]) Barnum, always looking for good press, had been unsuccessfully asking Samuel Clemens (Mark Twain) to "notice" his show in the articles he wrote for *Harper's Weekly*.[30] By the fall of 1875, Barnum was bored with the show, which had likely reached its saturation point and was no longer generating a decent profit, so he reinvented himself and his show again. This time, Barnum's idea was to travel by railroad, exhibiting his most popular acts under a "Big Top" tent to fresh audiences in different cities. No longer needing the Hippodrome livestock, equipment, and menagerie, on November 30, he auctioned most of it off in Bridgeport, including the hunt costumes, foxhounds, and the stag.[31] (Barnum's circus would combine with two others to become the Ringling Brothers, Barnum & Baily Circus—still "The Greatest Show on Earth.")

During Armstrong's whirlwind of socializing, it is not clear whether he expressed interest in the Hippodrome hounds or if Barnum offered them to him, but before the auction, he gave Armstrong three of the best.[32] On November 29, 1875, the day before the sale, Barnum (who was then also mayor of Bridgeport, Connecticut) wrote:

> My Dear General Custer—I take pleasure in sending you by Express, three of my English Fox Hounds. I bought them in London from the best kennels known in England & have no doubt by breeding in with your own stock, you will find that "blood tells." I am still under great obligations to you for past courtesies & shall be glad to have a chance to pay another installment. Truly yours, P.T. Barnum.[33]

Barnum was certainly the one who sent announcements about the dog deal to the newspapers. An article in the *Philadelphia Inquirer* on December 10, noted that Gen. Custer was given "several English fox hounds for use on the plains."[34] The *Bismarck Weekly Tribune* repeated the item under "Local Affairs" on December 29: "Barnum, the great showman, made him a present of his pack of fox hounds."[35]

The five remaining hounds were sold to a New Yorker for $35 (about $700 in today's dollars). Barnum had emphasized the purity of his foxhounds, and this aligned perfectly with Armstrong's aristocratic attitude about his horses and hounds. He intended to hunt with his new dogs in the spring and summer and was happy to have imported English hounds to breed with his existing stock. Barnum's agent was to send the hounds to John Hooey of the Adams Express Company who would in turn ship them west to Armstrong.[36] By then, the Custers were running low on money and moved out of their hotel to less expensive rooms across the street.[37] Probably to save dwindling funds (and because Barnum was fun), Armstrong and Libbie stayed for a while at his Bridgeport estate, Waldemere, in January 1876.[38]

The new year was America's Centennial, and Philadelphia would host a run of celebratory events and expositions from spring through fall, with the biggest hoopla on July 4. There were tributes from world nations and the thirty-seven states (Colorado, the thirty-eighth, would be admitted that August). Progress was the central theme and all manner of inventions and innovations were displayed along with industrial machinery and agricultural products. The Centennial Bench Show would run for four days beginning on Monday, September 4.[39] It was to be a national dog show like Barnum's in 1862, and exhibits would be sent from Great Britain and Ireland for competition. Several waggish editors volunteered to spare "about a hundred" dogs from their cities. As Armstrong had enthusiastically attended horse shows in Kentucky and St. Louis, and was now keen on purebred hounds, the Centennial Horse and Dog Shows would have attracted his attention.

As his leave was to end in February (but with no word on his third renewal due to winter travel difficulties), he had been negotiating what would have been a lucrative deal with the Redpath Lyceum Bureau for a series of lectures about his experiences in the Civil War and out West. It was a prestigious company which offered touring appearances by renowned authors and thinkers—and celebrities like Barnum. The income would be a much needed bolster for his personal finances, and the Redpath wanted him to start that spring, but Armstrong delayed signing in order to better prepare.[40] (Libbie knew her husband needed practice in public speaking. When excited or nervous, he talked faster and wouldn't notice her "slow down" wave—so she planned to stand up and raise her umbrella.[41]) To start lecturing so soon would involve yet another extension to his already lengthy leave. Also, Armstrong was just learning about the coming campaign against the Sioux, and he believed having a recent victory for the fall circuit would greatly increase his ticket sales.[42] The campaign might well be completed in time for him to attend the Centennial Horse and Dog Shows in September—although with the uncertainties of being in the field, he would have to miss its crescendo on July 4 in Philadelphia. As it turned out, Sherman (General of the Army since 1869) was finished with Armstrong's seemingly endless requests for leave, and despite snowdrifts on the rails, he was ordered to return to Fort Lincoln without delay. The Custers headed west on February 15 with Armstrong's three new foxhounds in the livestock car.

They made stops in the major cities but didn't begin the final leg until March. At St. Paul, General Terry, commander of the Dakota Territory, outlined the plan for the upcoming "Yellowstone Campaign" to force the Sioux back onto their reservations. On March 4, Armstrong excitedly telegraphed his friend, Lawrence Barrett, "We start to meet Sitting Bull tomorrow. Will reach Lincoln Monday."[43] Knowing the snow would be difficult, the Northern Pacific Railroad manager personally took extra measures to see that Armstrong's train had comfortable cars and the best chance of getting through. St. Paul to Bismarck was usually a one-day journey, but because of the snow it took much longer. Even with three engines with two snowplows and a crew of forty men with shovels, the train got stuck well outside of Bismarck. "Bucking the drifts" (ramming) failed, and the amount of digging needed was more than the workmen could manage. Each passenger car had a small stove, but there was not much food, and Libbie remembered hearing the unhappy "howling of our dogs" and the lowing cattle from the unheated livestock car. Fortunately, a portable telegraph set and glass jar battery were found and Mark Kellogg, a *Bismarck Tribune* reporter and amateur telegrapher, was able to climb up a pole, tap into the overhead line, and send a message from Armstrong to Fort Lincoln.[44] Upon hearing of his brother's predicament, Tom wired back, "Shall I come out? You say nothing about the old lady; is she with you?" He promptly organized a rescue mission by hiring a reliable driver and his team of mules and box sleigh, which Tom filled with straw, borrowed coats, and blankets.[45]

To the sound of jingling bells and the mules' steaming breath, they followed the telegraph line east for forty miles to find the snowbound train. Armstrong hauled the miserable foxhounds over to the sleigh where he settled them in the straw and returned for Libbie. "The drifts were too deep to drive near the cars, so my husband carried me over the snow and deposited me in the straw with the dogs. They were such strangers they growled at being crowded." Bundling up in loaned blankets and coats, the three Custers and foxhounds were cozy enough for the drive to the fort.[46] A couple of days after their arrival on March 12, Armstrong recieved a summons to testify in a Congressional hearing. On March 20, he left the new hounds with Libbie and Burkman who, mindful of Cardigan's unfortunate experience, were going to carefully integrate them into the rollicking pack.

The Belknap Scandal and the Start of the Great Sioux War

Congress was investigating corruption within the War Department—specifically how Secretary William Belknap made sutler appointments with expectations of continuing bribes. Armstrong, usually his own worst enemy in a political controversy, had been unwisely spouting opinions and hearsay evidence in the newspapers. As a result, the always newsworthy Indian fighter was called to testify. Congressman Heister Clymer was chairman and was determined to uncover the graft in what would be called "The Belknap Scandal."

Secretary of War Belknap was accused (and later proven guilty) of taking large kick-backs from his appointed post sutlers. As these positions had the sole right to sell goods on Army stations, they were potentially very lucrative. A post store was often the only place for officers and soldiers to buy liquor, tobacco, extra clothing, necessities and luxuries, so sutlers could charge what they liked and complaints be damned. It came out that these men often paid back more up the line than they kept in profits. In a time when a certain amount of graft was generally accepted as a benefit of government office, Belknap's corruption was so egregious that when revealed, it couldn't stand the light of day. The hearing began on February 29, and Belknap appeared on March 1 but didn't testify. The next day, he privately confessed to President Grant and resigned. Despite Belknap now being a civilian, Congress ruled they could still impeach him, and the proceedings continued. Although Armstrong had no hard evidence, at Fort Lincoln, his men had protested inflated post prices and taken to spending their money in Whiskey Point or Bismarck. When the sutler discovered this, he insisted he had the exclusive right to all sales to the soldiers and threatened enforcement via the War Department's chain of command. After hearing both sides, Armstrong confronted the sutler who admitted to making $15,000 per year on his sales but was sending $12,000 to Washington.[47] It was a hefty payment and only one from a great many Army posts. Despite his new role as whistleblower, Armstrong saw nothing wrong in accepting gifts from railroad companies—an expensive tent, free travel passes and special car accommodations, a holiday excursion, and, from a telegraph company, free messages (which were normally charged by word count and miles). Armstrong's dualistic attitude toward graft is reminiscent of the quip by Ashleigh Brilliant, "I either want less corruption, or more chance to participate in it."[48]

He continued to write editorial opinions and "leak" information to the papers—for which he was apparently paid.[49] An accusatory article, "Belknap's Anaconda," was published anonymously in the *New York Herald*, and while many thought Armstrong wrote the exposé, he always denied it. He testified twice on the corruption and even confirmed that the president's brother, Orvil Grant, was working dodgy business with the Department of the Interior.[50] The Committee on Military Affairs called him to testify on bribery and, with hearsay, he damned one of his own senior officers, Maj. Lewis Merrill, for taking bribes when stationed in South Carolina.[51] His rash charges against the administration (and by implication, the President) were tantamount to biting the hand which fed him. It was the same political blunder which McClellan had made in his failed presidential campaign against Abraham Lincoln.[52] With his cocksure attitude, Armstrong either didn't see the danger or presumed his name would give him immunity to repercussions. It was an election year and Grant hoped for a third term, but his government was plagued with scandals and with impeachment proceedings against his former secretary of war, the attack on his brother, public outcry, and rumblings of a political shake-up, the president's back was being pushed to the wall. Standing out in the crowd of accusers was the ever-flamboyant Armstrong. Grant exercised his perogative as commander in chief to get back at him in a perfectly legitimate way.

The Dakota Territory had been a thorn in President Grant's side for some time. With the unstoppable gold rush, he was going to have to either support the interloping miners or the treaty-protected and wronged Sioux. The government's offer to buy the Black Hills had been refused. A good many Sioux and Northern Cheyenne refused to live on a reservation or only went there when needing food. There was pressure to extend the railroad and the over-arching belief that Indians didn't know how to make proper use of land and therefore weren't entitled to it. In a White House meeting in early November 1875, President Grant, Generals Sherman and Crook, William Belknap, secretary of war, Zachariah Chandler, secretary of the Interior, and Edward Smith, commissioner of Indian Affairs, agreed the tribes needed to be forced to the reservations or attacked with the intent of completely eliminating their power. They would issue an ultimatum to the Sioux tribes to return to the reservations by January 31.[53] The tactic was a common, territory-grabbing gambit of many governments in many countries: issue an outrageous ultimatim to be complied with by an impossible date, and then "justifiably" declare war because the conditions hadn't been met.

Even if the Sioux tribes agreed to the ultimatum, moving villages in the dead of winter was physically impossible, and the government knew it. During peace, the Department of War, the Department of the Army, and the Bureau of Indian Affairs were all separate entities but with overlapping responsibilities and conflicts. With hostilities planned, control of the Indians switched from the Bureau of Indian Affairs (within the Department of the Interior) to the secretary of war and the Army. A campaign for late winter or early spring was planned by Sherman, and Sheridan was to execute it with three columns (any of them strong enough to defeat the number of Sioux they expected to find). The three forces would converge on the bands in their winter quarters. One column would drive the Sioux toward one or both of the others, catching it between hammer and anvil. Like Washita, the strategy was to encircle and surprise villages. For the campaign's leadership, Sheridan chose the commanding officers of the two relevant departments, Brig. General Alfred Howe Terry (Dakota) and Maj. General George R. Crook (the Platte). Terry was to command the Montana and Dakota columns, and Crook, himself a keen sportsman, had the Wyoming column. Only Crook was able to get his force moving for a winter campaign and had Col. Joseph Reynolds attack Cheyenne chief Old Bear's sleeping village on the Powder River on March 17. (The Oglala Sioux war leader, Crazy Horse, had periodically lived there.) The Powder River Fight accomplished almost nothing apart from getting Reynolds deservedly court martialed—and alerting the Northern Cheyenne and Sioux to the Army's intention. After that failure

12: The Last Dog Deals and the March to Little Bighorn

and logistical delays, the winter opportunity was missed, and the two generals would have to try for late spring or summer—when the tribes would be highly mobile.

Armstrong finally got to Fort Lincoln in melodrama-like circumstances. Having testified, he waited. On April 20 he went to Philadelphia to see the Centennial preparations but was recalled on the 24th. As it turned out, the committee didn't need him, so he asked Sherman if he could go to Fort Lincoln. Sherman asked the committee for his release, but this angered Grant, who ordered another commander be assigned to Fort Lincoln. Armstrong was cleared by the committee on May 1, but Sherman advised him to see the president and make amends. Grant, who considered the matter closed, refused to see him on three occasions and on the last, kept Armstrong waiting for five hours before sending him away. Indignant, Armstrong chose to interpret Grant's refusal for his audience as liberty to leave Washington. Stopping in Monroe, he collected his nephew and niece, Autie and Emma Reed, who were coming out for the season. On May 4 in Chicago, Sherman had him detained for leaving without permission. Armstrong was ordered to remain in Chicago while the 7th Cavalry proceeded on the campaign. That day, Sherman had three telegrams from Armstong trying to explain his situation. In his last message, he asked for detainment at his post so he could be with Libbie. Sherman was not wholly indifferent to his pleas and finally sent the near-frantic Armstrong to Fort Lincoln.

Even Armstrong's friend Sheridan was angry with his attacks on the government. Time was running short, as Terry was to leave St. Paul for Fort Lincoln in a few days. On May 6, Armstrong asked him to intercede. Terry, a former lawyer and capable commander during the war, had only been military commander of the Dakota Territory for a few years. He had never fought Indians but knew he could use Armstrong's experience. Having not seen Indian fighting since 1873, Armstrong was both eager for another round and worried about being left behind. Terry helped Armstrong to craft a soldier's appeal "...to spare me the humiliation of seeing my regiment march to meet the enemy and I not share its dangers."[54] As the commander, he endorsed Armstrong's letter and, reluctantly, so would Sheridan (who, despite everything, knew Armstrong was the right man for the campaign). By the time Grant received the plea, the newspapers were outraged at his personal vendetta against Armstrong. On May 8, Grant relented and cabled Terry that Armstrong could go on the campaign—*but* was to command nothing beyond his own regiment. (The beleaguered Grant announced at the end of May that he wouldn't run for a third term.) Two days after Armstrong's reprieve, he and Terry departed St. Paul for Bismarck, and a week later on May 17 the 7th Cavalry, as the largest part of the Dakota column, rode west to search for the Sioux somewhere in the Powder River country.

Over the Hills...

With the band playing, the Dakota column was led by Terry whose sedate uniform contrasted with Armstrong in fringed buckskins, with hunting rifle, two Webley Bulldog pistols (perhaps the gifts from Ainsworth and Townsend), and sheath knife. Prancing alongside their master were his deerhounds, Tuck, Swift, Kaiser, and Lady. Libbie rode alongside Armstrong, and Maggie and Emma Calhoun were in an ambulance. Boston, Autie Reed, and Richard Roberts (Annie Yates' brother) had been hired as herders, and they were determined to get Indian souvenirs. The march started out like other expeditions, with soldiers, Indian scouts, civilians, horses, Gatling guns, wagons, and beef cattle slowly grinding into motion—the two-mile-long column churning up prodigious amounts of dust. Libbie remembered the morning mist created a mirage—an illusion that the column was riding both on the earth and in the sky.[55] She would camp one last night with Armstrong for a protracted farewell. It was an easy march to the Heart River valley where the soldiers were paid their wages. Terry had delayed payday so he wouldn't lose any men at Whiskey Point. Of course, the sutler obliged the men with liquor, but they couldn't leave camp.

After a tearful farewell with Autie in the morning, Libbie watched them march out of sight, and she, Maggie, and Emma rode back in an ambulance with the sutler and paymaster. Both Armstrong and Libbie had hopes she could go upriver on the *Far West* to one of the supply depots on the Yellowstone. Despite her pleas, Capt. Marsh prudently wouldn't allow her and Nettie Smith to take passage upriver, citing the danger and lack of accommodations for ladies on a working freighter.[56]

Burkman's rambling memories have the hounds left behind at Fort Lincoln, but they escaped—"Thar was Tuck and Bleuch racin' to ketch up with the General, their tongues hangin' out, tails waggin', tickled to death to see him agin, skeered they'd be sent back."[57] Several times in his stories, Burkman gives a disclaimer about his memory, and about that day, he said, "It bein' more'n fifty years ago I ain't clear on some points. I disremember how fur we got that fust day."[58] While the four, Tuck, Kaiser, Swift, and Lady, *did* go with their master in 1876 (Armstrong never once mentions Blucher), Burkman misremembers them in the Little Bighorn valley—but in fairness to such a devoted dog man, over three years in Dakota Territory, he and Armstrong had taken the hounds over and into countless hills and valleys.

The three columns set out from Montana, Dakota, and Wyoming to converge on a large concentration of Sioux believed to be in the general area of the Powder, Tongue, Rosebud, and Big Horn rivers. Crook with his Wyoming column and fifteen companies of cavalry and five of infantry marched north from Fort Fetterman (near present-day Douglas, Wyoming). Col. John Gibbon's Montana column of six infantry and four cavalry companies moved east from Fort Ellis (near Bozeman) along the Yellowstone while Terry's Dakota column marched west from Fort Lincoln with all twelve companies of the 7th Cavalry, two companies of infantry and a Gatling gun detachment. Scouts were supposed to relay critical messages between the commanders but the difficult and dangerous territory made that nearly impossible. Indian agents estimated the maximum number of roaming warriors at 500 to 800, and Terry believed any of his columns could whip that many. Armstrong reckoned that if the agents reported 500, then he could face as many as 1,000 or 1,500. Even with the largest number, he was still convinced that the 7th Cavalry could handle the entire Sioux nation.

Having escaped Grant's wrath, Armstrong got cocky. In St. Paul, he told his friend Capt. William Ludlow he would "cut loose" from Terry as he had from Stanley on the Yellowstone expedition.[59] Sherman instructed Terry that Armstrong was *not* to have reporters with him, but he as commander was free to invite one. Mark Kellogg of the

Bismarck Tribune and Armstrong's acquaintance from the snowbound train incident got that invitation. He would cover the campaign for the *Tribune* and act as correspondent for the *New York Herald*. Kellogg happily filled in for his editor (whose wife was ill) and expected to file an exclusive battle story. Two days after the start, Kellogg made a note about Armstrong's pack, "Greyhounds after Jack Rabbit. Rabbit won the race."[60]

As usual, Armstrong was "on the scoot"—ahead of Terry and the column—but kept his promise to Libbie and rode with two companies. Despite the precaution, hunting with the staghounds nearly got him into the very trouble Libbie worried about. On May 23, Armstrong raced ahead of the advance party after an elk. Closing on it, he ran smack into a fresh campfire recently vacated by Sioux. Armstrong did an "about face" and galloped back with the news.[61] Naturally, he didn't frighten Libbie with this but rather told her about the mundane events of the expedition—horses and men stuck in river bottoms, preserving a bighorn sheep killed by Lonesome Charley Reynolds, and the pranks on his youngest brother. Boston was a good sport, and the three brothers ate together every day.[62]

So far, everything was pretty routine. In fact, Armstrong told Libbie the whole Yellowstone campaign was so ordinary that "…I have about made up my mind that when I go on expeditions like this you are to go too. You could have endured this as well as not…."[63] However, it was not quite a ride in the park. Relations were undoubtedly tense with Maj. Reno and Capt. Benteen—his two senior officers. Reno expected to lead the 7th Cavalry while Armstrong was in trouble and believed he was missing out on promotion because of him. Benteen had disliked Armstrong since Kansas (the feeling was mutual) and still blamed him for Maj. Elliott's death at Washita. On top of that, Armstrong bristled at being kept under Terry's watchful eye, even though it was he who had vouched for his good behavior to Grant. The late spring weather was rapidly changeable and the men experienced sunshine, rain, hail, and snow. Burkman remembered the bloody backs of the horses after one violent hail storm, and dry camps where there was only canteen water and none for horses and dogs.[64]

As with the 1874 expedition, Armstrong's hounds were no longer a novelty, and only a few mentioned them in memoirs. Trooper Peter Thompson of C Company remembered Armstrong had "a number of grey-hounds" and that he and Tom were always hunting with them. Lt. Edward Settle Godfrey, Company K, wrote about the staghounds amusing everyone with their futile attempts to catch antelope. One morning they tore after a large buck and Lt. Luther Hare rode after them, passing the hounds to shoot the antelope with his pistol.[65] One of three surgeons with the 7th, James DeWolf, in the early days of the march cynically noted, "the usual amount of chase of Antelope by the Hounds—[and the] band plays at every fish in the stream."[66] (DeWolf wasn't a dog person and just tolerated them at Fort Seward, east of Bismarck. "I am so sick of seeing dogs lying around & could see them all in—we *have* only sixteen or so."[67]) As on other treks, Armstrong's hounds were having a hard time with prickly pear cactus, and some historians believe they rode in the ambulance on this march too.[68] Officers and designated troopers had been hunting a day's march east of the Powder River on June 5 and hunters from Benteen's Company failed to return with fresh Indian signs, which was worrisome. A hilltop fire was risked, but the men didn't appear until the following day. Terry could not risk prematurely alerting the Sioux and halted all private hunting on June 6.[69] Riding ahead with four unleashed staghounds, Armstrong couldn't stop them from chasing game, but since sighthounds don't "give tongue," this hunting was comparatively silent—although they could be spotted by warriors.

Three companies of the 6th Infantry out of Fort Buford set up a supply depot at Terry's direction. On the south bank of the Yellowstone east of the Powder River was a large, open area above the river. It was flat with a few trees on the banks but plenty of scrub brush for firewood. With easy access from the shore to a steamboat, it was a good place for a supply depot and supporting troops and an excellent cavalry bivouac. The *Far West* offloaded the tons of supplies at the Powder River Supply Depot—canned rations, boxes of hardtack, horseshoes, fodder, ammunition, and everything else needed to keep the Army in the field. Two surgeons established a field hospital, and the sutler opened for business. The beef herd stayed there along with played out horses and mules. Counting soldiers and civilians, more than 500 men (some with dogs) made up the depot staff.[70]

Armstrong arrived there on June 11. Relaxing in the tent at night with Tuck and the rest of his hounds around him, he stayed up late writing his paid expedition reports for the *New York Herald*, an article for the *Galaxy*, and long letters to Libbie (he still hoped she might persuade a steamboat skipper to bring her upriver). He started one letter at 10:30 p.m. on the 11th and promptly wrote another before breakfast so it would make the mail. As Tuck had on the Yellowstone and Black Hills expeditions, she insisted on her master's attention regardless of what he was doing.

> Tuck regularly comes when I am writing, and lays her head on the desk, rooting up my hand with her long nose until I consent to stop and notice her. She and Swift, Lady, and Kaiser sleep in my tent. You need not be anxious about my leaving the column with small escorts; I scarcely hunt any more....[71]

Terry was going to send Armstrong and some of the 7th out to probe deeper for the Sioux. Armstrong remembered the futile pursuits in Kansas during the summer of 1867 and was only afraid he wouldn't find them—or in finding the Sioux, they would slip away before he could attack. To travel fast and light over difficult ground, he abandoned the wagons and took mules to carry food, grain, and ammunition. Left behind were tents, luggage, stoves, camp furniture, and the seldom-used sabers. (Lt. Edward G. Mathey of M Company, with the pack train, surreptitiously rolled his saber in a blanket and strapped it to a mule. Mathey survived the Reno-Benteen defense but never used his saber.[72] Lt. Charles DeRudio may have also had his saber tucked away but it wasn't used either.[73]) The men took only what they could carry or strap to their saddles, including personal items, overcoats, pup tent halves, and cartridges for their carbines and revolvers. The brass band's white horses were given to troopers with lame mounts. For good reasons, Armstrong refused a company of infantry (too slow) and the Gatling gun detachment (cumbersome and constantly getting stuck in gullies). Later on, Armstrong also turned down four companies of the 2nd Cavalry, saying Gibbon needed them.[74] Clearly, whatever lay ahead was to be an exclusive show for the 7th Cavalry.

As much as he loved being with his dogs, they were now a problem for him. Armstrong hoped to surprise the Sioux, and dogs could accidentally alert a village as they had at Washita, where he ordered a number killed to prevent their barking. Despite his best efforts to keep his own hounds out of danger, Blucher had been killed

12: The Last Dog Deals and the March to Little Bighorn

The Powder River Supply Depot where Armstrong was with his staghounds, Tuck, Kaiser, Swift, and Lady, for the last time. Looking northeast across the Yellowstone River, this view shows Pvt. William George's headstone and fenced grave in an expanse of prairie perfect for a cavalry camp and supply depot. Pvt. George was buried not far from where *Far West* would have loaded and unloaded supplies and soldiers. The site has changed little since the campaign, and the large tree on the left is old enough to have been there in 1876. Photograph by author.

there—and Armstrong had lost many other dogs in less perilous circumstances. Feeding the dogs was uncertain as there were only packed rations and no more hunting for game. Burkman couldn't be tasked with the dogs as he had to care for Armstrong's horses, Dandy and Vic. Perhaps as important as the other reasons, there were no ambulances for tired or injured dogs. The choice was either the devil or the deep blue sea—so in the end, Lady, Swift, Kaiser, and Tuck would have to wait for him at the Powder River Depot.[75]

If Armstrong had written more to Libbie about the dogs or his decision to leave them behind, those letters did not survive. For a self-centered man, he actually seems to have put his dogs' welfare ahead of his own wants for a change, or it may have been that the dogs would interfere with his objective—possibly both. Staying at the depot were 124 troopers of the 7th Cavalry and their officer to mind the regimental luggage and gear.[76] They were new recruits, troopers without horses, the sick, and the noncombatant brass band—plenty of men to look after his hounds. There were many other canines at the Powder River Depot. Pvt. Wilmot P. Sanford, who was with D Company, 6th Infantry there wrote in his journal, "We got a dog who sleeps with me. Plenty of others here."[77] When Armstrong rode out, his staghounds were tied to a wagon to prevent them from running after him.

On June 15, 1876, to the tune of "Garry Owen," the 7th Cavalry marched off to catch the Sioux—and that day was the last of George Armstrong Custer's life with dogs.

Many aspects of the Battle of Little Bighorn are understood, but the events leading up to Custer's Last Stand continue to be debated. What precisely happened to Armstrong and his battalion is a source of much study, speculation, and controversy, but as no soldier survived, their story on the ridge will never be known. It is certain that Armstrong's dogs were *not* there. While this book isn't about that battle, an overview is needed to provide context for the Last Stand dog rumors.

Little Bighorn

After the government's war ultimatum and the fight at the Powder River, word spread that the Army was coming, and Cheyenne bands moved north to join the Oglala Sioux war chief, Crazy Horse. They watched and harassed Gibbon's eastward moving column and eventually moved up along Rosebud Creek. Those and other bands converged on the village of the Hunkpapa Sioux holy man, Sitting Bull, and war chief, Gall. The Sioux and Northern Cheyenne formed an unusually large community with more warriors than any scout could have known. In six days, the number of lodges increased from 400 to 1,000, and besides the Sioux Hunkpapas, there were the Oglala, Brulé, Miniconjous, Sans Arc, Two Kettle, Blackfeet, other Sioux bands, Arapaho and the Cheyenne. There were probably 7,000 people, and of these, some 2,000 were well-armed warriors in peak fighting spirit. Such an enormous village couldn't last long as the game and grazing would rapidly be exhausted.[78] The warriors performed the power-giving sacred Sun Dance, and Sitting Bull's own blood sacrifice of fifty cuts on each arm produced a vision of soldiers falling upside down from the sky. It had been a peaceful spring for most of the bands, but with the might of their combined warriors and Sitting Bull's vision of victory, their spirit was high—and if they were not looking for a fight, neither would they run from one. Crook, moving on Rosebud Creek, discovered their resolve. On June 17 Crazy Horse's large war party of Sioux and Cheyenne fought him in a long and widespread battle on the Rosebud. Casualties were modest on both sides, but the Indians had the upper hand—although Crook held the battleground before retreating to care for his wounded and resupply. For seven weeks he waited for reinforcements with no way to communicate with Terry or Armstrong.

Before Armstrong arrived at the Powder River Supply Depot, Terry had gone upstream on the *Far West* on the 9th to confer with Gibbon. Halting his advance at the mouth of the Rosebud, Terry returned to the depot, still uncertain about the location of the Sioux, and sent Reno's wing off on a reconnaissance in force on the 10th. Armstrong got to the depot after Reno left and was annoyed the mission hadn't been saved for him. Finally, he was sent out from the depot on the 15th to combine forces with Reno and rejoin Terry. Reno had actually discovered the fresh trail of a village along the Rosebud but went too far toward the Tongue River. Terry recalled him to the mouth of the Rosebud, and Reno's news changed the game. After revising their strategy on board the *Far West* on the evening of June 21, Terry sent Armstrong and the 7th Cavalry to look for the Sioux in the valleys of the Tongue, Rosebud, and Little Bighorn—the most probable locations based on their intelligence. Terry and Gibbon would be at the confluence of the Big Horn and Little Bighorn rivers on the 26th or 27th, and Armstrong was to rendezvous there when his fifteen days of rations were depleted. Terry gave liberal instructions to act as he saw fit and, if finding Sioux, Armstrong was at liberty to attack. Crook was still believed to be moving north toward them, and Terry thought they would easily catch the Sioux between the columns. Armstrong's force consisted of 31 officers, 566 men, 49 scouts and civilians, and one reporter for a total of 647 souls.[79] They felt sure their flying moving column would overtake the Sioux, and young Autie Reed wrote home to his parents on the 21st, "Uncle Autie is now in full command...." Regardless of the coming fight, several animals had been caught and tamed. "We have all sorts of pets ... the latest is a tame Jack rabbit [sic] which Mary thinks all the world of. Mary is staying on the boat."[80] (Mary and Maria Adams were sisters and cooks for the Custers. Maria stayed with Libbie at home.) Mark Kellogg, certain he was going to see the Sioux whipped, rode off with Armstrong and, in his last dispatch, used an ironic fox hunting metaphor in assuring his readers of full coverage— "I go with Custer and will be in at the death!"[81]

Armstrong moved fast, and his scouts sent word about signs of a sizable number of Sioux. After a forced march in their probable direction, in the pre-dawn hours of Sunday, June 25, the Arikara and Crow scouts reported seeing the smoke of a huge village along the Little Bighorn River. Armstrong went up to the vantage point, but even with good binoculars, his eyes weren't sharp enough to see the massive, swirling pony herd in the morning haze. Despite the smoke from the morning cooking fires, Armstrong doubted there was a village, but scout Mitch Bouyer chided him, "Well, General, if you don't find more Indians in that valley than you ever saw together, you can hang me."[82]

With his scouts insisting there was a large village, Armstrong conceded. He intended to rest the regiment in a valley and attack early the next morning, but stray groups of Indians spotted them and it was presumed they were alerting the village (it turned out they weren't). Armstrong believed now a surprise attack was impossible but he still might prevent the Sioux from scattering. As tired as his men and horses were, the attack had to happen immediately. Armstrong split his force into four battalions: Maj. Reno and Capt. Benteen with three companies each, Capt. McDougall with one company for the pack train, and Armstrong himself with five companies to be commanded by Capts. Keogh and Yates. Needing a fresh horse, he swapped Dandy for Vic and told Burkman to stay with the pack mules and rest Dandy. Benteen and his battalion were ordered to scout on the north side of the twisting Little Bighorn to ascertain if there were other villages or war parties. Armstrong and Reno followed the Indian trail along a tributary of the Little Bighorn (now called Reno Creek), and McDougall's pack train slowly followed. The two battalions cautiously approached the southern end of the village, and Armstrong ordered Reno to cross the Little Bighorn and attack the village. Meanwhile, he would move to the east and north and hit the long village from the side. The fight they wanted was imminent, and Armstrong sent orders to Benteen and McDougall to rejoin him. All well and good—so far.

Fighting for their home and families, the Sioux and Cheyenne that Reno's men fired upon furiously counter-attacked—forcing the soldiers into a timber stand. Bloody Knife was shot through the head, his brains spattering Maj. Reno, who wasn't the same afterwards. Their firing line collapsed into a disorganized rout back across the river and up a bluff—the soldiers taking casualties all the way. At the top, they dug in. A few miles away on the east side of the river, Armstrong saw more warriors than he anticipated and sent a second and more urgent message for reinforcements and ammunition. It went unanswered for Benteen's battalion and the lagging pack train had met Reno's men on the exposed hilltop and stayed to reinforce them. They could hear Armstrong's volleys four miles away, but no man could get to him. Capt. Weir and a company rode a mile toward the gunfire, and through field glasses, Weir could see what appeared to be the end of a fight on a ridge about three miles distant—Indians were firing guns at objects on the ground. Approaching warriors chased Weir and his men back to the hilltop and strategically-positioned themselves to besiege the exposed soldiers. Benteen did much to organize the defense—ordering rifle pits dug and barricades built of supply boxes and dead horses. In full sight of the river, but with little water in their canteens, the men withstood sniper fire for nearly two days.

The Sioux and Cheyenne were relentless, shouting *"Hokahey!"*—popularly understood as "It is a good day to die!" but actually meaning closer to "Let's do it!" Wooden Leg, a Cheyenne warrior said, "The air was full of dust and smoke. Everybody was greatly excited. It looked like thousands of dogs might look if all of them were mixed together in a fight."[83] In a moving fight over ridges and ravines, Armstrong and his five companies had been cut off and overwhelmed, and they died a few at a time. He and his 209 men were killed (the number varies slightly depending upon the historian), including civilians Boston Custer, Autie Reed, and Mark Kellogg. The only survivors were the men at the Reno-Benteen Defense, and counting their dead, about 268 men from 7th Cavalry were casualties—a fair portion of the regiment. Late on the afternoon of the 26th, Sitting Bull's village split up and headed south. An exact number of Sioux and Cheyenne casualties could not be determined, as families retrieved their fallen warriors, but according to tribal histories, the numbers of their dead were slight compared to the soldiers.

One day later, Terry and Gibbon marched in from the north, looking for Armstrong's force, but found bodies decomposing in the sun. From Terry down to the lowliest private, no one could comprehend that Indians had defeated a modern cavalry regiment. Surely Lt. Col. Custer and the rest of the 7th were entrenched somewhere? Yet, there was only silence. Clustered on a hog-back ridge was a barricade of horse carcasses and the bodies of Armstrong and about forty men. That narrow ridge with its dead was quickly dubbed, "Last Stand Hill." The first rumor about a dog survivor of the so-called massacre appeared less than six weeks after the battle.

Tail Piece: Custer's First Stand

Newspaper humor about the defeat at Little Bighorn began appearing the month after the battle. It was a mechanism of both coping with the disaster and getting in digs at the Army and President Grant—who the public believed were responsible for the disaster. Puns were a particular favorite—the *Owensboro Examiner* wrote, "Custer's charge appeared to be Sioux-icide."[84] While troopers were never made fun of, Armstrong, the commander, was the butt of many of the jokes—with Sitting Bull haircuts being the obvious ones.

In time, even Custer family friends would have their private jokes. Henry McFadden, resident of Cadiz, Ohio (just south of Armstrong's birthplace), had two little girls playing piano duets but they were limited by only one stool. Henry went to Joseph R. Hunter's cabinet shop and asked for a simple seat. This was assigned to his young assistant, Armstrong, who turned four legs and joined them to a square plank for a top. After the McFadden girl outgrew her custom piano stool, the family used it through their generations to hold ashtrays and knickknacks. As late as the 1950s, it was still known in the family as "Custer's First Stand."[85]

Chapter 13

Dog Rumors and the Last Stand Hoax

"Three days after the fight, when a scouting party reached the battle ground where Custer and the few survivors had made their last stand, the greyhound was found lying down near his dead master."—Napoleon A. Comeau[1]

"The newspapers published all sorts of stories, some from eye-witnesses but others from people who had merely talked to a man whose wife's cousin had a friend in the fight; some of the stories were reliable, many were not, while a few were simply fantastic."—Edgar I. Stewart[2]

Despite what the press, Army, and first Little Bighorn historians proclaimed, the battle was not a massacre—it was a fight the Army started and lost badly. As Edgar Stewart stated, "…when the white man wins, it is a battle; if the Indian wins, it is a massacre."[3] In the aftermath of such an unimaginable disaster, the notion or hope that there was a human or animal survivor from "Custer's Last Stand" caught the public's imagination. Of course, there were many Sioux, Cheyenne, and Arapaho survivors, but in the egocentric world of 19th century white Americans, they didn't count. If there was a single survivor from Last Stand Hill, then the U.S. Army had not been completely defeated.

The stories of Last Stand survivors or eyewitnesses have four themes which Brian W. Dippie analyzed as variations on the literary theme of the "late hero"—the protagonist with help or information who arrives too late to prevent the tragedy. Dippie summarizes the survivor themes as the witness hiding in the Indian village as a prisoner/renegade; a trooper/scout with Reno, Benteen, or McDougall; Gen. Custer's final messenger; or a combatant who somehow escaped death in the Last Stand.[4] There is a great deal of published material on possible survivor stories with proofs for and against, but there is *no* one account accepted by historians as being true. An officer who served under Benteen once remarked, "It is astonishing the number of fakes who pose as 'heroes' as to Custer's last battle and campaign. The Plains and Rockies are full of them…."[5] Comparatively little has been written about the dog rumors and to evaluate those stories in context, it is important to understand what happened *after* the warriors left the battlefield.

On the afternoon of Monday the 26th, after nearly twenty-four hours of siege on the hilltop, the attacks on the Reno-Benteen defense slackened and stopped, but the soldiers remained warily entrenched. Acting Assistant Surgeon Henry R. Porter, the only surviving doctor, could now better treat the wounded surrounded by horses and mules (alive and dead) in his barricade. Volunteers, slung with canteens, scrambled down the steep ravine to get water (those who did it under fire were awarded the Medal of Honor). Burkman was caring for Armstrong's horse, Dandy, who had been shot in the neck. A few miles to the north, in the Last Stand area, the warriors had searched out and killed wounded troopers—often shooting arrows into dead bodies as a final gesture of contempt and to cripple them in the afterlife. They took guns, uniforms, and whatever caught their eye from the bodies. The wounded and dead warriors were carried away by their families, and women mutilated the troopers with knives and hatchets. Sitting Bull had warned his warriors to take nothing from the *wasi'chu* soldiers, but the entire village looted and left little of soldier clothing and gear behind.

The plunder and celebrations finished, the bands all packed up to leave, certain other soldiers would follow. Warriors, women, children, horses and dogs moved quickly away leaving a wide and dusty trail mixed with smoke from a deliberately set prairie fire. It was not until very late in the afternoon of the 26th that lookouts on the hilltop reported the uncertain activity in the Indian village. Cautiously, they stayed one more night in the entrenchment. The next morning, after nearly forty hours on the hill, Reno, believing Armstrong and his men to be similarly dug-in a few miles away, sent out scouting parties.

General Terry had hoped to meet Armstrong in this area on or about the 26th. The warnings from returning Arikaree and Crow scouts about something bad having happened were disbelieved. Not knowing what he was going to find, three miles from the village, Terry prudently camped in a defensive square with strategically placed Gatling guns.[6] The following morning, scouts went out searching for the 7th Cavalry about the time that Reno's men were seeking Armstrong. Terry's scouts approached from the north and crossing the Little Bighorn, began to see an increasing number of what appeared to be skinned buffalos. On riding closer, and finding bloody clothing and bodies—the awful truth sank in. Just below the peak of a hogback ridge, the bodies of Armstrong and Tom were found with Yates, Smith, Cooke, and others surrounded by a breastwork of dead horses. Forty-two bodies were found there. Boston Custer and Autie Reed were discovered down from the ridge, and Calhoun and his men had died on high ground to the southeast. Terry and Gibbon ran into Lts. Luther Hare and George Wallace coming from Reno Hill. Assuming the rest of the 7th had already joined the reinforcements, they asked, "Where's Custer?" Terry's eyes welled up with tears, "We have found him."[7]

Terry's men began a futile search for wounded and, finding none, they counted and marked the scattered dead. A number of grievously, wounded cavalry horses were found, and all but two were shot. Terry and Gibbon remained vigilant, and another uneasy night was spent near the battlefield. By Wednesday the 28th, Terry was certain there was no imminent danger and considered it safe to bury the dead. Maj. Reno, as the 7th's senior officer, claimed the right of the regiment to bury Armstrong's battalion. It was awful work, for horses and men had been decomposing in the heat for days. Mutilated bodies were covered with black flies, and the coyotes and birds had been at them. The stench was nauseating. John Stands in Timber (a respected cultural historian for the Northern Cheyenne) remembers being told as a boy that the battlefield reeked of carrion for months and was unapproachable.[8] As the Army didn't widely issue entrenching tools, digging graves in the hard dirt had to be done with a few shovels, hatchets, and picks. Without proper tools, men resorted to their hunting knives, tin cups, and even mess kits. Most of the troopers only had a shallow trench scooped out for them. It had been a running fight, and some bodies in tall grass or ravines remained undiscovered for years or even decades. Mark Kellogg's body was found in a ravine near the river, and only recognized by his unique boots. He was scalped with an ear cut off and had indeed been "in at the death with Custer." The reporter's body was forgotten by the warriors, and his personal possessions remained amazingly intact—including the diary with his entry about Armstrong's hounds. (Kellogg's diary is in the North Dakota State Historical Society Archives.[9])

The bodies of officers—when they were known—were buried a little deeper than those of the enlisted men. Friends identified them by facial features or possessions—but some officers would never be found. Keogh was recognized by the Catholic medal on his neck—which actually prevented his mutilation as the Indians thought it powerful medicine. Crittenden was identified by his glass eye, Algernon Smith by his dental fillings, and Cooke by one of his drooping side burns. Wooden Leg, a Cheyenne, had cut off the other as a novel scalp. If a body could be named, a note was inserted into an empty rifle cartridge, which was hammered into a wooden stake on the grave.

Near the top of the hogback ridge, Armstrong had been found naked, lying propped up against two soldiers with a relatively peaceful expression on his face—and un-scalped due to his short hair and bald spot. Apart from a bullet wound in his left temple and left chest, his body was comparatively intact, although he had a deep slash on his right thigh, a finger cut off, and an arrow had been rammed into his penis.[10] (The Indians believed mutilating an enemy prevented him from functioning in and enjoying the next life, so hands, feet, and trigger fingers could be cut off.) Libbie was spared the gruesome details and knew only of the bullet wounds. She came to believe (as did the public) that Armstrong was untouched because the Sioux respected "Long Hair" as a great warrior and chief. (No warrior could have known it was Armstrong, nor would they have recognized any soldier in the dirt, dust, and gunpowder smoke—a point agreed upon by credible Sioux and Cheyenne participants.) Tom fared worse, as his skull was bashed to a pulp and only recognized by a tattoo on his arm with his initials "T W C," the goddess of liberty on his left arm and eagles on his right arm.[11] (Gaining popularity during the Civil War, tattoos or "sailor's marks" were not uncommon in the Army.[12])

Sgt. John Ryan, M Company, helped bury Armstrong and Tom. They were wrapped in canvas and blankets in the same shallow grave, and a found *travois*-basket was placed over it and weighted with rocks to prevent scavenging wolves from getting at the bodies.[13] Ryan said it was the best burial they did, but the wolf "preventative" was completely futile. It was hard, repugnant work which needed finishing so the wounded could be carried to the *Far West*. Not all of Reno's men helped with burials—many were ordered to stay and destroy equipment to prevent it from being used by the Indians. The leather from saddles, boots, and belts (once so carefully polished) was slashed, rifles broken, and everything set ablaze. Surprisingly, John Burkman was denied permission to go to the battlefield and find his general. Absolutely crushed, he stayed behind with the wrecking detail and Dandy.

On the 27th, Crow scout Curly was the first of Armstrong's force to reach the *Far West* with the news. No one spoke Crow or knew sign language (or could understand his drawings and emotional pantomime), but it was clear something was very wrong. The next day, Terry's scouts explained what Curly was trying to say.[14] Capt. Marsh steamed upriver to get as close to the Little Bighorn as his draught would allow.

Two of the three surgeons with the 7th, James DeWolf and George Lord, had been killed, so Dr. Porter, assisted by medical personnel from Gibbon's column, was doing his best for the wounded. Transport was arranged by rigging blanket and horse-hide stretchers suspended between two mules (there was no shortage of dead horses). The column marched at night to spare the wounded from heat and slowly covered the 15-mile distance to the *Far West* which had anchored at the mouth of the Little Bighorn River on June 30. The troopers were laid on tarpaulin beds padded with freshly cut grass on the open boiler deck. Marsh ordered a full head of steam for the downstream run (at the very real risk of exploding the boilers) and set a standing record for river travel between the Little Bighorn and Bismarck. Despite Porter's ministrations, Pvt. William George died, and they made a hasty stop at the Powder River Depot on July 4 to bury him, collect the officers' luggage, and participate in a half-hearted celebration of the nation's birthday. After steaming 710 miles in fifty-four hours, the *Far West* docked at Fort Lincoln at 11 p.m. on July 5.

News of the disaster was tapped out over the wire in a marathon, twenty-two hour session by operator J.M. Carnahan and Clement Lounsberry (Kellogg's boss at the *Bismarck Weekly Tribune*). At Fort Lincoln, just before dawn on the 6th, two officers and the post surgeon knocked on the Custers' door. Only bad tidings came in this manner, and Libbie, Maggie Calhoun, and Emma Reed apprehensively met them in the parlor. Despite shock at the news her Autie was dead, Libbie knew as the commander's wife she had a duty to the wives and, grabbing a shawl to cover her nightgown, she set out with the three men to the other houses.

Armstrong's "Fighting 7th Cavalry" earned an unwanted nickname. They were now "The Bloody 7th," and the regiment was quickly characterized as having been "wiped out" with "all dead." Still, survivor stories began to percolate.

The Horse Survivors

Any cavalry horses which could walk were taken by the Sioux and Cheyenne as prizes. Napoleon or "Nap," a skittish gray horse from E Company, was either found at the village site or followed the marching soldiers. Back at Fort Lincoln, he was ridden by the children.[15] Nap lived for many years but never got the same kind of publicity as the celebrity horse survivor, Comanche.

Terry's men found Comanche near the river on his haunches with his saddle hanging below his belly. Captain Keogh of I Company was riding Comanche in the fight and died with his company on a ridge southeast of Last Stand Hill. With so many men scouring the field for survivors, it isn't surprising that several would claim to have found Comanche. The horse was in a bad way. Accounts say he had from five to thirteen wounds, although seven is generally accepted. (The taxidermist cataloged seven battle wounds as well as older ones.[16]) Because Comanche was the only live horse belonging to an officer, he wasn't euthanized. He was given water, and his wounds were cleaned, and, accompanying the wounded troopers, Comanche was led to the *Far West.* In the engine room at the stern, between the machinery which drove the paddle wheel, a grass bed was made, and Pvt. Gustav Korn, the blacksmith of I Company, tended to him. Dr. Porter would have done what he could for the horse. (John S. Gray cites a *Chicago Times* article of August 20 saying it was the *E.H. Durfee* which collected Comanche at the Rosebud Depot and delivered him to Fort Lincoln on August 10—although it mistakenly says Keogh rode Comanche during the Civil War.[17])

Comanche was suspended in a sling to take the weight off his legs while healing. Afterwards, he wandered freely around Ft. Lincoln, and visitors and guests were allowed to ride him. When the 7th was transferred to Ft. Meade, the rides became so frequent that Col. Samuel Sturgis (whose son Lt. James Sturgis was killed at Little Bighorn) finally ordered that, as Comanche was the "only living representative of the bloody tragedy of the Little Big Horn...," he was special to the regiment and should be given every comfort, never be ridden again, and be honored at ceremonial occasions.[18] With a pen stroke, Sturgis made Comanche the official mascot of the 7th Cavalry—which Armstrong's dogs never were. (Military mascots embody some admirable trait and proudly belong to the entire unit. Some even have heirs—the British Army's Irish Guards have had a succession of Irish Wolfhounds since 1902.)

When Comanche died in 1891, the officers of the 7th had him mounted as a tribute to General Custer and the regiment. Professor Lewis L. Dyche of the University of Kansas in Lawrence did the taxidermy work but when the officers capriciously balked at the bill, Dyche accepted the horse in exchange for the sum owed him. Comanche was then donated to the University Natural History Museum and displayed at the World's Fair in 1893. He remains on display at the university to this very day—amidst fossil skeletons and Dyche's mounted collection of North American animals. As he is safe behind glass, people can no longer pluck souvenir hairs from the mane and tail. At the time of mounting, Comanche's flesh and viscera had been given a military funeral with honors—one of only three such burials for U.S. Army horses—the others being Korean War combat veteran Staff Sgt. Reckless and Blackjack, the riderless horse in the funeral processions of Presidents Kennedy, Hoover, and Johnson, and Gen. Douglas McArthur.

Even with Comanche as a confirmed survivor, he was not widely known as such for decades after the battle. Eventually, the inevitable rumors sprang up—such as Comanche standing guard over Keogh's body or the glamorous story that he was Armstrong's horse. The latter was a much better story than the truth—which was that Armstrong's horse Vic was dead on Last Stand Hill and two officers cut off his hooves. Lt. John G. Bourke had his hoof made into an inkstand, and Col. Homer W. Wheeler lost his on campaign against the Nez Perce.[19]

In Dr. Elizabeth Lawrence's definitive history, *His Very Silence Speaks: Comanche, the Horse That Survived Custer's Last Stand,* she published part of a letter from a Custer aficionado who advocated Comanche's transfer from Kansas to the small museum at Little Bighorn and reinforced the dog survivor rumor.

> Since Comanche was the most famous of all living things, all animals, i.e., one dog, one grey horse that followed the Seventh down to the Yellowstone (or maybe only to the Yellowstone River) and several other wounded 7th Cavalry horses were mercifully shot, it [Comanche] should be given more and better exposure as "the last survivor."[20]

Nap, the other legitimate cavalry survivor of the battle (apart from the horses taken by the Indians), lived out his life in obscurity while Comanche was honored in poems and literature, paintings, sculpture, at least one song, and motion pictures. Given the clamor for survivors, this may seem unfair, but then Nap wasn't the mount of a dashing officer or a regimental mascot, nor was he stuffed and exhibited. Quite simply, Comanche had the better story—and it was one which few Hollywood press agents could have concocted.

There is a certain cachet to being a "sole survivor" (of any kind), but more than one diminishes the appeal of the story—not to mention the survivor's popular fame. One surviving equine from Little Bighorn was sufficient for the American public—but what of a canine survivor?

The Dog Survivor Stories

Unlike Comanche, the dogs in these stories are usually anonymous and never got lasting notice. Much as Armstrong's hounds were ignored in the papers when Black Hills gold was discovered, the sheer enormity of the 7th's defeat (and the search for a cause) overshadowed the dog stories for a long time. While there are comparatively few variations of Comanche's story, the accounts of dogs vary from plausible to improbable to impossible. The dogs of rumor range in type from bull-dogs to Irish Wolfhounds. Many Custer/Little Bighorn authors have repeated some of these stories, but for the first time, here are twenty-five published dog rumors spanning 1876 to 1948, collated, cited, and analyzed.

The First Rumors

#1 The "Fake News" Dog—published August 3, 1876. After Libbie left Fort Lincoln in July 1876, she asked a friend to find homes for her dogs, and he published an announcement to this effect (see Ch. 14). The story was reprinted around the country, but some newspaper editors appended the spurious header below.

> **Custer's Pack of Hounds**
> (Philadelphia Press)
> General Custer it will be remembered, was nearly always accompanied by a pack of hounds. They went with him on his Indian raids, and were terrible fighters. If we ever get at the whole truth of the "Little Big Horn Butchery: it may appear that some of his dogs took part in the affair."[21]

Analysis: In *My Life on the Plains* Armstrong mentions Maida and Blucher at the attack on Black Kettle's village—although neither he nor anyone else said his hounds had ever attacked Indians anywhere. At less than six weeks after the battle, it was pure sensationalism to suggest the hounds *might* have been participants at Little Bighorn.

#2 The Borrowed Dog—published August 5, 1876. The *Deadwood Hills Pioneer* first published this dog rumor without fanfare one month after the calamitous news reached Bismarck.

> Judge Ford, of this city, formerly of Bismarck, loaned General Custer a famous dog. The dog accompanied the General during the engagement against Sitting Bull. Ten days after the battle, the dog returned to Ft. Lincoln, a distance of 500 miles, in search of his master.[22]

Analysis: Judge J.B. Ford of Bismarck was variously a partner in Orlando Goff's photography parlor at Fort Lincoln, a gold prospector, and store owner. He claimed to have ridden out with Terry and Custer from Fort Lincoln to meet Gen. Gibbon, "at or near Crazy Horse or Powder River."[23]

There are no other accounts of anyone "loaning" Armstrong a dog for the expedition. If Ford did ride out with the column, then likely he returned after the first day's march before the Heart River with Libbie and company. The march from Fort Lincoln to the battlefield was more like 350 miles, so his quoted mileage of "500 miles" is an embellishment. While a hardy dog could have back-tracked by the column's scent trail, crossing rivers could have been problematic but not insurmountable. If the dog left the battlefield or the Powder River Depot on or shortly after June 26 and returned to Fort Lincoln ten days later on July 6 (the day after the *Far West* arrived), it would have been a speedy trek. (Several newspapers and a Society for the Prevention of Cruelty to Animals magazine reprinted Ford's story over the next few months.)

#3 Custer's Black Dog—private letter from 1877 published in 2011. In January 1877, Hinrich Glüsing, with Crook in the Wyoming column, wrote home to his father in Germany and said after the fight on the Rosebud Creek, another general (Köster) was wiped out with three companies. The dog rumor is translated as "No man and no mouse came out, just a big, black and tired dog which belonged to General Custer, came back to us."[24]

Analysis: Born in 1841 in Hannover, Germany, Hinrich Glüsing (or Heinrich Gluesing) immigrated to the United States and served in the Civil War. The translation of Glüsing's letter from 19th century German script, his unusual idioms, and difficult handwriting present a number of challenges, but he writes about being in Crook's Rosebud fight, the Starvation March, and the attack at Slim Buttes. From Glüsing's letter it is clear that the dog story was common knowledge among Crook's men.

There were at least two dogs with Crook's column—Capt. Thomas F. Tobey of the 14th Infantry had a greyhound-type named "Wollipes."[25] Tying in to Glüsing's letter was a found Newfoundland. During the pursuit of the Sioux in late August, Crook reached the Powder River, and in that vicinity his column acquired a Newfoundland—quite probably stolen from other soldiers. (The Powder River depot had been moved to Rosebud Creek on July 20 and christened Fort Beans.[26]) Newfoundlands, a popular breed, are typically black but also could be the Landseer variety of white with large black patches. On the Starvation march, Jack as he was named tried to catch prairie dogs, but his weight often collapsed the communal burrows and tumbled him into the hole.[27] The Newfoundland's appearance and Glüsing's "big, black and tired dog which belonged to Custer" seem too much of a coincidence to dismiss. Glüsing wrote his letter from Camp Robinson, Nebraska, where Crook ended up after Slim Buttes. (Glüsing's letter was privately shared among his family in Germany and Texas but not published in America until 2011.)

The I Company Bulldogs

#4 Rusty the Brindle Bulldog—published 1888. The *Sturgis Weekly*'s "Garrison Gossip" column printed a lengthy, rambling item, authoritatively claiming there were only two true survivors—Major Keogh's Comanche and Rusty, "a brindle, non-descript canine of no particular race, breed, or utility." In "The Only True 7th Cavalry Dog," the author claimed Rusty was with Keogh's I Company—barking furiously and biting Indians left and right. He was wounded twice but still continued to attack after the soldiers were dead. One of Gall's warriors shot and captured him. A prisoner for two years, Rusty rejoined the Army after Gall surrendered to Gen. Miles. He was kept at Fort Lincoln—the pet of the 11th Infantry, going with them to Fort Yates where he recognized Captain Godfrey's D Company of the 7th and "transferred his allegiance" to them. When they were transferred to Fort Meade, Rusty was sixteen years old, blind, toothless, and feeble. He pined away and was buried at Fort Yates by H Company, 7th Cavalry.[28]

Analysis: The omniscient and anonymous narrator not only knows all about Rusty after the troopers were killed but also the dog's emotions. (That sort of anthropomorphism was common enough—Libbie did it as well.) Aside from obvious logic holes, what motivation was there for a warrior to capture a small wounded dog, take it to Canada and back to the States over a two-year period? (Gall's band surrendered at Poplar River in 1881.) The name "Rusty" doesn't appear in other accounts of dogs supposed to be at Little Bighorn, nor is he mentioned with Keogh's I Company. If Rusty was sixteen years old when D Company was transferred to Fort Meade in late 1886 or early 1887, he would have been born in 1870 or 1871 when the 7th Cavalry was in Kansas or Kentucky. Possible but highly unlikely. (A company of the 11th Infantry was at Poplar River, and detachments were stationed at both Fort Yates and Fort Lincoln. Godfrey's D Company was at Fort Yates from 1881 through October 1886, then at Fort Meade for a year. H Company was at Fort Meade from 1880 to 1886 and at Fort Yates until July 1888. See the *Tail Piece* for the full text of Rusty's story.)

#5 **The Brindle Bull-dog Again—published 1897.** This same brindle dog story (without the details of the Indian capture and repatriation) was repeated by Walter C. Gooding and published as "Incidents Connected with Fort Abraham Lincoln" in Fargo's historical magazine, *The Record*.

> Capt. Keogh's horse, "Comanche," sorely wounded, was one living thing recovered from that disastrous field and brought back to Fort Lincoln to spend the rest of his days in peace. Also a brindle colored bull dog belonging to one of the cavalry men, was found alive, but badly shot. The dog was carefully cared for and also came back to his old home at the fort, and for years was a great pet, spending most of his time with the prisoners at the guard house. When the last of the Seventh cavalry vacated the post the dog went with them. The horse "Comanche" went to the headquarters of the Seventh cavalry, and whether he is alive yet, I cannot say. I think the poor dog died at Fort Yates shortly after leaving this place.[29]

Analysis: Gooding was appointed post trader in January 1884 and on good terms with veterans of the Indian Wars. His version repeats the essence of the 1888 dog story— that a wounded brindle bull-dog was brought back to Fort Lincoln. Gooding's belief that the dog died at Fort Yates was probably second- or third-hand information. In the same article, he also talked about the decline of Fort Lincoln and told dubious stories about Little Bighorn.

#6 **The Dog Who Came Back—story collected 1908–1924.** Walter Camp recapped this dog story from his undated interview with Gen. Edward Godfrey.

> One of Custer's dogs jumped on Godfrey's porch at Ft. Yates on June 25, 1885. This dog came back nearly starved to Ft. Lincoln from 1876 expedition. He was kept around the guardhouse at

Ft. Lincoln, and after the cavalry moved to Ft. Yates, this dog was taken along and kept with the guardhouse. Dog recognized Godfrey and acted friendly with him and Godfrey's children.[30]

Analysis: Walter Mason Camp was a railroad employee fascinated by Little Bighorn and between 1908 and 1924 tracked down participants from both sides for interviews. While Camp was meticulous about cross-referencing incidents and people, he tended to *summarize* interviews—rather than taking down the informants' words verbatim. Four of his participant notes have dog survivor stories, and he did try to verify them.

Having been in the Reno-Benteen siege as a lieutenant, Gen. Godfrey was considered a leading expert on the battle. This account doesn't suggest this dog had been missing for nine years, but rather that the dog came back hungry. As do the first two bull-dog stories, Godfrey says the dog went from Fort Lincoln to Fort Yates (Godfrey was there in June 1885). That the dog frequented the guardhouse tallies with Gooding's story and to a certain extent with Rusty's story. While the dog's breed is not specified, Camp's phrase "One of Custer's dogs" could mean either one belonging to Armstrong or a regimental dog. Godfrey would have known, but Camp doesn't elaborate. As with Judge Ford's loaner dog, it *could* have walked back to Fort Lincoln.

General Edward Settle Godfrey, who as a lieutenant was in the Reno hilltop fight and became one of the leading experts on the battle of Little Bighorn and an ally of Libbie as she advocated her husband's blamelessness. A dependable memoirist, Godfrey said definitively that Armstrong's four staghounds were left behind at the Powder River Supply Depot—but this fact is often overlooked. Courtesy of the National Park Service, Little Bighorn Battlefield National Monument, LIBI_00019_00195. Photographed by Joseph Judd Pennell about 1907.

#7 Joe Bush, the Black and White Bulldog—story collected 1908–1924. From another undated Camp interview, Pvt. Francis J. Kennedy, I Company, said, "The name of the bulldog of I Company, Seventh Cavalry, was *Joe Bush*. He was a black and white bulldog. He would make friends with a soldier in uniform or an Indian, but not with a man in civilian clothes."[31] Camp later added to the Joe Bush story, "He was recovered from Indians years after the battle."[32]

Analysis: Kennedy was clearly answering a question about the dog—but he doesn't say he witnessed the dog in the battle. Camp acquired enough testimony to convince him of an I Company, bull-dog survivor. He wrote to Gen. Godfrey in 1920 saying he had been told by "several 7th Cavalry men who were there on the Little Big Horn" that the I Company dog, Joe Bush, was captured and repatriated three years later. He affirmed that Gen. Winfield Scott Edgerly (who had been a lieutenant in D Company), was one of these informants.³³ (There was a steam engine operator named Joe Bush from Fort Buford who helped salvage a steamboat after it ran aground below Fort Lincoln.³⁴ There was also Capt. Joe Bush of the 22nd Infantry at Fort Sully, who was a popular fellow throughout Dakota.)

#8 Red the Bulldog—story collected 1908–1924. The indefatigable Camp uncovered yet another story, this one from Pvt. John C. Creighton of K Company. In an undated interview, Camp paraphrased Creighton as "Bulldog 'Red' liked by soldiers and fondled as an old veteran after the battle of Little Bighorn."³⁵

Analysis: Creighton (enlisted as Charles Chesterwood) was in the Reno-Benteen fight, and this statement has the feel of personal experience, although it lacks details which can be corroborated. Presumably, Red was indeed reddish in color. It is also possible Creighton was thinking of "Rusty" the brindle bulldog but misremembering his name.

#9 The Yellow Bulldog—collected before 1925 and published in 1934. There is one more survivor dog attributed to I Company as described by Pvt. John Burkman, Armstrong's striker and dog tender, to his friend I.H. "Bud" O'Donnell.

> They was a little yellow dog, though, that trotted off with the troops. I whistled to him but he didn't pay no attention. Two days arterwards, when they begun buryin' the dead, that little bulldog was still up on the hill, sniffin' 'round among the mutilized bodies fur his master. I never heerd what become of him. Off and on fur years I get to thinkin' about the leetle fellow, wishin' I could've held him back.³⁶

Later, Burkman noted the dog's owners in a brief repetition of this memory—"A little yellow bulldog came out of the fight. It belonged to I Troop."³⁷

Analysis: As Burkman was with the pack train when the battalions separated, he could have seen the dog follow I Company in Armstrong's Battalion. However, as he wasn't allowed on Last Stand Hill for the burials, the part about the dog among the bodies must have come from someone on the burial detail or who heard it from another. Without certainty, Burkman says the dog with I Company was the same one found on the battlefield. In his transcribed memories, those are the only mentions of the yellow dog.

#10 Another Possible Bulldog—published 1931. Wooden Leg, a battle veteran, seems to corroborate Burkman's statement about the bulldog as he saw the dog among the bodies.

> A dog was following one of the Sioux women among the dead soldiers. I did not see any other dog there, neither on that day nor on the day before, when the fight was on. There were some Indian dogs tangling among the feet of the horses at the time of the fighting of the first soldiers, on the valley above the camps. But even here most of them were called away by the women and old people going to the western hilltops.³⁸

Analysis: Wooden Leg, a Northern Cheyenne member of the Elk Warrior Society (named because he could walk tirelessly as if his legs were wood), mentions no other dogs in his battle recollections. His first sentence about the dog sounds like a random memory popping up, but the second reads like a reply to a question about the presence of dogs. The Indian dogs in the first fighting "above the camps" almost certainly refers to Reno's attack coming from upriver toward the Cheyenne teepees. Wooden Leg doesn't say whether the dog among the dead was a village or soldier dog—nor does he specify color. Thomas Marquis, M.D., collected Wooden Leg's stories in sign language—in which Marquis was fluent. Signs can vary slightly by tribe and tend to convey concepts which can be modified by descriptors. There was no sign (or word) for a specific breed of dog. However, adjectives noting size, color, shagginess, etc., could be added to the dog sign—two slightly extended fingers of the right hand dragged left to right to indicate the dog's original function of pulling a *travois*.

Both the Wooden Leg and John Burkman dog stories became so widely accepted that in 1955, the Western artist J.K. Ralston combined them in his detailed painting *After the Battle*. Ralston carefully studied participant accounts and pulled together thirty-six incidents in his expansive composition. The Burkman–Wooden Leg dog stories were merged to show a yellow bulldog following an Indian woman during the looting. (Currently on display at the Little Bighorn Battlefield National Monument visitor's center.)

#11 The Yellow Dog Is Killed—undated newspaper clipping (but published before Two Moons' death in 1917 at the age of 75). Two Moons was a lesser chief in the Fox Warrior Society of the Northern Cheyenne who fought at Little Bighorn. He told an interviewer, "We didn't allow even a yellow dog to escape. One ran out from somewhere, and the Indian boys killed it."[39]

Analysis: Two Moons spoke only broken English, and this article paraphrases his statement through an interpreter. The only *direct* quote from Two Moons in the article is the one about killing the yellow dog. The use of the phrase "Indian boys" suggests the youths who came up after the battle was over.

Two Moons told many stories about his importance in the battle and apparently just made things up to impress his white audiences. Wooden Leg remembered, "He filled the ears of his hearers with lots of other lies while the rest of us laughed among ourselves about what he was saying." After hearing Two Moons' stories told in public, Wooden Leg's friend, Black Wolf said, "You are the biggest liar in the whole Cheyenne tribe." Two Moons answered, "I think it is not wrong to tell lies to white people."[40] By 1914, the press was reporting Two Moons had "commanded the Northern Cheyenne" at Little Bighorn.[41] Apart from the undated newspaper clipping saved by Walter Camp, the yellow dog is not mentioned in ten other interviews with Two Moons given between 1898 and 1913.[42]

From the testimonies of Gooding, Creighton, Kennedy, Burkman, and Wooden Leg (and possibly Two Moons), it seems clear that a dog from I Company was at Little Bighorn and either repatriated or killed. Whether it was Rusty the brindle, Red, the black and white Joe Bush, or the yellow dog (or more than one of these) remains hidden.

The Sioux/Cheyenne Dogs

There are two soldier accounts of village dogs in the aftermath of the battle. While they are not cavalry dog survivors, the stories are worth including.

#12 The Skye Terrier Littermates—published 1910. This puzzling story appeared around the 1910 unveiling of General Custer's impressive memorial in Monroe.

> Canine Survivor of Custer's Last Battle is Buried Here: …it is interesting to know that Detroit was for a time the home, and is the burial place of one of the two survivors of the battle of Little Bighorn. This was a pretty blue skye [sic] terrier, called Smoke." [The story is told by the widow of Capt. Gibbs who was with Gen. Terry's relief column.] "The dog's Indian master had been killed in the fight. The dog refused to come near the captain until several hours later, when he came limping back with a cactus thorn in his paw. After the wound was dressed, the dog made friends with the captain who sent him home to his wife…. The other survivor of the battle was Smoke's brother, who was given to another member of Gen. Terry's command.[43]

The article gives further details about Smoke's life with the Gibbs family. After her husband's death, Mrs. Gibbs and Smoke moved to Detroit. Apart from her, the dog hated women but was a "well known character" in the Erskine Street neighborhood until his death at fourteen.

Analysis: Lt. Eugene Beauharnais Gibbs, C Company, 6th Infantry, was aide-de-camp to Gen. Terry and with the relief column. Gibbs was promoted to captain and working for the Quartermaster Department in New York when he died in 1882. His widow Mary moved to Detroit in 1883 to live with her sister. Buried in Detroit, Smoke had to have died after the relocation—and since his age couldn't have been known when found, fourteen years would be an estimate. That second village dog probably resembled Smoke but his being a "brother" is doubtful. Mrs. Gibbs notes that Lucy C. Little told Smoke's story in the *Chicago Inter Ocean*. Interestingly, Comanche is ignored by or unknown to Mrs. Gibbs and the reporter as the dogs are said to be the *only* survivors. No account of Smoke's "brother" is known. The Little Bighorn area is peppered with prickly pear cactus, but Gibbs removing a thorn from Smoke's paw to win his affection is the Great Sioux War version of the Androcles and the lion fable.

The *Detroit Free Press* ran Smoke's story and photograph as a local interest piece. The shaggy little dog resembles a poodle more than a long-backed and low-slung Skye Terrier—popular in the East but a highly unusual breed to be kept by Indians—even if captured from white settlers. (Skye Terriers were displayed at P.T. Barnum's dog show in 1862 but not recognized by the AKC until 1887.)

#13 The Dog the Sioux Left Behind—published 1940. After the 7th were relieved, the unwounded troopers were moved to the site of the Sioux village. There, Sgt. Charles Windolph of H Company (who briefly mentioned Armstrong's "wolf-hounds" in his memoirs) was poking around in the brush and found a handsome pair of Sioux saddle bags.

> Also, I came across a dog which had been left behind when the Sioux pulled out. He was frightened, cross and surly but finally made friends and I kept him for a long time. Someone stole him later at Ft. Berthold.[44]

Analysis: Charles Windolph was a German immigrant who enlisted in the 7th Cavalry in 1871 and was on the Yellowstone and Black Hills expeditions and in Benteen's company on Reno Hill (and awarded the Medal of Honor). After Little Bighorn, he was on the Nez Perce campaign and left the Army in 1883. A reliable witness, his remembrances were published as *I Fought with Custer: The Story of Sergeant Windolph* (1947). Windolph's story about the abandoned dog is entirely plausible—several troopers had adopted dogs from Black Kettle's camp on the Washita. (Soldiers adopting dogs in wartime is a common story, and perhaps the most famous example is Corp. Leland "Lee" Duncan's finding a litter of German Shepherd puppies during World War I. The pup Lee chose became Rin Tin Tin the movie star.[45])

The Messenger Dogs

#14 The Dog with a Note—story collected 1908–1924, published in 1997. The boy Charging Hawk stayed in the village but learned the warriors' stories about the fight. He told Walter Camp, "…he had often heard how, after the fight on Custer Ridge, one of the cavalry dogs was seen with a note tied to its neck, going back on the trail. The indians [sic] shot at him, but the dog escaped."[46]

Analysis: Living in Chicago, Charging Hawk was middle-aged when Camp was collecting stories (he was eight in 1876). Likely, the interview was done before 1912 (see #15 below) and would have been conducted through an interpreter. Largely unknown until Richard Hardorff found it in Camp's papers at Indiana University, it was published in 1997. Charging Hawk relays his elders' accounts of a dog running away (presumably south on the cavalry's trail). Simple enough on the surface, but how did they know the paper was a "note" if it escaped, and how could warriors miss hitting at a tired, panicky dog? Significantly, when Charging Hawk tells this story a second time, it is considerably embellished.

#15 The Dog with the Papers—published 1912. Charging Hawk, now saying he was a former Army scout and regular soldier, visited artist Ed Borein's studio in Times Square, New York, and told him tribal stories. Borein had been a cowboy and supposedly lived with Indians, so he was keen to collect stories and artifacts of the Old West. Charging Hawk's dog story was now:

> … a big black dog which escaped the fight just as the last white man went down. The Indians first saw the animal running around among the horses with a bundle of papers tied to its collar. Finally, it took off north. They gave chase but could neither catch nor kill it. For 20 miles they chased it, and then lost the track. What was on those papers? Where they government documents or the last letters from a soldier to the folk back home? It is one of the unsolved mysteries of the West.[47]

Analysis: It is possible that as an adult, Charging Hawk did serve as an Army scout or reservation policeman but that doesn't affect his Little Bighorn story. Borein told this story to A.R. Stewart, who first published it in "Stories of the Old West as Told and Painted by the Cow Puncher and Artist, Ed Borein" in the art and architecture magazine *The Craftsman* in November 1912. One month later, *The Detroit Free Press* excerpted it as "Echoes of Custer's Last Fight" and repeated the "bundle of papers" story.[48]

Charging Hawk's story was filtered through an interpreter, Borein, and Stewart. Now, the dog is big and black, and where it carried "a note" and ran south before, it has "a bundle of papers" and runs north. The questions raised by this augmentation are substantial. Why would papers be tied to a dog's collar during the fight? To what purpose, and whom could they exonerate or condemn? Why couldn't warriors on horseback shoot a worn out dog during a twenty-mile chase—and why would they even bother to try with looting and a victory celebration going on?

His credibility is further tainted when he says in that same story that "Long Hair" (Armstrong) was recognized in the fight and the Sioux chief offered five ponies to the warrior who killed him. Camp, having collected Charging Hawk's first story before 1912, came across the second version in *The Craftsman* or the *Detroit Free Press* and wanted to know more. In May 1920, he wrote to Gen. Godfrey, and among other questions, specifically asked about the dogs. "Query—Do you recall whether there were several dogs with the command as you approached the Little Bighorn, on June 25, 1876?" Camp goes on:

> ... the Sioux tell me of a dog found on Custer ridge, after Custer's fight was over, with a message tied to a string around its neck. This information came from a reliable source, and I asked them if it was a bulldog, but were not prepared to dispute that it was a dog of such breed.[49]

Curiously, Camp does not seem to have recorded any other Sioux describing a dog with "notes" except Charging Hawk.

Custer's Hounds

#16 Custer's Black Dog—published 1929. Three years after the fiftieth anniversary of the battle, this dog story was published in a Custer biography.

> A spotted horse ridden by an Indian scout who was killed arrived at his home tent miles away, without his rider. The Indians composed a song to this horse. There is also the story of a black dog, a pet of Custer's, that was in the fight and went cross country home to Fort Lincoln. Former residents of Bismarck recently said that this dog was known as a survivor of the battle and lived for years, a pet of all.[50]

Analysis: Milton Ronsheim was a newspaperman in Cadiz, Ohio, who turned a series of articles about Armstrong into a flattering biography. Like his first biographer, Frederick Whittaker, he doesn't give sources, but then it was written at a time when citations were optional. Ronsheim includes several preposterous stories about the battle, but arguably the most egregious has Sitting Bull, who had a brotherhood pact with Custer, finding his body. In despair, Sitting Bull sat with him, placing a silk handkerchief (given to him by Custer!) over his face and uttered a poem: "This handkerchief will guard your features against the desert's blackening heat. Farewell, great Custer, till we meet!"[51]

Black dogs do seem to crop up in survivor stories. Ronsheim and Glüsing, both say Armstrong had one, and Charging Hawk's second version has a generic one. (It is worthwhile noting Armstrong's sighthounds were not the only ones in the area. Not far away that spring, a greyhound was kept at the trapper's outpost, Fort Pease.[52])

#17 Queen Victoria's Gift Greyhound—published 1907. While not a Last Stand dog story, this summary of a long letter to *Forest and Stream* ties in with the next rumor.

A military expedition from Fort Harker, Kansas, was camping along the Republican River and Farley, their scout, went hunting with the man who wrote the letter—C.B. D.W. (referred to as C.W.). Farley had ill-advisedly borrowed one of Gen. Custer's greyhounds—a brindle said to be one of a pair from Queen Victoria. Farley and C.W. set off with escort and wagon to shoot game. While stalking antelope, Farley accidentally shot the greyhound. The bullet entered the base of his tail and exited through the shoulder. He begged C.W. to end the dog's suffering, but neither man could bear to pull the trigger. A grassy bed was made beside a stream and the greyhound was left to die. Two weeks later, the wounded greyhound tottered into camp, having fought his way through a pack of coyotes to return.[53]

Analysis: This letter was published at a time when the Last Survivor dog rumors were beginning to appear in force. C.B.D.W. was a buffalo hunter out with Capt. Keogh at Fort Harker and Farley, a scout.[54] While the author doesn't specifically say it, he is describing a cavalry mission, and I Company was stationed at Fort Harker during fall 1868. (Neither Armstrong nor Libbie mentions C.B.D.W. or Farley in their writings.) That the greyhound was able to recover after such a wound (and the inevitable infection) is consistent with other stories of the recuperative powers of dogs. There is no record or mention of the Custers being given a dog by Queen Victoria (more on that point below)—and one would think Armstrong would have written about his greyhound's toughness to either *Turf, Field,* or even Barker. The unlucky Farley died "...with his boots on after assisting horse thieves to get away with six of the troop horses." The troopers retrieved their horses but didn't want to be asked about Farley.[55]

#18 Queen Victoria's Vigilant Greyhound—published 1908. In response to C. B.D.W.'s letter, Nap. A. Comeau wrote about being at Fort Washakie, Wyoming, in 1882, and seeing an aged, one-eyed greyhound said to have been found with Custer's body on Last Stand Hill. Comeau said the greyhound was one of the pair given to Gen. Custer by Queen Victoria, and he wondered if it was the same one which C.B.D.W. had described. Comeau asserted the greyhound and Curly the Crow scout were the only survivors of Little Bighorn.

> Three days after the fight, when a scouting party reached the battle ground where Custer and the few survivors made their last stand, the greyhound was found lying down near his dead master. A rifle bullet had struck him near the eye which made him blind on that side, but otherwise he was uninjured. He was taken care of by the party and finally found a master in Lt. R.E. Thompson, of the Sixth Infantry, who was stationed at Fort Washakie when I was there. It was the lieutenant himself who gave me the above details about the dog.

Comeau thought the one-eyed hound was about twelve and saw him give "a good account of himself" in a coyote hunt. Comeau closed the letter wondering where and how Thompson's hound died.[56]

Analysis: Lt. Richard E. Thompson of the 6th Infantry was with Terry's relief column, had known Armstrong and was photographed several times with the officers at Fort Lincoln in July 1875. He was also with Terry's relief column. It is entirely possible that Thompson gave a home to one or more of Armstrong's hounds—as did other officers (see Ch. 14). Napoléon-Alexandre "Nap" Comeau (1848–1923) was a prominent Canadian naturalist who did go hunting in Wyoming in 1882. Comeau noted Lt. Thompson hunted with this greyhound and a smaller hound. If the one-eyed greyhound was the same one Farley shot during Armstrong's years in Kansas (1866–1871), then the hound could have been twelve years old in 1882—although that's an advanced age to be killing coyotes.

While faithful dogs have been known to guard their masters' bodies or graves (there are several examples from the Civil War), Armstrong's hounds were never anywhere near the battlefield. While he was given Scottish Deerhounds (and possibly some greyhounds) by an English peer and member of Parliament, there is no evidence Queen Victoria presented him with a dog or dogs—or indeed that she was even aware of a General Custer. Both Custers were inveterate namedroppers, and *if* they had a greyhound from the Queen, it would have been trumpeted in publications, letters, and Libbie's three books (and should appear in other Custer rumors). The "royal gift" notion almost certainly originated from Armstrong's own braggadocio about his deerhounds—as well as the first Westminster Kennel Club show where his re-homed hounds competed alongside two deerhounds from Queen Victoria's kennels in 1877. (Oscar and Dagmar had been shipped over for the dog show, and the *Daily Graphic* featured a vignette of the royal pair along with some of the other exhibits.[57])

#19 The Custer Hound Bequest—published 1921. James H. "Dog" Kelley, the second elected mayor of Dodge City, was known throughout Kansas for his pack of "Custer greyhounds." In 1921 it was said, "After Custer had been transferred to the northwest where he met his death in such a tragic manner, Kelly fell heir to the Custer pack,"[58] and by the following decade, "Custer… left his dogs with 'Dog Kelly,' with the understanding that if he did not return, he was to keep them."[59]

Analysis: Irishman James H. "Dog" Kelley (also Kelly) was short of stature, perpetually rumpled, and sported a drooping mustache. He immigrated to America and eventually ended up running saloons in Hays City and Dodge City. Kelley had four raucous terms as mayor of Dodge City, "the toughest town on the map," and was known for his congeniality and generosity as well as drunken hijinks and fisticuffs. "Dog" Kelley seems

James H. "Dog" Kelley and his greyhounds in Dodge City about 1900. Kelley had many variations of his life story, but all involved being a scout for Armstrong in Kansas and being given one or several greyhounds as a mark of his esteem. Sometimes he intimated that Armstrong charged him to take over his pack if he didn't return from Dakota. Kelley *did* have a large pack of greyhounds in Dodge City, but there is no way to be certain that any of them were from the Custers' pack. Boot Hill Museum, Dodge City, Kansas.

to have told as many versions of his personal history as he had listeners. He was born in Ireland or England, immigrated to New York or Connecticut, and fought for the South or the North. Kelley's connection with Armstrong is variously given as a civilian volunteer, a scout, a dog-horse orderly, an enlisted man—and even an officer. Kelley also claimed he knew about dog husbandry from an English lord or Armstrong—which was how he got his nickname, "Dog" (actually, a visiting newspaper man came up with it). Kelley boasted that in recognition of his scouting and doggy service, Armstrong presented him with a pair of his best greyhounds (or a whole pack), a fine horse, a commendation, and an inscribed silver (or gold) watch. One of the stories has the "Custer-Kelly" pack being recruited for Grand Duke Alexis's buffalo hunt.[60]

Amidst all this blarney, a few things are true. Armstrong and Kelly were both at Fort Hays and Hays City from 1869 through 1870. After moving to Dodge City, in 1872, Kelley had a large and well-known pack of hunting greyhounds, and while Armstrong did occasionally give some of his hounds to people he admired, there is no evidence whatsoever that Armstrong was that close to "Dog" Kelley. The Irishman's stories are too colorful to fade from Fort Dodge lore—and as the Irish used to say, "By the contints of all the books that ever wor opened an' shut, it's as thrue as the sun to the dial."[61]

#20 The Found Staghound—private letter, September 24, 1921, published 2002. At the Old Soldiers' Home in Sawtelle, Los Angeles, 78-year-old W.F. Towers wrote Libbie about finding a "stag dog" after Little Bighorn and recovering Tom Custer's ring. The poorly written letter is paraphrased here but can be read in full in the accompanying illustration.

Towers claimed he had been in the 6th Infantry and remembered being at Fort Buford when Hazen and Reno were arrested for intending to fight a duel, Curly bringing news of the battle, and bringing one of Armstrong's "stag dogs" to camp. He claimed to have purchased a gold ring said to be Tom Custer's and sold it to a post trader who supposedly sent it to Libbie—and said that he was Armstrong's mounted orderly during the Civil War.[62]

Analysis: For decades after the battle, Libbie came to be inundated by letters from people wanting to contribute their memories of the general, asking questions or for favors. On correspondence she intended to answer, Libbie penciled a short note of intent to herself on the first page or envelope. Libbie left no such note on Towers' letter, indicating she didn't take it seriously.

William F. Towers (alias John R. Bradford) was born in Massachusetts about 1843 and served in the Civil War with the 43rd Massachusetts Volunteer Infantry, C Company. On one of his pension documents, three other units are appended: C Company, New York Infantry, B Company, 6th U.S. Cavalry, and C Company, 6th U.S. Infantry.[63] If Towers was in the 6th Cavalry during the war, he wouldn't have served with Armstrong, who as a major general of volunteers only commanded state cavalry and not regular cavalry regiments.[64] However, the 6th Cavalry were garrisoned in Austin in November 1865 when Armstrong was chief of cavalry of the Department of Texas.[65] In none of his writing does Armstrong mention an orderly by the name of Towers (or Bradford).

Towers' pension records indicate he was in the 6th Infantry, C Company, at the time of the Little Bighorn campaign, although the official rosters do not show a Tow-

```
P. O. BX. 15. SOLDIERS. HOME CALIF. SEPT. 24th, 1921,

MRS. G. A. CUSTER.
NEW. YORK. CITY N. Y.
                    Dear Friend,
                                Years ago I. was ordered to go,
to help your Husband in his last fight, but Gen Hazen &. Gen, -
Reno had some trouble in regard of Rank & gen Reno challenged Gen -
Hazen to fight a Duel ,When we reached  FT Bufort N. ORTH DEkota,
The officers interfered & they were placed under arrest laid two day
 when Curley a scout came in & said all were killed I. brought in one
of his stag dogs in camp I. also bought from a Indian a gold ring
for one dollar said to belong Tom, Custer made out of native gold &.
I. sold it to the Post Trader at FT BUFORT  N. DAKOTA. After wards
he told me you recd it from him O. K. is that true, ?. I. was in the,
Sixth  U. S. Infintry at that time, , I. was your Husband Mounted -
Orderly During the civel war, I. saw your AD in the VETERNS -
ENTERPRISE ,of Sawtelle CAL. would likePAMPHLET. REVIEWED . NATL. TRIBE
              YOURS VERY TRULY.
                              W. F. TOWERS.
```

In 1921, veteran William F. Towers wrote a far-fetched letter to Libbie Custer about a Hazen-Reno duel, finding a staghound *and* Tom Custer's ring, and his service as Armstrong's mounted orderly during the Civil War. Libbie received many hundreds of inquiries after Armstrong's death and made a point to respond to the serious letters but ignored implausible ones like this. Courtesy of the National Park Service, Little Bighorn Battlefield National Monument, LIBI_00019_3596.

ers/Bradford in C, D, or I Companies stationed at Fort Buford in 1876. If his claim is genuine, Towers would have been at Buford when those three companies were sent downriver to join Terry's column. C Company arrived at the Powder River Supply Depot on June 6.[66] In addition, D and I companies of the 6th were also assigned to garrison the depot.[67] No other soldier mentions a staghound being "found" and returned (the other supposed returning hounds came back on their own).

There are numerous problems with Towers' letter—prime among them, the extremely improbable "duel" to which Maj. Marcus Reno challenged Col. William Hazen. Both were classmates at West Point and before the campaign, Hazen was at Fort Buford and Reno at Fort Lincoln. Both disliked Armstrong, and *if* there had been a disagreement between them, a duel would have been a breech of discipline (not to mention illegal) during what was effectively a time of war. (No record of any such duel or challenge exists.) The phrasing and broken syntax of the letter suggest the inattentiveness and wandering thought which can come with advanced age. Towers made no handwritten corrections in the letter, but writing of that sort was common enough in men of his time. He died seven years later in 1928 and is buried in the National Cemetery in Los Angeles. His tombstone records only C Co. of the 43rd Massachusetts Militia Infantry. (Roy Bird in *In His Brother's Shadow: The Life of Thomas Ward Custer* mistakenly has W.F. Towers as "W.W. Fowers" and erroneously cites the parts about the stag dog and Tom's ring as being taken from Robert M. Utley's article "The Enduring Custer Legend" in *American History Illustrated*. Coincidentally in 1877, a gold ring with the carved "blood stone" [jasper] seal of Lt. William Van W. Reilly, who fell near Armstrong, was retrieved from a Sioux warrior and returned to Reilly's mother.[68])

#21 The Dog Survivor Burial Which Never Happened—newspaper article, 1923.
In March 1923, a series of articles in the *Minneapolis Morning Tribune* attempted to sort out the fate of Cardigan, Libbie's favorite hound who was claimed to be a survivor.

> Mrs. M. H. French, 3338 West Thirty-second street, said yesterday that Cardigan was buried with military honors at Madison Barracks, N.Y., in 1889. According to Mrs. French, Cardigan, one mule, and one man were the only survivors of the battle of the Little Big Horn. After battle, she said, Cardigan was taken to Fort Abraham Lincoln and presented to Eleventh Infantry, accompanied that regiment to New York, and died there of old age.[69] [Mrs. M.H. French is not related to Capt. Thomas H. French, who fought in the Reno-Benteen Defense.]

Analysis: It is curious that in 1923, some rumors still had the equine survivor as a mule, but the 11th Infantry *was* in the Dakota Territory in August and September of 1876. Its companies were stationed at several posts during the Indian Wars. In 1886, only G Company remained at Fort Lincoln, and in 1887, G and three other companies were transferred to Madison Barracks, Sacketts Harbor, New York.[70] So far, Mrs. French's remembered dates are within the realm of possibility, and it is interesting that again the 11th Infantry at Fort Lincoln is said to have been given one of Armstrong's dogs. (See #4 Rusty the Brindle Bulldog.)

It seems a bit odd that a surviving Custer hound would be "presented" (and by whom?) to a newly arrived infantry unit when there is no demonstrable connection between that regiment and Armstrong's. (That said, the adoption could have been politely called a "presentation"—and there were a number of the 11th stationed at the newly established Fort Custer near the battlefield.) Cardigan was probably at least a year old on the 1873 Yellowstone expedition, so living until 1889 makes him seventeen years on his "death" at Madison Barracks—an extremely advanced age for any dog. As it turned out, Mrs. French's letter provoked several people to write in with solid facts about Cardigan, who actually died in St. Paul in 1881 (see "Epilogue: Custer's Last Hound").

#22 Tuck, Bleuch, Swift, Lady and Kaiser: The Dogs Who Were Nearly There—collected prior to 1925 and published in 1934.
Burkman's statements about Arm-

strong's staghounds on the Little Bighorn campaign are peppered in small doses throughout his memoirs. He said the staghounds escaped their constraints at Fort Lincoln and Blucher (Bleuch) and Tuck raced after Armstrong, and "They went with him on into the valley of the Little Big Horn."[71] Elsewhere, he appears to contradict himself by saying that the hounds were prevented from going farther when the battalions separated before the battle: "A few of 'em, Bleuch and Tuck and Lady, was with us that last day on the Little Big Horn. They whined and couldn't understand why I held 'em back when Custer went ridin' away at the head of the Seventh." (Burkman says this a second time in his *Old Neutriment* stories.[72]) In the aftermath of the Reno-Benteen siege, Burkman's final words on Armstrong's dogs were, "And whilst I worked funny thoughts went runnin' through my head, same's [sic], 'Wonder what'll become of the hounds now?' Or, 'Wonder can I make Bleuch and Tuck understand?' ... 'Then all of a sudden it come to me that I wouldn't never agin hear the General laughin' and jokin'. Seemed like they want no use me goin' on.'"[73]

Analysis: Due to an injury from a horse fall, Burkman was honorably discharged from the Army in 1879. He worked as a teamster but for the rest of his life was wracked with guilt because he didn't die with Armstrong or bury him—"Agin, I was left behind."[74] (His orders to stay on Reno Hill may not have been capricious, as Armstrong's horse Dandy was wounded in the siege and needed care.) Burkman was a bitter, distrustful old man when he told his stories to I.H. "Bud" O'Donnell in Billings, Montana. It took him years to win Burkman's trust and coax the Custer stories out of him. In fact, Burkman, being illiterate, nearly deaf, and suspicious, didn't want his stories written down at first. O'Donnell took surreptitious notes, but Burkman eventually agreed that the stories were important for posterity. With no friends but the O'Donnells, Burkman worked his memories over and over in his mind until they eventually unhinged him. His words about preventing the eager hounds from following their master seem to mirror his own frustration when ordered to stay behind with Dandy and the pack train. Unable to cope with his mental demons any longer, in 1925 at the age of eighty-six, Burkman shot himself.

O'Donnell gave his Burkman notes to Glendolin Wagner, who reworked the stories into book form by polishing the interview notes and adding colorful Western vernacular.[75] *Old Neutriment* (1934) is a delightful read which gives insight into the Custers and cavalry life, but those stories are two jumps away from Burkman's original words. Making historical sense out of Burkman's rambling stream of consciousness memories (told third-hand) is a problem. Western scholar and Custer historian Brian W. Dippie, in the introduction to the 1989 edition, wrote, "In truth, Burkman misremembered much of what he did at Little Big Horn, and Old Neutriment's mixture of opinion and observation is muddled indeed."[76] Burkman himself frequently admitted his memory was faulty—"A good many things I disremember, it bein' more'n fifty years ago."[77] Still, he was Armstrong's dog tender, and apart from Libbie, one can't get any closer to the man and his hounds than that.

Burkman had been Armstrong's striker since Kentucky and cared for the hounds all through the Dakota Territory—where one valley can look very much like another. When Burkman says the hounds went "...into the valley of the Little Big Horn," he had nearly two thousand miles of landscape to misremember. With his age and precarious state of mind, it is probable Burkman's dog recollections blended and became idealized and that his memories of Bleuch and Tuck beyond the Powder River Depot were subconsciously manufactured.

Certain points teased out of Burkman's stories actually confirm the dogs stayed at the Powder River Supply Depot. Armstrong wrote to Libbie on June 12 about Tuck and the dogs in the tent, and he left the depot on the 15th. Burkman says, "Tuck... was with us up on the Little Big Horn. He was in the tent with Custer the last night we camped."[78] Burkman describes the 7th marching out to the band's music—which happened at the depot. However, his memory plays him false when he says Tuck and Bleuch were sleeping on the cot in the tent and Tuck howled mournfully on the evening of the 21st—after the officers' conference at the mouth of the Rosebud.[79] Burkman attributed Tuck's howl to the coming tragedy, but after the battle, many survivors had 20–20 hindsight, saying they felt bad luck was ahead and Armstrong had been uncharacteristically melancholy. (Libbie included Armstrong's letter of June 12, 1876, in her 1885 book *Boots and Saddles* making it the first published record of his hounds on the campaign.)

No battle veteran mentions Armstrong's hounds *after* the Powder River Depot. In 1911, Burkman wrote Libbie (through O'Donnell) and described the hilltop siege, talking about the horses, but he made no mention of the hounds.[80] Nor did anyone say the hounds were on the steamboat with the wounded—which surely would have been worthy of remark. It is exceedingly curious that of the approximately five hundred men stationed at the Powder River Depot during its forty-five-day existence, no mention of Armstrong's pack being kept there has come to light. (The *Far West, Josephine,* and *E.H. Durfee* were making regular runs downriver, and any of them could have collected Armstrong's hounds from the depot.)

The first serious inquiry about Armstrong's hounds being in the fight came from an artist wanting to include them in a painting *if* they had been there. Edgar S. Paxson was gathering research for a massive painting he titled *Custer's Last Battle on the Little Bighorn* (later titled *Custer's Last Fight* and finally, *Custer's Last Stand*). In 1896, he wrote to Gen. Godfrey with a number of questions about the 7th's clothing and weapons and specifically asked about the staghounds. Godfrey sent back a six-page, typescript letter with specifics like:

> General Custer carried a Remington sporting rifle, octagonal barrel; two Bulldog, self cocking, English, white handled pistols, with a ring in the butt for a lanyard; a hunting knife, in a beaded fringe scabbard; and a canvas cartridge belt. He wore a whitish gray hat, with broad brim and rather low crown, very similar to the Cowboy hat; buckskin suit, with fringed welt in outer seams of trousers and arms of blouse: the blouse was double breasted military buttons, lappels [sic] general open, turndown collar, and fringe on bottom of skirt.[81]

Before Godfrey mailed the letter, he realized he had forgotten Paxson's question about the staghounds and wrote in ink, "*The dogs were left with the wagon train.*"

#23 The Hound Race—published 1941. In *Canines & Coyotes*, Leon V. Almirall gives an anecdotal history of hunting coyotes with sighthounds and crossbreds and says, "Until fairly recently the methods of the coyote hunt have remained the same as they were in the time of General Custer (who, incidentally, owned a fine pack of running dogs, and was about to run them in a matched race for a purse the day he left, never to return.")[82]

Analysis: Often repeated in articles, books, and websites to this day, Almirall's quote is still seized upon by hunters and coursing people to mean that this "matched race" was to have happened the night before Little Bighorn (impossible with the hounds back on the Powder River). Or, "the day he left, never to return" could mean either the departure from the Powder River Depot or Fort Lincoln, but none of these are plausible. Almirall gives no source, but this myth seems to have evolved from a description in *Old Neutriment* by Burkman about Armstrong's plan to match his horse Vic against Lt. William Cooke's horse in a thousand-yard race for a $500 stake (a staggering amount of money in 1876)—*after* they returned from the Little Bighorn expedition.[83]

As to staging a fair race for coursing hounds, there is considerable difficulty in doing so. Unlike a horse race with jockeys on a measured track, sighthounds don't run at top speed unless they are chasing game—which run long distances with course changes and don't stay in front of judges. (The mechanical rabbit for track greyhounds to chase wouldn't be invented until the decade before World War I.[84]) Sighthound performance could be compared only by observing who was fastest on the "run-up" to the hare and could force the first turn, who brought down the quarry first, or who caught the most. Armstrong never writes about his hounds winning "a matched race for a purse"—and his ego wouldn't let him mention losing the Fort Sully contest.

#24 Bran the Avenging Staghound—published 1948. In Fairfax Downey's novel for young adults, *The Seventh's Staghound*, he tells of Bran, a young staghound from Armstrong's pack adopted by Trumpeter Peter Shannon. Bran, chews through his tether at the Powder River Depot, follows the soldiers, arriving at Little Bighorn in time to save Peter (carrying the last message to Capt. Benteen) from being killed by a traitorous Army deserter. Bran is shot in the struggle and, thinking him dead, Peter rides on to Benteen and survives the hilltop siege. After the battle, the wounded Comanche and Bran are found and taken to Fort Lincoln on the *Far West*. Peter is promoted to 2nd lieutenant, awarded the Congressional Medal of Honor, and marries his sweetheart with Bran standing nearby.

Analysis: This fictional work contributed somewhat to the myth that there was a staghound in the battle. In his Afterword, Downey says he combined the incidents of the dogs at the Powder River Depot, the yellow dog running after the soldiers, and the dog following a Sioux woman on Last Stand Hill. Downey also liberally borrowed hound stories from Libbie Custer's books and Sir Walter Scott's novels.

To add to the list of stories and rumors, there was one dog hoax which should have been easily detected but which was overlooked in the public's desire to believe they were seeing a living canine survivor of Little Bighorn.

#25 The Dog Who Wasn't There—published 1887. One dog survivor rumor manifested itself in a manner which P.T. Barnum would have appreciated. In late 1887, people attending a dog, cat, and poultry show were greatly impressed by "General Custer's staghound 'Brutus,' a survivor of the Custer massacre, [who] was the center of much interest at the Madison Square Garden, New York, last week."[85]

Analysis: Brutus was an Irish Wolfhound who belonged to the daughter of

Gen. William D. Whipple of Governor's Island off the tip of Manhattan. Brutus had been a favorite with the troops, and while of imposing size, he was quite meek. When attacked by two dogs on post, he got the worst of it, so to prevent another incident, Brutus was sent to Bedloe's Island in the care of a sergeant with the 5th Artillery. (Irish Wolfhounds were a rare breed in America, having only been recently re-created in Britain. With the extinction of wolves in Ireland in the mid–1700s, the Irish Wolfhound nearly died out in the early 1800s. Henry Hastings Sibley, the first governor of Minnesota, hunted with two Irish Wolfhounds in the 1830s and 1840s near Fort Snelling,[86] and one "Irish wolf-dog" was exhibited at Barnum's National Dog Show in 1862.[87])

For a laugh and making fun of the dog's lack of pluck—"...he is a terrible coward and wouldn't fight a lady's pet poodle"—the soldiers started the rumor that the four-year-old wolfhound was one of General Custer's hounds and the *only* survivor of Little Big Horn. As such, he was shown to visitors who came to marvel at the island's famous attraction, "the Bartholdi statue"—the Statue of Liberty.

The wolfhound was a medal winner at dog shows but, loathing baths, Brutus would disappear if he spotted the preparations. A week before the 1887 Madison Square Garden event, the dog show manager's wife sought out Gen. Whipple and asked if the Last Stand hound could be exhibited. He agreed, saying, "The only earthly thing that dog is good for is to take prizes. He is very good for that purpose, however, and I think rather prides himself on it." Brutus was on Governor's Island when he got wind of the bath and took off running. The whole garrison spent three hours searching until at last he was discovered up in the old brick fort, hiding under a soldier's bed (no mean feat for a giant breed dog). Apprehended, bathed, and ferried over to Manhattan, Brutus, was put on display in a stall with a description of the battle providing "proof" of the sole survivor claim.[88] (That the hound belonged to a local general gave the story further credence.) The New Yorkers marveled at Brutus and doubtless imagined him first snarling in defiance at the attacking Sioux and Cheyenne—and perhaps then guarding his master's body on the hill.

The hoax about four-year-old Brutus was revealed by the *New York Sun* in January 1888. (The story was in the *Sturgis Weekly Record* as a lead-in to their story about Rusty, one of the "two survivors"[89]). What is so curious about this Last Stand Survivor hoax is that no one bothered to do the simple math. A puppy born in the first six months of 1876 would have been 11 years old in 1887—old for a hound in the days before distemper vaccines. Of course, Armstrong wouldn't have taken a youngster on the expedition, and a hound born before 1876 would be proportionately older and even less likely to be alive in 1887. Willingly throwing away disbelief, the audience accepted the story, and their wonderment at seeing the giant hound firmly pushed questions aside. (The American Kennel Club recognized the breed in 1897. It is interesting to contemplate that had Irish Wolfhounds been more available, they should have appealed to Armstrong because of their size, purpose, and heritage. The year following Brutus' exhibition, the Irish Brigade's monument at Gettysburg was unveiled, and at the base of the large Celtic cross is a reclining Irish Wolfhound.)

A dog claimed as a Last Stand Survivor wasn't always easy to prove or disprove and any dispute must come down to questioning the integrity of the dog's owner and the story. In fact, much like Brian Dippie's four essential plots for human survivor stories, all the Little Bighorn dog stories could derive from one formulaic flow chart: The dog is in the fight (wounding optional) → found at grave/village or captured → treks home alone or repatriated → welcomed back to fort → lives out rest of life as pampered survivor (honorable burial optional). Several of the rumors combine one or more of these plotlines, making them even more difficult to evaluate.

As to any physical evidence of dogs at Little Bighorn, the relief column and burial party didn't note any cavalry dogs alive or dead on the field, nor did the several reburial and interment missions occurring between 1877 and 1881. Modern archeological investigations have found no canine skeletal fragments on the battlefield—not even wolf or coyote remains.[90] However, at the Powder River Depot, where there were a number of dogs, in 1986, archeologists found the nearly complete skeletal remains of a dog in a trash pit. Definitely not wolf or coyote, it was of medium size and had two of its cervical vertebrae broken by three chops of a heavy, steel tool such as an axe, cleaver, or tomahawk. (There were no bone marks to indicate butchering for food.[91]) The date of the dog's death is uncertain, but the rest of the items in the pit (buttons, bottle fragments, etc.) were available to the Army in 1875–76.[92] This is the only extant, hard evidence of a dog which *may* be connected with this campaign.

From Gooding, Creighton, Kennedy, Burkman, and Wooden Leg's testimonies, it seems that there was at least one bulldog from Capt. Keogh's I Company in the valley of the Little Bighorn, and it may or may not have lived. However, the question of whether or not a dog was in the fight is entirely inconsequential to both the outcome of the battle and the consequences—which led to the 1890 Wounded Knee massacre and ultimately ended the Plains Tribes' way of life. Nonetheless, the dog in question is one which many have tried to answer in establishing even minor facts about a battle which, as historian Edgar Stewart said in 1955, "...has been almost completely engulfed in myth and legend, and the blood spilled on that eventful Sunday has been exceeded many times over by the ink from the fountain pens of historians and military experts who have written about it."[93]

So, why did Americans want desperately to believe a dog had survived Little Bighorn? Toward the end of the 19th century, middle and upper class Victorian attitudes toward dogs were changing, and they were no longer just a working component of livestock management or a hunting aid—they were becoming pets. Perhaps more significant than that shift of attitude is a basic connection. Man, horse, and dog are the trinity partnership of civilization. Dogs (rather than horses) are the embodiment of fidelity, protection, hunting, and companionship to humankind. The idea of a dog survivor had enormous appeal to the public, and people must have imagined how their own dogs might fare in such adverse circumstances. To cope with a disaster's aftermath, people need to salvage something (no matter how small)—a bit of hope, a reason, an undamaged possession, or better yet, a life saved. A dog could be all of these. (The "hero" dog survivor resurfaced in the immensely popular 1950s TV series *The Adventures of Rin-Tin-Tin*. Rusty, a little boy, and his German Shepherd "Rinty" are the sole survivors of a wagon train massacre and become mascots of the 101st Cavalry at Fort Apache. That the German Shepherd breed was unknown in America in the 1800s was conveniently overlooked because of Rin Tin Tin's box office draw.)

Apart from a presidential assassination or a massive natural disaster, it would be hard to imagine a bigger blow to America's ego at the peak of our Centennial celebrations than the nation's favorite Indian fighter being killed along with a fair amount of his regiment. As General George Armstrong Custer's final fight grew into legend, so also did the dog survivor stories. For Little Bighorn, Americans needed to believe in a survivor (even a dog) because if there is one, it wasn't a total defeat—and even a source of some pride. Comanche and the mythical dog survivor were the small victories at Little Bighorn. People don't like to let a good story go, despite facts and evidence to the contrary. Even today, the idea of a steadfast dog on Last Stand Hill is such a good story that it is continually repeated on the internet.

> "This is the West, sir. When the legend becomes fact, print the legend."
> —*The Man Who Shot Liberty Valance* (1962)

So, what really happened to Armstrong's hounds after being left at the Powder River Depot?

Tail Piece: Rusty's Improbable History

Given the number of wild rumors about a dog at Little Bighorn, it seems worthwhile to reprint the most preposterous one. From the Garrison Gossip column of the January 27, 1888, edition of *The Sturgis Weekly Record*, here is "THE ONLY TRUE 7TH CAVALRY DOG."

> Perhaps it is not generally known that only two living things survived Custer's ill starred charge on the Little Big Horn in '76. One was Capt. Keogh's war horse Comanche, the other was a dog, Rusty by name—the child of the regiment. ...Rusty, the other survivor, was a brindle nondescript canine of no particular race, breed or utility. His only redeeming quality was his devotion to the troop (I, of the Seventh cavalry) which adopted him. When that gallant troop made its disastrous charge, Rusty was in the van, cheering on the troop by his barking and determined sallies; and many of the redskins felt his bite. He was wounded shortly after the conflict began and lay on the field till most of his troop were annihilated, when he arose and literally fought like a mad dog until one of Gaul's [sic] men put a bullet into him and placed him *hors de combat*, when his capture was easily effected. For two years he was captive in Gaul's camp, but all the kindness they could lavish on him was to no effect; he was a changed dog. He would mope around the teepee, take whatever food was given to him or what he could steal. The veriest poodle in the camp would whip or drive him away from the succulent bone on which he was dining and he would not resent it in the least, but go rustling for himself. When Gen. Miles at the head of his column arrived to receive the surrender of Gaul and his band, Rusty saw and recognized the boys in blue coming two miles away and started on a full run for them. He was not satisfied until he had welcomed nearly every man in the line by joyously barking and wagging his tail. Finally, he again placed himself in the van of the advancing lines, expecting no doubt that he was in for it again and determined to wipe out the disgrace of having survived the troop to which he belonged. He seemed disgusted with the proceedings of the surrender, and up to the day of his death neither Indian nor Indian dog dare come near him. He was transferred to Fort Lincoln and lived there for a long time, drawing rations from the government. Although he was petted and treated with great kindness by the Eleventh infantry stationed there, yet he was never perfectly satisfied and when the companies of that regiment

were transferred to [Fort] Yates, he followed them down. There he recognized Capt. Godfrey's troop (D, of the Seventh cavalry,) which was under Major Reno in that memorable conflict, and immediately took up his quarters with their troop.

When the troop started for it journey to [Fort] Meade he was quite impossible. He tried to follow them, but owing to his age and feeble condition it was impossible to do so. He pined away until his death, when he was buried by some tender hearted boys of Troop H, Seventh cavalry, who knew him of yore.

He was at least 16 years old, blind and toothless.[94]

It is quite a tale and only needs a precocious boy to make it right for the old Disney genre of dog films.

Chapter 14

The Widow Custer's Burden

"...any person who takes the dogs can feel that he is doing a genuine service to the widow of a dead hero."—New York Herald, *July 22, 1876*[1]

As far as the Army was concerned, the widow of the commanding officer of Fort Lincoln, Lt. Col. of the 7th Cavalry, and Brevet Maj. Gen. U.S. Army had status no different than a trooper's widow. Libbie wanted to go home as quickly as she could. Devastated with grief, she still took the lead in comforting the other widows and tending to the wounded. In particular, she looked after "my widows"—Maggie Calhoun, Annie Yates, and Nettie Smith.[2] With Autie and Tom dead, she would never again be "the Old Lady."

Re-Homing the Dogs

As a new widow, Libbie was expected to send the news to family and friends, don mourning clothes, pack her possessions, and make travel arrangements to Monroe. She was an old hand at moving households, but this time it was different, as she had to pack Armstrong's uniforms, papers, swords, guns, dog horns, and hunting trophies. And then there was the problem of the dogs themselves.... At that time, there were some forty staghounds and foxhounds. (Once she said they had as many as fifty at Fort Lincoln.[3]) Libbie turned to the officers and her friends for help. Less than ten days after learning about Armstrong's death, Libbie wrote to her friend, Charles W. McIntyre in St. Paul, explaining her plight. McIntyre was a government agent and manager for two express companies and could arrange for shipping the crated dogs to new owners. On July 14, the same day he received Libbie's letter, McIntyre wrote to an upper class sporting magazine, *Spirit of the Times*.

> DEAR SPIRIT:—I am to-day in receipt of a letter from Mrs. Custer, widow of General Custer, asking me if I could provide homes for a pack of stag hounds and a pack of fox hounds. Our State laws forbid the running of deer with dogs; besides, the Indians shoot them, so that hounds are no use here; but I have written to Mrs. Custer to ship them all to me at once, as she wishes to leave the fort as soon as possible. Can you, to oblige Mrs. Custer, send me the names of some gentlemen who would like the dogs, and pay the express charges on them to New York, and provide them with a good home. I will ship the dogs, on your Recommend [sic], to any gentlemen you may suggest, provided they are not disposed of before I hear from you. Yours respectfully. C. W. McINTYRE.[4]

The letter was published in the July 21 edition of the *Spirit*, and the *New York Herald* reprinted it the next day along with this encouragement:

> We trust that we will at once receive a response to this letter from some party who can conveniently take care of such packs of hounds. The animals could be used in New Jersey when the fox-hunting season opens, and any person who takes the dogs, can feel that he is doing a genuine service to the widow of a dead hero.[5]

On Sunday, July 30, Libbie, her sister-in-law, Maggie Calhoun, friends Nettie Smith, and Annie Yates (with her three children and brother, Richard), and Armstrong's niece, Emma Reed, left Fort Lincoln. Armstrong had done much for the Northern Pacific, and they provided a special car for Libbie and her party. Reaching St. Paul at 6 a.m. on August 2, they spent the day secluded with very close friends.[6] Their progress eastward was noted by newspapers, frequently under the headline, "The Widows" or "Mrs. Custer's Party." Arriving in Chicago on August 3, they rested at the opulent Palmer House hotel. McIntyre's notice was paying off for William H. Emery of Athol, Massachusetts, wrote to Mrs. General Custer on August 4 asking for a foxhound. He could pay for the express shipping, but she would have to arrange the crate. Young William promised, "I will give the dog one of the best of homes."[7] It was an act of pure kindness, for if he had been intending to breed Custer hounds, he would have specified the wanted gender. Meanwhile, the dog notice was being picked up by other papers and reached beyond the Dakota, Montana, and Wyoming Territories to Colorado, Minnesota, Michigan, Missouri, Illinois, Ohio, Pennsylvania, and New York. It was America's first national dog rescue effort.

Word about the hounds reached the Thornes of Millbrook, New York. Ten-year-old Oakleigh and his father Edwin were breeding Scottish Deerhounds from the Custer/Barker stock and had at least one adult pair. The editor of *Forest and Stream* had admired the fine brace of "Chiefton" and "Dutchess" which were bred from that line. He noted this on June 15 along with a reminder that Oakleigh had been selling the Custer deerhound puppies at very low prices.[8] (Coincidentally, June 15 was the last day Armstrong was with his hounds at the Powder River Depot.) The Thornes were still keen on having some of Armstrong's hounds and arranged to take Stanley and Madgie—the two Russian Wolfhounds from Grand Duke Alexis.[9] That was a start on resolving Libbie's dog problem.

In Monroe, Libbie pondered a future without her husband on the Army's miserly pension. She was shocked to learn Armstrong had concealed debts from his failed business enterprises. How would she make ends meet and perhaps more importantly, what was she to do with herself? In August, Libbie had expressed interest in having her husband's horse, Dandy, and the officers of the 7th purchased him from the Army as a gift.[10] Libbie gave him to Armstrong's father as a living memento of his son. Still an excellent rider, the snowy bearded Emanuel Custer proudly rode Dandy around Monroe and in patriotic parades.

In printing McIntyre's call for dog homes, one editor speculated about "General Custer's hounds" being in the battle. (See Ch. 13, Rumor #1.) This "fake news" became a preamble to the announcement and then was circulated by other papers. Only six weeks after the calamity, Armstrong's adversaries were already blaming him. One newspaper ran a clarification that "General Custer's hounds" *didn't* mean his detractors, but rather "certain valuable stag and fox hounds which his friends wish to sell at the request of Mrs. Custer."[11] An anonymous source, claiming to be a three-year veteran of the 7th Cavalry, said he was with General Custer while fighting the "Chippewas on the Washita river" when he ruthlessly choked one his "magnificent Scotch grayhounds [sic]" to death" to prevent them from waking the village. Supposedly only a few soldiers standing near him saw this in the night's gloom.[12] The average reader wouldn't have known enough to detect the inaccurate details of this story. (See Chapter 7's *Tail Piece*.)

At Libbie's request, at the end of August McIntyre shipped two four-month-old Scottish Deerhound puppies to Col. Frank E. Howe of New York. Howe was the government pension agent for the city and trying to secure Libbie a government job as a postmistress of Monroe. He had been Armstrong's friend from his first New York business forays in 1866 and apparently kept in touch over the years. Perhaps inspired by the first murmurings about a Centennial Dog Show, in the spring of 1876, Howe asked for a pair of deerhounds. Armstrong replied on May 14 in the middle of the seven days he was at Fort Lincoln between the Belknap Hearings and marching with his regiment for the last time.

> My dear Colonel Howe: I have just returned from the East and find your letter awaiting me. I intended to send you the dogs at once, but find that I have lost some of my best ones and I do not want to send you a pair until they can show in every particular the breed.
>
> I have a nice lot of puppies showing the good points admirably. As soon as I return from the expedition I shall at once forward them to you. Had I not lost so many from distemper there would have been no delay but those I now have are not as fine as I wish you to have.
> Yours truly,
> CUSTER[13]

(Published in the *New York Herald Tribune* in 1926, the letter's date was erroneously given as 1875. It was a misprint or a poor transcription of Armstrong's sometimes-difficult handwriting, for in May 1875, Armstrong was in New York—and there was no expedition that year). Howe died in 1883, so the letter was probably given to the newspaper by his son in the anticipation of the 50th anniversary events at Little Bighorn. It is interesting that Armstrong mentions dogs dying of distemper in the winter of 1875–76 when in 1873 he boasted to *Turf* his own vaccination practices had stopped disease in his kennel.

Howe finally did get his Scottish Deerhound pups and settled the pair at Henry Gardner's boarding kennel by September 3. As the Centennial Dog Show was happening the following week, the former Custer hounds were mentioned in an interview with Gardner, a black man who inherited the mantle of a Manhattan dog expert from his late employer, Francis Butler, dog seller and trainer, teacher, and the manager of Barnum's National Dog Show in 1862. Gardner regularly advertised sporting dogs for sale and his training services and remedies. He kept his kennel and ersatz veterinary clinic at a rambling old cottage and garden at 50th and Broadway (near Times Square) and was planning to attend the Centennial Dog Show. He valued adult Scottish Deerhounds at $100 to $200 apiece and noted Howe's puppies "...are of a good strain. Gen. Custer always had the best." After hearing their story, the reporter mused:

> I looked at the two clumsy puppies for a while. Solemn, unformed, awkward brutes, with snake-like heads and big-jointed, clumsy limbs. I thought of him to whom they owed allegiance, and how he had fallen, and then the smallest dog drew up near me and laid his head on my knee. My hand rested on the grizzled head, and for a while nothing was said. The room was blurred with a mist that did not rise from the earth, and the thoughts of all were far away on the Western border land where a hero lies entombed on the battle-field where glory gave him death.[14]

The following month, another of Armstrong's staghound puppies went to Charles McCormick "Mc.C" Reeve, a young banker and businessman in Minneapolis. The nine-month-old hound "responds to the name of 'Reno,' given him by Gen. Custer before he went into the fatal fight."[15] (Considering Armstrong's dislike of Maj. Reno, the dog's name had to be a joke perpetrated by someone involved in the transfer. Reeve had been with George Bird Grinnell on Prof. O.C. Marsh's 1870 fossil expedition in Nebraska and was colonel of the 13th Minnesota Volunteer Infantry during the Spanish American War.) A year later, in November 1877, a nearly jet-black "fine European greyhound" came into the possession of David Donnelly of Stockton, Minnesota, who claimed it was the hound which Grand Duke Alexis brought to America and gave to Armstrong after the buffalo hunt in Nebraska. After Little Bighorn, Libbie supposedly sent the greyhound to a relative in St. Paul who gave him to a brother in Madelia, who in turn gave him to a Donnelly in Stockton, Minnesota.[16] This was even more malarkey than the Reno name as Alexis didn't bring dogs with him in 1872—nor did Libbie have relations in Minnesota. In August of 1879, J.W. Howard of Detroit, was noted as the "present owner of one of the late Gen. Custer's famous stag hounds"—suggesting the dog had been re-homed more than once.[17] There were other shuffles of the Custer hounds—in 1881, George W. Turney of Marion, Ohio, was visiting Colorado Springs and while there was given a pair by friends who were returning East.[18]

Any tangible connection to General Custer was something of a cachet and social coup, and people boasted they had his Dakota hounds or one of their puppies. Rightly or wrongly, he was considered by many to be an American martyr, and condolences and tributes filled Libbie's mailbox. The state of Texas had always thought well of Armstrong for his Reconstruction service, and their legislature sent Libbie a "Resolution of Condolence."[19] The press, demanding to know the cause of the 7th Cavalry's defeat, printed every wild account of the battle—without confirming the source. There were many "eyewitness" accounts with the minute details of General Custer's last fighting moments, and as with the improbable Last Stand Hill dog survivor rumors, the public was willing to believe any ink on the page. As it did frequently during his life, in death, Custer's name polarized Americans and churned up controversy. Everyone down to the lowliest beer-soak in the streets had an opinion—peaceful Indians had been attacked on their treaty land, the 7th were grossly outnumbered, the Indians had better rifles than the Army, the Gatling guns were left behind, Custer disobeyed Terry's orders and refused to wait for Gibbon's column, Reno and Benteen failed to come to his aid—or even that President Grant had deliberately scuppered the campaign by withholding full command from Custer. While all this was being debated in newspapers, barbershops, and saloons, there was another inquiry—"Who slew Custer?"—in the belief that a single warrior vanquished the noble Armstrong in chivalric combat. For Libbie, it was painful to read, and eventually she sought out supporters who were willing to write their own letters and articles proving his blamelessness. That controversy continued for the rest of Libbie's life—and still does today.

Frederick Whittaker, a former lieutenant in the 6th New York Volunteer Cavalry who wrote dime novels, rushed into print the first biography of George Armstrong Custer just before the year ended. He had Libbie's consent and nominal assistance as she loaned him family letters—and he advertised for anecdotes about General Custer (a portion of his profits were to go to Libbie).[20] Later, she distanced herself from him as she thought the book poorly written and even sometimes denied she'd read it.

Oddly enough, she would eventually take Whittaker's advice to write a memoir about her life with Armstrong. Despite her reluctance because she lacked formal training, Whittaker sensibly urged Libbie to write as if she were having a conversation with a friend—"talk on paper as you talk *via voce*, and you conquer all mankind." It would prove sound advice, but any thought about writing a memoir was years away. The most pressing problem for Libbie was the need to supplement her meager pension.

In a bold stroke, Libbie reinvented herself by moving to New Jersey and then New York to find employment. Libbie considered teaching, nursing, and charity work but in May 1877, she found a part-time job as a secretary for the Society for Decorative Arts, a charitable organization which instructed women in handicrafts and employed them to sell their work. Libbie also supplemented her wages by writing articles for newspapers and magazines. Over the years, she had increases to her widow's pension—but each had to be approved by Congress. It took Little Bighorn for the public to notice how little was paid to women widowed by the Army. Armstrong had life insurance which eventually paid Libbie $5,000 (despite delinquent premiums at the time of his death). Fund raising campaigns, corporate and private, sprouted up to benefit the widows. A "Woman's Relief Fund" was called for by the *Army and Navy Journal*, and soldiers, sailors, and civilians sent in money. Contributions were duly noted from such units as the Soldiers' Home in Washington, the Mare Island Naval Station sailors and marines, and even the Fort Cameron Minstrel and Alcatraz Prison Variety Troupes.[21] When the Grand Duke Alexis returned to New York in March of 1877 he quietly gave $500 to Libbie.[22] She thanked him, and he replied with condolences and a warm remembrance of Armstrong.[23] Alexis was offered a buffalo hunt and while he couldn't spare the time,[24] he did go squirrel shooting and fox hunting in Virginia.[25] He had brought his bull-terrier along and, incognito as "Mr. Parker" took him for unleashed walks in New York.

The Centennial Dog Show was so popular, a group of pointer-owning sportsmen in New York decided to match it with their own show in May 1877. It was dubbed the First Annual New York Bench Show, but by the 1890s it was more commonly known as the Westminster Kennel Club Show. It ran from the 8th to the 10th in Gilmore's Garden (formerly Barnum's Hippodrome and soon to be the first Madison Square Garden). The 1,201 dogs entered would be displayed in benches or stalls for three days.[26] Up until then, the nascent regional dog shows were almost exclusively for gun dogs—pointers and setters. In this much larger show, about half of the entries were pointers and setters, but other breeds included the giant Siberian bloodhound, mastiffs, terriers, lapdogs, and even a performing two-legged dog. While awards for Best of Breed, Best in Group, or Best in Show did not yet exist, sporting clubs, magazines, and gentlemen offered silver cups or cash prizes for the best dogs in individual classes. (The governing body was the National American Kennel Club, founded in the year of the Centennial Dog Show. They would simplify their name in 1884 to the American Kennel Club.)

Three months before the show, the Thornes transferred the Russian Wolfhounds Stanley and Madgie to Mr. John B. Miller, Esq., an attorney from Newburgh, who showed, bred, and sold dogs under the kennel name Windsor. (Newburg is about forty miles south of the Thornes' home in Millbrook.) The transfer happened in time for the Bench Show and a press release anticipated that "Mr. Thorne's fox hounds, and

Gen. Custer's deer hounds" would be there—and Grand Duke Alexis would be showing his bull-terrier.[27] The *New York Herald* ran a column titled "Towser's Big Show," which also called attention to "General Custer's celebrated pack of hounds, including those presented to him by the Grand Duke Alexis...."[28] (As it transpired, Alexis didn't get to show his dog, as he was recalled for military duties after Russia declared war on the Ottoman Empire on April 24, 1877.)

In "Class 24.—Staghounds (Dogs or Bitches)," J.B. Miller competed with both Russian Wolfhounds against four other "staghounds," and the catalog noted they were "...imported by the Grand Duke Alexis and presented to the late Gen. Custer." (The class was based on function rather than breed.) Stanley at seven years won first prize of $15 and six-year-old Madgie won the $10 second prize. Miller exhibited other dogs, including a greyhound who got a minor placement in the entry of sixteen.[29] It must have been gratifying for him to win with Stanley and Madgie, for he almost didn't make it to the show. While the Westminster officials arranged with some fifteen northeastern railway lines (and two Canadian ones) for free transportation of dogs entered, the stationmaster at Newburgh refused to allow his dogs on the train. Miller resorted to a river barge to get to Manhattan.[30]

There were nine Scottish Deerhounds entered in the class, "Deerhounds (Dogs or Bitches)." Young Oakleigh Thorne showed Muggins, an ash-colored dog of two years who was sired by "the late Gen. Custer's Kirk, out of the Hon. K.C. Barker's Fanny of Detroit," listing a $75 value. (H.M. "Muggins" Taylor was one of Gibbon's scouts and brought the disastrous news to Bozeman.) Robert Tallant, a twenty-one-year-old from San Francisco, who was a naturalist, Harvard student (class of '77), and member of the Harvard Rifle Club, showed Custer, a 16-month-old litter mate to Muggins valued at $250. The class favorites were two deerhounds, Oscar and Dagmar, from Queen Victoria's kennel (with a published value of £10,000 each). The winner of the $15 first prize was a five-year-old blue deerhound owned by Paul Dana of New York. Oscar won the $10 second prize, Dagmar was Very Highly Commended, and Oakleigh's Muggins was just Highly Commended.[31] (Each dog entered was technically required to be for sale and hence the listed values. An extreme price indicated the owner didn't want to sell. After the show, the public could buy exhibited dogs at auction.)

Burials and Monuments

After Little Bighorn, commanders Terry, Gibbon, Crook, and Miles spent the summer and fall chasing the separated bands of Sioux and Cheyenne. William F. Cody was scouting for Col. Wesley Merritt's 5th Cavalry when, in a skirmish on Warbonnet Creek on July 17, 1876, he shot the Cheyenne chief, Yellow Hand. Cody claimed a gory trophy as "The first scalp for Custer!"—an incident highly embellished in dime novels and his own Wild West Show. A good many of the Sioux went into Canada where the U.S. Army could not follow. In calmer times, they returned to their reservations. Some Sioux leaders were singled out for retribution—Crazy Horse was arrested and would be fatally stabbed with a guard's bayonet in September 1877 at Camp Robinson, Nebraska. Back from Canada, Sitting Bull was arrested and released, became a star in Cody's show for a time, and then at the Standing Rock Reservation, he was shot in a scuffle between his supporters and Indian Agency police in 1890.

The bodies of Armstrong and his troopers remained in their hasty graves. Terry's men had taken care to identify every officer they could and hoped the stake-marked graves would escape Indian notice and desecration. The *Army Navy Journal* noted in early August 1876 (as did the national papers), that their improvised marking method would allow the officers' bodies to be "...easily identified by means of the sticks any time friends may wish to remove them East."[32] The Army had no plans to spend money on removing the bodies, but a private citizen could exhume a relative—*if* they could get to the remote battlefield. In fairness to the Army, they had more pressing matters with the Sioux. Libbie was anxious for the return of Armstrong's body for she well knew bodies in the wilderness could be dug up by wolves, coyotes—and warriors who wanted trophies of clothing, scalps, and fingers. Fueling this worry, urban grave robbing was not uncommon at the time. (In November 1876, there was a bizarre attempt to kidnap Abraham Lincoln's body from its vault and ransom it. The bungling thieves might have succeeded if they had made better plans for moving the 500-pound, lead-lined coffin— and had not taken a Secret Service informer into their gang.)

In the early spring, the officers' widows, led by Libbie, were pressing the Army for the bodies to be retrieved and given proper burials—even though she knew that until the ice broke up on the rivers, transporting bodies would be impossible. In April, Gen. Sheridan's brother and aide-de-camp, Col. Michael V. Sheridan (also a captain in L Co., 7th Cavalry), assured her that plans were being made to bring the officers back and bury them at an Army cemetery or release them to their families.[33] Sheridan left Chicago on May 21 but couldn't reach the battlefield with his coffin-loaded wagons until July 3.[34] The bones of Armstrong and Tom and the other officers were collected and taken back for burials— several of them going to Fort Leavenworth. Because his parents wished it, Lt. John Crittenden was reinterred in a coffin where he fell. Apart from efforts to cover up some of the exposed bones, the 7th's troopers received little attention on that trip.

West Point had always been one of Armstrong's favorite places, and Libbie requested he be buried there. Originally, this was to happen in the summer, but she believed many of the cadets would be away on furlough—which might make attendance poor. Adamant that her husband's funeral service have the attention it deserved, she postponed it until October 10. Her instincts were right, and the chapel was full to bursting. Armstrong's casket was draped with the American flag and topped with his dress helmet and saber. After the service, it was taken to the gravesite on a caisson and followed by the riderless horse with reversed boots in its stirrups. Officers' wives could be buried there too, and Libbie was glad to know her last resting place would be beside Autie. (Tom Custer's body remained at Fort Leavenworth, while Boston Custer and Autie Reed were eventually reburied in Monroe.)

Having properly buried Armstrong, Libbie next devoted her energies to securing a fitting memorial for him. When the funds were subscribed in 1879 (the government, Theodore Roosevelt, Jr., John Jacob Astor, and Albert Bierstadt were among those who contributed), at West Point a bronze figure of Armstrong was placed atop a granite pediment featuring bronze *bas relief* plaques. Libbie had not been consulted, and while the likeness was decent, he was depicted standing in full dress uniform but with field boots and holding his pistol and saber like an operetta pirate. Libbie (and the cavalry) disliked it intensely, and campaigned to have it removed, later saying, "I literally cried it off its pedestal."[35] In 1884 the statue was removed and stored, and it eventually disappeared.[36] The original pediment with plaques was placed on Armstrong's grave and topped by a simple granite obelisk. Libbie was content but pressed for a worthier memorial to Armstrong, who in his Good Death, was thought to have been honored by both his troops and Sioux enemies.

During Libbie's life, there would be other bronzes of Armstrong—fittingly at Gettysburg in 1889, a *bas relief* bust was incorporated on the Michigan Cavalry Brigade's monument; in 1902, a new mining town, Custer City, Colorado, had a standing figure erected (which also disappeared); in 1910 there was a magnificent equestrian statue in Monroe; there was a plaque in Hardin, Montana in 1926 (the town nearest to the battlefield); and finally in 1932, a standing figure was erected in his birthplace, New Rumley, Ohio. For Libbie, the Monroe memorial's dedication (attended by President Taft and John Burkman) was the triumph she desired. However, the statue's prominent placement would become a traffic hazard, and it was moved. Libbie was so upset she never returned to the town of her birth. The Custer statue was moved once more to the side of a major intersection in 1955. The statue of General Custer now fittingly (or ironically) faces a veterinary clinic on the opposite corner. (Libbie's initial choice for the artist was Solon Borglum, the younger brother of the Mount Rushmore sculptor, but the design of Edward Potter, known for the famous lions at the New York Public and Morgan Libraries, won the commission.)

Being Armstrong's widow was Libbie's only job. Where she had been the sideline supporter of his career, after his death, she became the public face of his memory and worked tirelessly to "keep the general's name before the public." Libbie eventually solidified his image as an American hero-martyr. In her lifetime, the name of George Armstrong Custer would be added to Army posts, veterans' associations, counties, towns, public buildings, roads, national parks, an astronomical observatory on Long Island, and even dogs—C.S. Miller of Ann Arbor, incongruously named his diminutive Italian Greyhound Custer.[37] John Philip Sousa renamed an existing tune to "Custer's Last Charge."[38] (The verses were brimming with mythic symbolism and ended with Custer dead—but in possession of the battlefield.) Walt Whitman and Henry Wadsworth Longfellow wrote sonnets, and people who had never attempted verse, suddenly composed poems, odes, and songs. The *Rocky Mountain Herald* wryly commented, "Custer, after all, is better off than most of us, as the fortunes of war saved him from the awful fate of having to read the poems written on the massacre."[39]

From the heroic and defiant to the desperate and tragic, "Custer's Last Stand" has never lost fascination with artists. A seemingly endless line of artistic depictions began to appear—and have continued. The first, published on July 19, 1876, in a newspaper, was luridly titled "The Death Struggle of General Custer."[40] In 1886, Cassilly Adams' "Custer's Last Fight" wound up hanging in a St. Louis saloon where it was acquired by the Anheuser-Busch Brewing Company. They commissioned F. Otto Becker to turn it into a color lithograph in 1895 to distribute as an advertisement for Budweiser beer (Becker substantially altered Cassilly's version). Much of what American men knew about Little Bighorn and Custer's Last Stand was derived from that fantastical print hanging in saloons.[41] The wildly inaccurate image depicted far too many war-bonneted Indians carrying accoutrements which included beadwork from Eastern Woodland tribes to Zulu-style shields. Scalping and stripping bodies were shown in progress, and of course, General Custer was shown with long hair, full buckskins, and a saber and clubbed pistol just seconds before death. (As a boy, the author remembers sitting under the Becker print at the Silver Queen Saloon in Virginia City, Nevada.)

During Libbie's life, famous Western painters who tackled the subject included Frederic Remington and Charles Russell. Edgar S. Paxson wanted to include Armstrong's staghounds fighting beside him or wounded at his feet in his own *Custer's Last Stand*, until Gen. Godfrey confirmed they were left at the Powder River Depot. The hounds would have been an interesting feature in the crowded composition, but Paxson moved on to other details, completing the painting in 1899. Both Godfrey and Libbie were moved to tears when they stood in front of it for the first time—and she made an effort to see it on several other occasions.[42] (The painting is on display at the Buffalo Bill Center of the West in Cody, Wyoming.)

In January 1879, the raging controversy over who was to blame for the disaster led to a Court of Inquiry on Maj. Reno's behavior as second in command. After two weeks and 1,300 pages of written testimony, Reno was found to be blameless, although it was strongly suggested by the presiding officers that he could have done much more for "the safety of the command."[43]

Libbie was disappointed that while there were implications, no official fault could be assigned to Reno. Ironically, that same month a large force of British Army regulars and colonials were killed by a highly disciplined Zulu army armed with spears and clubs. The Battle of Isandlwana became the British equivalent of Little Bighorn, for they also had underestimated their enemy's fighting spirit and numbers, had insufficient intelligence, split their forces, and suffered from poor resupply of ammunition. As at Little Bighorn, there was a dog there—a colonial officer's setter bitch was stabbed to death when the camp was overrun.[44]

The condolence letters which Libbie had first received were gradually replaced by a stream of requests for photographs, autographs, and mementos (even locks of Armstrong's hair), and notes from veterans sending their memories of Armstrong. Libbie did her best to answer each serious letter while ignoring the obvious crackpots. It was a never-ending task, as every time a newspaper article mentioned Armstrong or Little Bighorn, the deluge would begin again. As it was usual for one or more New York papers to interview Libbie before the anniversary of the battle, the volume of letters had an annual peak. (In 1920, she spent six months in Europe and on her return found 800 letters waiting for her.[45])

The Hounds' Diaspora

At the Westminster Show in 1878, the year after the Romanoff/Custer Russian Wolfhounds were debuted by John Miller, General David Stanley, late of the Fort Sully Sporting Club, entered two of his English Greyhounds, Fleet and Pencawon, in a class of twenty-three.[46] (It is tempting to speculate that if Armstrong had returned from the Little Bighorn Campaign, he might well have competed in the show ring against Stanley, his former coursing rival from Fort Sully and the Yellowstone expedition.) In May, one of Armstrong's pack was a featured display at the New York Aquarium and billed as "Gen. Custer's stag hound"—as if he were the only one.[47] By September, there were apparently still a few of Armstrong's hounds which needed placing. Libbie must have been communicating with McIntyre, so her favorites went to special homes. That month, "the brace of imported Scotch staghounds, Swift and Tuck, given to the late General Custer by a Scotch nobleman," went to a wealthy Detroit friend and dog fancier, Mr. C. E. Mason, a member of the Lake St. Clair Shooting and Fishing Club. Apparently, the two deerhounds were already chasing deer at Mason's country home.[48] As Libbie's first book, *Boots and Saddles,* was years away from publication, the public couldn't have known that Tuck and Swift were with Armstrong at the Powder River Depot. About Lady's and Kaiser's fates, no information has surfaced.

That same year, Miller had bred the Romanoff/Custer Russian hounds, Stanley and Madgie, and put two of their six-month-old puppies at auction on October 5. Despite their distinguished lineage, they sold for the asking price of $5.50 and $5.75 (about $125 in today's dollars), and his other dogs went for lower amounts. Contrastingly, two field-tested Irish Setters sold for $59 and $70 (upwards of $1,000 today). George Bird Grinnell, now the editor of *Forest and Stream*, noted it could hardly have been worth Miller's while to bring all those dogs from Newburgh for the pittance he made.[49] In April 1879, at the third annual post–Westminster sale at Charles W. Barker's auction house and horse stables, Miller sold Stanley and Madgie's nine-month-old pups, Stanley II, Prince, and Magus, for low prices again. (At eight, Madgie was old for a brood bitch.) Stanley II went to W. V. Mangam of Manhattan, and Prince and Magus went to Boston racehorse fancier Wesley P. Balch—who also bought a bull-terrier and a pointer.[50]

An enigmatic mention of Armstrong's hounds appears in April 1880 just before the 4th Westminster Show. Brooklynite Col. Bradley acquired and intended to show "two magnificent" greyhounds, bred by DeWolf, of Manitoba, from stock obtained from the Indians, and originally imported by Gen. Custer. These dogs are lineal descendants of the famous English champion, descendants from Master McGrath."[51] *If* the statement of the greyhounds' origin is true, it presents a puzzle. The Dakota Territory abutted Canadian provinces Manitoba and Saskatchewan, and the Sioux did flee across the border after Little Bighorn. How Armstrong's greyhounds could have come to a tribe who only mated them with other purebreds before passing their offspring on to DeWolf in Manitoba is obscure. The tantalizing reference to Armstrong owning a descendant of Master McGrath came up again that year. (Master McGrath, a famous Irish-bred greyhound, he won the Waterloo Cup an astonishing three times in 1868, 1869, and 1871. Born in 1866, he stopped siring puppies after 1871 and died in 1873. His bronze effigy stands today in the center of Lurgan in Northern Ireland.)

Mr. L.C.F. Lotz of Chicago tried to ascertain the lineage of a greyhound acquired in the re-homing of the Custer hounds and published his results in June 1880. (Given the four-year lag between McIntyre's announcement and Lotz's pedigree inquiry, he was probably not the dog's first owner.) Tippecanoe was white with blue-gray spot, and claimed as both belonging to Armstrong and being Master McGrath's grandson. Lotz was having trouble finding pedigree documentation and wrote to B.C. Everleigh, the coursing correspondent for *The Field* in England, for information. (Established in 1853, *The Field* is Britain's oldest sporting magazine.) Everleigh found nothing about

Tippecanoe—even after consulting Lord Lurgan, Master McGrath's owner. Lotz wrote to Libbie, and she acknowledged Armstrong's ownership of the hound (suggesting it was indeed Scottish) but had no proof of lineage.

> New York, April 12th 1879
>
> Mr. Lotz—Sir—I regret to say the pedigree of the imported hound General Custer received from Scotland has been mislaid among the papers in our home in Monroe, Mich. The pedigree of the dogs sent him from Canada we never had. I do not know whether the dog you own is from the Scotch or Canadian dog. We often had fifty in the pack of hunting hounds. I thank you for your kindness to the dog, and I am glad he has a good home.
>
> Very respectfully,
> ELIZABETH B. CUSTER[52]

Lotz was not only a dog show exhibitor, but also an organizer of field coursing meets for greyhounds in the 1870s. He considered Libbie's statement proof of Tippecanoe's ancestry and published the full pedigree of Master McGrath—skipping the missing connection to "grandson" Tippecanoe.[53] (Lt. Javan Irvine of the Fort Sully Sporting Club found Lotz's item about Tippecanoe interesting enough to save with the other pedigrees in his greyhound papers. A note indicates the clipping was received on October 27, 1880, in Fort Griffin, Texas—the 22nd Infantry's station after leaving Fort Sully.) Interestingly, Lotz later stopped claiming Tippecanoe was a Custer hound in favor of boasting descent from Master McGrath, as such a distinguished ancestor would bring in hefty stud fees and help Lotz sell puppies. As the Custers had been great namedroppers, *if* they had owned a grandson of Master McGrath, Armstrong would have talked about it incessantly with Libbie noting it in her writings. (The Battle of Tippecanoe was an 1811 Army victory by future president William Henry Harrison against Chief Tecumseh's confederation of tribes. As such, Tippecanoe was a name Armstrong might well have given to a dog.)

In the East, Armstrong's dogs had gone to pet homes, but in the Territories their new owners worked them against wolf, coyote, and jackrabbit. Lt. Richard Thompson of the 6th Infantry at Fort Washakie said he had a one-eyed Custer hound in 1882 which could still course. (See Ch. 13, Rumor #18.) Some of the

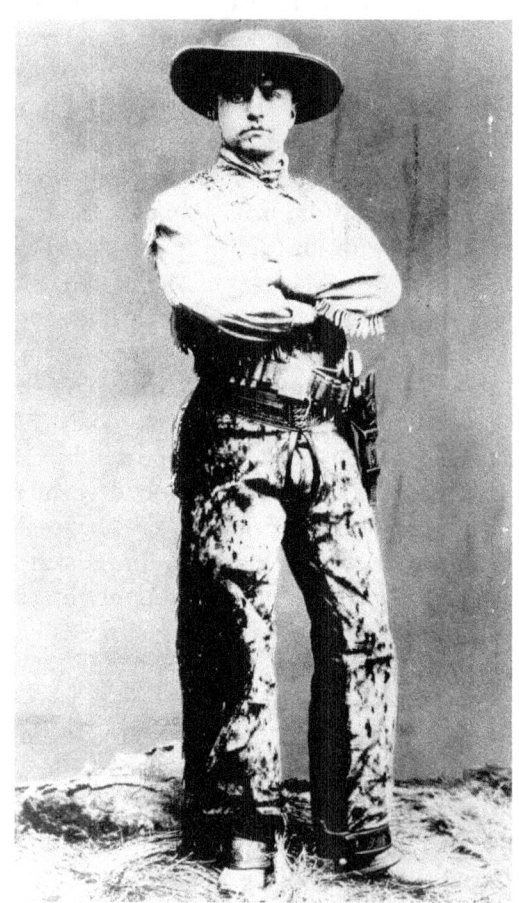

Dakotan cattle rancher Theodore "Teddy" Roosevelt, Jr. (who would become the 26th president) was proud to have hunted with descendants of Armstrong's deerhounds. Roosevelt R500.P69a-012, Houghton Library, Harvard University.

hounds stayed in Dakota Territory and were used by cattle ranchers for hunting and stopping wolf depredations. Up-and-coming New York politician and future president Theodore "Teddy" Roosevelt, who began ranching in Dakota in 1883, proudly stated, "I have myself hunted with many of the descendants of Custer hounds." Roosevelt was eighteen at the time of Little Bighorn and greatly admired Armstrong as a consummate frontiersman and American.[54]

Three Books and the Bugle's Last Call

In the summer of 1881, the three sections of a massive granite obelisk were hauled out to Little Bighorn and erected on the flattened-off ridge of Last Stand Hill. It had the names of the dead soldiers, scouts, and civilians engraved on all four sides. The remaining bones of the soldiers, such as could be found, were reburied in a trench surrounding the obelisk. Despite her job of being Custer's Widow, Libbie needed to escape periodically. In 1882, she sailed to England for the first time on the S.S. *Adriatic* (a steamship with sails) with her old friend, Gen. Gibbs' widow Peggy.[55] She went again in 1885 with free passage arranged by Samuel Graves (member of Parliament, industrialist, and guest buffalo hunter).[56] Despite the English hunters' standing invitations, Libbie never went fox hunting. Three years later, she met another of their English guests, T. Sutton Townsend, M.D., who was then a prominent medical man in London. Townsend recalled Armstrong and Tom's kindness in sending rattlesnakes for the London Zoological Gardens and assured Libbie that the snakes were still alive.[57] Libbie made many trips abroad, visiting France, Italy, Germany, Russia, India, China, and Japan, and she was once allowed on British Army transport from London to India only because she was General Custer's widow.[58] In 1914, she was in Germany when Archduke Ferdinand was assassinated and, along with the other Americans, she had to scramble to get home while the European war was erupting. (Samuel Graves was a partner in the White Star Line, whose ships included the *Adriatic, Oceanic,* and *Titanic.* In March 1912, Libbie sailed on the *Oceanic* from Cherbourg to New York—but if her return had been a month later, she might have been on the *Titanic* sailing that exact route when it struck an iceberg and sank on April 14, 1912.)

There were ceremonies on the battlefield to mark the major anniversaries—notably the tenth, twenty-fifth, and fiftieth. Aging veterans and warriors and the eager public listened to *de rigueur*, hero-worshiping speeches made by politicians (who were glad they hadn't been at Little Bighorn). The events included battle reenactments (small scale), attendance by surviving Army and Indian veterans, and on the 50th anniversary, a contingent of the 7th Cavalry as well as Crow, Sioux, and Cheyenne in feathered regalia. There were parades, rodeo-style events, fireworks, concerts, and souvenirs. The remains of a soldier from Reno's battalion had been unearthed by road workers a month before, and during the ceremonies he was reburied with military honors and a ceremonial hatchet. Participants Gen. Godfrey and Red Tomahawk shook hands over the grave. The speeches and battle reenactment were recorded on motion picture film and radio. Libbie was always invited to these anniversary ceremonies, and while she could never bear to attend any, from New York she did listen to the radio

Three unidentified men and a dog at the Little Bighorn monument on Last Stand Hill a few years after it was erected in 1881. The troopers were reburied in a trench around its base, which had not yet been leveled. The granite obelisk shows chipping by souvenir hunters and fractures from winter ice. Denver Public Library, Western History Collection, B0244. Photograph by D.F. Barry.

broadcast of the mock battle. (On one day, the crowds were estimated at 40,000 to 50,000—a figure obtained by counting cars from an airplane.[59])

William F. Cody wrote to Libbie ten years after Little Bighorn in August 1886, graciously asking her to attend the premier of a new addition to his Wild West show—the depiction of "Custer's last fight" at Madison Square Garden. In the finale, the long-haired General Custer died theatrically with saber in hand twice daily at "3 and 8 P.M.— ALL WEATHER."[60] Naturally, the real finale was the avenging Cody riding in to fight the murderous Yellow Hand—lifting up his feather bonnet as "The first scalp for Custer." Surprisingly, Libbie agreed to this idealistic simulation and went to many performances, becoming good friends with one of the stars, markswoman Annie Oakley.[61] (In 1913, Annie Oakley was still performing trick shots at age fifty-three and regularly shot apples off her setter Dave's head.)

The continuing interest in General Custer's life motivated Libbie to take Whittaker's advice and write a memoir of the man she loved. She eventually wrote three books which portrayed her husband "in his private life"—as a son, a brother, and a husband.[62]

Besides their focus on Armstrong, they were also engaging descriptions of a woman's life on the frontier. It was emotionally difficult for Libbie to wade through Armstrong's letters and memorabilia to write the narrative of their Dakota years. *Boots and Saddles or Life in Dakota with General Custer* was published in 1885 to excellent reviews. The first edition of 2,000 copies sold out, and ultimately some 31,000 copies would be sold.[63] (Publishers assumed that at least two people read each copy, so readership was double the sales number.) Naturally, the book abounded with stories of Old Rover, Lucy Stone, Tuck, Cardigan, and their other dogs. (Like Armstrong, Libbie didn't always name the dogs when relating their escapades, so it can be difficult deciding which dogs were at a particular post or expedition.)

Still in mourning, Libbie Custer embarked on an ocean voyage to Europe, Egypt, Turkey, India, and the Far East. Many adventures came her way as a renowned author, speaker, and widow of the famous General. Courtesy of the National Park Service, Little Bighorn Battlefield National Monument, LIBI_00019_00465. Photograph taken 1903–1906.

Her book was such a success that she began a second, *Tenting on the Plains or General Custer in Kansas and Texas*. This one touched on the end of the Civil War but focused on Texas and the first years on the Kansas prairie (Eliza helped Libbie with some of the anecdotes). To write the manuscript, she escaped to the Catskills, where she enjoyed again the pleasure of sleeping in a tent. Libbie included many dog stories—the first pack in Hempstead, sweet Ginnie, Byron the thief, Turk the pugilist, and Old Rover the snorer. While the first edition of *Boots and Saddles* had no illustrations (subsequent ones had a portrait of Custer and a Dakota Territory map), Libbie commissioned several drawings for *Tenting*, and Western artist Frederic Remington did two illustrations of exciting incidents—Armstrong lifting her from the saddle at full gallop and the standoff with the buffalo after he shot Custis Lee. There were also drawings by Albert Berghaus, who worked for *Frank Leslie's Illustrated Newspaper*. He produced a warm portrait of Armstrong surrounded by his horse, deerhounds, and foxhounds (see the cover illustration). Berghaus also created poignant images of a pensive Armstrong at his desk with a companion staghound and a solitary hound sleeping on the library couch with his master's hat nearby. Libbie also had the photo of the buffalo at bay surrounded by riders and blurry hounds, turned into an engraving with ten hounds clearly shown.[64] That she made the effort to include these drawings of their dogs is a wonderful testament to her feelings for them.

Tenting on the Plains (1887) was another smash hit and led to her third memoir, *Following the Guidon,* published in 1890. This one included bits and pieces not included in the first two. There were a number of dog stories in the chapters, "Pets of the Camp," "Hunting Records," and "'Garryowen' Leads the Hunt" (the latter telling of Maida's death). This book had just one dog illustration. Titled *General Custer and His Scouts*, it was a rendering of the photograph of Armstrong, Bloody Knife, two scouts, a greyhound, and a deerhound. Libbie had the drawing significantly altered to show a fourth Indian reporting to a beardless but mustachioed Armstrong, a second deerhound to replace the greyhound—and dramatically added teepees, horses, and burial scaffolds to help the composition.[65]

Armstrong posed for this pensive portrait in his library at Fort Lincoln. At the back of his desk, below the lamp is the sculpture of a hound's head, and between the antlers on the wall is a photograph of Libbie in her wedding dress (and there are two smaller ones of her on his desk). Besides his favorite Brady portrait of himself, there were framed photographs of Generals McClellan and Sheridan. For *Tenting on the Plains*, Libbie had Albert Berghaus draw the desk to include objects from elsewhere in the room and a waiting staghound. Courtesy of the National Park Service, Little Bighorn Battlefield National Monument, LIBI_00011_000268 and Elizabeth B. Custer's *Tenting on the Plains*.

Following the Guidon was also well received, and the income appreciably helped her financial situation. (Libbie's Civil War memoir was never finished.) Based on her books' popularity, the Redpath Lyceum Bureau (who had wanted Armstrong to lecture) contracted with her in 1890 to give lectures, which paid better than writing articles. As an author and lecturer, Libbie proudly considered herself a "working woman." Always charitably minded, in 1908, she purchased sixteen lots in north Manhattan to create a home for "aged literary women" and honor her husband.[66] Her speaking engagements had glowing reviews. Whittaker had been right about Libbie's natural style of talking and, with some elocution lessons, her ability to perform in lecture halls improved considerably. Listening to Libbie speak was like sitting down with a friend to catch up on her doings. She talked about Civil War and Indian War experiences, "Buffaloes and Buffalo Hunting," "Garrison Life on the Plains," and "Dogs on the March." The latter was based on eight pages of rambling notes where she more than once emphasized *attempting* to keep dogs out of the tent and off the wet mattresses while trying to resist their soulful, pleading eyes.[67] From one of her scrawled jottings, she was even going to talk about removing ticks from the dogs' ears in Texas.[68]

Life with Armstrong and the dogs provided an amazing amount of raw material for lectures, and Libbie frequently scribbled ideas for lectures on notepads, postmarked envelopes, or whatever scraps of paper were handy. After years of telling the stories without anyone to correct her, Libbie's memory slipped from time to time. In her "Dogs on the March" notes, she mixed up Byron and Blucher—mistakenly saying was it was the "well-named" Blucher who wouldn't let her into bed and was chased by Eliza after stealing the hot steak—while Armstrong chuckled about some dogs being smarter than most people.[69] Blucher was the only dog name from these notes, which included:

> Now swift—powerful—taking hold of a buffalo's jaw—thrashed from side to side but hanging on 'till the Genl brought the animal down. Scotch Stag hounds—Sent us from Scotland by Lord Paget & Lord Waterpark?
> A. so amused watching their performance—remarking how intelligent dogs became with constant association with humans. No acknowledgement that the impudent assertive dog needed a whipping—they knew so well what they were up to—but squealed a little, stretched—yawned when trying to be especially crafty but their eyes betrayed them and the lofty Scotch Stag hounds "descended from a hundred Kings" as far as pedigrees went were what Eliza called oudacious [sic].

On one of the last pages, Libbie said that their camp bedding was rolled up each day in a "poncho"—and then made a note to herself, "Is poncho Spanish?"

The Great Sioux War began with the Powder River Fight of 1876, but it was the disaster at Little Bighorn which galvanized the Army and the U.S. government into finally ending the Indian nation's autonomy and their way of life. The Army successively crushed the last of the rebellious tribes, relocating them to reservations where they were to live like white men. The last flicker of resistance was the spiritual Ghost Dance movement which ended in the winter of 1890 with a massacre that started accidentally. Over 200 and perhaps as many as 300, Oglala Sioux men, women, and children died at Wounded Knee (compared to Army fatalities of twenty-nine soldiers and an Indian scout).[70] Coincidentally, it was the 7th Cavalry (with an artillery detachment) that was sent to disarm the Sioux, and several Little Bighorn veterans were there. At that time, the Wounded Knee "battle" was characterized as the 7th's revenge upon the Sioux. Twenty soldiers received the Congressional Medal of Honor, which the Sioux have asked to be rescinded.

Libbie soldiered on in a strange mixture of sadness and pleasure from her memories of Armstrong and life with horses and dogs. In 1891, people were still spreading the Little Bighorn rumor that no survivor was left "...to tell the story save Keogh's horse and Custer's only hound."[71] (Curiously, Libbie never addressed the rumors of Armstrong's dogs being with him on Last Stand Hill.) Controversy about the battle seethed continuously, but serious inquiries into the events and causes were delicately avoided (or at least unpublished) for fear of offending Libbie Custer. The real research didn't begin until after her death but then was handicapped by clouded memories and the fact that many of the 7th had died. (The rich oral histories of the Sioux and Cheyenne warriors weren't yet considered useful by historians.) National opinion of Armstrong would swing from hero to perpetrator of genocide and everything in between, but the rumors about one of his dogs on Last Stand Hill persisted—despite whichever virtues and vices people assigned to George Armstrong Custer.

John Burkman lived the last decades of his solitary life in Billings, Montana, spending his mornings at the train depot and the afternoons in front of his shack—remembering the General and Miss Libbie. He sent this photograph to her about 1923. Two years later, after committing suicide, he was buried in the Custer National Cemetery at Little Bighorn. Courtesy of the National Park Service, Little Bighorn Battlefield National Monument, LIBI_00019_00177.

The long years went by, and Libbie's family, friends, and comrades from the 7th Cavalry faded away. Like the knot of men on Last Stand Hill, her circle grew smaller and smaller. Before Burkman shot himself in 1925, she corresponded with him periodically through Bud O'Donnell, warmly inquiring after his health, offering assistance, and reminiscing fondly, "How faithful you were to the General, Burkman and how he trusted you! And how happy he was with the horses and dogs!"[72]

Apart from the occasional ball gown (restrained in hue), Libbie wore somber clothes in memory of Armstrong to the end of her life. At nearly ninety-one years, her memory was failing her, and she had become frail and had trouble walking. She could no longer travel to the Catskills and sleep in her tent or go to Florida in the winter to escape arthritis pain, but she still enjoyed her life and wouldn't surrender. Libbie was always a good planner, and her will stipulated her papers and collection of Custer memorabilia would go to certain institutions—the final action to keep Armstrong's memory alive. Libbie died on April 4, 1933, and was buried unobtrusively next to Armstrong's granite obelisk at West Point. (Many visitors to his grave don't notice her name on the large stone slab.) Libbie never went to Little Bighorn. It would have been too painful, and she probably knew she would have been out of place at the anniversary events—a relic who could only bless the proceedings while being pressed by strangers with claims of soldiering with her husband. In her solitude, she did yearn for the dogs. In a stream of consciousness from *Tenting on the Plains*, Libbie gives us her canine manifesto.

> A dog is so human to me, and dogs have been my husband's chosen friends for so many years, I cannot look upon the commonest cur with indifference. Sometimes, as I stand now at my window, longing for the old pack that whined with delight, quarreled with jealousy for the best place near us, capered with excitement as we started off on a ride or walk, my eyes involuntarily follow each dog that pass on the street. I look at the master, to see if he realizes that all that is faithful and loving in this world is at his heels. If he stops to talk to a friend, and the dog leaps about him, licks his hand, rubs against him, and tries, in every way that his devoted heart teaches him, to attract the attention of the one who is all the world to him, all my sympathies are with the dog. I watch with jealous solicitude to see if the affectionate brute gets recognition. And if by instinct the master's hand goes out to the dog's head, I am quite as glad and grateful as the recipient. If the man is absorbed, and lets the animal sit patiently and adoringly watching his very expression, it seems to me that I cannot refrain from calling his attention to the neglect.[73]

Before she married Armstrong, Libbie lived a quiet, decorous girlhood in her father's house without pets. Yet, during her marriage, Elizabeth Bacon Custer rode with hunting deerhounds and foxhounds, broke up their fights and sutured the wounds, had her lap affectionately crushed by their bulk, raised their puppies, and mourned their deaths. She dearly loved the rough and tumble pack—one which would have pleased a Scottish laird or medieval baron. Libbie only had dogs for the twelve years she was married to Armstrong and lived the last fifty-seven years of her life without even a lap dog such as he tried twice to get for her. No matter how sweet tempered or handsome, any dog would have been a daily, anguishing reminder of those intense dog years with her Autie—of which she wrote, "Our dogs give us such pleasure…."

Epilogue

Custer's Last Hound

"Who will bring forth the dusty carcass from its hiding place—if any?"
—Minneapolis Morning Tribune, 1923[1]

One Custer hound shared a fate somewhat similar to the more well-known Comanche. He was Libbie's favorite and had the name which British newspapers trumpeted after the disastrously heroic Charge of the Light Brigade—Cardigan!

> I will anticipate a moment and speak of the final fate of Cardigan. When I left Fort Lincoln I asked some one to look out for his welfare, and send him, as soon as possible, to a clergyman who had been my husband's friend. My request was complied with, and afterwards, when the poor old dog died, his new master honored him by having his body set up by the taxidermist, and a place was given him in one of the public buildings in Minneapolis. I cannot help thinking that he was worthy of the tribute, not only because of the testimony thus given to the friendship of the people for his master, but because he was the bravest and most faithful of animals.[2]

After the dedication of Armstrong's memorial in Monroe in 1910, interest in General Custer lessened, but new readers of *Boots and Saddles* would be intrigued by the reference to Cardigan preserved somewhere in Minneapolis. Residents periodically resurrected the quest to learn his location—but the answer remained elusive until 1923.

Armstrong and Libbie knew the Rev. Cassius Marcellus Terry (1845–1881) of St. Paul's Congregational Plymouth Church. Going into or out of the States, the Custers often broke their journey there before moving on. Armstrong more frequently traveled through St. Paul than did Libbie, and that may explain why she called Terry "my husband's friend" rather than "our" friend. After leaving Fort Lincoln, Libbie and her fellow widows spent the day secluded with "intimate friends" in St. Paul before continuing east. Terry's church and residence were less than a mile and a half from Union Depot, and his house would have been a natural refuge for Libbie's group. Finding homes for the dogs was still on her mind, and perhaps Terry offered to take one at that time. (The Rev. Terry was distantly related to Gen. Alfred Terry—Armstrong's commander on the Little Bighorn Expedition and whose headquarters were in St. Paul.[3])

The cream-coated Cardigan, first mentioned on the 1873 march to Fort Rice and the Yellowstone expedition, was either bred by or sent to the Custers. Sighthound youngsters attain most of their adult body size and weight by the time they reach twelve months (mental and emotional maturity take a little longer), so it isn't unreasonable to suggest that Cardigan was perhaps one year old in early 1873—particularly as he was in the "Landseer" water battle with the bull elk. This would make him at least four years

Custer's Last Hound—Cardigan. Libbie took pains to see that her favorite staghound was re-homed with the Rev. Cassius Terry, a friend of Armstrong's. Terry had Cardigan's body mounted, and for many years, the staghound was on display in two different museums in Minneapolis before eventually disappearing. *Minneapolis Morning Tribune,* **March 25, 1923.**

at the time of Little Bighorn—but he stayed with Libbie because she was so attached to him, or perhaps he was no longer a good hunter or trekker (whether he recovered fully from his wounds in the pack fight was never mentioned). The friend Libbie asked to see to Cardigan's transfer to the Rev. Terry was certainly C.W. McIntyre, who handled the pack's dispersal.

Cardigan and his new master bonded, and the hound was a local celebrity. In May 1878, Terry was hired by the Geological and Natural History Survey of Minnesota and went on specimen-collecting field expeditions in 1879 and 1880.[4] Despite poor health, he was fond of camping and fishing, and Cardigan may have accompanied him rather than being left with his wife Emily. Together, master and dog posed for a photograph in their parlor about 1880. When Cardigan died soon after at about nine years of age, Terry had him mounted as a tribute to both Armstrong and the staghound himself and then presented Cardigan to the University of Minnesota's Natural History Museum. (In 1939, it became the Bell Museum.) Terry succumbed to tuberculosis at age thirty-six in August of 1881—not long after Cardigan's death. (His wife Emily Hitchcock Terry was a preeminent botanist in Minnesota, Vermont, and Massachusetts. In 1992, the

Rev. Terry-Cardigan photo was published in *A Painted Herbarium: The Life and Art of Emily Hitchcock Terry, 1838–1921.*)

While it may seem odd today, Victorians and Edwardians had no problem with stuffing pet dogs as a tribute—often having their small ones mounted in a glass dome or display case. (The Adams Museum in Deadwood, South Dakota, has *two* 19th century lapdogs on display.) A taxidermy manual of 1908 had instructions on mounting wild animals and different sizes of dogs.[5] After the carcass was measured, it was skinned and the hide was tanned, and it was treated with arsenical soap against insect damage. A wire or wood armature was filled out with bundled excelsior, tow, or oakum, and the hide stretched over it and carefully sewn together. The stuffing was manipulated to more closely resemble musculature, and the nose and mouth were painted or replicated in wax. Heads could be shaped of plaster and clay applied to the skull, but as weight was a consideration, a *papier mâché* form was often substituted. (The mounted dogs in the Natural History Museum at Tring, U.K., were separated from their skeletons.) The taxidermist would work from photographs or drawings to make the pose and expression lifelike. Cardigan was said to have been "very finely mounted" for his display at the museum. However, despite the best techniques, harsh preservative chemicals and exposure to unfiltered sunlight over the years faded the fur's natural colors.

For many years, Cardigan was displayed as one of General Custer's hounds, along with several of his 1874 Black Hills expedition trophies (removed from the collection long ago). In 1882, Mrs. O'Brien, a visitor from Ireland, saw "…in the Museum at Minneapolis, Minnesota, a stuffed specimen, labelled 'Irish Wolf hound'; it was rough, pure white in colour, and of good size."[6] With the passing years, the public lost interest in General Custer, and the exhibits were changed out for better specimens or as the collection's emphasis changed. Cardigan was eventually removed and largely forgotten among the Bell's stored pelts and mounted specimens. There were surges of interest in his whereabouts (with little result), until the 1923 Twin Cities Kennel Club show (April 4–6, 1923), which sparked a six-day whirlwind of articles in the *Minneapolis Morning Tribune.*

"Mounted Pelt of General Custer's Dog Sought Here." On March 21, a reporter repeated the rumor that Cardigan was on display in the university museum and disappeared when the museum moved. Nicholas R. Murphy, a veteran who was with Gibbon at the Little Bighorn aftermath, doubted the hound ever got to Minneapolis but conceded there were so many true and false stories about General Custer that it just might be "a part of the romantic pioneer history of the wonderful Northwest." He called for anyone knowing the "present resting place of the relic" to make it known.[7] (Nicholas Murphy was a private in I Company, 7th Infantry with Gibbon's column.[8])

"Custer's Dog Was in Old Museum, Graduate Writes." On March 22, the *Tribune* quoted a letter from a University of Minnesota graduate (class of 1885) who remembered the dog belonging to the Rev. C.M. Terry and his wife and that he was "a pet to the neighborhood and when it died there was much childish grief." She said when couples were courting at the obelisk alongside the old museum, through a window, they could see Cardigan "standing in state" in a glass case.[9] At this point, Cardigan's whereabouts were still unknown, but a subsequent mention of Armstrong's other hounds added further confusion.

"Custer's Lost Hound Mystery Complicated by Three New Entries." On the 23rd, a short piece said that George P. Flannery, president of the Northwestern Trust Company, stated General Custer had owned not one but *four* such hounds (he had read *Boots and Saddles*). Flannery and Teddy Roosevelt had gone hunting with two that had been given to Clinton R. Fealm, who owned a ranch near "Madan" (almost certainly Mandan, near Fort Lincoln). Flannery didn't recall that the hounds had any particular names, but one was later given to Mr. Cook of Minneapolis.[10]

"Search for Custer's Pet Hound Is Brought Back to Minneapolis." Prompted by the previous articles, six more people made contributions to the mystery. Dr. Thomas Sadler Roberts, director of the Zoological Museum at the university, said that in 1921 collection items no longer of general interest were removed. He had seen Cardigan then, and because of the mount's very poor condition after four decades in a window, it was thrown onto a trash heap. "That, at least, was the last I saw of the dog." (After becoming head of the museum in 1915, Roberts did remove a large number of decaying mounts.[11]) Prof. H.F. Nachtrieb, head of the Animal Biology Department, remembered Cardigan's ignominious disposal but added that a janitor named Olson "was ordered to retrieve the mount and pack it up." Mrs. M.H. French wrote that only Cardigan, a mule, and one man were survivors of Little Bighorn, and that the hound was given to the 11th Infantry and subsequently died in Madison Barracks, New York, where he had a full military funeral. (For the analysis of her story, see Ch. 13, #21.) Veteran Nicholas Murphy, who had written on the 21st, rejoined the conversation and stated that no pets had been allowed on Gibbon's march to Little Bighorn for fear their noise would alert the Indians. He thought Cardigan had been left with the supply train or with Mrs. Custer at Fort Lincoln.

Henry F. Douglas, president of the Great Western Grain Company in Minneapolis (and a former post trader at Fort Yates), recalled that several of General Custer's staghounds were brought to Yates in 1876 from Fort Lincoln and were kept there for a year or so until "...distributed among various friends by the widow. The dogs were very large... one of them being very much larger than the rest. They were white in color, with black and tan markings, the head somewhat on the pointer type, but the ears more pendulous and set lower." (For the "returning hound" rumors, see Ch. 13, #s 2, 6, 7, and 16.) The last informant in this installment of the story was Walter A. Eggleston, vice president of the David C. Bell Investment Company, whose account refuted that of Mrs. French by stating that Cardigan definitely died in Minneapolis and, in a brighter note, that he owned one of his puppies—"Lord Cardigan Jr." Eggleston added that another of Cardigan's offspring was owned by Fred D. Brown of the South Side neighborhood. At the close of this barrage of testimony, the reporter injected some levity into the article by quoting Prof. Nachtrieb: "It's a doggone story, I guess."[12]

"Photograph Strengthens City's Claim on Cardigan, Missing Custer Hound." On Sunday, the 25th, the *Tribune* published the photograph of the Rev. Terry and Cardigan, which had been given to Dr. Roberts by Terry himself. Roberts made a definite statement about Cardigan's death by saying he was presented with the mounted hound *before* Terry's death in August 1881. The photograph was proof Cardigan hadn't been buried in Madison Barracks. Dr. Addie R. Haverfield, Mrs. C.W. Kerr, and E.E. Van

Cleve all wrote saying they had seen the mounted dog long after its alleged burial date. All well and good, but where was Cardigan now?

While the reporter didn't reveal his source (possibly Dr. Roberts), he said the janitor who rescued Cardigan's mount made some repairs and sold it to Mr. Horner, the owner of the "old Dime Museum" on Hennepin Avenue (one of several such museums in the city). William Horner's small museum featured a collection of mammals and birds, but Cardigan was just a giant stuffed dog and apparently not labeled as General Custer's. A veteran police officer whose daily rounds took him past the museum remembered seeing Cardigan there amongst the other exhibits. On Horner's death the museum was sold to David C. Broderick, who did not remember Cardigan in the collection. (The 1899 Minneapolis City Directory lists Broderick as the manager.) The curious collection would change hands many times. The article ended with the hopeful note that the superintendent of the university's grounds and buildings, H.A. Hildebrandt, was searching for the former janitor to confirm the rescue and disposition of Cardigan's mount.[13] (Dime museums were quite popular in the late 1800s. Following the model of Barnum's American Museum, for 10¢ people could see "educational" and titillating curiosities.)

"The Clouded Ruins of Cardigan." Apparently that janitor was never found. On March 27, the editor summarized the various claims about Cardigan and inflated the mystery to the level of the Mona Lisa, the Kohinoor diamond, the golden tablets of Joseph Smith, and Homer's birthplace:

> ... and where, dear reader, did Cardigan die, and where his sepulture—if any? Who will bring forth the dusty carcass from its hiding place—if any? And who, once it is brought forth, can say finally and indisputably: "Behold the stuffed ruins of what was once the great Cardigan!"[14]

The *Tribune*'s quest lost steam, but it produced a few facts. At Libbie's direction, Cardigan was sent to the Rev. Cassius Terry, who owned him for about five years. On the hound's death, he was mounted by a taxidermist and presented to the University's Natural History Museum. After a few decades, the mount was in such poor condition that it was discarded—but rescued and sold to a curiosity museum. From there, Cardigan's mount was sold off and eventually lost.

In 1973, Indian War scholar Paul L. Hedren resurrected the search and wrote to the *Minneapolis Star* about Cardigan. His inquiry was passed on to the Minnesota Historical Society reference librarian and chief archeologist. The two men *believed* the hound's mount had initially been given to the Minnesota Academy of Natural Sciences and finally transferred to the old Minneapolis Public Library for display. They speculated that Cardigan "probably was moth-eaten and destroyed long ago."[15] Hedren learned the library had housed selected items from the Academy but had no record of Cardigan's presence. (While neither of the professors who wrote to the *Morning Tribune* fifty years earlier mentioned Cardigan at the library, it is possible the mount was there for a while on loan.) The best information from the Historical Society was that the hound had disappeared around 1890.[16] Hedren's article on Cardigan appeared in a 1974 edition of the Little Big Horn Associates' *Research Review*, and historian/artist Lisle Reedstrom contributed a line drawing of Cardigan being admired by a crowd.

Eighteen years later, Scottish Deerhound owner and Custer scholar Stephen D.

Youngkin took up the challenge and in November 1991 contacted the Minnesota Historical Society. They sent him copies of the *Minnesota Morning Tribune* articles but had no records of any of Armstrong's hunting trophies or Cardigan. On their recommendation, in January 1992, he wrote directly to the University Archives to see what they might know. Head of the Archives Penelope Krosch confirmed the Reverend Terry's ownership of Cardigan as well as the presentation of the mounted hound to their museum. (Her thinking was that the mount was discarded in 1916 when the Natural History collections were moved from the "Old Main" into a new building—coinciding with the advent of Dr. Roberts' tenure as director and the first "weeding" of the collection.)

Interestingly enough, Krosch related to Youngkin that her friend had seen Cardigan's skull in the Bell Museum's storage during the 1960s, and it was "marked on the underside in ink as belonging to Custers' dog." The fellow thought the skull more properly belonged in the museum at Little Bighorn Battlefield but did not pursue the transfer (somewhat surprising during a resurgence of popular interest in General Custer). Krosch speculated that a subsequent curator had disposed of the skull, but said the current mammal curator was going to check the collection. Youngkin had no further word from Krosch, so that apparently didn't happen.

Krosch thought if the skull existed in the collection, then it must have been removed *prior* to the discard, so the rescue of his *intact* mount from the trash heap was improbable. Yet people saw Cardigan afterwards in the dime museum. (As previously described, during the taxidermy process, his skeleton was quite probably not used, so his skull could have been separately preserved for study.) She confirmed there were annual inquiries about Cardigan from "Custer or Scottish Deerhound fanciers." Apart from the hound going from the Rev. Terry to the museum, the collection weeding, and the existence of Cardigan's skull, Krosch said, "The rest is rather apocryphal but great fun."[17]

That seems to be the end of Cardigan's story, although Dr. Sharon Jansa, current curator of mammals at the Bell Museum, made another fruitless search for traces of the hound—stranger things have happened than for the skull to be stashed in a long-forgotten box or to have disappeared into private hands. If the skull of Libbie's Cardigan is truly lost, then there can be some satisfaction in knowing his remote descendants may still be going for walks in the neighborhoods of the Twin Cities.

Appendix

General Custer's Dogs in Art, Literature and Film

> CADET CORPORAL SHARP: "I'm sorry we can't make arrangements for the dogs until tomorrow, though."
> CADET CUSTER: "Oh, think nothing of it, Mr. Sharp. They're accustomed to sleeping with me anyway."—*They Died with Their Boots On* (1941)

Nearly all the artistic attention to animals in the 7th Cavalry goes to a horse which had no connection to George Armstrong Custer. Comanche, as the sole cavalry horse survivor of Little Bighorn, was the subject of poems, songs, paintings, and films. If there were songs or poems about Armstrong's dogs, they've vanished into obscurity. The pendulum of popular opinion swings back and forth on Armstrong, and by association, his dogs too—but the few creative representations of them are worth noting. (For clarity here, I'll use "Custer" when speaking of his depictions and "Armstrong" or "General Custer" for the man himself.)

The Artist's Eye

Despite the fact that Armstrong's dogs were constantly with him out West, they are infrequently shown with him on paper or canvas. In 1969, Don Russell made a bibliographic listing of 967 painted or drawn images of Custer and Little Bighorn, and a considerable number of others have been made since.[1] Some of his more famous horses are represented—but only because he is riding them—and his hounds are largely neglected. The first artistic "Custer dog" would be Libbie's 1866 sketch of a pipe-smoking bull-dog (see Ch. 6). In a somewhat similar vein, an unintentional parallel of that bulldog/human hybrid image appeared recently in a fad for superimposing dog heads onto famous portraits (arguably started by Thierry Poncelet's whimsical paintings). Michele Lyon, inspired by Poncelet and a Mathew Brady portrait of Armstrong as a general,[2] cleverly substituted a blonde, blue-eyed dog's head for Armstrong's. The dog's hairy muzzle and ears mimic Armstrong's mustache and long curls, and the eyes even look off in the same direction that Armstrong does.

Of Armstrong's hounds at the time, there seem to be only a few period illustrations extant. In his 1867 *Harper's Weekly* sketch *Camp Pets of the Seventh United States Cavalry*, Theodore Davis included two greyhounds, one bull-dog, and two nondescript dogs—but these were breed-generic caricatures rather than portraits of individuals (see Ch. 6). However, it is possible the detailed bull-dog represents Turk or Brandy, which could make the sketch the only image of either. In 1873, a newspaper engraving of Armstrong, entourage, and foxhounds on the Yellowstone expedition was a stock illustration which was only personalized by superimposing Armstrong's head on the leader (see Ch. 10).

Armstrong seems to have commissioned James H. Beard for a hunting portrait based on the 1874 Illingworth photograph of himself and the grizzly (see Ch. 11). The painting was reproduced in *Recreation Magazine*, October 1894, with this text:

> Painting of Grizzly photo Custers First Grizzley [sic]—"The picture here referred to was painted from a photograph, taken on the spot, by James H. Beard, N. A., the father of Dan C. [Daniel Carter], J. [James] Carter and Frank Beard, of this city, under the personal direction of General Custer, so that each face shown in it is an actual portrait. With the General are his brother, Boston Custer, and Chief Bloody Knife. The dog is General Custer's famous deerhound, Tuck, who, the General states elsewhere, caught and pulled down several antelope, at different times, in straight-away races. The original painting is 24 × 36 inches in size and is offered for sale, by the widow of the deceased artist."[3]

Beard lived in New York and was a well-known painter of people and animals who lived in New York when Armstrong frequented the city. The painting of Tuck and the bear does not match Beard's sophisticated style, and one wonders if it is actually his. The photo's elements were changed considerably so that Armstrong now stands as the central figure. The sleeping hound on the left was replaced by a seated deerhound on the right, and the mustachioed Col. Ludlow has been moved to the far rear and renamed as Boston. The standing private has been removed, and the background tents and wagons were replaced by dramatic mountain peaks and a large tree. The only elements in the photograph which the painter didn't change are the dead bear and Bloody Knife. Presumably Beard's widow sold the painting in 1894, but nothing further is known of it. As the photograph was taken in the summer of 1874, Armstrong could have only commissioned this painting between then and the fall of 1875, after which he would have been too busy with his activities in New York and the Belknap Hearings before his last campaign. Subsequent images of the Custers' hounds in this period are confined to the illustrations Libbie commissioned in 1887 and 1890 for *Tenting on the Plains* and *Following the Guidon* (see pp. 277–278). As noted in Ch. 14, Edgar S. Paxson would have included Armstrong's deerhounds in his 1899 painting *Custer's Last Stand* were it not for Gen. Godfrey's definitive statement that the hounds were left at the Powder River Depot.

In 1948, the line drawings for Fairfax Downey's young adult novel *The Seventh's Staghound* were done by Paul Brown, and twelve featured the staghounds in vignettes from the story. The drawing of two staghounds fighting on their hind legs was inspired by Libbie's description of Cardigan's mauling in *Boots and Saddles.*

Western and Civil War historian, illustrator, and dog man E. Lisle Reedstrom created a series of pen and ink illustrations for the chapter headers in Frost's *General Custer's Libbie* (1976). Of the thirty-nine illustrations, four included dogs. Reedstrom did a larger illustration of Armstrong hunting with his pack for the cover of Brian W.

Appendix: General Custer's Dogs in Art, Literature and Film 291

Dippie's *Nomad: George A. Custer in Turf, Field and Farm* (1980) as well as smaller drawings for the fifteen chapter headers (three of which feature the dogs). Another large illustration, *Blucher and Maida Lead the Chase*, illustrated Don Schwarck's "Campaigning in Kansas with Maida and Blucher, General Custer's Staghounds" in the Little Big Horn Associates' *Research Review* (1991). Reedstrom's vigorous drawings are arguably the only depictions of Armstrong's hounds actually running in hunts. In 1980, Scott Meyer re-imagined the 1887 Berghaus line-drawing of Custer, Vic and the pack as a more intimate pencil portrait of just man, horse, and two Scottish Deerhounds. (The drawing was printed on limited edition note cards.) Western and wildlife artist Jerry Thomas of Scott City, Kansas, painted *One Perfect Day*, in 2016 to commemorate the 150th anniversary of the 7th Cavalry's inception at Fort Riley. The detailed acrylic painting shows Custer in uniform, Libbie in her gold-braided, riding habit, an orderly, and their greyhound returning from hunting along the Kansas River.

Much rarer are three-dimensional representations. In 1995, sculptor and historian Glenwood Swanson felt dogs were such a big part of Armstrong's personality that he

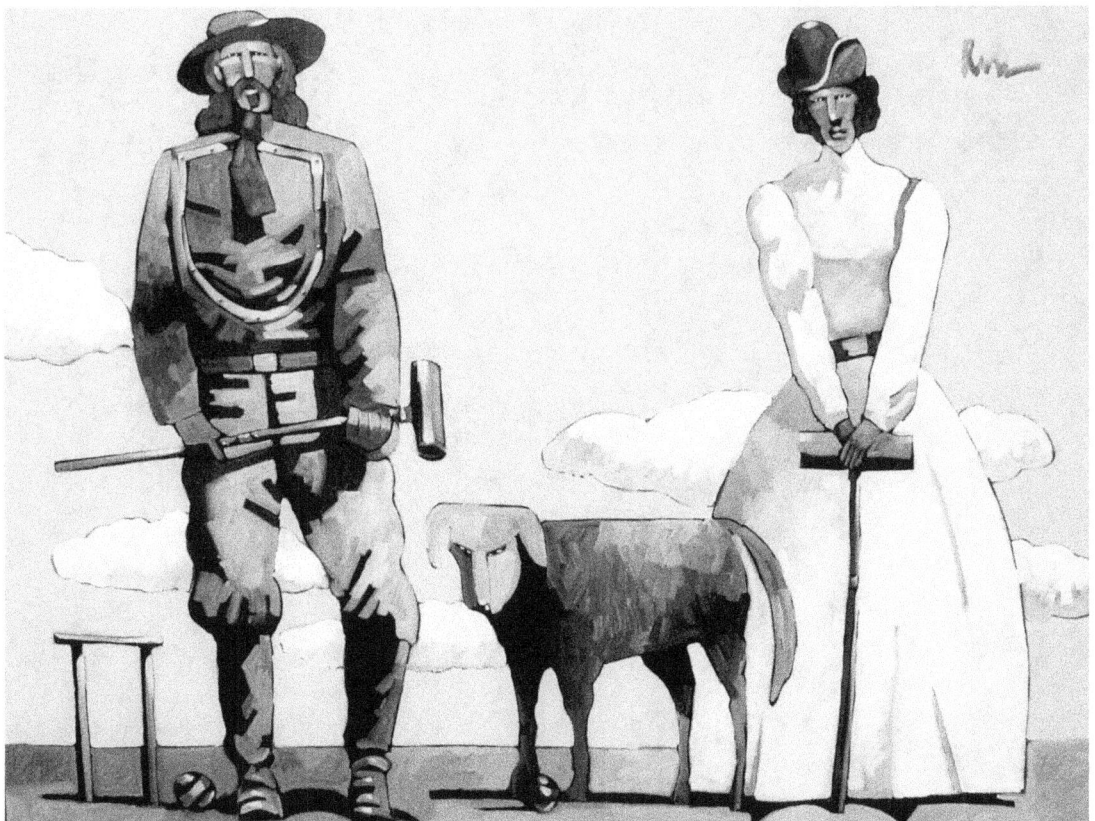

Custer & Libbie Playing Croquet (2008) by Thom Ross. The artist wanted to emphasize Armstrong as a human being by painting him with his wife and dog playing a game—aspects of Armstrong's character which people rarely think about when the name "Custer" is mentioned. Armstrong and Libbie actually did play croquet in Kansas while Maida looked on. Courtesy of Thom Ross and the Gunnar Nordstrom Gallery, Bellevue, Washington.

Blucher and Maida Lead the Chase, **a pen and ink by E. Lisle Reedstrom. A trained illustrator and historian by avocation, Reedstrom actually shows Armstrong's hounds in action in several of his drawings. Courtesy of Don Schwarck.**

created a limited edition of *Custer and the Pup*—a bronze of Custer wearing buckskins, seated on a rock with rifle against his leg and a resting deerhound puppy between his feet. (The hound was modeled from the 1874 photograph of Armstrong with his scouts and two hounds.) A life-size figure of Libbie's favorite was created in 2009 by artist Brandon Martz. Titled *Cardigan: General Custer's Last Staghound*, the wild-eyed, snarling figure with shaggy gray fur was constructed out of natural materials and draped with a red, white, and blue banner. *Cardigan* was on display in the 2010 exhibition *An Archive, a Forest*, at the University of Minnesota's Bell Museum—the same institution where Cardigan had first been on display. Like the mounted staghound, the sculpture no longer exists.

A different take on representing Armstrong and his relationship with dogs is seen in the acrylic paintings of Thom Ross, who creates art which causes the viewer to re-examine what they *think* they know about history—particularly the mythic folk heroes of the Old West. To accomplish the deconstruction and humanizing of stereotypes, Ross portrays historical situations with seemingly contradictory elements and uses bright colors in a contemporary style to "update" our sepia-toned visualization of the past. Dogs frequently appear in Ross's work—including his paintings of General Custer. In one, he is returning from the buffalo hunt after accidentally killing Custis Lee with his three hounds trailing behind, their heads drooping in embarrassment. In *Custer's Three Dogs*, they are lying, sitting, and standing on the prairie, gazing out of frame for their master's return. *Custer and Libbie Playing Croquet* (2008) contains the elements from the Big Creek camp photograph of Armstrong, Libbie, Maida, and their croquet set (see Ch. 8). After studying the photo, Ross saw it as an image which transformed the mythic General Custer into a husband being playful with his wife and dog.

> So I did that painting and added Libbie to show that he was a family man who had a wife who loved him... and I added the dog because, well, a hound appears in that photo, but also because dogs, in artwork, represent loyalty. A dog in a painting often MEANS something other than the presence of a damn dog.... And here, in my painting, Armstrong is doing something that we all have done: playing a game of croquet. This humanizes him as well as making him appear almost comical if only because alongside every other painting of him (which shows him killing people) this painting suggests something of his humanity.... George Custer was a person, first and foremost.

The Printed Page

Armstrong's dogs do appear in a few novels where it is easy for the author to insert a pack of staghounds as verisimilitude or evidence of character (e.g., his love of dogs). Apart from Armstrong's plagiarized tribute to Maida (see Ch. 8), any poetry about his hounds now lies hidden from sight. Very few plays have been written about Armstrong, but one definitely mentioned dogs. *Trails of the West* by W.T. Chichester and Robert Walsh was performed from 1957 to 1958 at Fort Abraham Lincoln and was substantially re-written by George Poletes and re-titled *The Custer Drama*. Performed by the Mandan Development Association on the grounds of Fort Lincoln from 1958 through 1968, it focused on Armstrong's life there. In a night scene, Tom Custer and a sergeant speak about the dogs no longer barking as a good sign that an Indian reconnaissance inside the fort was over.[4] Whether the author meant Custer's or the post's dogs is neither clear nor important to the plot.

Unlike proper dog stories, Armstrong's dogs don't contribute to a novel's storyline and aren't used as plot devices. Examples of this may be seen in several works. *The Court-Martial of George Armstrong Custer* (1976) by Douglas C. Jones is an alternative history where Custer survived Little Bighorn and was court martialed for the loss of his regiment. The staghounds are mentioned a few times (Turk and Rover have a single instance) but have no significance. Likewise, in Will Henry's *No Survivors* (1950) and G.G. Boyer's *Custer, Terry, and Me* (2004), brief appearances of the hounds are inconsequential to the stories. However, in the first two novels of Terry C. Johnston's trilogy, *Long Winter Gone* (1990) and *Seize the Sky* (1991), Custer's hounds are given more character than usual—not only based on Libbie and Burkman's descriptions but also from Johnston's own experience with dogs. Michael Blake's well written *Marching to Valhalla: A Novel of Custer's Last Days* (1996) unfolds as Custer writes his autobiography while approaching Little Bighorn. His dogs come up periodically as they would in a stream of consciousness memoir. Blake changed some dog facts for the sake of the story. Notably, Pvt. Burkman was the dog tender at Washita in 1868—two years before he enlisted in the 7th Cavalry. Custer has the noisy dogs killed long before the battle, saying only, "Two of my own animals had to be destroyed," and also records having his suffering dogs shot on the "deserter" march. (There is no evidence that Armstrong shot his dogs then.) Still, Blake deserves *kudos* for getting it right when he has Custer call the dogs "my canine friends."[5]

In the young adult genre, *Turk: The General's Dog* by Maurine Bergland Saylor (1981) is structured around the Custers' bull-dog and their adopted waif, Johnny Cisco. Told in an omniscient voice, the thoughts of Turk and everyone else are heard (except Byron the greyhound) as he campaigns with the 7th Cavalry in Kansas—and even saves the lives of Johnny and Custer at Washita. The other entry in this literary niche is Fairfax Downey's *The Seventh's Staghound*, where young bugler Peter Shannon and MacTavish the striker (taking Burkman's role) secretly nurse a runt puppy from Maida's litter to health. Named Bran, the grown Scottish Deerhound eventually saves Peter from a murderous traitor at Little Bighorn. Downey had carefully read Libbie's books and included Blucher, Cardigan, and Lucy Stone in his story. Both of these novels would have been good material for a film treatment such as Disney's story of Comanche, *Tonka* (1958), and the "boy and his dog" coming of age in the West, *Old Yeller* (1957).

As a curious literary aside, Edgar Rice Burroughs, the author of the *Tarzan* and *John Carter of Mars* books, was himself in the 7th Cavalry in Arizona but discharged with heart trouble in 1897. It cannot be a coincidence that a veteran of the 7th created a character named Bernard "Barney" Custer, Jr., of Beatrice, Nebraska, in his novel *The Eternal Lover* (serialized in 1914 and later published in 1925 as *The Eternal Savage*). Barney and his sister Victoria are in Africa as guests of Lord Greystoke (Tarzan) who keeps wolfhounds at his home, and one of them, Terkoz, attaches himself to Victoria as her protector against African dangers. (Barney Custer also appears in Burroughs' *The Mad King*, whose plot is loosely based on Anthony Hope's 1894 novel *The Prisoner of Zenda*.)

The Silver Screen

The widowed Libbie Custer is seldom imagined in a darkened cinema watching a movie, but the sprightly 81-year-old did see *The Covered Wagon* in 1923 and spoke highly of its authenticity. (Presumably this was not the only motion picture she saw.) In 1926, the year before the first talking picture, a reporter interviewing her about the semi-centennial anniversary of Little Bighorn asked if she could have made a movie of *Boots and Saddles*. Libbie replied, "I should like to."[6]

Beginning in 1909, there have been many films about Little Bighorn and General Custer, and while a great number of the early silent films have been lost, John Phillip Langellier in *Custer: The Man, the Myth, the Movies* records that there may have been as many as twenty-one films on the topic between 1909 and Libbie's death in April 1933.[7] Actually, two films with the title *Boots and Saddles* had been made—a short in 1909 and one in 1916—but from the available information, neither was about the Custers. (Whether or not Libbie saw any of these early films isn't known, but one has to be curious about her reaction to the 1914 slapstick comedy *Colonel Custard's Last Stand*.) Characteristic of her adventurous spirit, Libbie did accept a role in documentary filmmaker Robert Flaherty's second film, the 1925 short *The Potterymaker*, and played Grandma.[8] (Flaherty was well known at the time for his 1922 documentary *Nanook of the North* and later for *Man of Aran* in 1934.)

Of those many films, serials, and television programs about Armstrong since 1909 (Langellier documented ninety-four in 2000, and more have been made since then[9]), there are screenplays which specifically portray him, those where he is a secondary character, and others whose plots are derived from the defeat of Little Bighorn. The conspicuous absence of his hounds from biographic films is curious as they were such an integral part of his life. They are so well documented in books by the Custers and John Burkman that no scriptwriter or set designer worth their salt could or should neglect the dogs—but there are many reasons why the dogs might *not* have been included in a production.

The practicalities of filmmaking frequently outweigh attention to historical detail despite the best intentions—especially when accuracy involves extra expense or presents an impediment to the production. If a Scottish Deerhound (or any animal) is wanted, the studio production crew would have to find them through a trainer who supplies animals for productions. Assuming the dogs have no on-screen action (and most Custer film dogs didn't) then filming can be as normal as it ever is. However, if the dogs have to perform behaviors critical to the plot or scene, even if they are trained, re-takes and delays happen. Sometimes it is just easier to leave them out. A further complication for productions over the last two decades is the growing (and laudable) monitoring of animal treatment on set. Apart from the obligatory horses and mules, the cinema's Army posts are mostly devoid of the animals known to have been there—dogs, cats, cows, sheep, pigs, and chickens.

Armstrong's hounds, when present in film or video, are likely to be set dressing, but there are four dramas which depict Armstrong with his hounds. Two are correct as to breeds but only one accurately portrays his intimate relationship with them—and it shouldn't be surprising to learn it was Errol Flynn who got that right.

They Died with Their Boots On (1941)

In terms of Armstrong's interaction with his dogs, the screenwriters Wally Kline and Æneas MacKenzie and director Raoul Walsh were very much on target. Young Custer (Errol Flynn) arrives at West Point wearing an over-the-top uniform with his five foxhounds. Cadet Corporal Sharp (Arthur Kennedy) dislikes the cocky Custer and takes him to his supposed quarters (a senior officer's suite). Armstrong makes himself at home as do Caesar, Hannibal, Cleopatra and the other hounds. He gives them meaty bones and they take over the bed and rooms in joyful chaos. (The writer nailed Armstrong's habit of naming dogs after heroes.) Major Taipe (Stanley Ridges) arrives to find Custer and two hounds napping on the bed and throws them all out. The pack makes no further appearances. Armstrong's wild hunts and contemplative moments with them are absent from the film, and Libbie (Olivia de Havilland) never meets her husband's dogs.

Flynn's easy rapport with the dogs is an excellent visualization of Libbie's description of Armstrong with his pack. A dog man himself, he was clearly having a good time with the hounds and they with him. (In *Santa Fe Trail*, released the previous year, Cadet Custer [Ronald Reagan] didn't have dogs in his West Point barracks, but then, the film was really about J.E.B. Stuart [Errol Flynn].)

Custer (1967)

Film and television producers are often unsatisfied with perfectly good historical facts, and want something "better"—in this production, the larger Irish Wolfhounds were substituted for Armstrong's Scottish Deerhounds.

In the seventeen-episode series, the hounds only appear in the first episode, "Sabers in the Sun." Custer (Wayne Maunder) is newly returned from his suspension to the 7th Cavalry at Fort Hays, Kansas. He arrives at night and orders a sergeant to the station to get his luggage and hounds, "Don't be nervous about the dogs. They are quite gentle." The wolfhounds are in two scenes where Custer hands them off to a trooper, saying, "Trooper, take these animals to the cook house and see that they are fed" and "Take care of these monsters for me, will you?" (The wolfhounds are clearly uncomfortable with the actors.) The most faithful use of them is Armstrong in his quarters at night, stroking one hound while he thinks. They do not appear again, but in a few other scenes, their presence is implied by a basic filmmaking illusion—the sound of their barking off camera.

Of course, Armstrong didn't have Irish Wolfhounds. That they were cast speaks to Hollywood's predilection for denoting on-screen characters in a film by the type of dog the actor had—"staghounds and borzois for kings."[10] Irish Wolfhounds belong to the good guys in *Ivanhoe* (1952), *The Fighting Prince of Donegal* (1966), and *Robin Hood: Prince of Thieves* (1991). In fact, one breed characteristic in the AKC Irish Wolfhound standard might well apply to Armstrong himself—"commanding appearance...."[11]

Publicity still from the 1967 TV series *Custer* (and its derivative film *The Legend of Custer*) starring Wayne Maunder. Through Hollywood's predilection for "bigger is better," these Irish Wolfhounds were substituted for Armstrong's Scottish Deerhounds—but only appeared in the first episode. The hounds and Maunder were not comfortable with each other in their few scenes together and gave no sense of Armstrong's close bond with his dogs.

Son of the Morning Star (1991)

Based on Evan S. Connell's book of the same name, director Mike Robe along with historical consultant John M. Carroll, a Custer historian and author, actually got a Scottish Deerhound for the production (noteworthy as producers and directors do not always heed their historical consultants). The deerhound is seen four times—twice in the Custer house in Kansas in 1866 and once at Fort Lincoln in 1876. In both, Custer (Gary Cole) and Libbie (Rosanna Arquette) ignore the hound. (Armstrong didn't get his first deerhounds until 1868.) The deerhound appears even more briefly in two distant shots of Custer riding across the prairie in 1868. At first it is following the horses toward the camera but quickly trots out of frame. Robe and Carroll earn *kudos* for showing Armstrong in the field with at least one Scottish Deerhound. (Regardless of the poor use of Custer's hound, throughout the production, Army and Indian dogs are appropriately seen and heard in a number of scenes.)

Into the West (2005)

Three decades after *The Legend of Custer*, Hollywood was more attentive to historical details but still insisted on using Irish Wolfhounds for General Custer. Production staff contacted Deborah Sanders of Niobrara Irish Wolfhounds in New Mexico about using a brace of her hounds in the miniseries *Into the West*. Sanders explained to them that Scottish Deerhounds were what was needed, but they were adamant. Having done her bit for historical accuracy, Sanders sent four wolfhounds to the set in the care of her husband, who would hold the dogs as Custer's kennel man. Sanders noted, "The pay wasn't anything to speak of, but the hounds were paid handsomely in adulation and attention."[12]

Production designer Marek Dobrolowsky wanted absolute authenticity in everything—even the Lakota, Crow, and Cheyenne languages. The crew worked hard to achieve this, and Justin Falvey, co-executive producer, said, "The accuracy of the set design from the teepees to the wagons to the props and the guns, all that stuff is 100% accurate."[13] With this attention to accuracy, it is indeed curious that they ignored Sanders about the correct breed—but perhaps the larger Irish Wolfhounds would stand out better in crowded camp scenes.

In Chapter 4, "Casualties of War," on the 1874 Black Hills expedition, the film's Custer (Jonathan Scarfe) talks to reporters about the virtues of the Black Hills for settlement while the dog-tender follows closely with two leashed wolfhounds. One of the wolfhounds extends his head toward Custer but recoils slightly after he reaches out his gloved hand to pet the hound. There is a cry of "Gold!" from the adjacent creek, and the press conference ends abruptly. The wolfhounds appear once more in a bustling camp on June 14, 1876. All four of the Niobrara hounds are briefly seen alongside the tent where General Terry is strategizing with Custer and Gibbon about the advance to the Little Bighorn. With no meaningful interaction, the wolfhounds are merely extras—although the producers did get the correct number of hounds Armstrong had on his last campaign. (While the column was at the Powder River Supply Depot on June

14 where the hounds were left, this scene depicts the officers' meeting at the mouth of the Rosebud on June 21—a not unreasonable compression of events for the film.)

Given all Libbie wrote about their dogs, it's a pity that the on-screen Libbies have no relationships with the hounds in these films—apart from the suggested tolerance of the deerhound in their Kansas and Dakota homes in *Son of the Morning Star*. In fact, most writers of screenplays, novels, and print or internet articles only scratch the surface of the Custers' and Burkman's stories. In none of these films do any of Armstrong's dogs "act" (behavioral training to perform tasks, communicate, or simulate emotion) or serve as plot devices. Apart from *They Died with Their Boots On*, films include Custer's hounds as one checkbox on the list of film props. In describing this common passive appearance of dogs on screen, animal behaviorist and author Alexandra Horowitz might have well described these cinematic Custer dogs when she wrote, "Given the use of these dogs, one is left with the impression that they are included to lend an air of authenticity to the scene."[14]

Whether by design or happy accident, John Ford was perhaps the only director to capture an accurate portrayal of U.S. Cavalry dogs.

In *She Wore a Yellow Ribbon* (1949), a cavalry outpost in the southwest receives the news of the Custer massacre and prepares for a local Cheyenne and Arapaho uprising. Captain Nathan Brittles (John Wayne) and Top Sergeant Quincannon (Victor McLaglen) assemble their company on parade, and three dogs are seen lounging happily on the ground alongside the troopers' feet. Quincannon berates the soldiers and affects to notice one dog for the first time, demanding, "Whose dog is this?"—before stooping to pet the sleeping dog. These were actually Navajo sheep dogs which wandered around the set as they pleased, and while Ford was a martinet in the director's chair, he was glad to have them on camera. The dogs are seen (and heard) periodically inside the fort, running after buggies and horses, and when the column is riding across the desert, one dog can be seen happily running alongside the trotting horses.

Having looked at the three dramatic films and one television series which depict his dogs, at the opposite end of the spectrum there are three comedic meetings of Armstrong and dogs.

Touche Pas à La Femme Blanche or *Don't Touch the White Woman* (1974) is "A highly stylized surreal farce about the events leading up to Custer's Last Stand anachronistically reenacted in an urban renewal area in modern Paris."[15] Marcello Mastroianni is Custer (wearing a brown ponytail wig when in dress uniform), and Catherine Deneuve plays the White Woman (Marie-Hélène). The film uses a sprinkling of historical facts in absurd ways between crazy nonsequiturs (on his desk next to his ivory-handled pistol, Custer has a Coca-Cola advertisement and a photo of Richard Nixon). With the characters of Buffalo Bill, Sitting Bull's father, and a CIA agent, the film recalls the anti-establishment, guerrilla theater of the Vietnam War and cultural spoofs like *The Groove Tube* (1974). The solitary item which merits inclusion here is a scene where scout Mitch Bouyer (Ugo Tognazzi) holds a leashed greyhound which Custer points out as "My dog. He was given to me by the Tsar of Russia."

Set in 1924, *Won Ton Ton: The Dog That Saved Hollywood* (1976), the parody on Hollywood and the immensely popular Rin-Tin-Tin films, has a silent movie producer,

J.J. Fromberg (Art Carney) and director Grayson Potchuck (Bruce Dern) working out an idea to cast the desert sheikh specialist, Rudy Montague (Ron Liebman), with Won Ton Ton, a German Shepherd.

> POTCHUCK: "So, suppose that we give the public Rudy Montague as somebody that they can *really* identify with? Like Custer."
> FROMBERG: "Custer... the ice cream?"
> POTCHUCK: "No, Custer the *general*—and we make Won company mascot and in the end he saves him!"
> FROMBERG: "Now, wait a minute, wait a minute, wait a minute! Custer got killed at the end!"
> POTCHUCK: "So what?"
> FROMBERG: "You're right. History is not the Bible."

There are only two scenes shown from the film within the film, *Custer the Brave*. Won saves Custer (the clean-shaven and brown-haired Ron Liebman) from being burned at the stake and then, wearing a kepi, he leads an Indian maiden (Madeline Kahn) to Little Bighorn, where Custer is shot with arrows amidst the dead. Won licks Custer's ear as he is revived and in the maiden's embrace, and the end title promises a sequel—*Custer Returns*.

The exceptional dog who *does* have a relationship (albeit comedic) with Custer is animated. In the 1960s, the popular cartoon show *The Adventures of Rocky and Bullwinkle and Friends* featured regular episodes of "Peabody's Improbable History." The genius talking dog Mr. Peabody and his boy Sherman travel in their "Way Back" time machine to visit historical personalities. In the Black Hills of 1875, they find Custer searching for Indians but drastically outnumbered. Of course, Peabody's brainpower saves the day, and the segment ends with a signature bad pun—this one involving Custer's Last Hot Dog Stand.[16]

Chapter Notes

Preface

1. George MacDonald Fraser, *Flashman and the Redskins* (New York: Alfred A. Knopf, 1982), 455.
2. Robert M. Utley, ed., *Life in Custer's Cavalry: Diaries and Letters of Albert and Jennie Barnitz, 1867–1868* (Lincoln, NE, & London: University of Nebraska Press, 1987), 198.
3. Paul Andrew Hutton, ed., *The Custer Reader*. Lincoln (NE: University of Nebraska Press, 1992), 420.
4. Edgar I. Stewart, *Custer's Luck* (Norman, OK: University of Oklahoma Press, 1985), vii.

Chapter 1

1. Marguerite Merington, *The Custer Story: The Life and Intimate Letters of General George A. Custer and His Wife Elizabeth* (New York: The Devin Adair Co., 1940), 43.
2. Lawrence A. Frost, *General Custer's Libbie* (Seattle, WA: Superior Publishing Co., 1976), 15.
3. Merington, 17–18.
4. Frost, 16.
5. Merington, 20.
6. *Ibid.*, 22.
7. *Ibid.*
8. *Ibid.*
9. Frost, 19.
10. *Ibid.*, 21.
11. Elizabeth Bacon Custer, *Diary 1852–1860*, May 12, 1852, & January 12, 1854, Elizabeth Bacon Custer Papers. Western Americana Collection, Beinecke Rare Book and Manuscript Library, Yale University. Accessed on September 17, 2016, http://search.library.yale.edu/catalog/3156258.
12. *Ibid.*, November 6, 1860.
13. *Ibid.*, April 19, May 6, & May 16, 1852.
14. *Ibid.*, May 11, 1852.
15. *Ibid.*, August 27, 1854.
16. Custer, August 27, 1854.
17. Merington, 38.
18. *Ibid.*, 40.
19. *Ibid.*, 41.
20. Frost, 36.
21. Custer, November 6, 1860.
22. Frost, 34.
23. *Ibid.*, 37.
24. Arlene Reynolds, *The Civil War Memories of Elizabeth Bacon Custer* (Austin, TX: University of Texas Press, 1994), 4.
25. Frost, 38–39.
26. *Ibid.*, 41.
27. *Ibid.*, 42.
28. Merington, 44.
29. *Ibid.*
30. Frost, 43.
31. Merington, 46–47.
32. "Henry Munson Utley," *Library Journal* 42, no.1 (January—December 1917), 190, accessed January 24, 2018, https://archive.org/details/libraryjournal11assogoog.
33. Merington, 47.
34. *Ibid.*
35. Frost, 44.

Chapter 2

1. Elizabeth B. Custer, *Tenting on the Plains or General Custer in Kansas and Texas* (New York: C.L. Webster & Co. 1887), 298, accessed online January 25, 2018, http://hdl.handle.net/2027/loc.ark:/13960/t8nc6bj65.
2. Carl F. Day, *Tom Custer: Ride to Glory* (Norman, OK: University of Oklahoma Press, 2005), 18; Findagrave.com for Paulus Van Haren Küster & descendants through Emanuel Henry Custer, accessed on January 4, 2017, http://www.findagrave.com/cgi-bin/fg.cgi?page=gr&GRid=5582039.
3. Charles Augustus Hanna, *Historical Collections of Harrison County in the State of Ohio* (New York: privately printed, 1900), 114, accessed on November 1, 2016, https://books.google.com/books?id=V-ouAAAAYAAJ&pg=PA114#v=onepage&q&f=false & Charles B. Wallace, *Custer's Ohio Boyhood* (Cadiz, OH: Harrison County Historical Society, 1987), 7.
4. Wallace, 9.
5. Wallace, 10–11.
6. Day, 20.
7. *Ibid.*
8. Wallace, 20.
9. Day, 21.
10. Marguerite Merington, ed., *The Custer Story: The Life and Intimate Letters of General George A. Custer and His Wife Elizabeth* (New York: The Devin-Adair Company, 1950), 6.
11. Custer, 298.
12. *Ibid.*
13. *Ibid.*
14. Arlene Reynolds, *The Civil War Memories of Elizabeth Bacon Custer* (Austin, TX: University of Texas Press, 1994), 36.

15. Custer, 180.
16. Wallace, 20.
17. Custer, 180.
18. Brian W. Dippie, ed., *Nomad: George A. Custer in Turf, Field and Farm* (Austin, TX: University of Texas Press, 1980), 9–10.
19. Wallace, 22.
20. Lawrence A. Frost, *The Custer Album: A Pictorial Biography of General George A. Custer* (New York: Bonanza Books, 1984), 19.
21. Wallace 23, 24, 26.
22. Merington, 7.
23. Wallace 31.
24. Merington, 7–8.
25. Wallace, 33, 34.
26. Shirley A. Leckie, *Elizabeth Bacon Custer and the Making of a Myth* (Norman, OK: University of Oklahoma Press, 1993), 23.
27. Jay Monaghan, *Custer: The Life of General George Armstrong Custer* (Lincoln, NE: University of Nebraska Press, 1959, Bison Books, 1971), 22.
28. Frederick Whittaker, *A Popular Life of Gen. George A. Custer* (New York: Sheldon & Co., 1876), 19.
29. Carelton Mays, "The Romping Custers," *Real West*, February 1959, 29.
30. Merington, 84.
31. Jeffry D. Wert, *Custer: The Controversial Life of George Armstrong Custer* (New York, Touchstone, 1997), 30.
32. Wert, 29.
33. Tom O'Neil, *Cadet George Armstrong Custer: Demerits & Academics* (Brooklyn, NY: Arrow and Trooper, 1992), 2–12.
34. Wert, 33.
35. T. J. Stiles, *Custer's Trials: A Life on the Frontier of New America* (New York: Alfred A. Knopf, 2015), 18.
36. Thomas H. Sternberg, M. D., Ernest B. Howard, M. D., Leonard Dewey, M. D., and Paul Paget, M. D., "Venereal Diseases," *Preventative Medicine in World War II, Vol. V, Communicable Diseases*, U.S. Army Medical Dept., Office of Medical History, accessed on November 17, 2016 http://history.amedd.army.mil/booksdocs/wwii/communicablediseasesV5/chapter10.htm.
37. W. A. Newman Dorland, *The American Illustrated Medical Dictionary* (Philadelphia, PA: W. B. Saunders Co., 1927), 307.
38. Wert, 37.
39. Reynolds, 22.
40. Wert, 39.
41. *Ibid.*
42. "Here Is Custer," undated clipping. *Custer File and Scrapbooks*, 81. Montana Room, Billings Public Library, Billings, MT.
43. Marlana Cook, Curator of Art, West Point Museum, email message to author, April 19, 2017.

Chapter 3

1. Frederick Whittaker, *A Popular Life of Gen. George A. Custer* (New York: Sheldon & Co., 1876), 148, accessed on January 3, 2017, http://hdl.handle.net/2027/uc2.ark:/13960/t3dz03w59.
2. Jay Monaghan, *Custer: The Life of General George Armstrong Custer* (Lincoln, NE: University of Nebraska Press, 1959, Bison Books, 1971), 46.

3. Monaghan, 48.
4. Elizabeth B. Custer, *Tenting on the Plains or General Custer in Kansas and Texas* (New York: C.L. Webster & Co. 1887), 5, accessed online July 14, 2018, http://hdl.handle.net/2027/loc.ark:/13960/t8nc6bj65.
5. Monaghan, 55.
6. Monaghan, 56–57.
7. John M. Carroll, *Custer in the Civil War: His Unfinished Memoirs* (San Rafael, CA: Presidio Press, 1977), 110.
8. Jeffry D. Wert, *Custer: The Controversial Life of George Armstrong Custer* (New York: Touchstone, 1997), 44–45.
9. Whittaker, 82.
10. Carroll, 117.
11. Wert, 48.
12. Wert, 45
13. Doris Kearns Goodwin, *Team of Rivals: The Political Genius of Abraham Lincoln* (New York: Simon & Schuster, 2005), 428.
14. GAC to Parents, March 17, 1862, LIBI-00019–2780. National Park Service, Little Bighorn Battlefield National Monument. Also held by the Lawrence A. Frost Collection of the Monroe County Library System, Monroe, MI.
15. Webb Garrison, *Civil War Curiosities: Strange Stories, Oddities, Events, and Coincidences* (Nashville, TN: Rutledge Hill Press, 1994), 78–79.
16. Michael Zucchero, *Loyal Hearts: Histories of American Civil War Canines* (Lynchburg, VA: Schroeder Publications, 2010), 110, 141.
17. *Ibid.*, 31–32.
18. Henry W. Boynton, ed., *The Complete Poetical Works of Alexander Pope* (Boston & New York: Houghton Mifflin, 1903), 131.
19. "From the Thirteenth Regiment," *Lamoille Newsdealer*, Hyde Park, VT, March 12, 1863, p. 2, accessed on January 25, 2017, https://chroniclingamerica.loc.gov/lccn/sn84023428/1863-03-12/ed-1/seq-2/.
20. Zucchero, 45–46.
21. American Kennel Club, *The New Complete Dog Book, 21st Edition* (Irvine, CA: Irvine, i-5 Publishing, LLC, 2015), 202.
22. Wert, 48–49.
23. Whittaker, 100.
24. Monaghan, 69.
25. Wert, 53.
26. *Ibid.*
27. Carroll, 143.
28. Marguerite Merington, ed., *The Custer Story: The Life and Intimate Letters of General George A. Custer and His Wife Elizabeth* (New York: The Devin-Adair Company, New York, 1950), 326.
29. "George Armstrong Custer: McClellan and Pleasonton," *Wikipedia*, accessed on January 2 2017, https://en.wikipedia.org/wiki/George_Armstrong_Custer.
30. "General McDowell on Little Mac, *Wilke's Spirit of the Times and the New York Sportsman*, Vol. 9–11, Vo. 11, No. 15, December 10, 1864, 232, accessed on July 14 2017, https://books.google.com/books?id=m5M6AQAAMAAJ.
31. Anonymous, "Custer's Last Stand Near 'Togany," *Wood County Sentinel-Tribune*, Ohio, May 15 1968. Lawrence A. Frost Collection, Ellis Library & Reference Center, Monroe County Library System.

32. Whittaker, 125–126.
33. Wert, 52.
34. Monaghan, 90–92.
35. Whittaker, 128, 129.
36. Whittaker, 345.
37. D. Mark Katz, *Custer in Photographs* (New York: Bonanza Books, 1990), 8.
38. Merington, 46.
39. Shirley A. Leckie, *Elizabeth Bacon Custer and the Making of a Myth* (Norman: University of Oklahoma Press, 1993), 24.
40. Merington, 48, 49.
41. Arlene Reynolds, *The Civil War Memories of Elizabeth Bacon Custer* (Austin: University of Texas Press, 1994), 5.
42. Custer, 261.
43. Lawrence A. Frost, *General Custer's Libbie* (Seattle: Superior Publishing Co., 1976), 57.
44. *Ibid.*, 57–58.
45. Leckie, 24–25.
46. Merington, 48.
47. Leckie, 25; Merington, 50–51.
48. Merington, 51.
49. Wert, 70.
50. Frost, 63.
51. Whittaker, 148.
52. *Ibid.*
53. Custer, 478.
54. Merington, 52.
55. "Amusements," *New York Times*, May 11, 1862, 7.
56. "Amusements," *New York Times*, May 19, 1862, 8.
57. "Amusements," *New York Times*, May 11, 1862, 7.
58. "Amusements," *New York Times*, May 15, 1862, 7.
59. Brian Patrick Duggan, "America's First National Dog Show," *AKC Family Dog*, January/February 2016, 37, accessed on January 9, 2018 http://viewer.zmags.com/publication/d41bcb3c#/d41bcb3c/28.

Chapter 4

1. Reynolds, Arlene, *The Civil War Memories of Elizabeth Bacon Custer* (Austin, TX: University of Texas Press, 1994), 115.
2. Shirley A. Leckie, *Elizabeth Bacon Custer and the Making of a Myth* (Norman: University of Oklahoma Press, 1993), 56.
3. Leckie, 31.
4. Jeffry D. Wert, *Custer: The Controversial Life of George Armstrong Custer* (New York: Touchstone, 1997), 83.
5. George MacDonald Fraser, *Flashman and the Redskins, Fraser* (New York: Alfred A. Knopf, 1982), 474.
6. Wert, 106.
7. Wert, 97–99.
8. James Christiancy to Daniel S. Bacon, August 27, 1863, LIBI-00019–2791. National Park Service, Little Bighorn Battlefield National Monument.
9. Leckie, 30.
10. Marguerite Merington, ed. *The Custer Story: The Life and Intimate Letters of General George A. Custer and His Wife Elizabeth* (New York: The Devin-Adair Company, 1950), 65; Leckie, 33.
11. Merington, 72.
12. Merington, 70.
13. Leckie, 35.
14. Merington, 79.
15. Merington, 82–83
16. Merington, 84.
17. Leckie, 38.
18. Reynolds, 39.
19. Leckie, 40.
20. Merington, 117.
21. Leckie, 44.
22. Leckie, 50.
23. Reynolds, 93.
24. T. J. Stiles, *Custer's Trials: A Life on the Frontier of New America* (New York: Alfred A. Knopf, 2015), 185.
25. Leckie, 41, 48, 58.
26. Merington, 119; Monaghan, 204–205.
27. Leckie, 59–60.
28. Merington, 123.
29. Merington, 129.
30. Merington 131.
31. Merington, 135.
32. Elizabeth B. Custer manuscript notes, on Tom Custer's medals and Civil War, undated, LIBI-00019–5496. National Park Service, Little Bighorn Battlefield National Monument.
33. Merington, 131.
34. Merington, 132.
35. Reynolds, 62.
36. Merington, 131.
37. Custer, 134.
38. Merington, 134.
39. Reynolds, 110.
40. Reynolds, 102.
41. Reynolds, 63–64.
42. Reynolds, 114–115.
43. Leckie, 61.
44. Leckie, 50.
45. "Notes regarding Barnum's Mummy," undated, LIBI-00019–3528. National Park Service, Little Bighorn Battlefield National Monument.
46. D. Mark Katz, *Custer in Photographs* (New York: Bonanza Books, 1990), 35.
47. Philip Sheridan, *Personal Memoirs of P. H. Sheridan, General United States Army*, Vol. II (New York: Charles L. Webster & Co., 1888), 114, accessed on January 9, 2017, https://archive.org/details/personalmemoirso02sher.
48. Reynolds, 128.
49. Fred Streever, *The American Trail Hound* (New York: A. S. Barnes & Co., 1948), 144–145.
50. Sheridan, 112.
51. Brian Patrick Duggan, *Saluki: The Desert Hound and the English Travelers Who Brought It to the West* (Jefferson, NC: McFarland, 2009), 103–104.
52. Leckie, 64–65.
53. Merington, 147.
54. Wert, 224–225.
55. Leckie, 67.
56. Merington, 159.
57. John K. Mahon, *History of the Second Seminole War, 1835–1842* (Gainesville: University of Florida Press, 1992), 265–266.
58. John Ensminger, "Dogs in the Economy and Operation of the Peculiar Institution: Evidence from Slave State Case Law," February 23, 2012 posted on *Dog Law Reporter: Reflections on the Society of Dogs and Men*, accessed on October 21, 2017, http://doglawreporter.blogspot.com/2012/02/dogs-in-economy-and-operation-of.html.
59. David Nevin, *The Civil War: Sherman's March:*

Atlanta to the Sea (Alexandria, VA: Time-Life Books, 1986), 59–60.
  60. Marilyn W. Seguin, *Dogs of War and Stories of Other Beasts of Battle in the Civil War* (Boston: Branden Publishing Co., 1998), 108.
  61. Seguin, 110–111.

Chapter 5

  1. GAC to Daniel & Rhoda Bacon, October 5, 1865, #6351, Marguerite Merington papers. New York Public Library. Manuscripts and Archives. Astor, Lenox, and Tilden Foundations.
  2. Shirley A. Leckie, *Elizabeth Bacon Custer and the Making of a Myth* (Norman: University of Oklahoma Press, 1993), 67–68.
  3. Marguerite Merington, ed. *The Custer Story: The Life and Intimate Letters of General George A. Custer and His Wife Elizabeth* (New York: The Devin-Adair Company, 1950), 163–164.
  4. Ibid.
  5. Philip Sheridan to GAC, May 7, 1865, LIBI-00019–1842. National Park Service, Little Bighorn Battlefield National Monument.
  6. Daniel Clarke, *Lieutenant Henry H. Young: Sheridan's Chief of Scouts* (Amazon Digital Services, LLC, Daniel Clarke Publisher, 2012), loc 406 of 593; Phillip Sheridan, *Personal Memoirs of P. H. Sheridan, General United States Army*, Vol. II (New York: Charles L. Webster & Co., 1888), 222, accessed on July 19 2017. Available online at https://archive.org/details/personalmemoirso02sher.
  7. William B. Styple, ed., *Generals in Bronze: Interviewing the Commanders of the Civil War* (Kearny, NJ: Belle Grove Publishing Co., 2005), 268–269.
  8. Lawrence A. Frost, *General Custer's Libbie* (Seattle: Superior Publishing Co., 1976), 139, fn 33.
  9. Frost, *Custer's Libbie*, 136.
  10. Lawrence A. Frost, *The Custer Album: A Pictorial Biography of General George A. Custer* (New York: Bonanza Books, 1984), 72.
  11. Elizabeth B. Custer, *Tenting on the Plains or General Custer in Kansas and Texas* (New York: C.L. Webster & Co., 1887), 66, accessed online July 20, 2018, http://hdl.handle.net/2027/loc.ark:/13960/t8nc6bj65.
  12. Jeffry D. Wert, *Custer: The Controversial Life of George Armstrong Custer* (New York: Touchstone, 1997), 232.
  13. *Ibid.*
  14. John M. Carroll, *Custer in Texas: An Interrupted Narrative* (New York: Sol Lewis & Liveright, 1975), 90–91.
  15. Wert, 233.
  16. Don Rickey, Jr., *Forty Miles a Day on Beans and Hay* (Norman: University of Oklahoma Press, 1963), 155.
  17. *Ibid.*
  18. *Baton Rouge Tri-Weekly Gazette & Comet*, Oct. 12, 1865, 1, accessed on February 12, 2017, https://chroniclingamerica.loc.gov/lccn/sn86053661/1865-10-12/ed-1/seq-1/.
  19. Custer, 97–98.
  20. D. Mark Katz, *Custer in Photographs* (New York: Bonanza Books, 1990), xv.
  21. Frost, *General Custer's Libbie*, 138.
  22. Custer, 119.
  23. Custer, 129.
  24. Custer, 134–135.
  25. Carroll, 98.
  26. Philip Thomas Tucker, *Exodus from the Alamo: The Anatomy of the Last Stand Myth* (Philadelphia & Newbury: Casemate, 2010), 35–36.
  27. "Liendo Plantation," *Texas History Online*, Texas State Historical Association, accessed on March 1, 2017, https://tshaonline.org/handbook/online/articles/ccl01.
  28. Vernon Loggins, *Two Romantics and Their Ideal Life* (New York: The Odyssey Press, 1946), 198–199.
  29. Loggins, 206–207.
  30. Loggins, 208.
  31. Steve Tunnell, "Custer's Occupation of Hempstead Texas: George & Libbie at Liendo," *Research Review: The Journal of the Little Big Horn Associates*, vol. 10, no.1 (January 1996), 12.
  32. Carroll, 98.
  33. Carroll, 61.
  34. Custer, 155–156.
  35. Custer, 161.
  36. Custer, 162.
  37. Charlotte Libov, "Auctioneers as Rare as Their Wares," *New York Times*, March 8, 1987.
  38. GAC to Mr. & Mrs. Bacon, October 5, 1865, #6351, Marguerite Merington papers. New York Public Library. Manuscripts and Archives. Astor, Lenox, and Tilden Foundations.
  39. Custer, 188.
  40. *Ibid.*
  41. Custer, 252.
  42. EBC to Rebecca Richmond, November 17, 1865, Lawrence A. Frost Collection, Ellis Library & Reference Center, Monroe County Library System.
  43. Brian Patrick Duggan, "Yankee Dudu: The First Saluki in America," *American Saluki Association Newsletter*, Winter 2015, 25, 28.
  44. Brian Patrick Duggan, "Of Coursing Hounds and Cowboys, *AKC Family Dog*, November-December 2013, 27, accessed on March 7, 2017, http://viewer.zmags.com/publication/61d65aa3#/61d65aa3/26.
  45. Custer, 334.
  46. Custer, 204.
  47. Custer, 205.
  48. Custer, 210.
  49. *Ibid.*
  50. Custer, 206.
  51. Custer, 206–208.
  52. *Ibid.*
  53. Custer, 205.
  54. Custer, 191.
  55. Custer, 251.
  56. Custer, 206.
  57. Elizabeth B. Custer, "A Note Concerning Dogs and Taking Ticks from Their Ears," undated, LIBI-00019–5860, National Park Service, Little Bighorn Battlefield National Monument.
  58. Custer, 165.
  59. Custer, 258–259.
  60. *Ibid.*
  61. Custer, 257.
  62. GAC to his brother and sister, October 15, 1865, Lawrence A. Frost Collection, Ellis Library & Reference Center, Monroe County Library System.
  63. Custer, 164.
  64. GAC to Daniel & Rhoda Bacon, October 5,

1865, #6351, Marguerite Merington papers. New York Public Library. Manuscripts and Archives. Astor, Lenox, and Tilden Foundations.
65. GAC to brother and sister, October 15, 1865, and Custer, 181.
66. Merington, 175.
67. Charles H. Lothrop, *A History of the First Iowa Cavalry Veteran Volunteers* (Lyons, IA: 1890), 280, accessed on March 8, 2017, https://archive.org/details/firstregiowacava00lothrich.
68. Custer, 256.
69. Carroll, 250.
70. Lothrop, 280.
71. EBC to Rebecca Richmond, November 17, 1865, Lawrence A. Frost Collection, Ellis Library & Reference Center, Monroe County Library System.
72. Samuel I. Grey and John M. Carroll, *Custer's Private Orderly in Texas: Samuel I. Grey*, Harrison Pamphlets E467.1.C99 G73 1987, ca. 1987, Special Collections, Shields Library, University of California, Davis, 17–38.
73. Custer, 181.
74. Custer, 226–227.
75. Custer, 171–173.
76. Custer, 192.
77. EBC, Handwritten manuscript of her life, October 1868–January 1869, LIBI-00019–3310, National Park Service, Little Bighorn Battlefield National Monument.
78. Carroll, 228, 232, 236.
79. John M. Carroll, *Custer's Cavalry Occupation of Hempstead & Austin, Texas and the History of Custer's Headquarters Building* (Glendale, CA, The Arthur H. Clark, Co., 1983), 28.
80. Custer, 258.
81. EBC to Rebecca Richmond, November 17, 1865.
82. Custer, 253–254.
83. Custer, 256.
84. *Ibid*.
85. Malone Shannon, "Those Bumptious Custers," *Golden West*, November 1973, 11.
86. EBC to Rebecca Richmond, November 17, 1865.
87. GAC to Jacob Greene January 8, 1866, Jacob Greene Papers, U.S. Army Museum,
88. American Kennel Club, *The New Complete Dog Book, 21st Edition* (Irvine, CA: i-5 Publishing, LLC, 2015), 556.
89. *Catalogue of the 9th Annual New York Bench Show, 1885* (Westminster Kennel Club Show), 56, American Kennel Club Library, New York.
90. Custer, 263.
91. Loggins, 210.
92. Webb Garrison, *Civil War Curiosities: Strange Stories, Oddities, Events, and Coincidences* (Nashville, TN: Rutledge Hill Press, 1994), 169–170.
93. Duggan, "Yankee Dudu," 62–65.
94. Brian Patrick Duggan, "America's First National Dog Show," *AKC Family Dog*, January/February 2016, 28–30, accessed on March 6 2017, http://viewer.zmags.com/publication/d41bcb3c#/d41bcb3c/28.

Chapter 6

1. G. A. Custer, *My Life on the Plains or, Personal Experiences with Indians* (New York: Sheldon & Co., 1876), 37, accessed on March 15, 2017, http://hdl.handle.net/2027/uc2.ark:/13960/t5k932625.

2. Elizabeth B. Custer, *Tenting on the Plains or General Custer in Kansas and Texas* (New York: C.L. Webster & Co. 1887), 297, accessed March 15, 2017, http://hdl.handle.net/2027/loc.ark:/13960/t8nc6bj65.
3. Robert M. Utley, *Cavalier in Buckskin: George Armstrong Custer and the Western Military Frontier* (Norman: University of Oklahoma Press, 1988), 39.
4. Gregory J.W. Urwin, *Custer Victorious: The Civil War Battles of General George Armstrong Custer* (Lincoln: University of Nebraska Press, 1990), 240.
5. EBC, *Tenting*, 308–309.
6. *Ibid*.
7. Marguerite Merington, ed., *The Custer Story: The Life and Intimate Letters of General George A. Custer and His Wife Elizabeth* (New York: The Devin-Adair Company, 1950), 183–184.
8. Jeffry D. Wert, *Custer: The Controversial Life of George Armstrong Custer* (New York: Touchstone, 1997), 241.
9. T. J. Stiles, *Custer's Trials: A Life on the Frontier of New America* (New York: Alfred A. Knopf, 2015), 245.
10. Stiles, 248.
11. F.A. Barnard, *American Biographical History of Eminent and Self Made Men of the State of Michigan, Vol. 1* (Cincinnati, OH: Western Biographical Publishing Company, 1878), 9–10, accessed on March 15, 2017, https://babel.hathitrust.org/cgi/pt?id=miun.bad6019.0001.001;view=1up;seq=33.
12. Minnie Dubbs Millbrook, "Mrs. General Custer at Fort Riley, 1866," *Kansas Historical Quarterly*, Kansas Historical Society, vol. 40, no. 1 (Spring 1974), 64.
13. Lawrence A. Frost, *General Custer's Libbie* (Seattle: Superior Publishing Co., 1976), 152.
14. Don Schwarck, "Campaigning in Kansas with Maida and Blucher, General Custer's Staghounds," *Research Review: The Journal of the Little Big Horn Associates*, vol. 6, no. 2 (June 1992), 16.
15. Stiles, 246, 252.
16. Stiles, 245.
17. EBC, *Tenting*, 36–37.
18. Jay Monaghan, *Custer: The Life of General George Armstrong Custer* (Lincoln: University of Nebraska Press, 1959, Bison Books, 1971), 272.
19. Stiles, 253.
20. Stiles, 245.
21. EBC, *Tenting*, 334.
22. Millbrook, 67.
23. EBC, *Tenting*, 335–336.
24. American Kennel Club, *The New Complete Dog Book, 21st Edition* (Irvine, CA: i-5 Publishing, LLC, 2015), 642. 556.
25. Elizabeth B. Custer, *Following the Guidon* (New York: Harper & Brothers, 1890), 126, accessed on March 17, 2017, http://hdl.handle.net/2027/coo1.ark:/13960/t4kk9vn09.
26. GAC to C. F. Hatch, October 1, 1866, George Armstrong Custer Papers, WA MSS S-1643, Box 1, folder 2, Beinecke Rare Book and Manuscript Library, Yale University.
27. Stiles, 259.
28. EBC, *Tenting*, 368–370.
29. EBC, *Tenting*, 411–412.
30. EBC, *Tenting*, 537.
31. Elizabeth Atwood Lawrence, *His Very Silence Speaks: Comanche—The Horse Who Survived Custer's*

Last Stand (Detroit, MI: Wayne State University Press, 1989), 289.
32. John P. Langellier, Kurt Hamilton Cox, and Brian C. Pohanka, eds., *Myles Keogh: The Life and Legend of an "Irish Dragoon" in the Seventh Cavalry* (El Segundo, CA: Upton and Sons, 1998), 96.
33. Fred Dustin, *The Custer Tragedy* (Ann Arbor, MI: Edwards Brothers, Inc., 1939), 236.
34. Langellier, et al, 187–188.
35. Wert, 247.
36. Langellier, et al, 46.
37. Millbrook, 67.
38. EBC, *Tenting*, 380.
39. *Ibid.*
40. Richard Irving Dodge, *The Plains of the Great West and Their Inhabitants* (New York: Archer House, 1883), 111–112.
41. EBC, *Tenting*, 515–516.
42. EBC, *Tenting*, 517–518.
43. EBC, *Tenting*, 520.
44. Merington, 199.
45. GAC, 81.
46. Merington, 199; GAC, 82.
47. EBC, *Tenting*, 529–530.
48. EBC, *Tenting*, 253.
49. EBC, *Tenting*, 499–500.
50. John G. Bourke, *On the Border with General Crook* (New York: Skyhorse Publishing, 2014), 27.
51. Donald F. Danker, ed., *Man of the Plains: Recollections of Luther North 1856–1882* (Lincoln: University of Nebraska Press, 1961), 93.
52. James Parker, *The Old Army Memories 1872–1918* (Philadelphia: Dorrance & Company, 1929), 94.
53. Sandy Barnard, ed., *Ten Years with Custer: A 7th Cavalryman's Memoirs* (Terre Haute, IN: AST Press, 2001), 31.
54. EBC, *Tenting*, 564–570.
55. *Ibid.*
56. Brian W. Dippie, ed., *Nomad: George A. Custer in Turf, Field and Farm* (Austin, TX: University of Texas Press, 1980), 10–12.
57. G. A. Custer, "My Life on the Plains," *The Galaxy*, vol. 13, no. 4, April 1872, 477–479, accessed on Mar 22, 2017, http://ebooks.library.cornell.edu/cgi/t/text/pageviewer-idx?c=gala;cc=gala;rgn=full%20text;idno=gala0013-4;didno=gala0013-4;view=image;seq=0477;node=gala0013-4%3A6; GAC, *My Life*, 37–39.
58. Elizabeth B. Custer, 8-page MS on her recollections of her husband, etc., undated, LIBI-00019-2879. National Park Service, Little Bighorn Battlefield National Monument.
59. EBC, *Tenting*, 570.
60. GAC, *My Life*, 227, accessed on January 14, 2018, http://hdl.handle.net/2027/uc2.ark:/13960/t5k932625
61. EBC, *Tenting*, 533, 537–538.
62. "Breeds by Year Recognized," American Kennel Club web site, accessed March 27, 2017, http://www.akc.org/press-center/facts-stats/page-3/.
63. GAC, *My Life*, 53.
64. Dippie, 9.
65. EBC, *Tenting*, 575–576.
66. Merington, 198.
67. EBC, *Tenting*, 580.
68. Frost, 163.
69. Wert, 256.
70. Theodore R. Davis, "Summer on the Plains," *Harper's New Monthly Magazine*, February 1868, vol. 36, no. 213, 303, accessed on April 4, 2017, http://ebooks.library.cornell.edu/cgi/t/text/pageviewer-idx?c=harp;cc=harp;rgn=full%20text;idno=harp0036-3;didno=harp0036-3;view=image;seq=0302;node=harp0036-3%3A4; EBC, *Tenting*, 579.
71. EBC, *Guidon*, 161.
72. GAC, *My Life*, 69.
73. Wert, 260.
74. Davis, 306.
75. Elwood L. Nye, *Marching with Custer* (Glendale, CA: Arthur H. Clark Co., 1964), 19.
76. Elizabeth B. Custer, *Boots and Saddles* (New York: Harper & Brothers, 1885), 56, accessed on April 4, 17, http://hdl.handle.net/2027/uc2.ark:/13960/t3fx77t65.
77. Theodore R. Davis, "Indian War Scenes," *Harper's Weekly*, August 17, 1867, vol. XI, no. 555, 513–514, accessed on April 5, 2017, https://archive.org/stream/harpersweeklyv11bonn#page/514/mode/1up.
78. Dodge, 209.
79. Davis, "Indian War Scenes," 516.
80. Davis, "Indian War Scenes," 514.
81. Addressee unknown, undated 1868 letter fragment labeled "Summer 67 I think," and "5th," Marguerite Merington papers. New York Public Library. Manuscripts and Archives. Astor, Lenox, and Tilden Foundations.
82. EBC, *Tenting*, 702.
83. Lawrence A, Frost, *The Court Martial of General George Armstrong Custer* (Norman: University of Oklahoma Press, 1987), 101–102.
84. Wert, 261.
85. Merington, 214.
86. Merington, 215.
87. *Catalogue of the Second Annual New York Bench Show of Dogs Catalog, 1878* (2nd Westminster Kennel Club Show), 39, American Kennel Club Library, New York.
88. C. B. D. W., "Tales of the Plains: III. Custer's Dog," *Forest and Stream*, December 14, 1907, 935.

Chapter 7

1. G. A. Custer, *My Life on the Plains or, Personal Experiences with Indians* (New York: Sheldon & Co., 1876), 125, accessed on March 22, 2017, http://hdl.handle.net/2027/uc2.ark:/13960/t5k932625.
2. GAC, 124.
3. D. Mark Katz, *Custer in Photographs* (New York: Bonanza Books, 1990), 73.
4. General Order No. 6, Bvt. Maj. Gen. Alfred Gibbs, Ft. Leavenworth, April 18, 1868, LIBI-00019-3291. National Park Service, Little Bighorn Battlefield National Monument.
5. W. S. Nye, *Carbine & Lance: The Story of Old Fort Sill* (Norman: University of Oklahoma Press, 1962), 285.
6. Tom Custer to GAC, July 13, 1868, LIBI-00019-3290, National Park Service, Little Bighorn Battlefield National Monument.
7. Addressee unknown, undated 1868 letter fragment labeled "Summer 67 I think," and "5th," Marguerite Merington papers. New York Public Library.

Notes—Chapter 7

Manuscripts and Archives. Astor, Lenox, and Tilden Foundations.

8. *Ibid.*

9. Frederick Whitaker, *A Popular Life of Gen. George A. Custer* (Sheldon & Co., New York, 1876), 345, accessed on April 25, 2017, http://hdl.handle.net/2027/uc2.ark:/13960/t3dz03w59

10. Blaine Burkey, *Custer Come at Once!* (Hays, KS: Thomas More Prep, 1976), 42.

11. GAC to EBC, October 4 & October 10, 1868, contained in EBC's MS of Oct 1868—Jan 1869, LIBI-00019–3310, National Park Service, Little Bighorn Battlefield National Monument.

12. GAC to K. C. Barker, October 8, 1868, Marguerite Merington papers, New York Public Library, Manuscripts and Archives, Astor, Lenox, and Tilden Foundations.

13. GAC to EBC, October 2, 1868, LIBI-00019–03310.

14. GAC to K. C. Barker, October 8, 1868.

15. Letter to General Custer, Fort Hays, Kansas, from the secretary of the Audubon Club of Detroit announcing his honorary membership in the club, October 7, 1868. George Custer Papers, Burton Historical Collection, Detroit Public Library.

16. Robert M. Utley, ed., *Life in Custer's Cavalry: Diaries and Letters of Albert and Jennie Barnitz, 1867–1868* (Lincoln, NE, & London: University of Nebraska Press, 1987), 198.

17. GAC to EBC, October 10, 1868, LIBI-00019–03310.

18. GAC to EBC, October 18, 1868, LIBI-00019–03310.

19. GAC to K. C. Barker, undated letter fragments, Marguerite Merington papers. New York Public Library. Manuscripts and Archives. Astor, Lenox, and Tilden Foundations.

20. GAC to K. C. Barker, undated letter fragments.

21. EBC, *Following*, 9.

22. GAC to EBC, October 22, 1868, LIBI-00019–3310.

23. GAC to EBC, October 24, 1868, LIBI-00019–3310.

24. "Gen. Custer with Stag Hounds at Fort Dodge, 1868," card mounted photograph, LIBI-00019–0576, National Park Service, Little Bighorn Battlefield National Monument.

25. GAC to K. C. Barker, Undated Letter Fragments.

26. GAC to EBC, October 28, 1868, LIBI-00019–3310.

27. K. C. Barker to GAC, November 3, 1868. Brice C. W. Custer Collection.

28. GAC to EBC, November 4, 1868, LIBI-00019–3310.

29. GAC to K. C. Barker, November 8, 1868, Marguerite Merington papers, New York Public Library, Manuscripts and Archives, Astor, Lenox, and Tilden Foundations.

30. GAC to KC Barker, November 8, 1868.

31. Katz, 75.

32. GAC, *My Life*, 149–150.

33. Richard G. Hardorff, ed., *Washita Memories: Eyewitness Views of the Custer's Attack on Black Kettle's Village* (Norman, OK: University of Oklahoma Press, 2006), 135–136.

34. Hardorff, 207.

35. Peter Harrison, *The Eyes of the Sleepers: Cheyenne Accounts of the Washita Attack* (Southampton, UK: The English Westerners' Society, 1998), 3.

36. Utley, 220.

37. Sandy Barnard, ed., *Ten Years with Custer: A 7th Cavalryman's Memoirs* (Terre Haute, IN: AST Press, 2001), 74.

38. William C. Stair interview by Walter Camp, undated, Walter Mason Camp Papers, MSS 57 Box 3, SCM 000 827, L. Tom Perry Special Collections, Brigham Young University Library.

39. Hardorff, 186.

40. Dennis Lynch interview by Walter Camp, undated, 98, SCM 000 827-MSS 57 Box 3, Walter Mason Camp Papers, L. Tom Perry Special Collections, Brigham Young University Library.

41. Hardorff, 307.

42. Utley, 225.

43. Hardorff, 139.

44. Hardorff, 419.

45. Jerome A. Greene, *Washita: The U.S. Army and the Southern Cheyennes, 1867–1869* (Norman: University of Oklahoma Press, 2004), 119–120.

46. Stan Hoig, *The Battle of Washita: The Sheridan-Custer Indian Campaign of 1867–1869*. (Lincoln: University of Nebraska Press, 1979), 134.

47. Greene, 122–123.

48. Lorne Langley, "A Brevet or a Coffin for Doing All You Can," *Research Review, The Journal of the Little Bighorn Associates*, vol. 30 (2016): 23.

49. Greene, 136–137.

50. Hoig, 147.

51. Hardorff, 80–81.

52. Hoig, 137.

53. Paul L. Hedren, *Powder River: Disastrous Opening of the Great Sioux War* (Norman: University of Oklahoma Press, 2016), 166.

54. Hoig, 138.

55. Hardorff, 331.

56. GAC, *My Life*, 173.

57. John Stands in Timber and Margot Liberty, *Cheyenne Memories* (New Haven & London: Yale University Press, 1967). 172.

58. John K. Mahon, *History of the Second Seminole War, 1835–1842* (Gainesville, FL: University of Florida Press, 1992), 262.

59. Greene, 209–211.

60. GAC, *My Life*, 174.

61. Col. Henry Inman, *Tails of the Trail* (Topeka, KS: Crane & Co., Publishers, 1898), 177.

62. Lawrence A. Frost, *The Custer Album: A Pictorial Biography of General George A. Custer* (New York: Bonanza Books, 1984), 101.

63. Greene, 178.

64. Barnard, 74.

65. GAC, *My Life*, 194.

66. Utley, 220.

67. Utley, 223–224.

68. *Ibid.*

69. Barnard, 74.

70. Stair interview.

71. Lynch interview.

72. Richard E. Jensen, ed., *Voices of the American West, Volume 2: The Settler and Soldier Interviews of Eli S. Ricker, 1903–1919* (Lincoln: University of Nebraska Press, 2005). 365.

73. "Custer and His Greyhound," *The Somerset Herald*, Pennsylvania, August 23, 1876, 1. Accessed on De-

cember 15, 2017, https://chroniclingamerica.loc.gov/lccn/sn84026409/1876-08-23/ed-1/seq-1/.

Chapter 8

1. Anonymous, "The K. P. Excursion: A Two Day's Buffalo Hunt," *Chicago Tribune*, September 26 1870.
2. Elizabeth B. Custer, *Following the Guidon* (New York: Harper & Brothers, 1890), 77, accessed on July 15, 2017, http://hdl.handle.net/2027/coo1.ark:/13960/t4kk9vn09.
3. Elizabeth B. Custer, *Boots and Saddles* (New York: Harper & Brothers, 1885), 312, accessed on January 15, 2018, http://hdl.handle.net/2027/uc2.ark:/13960/t3fx77t65
4. Sandy Barnard, ed., *Ten Years with Custer: A 7th Cavalryman's Memoirs* (Fort Collins, CO: Citizen Printing, 2001), 103; EBC, *Following...*, 154.
5. EBC, *Following*, 159.
6. EBC, *Following*, 62–63.
7. EBC, *Following*, 122–123.
8. Barnard, 104.
9. *Ibid.*
10. Letter fragment, May 13, unknown year and author, LIBI-00019–3016. National Park Service, Little Bighorn Battlefield National Monument.
11. EBC, *Following*, 113–115, 125.
12. EBC, *Following*, 119–123.
13. EBC, *Following*, 119.
14. Jay Monaghan, *Custer: The Life of General George Armstrong Custer* (Lincoln, NE: University of Nebraska Press/Bison Book, 1971), 331.
15. EBC, *Following*, 220.
16. Brian C. Pohanka, ed., *A Summer on the Plains with Custer's 7th Cavalry: The 1870 Diary of Annie Gibson Roberts* (Lynchburg, VA: Schroeder Publications, 2004), 41.
17. EBC, *Following*, 221, 127–128.
18. "Camp on the Big Creek, near Fort Hays, Kansas, summer 1869," photograph, LIBI-00019–0495, National Park Service, Little Bighorn Battlefield National Monument.
19. "Mealtime on the Big Creek, near Fort Hays, Kansas, summer 1869," photograph, LIBI-00019–00496, National Park Service, Little Bighorn Battlefield National Monument (the blurry dog version of this photo is LIBI-00015–00600).
20. "Gen. Custer with Stag Hounds at Fort Dodge, 1868," photograph, LIBI-00019–0576 National Park Service, Little Bighorn Battlefield National Monument.
21. Jeffry D. Wert, *Custer: The Controversial Life of George Armstrong Custer* (New York: Touchstone, 1997), 289.
22. Elizabeth B. Custer, *Tenting on the Plains or General Custer in Kansas and Texas* (New York: C.L. Webster & Co., 1887) 403, accessed on July 15, 2017, http://hdl.handle.net/2027/loc.ark:/13960/t8nc6bj65.
23. EBC to Rebecca Richmond, October 16, 1870, LIBI-00019–003548, National Park Service, Little Bighorn Battlefield National Monument.
24. Paul Andrew Hutton, *Phil Sheridan & His Army* (Norman: University of Oklahoma Press, 1999), 246.
25. Anonymous, "The K. P. Excursion: A Two Day's Buffalo Hunt."
26. EBC, *Following*, 118–119, 173.
27. Lilah Pengra, *Corporals, Cooks, and Cowboys: African Americans in the Black Hills* (Buffalo Gap, SD: Lune House Publishing, 2006), 125.
28. EBC notes on buffalo hunting and Grand Duke Alexis, undated, LIBI-00019–002744, National Park Service, Little Bighorn Battlefield National Monument. (Also held by the Lawrence A. Frost Collection of the Monroe County Library System, Monroe, MI).
29. Brian W. Dippie, ed., *Nomad: George A. Custer in Turf, Field and Farm* (Austin & London: University of Texas Press, 1980), 50.
30. John I. Merritt, *Baronets and Buffalo: The British Sportsman in the American West 1833–1881* (Missoula, MT: Mountain Press Publishing Co., 1985), 130.
31. EBC, *Following*, 200.
32. EBC, *Following*, 209.
33. Nelson A. Miles, *Personal Recollections and Observations of General Nelson A. Miles* (Chicago & New York: The Werner Co., 1896), 151, accessed August 10, 2017, https://archive.org/details/personalrecollec00milerich.
34. Blaine Burkey, *Custer Come at Once!* (Hays, KS: Thomas More Prep, 1976), 99.
35. Eugene F. Ware, *The Indian War of 1864* (New York: St. Martin's, 1960), 35.
36. Dippie, 44–45.
37. Charles Leedham, "Lord Waterpark," *Bailey's Monthly Magazine of Sports and Pastimes*, London: A.H. Bailey & Co., vol. 25, no. 169, March 1874, 1–2, accessed on January 31 2018, https://archive.org/details/bailysmagazineof25gilbuoft.
38. Dippie, 45.
39. "Obituary for Sir Augustus Paget," *The Times* London, July 13, 1896; The Rt. Hon. Sir Augustus Berkeley Paget, at The Peerage.com, accessed on July 16, 2017, http://www.thepeerage.com/p3391.htm#i33906.
40. Dippie, 45.
41. EBC to Laura Noble, September 19, 1869, LIBI-00019–003553, National Park Service, Little Bighorn Battlefield National Monument.
42. Dippie, 46–47.
43. Minnie Dubbs Millbrook, "Big Game Hunting with the Custers, *Kansas Historical Quarterly*, Vol. XLI, No. 4 (Winter 1975): 437–438.
44. *Ibid.*
45. Dippie, 47.
46. Dippie, 48.
47. Dippie, 50.
48. Dippie, 48–50; EBC to Laura Noble, September 19, 1869.
49. EBC to Laura Noble, September 19, 1869.
50. Pohanka, 144–145.
51. Cecil Woodham-Smith, *The Reason Why* (New York: McGraw-Hill Book Co., Inc., 1954), 233–234.
52. Dippie, 50.
53. Letter from Sir Berkeley Paget to GAC, September 13, 1870, LIBI-00019–003470, National Park Service, Little Bighorn Battlefield National Monument.
54. Dippie, 49–50.
55. *Ibid.*
56. "Buffalo hunt, near Big Creek, Kansas, September 1869 by W. J. Philips, Preston, MO," photograph, Edward S. Godfrey Papers, Special Collections, United States Military Academy Library. (A copy is also held

by the Sternberg Memorial Museum, Fort Hays State University, Hays, KS.)
57. Dippie, 52.
58. "Buffalo near Ft. Hays," Photograph, LIBI-00019–00499. National Park Service, Little Bighorn Battlefield National Monument.
59. Dippie, 51.
60. Dippie, 139.
61. EBC to Laura Noble, September 19, 1869.
62. Dippie, 55–56.
63. Burkey, 88.
64. Dippie, 56.
65. Dippie, 58.
66. Dippie, 62–63.
67. J. C. Pickens to EBC, June 29, 1921, LIBI-00019–003482, National Park Service, Little Bighorn Battlefield National Monument.
68. Dippie, 56–57; EBC, *Following*, 265–266.
69. J. C. Pickens.
70. Dippie, 59–60.
71. J.C. Pickens.
72. Dippie, 60–62.
73. EBC, *Following*, 272–276.
74. Dippie, 63.
75. K C Barker to GAC, November 3, 1868. Brice C. W. Custer Collection.
76. EBC, *Following*, 276–277.
77. *Ibid.*
78. Stephen Youngkin, "Custer and His Staghounds," *The Claymore: Newsletter of the Scottish Deerhound Club of America*, March/April 1991, 42.
79. Don Schwarck, "Campaigning in Kansas with Maida and Blucher: General Custer's Staghounds," *Research Review: The Journal of the Little Bighorn Associates*, vol. 6, no. 2 (June 1992): 15.
80. EBC, *Following*, 312–314.
81. *Ibid.*
82. Lawrence A. Frost, *General Custer's Libbie* (Seattle: Superior Publishing Co., 1976), 187.
83. Minnie Dubbs Millbrook, "Rebecca Visits Kansas and the Custers," *Kansas History*, vol. 42, no. 2 (Winter 1976): 366–402, accessed on July 24, 2017, http://www.kshs.org/p/rebecca-visits-kansas-and-the-custers/13262.
84. *Ibid.*
85. *Ibid.*
86. Shirley A. Leckie, *Elizabeth Bacon Custer and the Making of a Myth* (Norman: University of Oklahoma Press, 1993), 123.
87. Millbrook, "Big Game Hunting with the Custers," 447.
88. T. S. Townsend to GAC, July 31, 1870, LIBI-00019–03339, National Park Service, Little Bighorn Battlefield National Monument.
89. Brian Patrick Duggan, *Saluki: The Desert Hound and the English Travelers Who Brought It to the West* (Jefferson, NC: McFarland, 2009), 42.
90. T. S. Townsend to GAC.
91. J. S. Ainsworth to GAC, September 12, 1870, LIBI-00019–03397, National Park Service, Little Bighorn Battlefield National Monument.
92. J. S. Ainsworth to GAC, February 25, 1872, LIBI-00019–03398, National Park Service, Little Bighorn Battlefield National Monument.
93. T.S. Townsend to GAC February 25, 1872, LIBI-00019–03398, National Park Service, Little Bighorn Battlefield National Monument.
94. J. S. Ainsworth to GAC, Jan 5 1873, LIBI-00019–03396, National Park Service, Little Bighorn Battlefield National Monument.
95. General E. S. Godfrey to E. S. Paxson on the Battle of Little Bighorn, January 16, 1896. MS 007.01.04, George Armstrong Custer Collection, McCracken Research Library, Buffalo Bill Center of the West, accessed on November 17, 2017, http://cdm17097.contentdm.oclc.org/cdm/compoundobject/collection/MS007/id/52/rec/1.
96. J. S. Ainsworth to GAC, February 25, 1872.
97. GAC 1868 Pocket Diary, LIBI-00019–01973–11A, National Park Service, Little Bighorn Battlefield National Monument.
98. William Goodwin to GAC, November 8, 1870, LIBI-00019–03469, National Park Service, Little Bighorn Battlefield National Monument.
99. William Goodwin to GAC.
100. Matthew Calbraith Perry and Francis L. Hawks, *Narrative of the Expedition of an American Squadron to the China Seas and Japan* (New York: D. Appleton & Co., 1857), 556–557, accessed on July 25, 2017, https://archive.org/details/narrativeofexped04perr.
101. "News of the Day," *Charleston Daily News*, September 12, 1870, 2, accessed on August 11, 2017, http://chroniclingamerica.loc.gov/lccn/sn84026994/1870-09-12/ed-1/seq-2/.
102. EBC to Rebecca Richmond, October 16, 1870, LIBI-00019–03548, National Park Service, Little Bighorn Battlefield National Monument.
103. Dippie, 70.
104. Anonymous, "The K. P. Excursion: A Two Day's Buffalo Hunt."
105. EBC to Rebecca Richmond, October 16, 1870.
106. "The West," *The New North-West*, November 18, 1870, 1, accessed on July 26, 2017, http://chroniclingamerica.loc.gov/lccn/sn84038125/1870-11-18/ed-1/seq-1/#date1=1870.
107. "Notes regarding Barnum's mummy," undated, LIBI-00019–03528, National Park Service, Little Bighorn Battlefield National Monument.
108. Merington, 181; "*Bal d'Opera*," *Harper's Weekly*, April 14, 1866, 232–233, accessed on May 2, 2017, https://archive.org/stream/harpersweeklyv10bonn#page/232/mode/2up/search/devil accessed on May 2 2017.
109. "Barnum on Buffalo Hunting," *The Evening Telegraph*, Philadelphia, November 4, 1879 4th edition, p. 6, accessed on July 26, 2017, http://chroniclingamerica.loc.gov/lccn/sn83025925/1870-11-04/ed-1/seq-6/.
110. Phineas T. Barnum, *The Life of P. T. Barnum Written by Himself* (Buffalo, NY: The Courier Co., 1888), 283, accessed on July 25, 2017, http://www.archive.org/details/lifeofptbarnum00barn.
111. "Barnum on Buffalo Hunting."
112. P. T. Barnum to GAC, November 29, 1875, LIBI-00019–003748, National Park Service, Little Bighorn Battlefield National Monument.
113. EBC to Rebecca Richmond, October 16, 1870.
114. Leckie, 125–128.
115. S. R. Graves to GAC, December 1, 1870, LIBI-00019–03378, National Park Service, Little Bighorn Battlefield National Monument.
116. A. Llewelyn Pratt, ed., *Our Friend the Dog in Verse* (London: The Guide Dogs for the Blind Assn., 1946), 49–50.

117. Phineas Taylor Barnum, *The Life of P. T. Barnum Written by Himself* (Buffalo, NY: The Courier Co., 1888), 66.

Chapter 9

1. Glendolin Damon Wagner, *Old Neutriment* (Lincoln: University of Nebraska Press, 1989), 57.
2. Sir Berkeley Paget to GAC, September 13, 1870, LIBI-00019–003470, National Park Service, Little Bighorn Battlefield National Monument.
3. Lawrence A. Frost, *Custer's 7th Cav and the Campaign of 1873* (El Segundo, CA: Upton & Sons, 1986), 152, 153.
4. Sir Berkeley Paget to GAC, September 13, 1870.
5. "The New York Bench Show," *Forest and Stream and Rod and Gun*, New York, May 24, 1877, 246, accessed on August 10 2017, https://archive.org/stream/Forestream8#page/246/mode/2up.
6. A. B. Snyder, *Pinnacle Jake* (Lincoln: University of Nebraska Press, 1951), 187.
7. Frost, *General Custer's Libbie*, 272.
8. Carl F. Day, *Tom Custer: Ride to Glory* (Norman: University of Oklahoma Press, 2005), 152–154.
9. Sandy Barnard, ed., *Ten Years with Custer: A 7th Cavalryman's Memoirs* (Terre Haute, IN: AST Press, 2001), 166.
10. Marguerite Merington, ed., *The Custer Story: The Life and Intimate Letters of General George A. Custer and His Wife Elizabeth* (New York: The Devin-Adair Company, 1950), 235.
11. Merington, 233–237.
12. T. J. Stiles, *Custer's Trials: A Life on the Frontier of New America* (New York: Alfred A. Knopf, 2015), 347.
13. Stiles, 344.
14. Elizabeth B. Custer, *Tenting on the Plains or General Custer in Kansas and Texas* (New York: C.L. Webster & Co. 1887), 527–528, accessed on August 21, 2017, http://hdl.handle.net/2027/loc.ark:/13960/t8nc6bj65.
15. Stiles, 348–349.
16. Stiles, 345–346.
17. L. P. Morton to GAC, February 9, 1871, LIBI-00019–03411, National Park Service, Little Bighorn Battlefield National Monument. Also held by the Lawrence A. Frost Collection of the Monroe County Library System, Monroe, MI.
18. J. W. Hall to GAC, June 3, 1875, LIBI-00019–03414; J. W. Hall to GAC, May 20, 1875, LIBI-00019–03415, National Park Service, Little Bighorn Battlefield National Monument.
19. W. Powell to GAC, April 21, 1871, LIBI-00019–03393, National Park Service, Little Bighorn Battlefield National Monument.
20. Powell to GAC, April 21, 1871.
21. A. McDonald to W. Powell, April 5, 1871, LIBI-00019–03394, National Park Service, Little Bighorn Battlefield National Monument.
22. S. R. Graves to GAC, August 18, 1872, LIBI-00019–03375, National Park Service, Little Bighorn Battlefield National Monument.
23. Powell to GAC, April 21, 1871.
24. William Scrope, *The Art of Deer-Stalking* (London: John Murray, 1839), 406–407.
25. Lawrence A. Frost, *General Custer's Libbie* (Seattle: Superior Publishing Co., 1976), 194–195.
26. Frost, 195–196.
27. Philip Henry Sheridan, *Personal Memoirs of P.H. Sheridan, General U.S. Army* (London: Chatto & Windus, 1888, v. 2), 440–441, accessed on August 20, 2017, https://catalog.hathitrust.org/Record/000204767.
28. Frost, 197.
29. Jeffry D. Wert, *Custer: The Controversial Life of George Armstrong Custer* (New York: Simon & Schuster, 1997), 295.
30. R. Gerald McMurtry, "The Two-Year Residence of General George A. Custer in Elizabethtown," *Kentucky Progress Magazine*, vol. V, no. 4 (Summer 1933): 32–33, Lawrence A. Frost Collection of the Monroe County Library System, Monroe, MI.
31. Theodore J. Crackel, "Custer's Kentucky: General George Armstrong Custer and Elizabethtown, Kentucky, 1871–1873," *The Filson Club Quarterly*, vol. 48, no. 2 (April 1974): 146, Lawrence A. Frost Collection of the Monroe County Library System, Monroe, MI.
32. Merington, 240–241.
33. Merington, 242.
34. Elizabeth B. Custer, *Boots and Saddles* (New York: Harper & Brothers, 1885), 26, accessed on August 29, 2017, http://hdl.handle.net/2027/uc2.ark:/13960/t3fx77t65.
35. Henry E. Davies, *Ten Days on the Plains* (Dallas, TX: Southern Methodist University Press, 1985), 78, 86, 103, 109.
36. Brian W. Dippie, ed., *Nomad: George A. Custer in Turf, Field and Farm* (Austin & London: University of Texas Press, 1980), 75.
37. Dippie, 87.
38. Dippie, 109–110.
39. EBC, *Following*, 331.
40. Wagner, 56.
41. Elizabeth B. Custer, *Boots and Saddles* (New York: Harper & Brothers, 1885), 68–69, accessed on August 21, 2017, http://hdl.handle.net/2027/uc2.ark:/13960/t3fx77t65.
42. EBC, *Tenting*, 340, accessed on August 21, 2017. http://hdl.handle.net/2027/loc.ark:/13960/t8nc6bj65.
43. Wagner, 57.
44. *Ibid.*
45. Wagner, 57–59.
46. Wagner, 59–60.
47. Wagner, 56–57.
48. Dippie, 101.
49. S. R. Graves to GAC, August 18, 1872.
50. David Chavchavadze, *The Grand Dukes* (New York: Atlantic International Publications, 1990), 114.
51. *Ibid.*
52. *Ibid.*
53. Douglas D. Scott, Peter Bleed, and Stephen Damm, *Custer, Cody, and Grand Duke Alexis: Historical Archeology of the Royal Buffalo Hunt* (Norman: University of Oklahoma Press, 2013), 27.
54. Lee A. Farrow, *Alexis in America: A Russian Grand Duke's Tour, 1871–1872* (Baton Rouge: Louisiana State University Press, 2014), 145.
55. Paul Andrew Hutton, *Phil Sheridan & His Army* (Norman: University of Oklahoma Press, 1999), 206–207.
56. William F. Cody, *The Life of Hon. William F. Cody Known as Buffalo Bill* (New York: Indian Head Books, 1991), 315.
57. Scott et al., 44.
58. Farrow, 149.

59. Scott et al., 57–58.
60. *Ibid.*
61. "Nimrod Alexis," *The New York Herald*, January 22, 1872, 7.
62. Frost, 267.
63. Frank Wallace, "The Grand Duke Nicholas as a Sportsman," *Country Life Magazine*, June 12, 1915, 804–806.
64. Farrow, 155.
65. Farrow, 160.
66. "Off to the Cave" and "Elizabethtown Ahead of Cincinnati—He Stops and Reviews Fine Stock," *Louisville Daily Ledger*, February 2, 1872.
67. McMurtry, 32–33; Crackel, 148.
68. EBC, *Tenting*, 442.
69. Shirley A. Leckie, *Elizabeth Bacon Custer and the Making of a Myth* (Norman: University of Oklahoma Press, 1993), 135.
70. "Confidential Communications: Allusion to Alexis," *Chicago Tribune*, March 31, 1872, 4.
71. Farrow, 215–216.
72. Frank Wallace, "The Grand Duke Nicholas as a Sportsman," *Country Life Magazine*, London, June 12, 1915, 806.
73. S. R. Graves to GAC, August 18, 1872.
74. *Ibid.*
75. S. R. Graves to GAC, November 21, 1872, LIBI-00019–03377, National Park Service, Little Bighorn Battlefield National Monument.
76. EBC to GAC from Elizabethtown, KY, undated, LIBI-00019–03547, National Park Service, Little Bighorn Battlefield National Monument. (Also held by the Lawrence A. Frost Collection of the Monroe County Library System, Monroe, MI).
77. Warwick, "Distemper in Dogs—Vaccinations," *Turf, Field and Farm*, vol. XV, no. 26, December 27, 1872, 403.
78. Ian Tizard, "Grease, Anthraxgate, and Kennel Cough: A Revisionist History of Early Veterinary Vaccines," *Advances in Veterinary Medicine*, vol. 41, no, 7 (1999): 17–18; Ian Tizard and M. Tawfik Omran, "*Syphilization and Civilization: Early Adventures in Vaccination*," presented at International Veterinary Vaccines Conference, Madison, WI, 2009.
79. Dippie, 101.
80. EBC, *Boots*, 11–12.
81. Kim Dennis-Bryan, and Juliet Clutton-Brock, *Dogs of the Last Hundred Years at the British Museum (Natural History)* (London: The British Museum, 1988), 30.
82. A. Croxton Smith, "Dogs of Tsars and Grand Dukes," *Country Life Magazine*, London, October 8, 1932, 413.
83. "Across the Plains," *The Leavenworth Weekly Times*, March 21, 1872, 3, accessed on August 26, 2017, http://chroniclingamerica.loc.gov/lccn/sn84027691/1872-03-21/ed-1/seq-3/.
84. Luther North, *Man of the Plains: Recollections of Luther North, 1856–1882* (Lincoln: University of Nebraska Press, 1961), 246.
85. Brian Patrick Duggan, "Army Hounds," *Sighthound Review*, vol. 3, no. 2, Summer/Fall 2012, 48.

Chapter 10

1. Katherine Gibson Fougera, *With Custer's Cavalry* (Caldwell, ID, The Caxton Printers Ltd., 1942), 110.
2. Elizabeth B. Custer, *Following the Guidon* (New York: Harper & Brothers, 1890), 14, accessed on August 28, 2017, http://hdl.handle.net/2027/coo1.ark:/13960/t4kk9vn09.
3. Glendolin Damon Wagner, *Old Neutriment* (Lincoln: University of Nebraska Press, 1989), 68–69.
4. *Ibid.*, 76
5. *Ibid.*, 69–70.
6. *Ibid.*, 71.
7. *Ibid.*, 73.
8. Fougera, 213.
9. Jeffry D. Wert, *Custer: The Controversial Life of George Armstrong Custer* (New York: Touchstone, 1997), 297.
10. Wagner, 71.
11. *Ibid.*, 76.
12. *Ibid.*, 74.
13. *Ibid.*, 80–81.
14. Elizabeth B. Custer, *Boots and Saddles* (New York: Harper & Brothers, 1885), 29, accessed on September 2, 2017, http://hdl.handle.net/2027/uc2.ark:/13960/t3fx77t65
15. Wagner, 82.
16. Elizabeth B. Custer, *Boots and Saddles* (New York: Harper & Brothers, 1885), 18, accessed on September 1, 2017, http://hdl.handle.net/2027/uc2.ark:/13960/t3fx77t65.
17. Wert, 297.
18. *Ibid.*, 298.
19. Asel Keyes to EBC, August 22, 1907, LIBI-00019–03111, National Park Service, Little Bighorn Battlefield National Monument.
20. Roger Darling, *Custer's Seventh Cavalry Comes to Dakota* (El Segundo, CA: Upton & Sons, 1989), 152–153.
21. *Ibid.*
22. *Ibid.*
23. Wagner, 43; EBC, *Boots*, 41.
24. *Ibid.*, 80.
25. Wagner, 83.
26. Fougera, 109.
27. Wagner, 56.
28. EBC, *Boots*, 43.
29. *Ibid.*, 73–75.
30. Fougera, 113.
31. *Ibid.*, 103.
32. *Ibid.*, 127–130.
33. Frazier and Robert Hunt, *I Fought with Custer: The Story of Sergeant Windolph* (New York: Charles Scribner's Sons, 1953), 18.
34. Louis E. Hills, "Surveying Expedition in 1873 by Bugler Hills," undated manuscript, 8–9, Lawrence A. Frost Collection of Custeriana, Monroe County Library System; Louis E. Hills, "With Gen. G. A. Custer on the Northern Pacific Surveying Expedition of 1873," *Journal of History*: Board of Publication of the Reorganized Church of Jesus Christ of Latter-Day Saints, Lamoni, IA, vol. 8, no. 2 (Apr 1915): 143–160.
35. Wagner, 103–104.
36. EBC, *Boots*, 55–56.
37. Wagner, 90–91.
38. Joseph Mills Hanson, *The Conquest of the Missouri: Being the Story of the Life and Exploits of Captain Grant Marsh* (Chicago: A.C. McClurg & Co., 1916), 177.
39. EBC, *Boots*, 57.
40. *Ibid.*, 57–58.
41. Wagner, 59.

42. EBC, *Boots*, 71.
43. Fort Sully Sporting Club Record Book, 1871–1874, H23–001, 50–51, South Dakota State Historical Society.
44. Fort Sully, 8.
45. *Ibid.*, 54.
46. *Ibid.*, 57.
47. Javan Bradley Irvine, Jr., Diaries 1870–1873, May 28, 1873, H75–016, South Dakota State Historical Society.
48. Javan Bradley Irvine, Jr., June 13, 1873,
49. *Ibid.*
50. J. B. Irvine, Jr., "A Hunt with General Custer," *Outdoor Life*, May 1923, in *A Seventh Cavalry Scrapbook #5*, ed. John M. Carroll (Bryan, TX: Privately printed, 1979), 9–10.
51. Javan Bradley Irvine, Jr., Diaries, May 29, 1873.
52. J. B. Irvine, Jr. "A Hunt with General Custer," 10.
53. Javan Bradley Irvine, Jr., Diaries.
54. J. B. Irvine, Jr. "A Hunt with General Custer," 10.
55. Javan Bradley Irvine, Jr., Diaries.
56. *Ibid.*
57. Fort Sully, 182.
58. EBC, *Boots*, 72.
59. Javan Bradley Irvine, Jr., Diary, July 24, 1873.
60. EBC, *Boots*, 86.
61. Herbert M. Hart, *Old Forts of the Northwest* (New York: Bonanza Books, 1963), 58.
62. William V. Wade, "Reminiscences of William V. Wade, Shields, N. D.," 70, MSS 20028. Small Manuscripts Collection Ms. 2100, State Historical Society of North Dakota.
63. Hanson, 394–395.
64. Wade, 70–71.
65. Wert, 303.
66. Fort Sully, 55.
67. Biographies for Lewis Henry Hugh Clifford, 9th Baron Clifford of Chudleigh, http://www.thepeerage.com/p7598.htm#i75977; Sir William Molesworth, 11th Baronet of Pencarrow, http://www.thepeerage.com/p51504.htm#i515032, from *The Peerage*, www.thepeerage.com, accessed September 3, 2017.
68. Letter from Lewis Clifford to his father, June 6 1873, 4, Lewis Clifford's Letters, May 11–June 29 1873, Box 9, Ugbrooke House Archives, Devon, U. K.
69. Anita Leslie, *Mr. Frewen of England* (London: Hutchinson & Co. 1966), 37.
70. Lewis Clifford's Letters, June 6, 1873, 5.
71. Fort Sully, unnumbered page.
72. EBC, *Boots*, 272.
73. *Ibid.*, 277.
74. Fort Sully, 154, 170.
75. Hanson, 176–178.
76. Fort Sully, 154.
77. Lewis Clifford's Letters, June 6, 1873, 6.
78. *Ibid.*
79. Lawrence A. Frost, *Some Observations on the Yellowstone Expedition of 1873* (Glendale, CA: Arthur H. Clarke Company, 1981), 43.
80. Wert, 306.
81. Wert, 309.
82. EBC, Boots, 279.
83. "Military News," *Forest and Stream*, August 14, 1873, 13, accessed on October 28, 2017, https://archive.org/stream/ForeststreamI#page/12/mode/2up.

84. "The Yellowstone Expedition," *Bismarck Tribune*, July 11, 1873, 1, accessed on September 3, 2017, http://chroniclingamerica.loc.gov/lccn/sn84022127/1873-07-11/ed-1/seq-1/.
85. Newspaper fragment, "Incidents of the Yellowstone Expedition," undated, LIBI-00019–03105. National Park Service, Little Bighorn Battlefield National Monument.
86. M. John Lubetkin, *Jay Cooke's Gamble: The Northern Pacific Railroad, the Sioux, and the Panic of 1873* (Norman, OK: University of Oklahoma Press, 2006), 185–186.
87. Wert, 304–305.
88. Ben Innis (Richard E. Collin, ed.), *Bloody Knife: Custer's Favorite Scout* (Bismarck, ND: Smokey Water Press, 1994), 19, 22.
89. Elizabeth B. Custer, *Boots and Saddles* (New York: Harper & Brothers, 1885), 236, accessed on September 14, 2017. Available online http://hdl.handle.net/2027/uc2.ark:/13960/t3fx77t65
90. Lewis Clifford's letters, August 28, 1873, 2.
91. Wert, 306–307.
92. Lawrence A. Frost, *Custer's 7th Cav and the Campaign of 1873* (El Segundo, CA: Upton & Sons, 1986), 75–77.
93. Frost, *Custer's 7th Cav*, 86.
94. Hills, "Surveying Expedition in 1873," 29.
95. *Ibid.*
96. Lewis Clifford's letters, August 28, 1873, 5.
97. Wert 308.
98. Louis E. Hills, "Surveying Expedition in 1873," 30.
99. Lewis Clifford's letters, August 28 1873, 5.
100. *Ibid.*
101. Wert, 307–308.
102. Frost, *Custer's 7th Cav*, 87.
103. *Ibid.*, 96, 98.
104. *Ibid.*, 90.
105. *Ibid.*
106. Frost, *Some Observations*, 51.
107. 2-page fragment attributed to GAC to K. C. Barker, September 6, 1873. Marguerite Merington Papers, New York Public Library, Manuscripts and Archives, Astor, Lenox, and Tilden Foundations.
108. "The Yellowstone War," *New York Tribune*, September 9, 1873, 4.
109. *Ibid.*
110. Lewis Clifford's Letters, August 28, 1873, 6.
111. *Ibid.*
112. Frost, *Custer's 7th Cav*, 96.
113. Frost, *Some Observations*, 132–133.
114. Frost, *Custer's 7th Cav*, 101.
115. *Ibid.*
116. GAC to K. C. Barker, September 6, 1873.
117. Dippie, 105–108.
118. Dippie, 108; GAC to EBC September 6, 1873; GAC to K. C. Barker, September 6, 1873. Marguerite Merington Papers. New York Public Library. Manuscripts and Archives. Astor, Lenox, and Tilden Foundations.
119. *Ibid.*
120. GAC to EBC September 6, 1873.
121. GAC to K. C. Barker, September 6, 1873, and 2-page fragment attributed to that letter, Marguerite Merington Papers, New York Public Library, Manuscripts and Archives, Astor, Lenox, and Tilden Foundations.
122. Dippie, 107.

123. Frost, *Custer's 7th Cav*, 101.
124. GAC to EBC, July 26, 1873, Marguerite Merington Papers, New York Public Library, Manuscripts and Archives, Astor, Lenox, and Tilden Foundations.
125. Brian Patrick Duggan, "Of Coursing Hounds and Cowboys," *AKC Family Dog*, November/December 2013, 34–37, accessed February 11, 2018, http://viewer.zmags.com/publication/61d65aa3#/61d65aa3/27.
126. Robert M. Utley, ed., *Life in Custer's Cavalry: Diaries and Letters of Albert and Jennie Barnitz, 1867–1868* (Lincoln, NE, and London: University of Nebraska Press, 1987), 30.
127. George Frederick Howe, ed., "Expedition to the Yellowstone River in 1873: Letters of a Young Cavalry Officer," *The Mississippi Valley Historical Review: Journal of American History*, vol. XXXIX, no. 3. (December 1952): 528.
128. Frost, *Some Observations*, 46–47.
129. G. O. Shields, *Hunting in the Great West: Rustlings in the Rockies* (Chicago, IL: Donohue, Henneberry & Co., 1883), 146.
130. Hanson, 177.
131. Fort Sully, 182, 184.
132. James F. Meline, *Two Thousand Miles on Horseback: Santa Fé and Back* (New York: Hurd and Houghton, 1867), 17, accessed on September 7, 2017, https://archive.org/details/twothousandmiles00meli.
133. Richard Irving Dodge, *The Plains of the Great West and Their Inhabitants* (New York: Archer House, 1959), 203.
134. Donald F. Danker, ed., *Man of the Plains: Recollections of Luther North 1856–1882* (Lincoln: University of Nebraska Press, 1961), 105.

Chapter 11

1. Elizabeth B. Custer, *Boots and Saddles* (New York: Harper & Brothers, 1885), 57–58, accessed on September 1, 2017, http://hdl.handle.net/2027/uc2.ark:/13960/t3fx77t65.
2. *First Annual New York Bench Show Catalog, 1877* [1st Westminster Kennel Club Show] (New York: American Kennel Club Library), 13.
3. Lee A. Farrow, *Alexis in America: A Russian Grand Duke's Tour, 1871–1872* (Baton Rouge: Louisiana State University Press, 2014), 220.
4. William V. Wade, *Paha Sapa Tawoyyake* (Mandan, ND: Crescent Printing Co., 1965), 9.
5. EBC, *Boots* 170.
6. Javan Bradley Irvine, Jr., Diary, May 27, 1871, # H72-003, box 3347A, South Dakota State Historical Society.
7. Glendolin Damon Wagner, *Old Neutriment* (Lincoln: University of Nebraska Press, 1989), 59.
8. EBC, *Boots*, 229.
9. Lawrence A. Frost, *Some Observations on the Yellowstone Expedition of 1873* (Glendale, CA: Arthur H. Clarke Company, 1981), 81–82.
10. Marguerite Merington, ed., *The Custer Story: The Life and Intimate Letters of General George A. Custer and His Wife Elizabeth* (New York: The Devin-Adair Company, 1950), 270.
11. Lawrence A. Frost, *Custer's 7th Cav and the Campaign of 1873* (El Segundo, CA: Upton & Sons, 1986), 119.
12. EBC, *Boots*, 55.

13. Elizabeth B. Custer, *Following the Guidon* (New York: Harper & Brothers, 1890), 230–231, 307, accessed on September 9, 2017, http://hdl.handle.net/2027/coo1.ark:/13960/t4kk9vn09.
14. EBC, *Boots* 185.
15. "John Burkman Holding Reins of Dandy & Vic, Custer's Horses with 4 Scotch Staghounds," albumen photograph, LIBI-00019–0173. National Park Service, Little Bighorn Battlefield National Monument.
16. Charles Francis Bates, *Custer's Indian Battles* (New York: Bronxville, 1936), 29, accessed October 7, 2017, https://babel.hathitrust.org/cgi/pt?id=mdp.39015029551432;view=1up;seq=35.
17. Wagner, 12.
18. *Ibid.*, 65.
19. EBC, *Following*, 230.
20. EBC, *Boots*, 111.
21. Wagner, 62–63.
22. Shirley A. Leckie, ed., *The Colonel's Lady on the Frontier: The Correspondence of Alice Kirk Grierson* (Lincoln: University of Nebraska Press, 1989), 72.
23. Wagner, 48–49.
24. EBC, *Boots*, 106.
25. *Ibid.*, 44.
26. Wagner, 56.
27. *Ibid.*, 66–67.
28. EBC, *Boots*, 58.
29. *Ibid.*, 112.
30. *Ibid.*, 111–112.
31. *Ibid.*, 107.
32. EBC, *Following*, 232.
33. EBC, *Boots*, 109.
34. *Ibid.*, 110–111.
35. *Ibid.*, 109.
36. EBC, *Following*, 242–243.
37. EBC, *Boots*, 155.
38. Frost, *Custer's 7th Cav*, 123, 126; EBC, *Boots*, 115–117.
39. EBC, *Boots*, 116–117.
40. *Ibid.*, 175–178; "Gen. & Mrs. Custer in their Study at Fort Lincoln," photograph, LIBI-00019–0219; "Custer in His Study at Fort Lincoln," LIBI-00019–0341. National Park Service, Little Bighorn Battlefield National Monument.
41. EBC, *Boots*, 176.
42. Herbert Krause and Gary D. Olson, *Prelude to Glory: A Newspaper Accounting of Custer's 1874 Expedition to the Black Hills* (Sioux Falls, SD: Brevet Press, 1974), 102.
43. *Ibid.*, 47, 50.
44. Donald F. Danker, ed., *Man of the Plains: Recollections of Luther North 1856–1882* (Lincoln: University of Nebraska Press, 1961), 106.
45. Tim Brady, *Gopher Gold: Legendary Figures, Brilliant Blunders, and Amazing Feats at the University of Minnesota* (St. Paul: Minnesota Historical Society Press, 2007), 53, 56; Krause and Olson, 39–40.
46. John M. Carroll and Lawrence A. Frost, *Private Theodore Ewert's Diary of the Black Hills Expedition of 1874* (Piscataway, NJ: CRI Books, 1976), 6–7.
47. Jay Monaghan, *Custer: The Life of General George Armstrong Custer* (Lincoln: University of Nebraska Press/Bison Book, 1971), 353.
48. Lawrence A. Frost, *General Custer's Libbie* (Seattle: Superior Publishing Co., 1976), 212; Wert, 314.
49. Carroll and Frost, 10.

50. *Ibid.*, 11; Lawrence A. Frost, *With Custer in '74: James Calhoun's Diary of the Black Hills Expedition* (Provo, UT: Brigham Young University Press, 1979), 25.
51. Danker, 185.
52. EBC, *Boots*, 304.
53. Merington, 274.
54. Frost, *General Custer's Libbie*, 205.
55. Merington, 273–274.
56. EBC, *Boots*, 301.
57. "Custer," *Bismarck Tribune*, August 5, 1874, 1, accessed on September 23, 1874, http://chroniclingamerica.loc.gov/lccn/sn84022127/1874-08-05/ed-1/seq-1/.
58. "Gold," *Bismarck Tribune*, August 12 1874, 1, accessed on September 23 2017, http://chroniclingamerica.loc.gov/lccn/sn84022127/1874-08-12/ed-1/seq-1/.
59. Carroll and Frost, 50–52.
60. Frost, *With Custer in '74*, 24.
61. George Frederick Howe, ed., "Expedition to the Yellowstone River in 1873: Letters of a Young Cavalry Officer," *The Mississippi Valley Historical Review: A Journal of American History*, vol. XXXIX, no. 3 (December 1952), 520.
62. Krause and Olson, 20, 162.
63. *Ibid.*, 264–265.
64. Frost, *With Custer in '74*, 42; Carroll and Frost, 31–32; EBC, *Boots*, 193.
65. EBC, *Boots*, 300.
66. GAC to EBC, July 15, 1874. Marguerite Merington Papers, New York Public Library, Manuscripts and Archives, Astor, Lenox, and Tilden Foundations.
67. EBC, *Boots*, 302.
68. Wagner, 65.
69. "Gold," *Bismarck Tribune*.
70. Monaghan, 357.
71. EBC, *Boots*, 304.
72. *Ibid.*
73. Krause and Olson, 271.
74. Carroll and Frost, 58–59.
75. Sandy Barnard, ed., *Ten Years with Custer: A 7th Cavalryman's Memoirs* (Terre Haute, IN: AST Press, 2001), 204; "Custer with Grizzly Bear," photograph, Illingworth # 2015-11-30-307, South Dakota State Historical Society, accessed on September 20, 2017, http://sddigitalarchives.contentdm.oclc.org/cdm/singleitem/collection/photos/id/58388/rec/21.
76. EBC, *Boots*, 175.
77. *Ibid.*, 293.
78. *Ibid.*
79. Robert M Utley, *Cavalier in Buckskin: George Armstrong Custer and the Western Military Frontier* (Norman, OK, University of Oklahoma Press, 1988), 137–138.
80. Brady, 62.
81. "Custer with Three Indians, Guide, & Two Dogs," photograph, LIBI-00019–4321. National Park Service, Little Bighorn Battlefield National Monument.
82. Carroll and Frost, 67.
83. *Ibid.*, 11.
84. Krause and Olson, 76.
85. Carroll and Frost, 76.
86. Monaghan, 357; Frederic F. Van de Water, *Glory Hunter: A Life of General Custer* (Lincoln: University of Nebraska Press, 1988) 134.
87. Krause and Olson, 268–270.
88. Carroll and Frost, 32, 35, 68.

89. "Nuggets," *Bismarck Tribune*, August 26, 1874, 2, accessed on September 23 2017, http://chroniclingamerica.loc.gov/lccn/sn84022127/1874-08-26/ed-1/seq-2/.
90. "Custer Interviewed," Bismarck Tribune, September 2, 1874, 1, accessed on September 23, 2017, http://chroniclingamerica.loc.gov/lccn/sn84022127/1874-09-02/ed-1/seq-1/.
91. Krause and Olson, 263.
92. Wert, 317.
93. Peter Cozzens, "Grant's Uncivil War," *Smithsonian Magazine*, vol. 47, no. 7 (November 2016), 59.
94. EBC, *Boots*, 235.
95. William H. Illingworth, "Custer's Wagon Train, Black Hills South Dakota, Photograph #2015-11-23-301; #2015-11-30-305, Digital Archives, South Dakota State Historical Society, accessed September 28, 2017, https://sddigitalarchives.contentdm.oclc.org/digital/collection/photos.
96. EBC, *Boots*, 192; Carroll and Frost, *Private Theodore Ewert's Diary Expedition of 1874*, 10.
97. EBC, *Boots*, 193.
98. *Ibid.*, 232.
99. Shirley A. Leckie, *Elizabeth Bacon Custer and the Making of a Myth* (Norman: University of Oklahoma Press, 1993), 169.
100. GAC to Capt. Elliott Gray, Tecumseh, Mich., October 26, 1874. From the collection of Philip Downs.
101. EBC, *Boots*, 176.
102. "California Joe and His Dog, 1875," photograph, Rose #667, Western History Collections, University of Oklahoma Libraries.
103. Joe E. Milner, *California Joe: Noted Scout and Indian Fighter* (Lincoln: University of Nebraska Press, 1987), 236–237.
104. EBC, *Boots*, 237; *Following*, 99.
105. Douglas C. McChristian, *Regular Army O!: Soldiering on the Western Frontier 1865–1891* (Norman: University of Oklahoma Press, 2017), 356.

Chapter 12

1. Elizabeth B. Custer, *Boots and Saddles* (New York: Harper & Brothers, 1885), 310, accessed on December 4, 2018, http://hdl.handle.net/2027/uc2.ark:/13960/t3fx77t65.
2. Jeffry D. Wert, *Custer: The Controversial Life of George Armstrong Custer* (New York: Touchstone, 1997), 318–319.
3. Lawrence A. Frost, *Custer's 7th Cav and the Campaign of 1873* (El Segundo, CA: Upton & Sons, 1986), 131–134; Wert, 319.
4. Lawrence A. Frost, *The Custer Album: A Pictorial Biography of General George A. Custer* (New York: Bonanza Books, 1984), 135–136.
5. Lawrence A. Frost, *General Custer's Libbie* (Seattle: Superior Publishing Co., 1976), 216.
6. EBC, *Boots*, 233–234.
7. J. W. Hall to W. A. Travers, February 23, 1875, LIBI-00019–03417; J. W. Hall to GAC April 5, 1875, LIBI-00019–03416, National Park Service, Little Bighorn Battlefield National Monument.
8. J. W. Hall to GAC August 19, 1874, LIBI-00019–03418; J. W. Hall to GAC April 5, 1875, LIBI-00019–03416, National Park Service, Little Bighorn Battlefield National Monument.

9. J. W. Hall to GAC, May 20, 1875, LIBI-00019-03415, National Park Service, Little Bighorn Battlefield National Monument.

10. W. S. Salisbury, Exhaust Draft Nozzle, U.S. Patent No. 226, 204, accessed on October 5, 2017, https://docs.google.com/viewer?url=patentimages.storage.googleapis.com/pdfs/US226204.pdf.

11. J. W. Hall to GAC, June 3, 1875, LIBI-00019-3414, National Park Service, Little Bighorn Battlefield National Monument.

12. "Drowned," *Detroit Advertiser & Tribune*, May 21 1875; "Casualties: Detroit River Disaster," *Chicago Daily Tribune*, May 22, 1875, 10, accessed on October 24, 2017, http://chroniclingamerica.loc.gov/lccn/sn84031492/1875-05-22/ed-1/seq-10/.

13. F.A. Barnard, *American Biographical History of Eminent and Self Made Men, Vol. 1*, Western Biographical Publishing Company, Cincinnati, OH, 1878, Michigan Vol., 9–10, accessed on March 15, 2017, https://books.google.com/books?id=U-IBAAAA MAAJ&pg=PA9#v=onepage&q&f=false.

14. "Dog Trade," *Fayetteville Observer*, March 6, 1856, 2, accessed on October 23, 2017, http://chroniclingamerica.loc.gov/lccn/sn85033395/1856-03-06/ed-1/seq-2/.

15. "Scottish Deer Hounds For Sale," *Forest and Stream*, October 7, 1875, 143, accessed on October 31, 2017, https://archive.org/stream/Foreststream5#page/143/mode/1up/.

16. Brian W. Dippie, ed., *Nomad: George A. Custer in Turf, Field and Farm* (Austin & London: University of Texas Press, 1980), 109–110.

17. Dippie, 110–111.

18. Rose Lambart Price, *A Summer on the Rockies* (London, Sampson Low, Marston & Co., 1898), 39–40, accessed on March 3, 2018, https://catalog.hathitrust.org/Record/008684038.

19. Marguerite Merington, ed., *The Custer Story: The Life and Intimate Letters of General George A. Custer and His Wife Elizabeth* (New York: The Devin-Adair Company, 1950), 276.

20. Shirley A. Leckie, *Elizabeth Bacon Custer and the Making of a Myth* (Norman: University of Oklahoma Press, 1993), 125.

21. GAC to EBC July 15, 1875. Marguerite Merington papers, New York Public Library, Manuscripts and Archives, Astor, Lenox, and Tilden Foundations.

22. Kathleen Maher, "P. T. Barnum (1810–1891)— The Man, the Myth, the Legend," *The Barnum Museum*, accessed on November 1, 2017, http://www.barnum-museum.org/manmythlegend.htm.

23. Advertisement for P. T. Barnum's "Great Roman Hippodrome," *The Sun*, November 5, 1874.

24. "P. T. Barnum's Great Roman Hippodrome" playbill, April 27, 1874, EL 1988.41.1. The Barnum Museum, Bridgeport, CT.

25. Newspaper Advertisement for the "Great Roman Hippodrome," August 3 (no year given) Florida State University Digital Repository, Harrison Sayre Circus Collection, accessed on May 29, 2017, http://fsu.digital.flvc.org/islandora/object/fsu%3A846.

26. "The Big Show," *Omaha Daily Bee*, May 12, 1874, 3.

27. "P. T. Barnum's Great Roman Hippodrome" playbill.

28. Newspaper Advertisement for the "Great Roman Hippodrome."

29. Lee A. Farrow, *Alexis in America: A Russian Grand Duke's Tour, 1871–1872* (Baton Rouge: Louisiana State University Press, 2014), 198.

30. A. H. Saxon, ed., *Selected Letters of P. T. Barnum* (New York: Columbia Press, 1983), 188–189.

31. "Barnum's Sale," *Forest and Stream*, Vol. 5, no 18 (December 9, 1875), 276, accessed on August 29, 2017, https://archive.org/stream/Foreststream5#page/276/mode/2up/search/Barnum.

32. Ibid.

33. P. T. Barnum to GAC, November 29, 1875, LIBI-00019-03748, National Park Service, Little Bighorn Battlefield National Monument.

34. "Personal," *The Philadelphia Inquirer*, December 10, 1875, 4.

35. "Local Affairs," *Bismarck Weekly Tribune*, December 29, 1875, 1, accessed on November 12, 2016, http://chroniclingamerica.loc.gov/lccn/sn84022129/1875-12-29/ed-1/seq-8/.

36. P. T. Barnum to GAC, December 11, 1875, LIBI-00019-03373, National Park Service, Little Bighorn Battlefield National Monument.

37. Jay Monaghan, *Custer: The Life of General George Armstrong Custer* (Lincoln: University of Nebraska Press/Bison Book, 1971), 364.

38. Irving Wallace, *The Fabulous Showman: The Life and Times of P.T. Barnum* (New York: Alfred A. Knopf, 1959), 151; *Bismarck Weekly Tribune*, December 29 1875.

39. "Grand Bench Show of Dogs," *New York Times*, September 12, 1876.

40. T. J. Stiles, *Custer's Trials: A Life on the Frontier of New America* (New York: Alfred A. Knopf, 2015), 427.

41. EBC, *Boots*, 148.

42. Leckie, 179.

43. GAC to Lawrence Barrett, March 4, 1876, telegram, #3826.764, Thomas Gilcrease Institute of American History and Art, accessed January 19, 2018, https://collections.gilcrease.org/object/3826764.

44. Sandy Barnard, *I Go with Custer: The Life and Death of Reporter Mark Kellogg* (Bismarck, ND: The Bismarck Tribune, 1996), 104.

45. EBC, *Boots*, 253–259; Frost, *General Custer's Libbie*, 218.

46. EBC, *Boots*, 259–260.

47. Monaghan, 361.

48. Grenville Kleiser, ed., *Dictionary of Proverbs* (New Delhi: APH Publishing, 2005), 78.

49. Stiles, 434.

50. Ibid.

51. Ibid., 435.

52. Ibid., 439.

53. Paul L. Hedren, *Powder River: Disastrous Opening of the Great Sioux War* (Norman: University of Oklahoma Press, 2016), 2–44.

54. Wert, 324.

55. EBC, *Boots*, 263.

56. James Donovan, *A Terrible Glory: Custer and the Little Bighorn, the Last Great Battle of the American West* (New York & Boston: Back Bay Books/Little, Brown and Co., 2009), 158.

57. Glendolin Damon Wagner, *Old Neutriment* (Lincoln: University of Nebraska Press, 1989), 123.

58. Ibid.

59. Wert, 325.

60. Barnard, *I Go with Custer*, 200; Mark H. Kellogg Diary 1876, # 20017, North Dakota State Historical Archives, accessed on October 30, 2017, http://history.nd.gov/archives/Kelloggdiary.pdf.

61. Barnard, *I Go with Custer,* 201.
62. EBC, *Boots,* 307–308.
63. *Ibid.,* 309.
64. Wagner, 128–129.
65. E. S. Godfrey, "Custer's Last Battle," *The Century Magazine,* January 1892, 361.
66. Todd E. Harburn, ed., *A Surgeon with Custer at the Little Big Horn: James DeWolf's Diary and Letters 1876* (Norman: University of Oklahoma Press, 2017), 102.
67. *Ibid.,* 60.
68. Ernest L. Reedstrom, *Bugles, Banners and War Bonnets: A Study of George Armstrong Custer's Seventh Cavalry from Fort Riley to Little Bighorn* (New York: Bonanza Books, 1986), 114.
69. Edward Settle Godfrey, *The Field Diary of Lt. Edward Settle Godfrey* (Portland, OR: Champoeg Press, 1957), 5.
70. Gerald R. Clark, *Supplying Custer: The Powder River Supply Depot, 1876* (Salt Lake City: University of Utah Press, 2014), 74–75.
71. EBC, *Boots,* 310.
72. James V. Schneider and Richard Campbell, *Behind Custer at the Little Big Horn: The Story of Lieutenant Edward Mathey and the Packtrain* (Fort Wayne, IN: privately published, 1980).
73. Donovan, 167.
74. Wert, 336.
75. Edgar I. Stewart, *Custer's Luck* (Norman: University of Oklahoma Press, 1985), 229.
76. Clark, 74.
77. Michael D. Hill and Ben Innis, eds. "The Fort Buford Diary of Private Sanford, 1876–1877," *North Dakota History,* 52 (Summer 1985): 14.
78. Robert M. Utley, *Cavalier in Buckskin: George Armstrong Custer and the Western Military Frontier* (Norman: University of Oklahoma Press, 1988), 179.
79. Wert, 335.
80. Frost, *General Custer's Libbie,* 270.
81. Barnard, *I Go with Custer,* 207.
82. Wert, 339.
83. Thomas B. Marquis, *A Warrior Who Fought Custer* (Minneapolis: The Midwest Co., 1931), 237.
84. James Mueller, "Taking a Humorous Stand: 19th Century Newspaper Jokes About Custer and the Little Big Horn," *Custer Battlefield Historical & Museum Association, Inc., 23rd Annual Symposium Proceedings,* Hardin MT (June 26, 2009): 26.
85. Robbins Hunter, *The Judge Rode a Sorrel Horse* (New York: E. P. Dutton, 1950), 16–17.

Chapter 13

1. Nap. A. Comeau, "Custer's Dog," *Forest and Stream,* March 7 1908, 377.
2. Edgar I. Stewart, "The Reno Court of Inquiry," *The Montana Magazine of History,* Vol. II, no. 3 (July 1952): 32.
3. Edgar I. Stewart, *Custer's Luck* (Norman, OK: University of Oklahoma Press, 1985), ix.
4. Brian W. Dippie, *Custer's Last Stand: The Anatomy of an American Myth* (Lincoln: University of Nebraska Press, 1994), 76.
5. *Ibid.*
6. Rickard, A. Ross, *First to Arrive on Custer's Battlefield with the Montana Column: Frederick E. Server, Montana Pioneer, Soldier, and Explorer* (El Segundo, CA: Upton and Sons, 2010), 65.
7. *Ibid.,* 70.
8. John Stands in Timber and Margot Liberty, *Cheyenne Memories* (New Haven CT: Yale University Press, 1998), 210–211.
9. Mark H. Kellogg Diary 1876, #20017, North Dakota State Historical Archives, accessed on October 30, 2017, http://history.nd.gov/archives/Kelloggdiary.pdf.
10. Jeffry D. Wert, *Custer: The Controversial Life of George Armstrong Custer* (New York: Touchstone, 1997), 355.
11. Edward S. Godfrey, "Godfrey Diary of the 7th Cavalry Expedition, May 17 to Sept. 24, 1876," 1908, v. II, 33, Francis R. Hagner Collection, 1860–1946, Manuscripts and Archives, New York Public Library.
12. Kelly Gibson, "A Short History of Military Tattoos," *VFW: Veterans of Foreign Wars,* August 2016, 44.
13. Sandy Barnard, ed., *Ten Years with Custer: A 7th Cavalryman's Memoirs* (Terre Haute, IN: AST Press, 2001), 304.
14. James Donovan, *A Terrible Glory: Custer and the Little Bighorn, the Last Great Battle of the American West* (New York & Boston: Back Bay Books/Little, Brown and Co., 2009), 312–313.
15. Richard G. Hardorff, *Cheyenne Memories of the Custer Fight: A Source Book* (Spokane, WA: The Arthur H. Clark Co., 1995), 44; Richard G. Hardorff, *The Custer Battle Casualties, II: The Dead, The Missing, and a Few Survivors* (El Segundo, CA: Upton and Sons, 1999), 176.
16. Hardorff, *Custer Battle Casualties, II,* 174.
17. John S. Gray, "Veterinary Service on Custer's Last Campaign," *Kansas Historical Quarterly,* vol. 43, no. 3 (Autumn 1977): 249–263, accessed on January 2, 2018. http://www.kancoll.org/khq/1977/77_3_gray.htm.
18. Elizabeth Atwood Lawrence, *His Very Silence Speaks: Comanche—The Horse Who Survived Custer's Last Stand* (Detroit, IL: Wayne State University Press, 1989), 105.
19. Hardorff, *Custer Battle Casualties, II,* 178–179.
20. Lawrence, 167.
21. "Custer's Pack of Hounds," *The Highland Weekly News,* Hillsborough, Ohio, August 3, 1876, 3, accessed on December 15, 2017, https://chroniclingamerica.loc.gov/lccn/sn85038158/1876-08-03/ed-1/seq-3/.
22. "Local News," *Black Hills Weekly Pioneer,* August 5, 1876, 4.
23. "Local News," *Black Hills Weekly Pioneer,* June 17 1876, 4.
24. "Letter from Hinrich Glüsing (Gluesing) to his father in Germany," *Bighorn County News,* Hardin, MT, June 23, 2011, 3.
25. Paul L. Hedren, *With Crook in the Black Hills: Stanley J. Morrow's 1876 Photographic Essay* (Boulder, CO: Pruett Publishing Co., 1985), 54, 55.
26. Gerald R. Clark, *Supplying Custer: The Powder River Supply Depot, 1876* (Salt Lake City: University of Utah Press, 2014), 72.
27. John G. Bourke, *On the Border with Crook* (New York: Charles Scribner's Sons, 1892), 362, 366.
28. "The Only True 7th Cavalry Dog," *The Sturgis Weekly Record,* January 27, 1888, 2.
29. Walter C. Gooding, "Incidents Connected with

Fort Abraham Lincoln," *The Record*, vol. 2, 1897, 8–9, MSS 20380, Robert P. Gooding Collection, Small Manuscript Collection Ms21000, State Historical Society of North Dakota.

30. Hardorff, *Custer Battle Casualties, II*, 189.

31. *Ibid.*

32. Richard G. Hardorff, *Camp, Custer, and The Little Bighorn: A Collection of Walter Mason Camp's Research Papers on General George A. Custer's Last Fight* (El Segundo, CA: Upton and Sons, 1997), 93.

33. W. M. Camp to E. S. Godfrey, May 19, 1920, LIBI-00019–03648. National Park Service, Little Bighorn Battlefield National Monument.

34. William V. Wade, *Paha Sapa Tawoyyake* (Mandan, ND: Crescent Printing Co., 1965), 20.

35. Hardorff, *Camp, Custer, and the Little Bighorn*, 71.

36. Glendolin Damon Wagner, *Old Neutriment* (Lincoln: University of Nebraska Press, 1989), 152.

37. Hardorff, *Custer Battle Casualties, II*, 189.

38. Thomas B. Marquis, *A Warrior Who Fought Custer* (Minneapolis: The Midwest Co., 1931), 263.

39. "Indian Tells of Custer," undated, original newspaper clipping, MSS 57 Walter Mason Camp Papers, L. Tom Perry Special Collections, Harold B. Lee Library, Brigham Young University, Provo, Utah. Also summarized in Hardorff, *Custer Battle Casualties, II*, 188.

40. Marquis, 349, 360.

41. "Two Moons to See President Today," *The Washington Herald*, July 30, 1914, 10, accessed November 12, 2017, https://chroniclingamerica.loc.gov/lccn/sn83045433/1914–07-30/ed-1/seq-10/.

42. Two Moon's interviews, 1898, 1901 (two that year), 1907, and 1909, are reprinted by Richard G. Hardorff in *Cheyenne Memories of the Custer Fight*. In 1908, there is "Chief Two Moons' Story of the Fateful Day When Gen. Custer's Men Met Death," *Bismarck Daily Tribune*, January 26, 1908, 3. In 1913, three different interviews from March appear in *Indian Views of the Custer Fight*, by Hardorff. Again, in 1913, *The Vanishing Race: The Last Great Indian Council*, Joseph K. Dixon, gives another yet account by Two Moons (this version was reprinted in various newspapers).

43. "Canine Survivor of Custer's Last Battle is Buried Here," *Detroit Free Press*, May 29, 1910. 7.

44. Charles Windolph, "The Battle of the Little Bighorn as Related by Charles Windolph, Company H, Old Seventh Cavalry, U.S.A," *Saga of the Hills* (Hollywood, CA: Cosmo Press, 1940), 72.

45. Susan Orlean, *Rin Tin Tin: The Life and the Legend* (New York, Simon & Schuster, 2011, 28–29.

46. Hardorff, *Camp, Custer, and The Little Bighorn*, 93.

47. A. R. Stewart, "Stories of the Old West as Told and Painted by the Cow Puncher and Artist, Ed Borein," *The Craftsman*, October 1912, 50.

48. "Echoes of Custer's Last Fight," *Detroit Free Press*, November 10, 1912, 5.

49. W. M. Camp to E. S. Godfrey, May 19, 1920, LIBI-00019–03648. National Park Service, Little Bighorn Battlefield National Monument.

50. Milton Ronsheim, *The Life of General Custer* (Cadiz, OH: reprinted from the *Cadiz Republican*, 1929), loc. 1885, accessed on November 11, 2017, https://babel.hathitrust.org/cgi/pt?id=mdp.39015071171634;view=1up;seq=56

51. *Ibid.*

52. Ross, 40–41, 51.

53. C. B. D. W., "Tales of the Plains: III. Custer's Dog," *Forest and Stream*, December 14, 1907, 935.

54. C. B. D. W., "Tales of the Plains: I. My First Buffalo Tongue," *Forest and Stream*, November 23, 1907, 813.

55. *Ibid.*

56. Napoleon A. Comeau, "Custer's Dog," *Forest and Stream*, March 7, 1908, 377.

57. William F. Stifel, *The Dog Show: 125 Years of Westminster* (New York: The Westminster Kennel Club, 2001), 26.

58. "Racing Hounds Were Popular with Pioneers of Dodge City, Who Owned Numerous Fine and Famous Animals," *Dodge City Daily Globe*, February 24, 1921.

59. P. F. Fadden, "Dodge City a Dog Center," written for "Sports and Recreation" in *WPA American Guide, Dodge City, Kansas*, S-686, James "Dog" Kelly file," Kansas Heritage Center, Dodge City, Kansas.

60. "Racing Hounds Were Popular..."

61. Padraic Colum, ed., *A Treasury of Irish Folklore* (New York, Crown Publishers, 1967), 421.

62. W. F. Towers to EBC, September 24, 1921, LIBI-00019–03596. National Park Service, Little Bighorn Battlefield National Monument.

63. William F. Towers' service, pension, and burial records may be found at www.ancestry.com.

64. Gregory J.W. Urwin, *Custer Victorious: The Civil War Battles of General George Armstrong Custer* (Lincoln: University of Nebraska Press, 1990), 291–292.

65. Katz, D. Mark. *Custer in Photographs* (New York: Bonanza Books, 1990), xv.

66. Clark, 57.

67. John S. Gray, *Centennial Campaign: The Sioux War of 1876* (Norman: University of Oklahoma Press, 1988), 87.

68. James S. Hutchins, ed., *The Army and Navy Journal on the Battle of Little Bighorn and Related Matters, 1876–1881* (El Segundo, CA: Upton and Sons, 2003), 141.

69. "Search for Custer's Pet Hound Is Brought Back to Minneapolis," *Minneapolis Tribune*, March 24, 1923.

70. 11th Infantry Regiment (United States), Indian Wars Wikipedia entry, accessed on November 16, 2017, https://en.wikipedia.org/wiki/11th_Infantry_Regiment_(United_States).

71. Wagner, 123.

72. *Ibid.*, 57, 152.

73. *Ibid.*, 182.

74. *Ibid.*, 38.

75. *Ibid.*, xiii.

76. *Ibid.*, xii.

77. *Ibid.*, 116.

78. *Ibid.*, 65.

79. *Ibid.*, 132–137.

80. John Burkman to EBC, February 3, 1911, LIBI-00019–03655. National Park Service, Little Bighorn Battlefield National Monument.

81. General E. S. Godfrey to E. S. Paxson on the Battle of Little Bighorn, January 16, 1896. MS 007.01.04, George Armstrong Custer Collection, McCracken Research Library, Buffalo Bill Center of the West, accessed on November 17, 2017, http://cdm17097.contentdm.oclc.org/cdm/compoundobject/collection/MS007/id/52/rec/1.

Godfrey's letter was published in Albert J. Partoll's "After the Custer Battle," in *The Frontier and Midland*, vol. 19, no. 4 (1939), and the definitive note about Armstrong's dogs being left at the Powder River supply depot was cited in Edgar I. Stewart's excellent but often overlooked *Custer's Luck* (1955).
82. Leon V. Almirall, *Canines and Coyotes* (Caldwell, ID: The Caxton Printers, Ltd., 1976), 28.
83. Wagner, 119–120.
84. Gwyneth Anne Thayer, *Going to the Dogs: Greyhound Racing, Animal Activism, and American Popular Culture* (Lawrence: University Press of Kansas Press, 2013), 6–7.
85. "Personal Items," *Army and Navy Journal*, December 24, 1887.
86. Ann Marcaccini, ed., "Lion" (Mendota, MI: Friends of the Sibley Historic Site, 1997), 4–7.
87. *The Albion, A Journal of News, Politics, and Literature*, May 17, 1862.
88. "The Only True 7th Cavalry Dog."
89. *Ibid*.
90. Douglas D. Scott, Richard A. Fox, Jr., Melissa A. Connor and Dick Harmon, *Archeological Perspectives on the Battle of the Little Bighorn* (Norman: University of Oklahoma Press, 1989), 286.
91. Danny N. Walker, "Canid Remains from the Powder River Supply Depot, Prairie County, Montana (24PE231)," *Archeology in Montana*, vol. 36, no. 2 (1995), 63–64, 67.
92. Clark, 108.
93. Edgar I. Stewart, *Custer's Luck* (Norman: University of Oklahoma Press, 1985), vii.
94. "The Only True 7th Cavalry Dog."

Chapter 14

1. Brian W. Dippie, ed., *Nomad: George A. Custer in Turf, Field and Farm* (Austin & London: University of Texas Press, 1980), 166.
2. Lawrence A. Frost, *General Custer's Libbie* (Seattle: Superior Publishing Co., 1976), 270.
3. Fort Sully Sporting Club Record Book, 1871–1874, H23–001. South Dakota State Historical Society.
4. Dippie, 166.
5. *Ibid*.
6. "Mrs. Custer in Chicago," *New York Herald*, August 7, 1876, 3, accessed on December 13, 2017, available online: https://chroniclingamerica.loc.gov/lccn/sn83030313/1876-08-07/ed-1/seq-3/.
7. W. H. Emery to Elizabeth B. Custer, August 4, 1876. Brice C. W. Custer Collection.
8. "The Kennel," *Forest and Stream*, June 15, 1876, 302, accessed on December 6, 2017, https://archive.org/stream/Foreststream6#page/302/mode/2up.
9. *Forest and Stream*, February 8, 1877, 10, accessed on December 6, 2017, https://archive.org/stream/Foreststream8#page/10/mode/1up.
10. Frost, 237.
11. "Notes and Opinions," *The Times*, Philadelphia, July 25, 1876, 2.
12. "Custer and His Greyhound," *The Somerset Herald*, Pennsylvania, August 23, 1876, 1, accessed on December 15, 2017, https://chroniclingamerica.loc.gov/lccn/sn84026409/1876-08-23/ed-1/seq-1/.
13. "Custer's Widow Is Thrilled by Honor Paid Him," *New York Herald Tribune*, June 25, 1926.

14. "Canines Catalogued," *St. Louis Daily Globe-Democrat—Supplemental Sheet*, September 3, 1876, 11.
15. "Gossip About Town," *Minneapolis Tribune*, October 20, 1876, 4.
16. "Custer's Grey Hound," *Minneapolis Tribune*, November 16, 1877, 2.
17. "Local Matters," *Detroit Free Press*, August 28, 1879, 6.
18. "Of General Grant," *The Marion Star*, Ohio, December 7, 1895, 2.
19. John M. Carroll, *Custer in Texas: An Interrupted Narrative* (New York: Sol Lewis & Liveright, 1975), 202.
20. Jim Donovan, "The Man Who Martyred Custer: The Fascinating Frederick Whittaker," *Proceedings of the 22nd Annual Symposium of the Custer Battlefield Historical & Museum Assn.*, Hardin, MT (June 27, 2008); 43–45.
21. James S. Hutchins, ed., *The Army and Navy Journal on the Battle of Little Bighorn and Related Matters, 1876–1881* (El Segundo, CA: Upton and Sons, 2003), 85, 101, 103–104, 143.
22. Frost, 239.
23. Baron N. Schilling to EBC, March 25, 1877, Marguerite Merington Papers, New York Public Library, Manuscripts and Archives, Astor, Lenox, and Tilden Foundations.
24. "The Ducal Party," *New York Herald*, February 21, 1877, 7, accessed on December 23, 2017, https://chroniclingamerica.loc.gov/lccn/sn83030313/1877-02-21/ed-1/seq-7/.
25. *Forest and Stream*, February 8, 1877, 10, col. 3, accessed on December 12, 2017, https://archive.org/stream/Foreststream8#page/10/mode/1up.
26. William F. Stifel, *The Dog Show: 125 Years of Westminster* (NY: The Westminster Kennel Club, 2001), 22.
27. "The Bow-Wows," *Reading Times*, April 7, 1877, 4.
28. "Towser's Big Show," *New York Herald*, April 29, 1877, 9, accessed on December 13, 2017, https://chroniclingamerica.loc.gov/lccn/sn83030313/1877-04-29/ed-1/seq-9/.
29. *Catalogue of the First Annual New York Bench Show, 1877* (1st Westminster Kennel Club Show), 13, American Kennel Club Library, New York.
30. *Forest and Stream*, May 3, 1877, 198–199 and May 24, 1877, 246, 250, accessed on December 13, 2017, https://archive.org/stream/Foreststream8#page.
31. *Catalogue of the First Annual New York Bench Show, 1877*.
32. Hutchins, 71.
33. Frost, 240.
34. Hutchins, 149.
35. Marguerite Merington, ed., *The Custer Story: The Life and Intimate Letters of General George A. Custer and His Wife Elizabeth* (New York: The Devin-Adair Company, 1950), 237.
36. Frost, 255.
37. "The Kennel: Ann Arbor Bench Show," *Forest and Stream*, January 29, 1880, 1027, accessed on December 8, 2017, https://archive.org/stream/ForeststreamXIII#page/1027/mode/1up/.
38. Frost, 294.
39. James Mueller, "Taking a Humorous Stand: 19th Century Newspaper Jokes About Custer and the Little Big Horn," *Custer Battlefield Historical & Mu-*

seum Association, Inc. 23rd Annual Symposium Proceedings, Hardin MT (June 26, 2009): 26.

40. Brian W. Dippie, *Custer's Last Stand: The Anatomy of an American Myth* (Lincoln: University of Nebraska Press, 1994), 34.

41. *Ibid.*, 51.

42. William Edgar Paxson, Jr., *E. S. Paxson: Frontier Artist* (Boulder, Co: Pruett Publishing Co., 1984), 46–47.

43. Robert M. Utley, *Custer and the Great Controversy* (Pasadena, CA: Westernlore Press, 1980), 61.

44. Donald R. Morris, *The Washing of the Spears* (New York: Simon & Schuster, 1965), 419.

45. Frost, 310.

46. *Second Annual New York Bench Show Catalog, 1878* (2nd Westminster Kennel Club Show), 9, American Kennel Club Library, New York.

47. Column 3, *Newton Kansan*, May 23, 1878, 5.

48. "Dog Items in and Around Detroit," *Forest and Stream*, September 12, 1878, 111, accessed on December 13, 2017, https://archive.org/stream/Foreststream11#page/111/mode/1up/.

49. "Dogs at Auction," *Forest and Stream*, Oct. 17, 1878, 223, accessed on July 27, 2017, https://archive.org/stream/Foreststream11#page/223/mode/1up/.

50. "All the Dogs Gone Home," *New York Times*, April 13, 1879, accessed on December 10, 2017, http://query.nytimes.com/mem/archive-free/pdf?res=9F07E7D7123EE63BBC4B52DFB2668382669FDE.

51. "The New York Dog Show," *Forest and Stream*, April 15, 1880, 207, accessed on December 30, 2017, https://archive.org/stream/ForestreamXIV#page/207/mode/1up/search/Bradley.

52. Fort Sully Sporting Club Record Book, misc. inserts.

53. *Ibid.*

54. Theodore Roosevelt, *The Wilderness Hunter, Vol. II* (Philadelphia: Gebbie & Company, 1903), 160, accessed December 22, 2017, https://archive.org/details/wildernesshunter00roos.

55. Frost, GCL, 254.

56. Frost, GCL, 260.

57. Elizabeth B. Custer, *Following the Guidon* (New York: Harper & Brothers, 1890), 116, accessed December 22, 2017. http://hdl.handle.net/2027/cool.ark:/13960/t4kk9vn09.

58. Frost, *GCL*, 280.

59. Richard Upton, ed., *The Battle of the Little Bighorn & Custer's Last Fight: Remembered by the Participants at the Tenth Anniversary June 25, 1886 & the Fiftieth Anniversary June 25, 1926* (El Segundo, CA: Upton & Sons, 2007), 43, 49–50, 58, 71, 141, 165, 167.

60. "Buffalo Bill's Wild West," *The Brooklyn Daily Eagle*, August 15 1886, 13.

61. Frost, 261.

62. Leckie, 231.

63. Frost, 257.

64. Elizabeth B. Custer, *Tenting on the Plains or General Custer in Kansas and Texas* (New York: C.L. Webster & Co. 1887), 333, 387, 409, 451, 567, 573, accessed on December 22, 2017, http://hdl.handle.net/2027/loc.ark:/13960/t8nc6bj65.

65. EBC, *Following*, frontispiece.

66. "General Custer's Widow to Aid Literary Women," *Los Angeles Herald*, January 14, 1908, vol. 35, no. 194, 12.

67. Elizabeth B. Custer, Notes regarding "Dogs on the March," undated, LIBI-00019–3507. National Park Service, Little Bighorn Battlefield National Monument.

68. Elizabeth B. Custer, "Note Concerning Dogs and Taking Ticks from Their Ears," undated, LIBI-00019–5860, National Park Service, Little Bighorn Battlefield National Monument.

69. EBC, "Dogs on the March."

70. Jerome A. Greene, *American Carnage: Wounded Knee 1890* (University of Oklahoma Press, 2014), Appendix D.

71. "The Indian Question," *The St. Joseph Herald*, January 10, 1891, 4.

72. Wagner, 71.

73. EBC, *Tenting*, 251–252.

Epilogue

1. "The Clouded Ruins of Cardigan," *Minneapolis Morning Tribune*, March 27, 1923.

2. Elizabeth B. Custer, *Boots and Saddles* (New York: Harper & Brothers, 1885), 58–59, accessed on September 23, 2017, http://hdl.handle.net/2027/uc2.ark:/13960/t3fx77t65.

3. Beatrice Scheer Smith, *A Painted Herbarium: The Life and Art of Emily Hitchcock Terry, 1838–1921* (Minneapolis: University of Minnesota Press, 1992), 22.

4. *Ibid.*, 66.

5. Charles K. Reed and Chester A. Reed, *Guide to Taxidermy* [1908 facsimile edition] (New York: Skyhorse Publishing, 2012), 105–119.

6. The Rev. Edmund Ignatius Hogan, *The History of the Irish Wolf Dog* (Dublin, Ireland: Sealy, Bryers & Walker, 1897), 91, accessed on December 16, 2017, https://books.google.com/books?id=jBUxAQAAMAAJ&dq=%22The+Irish+Wolf+Dog%.

7. "Mounted Pelt of General Custer's Dog Sought Here," *Minneapolis Morning Tribune*, March 21, 1923.

8. James Willert, *To the Edge of Darkness: A Chronicle of the 1876 Indian War, General Gibbon's Montana Column and the Reno Scout, March 14–June 20, 1876* (El Segundo, CA: Upton and Sons, 1998). 182.

9. "Custer's Dog Was in Old Museum, Graduate Writes," *Minneapolis Morning Tribune*, March 22, 1923.

10. "Custer's Lost Hound Mystery Complicated by Three New Entries," *Minneapolis Morning Tribune*, March 23, 1923.

11. Tim Brady, *Gopher Gold: Legendary Figures, Brilliant Blunders, and Amazing Feats at the University of Minnesota* (St. Paul, MN: Minnesota Historical Society Press, 2007), 63.

12. "Search for Custer's Pet Hound Is Brought Back to Minneapolis," *Minneapolis Morning Tribune*, March 24, 1923.

13. "Photograph Strengthens City's Claim on Cardigan, Missing Custer Hound," *Minneapolis Morning Tribune*, March 25, 1923.

14. "The Clouded Ruins of Cardigan."

15. "Column 1," *The Minneapolis Star*, January 8 1973.

16. Paul L. Hedren, "On the Trail of Elusive Custeriana: Cardigan," *Research Review: The Journal of*

the Little Bighorn Associates, vol. VIII, no. 3 (Fall, 1974), 2–3.

17. Letter from Penelope Krosch, Archivist and Head of University Archives, University of Minnesota, to Stephen D. Youngkin, January 21, 1992.

Appendix

1. Bruce A. Rosenberg, "Custer: The Legend of the Martyred Hero in America," in *The Custer Reader*, ed. Paul Andrew Hutton (Lincoln, NE: University of Nebraska Press. 1992), 525.

2. Katz, D. Mark Katz, *Custer in Photographs* (New York: Bonanza Books, 1990), 47.

3. "General Custer and His Deerhounds" by Steve Tillotson, January 2013, *Irish Wolfhound Times*, accessed on February 1, 2018, http://www.irishwolfhoundtimes.com/custer.htm.

4. Poletes, George, *The Custer Drama* script (1959–1968), MSS 20601, Small Manuscripts Collection Ms. 21000, State Historical Society of North Dakota.

5. Michael Blake, *Marching to Valhalla: A Novel of Custer's Last Days* (New York: Villard Books, 1996), 148, 188, 221.

6. "Boston Writer Tells Mrs. Custer's View of Semi-Centennial," *The Billings Gazette*, June 25, 1926, 4.

7. John Phillip Langellier, *Custer: The Man, the Myth, the Movies* (Mechanicsburg, PA: Stackpole Books, 2000), 89–90.

8. Lawrence A. Frost, *General Custer's Libbie* (Seattle: Superior Publishing Co., 1976), 307.

9. Langellier, 89–94.

10. Adrienne L. McLean, ed., *Cinematic Canines: Dogs and Their Work in the Fiction Film* (New Brunswick, NJ: Rutgers University Press, 2014), 28, n. 13.

11. "Irish Wolfhound Standard of Excellence," Irish Wolfhound Club of America web page, accessed on February 4, 2018, https://www.iwclubofamerica.org/breed-standard.

12. Brian Patrick Duggan, "Custer and His Hounds," *Sighthound Review*, vol. 2, no. 2 (Summer 2011), 95.

13. "Production Design," *Into the West* DVD, Disc 4, 2005, Paramount Pictures.

14. Alexandra Horowitz, "The Dog at the Side of the Shot: Incongruous Dog (*Canis familiaris*) Behavior in Film," in *Cinematic Canines: Dogs and Their Work in the Fiction Film*, ed. Adrienne L. McLean, 230. New Brunswick, NJ: Rutgers University Press, 2014.

15. *Touche Pas à La Femme Blanche*, Internet Movie Database, accessed on March 10, 2018, http://www.imdb.com/title/tt0072305/?ref_=fn_al_tt_1.

16. "Peabody's Improbable History: George Armstrong Custer," *The Adventures of Rocky and Bullwinkle and Friends Complete Season 1*, DVD Show 14, Ward Productions, Inc., 2003, distributed by Classic Media Inc.

Bibliography

Books

Almirall, Leon V. *Canines and Coyotes.* Caldwell, ID: The Caxton Printers, Ltd., 1976.

American Kennel Club. *The New Complete Dog Book, 21st Edition.* Irvine, CA: Irvine, i-5 Publishing, LLC, 2015.

Anderson, Robert M. *A Reader's Guide to Custeriana: George Armstrong Custer, the Battle of the Little Bighorn and Other People, Places & Events of the Sioux-Cheyenne Indian Wars (1854–1890).* Parker, CO: privately published by Robert M. Anderson, third ed., 2015.

Ash, Edward C. *Dogs: Their History and Development.* London: Ernest Benn, Ltd., 1927.

Athern, Robert G. *Westward the Briton.* Lincoln: University of Nebraska Press, 1953.

Baker, William Henry. *A Dictionary of Men's Wear.* Cleveland, OH: William Henry Baker, 1908.

Barnard, F. A. *American Biographical History of Eminent and Self-Made Men, Michigan Volume 1.* Cincinnati, OH: Western Biographical Publishing Co., 1878.

Barnard, Sandy. *I Go with Custer: The Life and Death of Reporter Mark Kellogg.* Bismarck, ND: The Bismarck Tribune, 1996.

Barnard, Sandy, ed. *Ten Years with Custer: A 7th Cavalryman's Memoirs.* Terre Haute, IN: AST Press, 2001.

Barnum, Phineas T. *Funny Stories Told by Phineas T. Barnum.* New York: George Routledge and Sons, Ltd., 1890.

Barnum, P.T. *The Life of P. T. Barnum Written by Himself.* Buffalo, NY: The Courier Co., 1888.

Bartley, Oliver. *Hunting Dogs.* Columbus, OH: A. R. Harding, 1909.

Bates, Charles Francis. *Custer's Indian Battles.* New York: Bronxville, 1936.

Bauer, John E. *Dogs on the Frontier.* Fairfax, VA: Denlinger's Publishers, Ltd., second printing 1982.

Berkhofer, Robert T., Jr. *The White Man's Indian: Images of the American Indian from Columbus to the Present.* New York: Vintage Books/Random House, 1979.

Bourke, John G. *On the Border with Crook.* New York: Charles Scribner's Sons, 1892.

Boynton, Henry, W., ed. *The Complete Poetical Works of Alexander Pope.* Boston & New York: Houghton Mifflin, 1903.

Brady, Tim. *Gopher Gold: Legendary Figures, Brilliant Blunders, and Amazing Feats at the University of Minnesota.* St. Paul, MN: Minnesota Historical Society Press, 2007.

Brininstool, E. A. *Troopers with Custer: Historic Incidents of the Battle of the Little Big Horn.* Lincoln: University of Nebraska Press, Bison Books, 1989.

Broome, Jeff. *Custer into the West, with the Journal and Maps of Lieutenant Henry Jackson.* El Segundo, CA: Upton & Sons, Publishers, 2009.

Brown, Dee. *The Year of the Century: 1876.* New York: Charles Scribner's Sons, 1966.

Burkey, Rev. Blaine, *Custer Come at Once!* Hays, KS: Thomas More Prep, 1976

Carroll, John M. *Custer in Texas: An Interrupted Narrative.* New York: Sol Lewis & Liveright, 1975.

Carroll, John M. *Custer in the Civil War: His Unfinished Memoirs.* San Rafael, CA: Presidio Press, 1977.

Carroll, John M., and Lawrence A. Frost. *Private Theodore Ewert's Diary of the Black Hills Expedition of 1874.* Piscataway, NJ: CRI Books, 1976.

Chadwick, Winifred E. *The Borzoi Handbook.* London, Nicholson & Watson, 1952.

Chambers, Lee. *Fort Abraham Lincoln Dakota Territory.* Atglen, PA: Schiffer Publishing, Ltd., 2008.

Chavchavadze, David. *The Grand Dukes.* New York: Atlantic International Publications, 1990.

Chorne, Laudie J. *Following the Custer Trail of 1876.* Bismarck, ND: Printing Plus, 1997.

Chun, Clayton K.S. *U.S. Army in the Plains Indian Wars 1865–91.* Oxford, UK: Osprey Publishing, 2004.

Clark, Gerald R. *Supplying Custer: The Powder River Supply Depot, 1876.* Salt Lake City: University of Utah Press, 2014.

Clarke, Daniel. *Lieutenant Henry H. Young: Sheridan's Chief of Scouts.* Amazon Digital Services, LLC, Daniel Clarke Publisher, 2012.

Cody, William F. *The Life of Hon. William F. Cody Known as Buffalo Bill.* New York: Indian Head Books, 1991.

Colum, Padraic, ed. *A Treasury of Irish Folklore.* New York: Crown Publishers, 1967.

Connell, Evan S. *Son of the Morning Star*. New York: Promontory Press, 1993.

Custer, Elizabeth B. *Boots and Saddles*. New York: Harper & Brothers, 1885.

Custer, Elizabeth B. *Following the Guidon*. New York: Harper & Brothers, 1890.

Custer, Elizabeth B. *Tenting on the Plains or General Custer in Kansas and Texas*. New York: C.L. Webster & Co. 1887.

Custer, Gen. G. A. *My Life on the Plains or, Personal Experiences with Indians*. New York: Sheldon & Co., 1876.

Danker, Donald F., ed. *Man of the Plains: Recollections of Luther North 1856–1882*. Lincoln, NE: University of Nebraska Press, 1961.

Darling, Roger. *Custer's Seventh Cavalry Comes to Dakota*. El Segundo, CA: Upton & Sons, 1989.

Davies, Henry E. (Paul Andrew Hutton, ed.). *Ten Days on the Plains*. Dallas, TX: Southern Methodist University Press, 1985.

Day, Carl F. *Tom Custer: Ride to Glory*. Norman: University of Oklahoma Press, 2005.

Dennis-Bryan, Kim & Juliet Clutton-Brock. *Dogs of the Last Hundred Years at the British Museum (Natural History)*. London: The British Museum, 1988.

Dippie, Brian W. *Custer's Last Stand: The Anatomy of an American Myth*. Lincoln: University of Nebraska Press, 1994.

Dippie, Brian W., ed. *Nomad: George A. Custer in Turf, Field and Farm*. Austin & London: University of Texas Press, 1980.

Dodge, Richard Irving. *Plains of the Great West and Their Inhabitants*. New York: Archer House, 1959.

Donovan, James. *A Terrible Glory: Custer and the Little Bighorn, the Last Great Battle of the American West*. New York & Boston: Back Bay Books/Little, Brown and Co., 2009.

Donovan, Jim. *Custer and the Little Bighorn: The Man, The Mystery, the Myth*. New York, Crestline, 2001.

Dorland, W. A. Newman. *The American Illustrated Medical Dictionary*. Philadelphia: W. B. Saunders Co., 1927, 14th ed.

Duggan, Brian Patrick. *Saluki: The Desert Hound and the English Travelers Who Brought It to the West*. Jefferson, NC: McFarland, 2009.

Dustin, Fred. *The Custer Tragedy*. Ann Arbor, MI: Edwards Brothers, Inc., 1939

Eales, Anne Bruner. *Army Wives on the American Frontier: Living by the Bugles*. Boulder, CO: Johnson Books, 1996.

Ensminger, John J. *Police and Military Dogs: Criminal Detection, Forensic Evidence, and Judicial Admissibility*. Boca Raton, LA: CRC Press/Taylor & Francis Group, 2012.

Farrow, Lee A. *Alexis in America: A Russian Grand Duke's Tour, 1871–1872*. Baton Rouge: Louisiana State University Press, 2014.

Field, Ron. *Forts of the American Frontier, 1820–91: Central and Northern Plains*. Oxford, UK: Osprey Publishing Ltd., 2008.

Field, Ron. *U. S. Army Frontier Scouts 1840–1921*. Oxford, UK: Osprey Publishing, 2003.

Fougera, Katherine Gibson. *With Custer's Cavalry*. Caldwell, ID: The Caxton Printers Ltd., 1942.

Frazer, Robert W. *Forts of the West*. Norman: University of Oklahoma Press, 1965.

Frost, Lawrence A. *The Court Martial of General George Armstrong Custer*. Norman: University of Oklahoma Press, 1987.

Frost, Lawrence A. *The Custer Album: A Pictorial Biography of General George A. Custer*. New York: Bonanza Books, 1984.

Frost, Lawrence A. *Custer's 7th Cav and the Campaign of 1873*. El Segundo, CA: Upton & Sons, 1986.

Frost, Lawrence A. *General Custer's Libbie*. Seattle: Superior Publishing Co., 1976.

Frost, Lawrence A. *General Custer's Thoroughbreds*. Mattituck, NY: J. M. Carroll & Co., 1986.

Frost, Lawrence A. *Some Observations on the Yellowstone Expedition of 1873*. Glendale, CA: Arthur H. Clarke Company, 1981.

Frost, Lawrence A. *With Custer in '74: James Calhoun's Diary of the Black Hills Expedition*. Provo, UT: Brigham Young University Press, 1979.

Garrison, Webb. *Civil War Curiosities: Strange Stories, Oddities, Events, and Coincidences*. Nashville, TN: Rutledge Hill Press, 1994.

Godfrey, Edward Settle. *The Field Diary of Lt. Edward Settle Godfrey*. Portland: Champoeg Press, 1957.

Goodwin, Doris Kearns. *Team of Rivals: The Political Genius of Abraham Lincoln*. New York: Simon & Schuster, 2005.

Gray, John S. *Centennial Campaign: The Sioux War of 1876*. Norman: University of Oklahoma Press, 1988.

Greatorex, Eliza. *Old New York, from the Bowery to Bloomingdale*. New York: G.P. Putnam's Sons, 1875.

Greene, Jerome A. *American Carnage: Wounded Knee 1890*. Norman: University of Oklahoma Press, 2014.

Greene, Jerome A. *Washita: The U.S. Army and the Southern Cheyennes, 1867–1869*. Norman: University of Oklahoma Press, 2004 (paperback ed. 2008).

Hammer, Kenneth, ed. *Custer in '76: Walter Camp's Notes on the Custer Fight*. Norman: University of Oklahoma Press, 1990.

Hancock, David. *Sighthounds: Their Form, Their Function, and Their Future*. Ramsbury, Wiltshire, U. K.: The Crowood Press, 2012.

Hanson, Joseph Mills. *The Conquest of the Missouri: Being the Story of the Life and Exploits of Captain Grant Marsh*. Chicago: A. C. McClurg & Co., 1916.

Harburn, Todd E., ed. *A Surgeon with Custer at the Little Big Horn: James DeWolf's Diary and Letters 1876*. Norman: University of Oklahoma Press, 2017.

Hardorff, Richard G. *Camp, Custer and The Little Bighorn: A Collection of Walter Mason Camp's Research Papers on General George A. Custer's Last Fight.* El Segundo, CA: Upton and Sons, 1997.

Hardorff, Richard G. *Cheyenne Memories of the Custer Fight: A Source Book.* Spokane, WA: Arthur H. Clark Co., 1995.

Hardorff, Richard G. *The Custer Battle Casualties: Burials, Exhumations, and Reinternments.* El Segundo, CA: Upton and Sons, 1991.

Hardorff, Richard G. *The Custer Battle Casualties II: The Dead, The Missing, and a Few Survivors.* El Segundo, CA: Upton and Sons, 1999.

Hardorff, Richard G. *Lakota Recollections of the Custer Fight.* Spokane, WA: Arthur H. Clark Co., 1991.

Hardorff, Richard G. *Washita Memories: Eyewitness Views of Custer's Attack on Black Kettle's Village.* Norman: University of Oklahoma Press, 2006 (paperback 2008).

Hardorff, Richard G., ed. *Walter M. Camp's Little Bighorn Rosters.* Spokane, WA: Arthur H. Clark Co., 2002.

Hart, Herbert M. *Old Forts of the Far West.* Seattle: Superior Publishing Co., 1965.

Hart, Herbert M. *Old Forts of the Northwest.* New York: Bonanza Books, 1963.

Hart, Herbert M. *Old Forts of the Southwest.* New York: Bonanza Books, 1964.

Hartley, A. N. *The Deerhound.* Leeds, U.K.: The Moxon Press, Ltd., 1986.

Hedren, Paul L. *Powder River: Disastrous Opening of the Great Sioux War.* Norman: University of Oklahoma Press, 2016.

Hedren, Paul L. *Traveler's Guide to the Great Sioux War.* Helena, MT: Montana Society Historical Press, 1996.

Hedren, Paul L. *With Crook in the Black Hills: Stanley J. Morrow's 1876 Photographic Essay.* Boulder, CO: Pruett Publishing Co., 1985.

Heier, Vincent, A. *Little Bighorn* (Postcard History Series). Charleston, SC: Arcadia Publishing 2009.

Herr, John K. and Edward S. Wallace. *The Story of the U. S. Cavalry 1775–1942.* New York: Bonanza Books, 1984.

Hogan, Rev. Edmund Ignatius. *The History of the Irish Wolf Dog.* Dublin: Sealy, Bryers & Walker, 1897.

Hoig, Stan. *The Battle of Washita: The Sheridan-Custer Indian Campaign of 1867–69.* Lincoln: University of Nebraska Press, 1976, First Bison Book printing 1979.

Hook, Jason. *The American Plains Indians.* London: Osprey Publishing, 1985.

Horowitz, Alexandra. "The Dog at the Side of the Shot: Incongruous Dog (*Canis familiaris*) Behavior in Film," in *Cinematic Canines: Dogs and Their Work in the Fiction Film,* ed. Adrienne L. McLean, 219–234. New Brunswick, NJ: Rutgers University Press, 2014.

Hunt, Frazier, and Hunt, Robert. *I Fought with Custer: The Story of Sergeant Windolph.* New York: Charles Scribner's Sons, 1953.

Hunter, Robbins. *The Judge Rode a Sorrel Horse.* New York, E. P. Dutton, 1950.

Hutchins, James S., ed. *The Army and Navy Journal on the Battle of Little Bighorn and Related Matters, 1876–1881.* El Segundo, CA: Upton and Sons, 2003.

Hutchinson, Walter, ed. *Hutchinson's Dog Encyclopædia,* London: Walter Hutchinson, 1935.

Hutton, Paul Andrew. *Phil Sheridan & His Army.* Norman. OK: University of Oklahoma Press, 1999.

Hutton, Paul Andrew, ed. *The Custer Reader.* Lincoln: University of Nebraska Press, 1992.

Inman, Col. Henry. *Tails of the Trail.* Topeka. KS: Crane & Co., Publishers, 1898.

Innis, Ben, and Richard E. Collin, ed. *Bloody Knife: Custer's Favorite Scout.* Bismarck, ND: Smokey Water Press, 1994.

Jensen, Richard E., ed. *Voices of the American West, Volume 2: The Settler and Soldier Interviews of Eli S. Ricker, 1903–1919.* Lincoln: University of Nebraska Press, 2005.

Jesse, Edward. *Anecdotes of Dogs.* London: Bell & Daldy, 1870.

Katcher, Philip. *The American Indian Wars 1860–1890.* London: Osprey Publishing, 1977.

Katz, D. Mark. *Custer in Photographs.* New York: Bonanza Books, 1990.

Kimmel, Jay. *Custer, Cody & the Last Indian Wars: A Pictorial History.* Portland, OR: Cory/Stevens Publishing, 1994.

Kleiser, Grenville, ed. *Dictionary of Proverbs.* New Delhi: APH Publishing, 2005.

Knight, Oliver. *Life and Manners in the Frontier Army.* Norman: University of Oklahoma Press, 1993.

Kraft, Louis. *Custer and the Cheyenne: George Armstrong Custer's Winter Campaign on the Southern Plains.* El Segundo, CA: Upton & Sons, Publishers, 1995.

Krause, Herbert, and Gary D. Olson. *Prelude to Glory: A Newspaper Accounting of Custer's 1874 Expedition to the Black Hills.* Sioux Falls, SD: Brevet Press, 1974.

Langellier, John P., Kurt Hamilton Cox, and Brian C. Pohanka, eds. *Myles Keogh: The Life and Legend of an "Irish Dragoon" in the Seventh Cavalry.* El Segundo, CA: Upton and Sons, 1998.

Langellier, John Phillip. *Custer: The Man, the Myth, the Movies.* Mechanicsburg, PA: Stackpole Books, 2000.

Lawrence, Elizabeth Atwood. *His Very Silence Speaks: Comanche—The Horse Who Survived Custer's Last Stand.* Detroit, MI: Wayne State University Press, 1989.

Leckie, Shirley A. *Elizabeth Bacon Custer and the Making of a Myth.* Norman: University of Oklahoma Press, 1993.

Leckie, Shirley A., ed. *The Colonel's Lady on the*

Frontier: The Correspondence of Alice Kirk Grierson. Lincoln: University of Nebraska Press, 1989.

Leedham, Charles. *Bailey's Monthly Magazine of Sports and Pastimes,* London: A.H. Bailey & Co., vol. 25, no. 169, March 1874.

Leeds Castle Foundation. *Four Centuries of Dog Collars at Leeds Castle.* London: Philip Wilson Publishers, 1979.

Leighton, Robert. *The New Book of the Dog.* London & New York: Cassell, 1907.

Leslie, Anita. *Mr. Frewen of England.* London: Hutchinson & Co. 1966.

Loggins, Vernon. *Two Romantics and Their Ideal Life.* New York: The Odyssey Press, 1946.

Lothrop, Charles H. *A History of the First Iowa Cavalry Veteran Volunteers.* Lyons, IA: Beers & Eaton, 1890.

Lubetkin, M. John. *Jay Cooke's Gamble: The Northern Pacific Railroad, the Sioux, and the Panic of 1873.* Norman: University of Oklahoma Press, 2006.

Magnussen, Daniel O., ed. *Peter Thompson's Narrative of the Little Bighorn Campaign 1876: A Critical Analysis of an Eyewitness Account of the Custer Debacle.* Glendale, CA: Arthur H. Clark Co., 1974.

Mahon, John K. *History of the Second Seminole War, 1835–1842.* Gainesville: University of Florida Press, 1992.

Marquis, Thomas B. *A Warrior Who Fought Custer.* Minneapolis, MN: The Midwest Co., 1931.

Mattes, Merrill J. *Indians, Infants, and Infantry: Andrew and Elizabeth Burt on the Frontier.* Lincoln: University of Nebraska Press, Bison Books, 1988.

McChristian, Douglas C. *Regular Army O! Soldiering on the Western Frontier 1865–1891.* Norman: University of Oklahoma Press, 2017.

Meline, James F. *Two Thousand Miles on Horseback: Santa Fé and Back.* New York: Hurd and Houghton, 1867.

Merington, Marguerite, ed. *The Custer Story: The Life and Intimate Letters of General George A. Custer and His Wife Elizabeth.* New York: The Devin-Adair Company, 1950.

Merritt, John I. *Baronets and Buffalo: The British Sportsman in the American West 1833–1881.* Missoula, MT: Mountain Press Publishing Co., 1985

Miles, Nelson A. *Personal Recollections and Observations of General Nelson A. Miles.* Chicago & New York: The Werner Co., 1896.

Miller, Constance O. *Gazehounds: The Search for Truth.* Wheat Ridge, CO: Hoflin Publishing Ltd., 1988.

Milner, Joe E. *California Joe: Noted Scout and Indian Fighter.* Lincoln: University of Nebraska Press, 1987.

Monaghan, Jay. *Custer: The Life of General George Armstrong Custer.* Lincoln: University of Nebraska Press/Bison Books, 1971.

Morris, Donald R. *The Washing of the Spears.* New York: Simon & Schuster, 1965.

Nevin, David. *The Civil War: Sherman's March: Atlanta to the Sea.* Alexandria, VA: Time-Life Books, 1986.

Nye, Elwood L. *Marching with Custer.* Glendale, CA: Arthur H. Clark Co., 1964.

Nye, W. S. *Carbine & Lance: The Story of Old Fort Sill.* Norman: University of Oklahoma Press, 1962.

O'Neil, Tom. *Cadet George Armstrong Custer: Demerits & Academics.* Brooklyn, NY: Arrow and Trooper, 1992.

Orlean, Susan. *Rin Tin Tin: The Life and the Legend.* New York: Simon & Schuster, 2011.

Pagnamenta, Peter. *Prairie Fever: British Aristocrats in the American West 1830–1890.* New York & London: W. W. Norton & Co., 2012.

Parker, James. *The Old Army Memories 1872–1918.* Philadelphia: Dorrance & Company, 1929.

Paxson, William Edgar, Jr. *E. S. Paxson: Frontier Artist.* Boulder, Co: Pruett Publishing Co., 1984.

Pengra, Lilah. *Corporals, Cooks, and Cowboys: African Americans in the Black Hills.* Buffalo Gap, SD: Lune House Publishing, 2006.

Perry, Matthew Calbraith, and Francis L. Hawks. *Narrative of the Expedition of an American Squadron to the China Seas and Japan.* New York: D. Appleton & Co., 1857.

Pohanka, Brian C., ed. *A Summer on the Plains with Custer's 7th Cavalry: The 1870 Diary of Annie Gibson Roberts.* Lynchburg, VA: Schroeder Publications, 2004.

Pratt, A. Llewelyn, ed. *Our Friend the Dog in Verse.* London: The Guide Dogs for the Blind Assn., 1946.

Price, Rose Lambart. *A Summer on the Rockies.* London: Sampson Low, Marston & Co., 1898.

Price, S. Goodale, *Saga of the Hills.* Hollywood, CA: Cosmo Press, 1940.

Pride, W. F. *The History of Fort Riley.* Fort Riley, KS: U. S. Cavalry Museum and Fort Riley Historical and Archeological Society, 1926 (reprint 1987).

Prucha, Francis Paul. *A Guide to the Military Posts of the United States 1789–1895.* Madison, WI: The State Historical Society of Wisconsin, 1964.

Reed, Charles K., and Chester A. *Guide to Taxidermy* (1908 facsimile edition). New York: Skyhorse Publishing, 2012.

Reedstrom, Ernest L. *Bugles, Banners, and War Bonnets: A Study of George Armstrong Custer's Seventh Cavalry from Fort Riley to Little Bighorn.* New York: Bonanza Books, 1986.

Reynolds, Arlene. *The Civil War Memories of Elizabeth Bacon Custer.* Austin: University of Texas Press, 1994.

Rickey, Don, Jr. *Forty Miles a Day on Beans and Hay.* Norman: University of Oklahoma Press, 1963.

Roe, Francis M. A. *Army Letters from an Officer's Wife 1871–1888.* Lincoln, NE, New York & London: D. Appleton & Co., 1909.

Ronsheim, Milton. *The Life of General Custer.* Cadiz, OH: reprinted from the *Cadiz Republican*, 1929.

Roosevelt, Theodore. *The Wilderness Hunter, Vol. II.* Philadelphia: Gebbie & Company, 1903.

Roosevelt, Theodore, and George Bird Grinnell. *Hunting in Many Lands: The Book of the Boone and Crockett Club.* New York: Forest and Stream Publishing Co., 1895.

Rosenberg, Bruce A. "Custer: The Legend of the Martyred Hero in America," in *The Custer Reader*, ed. Paul Andrew Hutton, 525–547. Lincoln: University of Nebraska Press, 1992.

Ross, Rickard, A. *First to Arrive on Custer's Battlefield with the Montana Column: Frederick E. Server, Montana Pioneer, Soldier, and Explorer.* El Segundo, CA: Upton and Sons, 2010.

Samaha, Joel. *The New Complete Irish Wolfhound.* New York: Howell Book House. 1991.

Saxon, A. H., ed. *Selected Letters of P. T. Barnum.* New York: Columbia Press, 1983.

Schneider, James V. and Richard Campbell. *Behind Custer at the Little Big Horn: The Story of Lieutenant Edward Mathey and the Packtrain.* Fort Wayne, IN: privately published, 1980.

Scott, Douglas D. *Archeological Perspectives on the Battle of the Little Bighorn.* Norman: University of Oklahoma Press, 2000.

Scott, Douglas D., Peter Bleed, and Stephen Damm. *Custer, Cody, and Grand Duke Alexis: Historical Archeology of the Royal Buffalo Hunt.* Norman: University of Oklahoma Press, 2013.

Scott, Douglas D., Richard A. Fox, Jr., Melissa A. Connor and Dick Harmon. *Archeological Perspectives on the Battle of the Little Bighorn.* Norman: University of Oklahoma Press, 1989.

Scrope, William. *The Art of Deer-Stalking.* London: John Murray, 1839.

Seguin, Marilyn W. *Dogs of War and Stories of Other Beasts of Battle in the Civil War.* Boston: Branden Publishing Co., 1998.

Sheridan, Philip. *Personal Memoirs of P. H. Sheridan, General United States Army*, Vol. II. New York: Charles L. Webster & Co., 1888.

Shields, G. O. (Coquina). *Hunting in the Great West.* Chicago: Donohue, Henneberry & Co., 1883.

Shields, George O. *The American Book of the Dog.* Chicago: Rand, McNally, 1891.

Shillingberg, William B. *Dodge City: The Early Years, 1872–1886.* Norman: Arthur H. Clark Co., 2009.

Smith, Beatrice Scheer. *A Painted Herbarium: The Life and Art of Emily Hitchcock Terry, 1838–1921.* Minneapolis: University of Minnesota Press, 1992.

Smith, Sherry L. *The View from the Officer's Row: Army Perceptions of Western Indians.* Tucson: University of Arizona Press, 1995.

Snyder, A.B. *Pinnacle Jake.* Lincoln: University of Nebraska Press, 1951.

Stands in Timber, John, and Margot Liberty. *Cheyenne Memories.* New Haven, CT: Yale University Press, 1998.

Steffen, Randy. *The Horse Soldier 1776–1943, vol. II The Frontier, the Mexican War, the Civil War, the Indian Wars 1851–1880.* Norman: University of Oklahoma Press, 1978.

Stewart, Edgar I. *Custer's Luck.* Norman: University of Oklahoma Press, 1985.

Stifel, William F. *The Dog Show: 125 Years of Westminster.* New York: The Westminster Kennel Club, 2001.

Stiles, T. J. *Custer's Trials: A Life on the Frontier of New America.* New York: Alfred A. Knopf, 2015.

Streever, Fred. *The American Trail Hound.* New York: A. S. Barnes & Co., 1948.

Styple, William B. ed. *Generals in Bronze: Interviewing the Commanders of the Civil War.* Kearny, NJ: Belle Grove Publishing Co., 2005.

Thayer, Gwyneth Anne. *Going to the Dogs: Greyhound Racing, Animal Activism, and American Popular Culture.* Lawrence: University Press of Kansas Press, 2013.

Tucker, Philip Thomas, *Exodus from the Alamo: The Anatomy of the Last Stand Myth.* Philadelphia: Casemate Publishers, 2010.

Upton, Richard, ed. *The Battle of the Little Bighorn & Custer's Last Fight: Remembered by the Participants at the Tenth Anniversary June 25, 1886 & the Fiftieth Anniversary June 25, 1926.* El Segundo, CA: Upton & Sons, 2007.

Urwin, Gregory J.W. *Custer Victorious: The Civil War Battles of General George Armstrong Custer.* Lincoln: University of Nebraska Press, 1990.

Utley, Robert M. *Cavalier in Buckskin: George Armstrong Custer and the Western Military Frontier.* Norman: University of Oklahoma Press, 1988.

Utley, Robert M. *Custer and the Great Controversy.* Pasadena, CA: Westernlore Press, 1980.

Utley, Robert M. *Frontier Regulars: The United States Army and the Indian, 1866–1891.* Lincoln: University of Nebraska Press, Bison Books, 1984.

Utley, Robert M., ed. *Life in Custer's Cavalry: Diaries and Letters of Albert and Jennie Barnitz, 1867–1868.* Lincoln, NE & London: University of Nebraska Press, 1987.

Van de Water, Frederic F. *Glory Hunter: A Life of General Custer.* Lincoln: University of Nebraska Press, 1988.

Wade, William V. *Paha Sapa Tawoyyake.* Mandan, ND: Crescent Printing Co., 1965.

Wagner, Glendolin Damon. *Old Neutriment.* Lincoln: University of Nebraska Press, 1989.
Wallace, Charles B. *Custer's Ohio Boyhood.* Cadiz, OH: Harrison County Historical Society, 1987.
Wallace, Irving. *The Fabulous Showman: The Life and Times of P.T. Barnum.* New York: Alfred A. Knopf, 1959.
Ware, Eugene F. *The Indian War of 1864.* New York: St. Martin's Press, 1960.
Wert, Jeffry D. *Custer: The Controversial Life of George Armstrong Custer.* New York: Touchstone, 1997.
Whittaker, Frederick. *A Popular Life of Gen. George A. Custer.* New York: Sheldon & Co., 1876.
Wilke's Spirit of the Times and the New York Sportsman, Vol. 9–11, Vol. 11, No. 15, December 10 1864.
Willert, James. *Little Big Horn Diary: Chronicle of the 1876 Indian War.* La Mirada, CA: James Willert, Publisher, 1977.
Willert, James. *To the Edge of Darkness: A Chronicle of the 1876 Indian War, General Gibbon's Montana Column and the Reno Scout, March 14-June 20, 1876.* El Segundo, CA: Upton and Sons, 1998.
Windolph, Charles. "The Battle of the Little Bighorn as Related by Charles Windolph, Company H, Old Seventh Cavalry, U. S. A." In *Saga of the Hills,* ed. S. Goodale Price, Hollywood, CA: Cosmo Press, 1940.
Woodham-Smith, Cecil. *The Reason Why.* New York: McGraw-Hill Book Co., Inc., 1954.
Young, Frederic R. *The Delectable Burg: An Irreverent History of Dodge City—1872 to 1886.* Dodge City, KS: Frederic R. Young & the Kansas Heritage Center, 2009.
Young, Frederic R. *Dodge City Up Through a Century in Story and Pictures.* Dodge City, KS: Boot Hill Museum, 1972.
Zucchero, Michael. *Loyal Hearts: Histories of American Civil War Canines.* Lynchburg, VA: Schroeder Publications, 2010.

Archives

Billings Public Library, Billings, MT, Montana Room, Custer File and Scrapbooks
Boot Hill Museum, Dodge City, KS
Brigham Young University, Harold B. Lee Library, L. Tom Perry Special Collections, Walter Mason Camp Papers
Buffalo Bill Center of the West, McCracken Research Library, Cody, WY
California State University, Fresno, Henry Madden Library
Detroit Public Library, Burton Historical Collection, George Custer Papers
Harvard University, MA, University Archives & the Houghton Library, Theodore Roosevelt Collection
Kansas Historical Society, Topeka
Library of Congress, Washington DC
Little Bighorn Battlefield National Monument, MT, Elizabeth Bacon Custer Collection
Monroe County Historical Museum, MI
Monroe County Library System, Monroe, MI, Lawrence A. Frost Collection of Custeriana
New York Public Library, Manuscripts and Archives Division, Marguerite Merington Papers & Francis R. Hagner Collection
Smithsonian Institution, National Portrait Gallery, Washington, DC
South Dakota State Historical Society, Pierre, SD
State Historical Society of North Dakota, Heritage Center, Small Manuscripts Collection, Bismarck, ND
Thomas Gilcrease Institute of American History and Art, Tulsa, OK
United States Center of Military History, Carlisle, PA, Jacob Lyman Greene Papers
United States Military Academy, West Point, Museum & Library
University of California, Davis, Shields Library, Special Collections
University of Minnesota, Twin Cities, University Archives & the Bell Museum
Yale University, Beinecke Rare Book and Manuscript Library: Western Americana Collection, George Armstrong Custer Papers & Elizabeth Bacon Custer Papers

Periodicals/Journals

Anonymous, "Henry Munson Utley." *Library Journal* 42, no. 1 (January–December 1917): 190, accessed January 24, 2018, https://archive.org/details/libraryjournal11assogoog.
Boldareff, Artein. "The Colour of the Borzoi." *Country Life Magazine,* May 1, 1897, 460.
Bowlegs, Billy. "Coursing in the Good Old Days." *Outdoor Life,* Vol. LII, No. 2, Aug 1923, 93–98.
Cozzens, Peter. "Grant's Uncivil War." *Smithsonian Magazine,* November 2016, vol. 47, no. 7, 59.
Crackel, Theodore J. "Custer's Kentucky: General George Armstrong Custer and Elizabethtown, Kentucky, 1871–1873." *The Filson Club Quarterly,* vol. 48, no. 2 (April 1974), 144–155.
Duggan, Brian Patrick. "America's First National Dog Show." *AKC Family Dog,* January/February 2016, 34–37.
Duggan, Brian Patrick. "Army Hounds." *Sighthound Review,* vol. 3 no. 2, Summer/Fall 2012, 43–49.
Duggan, Brian Patrick. "Of Coursing Hounds and Cowboys." *AKC Family Dog,* November/December 2013, 34–37.
Duggan, Brian Patrick. "The P.T. Barnum–Custer Dog Deal & Little Big Horn," The Brian C. Pohanka 31st Annual Symposium, Custer Battlefield Historical & Museum, Assn., Hardin, MT (June 23 2017): 22–32.
Ensminger, John. "Dogs in the Economy and Operation of the Peculiar Institution: Evidence

from Slave State Case Law." February 23 2012, posted on *Dog Law Reporter: Reflections on the Society of Dogs and Men,* accessed on October 21 2017, http://doglawreporter.blogspot.com/2012/02/dogs-in-economy-and-operation-of.html.

Gibson, Kelly. "A Short History of Military Tattoos." *VFW: Veterans of Foreign Wars,* Aug 2016, 42–44, 46, 48.

Godfrey, E.S. "Custer's Last Battle." *The Century Magazine,* January 1892, 358–384.

Godfrey, E.S. "Some Reminiscences, Including the Washita Battle." *The Cavalry Journal,* vol. XXXVII, no. 153 (October 1928), 481–500.

Hedren, Paul L. "On the Trail of Elusive Custeriana: Cardigan." *Research Review: The Journal of the Little Big Horn Associates,* vol. VIII, no. 3 (Fall, 1974), 2–3.

Hill, Michael D., and Ben Inis, eds. "The Fort Buford Diary of Private Sanford, 1876–1877." *North Dakota History,* 52 (Summer 1985), 2–40.

Hills, Louis E. "With Gen. G. A. Custer on the Northern Pacific Surveying Expedition of 1873." *Journal of History.* Lamoni, IA: Board of Publication of the Reorganized Church of Jesus Christ of Latter-Day Saints, vol. 8, no. 2. (Apr 1915), 143–160.

Howe, George Frederick, ed. "Expedition to the Yellowstone River in 1873: Letters of a Young Cavalry Officer." *The Mississippi Valley Historical Review: Journal of American History,* vol. XXXIX, no. 3 (December 1952), 519–534.

Kush, George. "An Old Trooper's Tail." *Western Horseman,* May 2000.

Langley, Lorne. "A Brevet or a Coffin for Doing All You Can." *Research Review, The Journal of the Little Bighorn Associates,* vol. 30 (2016), 14–23.

Lawrence, Dr. Elizabeth A. "The Desperate Last Message: Another Custer Enigma." *Research Review: The Journal of the Little Big Horn Associates,* vol. 28, no. 2 (2014), 27–28.

Lindstedt, Stan L., James F. Hokanson, Dominic J. Wells, Steven D. Swain, Hans Hoppeler, and Vilma Navarro. "Running Energetics in the Pronghorn Antelope." *Nature* 353, no. 6346 (October 24, 1991), 748–750.

Maher, Kathleen. "P.T. Barnum (1810–1891)—The Man, the Myth, the Legend." Published by *The Barnum Museum,* accessed on October 21, 2017, http://www.barnum-museum.org/manmythlegend.htm.

Mays, Carelton. "The Romping Custers." *Real West,* Feb 1959, 29.

McMurtry, R. Gerald. "The Two-Year Residence of General George A. Custer in Elizabethtown." *Kentucky Progress Magazine,* vol. V, no. 4 (Summer 1933), 32–33, 49–50.

Millbrook, Minnie Dubbs. "Rebecca Visits Kansas and the Custers." *Kansas History,* Vol. 42, No. 2 (Winter 1976), 366–402. accessed on September 21, 2017, http://www.kshs.org/p/rebecca-visits-kansas-and-the-custers/13262

Minnie Dubbs Millbrook. "Mrs. General Custer at Fort Riley, 1866." *Kansas Historical Quarterly,* Kansas Historical Society, vol. 40, no. 1 (Spring 1974), 63–71.

Mueller, James. "Taking a Humorous Stand: 19th Century Newspaper Jokes About Custer and the Little Big Horn." *Custer Battlefield Historical & Museum Association, Inc., 23rd Annual Symposium Proceedings,* Hardin, MT (June 26 2009), 25–36.

Potter, James E. "Firearms Accidents in the Frontier Army, 1806–1891." *Nebraska History,* vol. 78 (Winter 1997), 175–185.

Potter, James E. "The Great Source of Amusement: Hunting in the Frontier Army." *Montana: The Magazine of Western History,* vol. 55, no. 3 (Autumn 2005), 34–47.

Schwarck, Don. "Campaigning in Kansas with Maida and Blucher, General Custer's Staghounds." *Research Review: The Journal of the Little Big Horn Associates,* vol. 6, no. 2 (June 1992), 14–22.

Smith, A. Croxton. "Dogs of Tsars and Grand Dukes." *Country Life Magazine,* October 8, 1932, 413.

Sternberg, Thomas H., M.D., Ernest B. Howard, M.D., Leonard Dewey, M.D., and Paul Paget, M.D. "Venereal Diseases," *Preventative Medicine in World War II, Vol. V, Communicable Diseases,* U. S. Army Medical Dept., Office of Medical History, accessed on November 17, 2016 http://history.amedd.army.mil/booksdocs/wwii/communicablediseasesV5/chapter10.htm.

Stewart, A.R. "Stories of the Old West as Told and Painted by the Cow Puncher and Artist, Ed Borein." *The Craftsman,* October 1912, 4–51.

Stewart, Edgar I. "The Reno Court of Inquiry," *The Montana Magazine of History.* Vol. II, no. 3 (July 1952), 31–43.

Tizard, Ian. "Grease, Anthraxgate, and Kennel Cough: A Revisionist History of Early Veterinary Vaccines." *Advances in Veterinary Medicine,* vol. 41, no, 7 (1999), 7–24.

Tizard, Ian, and M. Tawfik Omran, "Syphilization and Civilization: Early Adventures in Vaccination," presented at the International Veterinary Vaccines Conference, Madison, WI (2009).

Tunnell, Steve. "Custer's Occupation of Hempstead Texas: George & Libbie at Liendo." *Research Review: The Journal of the Little Big Horn Associates,* vol, 10, No. 1 (January 1996), 8–16.

Walker, Danny N. "Canid Remains from the Powder River Supply Depot, Prairie County, Montana (24PE231)." *Archeology in Montana,* vol. 36, no. 2 (1995), 63–82.

Wallace, Frank. "The Grand Duke Nicholas as a Sportsman." *Country Life Magazine,* June 12, 1915, 804–806.

Youngkin, Stephen D. "Custer and His Staghounds." *The Claymore: Newsletter of the Scottish Deerhound Club of America,* Mar/Apr 1991, 40–43.

Youngkin, Stephen D. "General Custer." *The Claymore: Newsletter of the Scottish Deerhound Club of America,* May/Jun, 1991, 47–53.

Youngkin, Stephen D., "General Custer—The Last Campaign." *The Claymore: Newsletter of the Scottish Deerhound Club of America,* Jan/Feb, 1991, 26–37.

Manuscripts, Monographs and Booklets

Carroll, John M. *Custer's Cavalry Occupation of Hempstead & Austin, Texas and the History of Custer's Headquarters Building.* Glendale, CA: Arthur H. Clark, Co., 1983.

Grey, Samuel I. & John M. Carroll. *Custer's Private Orderly in Texas: Samuel I. Grey.* University of California, Davis, Shields Library, Special Collections, Harrison Pamphlets.

Hanna, Charles Augustus. *Historical Collections of Harrison County in the State of Ohio.* New York: privately printed, 1900. Accessed on November 1, 2016, https://books.google.com/books?id=V-ouAAAAYAAJ&pg=PA114#v=onepage&q&f=false

Harrison, Peter. *The Eyes of the Sleepers: Cheyenne Accounts of the Washita Attack.* Southampton, U.K.: The English Westerners' Society, 1998.

Hills, Louis E. "Surveying Expedition in 1873 by Bugler Hills." Undated manuscript, Lawrence A. Frost Collection of Custeriana, Monroe County Library System.

Irvine, J. B., Jr. "A Hunt with General Custer," in *A Seventh Cavalry Scrapbook #5,* ed. John M. Carroll, 8–10. Bryant, TX: Privately printed, 1979.

Marcaccini, Ann, ed. "Lion." Mendota, MI: Friends of the Sibley Historic Site, 1997.

Olivia, Leo E. *Fort Hays.* Topeka, KS: Kansas State Historical Society, 1986.

Pope, James L. *Custer and His Dogs.* Plover, WI: The Phoenix Proprietary Publications, 1990.

Pratt, A. Llewelyn, ed. *Our Friend the Dog in Verse.* London: The Guide Dogs for the Blind Assn., 1946.

Stair, William C., undated interview by Walter Camp. Brigham Young University Library, Special Collection, Walter Mason Camp Papers, MSS 57 Box 3, SCM 000 827.

Private Collections

The Brice C.W. Custer Collection
The Collection of Philip Downs
The Ugbrooke House Archives, Devon, U. K.

Internet Resources

American Kennel Club, www. http://akc.org
Ancestry.com, www.ancestry.com
The Army Navy Journal, https://catalog.hathitrust.org/Record/008898673
California Digital Newspaper Collection: Center for Bibliographic Studies and Research, University of California, Riverside, http://cdnc.ucr.edu
Find a Grave, www.findagrave.com
Friends of the Little Bighorn Battlefield, 7th Cavalry Muster Rolls & Leadership Structure, www.friendslittlebighorn.com/Soldiers-Warriors.htm
Hathi Trust Digital Library, www.hathitrust.org
Hennepin County, Minnesota, Online Historical Directories, https://sites.google.com/site/onlinedirectorysite/Home/usa/mn/hennepin
Internet Archive, https://archive.org
Internet Movie Data Base, www.imdb.com
Library of Congress: Chronicling America, https://chroniclingamerica.loc.gov
Library of Congress: Prints & Photographs Online Catalog, www.loc.gov/pictures/
"Liendo Plantation," *Texas History Online,* Texas State Historical Association, https://tshaonline.org/handbook/online/articles/ccl01.
Little Bighorn Battlefield National Monument, Historic Photos www.nps.gov/libi/learn/photosmultimedia/photogallery.htm
The Making of America, http://collections.library.cornell.edu/moa_new/index.html
MeasuringWorth.com, www.measuringworth.com/uscompare/
Monroe County Library System, https://saturn.monroe.lib.mi.us
The New York Times Archive, www.archive.nytimes.com
Newspapers.com, www.newspapers.com
The Online Books Page, http://onlinebooks.library.upenn.edu
The Peerage, www.thepeerage.com
South Dakota Digital Archives, https://sddigitalarchives.contentdm.oclc.org/digital/
State Historical Society of North Dakota: Online Photo Archive, http://history.nd.gov/archives/whatphotos.html
University of New Hampshire, Digital Collections, www.library.unh.edu/find/digital

Fiction

Blake, Michael. *Marching to Valhalla: A Novel of Custer's Last Days.* New York: Villard Books, 1996.

Boyer, G.G. *Custer, Terry, and Me.* Waterville, ME: Five Star, 2004.

Burroughs, Edgar Rice. *The Eternal Lover.* Chicago: A. C. McClurg & Co., 1925.

Downey, Fairfax. *The Seventh's Staghound.* New York: Dodd, Mead & Co., 1948.

Fraser, George MacDonald. *Flashman and the Redskins.* New York: Alfred A. Knopf, 1982.

Henry, Will. *No Survivors.* Lincoln: University of Nebraska Press, 1950.

Johnston, Terry C. *Long Winter Gone.* New York: Bantam Books, 1990.

Johnston, Terry C. *Seize the Sky.* New York: Bantam Books, 1991.

Jones, Douglas C. *The Court-Martial of George Armstrong Custer.* New York: Warner Books, 1976.

Saylor, Maurine Bergland. *Turk, General Custer's Dog.* Place of publication unknown: Clarinda Publishing, 1981.

Filmography

The Adventures of Rin-Tin-Tin (Episode 1, Season 1; 1954)
The Adventures of Rocky and Bullwinkle and Friends Complete Season 1 (2003).
Colonel Custard's Last Stand (1914)
The Covered Wagon (1923)
Custer (TV series; 1967)
The Fighting Prince of Donegal (1966)
Fort Apache (1948)
Gone with the Wind (1939)
The Groove Tube (1974)
Into the West, Mini-Series (2005)
Ivanhoe (1952)
Little Big Man (1970)
Man of Aran (1934)
The Man Who Shot Liberty Valance (1962)
Nanook of the North (1922)
Old Yeller (1957)
The Potterymaker (1925)
Robin Hood: Prince of Thieves (1991)
Santa Fe Trail (1940)
She Wore a Yellow Ribbon (1949)
Son of the Morning Star (1991)
They Died with Their Boots On (1941)
Tonka (1958)
Touche Pas à la Femme Blanche or *Don't Touch the White Woman* (1974)
Won Ton Ton: The Dog That Saved Hollywood (1976)

Index

Numbers in ***bold italics*** indicate pages with illustrations

Academy of Natural Sciences of Philadelphia 206
Adams, Cassilly 271
Adams, Maria 235
Adams, Mary 147, 152, 172, 183, 186–187, 200, 235; son Charlie 147
Adams Express Company 225
Adams Museum, Deadwood, SD 285
The Adventures of Rin Tin Tin 261
The Adventures of Rocky and Bullwinkle 300
Africa, North 22
After the Battle (J.K. Ralston) 248
Ainsworth, John Stirling 138, 148–149, 168, 229
Alabama 19, 69; Larkinsville 38, Mobile 167
Alaskan Territory Purchase 164
Alcatraz Prison Variety Troup 268
Alexis, Grand Duke *see* Romanov, Alexis Alexandrovich, Grand Duke
Almirall, Leon V. 258–259
ambulances 52, 68, 107–108, 230, 233; dogs in 76–77, 79, 93, 102, 136–137, 160, 173, 212, 231, 233
American History Illustrated, "The Enduring Custer Legend" (Robert Utley) 256
American Kennel Club 38, 46, 83, 85, 91, 102, 114, 150, 170, 249, 260, 268, 296
American Library Association 21
American Society for the Prevention of Cruelty to Animals 152
Androcles and the Lion, fable of 249
Anglesey, Marquess of *see* Paget, Henry William
Anheuser-Busch Brewing Co. 271
antelope vs. sighthound, accounts of 97, 194–195, 206, 231
anthropomorphism and dogs 75, 245
Apache 99

Arapaho 117, 122; 234, 238
archeologic excavations and evidence of dogs 261
Arikara (Arikaree, Ree) 187, 212, 216–217, 239
Aristedes (Kentucky Derby winner) 161
Arkansas 19
Arlington National Cemetery 38
Army and Navy Journal 268, 270
Army of the Potomac 38, 41, 43
Around the World in Eighty Days (Jules Verne) 148
Arquette, Rosanna 296
art, works of *see After the Battle; Blucher and Maida Lead the Chase; Cardigan: General Custer's Last Staghound; Custer & Libbie Playing Croquet; Custer and the Pup; Custer's Last Battle on the Little Bighorn* (a.k.a *Custer's Last Stand*); *Custer's Last Fight* (Adams & Becker versions); *The Death Struggle of General Custer; One Perfect Day*
Asboth, Brig. Gen. Alexander and dog 38
Aster, John Jacob, Jr. 157, 270
Asylum for the Blind (Custer's headquarters in Austin) 79, 81, ***84***, 199
The Atlantic Monthly 159
Austin, Stephen 69

Bacon, Daniel Stanton 13–15, 16, 17, 18, 19, 20, 23, 37, 44–45, 46, 50–52, 57, 59, 76, 79, 87, 89, 156
Bacon, Edward Augustus 14, 15, 16, 17
Bacon, Eleanor Sophia (née Page) 14, 16, 17, 20
Bacon, Elizabeth Clift *see* Custer, Elizabeth Clift Bacon
Bacon, Harriet 15, 16
Bacon, Leonard 12
Bacon, Rhoda Wells (née Pitts) 17–18, 20, 59, 87
Bacon, Sophia 15, 16
Balch, Wesley P. 273
Baliran, Augustus 188, 218

Ball, Pvt. John 188
balloons, hot air 39, 158
Baltimore, Maryland 43
Banker, James H. 157
banks: Hongkong and Singapore Banking Corporation (HSBC) 150; L.P. Morton & Co. 156; Morton, Rose & Co. 156
Barker, Charles W., auctions 273
Barker, Jeanette 89, 220
Barker Kirkland 5, 7, 72, 88–89, 90, 91–92, 107, 111, 113, 115, 116, 118, 119, ***120***, 124, 127, 132, 138, 141, 143–147, 158, 160, 163, 189, 190, 191, 192, 219–220, 221, 252
Barnard, Brig. Gen. John G. 40
Barnitz, Capt. Alfred 6, 102, 115, 122, 123, 126, 128, 129, 194
Barnitz, Jennie 115
Barnum, Phineas Taylor 16, 39, 138, ***151***–152, 153, 216, 223–225, 226, 259; American Museum exhibits 37, 46–47, 59, 151, 287; First National Dog Show 37, 46–47, 85, 225, 249, 260, 266; "Greatest Show on Earth" 47, 224, 225: Roman Hippodrome 47, 223–225, 268
Barrett, Lawrence 92, 205, 207, 223, 226
Bartholdi Statue (Statue of Liberty) 260
baseball 197, 208
Bates, Agnes 204
Bates, Charles Francis 199
Beard, James H. 290
Beauregard, Gen. P.G.T., C.S.A. 35
Becker, F. Otto 271–272
Beckwith, Judge W.G. 143, 144
Belknap, William (Secretary of War) 164, 227–228
Belknap Hearings (Belknap Scandal) 11, 226–227, 229, 266, 290
Bell, Lt. James 122, 125, ***142***, ***143***, 147
Bell, The David C., Investment Co. 286
Belmont, August 157
Bent, George 124

331

Benteen, Capt. Frederick 94, 102, 122, 127, 128, *142*, 231, 235, 236, 238, 259, 267
Bergh, Henry: and ASPCA 152
Berghaus, Albert 277, 291
Berkeley, 5th Earl of 169
Bernardo Plantation 69
Beth Gelert: Or the Grave of the Greyhound (William R. Spencer) 146
Bierstadt, Albert 92, 164, 223, 270
Big Creek Camp *see* camps, Army
Big Horn Mountains 12
Big Man 123
Billings Public Library, MT 32
Bingaman, Josephus 129
Bingham, Congressman John 27–28, 35
Bird, Roy 256
Birdsong, Col. George Lawrence (foxhound breeder) 60
Bishop (Custer's orderly) 147, 161
Bismarck, Chancellor Otto von 197
Bismarck, town of *see* Dakota Territory
Bismarck Tribune 185, 188, 189, 206, 208, 209, 212, 213, 225, 226, 231, 241
Black Friday stock market crash 157
Black Hills 181, 205, 213, 215, 218, 223, 228, 243
Black Kettle, Chief 118, 122, 123, 124, 126, 127, 130, 243, 250
Black Wolf 248
blacks 78; Custer's opinion 76, 88, 89; Libbie and 101; *see also* Buffalo Soldiers
Blake, Michael 294
Blinn, Clara 124, 126
Blinn, Willie 124, 126
Bloody Knife 187, 206, 209, *210*, *211*, 212, 235, 278, 290
Blücher, Field Marshal Gebhard Leberecht 113
Blucher and Maida Lead the Chase (E. Lisle Reedstrom) 291, *292*; *see also* Custers' dogs
Bluegrass Country, Kentucky 160, 161, 162
Boatswain, epitaph of 146, 153
bobbery pack 133
Bolsheviks 170; Revolution of 164
Bone Wars 206
Booth, John Wilkes 64
Boots and Saddles (Elizabeth B. Custer) 5, 159, 209, 258, 273, 279, 283, 290
Boots and Saddles (films) 295
Borein, Ed 250
Borglum, Solon 271
Bourke, Lt. John G. 242
Bouyer, Mitch 235; parody of 299
Bowen, Lt. Nicholas 39–40, *40*

Bowers, (Custer's orderly) 147, 152, 153, 161
Boyd, Rev. Erasumus J. 15, 21, 215
Boyd, Florence 215, 218
Boyd's Seminary 15, 17, 18, 25
Boyer, C.G. 294
Bradford, John R. *see* Towers, William F.
Bradley, Col. 273
Brady, Mathew 41, 185–186, 289
Breckinridge, John C. 31
Brewster, Capt. *143*
Bridger, Jim 138
Brilliant, Ashleigh 227
British Army 36, 149, 169, 242, 272, 275; prisoner of war escape 60
British hunters *see* Ainsworth; Cavendish; Clifford; Goodwin; Graves; Molesworth; Paget; Powell; Price; Stewart (Sir William); Townsend; Wyndham-Quinn
British Museum 148
British Navy 50, 169
Broderick, David C. 287
Brown, Eliza 50, 52, 54, 55, 56, 57, 59, *65*, 66, 73–74, 78, 80, 81, *84*, 89, 90, 93, 101, 102, 103–104, 116, 132, 133, 147, 151, 200, 277, 279
Brown, Fred D. 286
Brown, Paul 290
Brown, Capt. William Henry 160
Brown-Pusey House, Elizabethtown, KY, 159
Budweiser beer 271
buffalo: destruction of herds 135; hunting of 93, 98, 99–101, 102, 103, 108, 111, 113, 121, *134–137*, *142*, 144–145, 148–151, 152, 153, 164–166, 277, 279
"Buffalo Bill" *see* Cody, William F.
Buffalo Bill Center of the West 272
Buffalo Soldiers (9th & 10th Cavalry, 24th & 25th Infantry) 88, 200
bugologists *see* scientists
Bull Bear 98
Burkman, Pvt. John W., "Old Neutriment" 5, 7, *161*–163, 171–172, 175, 176–177, 181, 182, 196, 197, 199–200, 201, 202, 209, *211*, *222*, 226, 230, 231, 233, 235, 238, 240, 247–248, 256–258, 259, 261, 271, *280*, 281, 294, 295, 299
Burnside, Maj. Gen. Ambrose 43, 46
Burroughs, Edgar Rice 294
Bush, Joe (the officer, the steam engineer, and the bull-dog) 247
Butler, Francis 266
Byron, Lord, (poet) 72, 146, 153; *see also* Custers' dogs, Byron

Cadet George Armstrong Custer: Demerits & Academics (Tom O'Neil) 30
Calhoun, Emma 230
Calhoun, Frederick 207
Calhoun, Lt. James 12, 26, 168, 187, 194, 199–200, *204*, 207, 208, 239
Calhoun, Margaret "Maggie" 113, 134, 173, *204*, 230, 241, 265
California 94, 213; Los Angeles 254, 256; San Francisco 141, 148, 150, 269; Yosemite Valley 141
"California Joe" *see* Millner, Joseph "Moses" E.
Camp, Walter Mason 128–129, 245, 247, 248, 250, 251
campaigns and expeditions: Black Hills 1873 206; Black Hills 1874 1, 205–*214*, 215, 223, 231, 232, 247, 249, 285; Black Hills 1875 207, 218; Hancock 1867 96–97, 98, 108, 107, 134, 165; Lewis and Clark Expedition 1804–1806 188; 197; Nez Perce War 1877 242, 249; Northwestern Expeditions 1864 and 1865 181; Sioux War 1876 ("Yellowstone Campaign/Little Bighorn Expedition") 11–12, 207, 225, 226, 228–236, 244, 245, 259, 279; Washita 1868 120–127, 144, 174, 188, 213, 228, 231, 232 (dogs at 12, 114–115, 120–123, 125–130, 232–233, 250, 265; in fiction 294); Yellowstone Surveying 1871 and 1872 181, 182; 3rd Yellowstone 1873 177, 182–192, 194, 207, 208, 210, 212, 230, 232, 249, 256, 272, 283, 290; *see also* wars; Little Bighorn, Battle of
Campbell, Sarah "Aunt Sally" 212
camps, Army: Big Creek 103–104, 113, 134, *135*, *142*, 176, 199, 293; Robinson 244, 269; Sandy Forsyth 121; Supply 121, 126, 127, 131, 216–217
Canada (British Possessions) 113, 130, 155, 164, 169, 245, 269, 274; Canadians 94, 252; Manitoba 273; Ontario 147; Saskatchewan 273; *see also* Cooke, Lt. William
Canines & Coyotes (Leon V. Almirall) 258–259
Cardigan, Lord 177, 283; *see also* the Custers' dogs, Cardigan; Light Brigade, Charge of
Cardigan: General Custer's Last Staghound (Brandon Martz) 293; *see also* the Custers' dogs, Cardigan
Carnahan, J.M. 241
Carney, Art 300

Carpenter, Lucy (née Hewlett) 41–42
Carr, Maj. Eugene A. 160, 195
Carroll, John M. 298
cattle, longhorns 77–78
Cave, Mammoth, KY 166
Cavendish, Henry Anson, Baron Waterpark 138–*143*, 155, 279
C.B.D.W. (un-named dog correspondent) 251–252
centennial celebrations, America's 225, 226, 229, 262
Chandler, Senator Zachariah 53–54, 64, 228
Charbonneau, Jean Baptiste "Pompey" (Sacagawea's son) 188
Charbonneau, Toussaint 188
Charging Hawk 250–251
Charles O'Malley, the Irish Dragoon (Charles Lever) 26, 29
Cherbourg, France 275
Chesterwood, Charles *see* Creighton, Pvt. John C
Cheyenne: Northern 205, 212, 228, 234, 235–236, 238, 240, 241, 247, 248, 269, 275, 280, 298; Southern 96, 98, 99, 103, 108, 116, 117, 122, 124, 130, 131, 216–217
Cheyenne Bad Lands, Dakota Territory 180
Chicago Inter Ocean 206, 208, 249
Chicago Times 241–242
Chicago Tribune 131, 151
Chichester, W.T. 293
China 275
Chippewa *see* Ojibwe
Chivington, Col. 117
Choctaw 45
Christiancy, Lt. James 50
C.I.A. (in film parody) 299
circus *see* Barnum, Phineas Taylor; Rice, Dan
Cisco, Johnny 46, 52, 54, 294
civil peacekeeping: Dakota 197, 218; Kentucky 159; Texas 70, 77, 81
Civil War 19, 22, 31, 24, 34, 36–37, 38–39, 40–43, 46–47, 48–49, 50, 52, 53, 54, 55, *56*, 60–62, 63, 64, 66, 67, 117, 164, 208, 242, 244, 252; battles and campaigns (Antietam 42, 43; Appomattox Courthouse 61; Appomattox Station 60, 61; First Bull Run (Manassas) 32, 35, 36, 43, 61; Cedar Creek 55; Chancellorsville 46; Culpepper Court House 50; Dinwiddie Courthouse 60; Five Forks 60; Gettysburg 48, 49, 50, 96, 260, 271; Namozine Church, 60; New Bern 37, 47; Pea Ridge 38; Sailor's Creek 60; Shenandoah Valley 49, 54–55, 58, 59; Texas 64, 65, 66; Tom's Brook 55;

Trevilian Station 54; Waynesboro 60; Wilderness 54; Third Battle of Winchester 55; Yellow Tavern 54); *see also* Custer, Elizabeth Bacon, campaigning; Custer, George Armstrong, Civil War actions; U.S. Army, Federal and State regiments
Clark, Capt. William 188
Clemens, Samuel (Mark Twain) 101, 224
Clifford, Lewis, 9th Baron Clifford of Chudleigh 183–184, 188, 189, 194, 208
Clift, Elizabeth 13
Clymer, Congressman Heister 227; *see also* Belknap Scandal
Coates, Dr. 105
Coca-Cola (in film parody) 299
Cody, William F. "Buffalo Bill" 99, 160, 163, 164–165, 195, 222, 269, 276; parody 299
Coldstream Stud *see* McGrath, Henry Price
Cole, Gary 298
Colgan, Joseph N. 32
Colonel Custard's Last Stand 295
Colorado Territory 81, 93, 103, 166, 193, 213, 225, 265, 267; Custer City 271; Denver 151; Georgetown 157, 170; Hall Valley 219
Comanche (tribe) 122
Comanche the horse survivor 241–243, 244, 245, 249, 262, 283, 289, 294; *see also* Little Bighorn, Battle of, survivor stories/rumors; Napoleon the horse survivor
Comeau, Napoléon-Alexandre 238, 252
Comstock, William "Medicine Bill" 102, 103
Confederate renegades 66, 70
Confederate States of America 19, 31, 61, 65, 66; *see also* Davis, Jefferson; Secession
Congressional Hearing *see* Belknap Hearings
Congressional Medal of Honor 49, 60, 116, 238, 259, 280
Connecticut 152, 254; Bridgeport 152, 225
Connell, Evan S. 298
Connor, Col. Patrick 117
"contrabands" *see* slaves, escaped
Cook, of Minneapolis 285
Cooke, Lt. William 94, 107, *143*, 147, 152, 200, *221*, 222, 239, 240, 259
Cooper, Maj. Wickliffe 94, 104
Cope, Prof. Edward Drinker 207
coursing competitions, hounds 179–181, 258–259, 274
The Court Martial of George Armstrong Custer (Douglas C. Jones) 294

Courtenay, Mrs. 122–123, 128
The Covered Wagon 295
coyotes mistaken for wolves 106, 116
The Craftsman 250–251
Crawford, Capt. Jack 222
Crazy Horse 11, 228, 234, 244, 269
Creighton, Pvt. John C. (Charles Chesterwood) 247, 248, 261
Crittenden, Brig. Gen. Thomas L. 179
Crittenden, Lt. John Jordan 179, 240
Crockett, Davy 38
Crook, Maj. Gen. George R. 12, 228, 230, 234, 235, 244, 269
Crow 131, 239, 240, 275, 298
Curly, Crow scout 240
Curtis, Lt. Col. Elwell S. 178
Curtis, W.C. *204*
Curtis, William E. 206
Custer, Bernard "Barney" (fictional character) 294
Custer, Boston 12, 26, 168, 207, 223, 230, 231, 236, 239, 270, 290
Custer, Brice William 23
Custer, Elizabeth Clift Bacon "Libbie" 8; aftermath of Little Bighorn 241, 243; anthropomorphism and dogs 75; as author 100, 258, 268, 276–279, 295; Civil War campaigning 48, 52, 54, 55–59, 60, 64, 277, 278; clothes and fashion 17, 20, 21, 51–52, 55–56, 57, *65*, 68–69, *82*, 95, 157, 159, 175, 202, 213, 220–221, 281; as conversationalist and diplomat 21, 53–54, 94–95, 163, 222, 279; courting 18–21, 43–45, 50–51; death and burial of 281; as dog lover 74–75, 76, 78–79, 80, 81, 83, *84*, 111, 132, 148, 150, 171, 176–177, 197, 201, 203, 274, 277, 281; education 15, 17, 20; and films 295; and floods 103–104; girlhood of 14–18, 23; and Grand Duke Alexis 167–168; hunting 74, 75, 76, 78, 80, 81, 95–96, 140, 175, 203; and husband's Army career 53–54, 108; and husband's dogs 46, 51, 52, 55, 57, 58, 64, 64, 71, 75, 95, 117; images 19, *53*, *65*, *82*, *84*, *112*, *135*, *143*, *204*, *221*, *277*, *291*; as lecturer 59, 279; her letters 45, 50, 51, 54, 76, 97, 101, *104–105*, *107*, 111, 117, 135, 153, 157, 159, 168, 199, 230, 254, 264, 272; as married couple 52, 55, 93, 102, 108, 153, 157, 168,185, 215, 281; pet names for 53, 54, 58, 168; rehoming their dogs 264–267, 272; roughing it 68–69, 132, 175; Sheridan's gift to 61; social

activities 147–148, 160, 197, 216; and Southern lifestyle 76, 84; and Tom Custer 53, 57–58, 113, 117, 133, 226; travel abroad 275; in Washington 52–54, 59, 60; wedding and honeymoon 51–52, *53*; as a widow 264–265, 268, 270–271, 274, 276, 280, 281; *see also* the Custers' dogs

Custer, Emanuel Henry 23, 24, 27, 51, 70–71, 75, 76, 79, 81, *84*, 87, 168, 207, 222, 265

Custer, George Armstrong: as an Anglophile 141, 147, 148, 150, 152, 208; appearance 48–49, 55, 57, *65, 82*, 157, 166, 175, 191, 202, 222, 258; Army career 27, 31, 34, 36, 43–44, 45, 46, 48, 49–50, 55, 64, 68, 81–82, 88, 93, 104, 107–108, 111, 114, 134, 162; blacks, opinion of 76, 88, 89; boyhood 23–26, 28, 29; burials and monuments 249, 269–271, 281, 283; campaigning with Libbie 52, 54, 55–57, 60, 64; caring for dogs and horses 66, 72, 75, 79–80, 91, 98–99, 105, 162, 171, 176–177; Civil War actions 7; 26, 35–36, 39, 41, 42, 59–60, 61, 66, 187; Civil War dogs 66; 37, 38–39, *40*, 41, *42*, 43, 46, 50, 54, 55, 57, 58, 66; Congressional hearings 226–228; courts martial 32, 107–109, 213; courtship and marriage 21, 43–45, 50–52, 55, 93, 102, 104–105, 107, 108, 153, 157, 168, 185, 231 281; dead body 239, 240; as disciplinarian 67–68, 79, 103, 105, 107, 108, 173, 212; as dog killer 122, 126–130, 174, 232, 265–266, 294; dogs, affection for 25, 89, 95, 97, 115, 117, 146, 153, 191–192, 193; 200–201, 209, 216, 232, 277; financial opportunities 87, 88, 134, 157–158, 168, 219, 220, 225–226, 265, 266; and Grand Duke Alexis 164–168; grievances against 67, 79, 105, 107, 108, 126, 127–130, 212; horses of 34–35, 49, 50, 54, 66, 72, 73, 77, 83–84, 90, 93, 115, 168, 180, 225 (Bluegrass 162; Custis Lee 66, 68, 79, 84, 90, 99–101, 102, 108, 277, 293; Dandy 199, 202, *222*, 233, 235, 238, 240, 257, 265; Don Juan 66, 90; Fanchon 84, 90; Frogtown 162, 168; Harry 46; Jack Rucker 66, 84, 90; Phil Sheridan 83, 90, 162; Vic 199, 221, *222*, 233, 235, 242, 291); as a hunter 25, 69, 70–72, 73, 75, 76–77, 79, 80, 95–96, 98, 115, 116, 120, 121, 144–145, 184–185, 190, 209–212; images *28, 33, 40, 42, 53, 65, 82, 83, 84, 106, 112, 118, 135, 142, 143, 166, 186, 192, 204, 210, 211, 214, 221, 223, 278, 291, 292*; jokes and pranks 23, 24, 30–31, 36, 55, 60, 69, 70, 76, 93, 96, 98, 99, 100, 102, 115, 131, 137, 140, 145, 172, 175–176, 209, 231; letters 30, 54, 97, 100–101, 102, 108, 114, 115, 116, 119, 120, 145, 146, 153, 157, 160, 169, 179, 185, 190, 191, 201, 207, 208, 209, 232, 274; library 95, 205, 277, *278*; myths about 242, 251, 262; in newspapers 21, 36, 67, 88, 108, 127, 141, 144, 151, 185–*186*, 206, 208, 213, 218, 227; nicknames 9, 24, 29, 43, 49, 50, 68, 105, 129, 203, 222, 240, 251; pets, unusual 55, 102, 156, 190, 208, 211, 212; and politics 27–28, 31, 44, 88, 89–90; popular interest in 283, 285, 288, 289; relations with officers 94, 126, 127, 159, 199–201; reputation 66, 117, 119, 126, 134, 136, 152, 157, 165, 185, 193, 215, 220, 227, 262, 267, 271, 275, 280, 293; romances and flirtations 27, 30, 44, 101, 157; Southern lifestyle and friendships 29, 31, 42–43, 70, 76, 84, 88; teacher, as a 26–27; temperance 37, 45, 77, 104, 145, 161; at West Point 27–28, *28*, 29–31, 32, *33*; as a writer 5, 100–101, 109, 145, 146, 147, 152, 159, 168, 169, 185, 190, 191–192, 193, 205, 216, 221, 232, 295; *see also* campaigns/expeditions, Black Hills 1874; Hancock 1867; Sioux War 1876: Washita 1868; Yellowstone 1873; the Custers' dogs

Custer, Hannah 23
Custer, Jacob 23
Custer, John A. 23, 24
Custer, Margaret "Maggie" Emma 24, 147–148, 159, 168
Custer, Maria (née Ward) 23, 74; previous children 24, 25, 27, 87, 222
Custer, Mathilda P. (née Veirs) 23
Custer, Nevin Johnson 24
Custer, Thomas Ward 12, 24, 26, 49, 50, *53*, 57–58, 60, 66, 67, 77, 81, *84*, 87, 91, 93, 94, 107, 115, *116*, 124, 126, 127, 129, 132, 133, *142, 143*, 144, 147, 155, 156, 159, 180, 187, 200, *204*, 209, 218, *221*, 222, 226, 231, 240, 254, 270, 275, 293; and dogs 59, 71, 91, 98–99, 107, 113, 115, 117, 121, 133, 140, 152, 156, 171, 182, 184, 199; and hunting 67, 70–71, 75–76, 111, 113, 176, 290; and Libbie Custer 53, 57–58, 113, 117

Custer (The Legend of Custer) TV series 296, *297*, 298

Custer & Libbie Playing Croquet (Thom Ross) *291*, 293

Custer and the Pup (Glenwood Swanson) 291, 293

Custer Bend Cemetery *see* Snakey Bend Cemetery

"Custer Circle" 94

The Custer Drama (George Poletes) 293

"Custer Luck" 48, 101, 119

Custer Storm of 1873 (the blizzard) 173

The Custer Story (Marguerite Merington) 76, 193; *see also* Merington, Marguerite

Custer, Terry, and Me (C.G. Boyer) 294

Custer: The Man, the Myth, the Movies (John Phillip Langellier) 295

Custer's Indian Battles (Charles Francis Bates) 199

Custer's Last Battle on the Little Bighorn (Edgar S. Paxson) 258

Custer's Last Charge (song by John Philip Sousa) 271

Custer's Last Fight (Cassilly Adams) 271

Custer's Last Fight (Otto Becker) 271–272

Custer's Last Stand: artistic depictions 271–272; myths 238; *see also* Last Stand Hill

the Custers' dogs: black dog myth 244, 251; Blucher 6, 12, 111, 114, 115, 116, *118*, 120, 121, 123, 125, 126, 127, 131, 146, 232–233, 243, 279, 294; Blucher II (Bleuch) 133, 171, 172, 173, 176, 182, 190, 193, 200, 201, 202, 206, 209, 230, 256–258; Brandy 71, Byron 5, 72–74, 79, 80–81, *82, 83*, 84, *84*, 89–90, 93, 96, 133, 277, 279, 294; Cardigan 8, 177, 182, 183, 190, 196, 201, 206, 209. 227, 256, 277, 283–*284*, 285–288, 294 (*see also* Cardigan, Lord); Chesapeake Bay Retriever, rumored ownership of 102; Chihuahua 82–83; Driver 159, 161, 221; Duke 133; Fanny 96, 97, 98, 100–101, 114, 120, 121; Ferguson 159, 161, 221; Flirt 114, 117, *118*, 120, 121, 132, 160; Flora, Old 181; foxhounds 79, 84, 90, 96, 99–101, 160, 215–216, 221, 226, 277, 290; Ginnie 5, 74–75, 79, 80, 84, 89, 90, 96, 102, 111, *112*, 113, 114, 121, 148, 172, 277; greyhounds 77–78, 80, 89, 96, 99–101, 107, 110, 116, 129, 210, *211*, 212, 231,

253, 273, 278; Grime 155–156, 162, 163, 171, 203, 206; imported dogs 138, 141, 150, 153, 155–156, 158, 160 (unsuitability of 107, 113); Jude 133; Juno 133; Jupiter 71; Lady 11, 229, 230, 232, 233, 256–258, 273; Kaiser 11, 159, 229, 230, 232, 233, 256–258, 273; Lu 96, 97, 98, 99–101, 102, 103, 105, *106*, 107, 113, 165; Lucy Stone 177, 277, 294; Lufra 133; Lulu 159, 162, 171–172, 173, 193; Madgie 196, 206, 265, 268, 269, 273; Maida 111, 114, 115, 116–117, *118*, 120, 121, 123, 125, 126, 127, 129, 131, 132, 133, 134, *135*, 144, 145–146, 147, 153, 162, 192, 193, 243, 277; Maida II and III 182, 190, 192, 193, 201, 293; personalities of 201; Possum 158, 162, 163, 171, 203, 206; purebreds, opinions about 10, 75, 114, 150, 153, 177, 221, 225; Rattler (Kansas) 96, 97, 98, 99–101; Rattler (Texas) 71; Rosa 114, 115, 121; Rover 91, 96, 97, 98, 99–101, 102, 103–104, 111, 114, 115, 120, 121, 126, 131, 132, 159, 171, 177, 203, 277, 294; Russian Wolfhounds 166, 167, 196, 199, 265, 268, 273; Scottish Deerhounds 111, 113–114, 117, *118*, 120, 122, 127, 132,133, 199, 208, *211*, 212, 221, *222*, 252, 266, 269, 277, 278, 279, 291, 296, 298; selling/giving away 83–84, 117, 162, 179–180, 216, 219, 254; Setters 102; Sharp 96, 97, 99–101, 102, 103, 105, *106*, 107, 165; 113; staghounds 114, 116–117, 141, 160, 179, 189–190, 231, 232, 258, 290, 294; Stanley 196, 206, 265, 268, 269, 273; Sultan 71; Swift 11, 229, 230, 232, 233, 256–258, 273; Tippecanoe 273–274; Tuck 11, 12, 171, 173, 182, 193, 200, 201, 206, 209, 218, 229, 230, 232, 233, 256–258, 273, 277, 290; Turk 90, 93, 96, 99, 101–102, 103–104, *106*, 111, 114, 131, 132, 160, 277, 290, 294; Tyler 71; "wolf-hounds" 249; *see also* dog breeds/types

The Daily Graphic 253
Dakota Territory 162, 169, 172, 173–174, 196–197, 202, 213, 215, 226, 228, 229, 230, 256, 257, 265, 273, 275, 277; Bismarck 171, 181, 182, 196, 197, 204, 205, 226, 227, 229, 230, 241, 243, 251; Deadwood 285; Greenwood 174; Mandan 286, 293; Yankton 171, 172, 173, 178, 201; *see also* Black Hills

Dalham, James B., and dog's death 125
Dana, Paul 269
Dansard, Joe 20
Darrah, Anna 90, 93, 102, 103, 104
Daugherty, Lt. Will Dirt 180, 194
David Copperfield (Charles Dickens) 15, 109
Davis, Lt. "Bill" 100
Davis, Jeff (captured dog) 37, 47
Davis, Jefferson (President of the Confederate State of America) 37, 47, 59, 61, 64, 65
Davis, Gen. Jefferson Columbus 100
Davis, Theodore R. 103, 105–*106*, 107, 290
Deadwood Hills Pioneer 243
The Death Struggle of General Custer 271
De Hart, Capt. of 9th New Jersey Inf. 47
de Havilland, Olivia 296
Delaware 129
Democratic Party 23, 27, 31, 44
Deneuve, Catherine 299
Dern, Bruce 300
De Rudio, Lt. Charles 232
Detroit Audubon Club 113, 115, 119, 120, 191, 192, 211
Detroit Free Press 20, 21, 249, 250–251
Devin, Brig. Gen. Casimer 60
De Wolf, of Manitoba 273
De Wolf, Surgeon James 231
Dickens, Charles 15, 109, 138, 141
Dime Museum, Minneapolis 287
Dippie, Brian W. 142, 160, 238, 257, 261, 290–291
disease: in dogs (distemper 110, 169, 177, 266; rabies 16, 110, 153; vaccination 169, 266); in horses 68; in humans (boils 68, 169; cholera 15, 108; diarrhea 68, 212; diphtheria 15; dysentery 16; fever 68; gonorrhea 30); *see also* dogs, medical care of
Disney films 263, 294
Dobrolowsky, Marek 298
Dodge, Col. Richard Irving 96, 194–195, 218
dog breeders, ill repute of 45–46
dog breeds/types 10, 109, 114, 176, 216, 269; Adirondack Deer Hound 109; Alpine Shepherd 109; Aztec-Toltec 83; Black and Tan Coon Hound 38; Bloodhound 78; "buffalo dog" 102; bull-dog 90–91, *91*, 101, *106*, 133, 176, 243, 244–248, 251, 256, 289, 290; Bull-Terrier 268, 269, 273; Catahoula Leopard Dog 45–46; Chesapeake Bay Retriever 102: Chihuahua 82–83, 150; Chinese Crested 83; Chinese Edible Dog 109; Clydesdale Terrier 109; Cuban Bloodhound 62–63, 109; English Greyhound 72–73, 77–78, 80, *81*, *82*, *83*, *84*, 89–90, 96, 97, 99–101, *106*, 107, 110, *167*, 176, 178, 179, 183–184, 185, 193, 194–195, 200, 238, 244, 251–*253*, 254, 267, 272, 273, 290; English staghound 109; feist 109, 134, 183; Foxhounds 38, 60, *71*, 91, 96, 97, 99–101, 128, 159, 168, 170, 176, 178, 193, 224, 225, 268; German Shepherd 250, 261; Great Bruno 109; Indian tribal dogs 98, 121, 122, 123, 125, 128, 216–217; Irish Wolfhound 74, 177, 242, 243, 259–260, 285, 296, *297*, 298; Italian Greyhound *167*, 271; Japanese Spaniel (Chin) 149–150; lapdog 109, 268; leopard dog *see* Catahoula Leopard Dog; lurcher 109, 141; Mastiff 268; Mexican Hairless 83; mongrel/cur 75, 177; Newfoundland 109, 146, 153, 146, 244; performing dogs 268; Persian Greyhound (Saluki) 8, 60, 85, 148, *167*, 170, 177; Plott Hound 38; Pointer 74–75, 102, 111, 221, 268, 273; police dog 83; Poodle 150, 249, 260, 262; pure blooded 10, 114, 141, 153, 159, 177, 221, 225; Retriever 109, 116; Russian Bloodhound 63; Russian Harrier 168; Russian Wolfhound (Borzoi) 156, 164, 165, *167*, 168, 170, 176, 196, 199, 200, 269, 272, 296; St. Bernard 109; Saluki *see* Persian Greyhound; scent hounds 38; Setter 96, 102, 176 217, 221, 268, 272, 276, Gordon 109, Irish 273; Scottish Deerhound (Scotch Staghound) 11, 72, 109, 111, 113–114, 119, *167*, 153, 158, 159, 163, 169, 176, 178, 184, 193, 194–195, 199, 200, 252, 265, 269, 287, 288, 295, 298; Siberian Bloodhound (Great Dane) 47, 268; Siberian Mastiff 109; Siberian Wolfhounds 170; Skye Terrier 90, 249; Spaniel 102; staghound 94, 109, 114, 116–117, 119, 141, 176, 224, 269, 296; tailless 216–217; terriers (rat annihilators) 47, 268; turnspit dog 109; Virginia Black and Tan 38; Whitlock Shaggy 109; *see also* the Custers' dogs; prisons; slaves; tracking hounds
dog horns 168, 180, 202; sale prices of Custer's 71
dog robber 50
dog shows 83, 102, 114, 260, 268,

274; Centennial Dog Show 1876 47, 225, 226, 266, 268; First National Dog Show 37, 46–47, 85, 249, 260, 266; international dog shows 47; Twin Cities Kennel Club 285; Westminster Kennel Club 3, 6, 47, 83, 91, 109, 196, 253, 268–269, 272
dogs: anthropomorphism 75; and archeological excavations 261; attitudes towards 85, 261; as a business 220; daily care 76, 200; fights 91, 93, 96, 103–104, 163, 200, 201, 284, 290; in film 295; meaning of in paintings 293; medical care of 105, 109–110, 169, 176–177, 201, 202–203, 266; pack hierarchy 201; recuperative powers of 110, 127, 252; shipping 83, 156, 264–265; sign language for 248; and soldiers 37, 38, **40**, **56**, 59–60, 62–63, 96, 107, 111, 122, 125, 126, 128, 176, 193, 200, 231, 248–249, 250, 252, 286, 299 (adoptions 63, 127, 250, 252); *see also* campaigns: Hancock 1867, Sioux War 1876, Washita 1868; disease; dog breeds/types; Little Bighorn Survivor stories/rumors
dogsbody 50
Donaldson, Prof. Aris B. 206
Donnelly, of Stockton, MI 267
Don't Touch the White Woman (*Touche Pas à La Femme Blanche*) 299
Douglas, Henry F. 286
Douglas, Stephen 31
Downey, Fairfax 259, 290, 294
Drew, Capt. 21, 44
Dublin University Magazine 26
Duff, James, 5th Earl of Fife 158
Duncan, Leland "Lee" and Rin Tin Tin 250
Dunraven, 4th Earl of *see* Wyndham-Quinn, Alexis Windham Thomas
Dutton, Mr. 20
Dyche, Prof. Lewis L. 242

Early, Maj. Gen. Jubal, C.S.A. 54, 55, 59, 60
Edgerly, Lt./Gen. Winfield **221**, 246
Eggleston, Walter A. 286
Eliot, George (Mary Anne Evans) 75
Elliott, Maj. Joel 94, 104, 107, 111, 119, 121, 123, 124, 125, 126, 127, 128, 231
Emerson, Ralph Waldo 148
Emory, William H. 265
England (Britain) 8, 65, 138, 164, 170, 178, 254, 260, 273, 275; Cornwall 183; Cumberland 148; Devon 183: Lambeth 150; Liverpool 65, 148, 153, 158; London 148, 155, 156, 183, 225, 275; Malmesbury; Tring 285; *see also* British Army; British hunters; British Museum; British Navy; ships; weapons, revolvers; zoos
Erie Canal 13
The Eternal Lover/The Eternal Savage (Edgar Rice Burroughs) 294
Everleigh, B.C. 273–274
Ewert, Pvt. Theodore 209–210, 212, 215
Expansion, Westward 88, 93–94

Falvey, Justin 298
Farley the scout 251–252
Farnsworth, Brig. Gen. Elon 48
Farragut, Adm. David 85, 89
fashion, military 44, 57, **65**, 159, 202, 220
Fealm, Clinton R. 286
Feejee Mermaid 46, 59, 152
Ferdinand, Archduke, assassination of 275
Fetterman Massacre 125
The Field 149, 252, 273
Fife, 5th Earl of 158
Fifield, Fanny 44, 45, 50, 121
The Fighting Prince of Donegal 296
films and television *see The Adventures of Rin-Tin-Tin*; *The Adventures of Rocky and Bullwinkle and Friends*; *Boots and Saddles*; *Colonel Custard's Last Stand*; *The Covered Wagon*; *Custer, Fort Apache*; *The Fighting Prince of Donegal*; *Gone with the Wind*; *The Groove Tube*; *Into the West*; *Ivanhoe*; *Little Big Man*; *Man of Aran*; *The Man Who Shot Liberty Valance*; *Nanook of the North*; *Old Yeller*; parodies of Custer 295, 299–300; *The Potterymaker*; *Robin Hood: Prince of Thieves*; *Santa Fe Trail*; *She Wore a Yellow Ribbon*; *Son of the Morning Star*; *They Died with Their Boots On*; *Tonka*; *Touche Pas à La Femme Blanche* or *Don't Touch the White Woman*; *Won Ton Ton: The Dog That Saved Hollywood*; *see also* Disney
firearms *see* weapons
Fisk, James "Diamond Jim," Jr. 157, 158, 219
Flaherty, Robert 295
Flannery, George P. 286
Flint, Mrs. Rose **112**
Florida 19, 281; Pensacola 167
Flynn, Errol 295, 296
Fogg, Phileas 148
Following the Guidon (Elizabeth B. Custer) 5, 146, 278–279, 290
Fonda, Henry 22
Ford, Judge J.B. 243–244
Ford, John 299
Ford's Theater 64
Forest and Stream 185, 205, 220, 251, 265, 273
Forsyth, Maj. George Alexander "Sandy" 207
Forsyth, Maj. Gen. James 149
Fort Apache 22
Fort Laramie Treaty *see* Lakota Sioux Treaty 1868
Fort Riley Hunt Pack 170
Fort Sully Sporting Club 178–181, 183, 184, 193, 194, 259, 272, 274
Fortress Monroe 39, 64,
forts: Abraham Lincoln 6, 11, 181, 184, 191, 192–193, 196–197, **198**, 199, 200, 201, 202, 203–**204**, 205, 207, 208, 212, 215, 216–217, 218–219, 220, 226, 227, 229, 230, 241, 242, 243–244, 245, 247, 251, 252, 256, 257, 259, 262, 264, 265, 266, 283, 286, 293, 298; Benton 183, 189; Berthold 249; Buford 232, 247, 254, 255–256; Cobb 126, 131; Cameron 268; Concho 200; Crawford 72; Dearborn 72; Dodge 115, 116, 118, 120, 134; Ellis 230; Fetterman 230; Griffin 100, 274; Harker 94, 107, 110, 152, 251–252; Hays 101, 102, 102, 103, 107, 113, 114, 131–132, 134, 137, 138, 139, 141, 143, 146, 148, 151–152, 155, 156, 159, 160, 197, 223, 254, 296; Kearney 72, 138, 168, 193, 194; Laramie 181; Larned 98; Leavenworth 91, 93, 95, 107, 108, 111, 113, 114, 115, 117, 120, 131, 143, 146–147, 149, 152–153, 156, 157, 190, 270; Lyon 81; Madison Barracks 256, 286; McKeen 196, 197; McPherson 103, 104, 160; Meade 242, 245, 263; Pease (trapper's post) 251; Rice 162, 169, 171, 175, 179, 181, 182, 183, 184, 188, 208, 212, 218, 283; Riley 6, 90, 91, 93, 94, 96, 97, 101, 102, 107, 108, 134, 167, 170, 291; Sedgwick 103, 104, 105; Seward 231; Sill 111; Snelling 260; Sully 169, 178–181, 182, 197, 247, 259, 274; Sumter 19, 31; Union 72, 193; Wallace 94, 103, 104, 105, 107; Washakie 252; 108, 274; Yates 245, 263, 286; *see also* camps, Army
Fougera, Katherine Gibson 171
fox hunting 25, 26, 59–60, 66, 138, 155, 170, **186**, 235, 265, 268; Barnum's fox hounds

224–225, 226–227; women
and 62
France 275 *see also* wars,
Franco-Prussian
Frank Leslie's Illustrated Newspaper 277
Fraser, George MacDonald 3, 49
French, Mrs. M.H. 256, 286
French, Capt. Thomas H. 256
French Foreign Legion 22, 66
Frewen, Morton 183
Frost, Brig. Gen. Daniel Marsh,
C.S.A. 183
Frost, Lawrence A. 7, 21, 153,
290
Frost, Robert Graham 183, 188,
189

The Galaxy magazine (later *The
Atlantic Monthly*) 101, 109,
147, 149, 159, 168, 185, 193,
205, 216, 232
Gall 234, 245, 262
Gardner, Henry 266
Garfield, Gen. James A. 138
Garrett, Katherine 175, 176
Gatling guns *see* weapons
General Custer's Libbie
(Lawrence A. Frost) 290
George, Pvt. William 241
Georgia 19, 69; total war and
Sherman's March to the Sea 55,
63; Upson 60
Germany 23, 161, 244, 275; *jäger*
clothing **166**; *see also* Prussia;
wars, Franco-Prussian
Ghost Dance *see* Wounded
Knee Massacre
Gibbon, Col. John 12, 230, 232,
234, 236, 239, 241, 244, 267,
269, 285, 286, in film 298
Gibbs, Maj./Gen. Alfred 93, 94,
95, 101, 111
Gibbs, Lt. Eugene Beauharnais
249
Gibbs, Mrs. Mary 249
Gibbs, Peggy 93, 97, 104, 115,
275
Gibson, Mrs. Fannie 134
Gibson, Lt. Francis **142**, 200
Gibson, Maj. George 134
Gilmore's Gardens 47, 268; *see
also* Barnum's Roman Hippodrome; Madison Square Garden; Westminster Kennel Club
Given, John 179, 184
Glüsing, Hinrich (Heinrich
Gluesing) 244, 251
Godey's Lady's Book 220
Godfrey Lt./Capt./Gen. Edward
Settle 123, 124, 207, 231, 245–
246, 251, 258, 263, 272, 275,
290
Godfrey, Mrs. **143**
Goff, Orlando 243
gold, in Black Hills 205–206,
208, 209, 212–213, 215, 218,
243

Gold Rush, California 213
Gone with the Wind 45
"Good Death" 121, 126, 271
Gooding, Walter C. 245, 248, 261
Goodwin, William 138, 149–150
Gore, Sir St. George, 8th Baronet
of Magherabegg 138, 179, 193
Gould, Jay 157
Governor's Island 260
Grant, Lt. Fred 183, 190, 207, 215
Grant, Orvil 227
Grant, Ulysses S.: as general 28,
54, 60–61, 65, 88, 89, 90, 107,
108, 114; as president 11, 119,
227–228, 229, 230, 231, 236,
267
grave robbing 146, 270
Graves, Samuel Robert, M.P. 138,
150, 153, 158, 163, 168, 275
Gray, Capt. Elliott 215–216
Gray, Maj. Horace 143, 145
Great Britain, dog show entries of
225; *see also* British; England;
Ireland
Great Western Grain Co. 286
"Greatest Show on Earth" 47,
224, 225; *see also* Barnum,
Phineas Taylor
Greene, Jacob 45, 50, 52, 61, 66,
70, 81, 82, **84**, 147, 150; *see also*
Humphrey, Mary Annette
"Nettie"
Grey, Pvt. Samuel Isadore
(Custer's orderly) 77
*The Greyhound: On the Art of
Breeding, Rearing, and Training Greyhounds for Public Running, and Their Diseases and
Treatment* (John Henry H.
Walsh "Stonehenge") 179
greyhounds, famous English 179,
183, 184, 273; *see also* the
Custers' dogs; dogs
breeds/types
Grierson, Col. Benjamin H. 200
Grinnell, Prof. George Bird 206,
209, 267, 273
Groce, Jared 69
Groce, Col. Leonard Waller 69–
70; daughter 69; hospitality of
70–71, 84; wife 70
The Groove Tube 299
The Guardsman (Charles Lever)
26

Hack, Charles 143
Hale, Capt. Owen 151, 152
Hall, Col. Jairus W. 157–158, 219
Hamilton, Alexander 94
Hamilton, Gov. Andrew Jackson
(Austin, TX) 79
Hamilton, Capt. Louis M. 94,
115, 123, 126
Hancock, Maj. Gen. Winfield
Scott 96, 98, 102, 108, 114, 179;
Indian expedition of 96–97,
98, 108, 114, 117, 134, 165; *see
also* campaigns, Hancock 1867

Hardorff, Richard G. 7, 250
Hare, Lt. Luther 231, 239
Harper's Bazaar 220
Harpers Ferry 54, 55, 58, 58
Harpers Weekly 105, 106, 224,
290
Harrison, President Benjamin
156
Harrison, Gen./President
William Henry 274
Harvard College 148, 269
Havelock, Sir Henry 22
havelocks 19, 22
Haverfield, Dr. Addie R. 286
Hazen, Col. William 213, 218,
254, 256
Hedren, Paul 124, 287
Henry, Dr. Thomas Y. 60
Henry, Will 294
Henry V (William Shakespeare)
185–186
Hickok, James Butler "Wild Bill"
97, 104, 134, 155, 194, 222
Hildebrandt, H.A. 287
Hill, "Aunt" Beck 159, 162
Hills, Bugler Louis E. 176, 188
His Very Silence Speaks: Comanche, the Horse That Survived Custer's Last Stand (Dr.
Elizabeth Lawrence) 242
Hodgson, Lt. Benny 200
Holland, Alexander 27
Holland, Mary Jane "Mollie" 27,
30
Hollywood 243, 296, 299
Honsinger, Dr. John 188, 218
Hooey, John 225
Hooker, Maj. Gen. Joseph 46
Hoover, President Herbert 242
Hope, Anthony 294
Horner, William 287
Horowitz, Alexandra 299
horses 95, 119, 131, 169, 212, 261;
military funerals for 242; *see
also* Comanche; Custer,
George Armstrong, horses of;
races, horse
Howard, J.W. 267
Howard, Gen. Rufus Lombard
143, 145
Howe, Col. Frank E. 266
Howlett Hill 13, 14, 17
Hughes, Thomas, M.P. 150
Humphrey, Gen. Levi S. 18
Humphrey, Mary Annette "Nettie" (later Mrs. Jacob Greene)
18, 45, 50, 52, 78, 81, **84**, 147
Hunter, Joseph R. 237
hunting 11, 25, 38, 60, 63, 70–
73, 75–78, 79, 80, **81**, 83, 85,
93, 94, 95–96, 97, 98, 99–101,
102, 103, 108, 109, 111, 113, 115,
116, 119–120, 121, 127, 132–
133, 134–146, 148–149, 150–
152, 158, 160, 164–166, 170,
176, 178, 179–181, 184–185,
190–191, 193, 194–195, 200,
202–203, 207, 208, 209–**210**,

215, 216, 218, 221, 223, 231–232, 233, 251–252, 254, 258, 260, 261, 268, 274–275, 281; dangers of 96, 97, 101, 102, 110, 111, 113–114, 115, 120, 121, 134, 136–137, 139–140, 142, 145, 151, 165, 175, 176, 180, 184, 189, 190, 202–203, 207; *see also* British Army, prisoner of war escape; fox hunting
Hutton, Paul Andrew 7
hydrophobia *see* disease, dogs

I Fought with Custer: The Story of Sergeant Windolph (Sgt. Charles Windolph) 249
Illingworth, William Henry 206, 208, 209–210, 212, 215, 290
Illinois 265; Cairo 171; Chicago 72, 91, 141, 147, 158, 215, 219, 220, 229, 250, 265, 270, 273; Chicago Fire, charity for victims 167
In His Brother's Shadow: The Life of Thomas Ward Custer (Roy Bird), error in 256
India 275
Indian Affairs, Bureau of 228; *see also* U.S. Government
Indian agents 96, 97,98, 218, 230
Indian dogs 98, 216–217, 247, 248–250, 262
Indian personalities *see* Big Man; Black Kettle; Black Wolf; Bull Bear; Charging Hawk; Crazy Horse; Gall; Little Rock; Medicine Woman; Old Bear; Pawnee Killer; Rain-in-the-Face; Red Tomahawk; Roman Nose; Sacagawea, Sitting Bull; Spotted Tail; Tecumseh; Two Moons; Wooden Leg; Yellow Hand
Indian Territory (Oklahoma) 93, 120
Indiana University 250
Indians 9, 11–12 55, 88, 93, 94, 95, 96, 97, 98, 99, 101, 102, 103, 104, 105, 107, 108, 114, 116, 117, 120–122, 126, 131, 135, 146, 149, 155, 165, 171,173–174, 175, 178, 181, 183, 187–188, 189, 196, 202, 203, 212, 213, 216–217, 218, 224, 230, 238, 240, 242, 243, 245, 246, 248, 249, 250, 251, 261, 264, 267, 271–272, 273, 279–280; *see also* Apache; Arapaho; Arikara (Arikaree, Ree); Cheyenne: Northern and Southern; Choctaw; Comanche; Crow; Delaware; Kiowa; Nez Perce; Ojibwe (Chippewa); Osage; Pawnee; Powatomi; Seminole; Shoshone; Sioux (sub-groups of: Blackfeet; Brulé; Gros Ventre; Hunkpapa; Lakota; Miniconjous; Oglala; Sans Arc); Two Kettle; Yankton (Ihanktonwan Dakota); Tecumseh's Confederation of Tribes; *see also* campaigns and expeditions; reservations
Ingalls, Gen. Rufus 38
Inman, Maj. Henry 94, 126
Into the West 298–299
Iowa, Keokuk 179, 184
Ireland 254, 260, 285; dog show entries from 225
Ireland, Northern 273
Irish Brigade Monument, Gettysburg 260
Irvine, Javan B., Jr. "Javi" 179–181
Irvine, Capt. Javan Bradley 178–181, 182, 197, 274
Isandlwana, Battle of 272
Italy 275; king of 158; Papal Wars 94; Pisa 158
Ivanhoe: film 296; novel by Sir Walter Scott 92

Jack Hinton (Charles Lever) 26
jackrabbit, species 80, 140
James, Henry 101
Jansa, Dr. Sharon 288
Japan 149–150, 275; Yokohama 149–150
Jenner, Dr. Edward 169
Jessie's Scouts (Sheridan's Raiders) 59
John Carter of Mars (Edgar Rice Burroughs) 294
Johnson (Custer's civilian cook) 212
Johnson, President Andrew 64–65, 67, 88, 89; Swing Around the Circle 89–90
Johnson, President Lyndon B. 242
Johnston, Terry C. 294
Jones, Douglas C. 294
Journal of History 176
Juarez, Benito 66, 82, 88
Jumbo the Elephant 46

Kahn, Madeline 300
Kaiser Wilhelm I 159
Kansas 55, 79, 90, 93, 94, 115, 152, 196, 242, 252, 253, 277; Dodge City 253–254; Hays City 132, 134, 139, 144, 147, 151, 155, 253–254; Leavenworth 159; Scott City 291; Topeka 147; Volunteer Cavalry of (19th) 114, 126, 129, 131
Kansas City Journal 94
Katz, D. Mark 80
Kearney, Brig. Gen. Vols. Philip 36
Keevan, Pvt. (Custer's orderly) 206, 213, 215
Kelley, James "Dog" **253**–254
Kellogg, Clara Louise 157
Kellogg, Mark 226, 230–231, 235, 236, 239–240, 241
Kennedy, Arthur 296
Kennedy, Pvt. Francis J. 246, 248, 261
Kennedy, President John F. 242
Kentucky 77, 156, 159, 190, 216, 225; Cave City 166; Elizabethtown 156, 159–160, 163, 165, 166, 168, 171; Lexington 156, 161, 162; Louisville 156, 159, 162, 166, 171; Mammoth Cave 166; Paducah 38
Keogh, Capt. Myles 94, 95, 108, 152, 200, 235, 240, 241, 242, 244–245, 252, 261, 262, 280
Kercheval, Charles 136
Kercheval, Mary 136
Kerr, Mrs. C.W. 286
Keyes, Asel 173
Kidder, Lt. Lyman 105, 107
King, Sgt., Bugler 99
Kiowa 101, 117, 122, 131
Kipling, Rudyard 138
Kirkpatrick, Lydia Ann 26; *see also* Reed, Lydia Ann
Kirkpatrick, Maria (née Ward) 23; *see also* Maria Custer
Kline, Wally 296
Korn, Pvt. Gustav 241
Krosch, Penelope 288
Ku Klux Klan 156, 159
Küster, Paulus Van Haren 23

Lady of the Lake (Sir Walter Scott) 133
Lake Erie 14, 111, 219
Lake St. Clair Shooting and Fishing Club 273
Lake Superior 130
Lakota Sioux (Fort Laramie) Treaty 1868 181, 205, 213, 228
Lambourne, Col. Charles Burleigh 151, 155, 158
Landon, Mary 20
Landseer, Sir Edwin 190–***191***, 283
Langellier, John Phillip 295
Langley, Lorne 124
Larned, Lt. Charles W. 188, 194, 208
Last Stand Hill *see* Little Bighorn, Battle of
lawlessness in Texas 70, 77, 81
Lawrence, Dr. Elizabeth 242
Lea, Capt. John "Gimlet," C.S.A. 42–43
Leckie, Shirley A. 27, 53, 153, 223
Lee, Gen. Robert E., C.S.A. 43, 46, 49, 60–61
Leeds, Duke of 158
Letters from an Army Officer's Wife, 1871–1888 (Francis M.A. Roe) *81*
Lever, Charles 26, 48, 141
Lewis, Samuel 143
libraries, New York Public and Morgan 271
Liebman, Ron 300
Liendo Plantation 69–70, 71, 76

Light Brigade, Charge of 141, 177, 283; *see also* Cardigan, Lord; wars, Crimean War 1853–1856
Lincoln, Abraham 19, 27, 31, 37, 41, 43, 54, 58, 59, 64–65, 85, 88, 89, 228, 270
Lind, Jenny, "the Swedish Nightingale" 46
Little, Lucy C. 249
Little Big Horn Associates *see* Research Review
Little Big Man 124
Little Bighorn, Battle of 6, 7–8, 10, 26, 32, 127, 130, 131, 162, 179, 187, 213, 234–236, 238; aftermath 234, 236, 238–241, 243–261, 274, 279, 285; anniversaries 266, 272, 275–276, 281; burials 270–271, 275; in fiction 259, 294; humor about 236–237; monument at 275, **276**; myths 240, 242, 261–262, 267; re-enactments 275, 276; survivor stories/rumors (dogs 8, 242, 243–261, 267, 280; horse 241–243, 256, 280, 286; human 238, 256, 261, 286); *see also* campaigns and expeditions, Sioux War 1876; mystique of the sole survivor
Little Bighorn Battlefield National Monument 242, 248, 288
Little Rock 124
London University 183
Long Winter Gone (Terry C. Johnston) 294
Longfellow, Henry Wadsworth 148, 271
Lookout Station 101
Lord, Surgeon George 240
Lotz, C.F. 273–274
Louisiana 19, 45–46; Alexandria 66, 67, 68, 68, 79; New Orleans 66, 69, 84, 167, 169, 224
Lounsberry, Clement 241
Ludlow, Capt. William 206, 207, 209, **210**, 230, 290
Lurgan, Lord 274
Lurgan, Northern Ireland 273
Lynch, Pvt. Dennis 128–129
Lyon, Mrs. Carrie 70, 78, 80, **83**
Lyon, Capt. Farnham 70, 76, 83
Lyon, Michele 289
Lyons, Pvt. (Custer's orderly) 77

MacKenzie, Æneas 296
The Mad King (Edgar Rice Burroughs) 294
Madison Square Garden 47, 224, 259, 260, 268, 276; *see also* dog shows, Barnum's Roman Hippodrome, Gilmore's Gardens, Westminster Kennel Club
Maida, Battle of 113
Man of Aran (Robert Flaherty) 295

The Man Who Shot Liberty Valance 262
Mangam, W.V. 273
Mar Forest (Marr) 158; *see also* Scottish Highlands
Marching to Valhalla (Michael Blake) 294
Marquis, Dr. Thomas 248
Marsh, Capt. Grant 183, 184, 240, 241 *see also* steamboat, *Far West*
Marsh, Prof. Othniel Charles 206, 267
Martin, Enos Thompson Throop 94; daughter Nelly 94; and staghound 94
Martz, Brandon 293
Maryland 23, 25, 59; Baltimore 43; Crespatown 23
mascots: dogs 27, 38, 170, 242, 261; horse 242 *see also* Comanche
Mason, C.E. 273
Massachusetts 254, 284; Athol 265; Boston 159, 167, 273; New Bedford 17
massacres 238; in film 22; *see also* Fetterman; Sand Creek; Wounded Knee
Master McGrath (Waterloo Cup winner) 179, 273–274
Mastroianni, Marcello 299
Mathey, Lt. Edward 232
Maunder, Wayne 296, **297**
Maximillian Affair, Mexico 1861–1867 22, 66; *see also* Mexico
Mayflower Colony 14
McArthur, Gen. Douglas 242
McClellan, Maj. Gen. George B. 21, 36, 37, 38, 41, 42, 43, 44, 45, 58, 205, 228
McClellan saddle 36
McCook, Gov. 138, 151
McDonald (Russian Wolfhound owner) 170
McDonald, Alastair 158
McDougall, Capt. Thomas 235, 238
McDowell, Brig. Gen. Irwin 34, 35, 36
McFadden, Henry 237
McGrath, Henry Price 161; McGrathiana stud farm 161
McIntosh, Lt. Donald 176, 200
McIntyre, Charles W. 264, 265, 266, 273, 284
McKay, William 206, 209
McLaglen, Victor 299
McLean, Wilmer 61; *see also* Civil War, Appomattox Courthouse
Meade, Maj. Gen. George 46
"Medicine Bill" *see* Comstock, William
Medicine Woman 123
Meline, Col. James F. 194
mercy killing: horses 122, 212; human 95, 175, 203

Merington, Marguerite 7, 20, 76, 153, 193, 223; *see also The Custer Story*
Merrill, Maj. Lewis 227
Merritt, Brig. Gen./Col. Wesley 48, 55, 66, 88, 89, 269
Messiter, Charles 137
Mexican Nationalist Rebellion 66, 82, 88
Mexico 22, 66, 67, 69, 70, 82–83, 88, 106; Chihuahua City 82; *see also* Brownsville, Texas; Juarez, Benito; Maximillian Affair; rivers and creeks, Rio Grande; Romero, Don Matias
Meyer, Scott 291
Meyers, Capt. 104–105, 122
Michigan 13, 14, 25, 57, 88, 143, 265; Ann Arbor 157, 184, 271; Bloomfield 13; Detroit 21, 51, 72, 91, 220, 249, 267, 272; Dundee 111, 144, 147; Grand Rapids 14, 17, 20, 222; Grosse Ile 158, 220; Jackson 219; Monroe 13, 15, 16, 18, 19, 20, 21, 25, 26, 29, 37, 43, 46, 50, 59; 61, 66, 70, 78, 83–84, 90, 91, 111, 113, 114, 115, 117, 156, 158, 159, 162, 168, 191, 215, 219, 222, 229, 249, 264, 265, 270, 271, 274, 283; regiments and brigades 19, 21, 41, 48, 49, 50, 51, 52, 271; Tecumseh 17, 215
Miles, Mrs. Mary 137, 140
Miles, Col./Gen. Nelson A. 132, 137–138, 245, 262, 269
military *see* fashion; music
Miller, C.S. 271
Miller, John B. 268–269, 272, 273
"millionaire's hunt" 160, 165
Millner, Joseph E. (grandson) 216
Millner, Joseph "Moses" E. (a.k.a. "California Joe") 115, 125, 216
mine *see* Stevens Lode Silver Mine
miners, on the Black Hills Expedition 206, 209
Minneapolis Morning Tribune 256, 283, 285–288
The Minneapolis Star 287
Minnesota 207, 260, 265, 284; Academy of Natural Sciences 287; Geological and Natural History Survey of 284, Historical Society of 287, 288; Minneapolis 266, 283, 285, 286, 287; Public Library of 287; St. Paul 204, 215, 216, 220, 226, 229, 230, 256, 264, 265, 283; Stockton 267; Twin Cities 285, 288; *see also* University of Minnesota
Mississippi 19, 64; Oxford 156
Missouri 265; Kansas City 93; Preston 141; St. Louis 91, 92, 183, 189, 271

Molesworth, Lewis William, 11th Baronet of Pencarrow 183, 188, 189, 208
Molesworth, Sady (greyhound) 183–184
Molesworth, Sir Paul, 10th Baronet of Pencarrow 183,
Monaghan, Jay 89, 212
Montana Territory 32, 193, 228, 230, 265; Billings 32, 257; Bozeman 230, 269; Helena 189; Prospect Valley 209
Morgan, Mrs. James 131
Morgan, J.H. 143, 145
Mormons 141, 148
Morton, Levi P. 155, 157
Mosby's Raiders 55, 59
Mount Bonnell, TX 80
Mount Rushmore, SD 271
mourning practices, Victorian 16, 89
Moylan, Lt. Myles 94, 111, 121, 139, *143*, *147*, *187*, *200*
mule skinners 183
mummies, Egyptian 59
Murphy, Nicholas R. 285, 286
museums *see* Dime; Little Bighorn National Monument; Natural History at Tring; University of Minnesota
music, military: *Ain't I Glad to Get Out of the Wilderness* 125; *Garry Owen* 95, 122, 123, 144, 188, 207, 215, 233; *The Girl I Left Behind Me* 95, 121, 207; *see also Custer's Last Charge* (song)
My Life on the Plains (George Armstrong Custer) 101, 130, 168, 216, 243
mystique of the sole survivor 238, 243, 261–262

Nactrieb, Prof. H.F. 286
Nanook of the North (Robert Flaherty) 295
Napoleon, the horse survivor 241, 242 *see also* Comanche
Nast, Thomas 151
National Land Company 152
National Union Convention 88
Natural History Museum at Tring, U.K. 285
Nebraska 72, 93, 137, 193, 267, 269; North Platte 165, Red Willow Creek 165
Nevada, Virginia City 272
New Jersey 36, 55, 265, 268; Hoboken 154; Trenton 20
New Mexico 72, 193, 298
New Orleans 66
New York 13, 94, 222, 265, 275; Aquarium 273; Auburn 94; Bedloe's Island 260; Brooklyn 273; Buffalo 14; Catskills 277, 281; Central Park Zoological Gardens 106, 156; City of 6, 16, 28, 30, 32, 37, 47, 51, 52, 59, 85, 87, 147, 147, 152, 155, 156, 157, 158, 164, 167, 216, 219, 220, 222, 254, 264, 266, 271, 272, 290; Governor's Island 260; Manhattan 59, 154, 224, 260, 266, 269, 273; Manhattanville 89; Millbrook 220; Newburgh 268, 269; Onondaga County 13; Sacketts Harbor 256; Syracuse 13; Times Square 250, 265
New York Citizen 141
New York Herald 218, 227, 231, 232, 264, 269
New York Herald Tribune 266
New York Sun 260
New York Times 47, 140
New York Tribune 206, 223
New York World 206, 208
newspapers and magazines *see Army and Navy Journal; The Atlantic Monthly; Bismarck Tribune; Chicago Inter Ocean; Chicago Times; Chicago Tribune; The Daily Graphic; Deadwood Hills; Pioneer; Detroit Free Press; Dublin University Magazine; The Field; Forest and Stream; Frank Leslie's Illustrated Newspaper; The Galaxy; Godey's Lady's Book; Harper's Bazaar; Harpers Weekly; Journal of History; Kansas City Journal; Minneapolis Morning Tribune; The Minneapolis Star; New York Citizen; New York Herald; New York Herald Tribune; New York Sun; New York Times; New York Tribune; New York World; Ohio State Journal; The Philadelphia Inquirer; Philadelphia Press; Post (Detroit); The Record (Fargo); Recreation Magazine; Research Review: The Journal of the Little Big Horn Associates; Rocky Mountain Herald; St. Paul Daily Pioneer; St. Paul Press; Spirit of the Times; Sturgis Weekly Record; Turf, Field and Farm; Vanity Fair*
Nez Perce 242
Nikolayeich, Grand Duke Nicholas 167–168
9/11 Memorial, New York City 59
Nixon, Richard (in film parody) 299
No Survivors (Will Henry) 294
Noble, Conway 21
Noble, Laura 140
Nomad: George A. Custer in Turf, Field and Farm (Brian W. Dippie) 5, 290
Noonan, Pvt. *210*
Norris, Gilman 189
North, Maj. Luther 195, 206, 207
North Carolina 19, 38, 89; New Bern 37, 47

North Dakota *see* Dakota Territory
North Dakota State Historical Society Archives 240
Northwestern Trust Co. 286
novels and poetry *see Beth Gelert: or the Grave of the Greyhound* (poem); *Boatswain's Epitaph* (poem); *Charles O'Malley, the Irish Dragoon; The Court Martial of George Armstrong Custer; Custer, Terry, and Me; Custer's Last Jump; David Copperfield; The Eternal Lover/The Eternal Savage; Flashman and the Redskins; The Guardsman; Ivanhoe; Jack Hinton; John Carter of Mars; Lady of the Lake; Long Winter Gone; The Mad King; Marching to Valhalla; No Survivors; The Prisoner of Zenda; Seize the Sky; The Seventh's Staghound; Tarzan; Tom Brown's School Days; Turk: The General's Dog*
Nowlan, Lt. 113, *142*, *143*, 147

Oakley, Annie 276
O'Brien, Mrs. (Irish visitor) 285
O'Donnell, I.H. "Bud" 247, 257, 258, 281
Ohio 23, 25, 26, 31, 38, 139, 265; Cadiz 237, 251; Cincinnati 162, 167; Cleveland 23, 52, 90; 11th Ohio Volunteer Inf. 38; Marion 267; New Rumley 23, 24, 26, 29, 271; Peru 13; Sandusky 13
Ohio State Journal 140
Ojibwe (Chippewa) 129, 265
Oklahoma *see* Indian Territory
Old Bear 228
Old Neutriment (Glendolin Wagner) 5, 7, 257, 259
"Old Neutriment" *see* Burkman, Pvt. John W.
Old Soldiers Home, Sawtelle, Los Angeles, Calif. 254
Old Yeller 294
Olson (janitor at University of Minnesota) 286
Omohundro, John "Texas Jack" 165
One Perfect Day (Jerry Thomas) 291
O'Neil, Tom 30
Oregon 94, 115
Osage 116, 123, 126
Ottoman Empire *see* Turkey
Ourosoff, Prince 134, 167
Outdoor Life 181
Owensboro Examiner 236

Page, Maj. Abel 14, 20
Page, Eleanor Sophia 14
Page, Zilphia 14, 20
Paget, Sir Augustus Berkeley 138–*143*, 153, 155, 279

Paget, Lord George Augustus 139, 141
Paget, Henry William, Marquess of Anglesey, Earl of Uxbridge 139, 141
Paha Sapa Tawoyakie (William Vose Wade) 181
A Painted Herbarium: The Life and Art of Emily Hitchcock Terry, 1838–1921 285
Palmer House 265
Panic of 1873 213
Papal Wars, Italy 94
Parliament, Members of *see* Graves, Samuel; Hughes, Thomas; Powell, Walter
Parsons, Capt. Charles 108, 113
Pawnee 206
Pawnee Killer 104
Paxson, Edgar S. 258, 272, 290
Peabody, Mr. (cartoon dog) 300
Pennington, Gen. Alfred 66
Pennsylvania 23, 49, 161, 265; Germantown 23; Gettysburg 48, 49, 50; Johnstown 90; Philadelphia 23, 88, 225, 226, 229
Perchina Kennels 168
Perry, Com. Matthew 150
Peter the Great 164; *see also* Russian nobility
The Philadelphia Inquirer 225
Philadelphia Press 243
Phillips, W.J. 141, 143
photography 15, 19, 27, 28, 45, 65, 141, 142, 143, 191, 196, **198**, 206; dogs and 37–38, 39–40, 41, 42, 59, 80–81, 82, 83, 84, 111, 112, 118, 134, 135, 199, 209–**210**, **211**, 212, **221**, **222**, 290, **276**, 293 *see also* Brady, Matthew; Goff, Orlando; Illingworth, William Henry; Phillips, W.J.; Pywell, William
Pickens, Pvt. J.C. 144, 145
Pickwick Papers (Charles Dickens) 15
Pierce, President Franklin 150
pistols *see* weapons
Pitts, Rhoda Wells 17
Pitts, Samuel 17
Plains of the Great West and Their Inhabitants (Col. Richard Irving Dodge) 218
Platte, Dept. of *see* Crook., Maj. Gen George R.
plays *see* *The Custer Drama*, *Henry V*; *Trails of the West*
Pleasant (Whiskey) Point at Fort Abraham Lincoln 197, 227, 230
Pleasonton, Maj. Gen. Alfred 45, 46, 48, 52, 54
Poland 165
Poletes, George 293
Pompey's Pillar, MT 188–189
Poncelet, Thierry 289
Pope, Alexander 38

Porter, Adm. David Dixon 64; and foxhounds 85
Porter, Com. David, importing Persian greyhounds 85
Porter, Gen. Fitz-John 39–40
Porter, Asst. Surgeon Henry R. 238, 241
Post (Detroit) 144
Potter, Edward 271
The Potterymaker (Robert Flaherty) 295
Powatomi 13
Powder River Fight 228, 234, 279
Powder River Supply Depot 6, 11–12, 218, 232, 233, **233**, 234, 241, 244, 254, 258, 259, 261, 262, 265, 272, 273, 290, 298; *see also* rivers and creeks, Powder; Rosebud Creek Depot
Powell, Walter, M.P. 138, 150, 153, 158, 163
prairie dogs: as pets 113; towns 97; in zoo 150, 153
presidential elections 31, 58
Price, Sir Rose Lambart 223
Prince of Wales *see* Wales, Prince of
The Prisoner of Zenda (Anthony Hope) 294
prisons, Confederate 62–63, 66, 69; use of slave tracking dogs in 63
prostitutes: New York 87; Pleasant (Whiskey) Point 197; Washington D.C. 52
Prussia 159
Pywell, William 178, 182, 191, 192

Quaker Gun Affair 37, 43
Queen Victoria 170, 251–253; Scottish Deerhounds of 269

rabies *see* disease in dogs
races 258–259, 274; foot 103, 197; horse 66, 77, 79, 90, 103, 153, 158, 160, 161, 162, 169, 197, 259; *see also* coursing competition, hounds; Custer, George Armstrong, horses of
railroads: Kansas Pacific 93, 150–151, 155; luxury cars 92, 143, 164; Northern Pacific 91, 171, 182, 185, 226, 265; Union Pacific 93
Rain-in-the-Face 218
Ralston, J.K. 248
ranks *see* U.S. Army
Reagan, Ronald 296
Reconstruction of Southern States 4, 71, 81, 82, 87, 88, 89, 92, 98, 152, 156, 157, 267
The Record (Fargo) 245
Recreation Magazine 290
Red Tomahawk 275
Redpath Lyceum Bureau 226–227, 279
Reed, David 26, 27

Reed, Emma 26, 229, 241, 265
Reed, Harry Armstrong "Autie" 12, 26, 46, 230, 234, 236, 239, 270
Reed, Lilla Belle 26
Reed, Lydia Ann (née Kirkpatrick) 26, 30, 37, 42
Reed, Maria 26
Reedstrom, E. Lisle 287, 290–291
Reeve, Charles McCormick "Mc.C" 266
Reilly, Lt. William Van W., recovered ring of 256
Remington, Frederic 100, 272, 277
Reno, Maj. Marcus 11, 231, 234, 235–236, 238, 239, 247, 254, 256, 263, 267, 272
Reno-Benteen Defense 236, 238, 239, 246, 247, 249, 256, 257
Republican Party 23, 27–28, 31
Research Review: The Journal of the Little Big Horn Associates 7, 287, 291
reservations: Great Sioux 205, Standing Rock 270
revolvers *see* weapons
Reynolds, "Lonesome" Charlie 189, 206, 207, 209, 218, 231
Reynolds, Col. Joseph 228
Rhode Island 59
Rice, Dan, circus of 224
Richmond, Mary 20
Richmond, Rebecca 18, 20, 44, 59, 60, 72, 80, 95, 108, 111, 135, 147–148, 151
Richmond, Virginia 35, 36, 41
Ricker, Judge Eli S. 129
Ridges, Stanley 296
Riff, Mr. (dog transfer agent) 158
rifles and carbines *see* weapons
Rin Tin Tin 250, 261, 299
Ringling Brothers, Barnum & Bailey Circus 225
riverboats *see* steamboats
rivers and creeks: Beaver Creek 102; Big Horn 188, 230, 234; Chickahominy 40–41; Colorado 80, 171; Detroit 219–220; Glendive Creek 189; Heart 193, 230, 244; Hudson 28, 89, 154; James 64; Kansas 291; Little Bighorn 9, 234, 235, 239, 240, 241, 246, 251, 257; Mississippi 66, 150–151; Missouri 6, 171, 175, 176, 181, 196, 197, 199, 203; Occoquan 38; Pawnee 98; Platte 105, 171; Poplar 245; Potomac 58; Powder 230, 231, 232, 244, 259 (*see also* Powder River Fight, Powder River Supply Depot); Raisin 13; Razor Creek 189; Red 66–67; Red Willow Creek 165; Reno Creek 235; Republican 104, 105, 251; Rio Grande 66, 82, 171; Rosebud 230, 234,

244, 258, 298 (*see also* Rosebud Creek, Battle of, Rosebud Creek Depot); Tongue 187, 230, 234; Walnut Creek 99; Warwick 39; Washita 118, 122, 123, 125; Yellowstone 188, 189, 230, 232, 242; *see also* campaigns and expeditions, Washita 1868; Sioux War 1876
Riverside Station 105
Robbins, Lt. Samuel 104–105
Robe, Mike 298
Roberts, Annie Gibson 134
Roberts, Richard 230
Roberts, Dr. Thomas Sadler 286, 287
Robin Hood: Prince of Thieves 296
Rocky Mountain Herald 271
Roe, Lt. Fayette Washington and Francis M.A. 81
Roman Nose 98
Romanov, Alexis Alexandrovich, Grand Duke 163–*166*, 167–168, 179, 196, 224, 254, 265, 268, 269; *see also* Russia; Russian nobility
Romero, Don Matias, Mexican minister 88, 89; *see also* Mexico
Ronsheim, Milton 251
Roosevelt, Theodore "Teddy," Jr. 270, *274*, 275, 286
Rosebud Creek, Battle of 234, 244
Rosebud Creek Depot ("Fort Beans") 244
Ross, Horatio 206, 209
Ross, Thom 291, 293
Rosser, Gen. Thomas Lafayette, C.S.A. 55, 183, 185, 186
Russell, Charles 272
Russell, Don 289
Russia 164, 165, 170, 196, 269, 275; St. Petersburg 166
Russian nobility *see* Nikolayeich, Grand Duke Nicholas; Ourosoff, Prince; Peter the Great; Romanov, Alexis Alexandrovich Grand Duke; Tsars Alexander II and Nicholas II
Ryan, Pvt./Sgt. John 100, 127, 128, 129, 132, 156, 210, 240

sabers *see* weapons
Sacagawea 188
St. Paul Daily Pioneer 206
St. Paul Press 206
St. Paul's Congregational Plymouth Church, MN 283
Salisbury, W.S. 219
Salt Lake City, UT 141, 148, 189
Sand Creek Massacre 117, 122, 123
Sanders, Deborah 298
Sanford, Pvt. Wilmot P. 233
Santa Fe Trail 93–94

Santa Fe Trail (film) 296
Saylor, Maurine Bergland 294
Scarfe, Jonathon 298
Schofield, Maj. Gen. 138, 143
Schwarck, Donald P. 146, 291
scientists, on expeditions 182, 184, 191, 206–207, 209; *see also* campaigns and expeditions, Black Hills 1874; Yellowstone 1873
Scotland 113, 149, 158, 190, 274, 279
Scott, Sir Walter 48, 92, 113, 114, 133, 141, 145, 259
Scott, Gen. Winfield 26, 34, 36, 37, 66
Scottish Highlands 113; *see also* Scotland
scouts, civilian 97, 103, 115–116, 121, 122, 123, 189, 194, 206, 230, 269; *see also* Bent; Bouyer; Cody; Comstock; Hickok; Millner; Norris; Reynolds; Taylor
scouts, Indian 116, 122, 196–197, 208, 235; Arikara (Arikaree, Ree) 187, 206, *211*, 215, 235, 239; Crow 235, 239, 240; Osage 116; Pawnee 206; Santee Sioux 206; *see also* Bloody Knife, Curly
Secession of Southern States 19, 31, 47
Secret Service 270
Seize the Sky (Terry C. Johnston) 294
Seminole 62
7th Cavalry *see* U.S. Army Federal regiments
The Seventh's Staghound (Fairfax Downey) 259, 290, 294
Seward, William, Secretary of State 64, 88, 164; *see also* Alaskan Territory Purchase
Shakespeare, William 185–186
She Wore a Yellow Ribbon 299
Sheridan, Col. Michael V. 270
Sheridan, Gen. Philip 54, 55, 58, 59, 60, 61, 65, 66, 67, 70, 79, 82, 88, 89, 94, 108, 114, 117, 122, 123, 125, 126, 127, 138, 143, 149, 158, 160, 163, 164–165, 179, 183, 205, 207, 228, 229, 270
Sheridan's Raiders (Jessie's Scouts) 59
Sherman, Maj. Gen. William Tecumseh 55, 104, 105, 114, 138, 164, 179, 226, 228, 229, 230; total war and March to the Sea 55, 63
Shields, G.O. 194
ships: S.S. *Adriatic* 275; U.S.S. *Black Hawk* 85; H.M.S. *Captain* 155; gunboat, President Lincoln's 64; S.S. *Oceanic* 275; C.S.S. *Shenandoah* 65; *Svetlana* 164, 167; R.M.S. *Titanic*

275; Union Army flotilla 38–39; *see also* steamboats
Shoshone 117
Sibley, Henry Hastings 260
sign language, Indian 103, 115, 240, 248
Silver Queen Saloon, Virginia City, NV 272
Sioux 11–12, 96, 98, 99, 103, 104, 116, 181, 182, 187, 205, 212, 213, 218, 226, 228, 230, 231, 232, 234–236, 238–240, 241, 244, 247, 251, 256, 259, 269, 271, 273, 275, 279–280; sub-groups (Blackfeet 234; Brulé 165–166, 234; Hunkpapa 187, 234; Lakota 181, 205, 213, 298; Miniconjous 234; Oglala 228, 234, 279; Sans Arc 234; Two Kettle 234; Yankton [Ihanktonwan Dakota]) 173–174
Sitting Bull 11, 226, 234, 236, 237, 239, 251, 269–270; his father in parody 299
skunks 115, 146, 134, 145, 146
slavery 19, 31, 63, 89,
slaves, escaped ("contrabands") 39, 50; terrorizing of 62–63; tracking hounds used to capture 62–63, 78
Slim Buttes, attack at 244
Smith, (Nebraska rancher with wolfhounds) 170
Smith, Lt. Algernon "Fresh" 94, 144, 159, 169, *182*, 183, 189, 199–200, 206, 239, 240
Smith, Col. Andrew Jackson 93, 97, 102, 107, 108
Smith, Edward (Commissioner of Indian Affairs) 288
Smith, Lt. Henry Walworth "Salt" 94
Smith, Nettie 159, 230, 265
Smith, U.S. Assistant Postmaster 138, 151
Smith, Gen. W.F. "Baldy" 39
Smithsonian National Museum of American History 61
Smokey Hill Trail 93–94, 105
Snakey Bend (Custer Bend) Cemetery 126
Snow, Frederick S. "Antelope Fred" 212
Snyder, "Pinnacle Jake" 156
Society for the Prevention of Cruelty to Animals Magazine 244
soldiers: alcoholism on posts 94; burials 145–146, 188; desertion 103, 105, 107, 108, 173; entertainments 132, 197, 208; as orderlies 37, 97, 103, 203; pets (wild) of 105–*106*, 235; punishment 67, 79, 200, 207; rations 67, 79; resentment of extended service 67–68; social life on posts 95, 147–148, 160, 197, 216; *see also* dogs and soldiers

Soldiers and Sailors Convention 90
Soldiers' Home, Washington D.C. 268
Sommereisen, Fr. Valentin 188
Son of the Morning Star (book by Evan S. Connell & film) 298, 299
Sousa, John Philip 271
South Carolina 19, 31, 227; Charleston 31, Darlington 156
South Dakota *see* Dakota Territory
Southerland, John B. 143
Southern States *see* Reconstruction of
Spencer, William R. 146
Spirit of the Times 264
Spotted Tail 165–166
Stair, Pvt. William C. 122, 128, 129
Standing Rock Reservation/Agency 218
Stands in Timber, John, Cheyenne historian 239
Stanley, Col. David S. *178*, 179–180, 181, 182, 183, 184, 186–187, 188, 189, 192, 196, 230, 272
"Stanley's Stockade" (Yellowstone Stockade) 189, 192
Stanton, Edwin, Secretary of War 60, 88
Statue of Liberty 260
steamboats 66–67, 173; *E.H. Durfee* 241–242, 258; *Far West* 184, 232, 234, 240, 241, 244, 258, 259; *F.Y. Batchelor* 181; *Josephine* 258; *Miner* 173 *see also* ships
Stebbins, Alfred 26; Stebbins' Academy 26
Stevens Lode Silver Mine 157–158, 168, 219
Stevenson, Robert Louis 138
Stewart, A.R. 250
Stewart, Edgar I. 238, 261
Stewart, Sir William Drummond, 7th Baronet of Blair and Balcaskie 138
Stiles, T.J. 30, 82
stock market crash, Black Friday 157
stockade *see* Stanley's
Stone, Lucy, suffragist 177; *see also* Custers' dogs, Lucy Stone
"Stonehenge" *see The Greyhound: On the Art of Breeding, Rearing, and Training Greyhounds for Public Running, and Their Diseases and Treatment* (John Henry H. Walsh)
Stoneman, Brig. Gen. George 36, 37–38, 46
striker *see* soldiers: as orderlies
Stuart, Maj. Gen. James Ewell Brown "Jeb," C.S.A. 49, 50, 54
Sturgis, Lt. James 242

Sturgis, Col. Samuel D. 138, *143*, 147, 155, 173, 174, 242
Sturgis Weekly Record 244–245, 260, 262
Sully, Gen. Alfred 94, 181
Sun Dance before Little Bighorn 234
sun protection 22, 42; *see also* Havelock; topee
survivor *see* mystique of sole
Swanson, Glenwood 291, 293
Swett, Leonard 204
Swing Around the Circle, Pres. Johnson's political tour 89–90

Taft, President William Howard 271
Tallant, Robert 269
Talmadge, Frank 139
Talmadge, Miss 140, 141, *143*
Talmadge, Mr. *143*
Tarzan (Edgar Rice Burroughs) 294
tattoos, Tom Custer's 240
taxidermy 8, 191, 209, 241, 242, 284–285, 287, 288
Taylor, H.M. "Muggins" 269
Tecumseh, Chief and his Confederation of Tribes 274; *see* Michigan for the city
Tennessee 19; Memphis 171
Tenting on the Plains (Elizabeth B. Custer) 73, 76, 100, 142, 277–278, 281, 290
Terry, Brig. Gen. Alfred Howe 11–12, 207, 226, 228, 229, 230, 231–232, 234, 235, 236, 239, 244, 249, 252, 255, 269, 270, 283; in film 298
Terry, Rev. Cassius Marcellus 283–*284*, 285, 286, 287, 288
Terry, Mrs. Emily Hitchcock 284–285
Texas 19, 64, 65, 66, 67, 68, 69, 70, 72, 77, 80, 81, 83, 87, 100, 106, 120, 183, 196, 197, 254, 267, 274, 277; Austin 76, 78, 79, 80, 81, 83, 89, 254; Brownsville 66; Galveston 66, 84; Hempstead 68, 69, 70, 76–77, 79, *82*, *83*, 277; Houston 66, 68; Reconstruction in 71, 81, 82, 87, 157; San Antonio 82–83; *see also* Texican Rebellion
"Texas Jack" *see* Omohundro, John
Texican Rebellion 1836 69
They Died with Their Boots On 29, 289, 299
Thieves Road in the Black Hills 213
Thomas, Jerry 291
Thompson, Charley *142*
Thompson, Pvt. Peter 231
Thompson, Lt. Richard E. *204*, 252, 274
Thompson, Capt. William 122, 123, *142*, *143*

Thorne, Edwin 220, 265, 268, 269
Thorne, Oakleigh 220, 265, 268, 269
Three Hundred Settlers, Stephen Austin's 69
Thumb, "General" Tom 16, 46
Thurber, Julia 147
Tippecanoe, Battle of 274; *see also* Custers' dogs, Tippecanoe
Tobey, Capt. Thomas F. 244
Tognazzi, Ugo 299
Tom Brown's School Days (Thomas Hughes, M.P.) 150
Tonka 294
topee 42; *see also* sun protection
Torbert, Maj. Gen. Alfred Thomas Archimedes 57
total war: in Georgia 55, 63; Indian Wars 117
Towers, William F. (alias John R. Bradford), letter of 254–*255*, 256
Townsend, Thomas Sutton, M.D. 138, 148–149, 168, 229, 275
Trails of the West (W.T. Chichester and Robert Walsh) 293
Travers, William R. 157
Tsars, Russian Alexander II and Nicholas II 164; *see also* Russian nobility
Tuebor, motto on Custer's personal badge 57, 65,
Turf, Field and Farm 100–101, 108, 115, 119, 134, 141, 142, 145, 146, 160, 169, 179, 190, 191, 193, 205, 210, 221, 252, 266
Turk: The General's Dog (Maurine Bergland Saylor) 294
Turkey 85, 269; Yozgut POW camp 60
Turney, George W. 267
Tutankhamun's tomb, discovery of and Salukis 85
Tuttle, Pvt. John H., (Custer's orderly) 182, 188
Twain, Mark *see* Clemens, Samuel
Two Moons 248
Tyler, President John 71

U.S. Army 228, 279; 1st Brigade of Horse Artillery *56*; 1st Iowa Cavalry 67; 1st Vermont Cavalry 52; 2nd Cavalry 32, 34, 35, 36, 37, 105, 165, 232; 2nd Wisconsin Cavalry 67; 3rd Infantry 81; 4th Infantry 159; 4th Michigan Cavalry 40–41; 4th Michigan Infantry 157; 5th Cavalry 37, 81, 160; 5th Infantry 137; 5th Missouri Mounted Infantry 161; 6th Cavalry 254; 6th Infantry 232, 233, 249, 252, 254, 255, 274; 6th New York Cavalry 267; 7th Cavalry 11–12, 88, 89, 90, 91, 94–95, 96, 100, 105–106, 114–

115, 119, 120, 126, 127, 131, 132, 143, 146, 148, 152, 156, 159, 161, 169, 171, 173–174, 176, 179, 182, 188, 192–193, 196, 205, 206, 207, 208, 213, 229, 230, 231, 232, 233, 234, 236, 239, 240, 242, 243, 245–246, 249, 258, 262–263, 265, 270, 275, 280, 281, 291; 7th Indiana Cavalry 67, 77; 7th Michigan Cavalry 51, 215; 9th Cavalry 88, 89; 9th New Jersey Inf. 47; 10th Cavalry 88, 200; 11th Infantry 245, 256, 262, 286; 12th Illinois Cavalry 67; 13th Minnesota Infantry 267; 13th Vermont Infantry 38; 14th Infantry 244; 20th Infantry 217; 21st Ohio Infantry 50; 22nd Infantry 169, 178, 182, 134, 247, 274; 23rd Infantry 218; 24th Infantry 88: 25th Infantry 88; 27th Infantry 170; 37th Infantry 97; animals of 105–*106*, 134, 290; Cavalry 5th Illinois Cavalry 67; Cavalry School 94, 170; Federal Regiments of 5th Artillery 260; in fiction 294; in film 296; horses, "coloring" of 119; Infantry 43rd Massachusetts 254, 256; mascot of 242; medals 49; New York Infantry 254: 11th Ohio Infantry 38; nicknames of 241; ranks, system of 9, 49; State Volunteer Regiments of: Artillery 1st Illinois Light Artillery 38; Topographical Engineers 39; uniform trends of 159; unit nomenclature 9

U.S. Government 19, 64–65, 89, 117, 135, 164, 181, 213, 227, 228, 229, 234, 270, 279; Indian Affairs, Bureau of 228; Interior, Dept. of 227, 228; Secretaries, of State 64, 88, 164; of War 60, 88, 164, 226–228

U.S. Military Academy (West Point) 26, 27–32, *33*, 35, 42, 52, 55, 61, 64, 82, 88, 89, 96, 107, 134, 141, 157, 183, 206, 213, 256, 281; in film 296

University of Kansas, Lawrence 242

University of Michigan (Ann Arbor College) 184

University of Minnesota 206; Animal Biology Dept. 286; Archives 288; Natural History Museum (Bell Museum) 211, 284, 285, 287, 288, 293; Zoological Museum 286

University of Texas, Austin 79, *84*

Utah Territory *see* Salt Lake City

Utley, Henry Munson 21

Utley, Robert M. 4, 7, 128, 256

Utley, Steven 3

Uxbridge, Earl of *see* Paget, Henry William

Van Cleve, E.E. 286–287

Van de Water, Frederic F. 212

Vanity Fair 151

Varnum, Lt. Charles 187

Veirs, Mathilda P. 23; *see also* Custer, Mathilda

Vermont 284; regiment 52

Verne, Jules 148

Victor Emanuel, King of Italy 158

Vietnam War (in film parody) 299

Virginia 19, 25, 38, 59, 66, 69; Alexandria 36; Amosville 50; Brandy Station *56*; Centreville 34, 37; 38; Charlotte 60; City Point 64, 85; Fairfax 38; Manassas 34, 37; Richmond 35, 36, 41, 64; Shenandoah Valley 49, 54–55, 58, 59; Stevensburg 52; Waynesboro 60; Williamsburg 42; Winchester 55, 57, 58–59

Waddell, Capt. of C.S.S. *Shenandoah* 65

Wade, William Vose 181–182, 196

Wadsworth, Emma *204*, 220, *221*

Wadsworth, Nellie *204*, 220, *221*

Wagner, Glendolin Damon *see Old Neutriment*

Wales, Prince of 38

Wallace, Lt. George 239

Walsh, John Henry H. "Stonehenge" 179

Walsh, Raoul 296

Walsh, Robert 293

wars: American Civil War 1861–1865 *see* Civil War; Crimean War 1853–1856 36, 139, 141, 155, 177; Custer George Armstrong, Civil War actions; Franco-Prussian 1870–1871 149, 153, 155, 158–159; Indian Mutiny of 1857–1858 22; Korean War 242; Mexican 1846–1848 26, 34, 61; Napoleonic 26, 113, 139, 141, 155; Papal Wars 94; Revolutionary 1775–1783 28, 138; 2nd Seminole War 1835–1842 61, 125; Sioux War 1876 1, 11–12, 207, 208; Spanish American War 1898 267; Tecumseh's War 1810–1812 274; Vietnam War 299; War of 1812 34, 85, 138; World War I 60, 259, 275; Zulu War 1879 272; *see also* campaigns and expeditions

Washington D.C. 32, 34, 35, 36, 39, 43, 44, 45, 49, 52, 54, 54, 55, 59, 60, 64, 66, 87, 147, 157, 164, 229, 268

Washita, attack on *see* campaigns and expeditions

Waterloo, Battle of 113, 141

Waterpark, 4th Baron *see* Cavendish, Henry Anson

Wayne, John 22, 299

weapons: artillery (Rodman guns) 188, 206; carbines 100; Gatling guns 12, 104, 206, 207, 230, 232, 239, 267; revolvers 99–100, 140, 149, 155, 205, 207, 229, 258; rifles 100, 114, *166*, 205, 207, 212, 258; sabers 12, 60, 66, 100, 106, 122, 132, 133, 147, 175, 201, 205, 232, 270; *see also* Quaker Gun Affair

Weir, Lt. Thomas 94, 134, *142*, *143*, 152, 200, 236

Wellington, Duke of 113, 141

Wert, Geoffrey 48, 94, 103

West, Capt. Robert 94, 108

West Point *see* U.S. Military Academy

West Virginia: Berryville 55; Harpers Ferry 54

Westward expansion 88, 93–94

Wheeler, Co. Homer W. 242

Whipple, Gen. William D. 260

Whistler, Maj. Joseph Garland 178

White, Sara 131

White Star Line 275

Whitman, Walt 101, 271

Whittaker, Frederick 43, 90, 113, 251, 267–268, 276, 279

Wichita Mountains, OK 120

"Wild Bill" Hickok *see* Hickok, James Butler

Wild West Show, William F. "Buffalo Bill" Cody's 99, 269, 276

Wilde, Oscar 138

Wiley, Jefferson 143, 144

Wilhelm I, Kaiser of Prussia 159

Williamsburg, Virginia 42

Wilson, Hill *142*

Winchell, Prof. Newton H. 206, 213

Windolph, Sgt. Charles 176, 249

Wisconsin, Prairie du Chien 72

Wolf Mountains, Dakota Territory 12

wolf, varieties of 106, 116

Wolfhound Regiment, The (U.S. 27th Infantry) 170

Wolverines, Michigan Cavalry Brigade nickname 41, 48, 49, 50, 67

Woman's Relief Fund 268

Won Ton Ton: The Dog That Saved Hollywood 299–300

Wood, William R. 209

Wooden Leg 236, 240, 247–248, 261

World's Fair 1893 242

Wounded Knee Massacre 137, 261, 279–280
W.P.A. (Works Progress Administration) Federal Art Project *33*
Wyndham-Quinn, Alexis Wyndham Thomas, 4th Earl of Dunraven 165, 223
Wynkoop, Indian Agent 98
Wyoming Territory 117, 193, 206, 228, 230, 252, 265; Cody 272; Douglas 230

Yale University 206

Yankton *see* Dakota Territory
Yates, Mrs. Annie Gibson, (née Roberts) 134, 230, 265
Yates, Capt. George 94, 134, 147, 152, 200, 218, 235, 239
Yates, Mrs. George *221*
Yellow Hand 269, 276
Yellowstone Campaign *see* campaigns and expeditions, Sioux War 1876
Yellowstone Lake 189
Yellowstone War *see* campaigns and expeditions, 3rd Yellowstone 1873

Young, Lt. Col. Henry H., of Sheridan's Raiders (Jessie's Scouts) 59, 60, 66
Youngkin, Stephen D. 146, 287–288

zoos: New York Central Park Zoological Gardens (menagerie) 106, 156, 190, 211; Zoological Society of London (Zoological Gardens) 148–149, 150, 153, 275
Zulu army 272

www.ingramcontent.com/pod-product-compliance
Lightning Source LLC
Chambersburg PA
CBHW080756300426
44114CB00020B/2741